Human Relations for Career and Personal Success

Eighth Edition

Human Relations for Career and Personal Success

Concepts, Applications, and Skills

Eighth Edition

Andrew J. DuBrin
Rochester Institute of Technology

PEARSON

Prentice
Hall

Upper Saddle River, New Jersey 07458

Library of Congress Catoging-in-Publication Data

DuBrin, Andrew J.
    Human relations for career and personal success : concepts, application, and skills / Andrew J. DuBrin. — 8th ed.
    p. cm.
    Includes index.
    ISBN: 0-13-179179-6
    1. Success in business. 2. Organizational behavior. 3. Psychology, Industrial. 4. Interpersonal relations.
    I. Title.
    HF5386.D768 2008
    650.1'3—dc22   2006022997

Editor-in-Chief: Vernon R. Anthony
Senior Acquisitions Editor: Gary Bauer
Editorial Assistant: Dan Trudden
Development Editor: Deborah Hoffman
Marketing Manager: Leigh Ann Sims
Marketing Coordinator: Alicia Dysert
Managing Editor—Production: Mary Carnis
Manufacturing Buyer: Ilene Sanford
Production Liaison: Denise Brown
Full-Service Production and Composition:
Judy Ludowitz/Carlisle Publishing Services
Permission Coordinator: Lori Bradshaw/
Carlisle Publishing Services

Manager of Media Production: Amy Peltier
Media Production Project Manager: Lisa Rinaldi
Director, Image Resource Center: Melinda Patelli
Manager, Rights and Permissions: Zina Arabia
Manager, Visual Research: Beth Brenzel
Manager, Cover Visual Research & Permissions:
Karen Sanatar
Image Permission Coordinator: Nancy Seise
Senior Design Coordinator: Christopher Weigand
Cover and Interior Design: Karen Quigley
Cover Images: Getty Images/Royalty Free
Printer/Binder: Banta/Menasha
Cover Printer: Phoenix Color

Photo Credits: Page 2: RON CHAPPLE, Getty Images, Inc. – Taxi, Page 4: © Mark Peterson / Corbis, Page 28: Tom McCarthy, PhotoEdit Inc., Page 30: eBay Inc. These materials have been reproduced with the permission of eBay Inc. COPYRIGHT (c) 2006 EBAY INC. ALL RIGHTS RESERVED, Page 52: STEPHEN SIMPSON, Getty Images, Inc. – Taxi, Page 54: Nelson Hancock © Rough Guides, Page 78: ARTHUR TILLEY, Getty Images, Inc. – Taxi, Page 80: Koester Axel, Corbis/Sygma, Page 102: Photolibrary.Com, Page 104: Getty Images - Stockbyte, Page 128: RON CHAPPLE, Getty Images, Inc. – Taxi, Page 130: Copyright © Eastman Kodak Company, Page 156: SuperStock, Inc. Page 158: SuperStock, Inc., Page 186: EyeWire Collection, Getty Images – Photodisc, Page 188: Kelvin Murray, Getty Images Inc. – Stone Allstock, Page 208: Alamy Images Royalty Free, Page 210: Robert Daly, Getty Images Inc. – Stone Allstock, Page 238: © BILL BACHMANN / DanitaDelimont.com, Page 242: Steve Gottlieb, The Stock Connection, Page 266: Photolibrary.Com, Page 270: Jeff Greenberg, PhotoEdit Inc., Page 294: Getty Images, Inc., Page 298: Mel Winer, The Stock Connection, Page 322: EyeWire Collection, Getty Images – Photodisc, Page 326: Wegmans Food Markets, Inc., Page 350: Ken Fisher, Getty Images Inc. – Stone Allstock, Page 354: David Oliver, Getty Images Inc. – Stone Allstock, Page 376: Getty Images – Digital Vision, Page 380: United Parcel Service, Page 408: Steve Cole, Getty Images, Inc.– Photodisc., Page 412: Getty Images – Stockbyte, Page 436: Getty Images – Stockbyte, Page 440: Vito Aluia, Index Stock Imagery, Inc.

Pearson Education Ltd.
Pearson Education Singapore, Pte. Ltd.
Pearson Education Canada, Ltd.
Pearson Education—Japan

Pearson Education Australia PTY, Limited
Pearson Education North Asia Ltd.
Pearson Educación de Mexico, S.A. de C.V.
Pearson Education Malaysia, Pte. Ltd.

10 9 8 7 6 5 4 3 2 1
ISBN 0-13-179179-6

To Rosie—and her sparkle

To Clare—and her spirit

To Camila—and her spontaneity

To Sofia—and her self-confidence

Brief Contents

Contents

" The hallmark of this text is the use of many real world examples of human relations issues and practices. "

—Darlean McClure, College of the Sequoias

"
The self-assessment quizzes
are excellent.
"

—Jim Wilhelm, South Plains College

> I really like . . . knowing
> oneself before you can
> begin to understand
> others and the environ-
> ment around you.

—Jewel Cherry, Forsyth Technical and
Community College

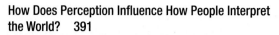

"One strength is the readability, second strength is the practical approach, third strength is the summary section, fourth strength concerns the case studies . . . ."

—Reginald St. Clair, Mountain Empire Community College

Welcome to the eighth edition of *Human Relations for Career and Personal Success: Concepts, Applications, and Skills*. This new edition has been expanded to emphasize developing effective human relations skills for the workplace, including material on teamwork and motivating and influencing others. The purpose of this book is to show you how you can become more effective in your work and personal life through knowledge of and skill in human relations. A major theme of this text is that career and personal success are related. Success on the job often enhances personal success, and success in personal life can enhance job success. Dealing effectively with people is an enormous asset in both work and personal life.

This text is written to help students deal with human relations problems on the job and in personal life. It is designed to be appropriate for human relations courses taught in colleges, career schools, vocational–technical schools, and other postsecondary schools. Managerial, professional, and technical workers who are forging ahead in their careers will also find this book immediately useful in improving workplace and personal relationships.

Organization of the Book

The text is divided into four parts, reflecting the major issues in human relations.

Part I covers four aspects of understanding and managing yourself: Chapter 1 focuses on the meaning of human relations, self-understanding, and the interrelationship of career and personal success. Chapter 2 explains how self-esteem and self-confidence are such important parts of human functioning. Chapter 3 explains how to use self-motivation and goal setting to improve your chances for success. Chapter 4 deals with the importance of emotional intelligence and attitudes, and factors associated with being happy. Chapter 5 explains the contribution of values and ethics to effective human relations. Chapter 6 explains the basics of solving problems and making decisions with an emphasis on creativity.

Part II examines the heart of human relations—dealing effectively with other people. The topics in Chapters 7 through 13 are, respectively, personal communication effectiveness; communication in the workplace; getting along with your manager, coworkers, and customers; managing conflict; becoming an effective leader; motivating others and developing teamwork; and developing cross-cultural competence.

Part III provides information to help career-minded people capitalize on their educations, experiences, talents, and ambitions. The topics of Chapters 14 through 16 are getting ahead in your career; learning strategies, perception, and life span changes; and developing good work habits.

Part IV deals with staying emotionally healthy. Chapter 17 covers managing stress and personal problems.

Changes in the Eighth Edition

The eighth edition of *Human Relations for Career and Personal Success* is the most significant revision to date with a major shift toward emphasizing human relations in the workplace. You will find added emphasis on research findings that support the text discussion, a focus suggested by reviewers. The following chapters are either new or include substantial changes:

Chapter 2: Self-Esteem and Self-Confidence

Chapter 4: Emotional Intelligence, Attitudes, and Happiness

Chapter 5: Values and Ethics

Chapter 8: Communication in the Workplace

Chapter 12: Motivating Others and Developing Teamwork

Chapter 14: Getting Ahead in Your Career (The new chapter consolidates three chapters from the previous edition: Chapter 10 on career choice, Chapter 11 on job search, and Chapter 13 on career advancement.)

Chapter 15: Learning Strategies, Perception, and Life Span Changes

All chapters are thoroughly updated wherever possible in terms of research and published opinions. Detailed chapter by chapter revisions and updates include the following:

Chapter 1, Human Relations and You

- Revised description of the human relations movement and overview of major concepts in human relations
- New description of major factors in job performance and behavior
- New self-assessment quiz about human relations skills

Chapter 2, Self-Esteem and Self-Confidence

- Consolidates and updates material found in previous edition Chapters 1 and 14

Chapter 3, Self-Motivation and Goal Setting

- New figure about ranking of job satisfaction factors by 600 employees with opportunity for students to self-apply the knowledge
- Added findings of research study about the relationship of self-discipline scores to career success and satisfaction

Chapter 4, Emotional Intelligence, Attitudes, and Happiness

- **New chapter** that includes information on happiness that appeared in the seventh edition Chapter 16
- New discussion of attitudes
- New Figure 4-1 on wisdom of Dale Carnegie in relation to positive attitudes
- New Core Self-Evaluation Scale that measures the strength of self-attitudes

Chapter 5, Values and Ethics

- New chapter
- New Figure 5-1 on the mission and values of Microsoft Corporation
- New Self-Assessment Quiz 5-1, the Ethical Reasoning Inventory
- New Figure 5-3 detailing excerpts from professional codes of conduct

Chapter 6, Problem Solving and Creativity

- Two brainteasers for improving problem-solving ability: Frame Games and Sudoko

Chapter 7, Personal Communication Effectiveness

- New Figure 7-1, modified model of the communication process
- New section on interpersonal communication and relationship building

Chapter 8, Communication in the Workplace

- **New chapter** that includes parts of Chapter 6 from the seventh edition
- New material on formal and informal communication channels
- New technologies to supplement e-mail messaging
- New material on the multitasking movement and conducting a business meeting

Chapter 9, Getting Along with Your Manager, Coworkers, and Customers

- New cultural diversity aspects added
- New Figure 9-1, Ten Major Personality Disorders (in the section on difficult people)
- New Figure 9-2, Service-Oriented Organizational Citizenship Behaviors

Chapter 10, Managing Conflict

- New material on culturally diverse teams and factional groups as sources of conflict
- New material on microinequities (unintended slights) as sources of conflict
- New section on managing anger moved from Chapter 5

Chapter 11, Becoming an Effective Leader

- New material includes crisis management, being a servant leader, leadership style, and style flexibility
- New Self-Assessment Quiz 11-2, What Style of Leader Are You or Would You Be?

Chapter 12, Motivating Others and Developing Teamwork

- **New chapter** on diagnosing motivating factors, theories, and tactics
- New coverage of development of team work, group dynamics, and characteristics of effective work groups
- New Self-assessment Quiz 12-1, Team Player Roles

Chapter 13, Diversity and Cross-Cultural Competence

- New section on multicultural identities and the cultural mosaic
- New coverage of cultural intelligence
- New Figure 13-3, Competencies for Successful Cross-Cultural Adaptation of Expatriates
- New coverage of gender differences in leadership as cultural differences
- New coverage of legal aspects of a culturally diverse environment

Chapter 14, Getting A head in your Career

- **New chapter** that consolidates three chapters from the seventh edition (Chapter 10 on career choice, Chapter 11 on job search, and Chapter 13 on career advancement)

Chapter 15, Learning Strategies, Perception, and Life Span Changes

- **New chapter**
- New coverage of learning strategies, learning styles, cognitive styles, individual differences in learning, continuous learning, perception
- New coverage of stages of the life cycle, responding to changes at different life stages, impact of life span on life and job satisfaction
- New coverage of dealing with career changes and coping with personal change, including new figure on sources of learning on the job
- New Self-Assessment Quiz 15-1 Visual, Auditory, and Kinesthetic Survey
- New discussion of Myers-Briggs Type® Indicator (MBTI), particularly as it relates to learning styles
- New coverage of Erickson's eight stages of development and associated crises
- New discussion of how the "flat world" might affect the reader's career

Chapter 16, Developing Good Work Habits

- New time-and-activity chart for scheduling activities
- New data about time wasting among U.S. workers, including Figure 16-3, Categories of Nonjob-Related Computer Surfing
- New Figure 16-4, Categories of Nonjob-Related Computer Surfing.

Chapter 17, Managing Stress and Personal Problems

- Consolidates and updates two chapters from the previous edition (Chapter 4 on wellness and stress and Chapter 5 on dealing with personal problems)

Human Relations for Career and Personal Success is not simply a textbook. The eighth edition contains a wealth of experiential exercises, including new cases and self-assessment quizzes, that can be completed in class or as homework.

New Chapter-Opening Cases Set the Stage

Following a list of the chapter objectives and the chapter outline, all chapters begin with a case scenario that deals with the chapter topic and sets the stage for the chapter narrative.

Pedagogical Features Relate Concepts to What's Happening Today, Personally and in the Workplace

- **Self-assessment quizzes** give students the opportunity to explore their own opinions, feelings, and behavior patterns as related to chapter topics. All chapters include one or more self-assessment quiz.

- **Human Relations in Practice** boxes in all chapters illustrate real human relations business practices in today's business world.

- **Motivational "words of wisdom"** from a wide variety of business and world leaders and experts are included in all chapters.

New, Expanded Assignment Material

End-of-chapter assignment material has been reorganized and expanded into two sections:

Concept Review and Reinforcement featuring exercises that focus on concept retention and developing critical-thinking skills and **Developing Your Human Relations Skills** focusing on developing skills that can be used immediately in life and on the job.

Concept Review and Reinforcement

Key Terms

Chapter Summary and Review provides an **excellent** detailed review of key chapter concepts

Check Your Understanding provides objective questions review key chapter topics and stimulate thinking about the issues

Web Corner provides informational websites and asks students to use the power of the web in researching outside resources

---

Developing Your Human Relations Skills

Two new Developing Your Human Relations Skills

Skills Exercises tie together chapter topics and allow students to apply what they have just learned.

Two Human Relations Case Studies put students into a realistic scenario so they can practice making decisions in tough situations.

Supplements for Teaching and Learning

Resources for Students: Need additional practice and support?

COMPANION WEB SITE

Go to *www.prenhall.com/dubrin* to access links to on-line resources for each chapter and to prepare for tests. Here you will find additional Web exercises and self-grading quizzes for each chapter, including multiple-choice questions, true/false questions, and essay questions, with immediate feedback and assessment.

PRENTICE HALL SELF-ASSESSMENT LIBRARY (S.A.L.)

S.A.L. is a CD-ROM product developed by Steve Robbins that contains 51 research-based self-assessments that provide students with insights into their skills, abilities, and interests. It is easy to use, self-scoring, and can be packaged with this text at a discounted price. Please contact your Prentice Hall representative to obtain a review copy.

Resources for Instructors

All instructor resources are available on the **Instructor's Resources CD** or you can download them from the **Instructor Resource Center** at *www.prenhall.com*. Register once and gain access to instructor materials for all of your Prentice Hall textbooks.

INSTRUCTOR'S MANUAL WITH TEST ITEM FILE

The instructor's manual for this text contains a large number of multiple-choice and true/false test questions, chapter outlines and lecture notes, answers to discussion questions and case problems, and comments about the exercises.

PRENTICE HALL TEST GENERATOR

The computerized test-generation system gives you maximum flexibility in preparing tests. It can be used to create custom tests and print scrambled versions of a test at one time, as well as to build tests randomly by chapter, level of difficulty, or question type. The software also allows on-line testing and record keeping and the ability to add problems to the database.

POWERPOINT LECTURE PRESENTATION PACKAGE

Lecture presentation screens for each chapter are available on-line and on the Instructor Resources CD.

INSTRUCTOR RESOURCES CD (IRCD)

The IRCD contains the Instructor's Manual with Test Item File, Prentice Hall Test Gen, and the PowerPoint Lecture Presentation Package.

JWA HUMAN RELATIONS VIDEOS

JWA videos on human relations and interpersonal communication topics are available to qualified adopters. Contact your local representative for details.

On-Line Course Support

OneKey Distance Learning Solutions: Convenience, Simplicity, Success

Ready-made **WebCT** and **Blackboard** on-line courses are available. If you adopt a OneKey course, student access cards will be packaged with the text at no extra charge to the student. OneKey courses include Research Navigator, a premium on-line research tool.

Pearson's **Research Navigator™** is the easiest way for students to start a research assignment or research paper. Complete with extensive help on the research process and four exclusive databases of credible and reliable source material including the EBSCO Academic Journal and Abstract Database, *New York Times* Search by Subject Archive, "Best of the Web" Link Library, and *Financial Times* Article Archive and Company Financials, Research Navigator helps students quickly and efficiently make the most of their research time.

Acknowledgments

A book of this nature cannot be written and published without the cooperation of many people. Many outside reviewers of this and the previous editions provided constructive suggestions for improving the book. The following reviewers provided detailed feedback that drove the refocusing of this edition:

Daniel Bialis, Muskegon Community College

Jewel Cherry, Forsyth Technical Community College

Claudia Cochran, El Paso Community College

Darlean McClure, College of the Sequoias

Michelle Meyer, Joliet Junior College

Alvin Motley, Metropolitan Community College

Debra Rowe, Oakland Community College

Reginald St. Clair, Mountain Empire Community College

Rudy Soliz, Houston Community College

Carol Thole, Shasta College

James Van Arsdall, Metropolitan Community College

Susan Verhulst, Des Moines Area Community College

Jim Wilhelm, South Plains College

Previous edition reviewers include the following:

Mary D. Aun, DeVry Technical Institute

Donna Ana Branch and H. Ralph Todd, Jr., American River College

Hollis Chaleau Brown, Oakton Community College

Sheri Bryant, DeKalb Technical Institute

Win Chesney, St. Louis Community College

Joy Colwell, Purdue University

Ruth Keller, Indiana Vo-Tech College

Robert F. Pearse, Rochester Institute of Technology

Steve Quinn, Olympic College

Bernice Rose, Computer Learning Center

Pamela Simon, Baker College

A special thanks goes to Therese Nemec and Kathy Lich at Fox Valley Technical College for assisting in the preparation of the instructors material for this edition.

Thanks also to my family members whose emotional support and encouragement assist my writing: Melanie, Will, Douglas, Gizella, Camila, Sofia, Drew, Rosie, and Clare.

Andrew J. DuBrin

Rochester, New York

An accomplished author, Andrew J. DuBrin, Ph.D., brings to his work years of research experience in human relations and business psychology. His research has been reported in *Entrepreneur, Psychology Today, The Wall Street Journal, Fortune Small Biz*, and more than 100 national magazines and local newspapers. He has published numerous articles, textbooks, and well-publicized professional books. Dr. DuBrin received his Ph.D. from Michigan State University and is professor emeritus at the College of Business, Rochester Institute of Technology, where he has taught organizational behavior, leadership, and career management.

Human Relations for Career
and Personal Success

1

Human Relations and You

Learning Objectives

Outline

After studying the information and doing the exercises in this chapter, you should be able to:

1 Describe the nature and importance of human relations.

2 Understand how studying human relations will help you.

3 Pinpoint how work and personal life influence each other.

4 Understand how effective human relations begins with self-understanding.

5 Understand the timeline and development of the human relations movement, plus the major concepts in human relations today.

6 Understand the major factors influencing job performance and behavior.

When David Neeleman, founder, chair, and Chief executive officer (CEO) of the highly successful airline JetBlue, was asked to describe his Golden Rule, he replied as follows:

My grandfather ran a general store, and if a customer needed something that wasn't in stock, he did whatever it took to get the item—even running across the street to a competitor— rather than asking the customer to take her business elsewhere. He never told me, "Take care of others, and they'll take care of you"—he didn't have to. I saw it happen.

When I entered the aviation business, I never thought in terms of "passengers" or "tickets sold" but of "people" and "customers." It was distressing to hear airline colleagues complain about the customers—even going so far as to say how much easier it would be for them if there were fewer passengers.

When JetBlue started flying in February 2000, my goal was to bring humanity back to air travel. We hire nice people and train them in the skills they require to help run the airline. . . . We are all servants in the best sense of the word, which brings amazing personal and professional rewards. [1]

The comments by the highly successful and much admired business executive David Neeleman focus on the importance of effective human relations. You have to be nice to begin with (have good human relations skills and a positive attitude), and then you have to treat your customers well (more good human relations skills.) This book presents a wide variety of suggestions and guidelines for improving your personal relationships both on and off the job. Most of them are based on systematic knowledge about human behavior.

What is the Nature and Importance of Human Relations?

■ **Learning Objective 1**

■ **Human relations**
the art of using systematic knowledge about human behavior to improve personal, job, and career effectiveness

In the context used here, **human relations** is the art of using systematic knowledge about human behavior to improve personal, job, and career effectiveness. Human relations is far more than "being nice to people" because it applies systematic knowledge to treating people in such a way that they feel better and are more productive, such as providing a more relaxed work atmosphere to enhance worker creativity.

Similar to the field known as *organizational behavior*, human relations studies individuals and groups in organizations. Human relations, however, is essentially a less technical and more applied version of organizational behavior. In this text we make some references to research and theory, but the emphasis is on a more personal and applied approach to the subject matter.

■ **Organizational effectiveness**
the extent to which an organization is productive and satisfies the demands of interested parties, such as employees, customers, and investors

From the standpoint of management, human relations is quite important because it contributes to **organizational effectiveness**—the extent to which an organization is productive and satisfies the demands of interested parties, such as employees, customers, and investors. Steve Kent, an equity analyst (not a human relations specialist) at Goldman Sachs & Co., made extensive observations about the importance of treating employees well (using principles of human relations). He found that treating employees with respect and paying them fairly contributes to developing an efficient and creative organization. Business firms that go the extra mile to treat employees well often derive tangible benefits, such as a high quality of customer service.

Kent notes that Starbucks Corporation is at the forefront of treating workers with respect. CEO Howard Schultz has set the tone from the top and made it clear that workers will not be neglected. For example, employees who work at least 20 hours per week are eligible for health benefits and may receive a chance to receive a stock option grant. (A stock option allows the employee to purchase stock at a specified price at a later date. So if the stock rises in price, the employee can buy it at a profit.) As a result of good human relations, Starbucks's employee turnover is low for the restaurant industry, and its customer service levels are high. [2]

Why does paying more attention to the human element improve business performance? Organizational behavior professor Jeffery Pfeffer at Stanford University notes that people work harder when they have greater control over their work environment, and when they are encouraged by peer pressure from teammates. Even more advantage comes from people working smarter. People-oriented management practices enable workers to use their wisdom and receive the training they need to perform better. Another contribution to improved performance stems from eliminating positions that focus primarily on watching and controlling people. [3] The accompanying Human Relations in Practice box insert provides additional information about the payoff from company management practicing good human relations.

Human Relations in Practice

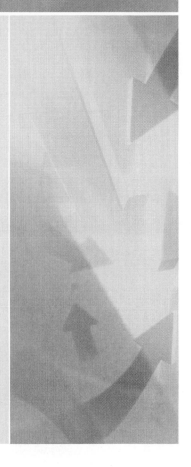

Growing a Technology Company by Focusing on People

When John Nix and Larry Spear founded a technology company as graduate business students, they were short on cash but big on ideas, including how to treat employees. Seven years later, as recipients of a Best Bosses award by Winning Workplaces and *Fortune Small Business*, the co-founders of Go2Call.com credit their employees for the company's ability to make money in the dot-com and telecom industries and achieve profitability at a time when many competitors failed.

At Go2Call, the company's 35 employees know exactly what they need to accomplish for the company to succeed, thanks to management's open-book philosophy, which involves sharing the company's financials with all workers at regular meetings. Staffers also have a stake in boosting the company's performance, by receiving bonuses based on profitability.

"It's the people who make the company," said Nix, recalling how his workers pulled together in 2001 to quickly launch a resellers platform, bringing the company a new revenue stream when it desperately needed it. Most of the staffers are still with the company. "Retention [of employees] has been really critical to our success," Nix said. "Our technology is complex. Our engineers have been building it for years—they understand it."

Question: So in what way are Nix and Spear practicing good human relations?

Source: Ann Meyer, "Firms Value Worker Morale as Asset: Employees' Ideas, Enthusiasm Can Have Effect on Bottom Line," *Chicago Tribune* on-line edition, September 26, 2005.

■ Learning Objective 2

How Can Studying Human Relations Help You?

Another way of understanding the importance of human relations is to examine its personal benefits. A person who carefully studies human relations and incorporates its suggestions into his or her work and personal life should derive the five benefits discussed next. Knowledge itself, however, is not a guarantee of success. Because people differ greatly in learning ability, personality, and life circumstances, some will get more out of studying human relations than will others. You may, for example, be getting along well with coworkers or customers so that studying this topic seems unnecessary from your viewpoint. Or you may be so shy at this stage of your life that you are unable to capitalize on some of the suggestions for being assertive with people. You might have to work doubly hard to benefit from studying that topic. The major benefits from studying human relations are the following:

1. **Acquiring valid information about human behavior.** To feel comfortable with people and to make a favorable impression both on and off the job, you need to understand how people think and act. Studying human relations will provide you with some basic knowledge about interpersonal relationships, such as the meaning of self-esteem, why goals work, and win–win conflict resolution. You will even learn such things as effective methods of dealing with difficult people.

2. **Developing skills in dealing with people.** People who aspire to high-level positions or enriched social lives need to be able to communicate with others, work well on a team, manage stress, and behave confidently. Relating well to diverse cultural groups is also an asset. Studying information about such topics, coupled with practicing what you learn, should help you develop such interpersonal skills. The accompanying Human Relations in Practice box insert illustrates how much employers value skills in dealing with people.

3. **Coping with job problems.** Almost everyone who holds a job inevitably runs into human relations problems. Reading about these problems and suggestions for coping with them could save you considerable inner turmoil. Among the job survival skills that you will learn about in the study of human relations are how to deal with difficult people and how to overcome what seems to be an overwhelming workload.

Human Relations in Practice

Personal Characteristics of Job Applicants Valued at Enterprise Auto

"We look for several attributes in potential employees, but, in short, Enterprise is made up of individuals who thrive on or being in charge or dream of being entrepreneurs. We look for individuals who have leadership skills and who have worked in some capacity to develop these skills. We also like to see individuals who are genuine team players, who are eager to share ideas, and who have demonstrated their enthusiasm and drive, and who have a customer service attitude."

Source: Andrew Taylor, CEO and Chairman of Enterprise Rent-A-Car, quoted in *BizEd*, July/August, 2003, p. 16.

4. **Coping with personal problems.** We all have problems. An important difference between the effective and the ineffective person is that the effective person knows how to manage them. Among the problems studying human relations will help you cope with are self-defeating behavior, dealing with a difficult coworker, overcoming low self-confidence, and working your way out of debt.

5. **Capitalizing on opportunities.** Many readers of this book will someday spend part of their working time taking advantage of opportunities rather than solving daily problems. Every career-minded person needs a few breakthrough experiences to make life more rewarding. Toward this end, studying human relations gives you ideas for developing your career and becoming a leader.

You are invited to take the accompanying Human Relations Self-Assessment Quiz 1-1 to think through your current level of human relations effectiveness.

How Do Work and Personal Life Influence Each Other?

■ **Learning Objective 3**

Most people reading this book will be doing so to improve their job effectiveness and careers. Therefore, the book centers on relationships with people in a job setting. Keep in mind that human relationships in work and personal life have much in common. Several studies have supported the close relationship between job satisfaction and life satisfaction. One such study conducted by Timothy A. Judge, psychology professor at the University of Florida, and Remus Ilies, psychology professor at Michigan State University, involved 74 university employees with administrative support positions, such as secretaries or office managers. The researchers collected reports of mood and job satisfaction at work, mood away from work, and job satisfaction. Data were collected using questionnaires posted on a Web site.

The major findings of the study were that mood influences job satisfaction, with a positive mood increasing satisfaction. The effect decreases rapidly because moods pass quickly. The researchers also found that employee's satisfaction with their jobs, measured at work, influences the mood at home. Workers who are more emotional by nature are more likely to experience these relationships, such as joy or anger, on the job spilling over to home life. A related finding was that a mood developed on the job spilled over to the home later in the day. [4] In short, this study confirmed the old cartoons about a worker who is chewed at by the boss coming home and swearing at his or her dog or kicking the furniture!

An earlier study by Judge and a colleague based on a nationwide sample supports the close relationship between job satisfaction and life satisfaction. The study also found that both job satisfaction and life satisfaction influence each other. Life satisfaction significantly influenced job satisfaction, and job satisfaction significantly influenced life satisfaction. The relationship between job and life satisfaction is particularly strong at a given time in a person's life. However, being satisfied with your job today has a smaller effect on future life satisfaction. [5]

Work and personal life influence each other in a number of specific ways. First, the satisfactions you achieve on the job contribute to your general life satisfactions. Conversely, if you suffer from chronic job dissatisfaction, your life satisfaction will begin to decline. Career disappointments have been shown to cause marital relationships to suffer. Frustrated on the job, many people start feuding with their partners and other family members.

Second, an unsatisfying job can affect physical health, primarily by creating stress and burnout. Intense job dissatisfaction may even lead to heart disease, ulcers, intestinal disorders, and skin problems. People who have high job satisfaction even

Human Relations Self-Assessment Quiz   1-1

Human Relations Skills

For each of the following statements about human relations skills, indicate how strong you think you are right now. Attempt to be as objective as possible, even though most of us tend to exaggerate our skills in dealing with people. To help obtain a more objective evaluation of your capabilities, ask someone who knows you well (family member, friend, or work associate) to also rate you on these factors. Use the following scale: (1) very weak, (2) weak, (3) average, (4) strong, (5) very strong.

	Self-Rating	Rating by Other Person
1. Listen carefully when in conversation with another person	_____	_____
2. Smile frequently	_____	_____
3. Tactful when criticizing others	_____	_____
4. Comfortable in dealing with people from a different generation from myself	_____	_____
5. Comfortable in dealing with a person from a different ethnic group from myself	_____	_____
6. Comfortable in dealing with a person from a different race than myself	_____	_____
7. Let my feelings be known when I disagree with another person	_____	_____
8. Let my feelings be known when I am joyful about something	_____	_____
9. Make a neat, well-groomed appearance	_____	_____
10. Congratulate the winner when I lose an athletic or any other type of contest	_____	_____
11. Concentrate on another person when in conversation instead of accepting a call on my cell phone, making use of call waiting, or responding to e-mail	_____	_____
12. Compliment others when the person merits a compliment	_____	_____
13. Good sense of humor	_____	_____
14. Patient with people who do not understand what I am saying	_____	_____
15. Cooperate with others in a team effort	_____	_____
16. Have controllable temper	_____	_____
17. Respected for being honest and dependable	_____	_____
18. Hug people when the situation is appropriate	_____	_____
19. Trusted by other people	_____	_____
20. Motivate others to do something they hadn't thought of doing	_____	_____
Total Score	_____	_____
Combined Score (self plus other)		_____

Interpretation

1. **Self-ratings:** If your self-rating is 85 or more, and your scoring is accurate, you have exceptional human relations skills. Scores between 60 and 84 suggest moderate, or average, human relations skills. Scores of 59 and below suggest below-average human relations skills in the areas covered in this quiz.
2. **Rating by other person:** Because people tend to judge us a little more critically than we judge ourselves in human relations skills, use the following scale: 80 or more suggests exceptional human relations skills; 55 to 79 suggests moderate, or average, human relations skills; 55 and below suggests below-average human relations skills.
3. **Combined ratings:** 165 or more suggests exceptional human relations skills; 115 to 163 suggests moderate, or average, human relations skills; 114 or below suggests below-average human relations skills.

Action plan: Whether you scored high, low, or medium on this quiz, there is always room for improvement, just as athletes, actors, and musicians are always looking to improve their art. Scores in the bottom category suggest a more urgent need for improvement in human relations skill.

tend to live longer than those who suffer from prolonged job dissatisfaction. These benefits may be attributed to better physical health and passion for life. Finding the right type of job may thus add years to a person's life.

Third, the quality of your relationships with people at work and in personal life influence each other. If you experience intense conflict in your family, you might be so upset that you will be unable to form good relationships with coworkers. Conversely, if you have a healthy, rewarding personal life, it will be easier for you to form good relationships on the job. People you meet on the job will find it pleasant to relate to a seemingly positive and untroubled person.

Personal relationships on the job also influence personal relationships off the job. Interacting harmoniously with coworkers can put one in a better mood for dealing with family and friends after hours. Crossing swords with employees and customers during working hours can make it difficult for you to feel comfortable and relaxed with people off the job.

Fourth, certain skills contribute to success in both work and personal life. For example, people who know how to deal effectively with others and get things accomplished on the job can use the same skills to enhance their personal lives. Similarly, people who are effective in dealing with friends and family members and who can organize things are likely to be effective supervisors. Can you think of other ways in which success in work and success in personal life are related to each other?

In What Way Does Human Relations Begin with Self-Understanding?

■ Learning Objective 4

Before you can understand other people very well, and therefore practice effective human relations, you must understand yourself. All readers of this book already know something about themselves. An important starting point in learning more about yourself is self-examination. Suppose that instead of being about human relations, this book were about dancing. The reader would obviously need to know what other dancers do right and wrong. But the basic principles of dancing cannot be fully grasped unless they are seen in relation to your own style of dancing. Watching a DVD of your dancing, for example, would be helpful. You might also ask other people for comments and suggestions about your dance movements.

Similarly, to achieve **self-understanding,** you must gather valid information about yourself. (Self-understanding refers to knowledge about you, particularly with respect to mental and emotional aspects.) Every time you read a self-help book, take a personality quiz, or receive an evaluation of your work from a manager or instructor, you are gaining some self-knowledge.

■ **Self-understanding**
gathering valid information about oneself; self-understanding refers to knowledge about oneself, particularly with respect to mental and emotional aspects

In achieving self-understanding, it is helpful to recognize that the **self** is a complex idea. It generally refers to a person's total being or individuality. A neuroscientist expressed wonder at the experience referred to as the self in these words:

■ **Self**
a complex idea generally refering to a person's total being or individuality

> *It is astonishing that we have a sense of self at all, that we have—that most of us have, that some of us have—come continuity of structure and function that constitutes identity, some stable traits of behavior we call a personality. Fabulous indeed, amazing for certain, that you are you and I am me.* [6]

To help clarify the meaning of the self, a distinction is sometimes made between the self a person projects to the outside world and the inner self. The **public self** is what the person is communicating about himself or herself and what others actually perceive about the person. The **private self** is the actual person you may be. [7] A similar distinction is made between the real self and the ideal self. Many people think of themselves in terms of an ideal version of what they are really like. To avoid

■ **Public self**
what a person communicates about himself or herself and what others actually perceive about the person

■ **Private self**
the actual person an individual may be

making continuous distinctions between the various selves throughout this text, we will use the term *self* to refer to an accurate representation of the individual.

Some scientific evidence suggests that the self is based on structures within the brain. According to the research of Joseph LeDoux at New York University, the self is the sum of the brain's individual components, or subsystems. Each subsystem has its own form of memory, along with its interactions with other subsystems. [8] Two examples of subsystems in the brain would be a center for speech and a center for hearing. The implication to recognize here is that the self could be an entity that is both psychological and biological.

Because we discuss the self in the first chapter, it does not imply that the other chapters do not deal with the self. Most of this text is geared toward using human relations knowledge for self-development and self-improvement. Throughout the text you will find questionnaires designed to improve insight. The self-knowledge emphasized here deals with psychological (such as personality traits and thinking style) rather than physical characteristics (such as height and blood pressure). Here we discuss five types of information that contribute to self-understanding, along with potential problems in self-evaluation.

GENERAL INFORMATION ABOUT HUMAN BEHAVIOR

As you learn about people in general, you should also be gaining knowledge about yourself. Therefore, most of the information in this text is presented in a form that should be useful to you personally. Whenever general information is presented, it is your responsibility to relate such information to your particular situation. One such general cause is limited resources, that is, not everyone can have what he or she wants. See how this general principle applies to you. An example involving others is, "That's why I've been so angry with Melissa lately. She was the one given the promotion, whereas I'm stuck in the same old job."

In relating facts and observations about people in general to yourself, be careful not to misapply the information. Feedback from other people will help you avoid the pitfalls of introspection (looking into yourself).

INFORMAL FEEDBACK FROM PEOPLE

■ **Feedback**
information that tells one how well he or she has performed

As just implied, **feedback** is information that tells you how well you have performed. You can sometimes obtain feedback from the spontaneous comments of others or by asking them for feedback. An order-fulfillment materials-handling specialist grew one notch in self-confidence when coworkers began to call him "Net Speed." He was given this name because of the rapidity with which he processed orders. His experience illustrates that a valuable source of information for self-understanding is what the significant people in your life think of you. Although feedback of this type might make you feel uncomfortable, when it is consistent, it accurately reflects how others perceive you.

With some ingenuity you can create informal feedback. (In this sense, the term *formal* refers to not being part of a company-sponsored program.) A student enrolled in a human relations course obtained valuable information about himself from a questionnaire he sent to 15 people. His directions were as follows:

> I am hoping that you can help me with one of the most important assignments of my life. I want to obtain a candid picture of how I am seen by others—what they think are my strengths, areas for improvement, good points, and bad points. Any other observations about me as an individual would also be welcome.
>
> Write down your thoughts on the attached questionnaire. The information that you provide me will help me develop a plan for personal improvement that I am writing for a course in human relations. Mail the form back to me in the enclosed envelope. It is not

necessary for you to sign the form. If you are not concerned about being anonymous, just fill out the questionnaire on the document in the e-mail I sent you.

A few skeptics will argue that friends never give you a true picture of yourself but, rather, say flattering things about you because they value your friendship. Experience has shown, however, that if you emphasize the importance of their opinions, most people will give you a few constructive suggestions. You also have to appear sincere. Because not everyone's comments will be helpful, you may have to sample many people.

FEEDBACK FROM SUPERIORS

Virtually all employers provide employees with formal or informal feedback on their performances. A formal method of feedback is called a *performance evaluation*. During a performance evaluation (or appraisal) your superior will convey to you what he or she thinks you are doing well and not so well. These observations become a permanent part of your human resources record. Informal feedback occurs when a superior discusses your job performance with you but does not record these observations.

The feedback obtained from superiors in this way can help you learn about yourself. For instance, if two different bosses say that you are a creative problem solver, you might conclude that you are creative. If several bosses told you that you are too impatient with other people, you might conclude that you are impatient.

FEEDBACK FROM COWORKERS

A sometimes-used practice in organizations is **peer evaluations,** a system in which teammates contribute to an evaluation of a person's job performance. Although coworkers under this system do not have total responsibility for evaluating each other, their input is taken seriously. The amount of a worker's salary increase could thus be affected by peer judgments about his or her performance. The results of peer evaluations can also be used as feedback for learning about yourself. Assume that coworkers agree on several of your strengths and needs for improvement. You can conclude that others who work closely with you generally perceive you that way.

Teammates might rate each other on performance dimensions such as cooperation with other members of the team, customer service attitude, productivity, and contributions to meetings. If several teammates rated you low in one of these dimensions, it could indicate a **developmental opportunity,** an area for growth, or weakness.

■ **Peer evaluations**
system in which teammates contribute to an evaluation of a person's job performance

■ **Developmental opportunity**
teammates rating one another on performance dimensions, such as cooperation with other members of the team, customer service attitude, productivity, and contribution to meetings

FEEDBACK FROM SELF-ASSESSMENT QUIZZES

Many self-help books, including this one, contain questionnaires that you fill out by yourself, for yourself. The information that you pick up from these questionnaires often provides valuable clues to your preferences, values, and personal traits. Such self-examination questionnaires should not be confused with the scientifically researched test you might take in a counseling center or guidance department or when applying for a job. Another source of useful self-assessment quizzes is ***www.queedom.com***, which offers a variety of tests that contribute to self-understanding, including the classical Intelligence quotient (IQ), mental toughness, risk-taking, and self-esteem among many others.

The amount of useful information gained from self-examination questionnaires depends on your candor. Because no outside judge is involved in these self-help

Human Relations Self-Assessment Quiz   **1-2**

The Written Self-Portrait

A good starting point in acquiring serious self-knowledge is to prepare a written self-portrait in the major life spheres (or aspects). In each of the following spheres, describe yourself in about 25 to 50 words. For example, under the social and interpersonal sphere, a person might write, "I'm a little timid on the surface. But those people who get to know me well understand that I'm filled with enthusiasm and joy. My relationships with people last a long time. I'm on excellent terms with all members of my family. And my significant other and I have been together for five years. We are very close emotionally and should be together for a lifetime."

A. Occupational and school: _____

_____

_____

_____

B. Social and interpersonal: _____

_____

_____

_____

C. Beliefs, values, and attitudes: _____

_____

_____

_____

D. Physical description (body type, appearance, grooming): _____

_____

_____

_____

quizzes, candor usually is not a problem. An exception is that we all have certain blind spots. Most people, for example, believe that they have considerably above-average skills in dealing with people.

As a starting point in conducting self-examination exercises, you already completed Human Relations Self-Assessment Quiz 1–1. Quiz 1-2 gives you an opportunity to write some things down about yourself.

TWO SELF-EVALUATION TRAPS

The theme of this section of the chapter is that self-awareness is a positive force in our lives. Yet self-awareness also has two negative extremes or traps. One of these extremes is that focusing on the self can highlight shortcomings the way staring into a mirror can dramatize every blemish and wrinkle on a face. Certain situations predictably force us to engage in self-reflection and become the object of our own attention. When we talk about ourselves, answer self-quizzes, stand before an audience or camera, or watch ourselves on DVD or videotape, we become more self-aware and make comparisons to some arbitrary standard of behavior. The comparison often results in negative self-evaluation in comparison to the standard and a decrease in self-esteem as we discover that we fall short of standards. [9] Keeping the self-awareness trap in mind will help you minimize needless underevaluation, thereby benefiting from gathering feedback about yourself.

In contrast to underevaluation, it is also true that many people tend to overestimate their competence, such as thinking they deserve a bigger raise or an A in every course. A particular area in which people overestimate their competence is in the moral domain. Many people suffer from a *"holier than thou"* syndrome. A study with college students, for example, found that they consistently overrated the likelihood that they would act in generous or selfless ways. For example, in one study 84 percent of the students initially predicted that they would cooperate with their partner but in reality only 61 percent did. [10]

Cultural differences help explain at least some of the differences in underevaluation versus overevaluation. Several studies have shown, for example, that East Asians tend to underestimate their abilities, with an aim toward improving the self and getting along with others. North Americans are more likely to overestimate their abilities and not be so prone to look for areas of self-improvement. [11] Cultural differences are stereotypes that apply to the average individual from a culture.

The antidote to the twin self-evaluation traps is to search for honest and objective feedback from others to help you supplement your self-evaluation. Competing against peers, such as in school, sports, and contests on the job (for example, a sales contest or creative suggestion contest) can help you evaluate yourself more realistically. Next, we look more at human relations from the standpoint of the workplace rather than the individual.

How Did the Human Relations Movement Develop?

■ **Learning Objective 5**

The **human relations movement** began as a concentrated effort by some managers and their advisors to become more sensitive to the needs of employees or to treat them in a more humanistic manner. In other words, employees were to be treated as human beings rather than as parts of the productive process. The human relations movement was supported directly by three different historic influences: the Hawthorne studies, the threat of unionization, and industrial humanism (see Figure 1-1). [12] Scientific management, which predated the growth of human relations in industry, contributed indirectly to the movement.

■ **Human relations movement**
movement that began as a concentrated effort by some managers and their advisors to become more sensitive to the needs of employees or to treat them in a more humanistic manner

SCIENTIFIC MANAGEMENT

The study of management became more systematized and formal as a by-product of the Industrial Revolution that took place from the 1700s through the 1900s. Approaches to managing work and people needed to be developed to manage all the new factories that were a central part of the Industrial Revolution. The focus of **scientific management** was on the application of scientific methods to increase individual workers' productivity. Frederick W. Taylor, considered the father of scientific management, was an engineer by background. He used scientific analysis and experiments to increase worker output. Taylor's goal was to remove human

■ **Scientific management**
theory that focuses on the application of scientific methods to increase individual workers' productivity

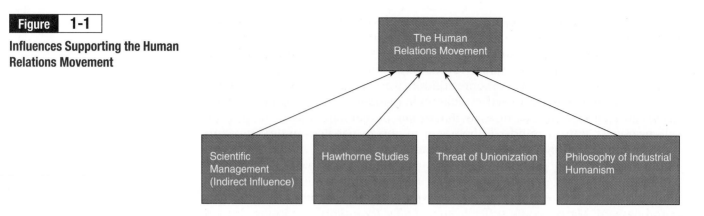

Figure **1-1**

Influences Supporting the Human Relations Movement

variability so each worker could become essentially an interchangeable part. His model for human behavior was a machine, with inexpensive parts, each of which has a specific function. Using the principles of scientific management, a worker might assemble a washing machine with the least number of wasted motions and steps. United Parcel Service (UPS) relies heavily on the principles of scientific management to get the most productivity from carriers and shipping personnel, including tightly timing their deliveries.

With scientific management sounding so dehumanizing, how could the movement have contributed to good human relations? Taylor also studied problems such as fatigue and safety. He urged management to study the relationship between work breaks and the length of the workday, and productivity. He convinced some managers that work breaks and shorter workdays could increase productivity. Furthermore, scientific management proposed that workers who produced more be paid more.

Scientific management also contributed to the human relations movement by creating a backlash against what many people thought was mistreatment of workers. The industrial engineer with his or her stopwatch and clipboard, hovering over a worker measuring each tiny part of the job and the worker's movements, became a hated figure. [13] The objection to this approach called for a better way to treat people, that came to be known as the human relations movement.

THE HAWTHORNE STUDIES

The human relations school of management is generally said to have begun in 1927 with a group of studies conducted at the Hawthorne plant of an AT&T subsidiary. These studies were prompted by an experiment carried out by the company's engineers between 1924 and 1927. Following the tradition of scientific management, these engineers were applying research methods to investigate problems of employee productivity.

Two groups were studied to determine the effects of different levels of illumination on worker performance. As prescribed by the scientific method, one group received increased illumination, whereas the other did not. A preliminary finding was that when illumination was increased, the level of performance also increased. Surprisingly to the engineers, productivity also increased when the level of illumination was decreased almost to moonlight levels. One interpretation of these findings was that the workers involved in the experiment enjoyed being the center of attention. In other words, they reacted positively because management cared about them. Such a phenomenon taking place in any work or research setting is now called the **Hawthorne effect.** [14]

As a result of these preliminary investigations, a team of researchers headed by Harvard professors Elton Mayo and Fritz J. Roethlisberger conducted a series of

■ **Hawthorne effect**

applying research methods to investigate problems of employee productivity using the scientific method; in the study, employees reacted positively because management cared about them experiments extending over a six-year period. The conclusions they reached served as the foundations for later developments in the human relations approach to management. It was found that economic incentives are less important than generally believed in influencing workers to achieve high levels of output. Also, leadership practices and work-group pressures profoundly influence employee satisfaction and performance. An example of an effective leadership practice would be coaching and encouraging workers to higher performance. The researchers noted that any factor influencing employee behavior is embedded in a social system. For example, to understand the impact of pay on performance, you have to understand the atmosphere that exists in the work group and how the leader approaches his or her job.

A major implication of the Hawthorne studies was that the old concept of an economic person motivated primarily by money had to be replaced by a more valid idea. The replacement concept was a social person, motivated by social needs, desiring rewarding on-the-job relationships, and more responsive to pressures from coworkers than to control by the boss. [15] Do you believe that workers are more concerned with social relationships than with money?

THE THREAT OF UNIONIZATION

Labor union officials and their advocates contend that the benefits of unionization extend to many workers who themselves do not belong to unions. Management in nonunion firms will often pay employees union wages in order to offset the potential advantages of unionization. A similar set of circumstances contributed to the growth of the human relations movement. Labor unions began to grow rapidly in the United States during the late 1930s. Many employers feared that the presence of a labor union would have negative consequences for their companies. Consequently, management looked aggressively for ways to stem the tide of unionization, such as using human relations techniques to satisfy workers. [16] Their reasoning is still valid today: dissatisfied workers are much more likely to join a labor union, in hope of improving their working conditions. [17]

Today the threat of unionization is primarily in the public sector. Although unionization has declined considerablly in manufacturing, about 36 percent of government workers, including those in education, are union members compared with about 8 percent of workers in private-sector industries. In 1945 about 36 percent of the U.S. workforce was unionized, versus about 12 percent today. [18] The decline of manufacturing jobs has contributed to the decline of union membership.

THE PHILOSOPHY OF INDUSTRIAL HUMANISM

Partly as a by-product of the Hawthorne studies, a new philosophy arose of human relations in the workplace. Elton Mayo was one of the two key figures in developing this philosophy of industrial humanism. He cautioned managers that emotional factors (such as a desire for recognition) were a more important contributor to productivity than physical and logical factors. Mayo argued vigorously that work should lead to personal satisfaction for employees.

Mary Parker Follett was another key figure in advancing the cause of industrial humanism. Her experience as a management consultant led her to believe that the key to increased productivity was to motivate employees, rather than simply ordering better job performance. The keys to both productivity and democracy, according to Follett, were cooperation, a spirit of unity, and a coordination of effort. [19]

THEORY X AND THEORY Y OF DOUGLAS MCGREGOR

The importance of managing people through more effective methods of human relations was advanced by the writings of social psychologist Douglas McGregor. His famous position was that managers should challenge their assumptions about the nature of people. McGregor believed that too many managers assumed that people were lazy and indifferent toward work. He urged managers to be open to the possibility that under the right circumstances people are eager to perform well. If a supervisor accepts one of these extreme sets of beliefs about people, the supervisor will act differently toward them than if he or she believes the opposite. These famous assumptions that propelled the human relations movement forward are summarized as follows:

Theory X Assumptions

1. The average person dislikes work and, therefore, will avoid it if he or she can.

2. Because of this dislike of work, most people must be coerced, controlled, directed, or threatened with punishment to get them to put forth enough effort to achieve organizational goals.

3. The average employee prefers to be directed, wishes to shirk responsibility, has relatively little ambition, and highly values job security.

Theory Y Assumptions

1. The expenditure of physical and mental effort in work is as natural as play or rest.

2. External control and the threat of punishment are not the only means for bringing about effort toward reaching company objectives. Employees will exercise self-direction and self-control in the service of objectives to which they attach high valence.

3. Commitment to objectives is related to the rewards associated with their achievement.

4. The average person learns, under proper conditions, not only to accept but also to seek responsibility.

5. Many employees have the capacity to exercise a high degree of imagination, ingenuity, and creativity in the solution of organizational problems.

6. Under the present conditions of industrial life, the intellectual potentialities of the average person are only partially utilized. [20]

The distinction between Theory X and Theory Y has often been misinterpreted. McGregor was humanistic, but he did not mean to imply that being directive and demanding with workers is always the wrong tactic. Some people are undermotivated and dislike work. In these situations, the manager has to behave sternly toward group members to motivate them. If you are a Theory Y manager, you size up your group members to understand their attitudes toward work.

RELEVANCE OF THE HISTORY OF HUMAN RELATIONS TO TODAY'S WORKPLACE

Many of the pioneering ideas described in the history of human relations are still relevant, partly because human nature has not undergone major changes. Most of the core ideas in the history of the human relations movement are still part of the human relations and organizational behavior curriculum today, even though they have more research substantiation and new labels. A good example is the push toward creativity and innovation based on the involvement of loads of workers, not only specialists from one department. The link to history is that Theory Y encourages empowering employees to use their ingenuity and creativity to solve organizational problems. Next is a bulleted summary of ideas from the human relations movement that still influence the practice of human relations today.

- Many principles of scientific management are useful in making workers more productive so business firms can compete better in a global economy.

- Ideas from the Hawthorne studies have helped managers focus on the importance of providing both congenial work surroundings and adequate compensation in order to motivate and retain workers.

- Industrial humanism is widely practiced today in the form of looking for ways to keep workers satisfied through such methods as flexible work arrangements, family leave, and dependent care benefits.

- Theory Y has prompted managers to think through which style of leadership works best with which employees. Specifically, a modern manager is likely to grant more freedom to employees who are well-motivated and talented. Spurred partially by Theory X, few managers today believe that being the "bull of the woods" is the best way to supervise all workers.

MAJOR CONCEPTS IN HUMAN RELATIONS TODAY

A major purpose of this text is to provide a presentation of major concepts or themes in human relations today. Ideas already presented in this chapter, including the modern-day spinoffs from the human relations movement, are major themes in human relations. Subsequent chapters in this text deal with these plus other major concepts in human relations today. In quick overview, here are the major themes and concepts of human relations you will be studying:

- **Self-understanding.** Practicing good human relations begins with self-understanding.

- **Self-esteem and self-confidence.** It helps to feel good about yourself when you are dealing with others.

- **Self-motivation and self-discipline.** You cannot succeed in today's world if you cannot light your own fire. Without being focused individuals usually accomplish very little.

- **Emotional intelligence and positive attitudes.** Having technical smarts is not enough. You need to be able to understand people and have a positive, can-do attitude.

- **Values and ethics.** Most of the greatest business flops in recent years can be attributed to warped values and low ethics.

- **Problem solving and creativity.** All types of workplaces seek imaginative and creative employees in professional and technical positions. If you can only provide standard solutions to problems, you are in danger of being replaced by software or a handbook.

- **Communication effectiveness.** A major requirement for success in both technical and nontechnical positions is being able to communicate effectively with other people. Organizations also have a responsibility to establish systems that enhance communication among people, including company blogs as a recent development.

■ **Getting along with others in the workplace.** When one cave-person grunted to the other, "Good job catching fish," the importance of constructive relationships with managers, coworkers, and customers began. Developing effective interpersonal relationships remains the major purpose of studying human relations and one of the major requirements for a successful workplace.

■ **Managing conflict.** Managing conflict is another major concern of human relations. Too much unresolved conflict results in such negative consequences as negative stress, strikes, and worker violence.

■ **Leadership.** The study of how to effectively lead others has become the hottest topic in human relations, organizational behavior, and management in the past decade. Effective leaders are in demand at every level of the organization from team leader to chief executive officer.

■ **Motivating others and developing teamwork.** Motivating employees to high standards of performance is still seen as a major pathway to productivity and competitiveness. At the same time, the leader must develop teamwork because business is a team sport.

■ **Diversity and cross-cultural competence.** The workplace has become increasingly diverse both domestically and in terms of working with people from other countries. Being able to work effectively with diverse individuals has become one of the major human relations competencies.

■ **Learning strategies, perception, and life-span changes.** Three significant topics in managing our life are understanding how we learn, how we make sense out of the world (perception) and how to deal with a variety of predictable challenges from adolescence to the final stages of physical life.

■ **Developing effective work habits.** A starting point in being productive is managing your work and time effectively, including overcoming the number-one form of self-defeating behavior—procrastination. Human relations emphasizes being productive as well as getting along well with others.

■ **Getting ahead in your career.** Another useful aspect of studying human relations is to strategize ways of getting the biggest return on your most important asset—you. Understanding how to become successful has become even more important as so many people's careers are threatened by moving some jobs to other countries.

■ **Managing stress and personal problems.** Staying mentally and physically healthy is a human relations issue because organizations need productive workers who are not so stressed out or distracted that they lose time from work and run up medical costs.

■ Learning Objective 6

What Major Factors Influence Job Performance and Behavior?

Part of understanding human relations is recognizing the factors or forces that influence job performance and behavior. In overview, the performance and behavior of workers is influenced by both factors related to the employee, manager, job, and organization as discussed next and outlined in Figure 1-2. Here we present a sampling of these many factors because a comprehensive understanding of them would encompass the study of human relations, organizational behavior, and management.

1. **Factors related to the employee.** The major influence on how a worker performs and behaves, or acts, on the job stems from his or her personal attributes.

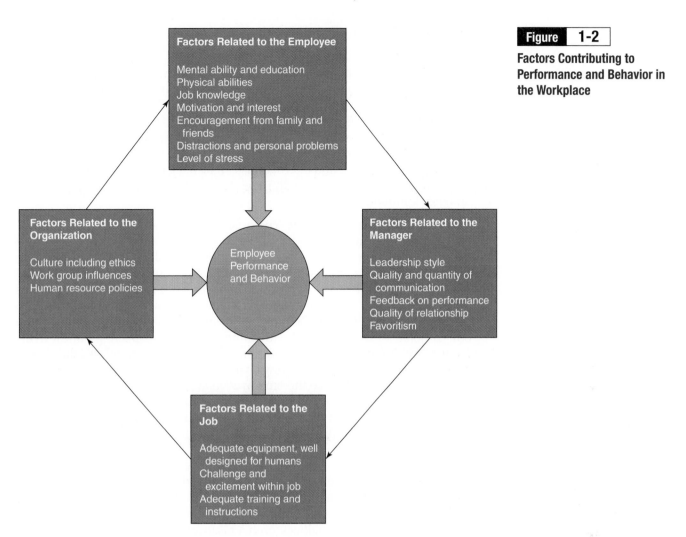

Figure 1-2

Factors Contributing to Performance and Behavior in the Workplace

The worker's mental ability influences how quickly and accurately he or she can solve problems. Physical ability would influence some types of performance, such as the ability to stand up for long periods of time as a store manager or lift boxes as a warehouse attendant. Job knowledge is obviously important, such as a financial consultant being knowledgeable about a variety of investments. Employees who are well motivated and interested in the work are likely to perform better and behave in a more professional manner. Workers who receive encouragement from friends and family are likely to perform better. Being distracted, such as Internet surfing during the workday or experiencing heavy personal problems, can influence performance negatively. Having the right amount of stress can boost performance, whereas being overstressed can lower performance and distracting behavior such as appearing confused.

2. **Factors related to the manager.** The manager, or supervisor, is another major influence on work behavior. A manager's whose style, or approach, is warm and supportive is likely to bring out the best in many employees. However, some workers required a more directive and demanding supervisor to perform at their best. Ample communication among the manager and group members is likely to enhance performance and guide employees toward doing what is expected of them. Most workers need considerable feedback from their supervisor to stay on track and be highly motivated. A high-quality relationship between the manager and group members leads to high performance, more loyalty, and lower absenteeism. Favoritism is another key factor related to the

manager. A manager who plays favorites is less likely to gain the cooperation of the entire group.

3. **Factors related to the job.** The job itself influences how well the worker might perform and behave. Given the right equipment, designed well for human use, a worker is likely to perform better, such as being less likely to have aches, pains, and wrist injuries as a result of many hours of keyboarding. A proven strategy for improving worker motivation is to give the employee an exciting, challenging job, such as the opportunity to make presentations to management about a project. Adequate training and instructions can be a big boost to job performance. For example, IBM invests annually more than $100 million in employee training and development.

4. **Factors related to the organization.** The organization as a whole can have a profound influence on the individual worker's performance and behavior. The *culture*, or atmosphere and values of a company, establishes an unwritten standard for how employees perform and behave. At Google, for example, employees are placed in an atmosphere where being creative and making suggestions is expected. And all Southwest Airlines employees know that having fun is supposed to be part of the job. The culture of the organization also influences the ethical behavior of employees, with some companies expecting honest treatment of workers and employees. Other companies are much less ethical, and encourage tactics such as deceiving customers. The work group, as part of the organization, can influence the employee in such ways as encouraging teamwork and high productivity. Human resource policies are another notable influence on the individual. If your company offers you generous medical and dental benefits, and allows time off for family emergencies, it becomes easier to concentrate on the job.

The four factors just listed often have a combined influence on the worker. Let us take an extreme example: Jack, a well-motivated and talented assistant hotel manager, reports to a manager with whom he has a great relationship, which includes giving Jack ample feedback on his performance. Jack finds his job challenging, and his hotel has the advanced equipment necessary for success. The hotel has a friendly climate, along with generous benefits. As a result of this combination of factors, Jack is an outstanding performer who approaches his job with a high degree of professionalism.

Concept Review and Reinforcement

Key Terms

Summary and Review

Human relations is the art and practice of using systematic knowledge about human behavior to improve personal, job, and career effectiveness. From the standpoint of management, human relations is important because it contributes to organizational effectiveness. Treating employees with respect and paying them fairly contributes to developing an efficient and creative organization.

Major benefits of studying human relations include:

- Acquiring information about human behavior
- Developing skills in dealing with people
- Coping with job problems
- Coping with personal problems
- Capitalizing on opportunities

Work and personal life often influence each other in several ways, as follows:

- Mood influences job satisfaction, but the effect passes quickly.
- Job satisfaction influences the mood at home, with more emotional employees more likely to experience this relationship.
- A high level of job satisfaction tends to spill over to your personal life. Conversely, an unsatisfactory personal life could lead to negative job attitudes.
- Your job can affect physical and mental health. Severely negative job conditions may lead to a serious stress disorder, such as heart disease.
- The quality of relationships with people in work and personal life influence each other.
- Certain skills (such as the ability to listen) contribute to success in work and personal life.

To be effective in human relationships, you must first understand yourself. Five types of information that contribute to self-understanding are as follows:

- General information about human behavior
- Informal feedback from people
- Feedback from superiors
- Feedback from coworkers
- Feedback from self-examination exercises

Be aware of the self-evaluation traps of highlighting your shortcomings and unrealistically overevaluating your competence. Cultural differences help explain some of the differences in underevaluation versus overevaluation.

The human relations movement was a concentrated effort to become more sensitive to the needs of employees or to treat them in a more humanistic manner. The movement was supported directly by three historic influences along with the indirect influence of scientific management:

- Scientific management applied scientific methods to increase worker productivity.
- The Hawthorne studies showed that concern for workers can increase their performance as much or more than improving physical working conditions.
- The threat of unionization, in which (management used human relations techniques to deter workers from joining a labor union.
- The philosophy of industrial humanism, in which motivation and emotional factors are important.

Many of the pioneering ideas described in the history of human relations are still relevant, partly because human nature has not undergone major changes. An example of a pioneering idea in use is that Theory Y has prompted managers to think through which style of leadership works best with which employees.

The major concepts in human relations today are reflected in the chapter topics of this text, including understanding the self, dealing effectively with people, developing career thrust, and staying emotionally healthy.

The major factors influencing job performance and behavior are related to the employee, manager, job, and organization.

Check your Understanding

1. Why do you think good human relations skills are so important for supervisors who direct the work activities of entry-level workers?
2. Give an example of a business executive, politician, athletic coach, or professor whom you think has exceptional human relations skills. On what basis did you reach your conclusion?
3. Give an example from your own experience of how work life influences personal life and vice versa.
4. How might a person improve personal life to the extent that the improvement would also enhance job performance?
5. How might a person improve his or her job or career to the extent that the improvement would actually enhance personal life?

6. Of the five sources of information about the self described in this chapter, which one do you think is likely to be the most accurate? Why?
7. How can your self-concept affect your career?
8. How might you improve your self-efficacy for a specific job that you are performing?
9. Imagine yourself as a manager or small-business owner. How might you apply the Hawthorne effect to increase the productivity of workers reporting to you?
10. In your current job, or any previous one, which set of factors had the biggest impact on your performance and behavior—those related to the employee, manager, job, or organization? How do you know?

Web Corner

The Dale Carnegie organization has long been associated with teaching human relations effectiveness. The company stemmed from the work of Dale Carnegie who many years ago popularized the idea of "winning friends and influencing people." Visit *www.dale-carnegie.com/* to understand what type of skills Dale Carnegie teaches. Compare the course listing to subjects listed in the table of contents in this text. What similarities do you see?

INTERNET SKILL BUILDER *The Importance of Human Relations Skills in Business*

One of the themes of this chapter and the entire book is that human relations skills are important for success in business. But what do employers really think? To find out, visit the Web sites of five of your favorite companies, such as www.apple.com or www.ge.com. Go to the employment section and search for a job that you might qualify for now or in the future. Investigate which human relations or interpersonal skills the employer mentions as a requirement, such as "Must have superior spoken communication skills." Make up a list of the human relations, or interpersonal skills, you find mentioned. What conclusion or conclusions do you reach from this exercise?

Developing Your Human Relations Skills

Human Relations Application Exercises

Applying Human Relations Exercise 1-1

Learning about Each Other's Human Relations Skills

A constructive way of broadening your insights about human relations skills is to find out what other people perceive as their strengths in dealing with others. Toward this end, each class member comes to the front of the class, one-by-one, to make a two-minute presentation on his or her best ability in dealing with people. To help standardize the presentations, each student answers the following question: "What I do best with people is _____."

In this exercise, and all other class presentation exercises contained in the text, students are asked to share only those ideas they would be comfortable in sharing with the class. Here, for example, you might be very good at doing something with people about which you would be embarrassed to let others know.

As the other students are presenting, attempt to concentrate on them and not be so preoccupied with your presentation that you can not listen. Make note when somebody says something out of the ordinary. When the presentation is over, the class will discuss answers to the following questions:

1. What was the most frequent human relations capability mentioned?
2. To what extent do classmates appear to be exaggerating their human relations skills?
3. What omissions did you find? For example, were there any important human relations skills you thought a few students should have mentioned but were not?

Applying Human Relations Exercise 1-2

My Human Relations Journal

A potentially important aid in your development as a person with effective human relations skills is to maintain a journal or diary of your experiences. Make a journal entry within 24 hours after you carried out a significant human relations action, or failed to do so when the opportunity arose. You, therefore, will have entries dealing with human relations opportunities both capitalized on and missed. Here is an example: "A few of my neighbors were complaining about all the vandalism in the neighborhood. Cars were getting dented and scratched, and lamplights were being smashed. A few bricks were thrown into home windows. I volunteered to organize a neighborhood patrol. The patrol actually helped cut back on the vandalism." Or, in contrast: "A few of my neighbors . . . windows. I thought to myself that someone else should take care of the problem. My time is too valuable." (Here, the key human relations skill the person exercised was leadership.)

Also include in your journal such entries as feedback you receive on your human relations ability, good interpersonal traits you appear to be developing, and key human relations ideas about which you read.

Review your journal monthly, and make note of any progress you think you have made in developing your human relations skills. Also consider preparing a graph of your human relations skill development. The vertical axis can represent skill level on a 1-to-100 scale, and the horizontal axis might be divided into time internals, such as calendar quarters.

Human Relations Case Study 1-1

We Can't Afford Good Human Relations around Here

Tammy Ho was happy to be hired by Bradbury Foods as a supervisor in the main food processing plant. It was apparent to her that being a supervisor so soon after graduation from career school would be a real boost to her career. After about a month on the job, Tammy began to make some critical observations about the company and its style of management.

To clarify issues in her own mind, Tammy requested a meeting with Marcus Green, plant superintendent. The meeting between Ho and Green included a conversation of this nature:

Marcus: Have a seat, Tammy. It's nice to visit with one of our new supervisors. Particularly so when you didn't say you were facing an emergency that you and your boss couldn't handle.

Tammy: (*nervously*) Marcus, I want to express my appreciation for your willingness to meet with me. You're right, I'm not facing an emergency, and I am not here to complain about my boss. But I do wonder about something. That's what I came here to talk to you about.

Marcus: That's what I like to see—a young woman who takes the initiative to ask questions about things that are bothering her.

Tammy: To be truthful, I am happy here and I'm glad I joined Bradbury Foods. But I'm curious about one thing. As you may know, I majored in business at my career college. A few of the courses I took emphasized using human relations knowledge and skills to manage people—you know, kind of psychology on the job. It seems like the way to go if you want to keep employees productive and happy.

Here at Bradbury it seems that nobody uses human relations knowledge and skills. I know that we're a successful company. But some of the management practices seem out of keeping with the times. The managers make all the decisions. Everybody else listens and carries out orders. Even professionals on the payroll have to use time recording devices for checking in and checking out. I've been here for almost two months and I haven't even heard the term "human relations" used once.

Marcus: Oh, I get your point. You're talking about using human relations around here. I know all about that. The point you are missing, Tammy, is that human relations is for big, profitable companies. That stuff works great when business is good and profit margins are high. But around here business is so-so, and profit margins in the food business are thinner than a potato chip. Maybe someday when we get fat and profitable we can start using human relations. In the meantime, we've all got a job to do.

Tammy: I appreciate your candid answer, Marcus. But when I was in career school, I certainly heard a different version of why companies use human relations.

Questions

1. What is your evaluation of Marcus' contention that human relations knowledge is useful primarily when a firm is profitable?
2. To what extent should Tammy be discouraged?
3. What should Tammy do next about her concerns about the application of human relations knowledge at Bradbury?
4. Based on your experiences, how representative of most managers is Marcus's thinking?

Human Relations Case Study 1-2

Critical Carrie of the Claims Department

Carrie Donahoe is one of five claims examiners in a regional office of a large casualty and property insurance

company. The branch is still thriving despite the insurer selling many policies on-line, and billing conducted by a centralized office. The sales group sells policies and services existing business, such as consulting with managers and business owners about upgrading their policies. The sales representatives also answer questions about policies, such as whether the policy owner is covered against a terrorist attack.

Carrie works with four other examiners, as well as her supervisor Michelle Pettigrew. The essential job of the claims examiner is to visit the site of a client with a demand for reimbursement for damages, such as a fire, flood, or industrial accident. The claims examiner then files a report with a recommendation for payment that is reviewed by the examiner's supervisor. Also, the home office reviews estimated payments beyond $15,000. Carrie has held her position for five years. She has received satisfactory performance evaluations, particularly for the accuracy and promptness of her insurance claim reports.

Carrie has frequent negative interactions with her coworkers who resent many of her suggestions and criticisms. Jim, a senior claims analyst, says his nickname for Carrie is "Ms. Pit Bull," although he has not shared this nickname with her. Asked why he refers to Carrie as a pit bull, he replied, "It's not that Carrie physically attacks people, but it's that she's so negative about so many things. I'll give you two recent examples.

"Carrie asked me to show her a sample claims report for mud damage. I e-mailed her a report. Two days later she sent me back the report, underlining six words or phrases she said were wrong. She didn't even thank me for the report.

"I came back from a two-day trip to inspect a building damaged by a runaway truck. When I returned to the office, Carrie asked me why it took me two days to investigate a simple claim."

Sharon, a junior claims examiner, says that at her best Carrie is a charming coworker. Yet at her worst, she grates on people's nerves. "Here's what I'm talking about. Last week I came to work wearing a blue skirt and a red blouse, on a day the vice president of claims was coming to visit our office. Carrie tells me that a person should never wear a red-and-blue combination for a special event. Not only is Carrie critical, her criticisms are sometimes way off base.

"Another time she told me that I should not waste my time studying for advanced certification in claims because it's a waste of time. She said that no manager in the company really cares about certification. Either you can do your job or you can't."

A human resource specialist from the home office asked Michelle Pettigrew how she was handling Carrie's personality clashes with coworkers and about her personal relationship with Carrie. Michelle said that she was mildly concerned about Carrie's personality problems but that Carrie still gets her work done. Yet Michelle did mention that several clients indicated that Carrie surprised them with some of her criticisms of their operation. She told one tool-and-die shop owner that a well-managed firm never has a serious accident. That was the company's first claim in 50 years being insured by us.

"When she's snippy with me, I just shrug it off unless it gets too personal. Then I tell Carrie that she's gone too far. For example, a week ago she told me that I don't do a good job of getting enough resources for our branch. That if I were a strong branch manager, we would have our offices refurbished by now. I told Carrie that our conversation was now over."

The human resources director said to Michelle, "I think you and I should talk about effective ways of dealing with Carrie and her problems."

Questions

Note to student: You might want to peak ahead to the section in Chapter 9 about dealing with difficult people to give you some more ideas for case analysis here.

1. What do you recommend that Michelle Pettigrew do to improve Carrie's human relations skills in the office?
2. What is your evaluation of Michelle's approach to dealing with Carrie so far?
3. What do you recommend that Carrie's coworkers do to develop more harmonious relationships with her?

REFERENCES

1. David Neeleman, "My Golden Rule: Never, Ever Forget That You Are a Servant," *Business* 2.0, December 2005, p. 122.
2. Steven Kent, "Happy Workers Are the Best Workers," *The Wall Street Journal*, September 6, 2005, p. A20.
3. Jeffery Pfeffer, *The Human Equation* (Boston: Harvard Business School Press, 1998), p. 59; Pfeffer, "Producing Sustainable Competitive Advantage through the Effective Management of People," *Academy of Management Executive*, November 2005, pp. 95–108.
4. Timothy A. Judge and Remus Ilies, "Affect and Job Satisfaction: A Study of Their Relationship at Work and Home," *Journal of Applied Psychology*, August 2004, pp. 661–673.
5. Timothy A. Judge and Schinichiro Watanabe, "Another Look at the Job Satisfaction–Life Satisfaction Relationship," *Journal of Applied Psychology*, December 1993, pp. 939–948.
6. A. R. Damasio, *The Feeling of What Happens: Body and Emotion in the Making of Consciousness* (New York: Harcourt Brace, 1999), p. 144.
7. C. R. Snyder, "So Many Selves," *Contemporary Psychology*, January 1988, p. 77.
8. Etienne Benson, "The Synaptic Self," *Monitor on Psychology*, November 2002, p. 40.
9. Saul Kassin, *Psychology*, 3rd ed. (Upper Saddle River, NJ: Prentice Hall, 2001), p. 74.
10. Research summarized in Tori DeAngelis, "Why We Overestimate Our Competence," *Monitor on Psychology*, February 2003, p. 61.
11. Ibid.
12. Robert Kreitner, *Management*, 5th ed. (Boston: Houghton Mifflin, 1992), pp. 51–52.
13. Edward G. Wertheim, "Historical Background of Organizational Behavior," available at *http://web.cba.neu.edu/~werthein/introd/history.htm* retrieved March 15, 2006.
14. Elton Mayo, *The Human Problems of Industrial Civilization* (New York: Viking Press, 1960).
15. James A. F. Stoner and R. Edward Freeman, *Management*, 4th ed. (Upper Saddle River, N.J.: Prentice Hall, 1989), p. 49.
16. Kreitner, *Management*, p. 50.
17. Alan B. Krueger, "Job Satisfaction Is Not Just a Matter of Dollars," *The New York Times*, available at nytimes.com, retrieved December 8, 2005.
18. "Union Members Summary," *Bureau of Labor Statistics News*, available at (*www.bls.gov/news*), retrieved January 27, 2005.
19. Kreitner, *Management*, p. 62.
20. Douglas McGregor, *The Human Side of Enterprise* (New York: McGraw-Hill, 1960), pp. 33–48.

2

Self-Esteem and Self-Confidence

Learning Objectives

After studying the information and doing the exercises in this chapter, you should be able to:

1 Describe the nature, development, and consequences of self-esteem.

2 Explain how to enhance self-esteem.

3 Describe the importance of self-confidence and self-efficacy.

4 Pinpoint methods of enhancing and developing your self-confidence.

Outline

Family members who are entrepreneurs helped Eran Dekel start his own fashion company. But it was a chance connection with an uncle who owns a clothing store that started him in the fashion business. "My uncle asked me to help him liquidate some designer suits on the Internet. Right away, I thought of eBay," Dekel says. "When the first suit sold for a 300 percent profit, a light went on in my head." The same uncle helped him find wholesale suppliers—one of the biggest hurdles for any beginning eBay seller.

eBay challenges individuals to do their own market research to select, price, and present merchandise. Dekel, who graduated from Cooper Union in New York City with a degree in engineering, saw such activities as an extension of his studies. "The problem-solving and analytical capabilities I learned in college really prepared me for this type of business," he says. "You have to perform both quantitative and qualitative reasoning in determining what products to sell and you need to know how to think outside the box when it comes to completing transactions."

After finding success on eBay, Dekel was able to launch his own DeCalo Fashion Web site (www.decalofashion.com), and he shows boundless enthusiasm. "The potential for success is within each individual," he says. "You can't be afraid to take risks or try something new." [1]

The story just presented illustrates how self-confidence, such as being willing to take risks and try something new, helps a person succeed in a competitive field. Dekel also has to have high self-esteem to think that his analytical skills are so good that he can compete in the world of fashion. Many other people you will meet in this book score high in self-esteem and self-confidence—otherwise they would never have been so successful. In this chapter the focus is on two of the biggest building blocks for more effective human relations: the nature and development of self-esteem and self-confidence.

What is the Nature of Self-Esteem? How Does it Develop, and What are its Consequences?

■ **Learning Objective 1**

Understanding the self from various perspectives is important because who you are and what you think of yourself influences many facets of your life both on and off the job. A particularly important role is played by **self-esteem,** the experience of feeling competent to cope with the basic challenges in life and of being worthy of happiness. [2] In more general terms, self-esteem refers to a positive overall evaluation of oneself. People with positive self-esteem have a deepdown, inside-the-self feeling of their own worth. Consequently, they develop positive self-concepts. Before reading further, you are invited to measure your current level of self-esteem by taking the Human Relations Self-Assessment Quiz 2-1. Next the nature of self-esteem and many of its consequences are examined.

■ **Self-esteem**

the experience of feeling competent to cope with the basic challenges in life and of being worthy of happiness

THE NATURE OF SELF-ESTEEM

The definition of self-esteem presented reveals a lot about it, yet there is much more to know about its nature. According to Nathaniel Brandon, self-esteem has two

Human Relations Self-Assessment Quiz 2-1

The Self-Esteem Checklist

Indicate whether each of the following statements is Mostly True or Mostly False as it applies to you.

	Mostly True	Mostly False
1. I am excited about starting each day.	_____	_____
2. Most of any progress I have made in my work or school can be attributed to luck.	_____	_____
3. I often ask myself, "Why can't I be more successful?"	_____	_____
4. When my manager or team leader gives me a challenging assignment, I usually dive in with confidence.	_____	_____
5. I believe that I am working up to my potential.	_____	_____
6. I am able to set limits to what I will do for others without feeling anxious.	_____	_____
7. I regularly make excuses for my mistakes.	_____	_____
8. Negative feedback crushes me.	_____	_____
9. I care very much how much money other people make, especially when they are working in my field.	_____	_____
10. I feel like a failure when I do not achieve my goals.	_____	_____
11. Hard work gives me an emotional lift.	_____	_____
12. When others compliment me, I doubt their sincerity.	_____	_____
13. Complimenting others makes me feel uncomfortable.	_____	_____
14. I find it comfortable to say, "I'm sorry."	_____	_____
15. It is difficult for me to face up to my mistakes.	_____	_____
16. My coworkers think I am not worthy of promotion.	_____	_____
17. People who want to become my friends usually do not have much to offer.	_____	_____
18. If my manager praised me, I would have a difficult time believing it was deserved.	_____	_____
19. I'm just an ordinary person.	_____	_____
20. Having to face change really disturbs me.	_____	_____

Scoring and Interpretation:

The answers in the high self-esteem direction are as follows:

1. Mostly True	8. Mostly False	15. Mostly False
2. Mostly False	9. Mostly False	16. Mostly False
3. Mostly False	10. Mostly False	17. Mostly False
4. Mostly True	11. Mostly True	18. Mostly False
5. Mostly True	12. Mostly False	19. Mostly False
6. Mostly True	13. Mostly False	20. Mostly False
7. Mostly False	14. Mostly True	

17–20   You have very high self-esteem. Yet if your score is 20, it could be that you are denying any self-doubts.

11–16   Your self-esteem is in the average range. It would probably be worthwhile for you to implement strategies to boost your self-esteem (described in this chapter) so that you can develop a greater feeling of well-being.

0–10   Your self-esteem needs bolstering. Discuss your feelings about yourself with a trusted friend or with a mental health professional. At the same time, attempt to implement several of the tactics for boosting self-esteem described in this chapter.

Questions: 1. How does your score on this quiz match your evaluation of your self-esteem?

2. What would it be like being married to somebody who scored 0 on this quiz?

■ **Self-efficacy**

confidence in your ability to carry out a specific task in contrast to generalized self-confidence

■ **Self-respect**

the second component of self-esteem, refers to how you think and feel about yourself

interrelated components: self-efficacy and self-respect. [3] **Self-efficacy** is confidence in your ability to carry out a specific task in contrast to generalized self-confidence. When self-efficacy is high, you believe you have the ability to do what is necessary to complete a task successfully. Being confident that you can perform a particular task well contributes to self-esteem. Hundreds of studies have shown that high self-efficacy improves performance on a variety of tasks. More recent evidence suggests, however, that on certain puzzlelike tasks developing high self-efficacy can lead to overconfidence and, hence, to making errors in logic. [4] In this way self-efficacy is like self-confidence. Watch out for feeling so good about your ability that you become careless in your thinking.

Self-respect, the second component of self-esteem, refers to how you think and feel about yourself. Self-respect fits the everyday meaning of self-esteem. Many street beggars are intelligent, able-bodied, and have good physical appearance. You could argue that their low self-respect enables them to beg. Also, people with low self-respect and self-esteem allow themselves to stay in relationships where they are frequently verbally and physically abused. These abused people have such low self-worth that they think they deserve punishment. Another noteworthy aspect of self-respect is that when individuals are secure with themselves (high self-respect), they are less likely to be self-absorbed. As a consequence, they are more likely to focus on the needs of other people. [5]

THE DEVELOPMENT OF SELF-ESTEEM

Part of understanding the nature of self-esteem is to know how it develops. Self-esteem comes about from a variety of early life experiences. People who were encouraged to feel good about themselves and their accomplishments by family members, friends, and teachers are more likely to enjoy high self-esteem. Early life experiences play a key role in the development of both healthy self-esteem, and low self-esteem according to research synthesized at The Counseling and Mental Health Center of the University of Texas. [6] Childhood experiences that lead to healthy self-esteem include the following:

■ being praised

■ being listened to

■ being spoken to respectfully

■ getting attention and hugs

■ experiencing success in sports or school

In contrast, childhood experiences that lead to low self-esteem include the following:

■ being harshly criticized

■ being yelled at or beaten

■ being ignored, ridiculed, or teased

■ being expected to be "perfect" all the time

■ experiencing failures in sports or school

■ often being given messages that failed experiences (losing a game, getting a poor grade, and so forth) were failures of their whole self.

A widespread explanation of self-esteem development is that compliments, praise, and hugs alone build self-esteem. Yet many developmental psychologists seriously question this perspective. Instead, they believe that self-esteem results from accomplishing worthwhile activities and then feeling proud of these accomplishments. Receiving encouragement, however, can help the person accomplish activities that build self-esteem.

Leading psychologist Martin Seligman argues that self-esteem is caused by a variety of successes and failures. To develop self-esteem, people need to improve their skills for dealing with the world. [7] Self-esteem, therefore, comes about by genuine accomplishments, followed by praise and recognition. Heaping undeserved praise and recognition on people may lead to a temporary high, but it does not produce genuine self-esteem. The child develops self-esteem not from being told he or she can score a goal in soccer but from scoring that goal.

Although early-life experiences have the major impact on the development of self-esteem, experiences in adult life also impact self-esteem. David De Cremer of the Tilburg University (Netherlands) and his associates conducted two studies with Dutch college students about how the behavior of leaders and fair procedures influence self-esteem. The focus of the leaders' behavior was whether they motivated the workers/students to reward *themselves* for a job well done, for example, giving self-compliments. Procedural fairness was measured in terms of whether the study participants were given a voice in making decisions. Self-esteem was measured by a questionnaire somewhat similar to Human Relations Self-Assessment Quiz 2-1 in this chapter. The study questionnaire reflected the self-perceived value that individuals have of themselves as organizational members.

The study found that self-esteem was related to procedural fairness and leadership that encourages self-rewards. When leadership that encouraged rewards was high, procedural fairness was more strongly related to self-esteem. The interpretation given of the findings is that a leader/supervisor can facilitate self-esteem when he or she encourages self-rewards and uses fair procedures. Furthermore, fair procedures have a stronger impact on self-esteem when the leader encourages self-rewards. [8] A take away from this study would be that rewarding yourself for a job well done, even in adult life, can boost your self-esteem a little.

> **"Parents need to fill a child's bucket of self-esteem so high that the rest of the world can't poke enough holes in it to drain it dry."**
> **—Alvin Price, child development specialist**
>
> (Adapted to the world of work, this quote reads: "Supervisors need to fill a worker's bucket of self-esteem so high that the rest of the world can't poke enough holes in it to drain it dry.")

THE CONSEQUENCES OF SELF-ESTEEM

No single factor is as important to career success as self-esteem, as observed by psychologist Eugene Raudsepp. People with positive self-esteem understand their own competence and worth, and have positive perceptions of their abilities to cope with problems and adversity. [9] Kendrick Melrose, former CEO of Toro, illustrates this fundamental point. Toro employees were bedraggled because of some rough time business years, and they were reluctant to make decisions. Melrose helped them learn how to make decisions as a team. He said, "The transformation in management philosophy built self-esteem. It built innovation, creativity, risk, ownership." [10]

One of the major consequences of high self-esteem is good mental health. People with high self-esteem feel good about themselves and have positive outlooks on life. One of the links between good mental health and self-esteem is that high self-esteem helps prevent many situations from being stressful. Few negative comments from others are likely to bother you when your self-esteem is high. A person with low self-esteem might crumble if somebody insulted his or her appearance. A person with high self-esteem might shrug off the insult as simply being the other person's point of view. If faced with an everyday setback, such as losing keys, the high-self-esteem person might think, "I have so much going for me, why fall apart over this incident?"

Positive self-esteem also contributes to good mental health because it helps us ward off being troubled by feelings of jealousy and acting aggressively toward others because of our jealousy. Particularly with adolescents, lower self-worth leads to jealousy about friends liking other people better. [11]

Although people with high self-esteem can readily shrug off undeserved insults, they still profit well from negative feedback. Because they are secure, they can profit from the developmental opportunities suggested by negative feedback. Workers with high self-esteem develop and maintain favorable work attitudes and perform at high levels. These positive consequences take place because such attitudes and behaviors are consistent with the personal belief that they are competent individuals. Mary Kay Ash, the legendary founder of a beauty products company, put it this way: "It never occurred to me I couldn't do it. I always knew that if I worked hard enough, I could." Furthermore, research has shown that high-self-esteem individuals value reaching work goals more than do low-self-esteem individuals. [12]

The combined effect of workers having high self-esteem helps a company prosper. Long-term research by Branden, as well as more recent studies, suggests that self-esteem is a critical source of competitive advantage in an information society. Companies gain the edge when, in addition to having an educated workforce, employees have high self-esteem, as shown by such behaviors as the following:

- being creative and innovative
- taking personal responsibility for problems
- feeling of independence (yet still wanting to work cooperatively with others)
- trusting one's own capabilities
- taking the initiative to solve problems [13]

Behaviors such as these help workers cope with the challenge of a rapidly changing workplace where products and ideas become obsolete quickly. Workers with high self-esteem are more likely to be able to cope with new challenges regularly because they are confident they can master their environments.

A potential negative consequence of low self-esteem is envying too many people. If you perceive that many individuals have much more of what you want and are more worthwhile than you, you will suffer from enormous envy. To decrease pangs of envy, it is best to develop realistic standards of comparison between you and other people in the world. If high school basketball player Joshua measures his self-esteem in terms of how well he stacks up with basketball superstar and super-millionaire Le Bron James, young Joshua will take a lot of blows to his self-esteem. However, if Joshua compares himself to other players on his team and in his league, his self-esteem will be higher because he has chosen a more realistic reference group.

According to economist Robert H. Frank of Cornell University, our own reference group has the biggest impact on self-esteem. He writes: "When you see Bill Gates' mansion, you don't actually aspire to have one like it. It's who is local, who is near you physically and who is most like you—your family members, coworkers and old high school classmates—with whom you compare yourself. If someone in your reference group has a little more, you get a little anxious." [14]

Low self-esteem can have negative consequences for romantic relationships because people with self-doubts consistently underestimate their partners' feelings for them. People with low self-respect distance themselves from the relationship—often devaluing their partner—to prepare themselves for what they think will be an inevitable breakup. John G. Holmes, a psychologist at the University of Waterloo in Ontario, Canada, says, "If people think negatively about themselves, they think their partner must think negatively about them—and they're wrong." [15]

The consequences of self-esteem are related to its source. People who evaluate their self-worth on how others perceive them and not on their value as human beings often suffer negative mental and physical consequences. In a series of studies, developmental psychologist Jennifer Crocker found that college students who based their self-worth on external sources reported more stress, anger, academic problems, and interpersonal conflicts. In addition, these students had higher levels of drug and alcohol use and symptoms of eating disorders. (External sources of self-worth include appearance, approval from others, and grades in school.) Students who based their self-esteem (or self-worth) on internal sources generally received higher grades and were less likely to consume alcohol and drugs or develop eating disorders. [16] (An internal source would be thinking of yourself as a kind and charitable person.)

How Do You Enhance Self-Esteem?

■ Learning Objective 2

Improving self-esteem is a lifelong process because self-esteem is related to the success of your activities and interactions with people. Following are approaches to enhancing self-esteem that are related to how self-esteem develops.

ATTAIN LEGITIMATE ACCOMPLISHMENTS

To emphasize again, accomplishing worthwhile activities is a major contributor to self-esteem in both children and adults. Social science research suggests this sequence of events: Person establishes a goal ➔ person pursues the goal ➔ person achieves the goal ➔ person develops esteemlike feelings. [17] ☺ The opposite point of view is this sequence: Person develops esteemlike feelings ➔ person establishes a goal ➔ person pursues the goal ➔ person achieves the goal. ☺ Similarly, giving people large trophies for mundane accomplishments is unlikely to raise self-esteem. More likely, the person will see through the transparent attempt to build his or her self-esteem and develop negative feelings about the self. What about you? Would your self-esteem receive a bigger boost by (1) receiving an A in a course in which 10 percent of the class received an A or by (2) receiving an A in a class in which everybody received the same grade?

BE AWARE OF PERSONAL STRENGTHS

Another method of improving your self-esteem is to develop an appreciation of your strengths and accomplishments. Research awhile back with more than 60 executives has shown that their self-concepts become more positive after one month of practicing this exercise for a few minutes every day. [18] A good starting point is to list your strengths and accomplishments on paper. This list is likely to be more impressive than you expected.

You can sometimes develop an appreciation of your strengths by participating in a group exercise designed for such purposes. A group of about seven people meet to form a support group. All group members first spend about 10 minutes answering the question, "What are my three strongest points, attributes, or skills?" After each group member records his or her three strengths, the person discusses them with the other group members.

Each group member then comments on the list. Other group members sometimes add to your list of strengths or reinforce what you have to say. Sometimes you may find disagreement. One member told the group, "I'm handsome, intelligent, reliable, athletic, self-confident, and very moral. I also have a good sense of humor."

Another group member retorted, "And I might add that you're unbearably conceited."

MINIMIZE SETTINGS AND INTERACTIONS THAT DETRACT FROM YOUR FEELINGS OF COMPETENCE

Most of us have situations in work and personal life that make us feel less than our best. If you can minimize exposure to those situations, you will have fewer feelings of incompetence. The problem with feeling incompetent is that it lowers your self-esteem. An office supervisor said she detested company picnics, most of all because she was forced to play softball. At her own admission, she had less aptitude for athletics than any able-bodied person she knew. In addition, she felt uncomfortable with the small-talk characteristic of picnics. To minimize discomfort, the woman attended only those picnics she thought were absolutely necessary. Instead of playing on the softball team, she volunteered to be the equipment manager.

A problem with avoiding all situations in which you feel lowly competent is that it might prevent you from acquiring needed skills. Also, it boosts your self-confidence and self-esteem to become comfortable in a previously uncomfortable situation.

TALK AND SOCIALIZE FREQUENTLY WITH PEOPLE WHO BOOST YOUR SELF-ESTEEM

Psychologist Barbara Ilardie says that the people who can raise your self-esteem are usually those with high self-esteem themselves. They are the people who give honest feedback because they respect others and themselves. Such high-self-esteem individuals should not be confused with yes-people who agree with others simply to be liked. The point is that you typically receive more from strong people than weak ones. Weak people will flatter you but will not give you the honest feedback you need to build self-esteem. [19]

MODEL THE BEHAVIOR OF PEOPLE WITH HIGH SELF-ESTEEM

Observe the way people who are believed to have high self-esteem stand, walk, speak, and act. Even if you are not feeling so secure inside, you will project a high-self-esteem image if you act assured. Raudsepp recommends, "Stand tall, speak clearly and with confidence, shake hands firmly, look people in the eye and smile frequently. Your self-esteem will increase as you notice encouraging reactions from others." [20] (Notice here that self-esteem is considered to be about the same idea as self-confidence.)

Choose your models of high self-esteem from people you know personally as well as celebrities you might watch on television news and interview shows. Observing actors on the large or small screen is a little less useful because they are guaranteed to be playing a role. Identifying a teacher or professor as a self-esteem model is widely practiced, as is observing successful family members and friends.

Building self-esteem is a major asset in life. Yet, as with self-efficacy, a danger exists in having highly inflated self-esteem. A controversial study conducted in England found that people with high self-esteem might have an unrealistic sense of themselves. "They expect to do well at things, discount failure, and feel beyond reproach." Furthermore, people with exaggerated self-esteem are sometimes intolerant of people who are different from them. [21]

What is the Importance of Self-Confidence and Self-Efficacy?

■ **Learning Objective 3**

Although self-confidence can be considered part of self-esteem, it is important enough to study separately. Self-confidence and self-efficacy are often more directly tied to task performance than is the self-respect part of self-esteem. Various studies have shown that people with a high sense of self-efficacy tend to have good job performance, so being self-confident is important for your career. They also set relatively high goals for themselves. [22] Self-confidence has also long been recognized as a trait of effective leaders. A straightforward implication of self-efficacy is that people who think they can perform well on a task do better than those who think they will do poorly.

The importance of self-confidence for your career can be illustrated by the tactics of Jack Welch, the former CEO of General Electric (GE), who is regarded by many business writers as one of the most influential leaders of all time. Welch has become a well-known business author and columnist, in addition to remaining active in directing several companies. Welch once said that his most important responsibility at GE was building the self-confidence of managers throughout the company. Although an intimidating and demanding boss, Welch would help managers develop their self-confidence by giving them lots of opportunities to succeed on major assignments.

An encouraging note is that self-efficacy can be boosted through training. In an experiment, 66 unemployed people participated in a self-efficacy workshop. The group included bookkeepers, clerks, teachers, skilled mechanics, and technicians. The workshop featured watching videoclips of successfully performing job search behaviors, followed by encouragement from the trainer and peers. In contrast to unemployed people who did not attend the workshop, the people who were trained in self-efficacy became more involved in job searches. [23] Being involved in job searches included telephoning about a job and obtaining an interview.

Research by college professors and psychological consultants George P. Hollenbeck and Douglas T. Hall suggests that our feelings of self-confidence stem from five sources of information. [24] The first source is the *actual experience,* or *things we have done.* Having done something before and succeeded is the most powerful way to build self-confidence. If you successfully inserted a replacement battery in your watch without destroying the watch, you will be confident in making another replacement.

The second source of self-confidence is the *experiences of others,* or *modeling.* You can gain some self-confidence if you have carefully observed others perform a task, such as resolving conflict with a customer. You might say to yourself, "I've seen Tracy calm down the customer by listening and showing sympathy, and I'm confident I can do the same thing." The third source of self-confidence is *social comparison,* or *comparing yourself to others.* If you see other people with capabilities similar to your own perform a task well, your will gain in confidence. A person might say to himself or herself, "If that person can learn how to work with enterprise software, I can do it also. I'm just as smart."

The fourth source of self-confidence is *social persuasion, the process of convincing another person.* If a credible person convinces you that you can accomplish a particular task, you will often receive a boost in self-confidence large enough to give the task a try. If the encouragement is coupled with guidance on how to perform the task, your self-confidence gain will be higher. So the boss or teacher who says, "I know you can do it, and I'm here to help you," knows how to build self-confidence.

Human Relations Self-Assessment Quiz   2-2

How Self-Confident Are You?

Indicate the extent to which you agree with each of the following statements. Use a 1-to-5 scale: (1) disagree strongly; (2) disagree; (3) neutral; (4) agree; (5) agree strongly.

	DS	D	N	A	AS
1. I frequently say to people, "I'm not sure."	5	4	3	2	1
2. I perform well in most situations in life.	1	2	3	4	5
3. I willingly offer advice to others.	1	2	3	4	5
4. Before making even a minor decision, I usually consult with several people.	5	4	3	2	1
5. I am generally willing to attempt new activities for which I have very little related skill or experience.	1	2	3	4	5
6. Speaking in front of the class or other group is a frightening experience for me.	5	4	3	2	1
7. I experience stress when people challenge me or put me on the spot.	5	4	3	2	1
8. I feel comfortable attending a social event by myself.	1	2	3	4	5
9. I'm much more of a winner than a loser.	1	2	3	4	5
10. I am cautious about making any substantial change in my life.	5	4	3	2	1

Total score: _____

Scoring and Interpretation:

Calculate your total score by adding the numbers circled. A tentative interpretation of the scoring is as follows:

45–50   Very high self-confidence with perhaps a tendency toward arrogance

38–44   A high, desirable level of self-confidence

30–37   Moderate, or average, self-confidence

10–29   Self-confidence needs strengthening

Questions: 1. How does your score on this test fit with your evaluation of your self-confidence?

2. What would it be like working for a manager who scored 10 on this quiz?

The fifth source of information for making a self-confidence judgment is *emotional arousal,* or *how you feel about events around you and manage your emotions.* People rely somewhat on inner feelings to know if they are self-confident enough to perform the task. Imagine a person standing on top of a high mountain ready to ski down. However, he or she is trembling and nauseous with fear. Contrast this beginner to another person who simply feels mildly excited and challenged. Skier number one has a self-confidence problem, whereas skier number two has enough confidence to start the descent. (Have your emotional sensations ever influenced your self-confidence?)

The more of these five sources of self-confidence are positive for you, the more likely your self-confidence will be positive. Human Relations Self-Assessment Quiz 2-2 provides some insight into your level of self-confidence.

How Do You Develop and Enhance Your Self-Confidence?

Self-confidence is generally achieved by succeeding in a variety of situations. A confident civil engineering technician may not be generally self-confident unless he or she also achieves success in activities such as forming good personal relationships, navigating complex software, writing a letter, learning a second language, and displaying athletic skills.

Although this general approach to self-confidence building makes sense, it does not work for everyone. Some people who seem to succeed at everything still have lingering self-doubt. Low self-confidence is so deeply ingrained in this type of personality that success in later life is not sufficient to change things. Following are seven specific strategies and tactics for building and elevating self-confidence. They will generally work unless the person has deep-rooted feelings of inferiority. The tactics and strategies are arranged approximately in the order in which they should be tried to achieve best results.

TAKE AN INVENTORY OF PERSONAL ASSETS AND ACCOMPLISHMENTS

Many people suffer from low self-confidence because they do not appreciate their own good points. Therefore, a starting point in increasing your self-confidence is to take an inventory of personal assets and accomplishments. This same activity was offered previously as a method of developing self-esteem. Personal assets should be related to characteristics and behaviors rather than tangible assets, such as an inheritance or an antique car.

Accomplishments can be anything significant in which you played a key role in achieving the results. Try not to be modest in preparing your list of assets and accomplishments. You are looking for any confidence booster you can find. Two lists prepared by different people will suffice to give you an idea of the kinds of assets and accomplishments that might be included.

Amy

Good listener; most people like me; good messaging skills; good posture; inquisitive mind; good at solving problems; above-average Internet search skills; good sense of humor; patient with people who make mistakes; better-than-average appearance. Organized successful fund drive that raised $40,000 for church; graduated tenth in high school class of 500; achieved first place in industrial bowling league; daughter has an excellent career.

Todd

Good mechanical skills, including automotive repair and computer repair; work well under pressure; good dancer; friendly with strangers; great physical health (drug and disease free); good cook; can laugh at my own mistakes; favorable personal appearance; respectful of authority. Made award-winning suggestion that saved company $45,000; scored winning goal in college basketball tournament; dragged child out of burning building.

The value of these asset lists is that they add to your self-appreciation. Most people who lay out their good points on paper come away from the activity with at least a temporary boost in self-confidence. The temporary boost, combined with a few success experiences, may lead to a long-term gain in self-confidence.

An important supplement to listing your own assets is hearing the opinion of others on your good points. This tactic has to be used sparingly, however, and mainly with people who are personal growth minded. A good icebreaker is to tell your source of feedback that you have to prepare a list of your assets for a human relations exercise. Because that person knows of your work on your capabilities, you hope that he or she can spare a few minutes for this important exercise. For many people, positive feedback from others does more for building self-confidence than does feedback from you. The reason is that self-esteem depends to a large extent on what people think others think about them. Consequently, if other people—whose judgment you trust—think highly of you, your self-image will be positive.

DEVELOP A SOLID KNOWLEDGE BASE

A bedrock strategy for projecting self-confidence is to develop a base of knowledge that enables you to provide sensible alternative solutions to problems. Intuition is very important, but working from a base of facts helps you project a confident image. Formal education is an obvious and important source of information for your knowledge base. Day-by-day absorption of information directly and indirectly related to your career is equally important. A major purpose of formal education is to get you in the right frame of mind to continue your quest for knowledge.

In your quest for developing a solid knowledge base to project self-confidence, be sensitive to abusing this technique. If you bombard people with quotes, facts, and figures, you are likely to be perceived as an annoying know-it-all.

USE POSITIVE SELF-TALK

■ **Positive self-talk**

saying positive things about yourself to yourself

A basic method of building self-confidence is to engage in **positive self-talk,** saying positive things about yourself to yourself. The first step in using positive self-talk is to objectively state the incident that is casting doubt about self-worth. [25] The key word here is *objectively.* Terry, who is fearful of poorly executing a report-writing assignment, might say, "I've been asked to write a report for the company, and I'm not a good writer."

The next step is to objectively interpret what the incident *does not* mean. Terry might say, "Not being a skilled writer doesn't mean that I can't figure out a way to write a good report or that I'm an ineffective employee."

Next, the person should objectively state what the incident *does* mean. In doing this, the person should avoid put-down labels such as *incompetent, stupid, dumb, jerk,* or *airhead.* These terms are forms of negative self-talk. Terry should state what the incident does mean: "I have a problem with one small aspect of this job."

The fourth step is to objectively account for the cause of the incident. Terry would say, "I'm really worried about writing a good report because I have very little experience in writing along these lines."

The fifth step is to identify some positive ways to prevent the incident from happening again. Terry might say, "I'll get out my textbook on business communications and review the chapter on report writing" or "I'll enroll in a course or seminar on business report writing."

The final step is to use positive self-talk. Terry imagines his boss saying, "This report is really good. I'm proud of my decision to select you to prepare this important report."

Positive self-talk builds self-confidence and self-esteem because it programs the mind with positive messages. Making frequent positive statements or affirmations about the self creates a more confident person. An example would be, "I know I can learn this new equipment rapidly enough to increase my productivity within five days."

Business coach Gary Lockwood emphasizes that positive self-talk is also useful for getting people past difficult times. "It's all in your head," he said. "Remember you are in charge of your feelings. You are in control of your attitude." Instead of berating yourself after making a mistake, learn from the experience and move on. Say to yourself, "Everyone makes mistakes," "Tomorrow is another day," or "What can I learn from this?" [26]

AVOID NEGATIVE SELF-TALK

As implied, you should minimize negative statements about yourself to bolster self-confidence. A lack of self-confidence is reflected in statements such as, "I may be stupid but . . .," "Nobody asked my opinion," "I know I'm usually wrong, but . . .," "I know I don't have as much education as some people, but . . . ." Self-effacing statements such as these serve to reinforce low self-confidence.

It is also important not to attribute to yourself negative, irreversible traits, such as "idiotic," "ugly," "dull," "loser," and "hopeless." Instead, look on your weak points as areas for possible self-improvement. Negative self-labeling can do long-term damage to your self-confidence. If a person stops that practice today, his or her self-confidence may begin to increase.

USE POSITIVE VISUAL IMAGERY

Assume you have a situation in mind in which you would like to appear confident and in control. An example would be a meeting with a major customer who has told you by e-mail that he is considering switching suppliers. Your intuitive reaction is that if you cannot handle his concerns without fumbling or appearing desperate, you will lose the account. An important technique in this situation is **positive visual imagery,** or picturing a positive outcome in your mind. To apply this technique in this situation, imagine yourself engaging in a convincing argument about why your customer should retain your company as the primary supplier. Imagine yourself talking in positive terms about the good service your company offers and how you can rectify any problems.

■ **Positive visual imagery**
picturing a positive outcome in your mind

Visualize yourself listening patiently to your customer's concerns and then talking confidently about how your company can handle these concerns. As you rehearse this moment of truth, create a mental picture of you and the customer shaking hands over the fact that the account is still yours.

Positive visual imagery helps you appear self-confident because your mental rehearsal of the situation has helped you prepare for battle. If imagery works for you once, you will be even more effective in subsequent uses of the technique.

SET HIGH EXPECTATIONS FOR YOURSELF (THE GALETA EFFECT)

If you set high expectations for yourself, and you succeed, you are likely to experience a temporary or permanent boost in self-confidence. The **Galeta effect** is a type of self-fulfilling prophecy in which high expectations lead to high performance. Similar to positive self-talk, if you believe in yourself, you are more likely to succeed. You expect to win, so you do. The Galeta effect does not work all the time, but it does work some of the time for many people.

■ **Galeta effect**
a type of self-fulfilling prophecy in which high expectations lead to high performance

Workplace behavior researchers D. Brian McNatt and Timothy A. Judge studied the Galeta effect with 72 auditors within three offices of a major accounting firm for a three-month period. The auditors were given letters of encouragement to strengthen their feelings of self-efficacy. Information in the letters was based on facts about the auditors, such as information derived from their résumés and company records. The results of the experiment showed that creating a Galeta effect bolstered self-efficacy, motivation, and performance. However, the performance improvement was temporary suggesting that self-expectations need to be boosted regularly. [27]

STRIVE FOR PEAK PERFORMANCE

■ **Peak performance**
exceptional accomplishment in a given task

A key strategy for projecting self-confidence is to display **peak performance,** or exceptional accomplishment in a given task. The experience is transient but exceptionally meaningful. Peak performance refers to much more than attempting to do your best. Experiencing peak performance in various tasks over a long time period would move a person toward self-actualization. [28] To achieve peak performance, you must be totally focused on what you are doing. When you are in the state of peak performance, you are mentally calm and physically at ease. Intense concentration is required to achieve this state. You are so focused on the task at hand that you are not distracted by extraneous events or thoughts. To use an athletic analogy, you are *in the zone* while you are performing the task. In fact, many sports psychologists and other sports trainers work with athletes to help them attain peak performance.

The mental state achieved during peak performance is akin to a person's sense of deep concentration when immersed in a sport or hobby. On days when tennis players perform way above their usual game, they typically comment, "The ball looked so large today, I could read the label as I hit it." On the job, focus and concentration allow the person to sense and respond to relevant information coming both from within the mind and from outside stimuli. When you are at your peak, you impress others by responding intelligently to their input. While turning in peak performance, you are experiencing a mental state referred to as *flow.*

Although you are concentrating on an object or sometimes on another person during peak performance, you still have an awareness of the self. You develop a strong sense of the self, similar to self-confidence and self-efficacy, while you are concentrating on the task. Peak performance is related to self-confidence in another important way. Achieving peak performance in many situations helps you develop self-confidence. Here are two representative examples of peak performance:

■ A real estate agent sells $17 million of homes in her region in one year, 40 percent higher than any other agent in her area.

■ A manufacturing technician becomes certified as a Black Belt in the quality-improvement process called Six Sigma, and then leads a team that moves a call center from a customer satisfaction rating of 75 to 98 percent.

BOUNCE BACK FROM SETBACKS AND EMBARRASSMENTS

Resilience is a major contributor to personal effectiveness. Overcoming setbacks also builds self-confidence. An effective self-confidence builder is to convince yourself that you can conquer adversity, such as setbacks and embarrassments, thus being resilient. The vast majority of successful leaders have dealt successfully with at least one significant setback in their careers, such as being fired or demoted. In contrast, crumbling after a setback or series of setbacks will usually lower self-confidence. Two major suggestions for bouncing back from setbacks and embarrassments are presented next.

Get Past the Emotional Turmoil

Adversity has enormous emotional consequences. The emotional impact of severe job adversity can rival the loss of a personal relationship. The stress from adversity

Human Relations in Practice

Eddie Lampert Uses Self-Confidence to Make Billions and Escape Kidnappers

By the time financier Eddie Lampert was 42 years old he had amassed a fortune estimated at nearly $2 billion. He is the owner of the private investment fund, ESL Investments. After his fund acquired the bankrupt discounter Kmart, Lampert then acquired Sears Roebuck & Co. to form Sears Holding Company—with Lampert as chair. In his dealings with business associates, Big Eddie brims with self-confidence in his decision making. During a meeting with Sears Executives, he asked again and again, "What's the benefit of that?" or "Why invest in that?" He shot down a modest $2 million proposal to improve lighting in the stores.

In 2003, he was kidnapped at gunpoint in a parking garage by four hoodlums who had been searching for wealthy people on the Internet. He was held bound in a bathtub at a motel. The men told Lampert they had been hired to kill him for $5 million but would let him go for $1 million. As the kidnappers became increasingly nervous, Lampert convinced them that if they would release him, he would pay them $40,000 a couple of days later. The hoodlums let him off on the side of a road in Greenwich, Connecticut. "It was very much like going to your own funeral," he says. Two days later Lampert was back in Kmart negotiations, with all the more confidence in his negotiating skills.

Source: Patricia Sellers, "Eddie Lampert: The Best Investor of His Generation," *Fortune, Investor's Guide* February 6, 2006; Robert Berner, "The Next Warren Buffet," *Business Week*, November 22, 2004, pp. 144–154.

leads to a cycle of adversity followed by stress, followed by more adversity. A starting point in dealing with the emotional aspects of adversity is to *accept the reality of your problem.* Admit that your problems are real and that you are hurting inside. The next step is *not to take the setback personally.* Remember that setbacks are inevitable as long as you are taking some risks in your career. Not personalizing setbacks helps reduce some of the emotional sting. If possible, *do not panic.* Recognize that you are in difficult circumstances under which many others panic. Convince yourself to remain calm enough to deal with the severe problem or crisis. Also, *get help from your support network.* Getting emotional support from family members and friends helps overcome the emotional turmoil associated with adversity.

A type of emotional turmoil that faces many people at some point in their careers is to be fired for what the company thinks is poor performance. Being fired hurts most people deeply, but by following the steps previously described the impact can be softened and can ultimately lead to heightened self-confidence. A surprisingly large number of successful entrepreneurs were at one time fired from a corporate job, often because they were seen as mavericks who would not follow rules well.

Find a Creative Solution to Your Problem

An inescapable part of planning a comeback is to solve your problem. You often need to search for creative solutions. Jason, a business student in Chicago ran a sub shop to earn a living and support himself through college. Layoffs at nearby companies had driven his sales way down below the point at which it paid to keep the sub shop open. In the process of exploring all the possibilities of what he could do in a hurry to earn a living, Jason observed that loads of old buildings in downtown Chicago were being rebuilt and turned into apartments and retail space. Jason then thought of starting an "interior demolition" company, combining efforts with two relatives in the home repair business. Jason's creative solution accomplished what needed to be done to regain his financial equilibrium. His self-confidence continues to surge as his interior demolition business has prospered. If the preceding steps work for you and you bring your level of self-confidence to where you want it to be, you will have achieved a major milestone in applying human relations to yourself.

Concept Review and Reinforcement

Key Terms

Self-esteem, 30

Self-efficacy, 32

Self-respect, 32

Positive self-talk, 40

Positive visual imagery, 41

Galeta effect, 41

Peak performance, 42

Summary and Review

- Self-esteem refers to feeling competent and being worthy of happiness. People with high self-esteem develop positive self-concepts.
- Self-esteem has two interrelated components: self-efficacy (a task-related feeling of competence) and self-respect. People with high self-respect are more likely to focus on the needs of others.
- Self-esteem develops from a variety of early-life experiences. People who were encouraged to feel good about themselves and their accomplishments by key people in their lives are more likely to enjoy high self-esteem.
- Of major significance, self-esteem also results from accomplishing worthwhile activities and then feeling proud of these accomplishments. Praise and recognition for accomplishments also help develop self-esteem.
- Self-esteem is important for career success. Good mental health is another major consequence of high self-esteem. One of the links between good mental health and self-esteem is that high self-esteem helps prevent many situations from being stressful.
- Workers with high self-esteem develop and maintain favorable work attitudes and perform at a high level. A company with high self-esteem workers has a competitive advantage.
- A potential negative consequence of low self-esteem is envying too many people. Our own reference group has the biggest impact on self-esteem.
- Low self-esteem can have negative consequences for romantic relationships because people with self-doubts consistently underestimate their partners' feelings for them.

- A series of studies showed that students who based their self-esteem on internal sources generally received higher grades and were less likely to consume alcohol and drugs or develop eating disorders.

Self-esteem can be enhanced in many ways:

- Attain legitimate accomplishments
- Be aware of your personal strengths
- Talk and socialize frequently with people who boost your self-esteem
- Model the behavior of people with high self-esteem

Exaggerated self-esteem can sometimes lead to intolerance of people who are different from you.

Various studies have shown that people with a high sense of self-efficacy tend to have good job performance, so self-confidence is important for your career. Our feelings of self-confidence stem from five sources of information:

- actual experiences, or things that we have done
- experiences of others, or modeling
- social comparison, or comparing yourself to others
- social persuasion, the process of convincing another person
- emotional arousal, or how people feel about events around them and managing emotions

A general principle of boosting your self-confidence is to experience success (goal accomplishment) in a variety of situations. The specific strategies for building self-confidence described here are as follows:

■ Take an inventory of personal assets and accomplishments
■ Develop a solid knowledge base
■ Use positive self-talk
■ Avoid negative self-talk

■ Use positive visual imagery
■ Set high expectations for yourself (the Galeta effect)
■ Strive for peak performance
■ Bounce back from setbacks and embarrassments

Check Your Understanding

1. Do you see any relationship between a person having loads of tattoos all over the body and his or her self-esteem? Explain your reasoning.
2. A study by economists indicated that workers with higher levels of self-esteem tended to be more productive. What would be an explanation for this finding?
3. Having workers with high self-esteem is supposed to give a company a competitive edge. If you were responsible for hiring a few new workers, how would you evaluate a given applicant's level of self-esteem?
4. How might you improve your self-efficacy for a specific job that you are performing?
5. A study mentioned in this chapter showed that people with high self-esteem are sometimes intolerant of people quite different from themselves. How would you explain these findings?

6. When you meet another person, on what basis do you conclude that he or she is self-confident?
7. What positive self-talk can you use after you have failed on a major assignment?
8. In what way does your program of studies contribute to building your self-esteem and self-confidence?
9. Many pharmaceutical firms actively recruit cheerleaders as sales representatives to call on doctors to recommend their brand of prescription drugs. The firms in question say that cheerleaders make good sales reps because they are so self-confident. What is your opinion on this controversial issue?
10. Interview a person whom you perceive to have a successful career. Ask that person to describe how he or she developed high self-esteem. Be prepared to discuss your findings in class.

Web Corner

Building Your Self-Esteem

www.More-Self-esteem.com

Integrating self-esteem into the fabric of society

www.self-esteem-nase.org

INTERNET SKILL BUILDER 2-1

Learning More about Your Self-Esteem

The Self-Esteem Checklist in this chapter gave you one opportunity to assess you self-esteem. To gain additional insights into your self-esteem, visit www.more-selfesteem.com. Go to "quizzes" under Free Resources, and take the self-esteem test. How does your score on this quiz compare to your score on *The Self-Esteem*

Checklist? If your level of self-esteem as measured by the two quizzes is quite different (such as high versus low), explain why this discrepancy might occur.

INTERNET SKILL BUILDER 2-2

Developing Your Self-Confidence On-Line

As described in this chapter, self-confidence is a major contributor to leadership effectiveness in a variety of situations. www.self-confidence.co.uk offers a free self-confidence course on-line. After you sign up for the course, you will receive your first installment immediately. After that you will receive one tutorial a week for six weeks. The lessons include self-confidence-boosting stories, information and quotes, and skill-development exercises. Sponsors of the site will invite you to take related courses for a fee.

Applying Human Relations Exercise 2-1

The Self-Esteem Building Club

You and your classmates are invited to participate in one of the most humane and productive possible human relations skill-building exercises: membership in the "self-esteem building club." Your assignment is for three consecutive weeks to help build the self-esteem of one person. Before embarking on the exercise, review the information about self-esteem development in the chapter. One of the most effective tactics would be to find somebody who had a legitimate accomplishment and give that person a reward or thank you. Record carefully what the person did, what you did, and any behavioral reactions of the person whose self-esteem you attempted to build. The incident could become part of your human relations journal. An example follows, written by a 46-year-old student of human relations:

Thursday night two weeks ago I went to the athletic club to play racquetball. Different from usual, I had a date after the club. I wanted to look good, so I decided to wear my high-school class ring. The ring doesn't have much resale value, but I was emotionally attached to it, having worn it for special occasions for 28 years. I stuffed the ring along with my watch and wallet in my athletic bag.

When I was through with racquetball, I showered and got dressed. My ring was missing from my bag even though my wallet and watch were there. I kind of freaked out because I hate to lose a prized possession. I shook the bag out three times but no luck. Very discouraged, I left my name, telephone number, and e-mail address at the front desk just in case somebody turned in the ring. I kept thinking that I must have lost the ring when I stopped at the desk to check in.

The next morning before going to class, I got a phone call from a front-desk clerk at the club. The clerk told me that Karl, from the housekeeping staff, heard a strange noise while he was vacuuming near the front desk. He shut off the vacuum cleaner immediately and pulled out my ring. To me Karl was a hero. I made a special trip to the club that night to meet with Karl. I shook his hand, and gave him a $10 bill as a reward. I also explained to Karl what a difference he had made in my mood. I told him that honest, hardworking people like him who take pride in their work make this world a better place. It made my day when Karl smiled and told me it was a pleasure to be helpful.

Your instructor might organize a sharing of self-esteem building episodes in the class. If the sharing does take place, look for patterns in terms of what seemed to work in terms of self-esteem building. Also, listen for any patterns in failed attempts at self-esteem building.

Applying Human Relations Exercise 2-2

Building Your Self-Confidence and Self-Efficacy

Most people can use a boost to their self-confidence. Even if you are a highly confident individual, perhaps there is room for building your feelings of self-efficacy in a particular area, for example, as a proud and successful business owner learning a new skill such as editing digital photos or speaking a foreign language. For this skill-building exercise enhance your self-confidence or self-efficacy in the next two weeks by trying out one of the many suggestions for self-confidence building described in the text.

As part of planning the implementation of this exercise, think about any area in which your self-confidence could use a boost. A candid human relations student, who was also a confident cheerleader, said, "Face it, I suck at PowerPoint presentations. I put up so many details on my slides that the audience is trying to read my slides instead of looking at me. I have to admit that my PowerPoint presentation consists mostly of my reading my slides to the audience. I'm much better at cheerleading." So this student studied information in her human relations text about making better graphic presentations.

She revamped her approach to using her slides as headlines and talking points. She tried out one presentation in class and one at her church. She received so many compliments about her presentations that she now has much higher self-efficacy with respect to PowerPoint presentations.

Your instructor might organize a sharing of self-confidence building episodes in the class. If the sharing does take place, look for patterns in terms of what seemed to work in terms of self-confidence or self-efficacy building. Also, listen for any patterns in failed attempts at self-confidence building.

Human Relations Case Study 2-1

Self-Esteem Building at Pyramid Remanufacturing

Pyramid Remanufacturing opened for business 10 years ago in a cinder block building with four employees. Today Pyramid is housed in an old factory building in a low-rent district. The company has 100 full-time employees and about 50 part timers. The nature of the company's business is salvaging parts from used or broken equipment sent to them by other companies. One of Pyramid's remanufacturing projects is to salvage the workable parts from single-use cameras and recycle the balance of the plastic parts. Despite the rapid decline in film photography, single-use cameras are still much in demand. Another large company contract is to salvage parts from children's toys that are returned to retailers because they do not function properly. Both contracts also call for making new single-use cameras and toys, incorporating the salvaged parts.

The basic remanufacturing jobs can be learned in several hours. The work is not complex, but it is tedious. For example, a remanufacturing technician would be expected to tear down and salvage, and assemble about 100 single-use cameras per day. The jobs pay about twice the minimum wage, and full-time workers receive standard benefits.

Derrick Lockett, the president and founder of Pyramid, believes that his company plays an important role in society. As he explains, "First of all, note that we are *remanufacturers*. We are helping save the planet. Think of the thousands and thousands of single-use cameras that do not wind up in landfills because of our recycling efforts. The same goes for plastic toys. Consider also, that we hire a lot of people who would not be working if it were not for Pyramid. A lot of our employees would be on welfare if they were not working here. We hire a lot of people from the welfare roles. We also hire a lot of

troubled teenagers and seniors who can't find employment elsewhere.

"Some of our other employees have a variety of disabilities which make job finding difficult for them. Two of our highest producers are blind. They have a wonderful sense of touch, and they can visualize the parts that have to be separated and assembled. Another source of good employees for us is recently released prisoners."

Lockett was asked if all Pyramid manufacturing employees were performing up to standard. He explained that about one-fourth of the workforce were either working so slowly or doing such sloppy work that they were poor investments for the company. "Face it," said Lockett, "some of our employees are dragging us down. After a while we have to weed out the workers who simply don't earn their salaries."

Next, Lockett gave his analysis of why some remanufacturing technicians are unable to perform properly. "Lots of reasons," said Lockett. "Some can't read; some have a poor work ethic; some have attention deficit disorders. But the big problem is that many of the poor performers have such rotten self-esteem. They don't believe in themselves. They think nobody wants them and that they are incapable of being valuable employees."

Lucy Winters, the director of human resources and administration, explained what Pyramid was attempting to do about the self-esteem problem. "You have to realize," she said, "that it's not easy for a company to build the self-esteem of entry-level employees. Derrick and I would both like to save the world, but we can't do everything. But we are taking a few initiatives to build the self-esteem of our employees.

One approach is that our supervisors give out brightly colored badges, imprinted with the words, 'I'm a real remanufacturer.' The supervisors are supposed to give out the badges when a technician looks to be down in the dumps. We also have a newsletter that features stories about our remanufacturing technicians. Each month we choose somebody to be the "Remanufacturer of the month." Usually it's an employee whose self-esteem appears to be hurting.

"Another approach is more informal. We ask our supervisors to remember to be cheerleaders. They're supposed to lift the spirits of employees who don't think much of themselves by saying things such as 'I know you can do it' or 'I believe in you.'"

When asked how the self-esteem-building program was working, Winters and Lockett both said it was too early to tell with certainty. Winters did comment, however, "I see a few bright smiles out there among our technicians.

And the turnover rate is down about 5 percent. So the program might be working."

Questions

1. What is your evaluation of Lockett's analysis that low self-esteem could hurt the work performance of entry-level remanufacturing technicians?
2. What is your evaluation of the self-esteem-building program at Pyramid?
3. What other suggestions can you offer for building the self-esteem of the Pyramid employees who appear to be having self-esteem problems?

Human Relations Case Study 2-2

Building Up Kristina

Kristina Wright entered the front door of the half of a house she was sharing with Wendy Lopez. Her housemate said, "I don't see a smile on your face. How did the job hunt go today?"

"Not too well," replied Wright. "I had two interviews, but I doubt I will be called back. After all there are dozens of applicants looking for administrative assistant positions with better qualifications than mine. In this economy you really have to know the right people to land a job."

"Will you please stop it, Kristina? You're as good or better than the competition. You have your degree, and you have experience as an administrative intern. Besides that, you look great."

"That's easy for you to say, Wendy. You have a good job, and people like you. I'm simply average, average,

average. Even Lucky [Kristina's cocker spaniel] has an average name. And thousands of girls are named Kristina."

"With an attitude like that," replied Lopez, "you won't get hired. Be proud of who you are. You are somebody special."

"Thanks for the ego boost, my ever-faithful friend. But I almost don't have the courage to go back out there tomorrow and face any more interviews."

Questions

1. What seems to be Wright's problem based on the brief information you have been given?
2. What recommendations can you make to Wright to boost her self-confidence enough to get through any upcoming job interviews she might have?
3. How helpful might be the words of encouragement and advice that Lopez has given Wright so far?

REFERENCES

1. Excerpted from Greg Holden, "Find Out How Entrepreneurs Tapped into the Power of eBay and Made Millions," *Entrepreneur*, May 2006, pp. 64–65.
2. Nathaniel Branden, *Self-Esteem at Work: How Confident People Make Powerful Companies* (San Francisco: Jossey-Bass, 1998).
3. Cited in Wayne Weiten and Margaret Lloyd, *Psychology Applied to Modern Life* (Pacific Grove, CA: Brooks/Cole Publishing, 1994), p. 51.
4. Jeffery B. Vancouver, Charles M. Thompson, E. Casey Tischner, and Dan J. Putka, "Two Studies Examining the Negative Effect of Self-Efficacy on Performance," *Journal of Applied Psychology*, June 2002, pp. 506–516.
5. Janis Miller, "The Value of Self-Respect," available at *www.foryoumagazine.com/summer02/selfrespect.html.* February 5, 2006.
6. "Better Self-Esteem," available at *www.utexas.edu/student/cmhc/booklets/selfesteem/selfest.html.* February 1, 2006.
7. Randall Edwards, "Is Self-Esteem Really All That Important?" *The APA Monitor*, May 1995, p. 43.
8. David De Cremer et al., "Rewarding Leadership and Fair Procedures as Determinants of Self-Esteem," *Journal of Applied Psychology*, January 2005, pp. 3–12.
9. Eugene Raudsepp, "Strong Self-Esteem Can Help You Advance," *CareerJournal.com* (*The Wall Street Journal*), August 10, 2004.
10. Larry Werner, "Coffee with Retired Toro CEO Kendrick Melrose," Minneapolis, Minnesota *Star Tribune*, May 23, 2005, as reprinted by Center for Ethical Business Culture, available at *www.cebeglobal.org.* February 7, 2006.
11. Research reported in Melissa Dittman, "Study Links Jealousy with Aggression, Low Self-Esteem," *Psychology Today*, February 2005, p. 13.
12. Jon L. Pierce, Donald G. Gardner, Larry L. Cummings, and Randall B. Dunman, "Organization-Based Self-Esteem: Construct Definition, Measurement, and Validation," *Academy of Management Journal*, September 1989, p. 623.
13. Branden, *Self-Esteem at Work*; Timothy A. Judge and Joyce E. Bono, "Relationship of Core Self-Evaluations Traits—Self-Esteem, Generalized Self-Efficacy, Locus of Control, and Emotional Stability—With Job Satisfaction and Job Performance: A Meta-Analysis," *Journal of Applied Psychology*, February 2001, pp. 80–92.
14. Quoted in Carlin Flora, "The Measuring Game: Why You Think You'll Never Stack Up," *Psychology Today*, September/October 2005, p. 44.
15. Cited in Julia M. Klein, "The Illusion of Rejection," *Psychology Today*, January/February 2005, p. 30.
16. Research reported in Melissa Dittmann, "Self-Esteem That's Based on External Sources Has Mental Health Consequences, Study Says," *Monitor on Psychology*, December 2002, p. 16.
17. Research mentioned in book review by E. R. Snyder in *Contemporary Psychology*, July 1998, p. 482.
18. Daniel L. Aroz, "The Manager's Self-Concept," *Human Resources Forum*, July 1989, p. 4.
19. Cited in "Self-Esteem: You'll Need It to Succeed," *Executive Strategies*, September 1993, p. 12.
20. Raudsepp, "Strong Self-Esteem."
21. Research reported in David Dent, "Bursting the Self-Esteem Bubble," *Psychology Today*, March/April 2002, p. 16.
22. Marilyn E. Gist and Terence R. Mitchell, "Self-Efficacy: A Theoretical Analysis of Its Determinants and Malleability," *Academy of Management Review*, April 1992, pp. 183–211.
23. Dov Eden and Arie Aviram, "Self-Efficacy Training to Speed Reemployment: Helping People to Help Themselves," *Journal of Applied Psychology*, June 1993, pp. 352–360.
24. George P. Hollenbeck and Douglas T. Hall, "Self-Confidence and Leader Performance," *Organizational Dynamics*, Issue 3, 2004, pp. 261–264.
25. Jay T. Knippen and Thad B. Green, "Building Self-Confidence," *Supervisory Management*, August 1989, pp. 22–27.
26. "Entrepreneurs Need Attitude: Power of Being Positive Can Help You to Succeed in Spite of Setbacks," Knight Ridder, September 16, 2002.
27. D. Brian McNatt and Timothy A. Judge, "Boundary Conditions of the Galeta Effect: A Field Experiment and Constructive Replication," *Academy of Management Journal*, August 2004, pp. 550–565.
28. Frances Thornton, Gayle Privette, and Charles M. Bundrick, "Peak Performance of Business Leaders: An Experience Parallel to Self-Actualization Theory," *Journal of Business and Psychology*, Winter 1999, pp. 253–264.

3

Self-Motivation and Goal Setting

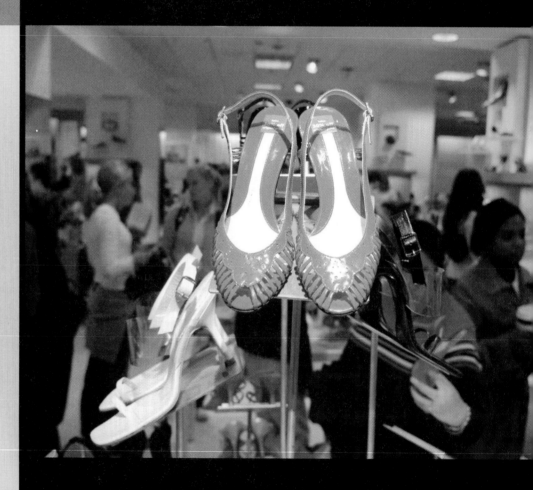

Learning Objectives

Outline

After studying the information and doing the exercises in this chapter, you should be able to:

1 Explain how needs and motives influence motivation.

2 Identify several needs and motives that could propel you into action.

3 Pinpoint how the hierarchy of needs could explain your behavior.

4 Explain why and how goals contribute to self-motivation.

5 Describe how to set effective goals and the problems sometimes created by goals.

6 Describe several specific techniques of self-motivation.

7 Apply the self-discipline model to achieving your goals.

Elizabeth Schweitzer represents the future of retailing. When the 21-year-old was planning to graduate from the Wharton School of the University of Pennsylvania, she was not following most of her classmates to investment banking or consulting. Instead, she would be joining the executive training program at Bloomingdale's, a job that many could perceive as less financially attractive. But her goals were at least as lofty; someday she wants to be CEO of Bloomingdale's parent, Federated Department Stores Inc.

"This is a ripe time for young talent to come up in the world of retailing. And I feel lucky," said the Larchmont, New York, native, who learned the ropes of merchandising at age 13 while working at a clothing store.

Schweitzer, who took a buying internship at Bloomingdale's one summer, said that she has made many contacts in the industry through the program, which provides a strong partnership with the industry. [1]

Maybe a career in upscale retailing is not your dream, and maybe you do not aspire to become the CEO of a major business corporation. Yet Schweitzer's comments emphasize an important truth. You have to be motivated and establish goals to achieve success in your career. Strong motivation is also important for personal life. Unless you direct your energies toward specific goals, such as improving your productivity or meeting a new friend, you will accomplish very little. Knowledge of motivation and goal setting as applied to yourself, therefore, can pay substantial dividends in improving the quality of your life. Knowledge about motivation and goal setting is also important when attempting to influence others to get things accomplished. Motivating others, for example, is a major requirement of the manager's job.

Being well motivated is also important simply to meet the demands of employers. Most organizations insist on high productivity from workers at all levels. Assuming that you have the necessary skills, training, and equipment, being well motivated will enable you to achieve high productivity.

The general purpose of this chapter is to present information that can help you sustain a high level of motivation, centering on the importance of needs and goals.

■ Learning Objective 1

How Do Needs and Motives Influence Motivation?

According to a widely accepted explanation of human behavior, people have needs and motives that propel them toward achieving certain goals. Needs and motives are closely related. A **need** is an internal striving or urge to do something, such as a need to drink when thirsty. It can be regarded as a biological or psychological requirement. Because the person is deprived in some way (such as not having enough fluid in the body), the person is motivated to take action toward a goal. In this case the goal might be simply getting something to drink.

A **motive** is an inner drive that moves a person to do something. The motive is usually based on a need or desire and results in the intention to attain an appropriate goal. Because needs and motives are so closely related, the two terms are often used interchangeably. For example, "recognition need" and "recognition motive" refer to the same thing.

■ **Need**

an internal striving or urge to do something, such as a need to drink when thirsty

■ **Motive**

an inner drive that moves a person to do something

THE NEED THEORY OF MOTIVATION

The central idea behind need theory is that unsatisfied needs motivate us until they become satisfied. When people are dissatisfied or anxious about their present status or performance, they will try to reduce this anxiety. This need cycle is shown in Figure 3-1. Assume that you have a strong need or motive to achieve recognition. As a result, you experience tension that drives you to find some way of being recognized on the job. The action you take is to apply for a position as the team leader of your group. You reason that being appointed as team leader would provide ample recognition, particularly if the team performs well. You are appointed to the position, and for now your need for recognition is at least partially satisfied as you receive compliments from your coworkers and friends. Once you receive this partial satisfaction, two things typically happen. Either you will soon require a stronger dose of recognition, or you will begin to concentrate on another need or motive, such as achievement. In either case, the need cycle will repeat itself. You might seek another form of recognition or satisfaction of your need for power. For example, you might apply for a position as department manager or open your own business. Ideally, in this situation your boss would give you more responsibility. This could lead to more satisfaction of your recognition need and to some satisfaction of your need for achievement. (The needs mentioned so far, and others, are defined next.)

The need theory suggests that self-interest plays a key role in motivation. [2] People ask, "What's in it for me?" or "WIIFM" (pronounced *wiff'em*) before engaging in any form of behavior. In one way or another people act in a way that serves their self-interest. Even when people act in a way that helps others, they are doing so because helping others helps them. For example, a person may give money to poor people because this act of kindness makes him or her feel wanted and powerful.

IMPORTANT NEEDS AND MOTIVES PEOPLE ATTEMPT TO SATISFY

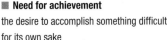

Work and personal life offer the opportunity to satisfy dozens of needs and motives. In this and the following section, important needs that propel people into action are described. As you read about these needs and motives, relate them to yourself. For example, ask yourself, "Am I a power-seeking person?"

Achievement

The **need for achievement** is the desire to accomplish something difficult for its own sake. People with a strong need for achievement frequently think of how to do

■ **Need for achievement**
the desire to accomplish something difficult for its own sake

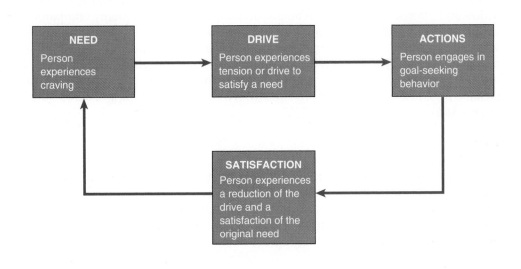

The Need Cycle

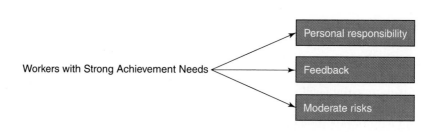

Figure   3-2

Preferences   of   Workers   with
Strong Achievement Needs

a job better. Responsibility seeking is another characteristic of people with a high need for achievement. They are also concerned with how to progress in their careers. Workers with a high need for achievement are interested in monetary rewards primarily as feedback about how well they are achieving. They also set realistic yet moderately difficult goals, take calculated risks, and desire feedback on performance. (A moderately difficult goal challenges a person but is not so difficult as to most likely lead to failure and frustration.) In general, those who enjoy building business, activities, and programs from scratch have a strong need for achievement. Figure 3-2 outlines the preferences of workers with strong achievement needs.

Power

People with a high power need feel compelled to control resources, such as other people and money. Successful executives typically have a high power motive and exhibit three dominant characteristics: (1) They act with vigor and determination to exert their power; (2) they invest much time in thinking about ways to alter the behavior and thinking of others, and (3) they care about their personal standing with those around them. [3] The power need can be satisfied through occupying a high-level position or by becoming a highly influential person. Or you can name skyscrapers and hotels after yourself, following the lead of Donald Trump.

Affiliation

People with a strong affiliation need seek out close relationships with others and tend to be loyal as friends or employees. The affiliation motive is met directly through belonging to the "office gang," a term of endearment implying that your coworkers are an important part of your life. Many people prefer working in groups to individual effort because of the opportunity the former provides for socializing with others.

Recognition

People with a strong need for recognition want to be acknowledged for their contribution and efforts. The need for recognition is so pervasive that many companies have formal recognition programs in which outstanding or long-time employees receive gifts, plaques, and jewelry inscribed with the company logo. The recognition motive can be satisfied through means such as winning contests, receiving awards, and seeing your name in print. A major reason the need for recognition is such a useful motivator is that most people think they are underappreciated (and overworked).

Order

People with a strong need for order have the urge to put things in order. They also want to achieve arrangement, balance, neatness, and precision. The order motive can be quickly satisfied by cleaning and organizing your work or living space. Occupations offering the opportunity to satisfy the order motive almost every day include accountant, computer programmer, and paralegal.

Risk Taking and Thrill Seeking

Some people crave constant excitement on the job and are willing to risk their lives to achieve thrills. The need to take risks and pursue thrills has grown in importance in the high-technology era. Many people work for employers, start businesses, and purchase stocks with uncertain futures. Both the search of giant payoffs and daily thrills motivate these individuals. [4] A strong craving for thrills may have some positive consequences for the organization, including willingness to perform such dangerous feats as setting explosives, capping an oil well, controlling a radiation leak, and introducing a product in a highly competitive environment. However, extreme risk takers and thrill seekers can create such problems as being involved in a disproportionate number of vehicular accidents and making imprudent investments. Take Human Relations Self-Assessment Quiz 3-1 to measure your tendency toward risk taking.

MASLOW'S NEED HIERARCHY

The best-known categorization of needs is **Maslow's need hierarchy.** At the same time, it is the most widely used explanation of human motivation. According to psychologist Abraham H. Maslow, people strive to satisfy the following groups of needs in step-by-step order:

1. *Physiological needs* refer to bodily needs, such as the requirements for food, water, shelter, and sleep.

2. *Safety needs* refer to actual physical safety and to a feeling of being safe from both physical and emotional injury.

3. *Social needs* are essentially love or belonging needs. Unlike the two previous levels of needs, they center around a person's interaction with other people.

4. *Esteem needs* represent an individual's demand to be seen as a person of worth by others—and to him- or herself.

5. *Self-actualizing needs* are the highest level of needs, including the needs for self-fulfillment and personal development. [5]

A diagram of the need hierarchy is presented in Figure 3-3. Notice the distinction between higher-level and lower-level needs. With few exceptions, higher-level

■ **Learning Objective 3**

■ **Maslow's need hierarchy**
the best-known categorization of needs; according to psychologist Abraham H. Maslow, people strive to satisfy the following groups of needs in step-by-step order: physiological needs, safety needs, social needs, esteem needs, and self-actualizing needs

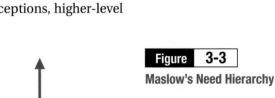

| Figure | **3-3** |

Maslow's Need Hierarchy

Human Relations Self-Assessment Quiz 3-1

The Risk-Taking Scale

Answer true or false to the following questions to obtain an approximate idea of your tendency to take risks, or your desire to do so:

	True	False
1. I eat sushi or other raw fish.	❑	❑
2. I would rather be a stock broker than an accountant.	❑	❑
3. I think that amusement park roller coasters should be abolished.	❑	❑
4. I enjoy doing creative work.	❑	❑
5. I enjoy (or did enjoy) the excitement of looking for new dates.	❑	❑
6. I don't like trying foods from other cultures.	❑	❑
7. I would choose bonds over growth stocks.	❑	❑
8. Friends would say that I do not like to take risks.	❑	❑
9. I like to challenge people in positions of power.	❑	❑
10. I don't always wear seat belts while driving.	❑	❑
11. I sometimes talk on my cell phone while driving at highway speeds.	❑	❑
12. I would love to be an entrepreneur (or I love being one).	❑	❑
13. I purposely avoid traveling overseas.	❑	❑
14. Most days are boring for me.	❑	❑
15. I would like helping out in a crisis such as a product recall.	❑	❑
16. On the highway, I usually drive at least 10 miles per hour beyond the speed limit.	❑	❑
17. I would like to go cave exploring (or already have done so).	❑	❑
18. I like to have a daily dose of simulation.	❑	❑
19. I would be willing to have at least one-third of my compensation based on a bonus for good performance.	❑	❑
20. I would be willing to visit a maximum security prison on a job assignment.	❑	❑

Scoring and Interpretation:

1. T	**5.** T	**9.** T	**13.** F	**17.** T
2. T	**6.** F	**10.** T	**14.** F	**18.** T
3. F	**7.** T	**11.** T	**15.** T	**19.** T
4. T	**8.** F	**12.** T	**16.** T	**20.** T

Give yourself one point each time your answer agrees with the key. If you score 16–20, you are probably a high risk taker. 10–15: You're a moderate risk taker. 5–9: You are cautious. 0–4: You're a very low risk taker.

Questions: 1. How does your self-evaluation of your risk-taking tendencies compare with your score on this quiz?

2. Do you see any needs for improvement in terms of becoming more (or less) of a risk taker?

Source: The idea of a test about risk-taking comfort, as well as several of the statements on the quiz come from psychologist Frank Farley.

needs are more difficult to satisfy. A person's needs for affiliation might be satisfied by being a member of a friendly work group. Yet to satisfy self-actualization needs, such as self-fulfillment, a person might have to develop an outstanding reputation in his or her company.

The need hierarchy implies that most people think of finding a job as a way of obtaining the necessities of life. Once these are obtained, a person may think of achieving friendship, self-esteem, and self-fulfillment on the job. When a person is generally satisfied at one level, he or she looks for satisfaction at a higher level. As Maslow describes it, a person is a "perpetually wanting animal." Very few people are totally satisfied with their lot in life, even the rich and famous.

The extent of need satisfaction is influenced by a person's job. Some construction jobs, for example, involve dangerous work in severe climates, thus frustrating both physiological and safety needs. Ordinarily there is much more opportunity for approaching self-actualization when a person occupies a prominent position, such as a top executive or famous performer. However, a person with low potential could approach self-actualization by occupying a lesser position. In the current era, workers at all levels are threatened with the frustration of security needs because so many companies reduce the number of employees to save money.

How do Maslow's needs and the other needs described in this chapter relate to self-motivation? First you have to ask yourself, "Which needs do I really want to satisfy?" After answering the question honestly, concentrate your efforts on an activity that will most likely satisfy that need. For instance, if you are hungry for power, strive to become a high-level manager or a business owner. If you crave self-esteem, focus your efforts on work and social activities that are well regarded by others. The point is that you will put forth substantial effort if you think the goal you attain will satisfy an important need.

Another way of understanding self-motivation as related to need satisfaction is to examine what work factors are important to you. A job satisfaction survey conducted by the Society for Human Resource Management and CNN found the factors listed in Figure 3-4 "very important" by 600 employees at a variety of companies. The list shows the order of importance of job satisfaction factors among employees as a group. [6] Two examples of how needs come into play are (4) job security and (9) opportunities to use skills/abilities. If 4 is important to you, it might reflect a strong need for security. If 9 is important to you, it might reflect a strong need for self-fulfillment.

How Do Goals Contribute to Motivation?

■ **Learning Objective 4**

At some point in their lives, almost all successful people have established goals, attesting to the importance of goals. A **goal** is an event, circumstance, object, or condition a person strives to attain. A goal thus reflects your desire or intention to regulate your actions. Here we look at five topics to help you understand the nature of goals: (1) the advantages of goals, (2) different goal orientations, (3) goal setting on the job, (4) personal goal setting, and (5) guidelines for goal setting, as well as potential disadvantages of goals.

■ **Goal**
an event, circumstance, object, or condition a person strives to attain

ADVANTAGES OF GOALS

Substantial research indicates that setting specific, reasonably difficult goals improves performance. One of many possible examples involves the American Pulpwood Association, which wanted to increase the productivity (employee cords per hour) of independent loggers in the southern United States. Based on goal-setting theory, Pulpwood crew supervisors assigned a specific high goal for the loggers. They also handed out tally meters to enable the workers to keep count of the number of tress they cut down. Productivity soared in comparison to those crews who were simply

The 2004 *Job Satisfaction Survey* conducted by the Society for Human Resource Management and CNN found the following factors "very important" by 600 employees at a variety of companies. The list shows the order of importance of job satisfaction factors among employees as a group.

Rank According to Employees	Rank According to You
1. Benefits	_____
2. Compensation/pay	_____
3. Feeling safe in the work environment	_____
4. Job security	_____
5. Flexibility to balance work/life issues	_____
6. Communication between employees and senior management	_____
7. Relationship with immediate supervisor	_____
8. Management recognition of employee job performance	_____
9. Opportunities to use skills/abilities	_____
10. The work itself	_____
11. Overall corporate culture	_____
12. Autonomy and independence	_____
13. Career development opportunities	_____
14. Meaningfulness of the job	_____
15. Variety of work	_____
16. Career advancement opportunities	_____
17. Contribution of work to organization's business goals	_____
18. Organization's commitment to professional development	_____
19. Job-specific training	_____
20. Relationship with coworkers	_____
21. Networking	_____

Question: Why do you think modern employees rank benefits (e.g., medical insurance and life insurance) as the most important job satisfaction factor?

Suggestion: Make your own ranking of the 21 factors. What big differences do you see between your ranking and the national ranking?

Source: Adapted from Pamela Babcock, "Find What Workers Want," *HR Magazine*, April 2005, p. 53.

Figure   3-4

Ranking of Job Satisfaction Factors by 600 Employees

urged to do their best. According to professor of organizational effectiveness, Gary Latham of the Rotman School of Management, goal setting instilled purpose, challenge, and meaning into what was previously seen as a boring, tiresome, task. [7]

Goals are useful for several reasons. First, when we guide our lives with goals, we tend to focus our efforts in a consistent direction. Your conscious goals affect what you achieve. Without goals, our efforts may become scattered in many directions. We may keep trying, but we will go nowhere unless we happen to receive more than our share of luck.

Second, goal setting increases our chances for success, particularly because success can be defined as the achievement of a goal. The goals we set for accomplishing a task can serve as a standard to indicate when we have done a satisfactory job. A sales representative might set a goal of selling $300,000 worth of merchandise for the year. By November, she might close a deal that places her total sales at $310,000. With a sigh of relief she can then say, "I've done well this year."

Third, goals serve as self-motivators and energizers. People who set goals tend to be motivated because they are confident that their energy is being invested in something worthwhile. Aside from helping you become more motivated and productive, setting goals can help you achieve personal satisfaction. Most people derive a sense of satisfaction from attaining a goal that is meaningful to them.

THE LEARNING AND PERFORMANCE ORIENTATIONS TOWARD GOALS

Another useful perspective on understanding how goals influence motivation is that goals can be aimed at either learning or hoping to perform well. [8] A learning-goal orientation means that an individual is focused on acquiring new skills and mastering new situations. For example, you might establish the goal of learning how to develop skill in making a computerized presentation package. You say to yourself, "My goal is to learn how to use PowerPoint [or similar software] so I know even more about how to apply information technology."

A performing-goal orientation is different. It is aimed at wanting to demonstrate and validate the adequacy of your competence by seeking favorable judgments about your competence. At the same time, the person wants to avoid seeking negative judgments. For example, your goal might be to make PowerPoint presentations that would highly impress whoever watched them. Your focus is on looking good and avoiding negative evaluations of your presentations.

A person's goal orientation usually affects his or her desire for feedback. People with a learning-goal orientation are more likely to seek feedback on how well they are performing. In contrast, people with a performing-goal orientation are less likely to seek feedback. If you focus too much on setting performance goals, you might have a tendency to overlook the value of feedback. Yet the feedback could help you improve your performance in the long run.

Goal orientation is also important because it can affect work performance. Attempting to master skills often leads to better results than does attempting to impress others. A study of the effects of the two different goal orientations was conducted with 167 salespeople working for a medical supplies distributor. The salespeople were paid mostly on the commission of the gross profits they generated. The researchers found that a learning-goal orientation was associated with higher sales performance. In contrast, a performing-goal orientation was unrelated to sales performance. An important implication of the study for managers and workers is that a focus on skill development, even for an experienced workforce, is likely to lead to higher performance. [9]

Another positive consequence of a mastery (or learning-goal) orientation is that it often prompts workers to develop better relationships with their supervisors. A study in a Dutch energy supply company found that workers with a mastery orientation had stronger job performance and job satisfaction than those workers with a performance orientation. The positive outcomes of stronger job performance and satisfaction appeared to take place because the workers developed better relationships with their supervisors. [10]

A recent synthesis of evidence points to a key reason why a learning- (or mastery) goal orientation is so important in today's business world. The purpose of a learning goal is to stimulate a person's imagination, to engage in discovery, and to think imaginatively. A performance goal focuses more on exerting effort to attain an objective using the knowledge one already possesses. When an effective strategy requires innovation that has yet to emerge—as is often the case—specific, high-learning goals should be set. [11] An example of a learning goal of high importance would be figuring out how to dispose of debris after a hurricane.

GOAL SETTING ON THE JOB

Virtually all organizations have come to accept the value of goal setting in producing the results they want to achieve. In most goal-setting programs, executives at the top of the organization are supposed to plan for the future by setting goals such as "Improve profits 10 percent this year." Employees at the bottom of the organization are supposed to go along with such broad goals by setting more specific goals. An example is "I will decrease damaged merchandise by 10 percent this year. I will accomplish this by making sure that our shelving is adequate for our needs."

You participate in the goal-setting process by designing goals to fit into the overall mission of the firm. A bank teller might set a personal goal of this nature: "During rush periods, and when I feel fatigued, I will double-count all the money that I handle." In some goal-setting programs, employees are requested to set goals that will lead to their personal improvement. An auditor for the state set this goal for herself: "Within the next 12 months, I will enroll in and complete a supervisory training course in a local college." This woman aspired toward becoming a supervisor.

A sample set of work goals is shown in Figure 3-5. The service and repair shop supervisor who set these objectives took into account the requirements of his boss and the automobile dealership. Even if you set goals by yourself, they must still take into account the needs of your employer.

PERSONAL GOAL SETTING

If you want to lead a rewarding personal life, your chances of doing so increase if you plan it. Personal goals heavily influence the formulation of career goals as well. For this reason, it is worthwhile to set personal goals in conjunction with career goals.

JOB TITLE AND BRIEF JOB DESCRIPTION

Manager, Service Department:
Responsible for supervision of service department of automobile dealership. Responsible for staffing service department with appropriate personnel and for quality of service to customers. Work closely with owner of dealership to discuss unusual customer problems. Handle customer complaints about mechanical problems of cars purchased at dealership.

Objectives for Scott Gilley

1. By December 31 of this year, decrease by 10 percent customer demands for rework.

2. Hire two general mechanics within 45 days.

3. Hire two body specialists within 45 days.

4. Decrease by 30 percent the number of repairs returned by customers for rework.

5. Reduce by 10 percent the discrepancy between estimates and actual bills to customers.

6. Schedule at least 20 percent of our service appointments through our Web site by January 15 of next year.

Figure **3-5**

Form used in Automobile Dealership for Statement of Goals

Ideally, they should be integrated to help achieve a balance between the demands of work and personal life. For example, if your preferred style would be to live in a rural area, a career in manufacturing would be more sensible than a career in advertising. This is true because manufacturing within North American has moved mostly to rural areas, whereas advertising remains mostly in large cities.

Types of Personal Goals

Personal goals can be subdivided into those relating to social and family life, hobbies and interests, physical and mental health, career, and finances. An example of each type follows:

Social and family life. "By age 30 I would like to have a spouse and two children."

Hobbies and interests. "Become a black belt in karate by age 28."

Physical and mental health. "Be able to run four miles without stopping or panting for breath by April 15 of next year."

Career. "Become office manager by age 28."

Finances. "Within the next four years be earning $70,000 per year, adjusted for inflation."

Other categories of personal goals are possible, yet the list presented represents convenient categories for most people.

ACTION PLANS TO SUPPORT GOALS

Ideally, reading this chapter and doing the exercises in it will start you on a lifelong process of using goals to help you plan your life. But before you can capitalize on the benefits of goal setting, you need a method for translating goals into action. An **action plan** describes how you are going to reach your goal. The major reason you need an action plan for most goals is that without a method for achieving what you want, the goal is likely to slip by. If your goal were to build your own log cabin, part of your action plan would be to learn how to operate a buzz saw, to read a handbook on log cabin building, to learn how to operate a tractor, and so forth. Some goals are so difficult to reach that your action plan might encompass hundreds of separate activities. You would then have to develop separate action plans for each step of the way.

> ■ **Action plan**
> describes how you are going to reach your goal

Some immediate goals do not really require an action plan. A mere statement of the goal may point to an obvious action plan. If your goal were to start painting your room, it would not be necessary to draw up a formal action plan such as "Go to hardware store; purchase paint, brush, and rollers; borrow ladder and drop cloth from Ken; put furniture in center of room"; and so on.

GUIDELINES FOR GOAL SETTING

> ■ **Learning Objective 5**

Goal setting is an art in the sense that some people do a better job of goal setting than others. Following are suggestions on setting effective goals—those that lead to achieving what you hoped to achieve.

Formulate Specific Goals

A goal such as "attain success" is too vague to serve as a guide to daily action. A more useful goal would be to state specifically what you mean by success and when you expect to achieve it. For example, "I want to be the manager of customer service at a telecommunications company by January 1, 2010, and receive above-average performance reviews."

Formulate Concise Goals

A useful goal can usually be expressed in a short, punchy statement, for example, "Decrease input errors in bank statements so that customer complaints are decreased by 25 percent by September 30 of this year." People new to goal setting typically commit the error of formulating lengthy, rambling goal statements. These lengthy goals involve so many different activities that they fail to serve as specific guides to action.

Set Realistic as Well as Stretch Goals

A realistic goal is one that represents the right amount of challenge for the person pursuing the goal. On the one hand, easy goals are not very motivational—they may not spring you into action. On the other hand, goals that are too far beyond your capabilities may lead to frustration and despair because there is a good chance you will fail to reach them. The extent to which a goal is realistic depends on a person's capabilities. An easy goal for an experienced person might be a realistic goal for a beginner. Self-efficacy is also a factor in deciding whether a goal is realistic. The higher your self-efficacy, the more likely you are to think that a particular goal is realistic. A person with high self-efficacy for learning Chinese might say, "I think learning two new Chinese words a day is realistic."*

Several goals that stretch your capability might be included in your list of goals. The goal of becoming the CEO of Federated Department Stores established by the college student in the chapter opener represents an extreme stretch goal. Another type of stretch goal is striving for a noble cause. A logging supervisor may not get excited about having the crew load a certain number of felled trees on a flatbed truck. However, she might get excited about the trees being used to build homes, schools, and hospitals.

* The accompanying Human Relations in Practice insert provides an example of the use of stretch goals.

Human Relations in Practice

Technology Executive Sets Challenging Goals

The best goals are a bit of a stretch according to technology executive Margaret Heffernan. She learned this lesson more than a decade ago when a software company hired her to manage the immediate launch of some newly acquired software. A big problem, however, was that the software did not function properly. So, Heffernan and her team decided to reengineer (or reconfigure and redesign) the product in only 90 days.

"The software specialists knew they had set themselves up for a tough challenge and that reaching it was a real coup," she says. "But everyone knew that with each process we rethought, we were closer to the goal. We created energy and optimism rather than quashing it."

Source: Adapted from Margaret Heffernan, "The Morale of the Story," *Fast Company*, www.fastcompany.com, as reported in "Goals Should Challenge, Not Overwhelm," *Manager's Edge*, May 2005, p. 1.

Set Goals for Different Time Periods

Goals are best set for different time periods, such as daily, short range, medium range, and long range. Daily goals are essentially a to-do list. Short-range goals cover the period from approximately one week to one year into the future. Finding a new job, for example, is typically a short-range goal. Medium-range goals relate to events that will take place within approximately two to five years. They concern such things as the type of education or training you plan to undertake and the next step in your career.

Long-range goals refer to events taking place five years into the future and beyond. As such, they relate to the overall lifestyle you wish to achieve, including the type of work and family situation you hope to have. Although every person should have a general idea of a desirable lifestyle, long-range goals should be flexible. You might, for example, plan to stay single until age 40. But while on vacation next summer, you might just happen to meet the right partner for you.

Short-range goals make an important contribution to attaining goals of longer duration. If a one-year work goal is to reduce mailing and shipping costs by 12 percent for the year, a good way to motivate workers is to look for a 1 percent saving per month. Progress toward a larger goal is self-rewarding.

PROBLEMS SOMETIMES CREATED BY GOALS

Despite the many advantages of goals, they can create problems. A major problem is that *goals can create inflexibility*. People can become so focused on reaching particular goals that they fail to react to emergencies, such as neglecting a much-needed machine repair to achieve quota. Goals can also make a person inflexible with respect to missing out on opportunities. Sales representatives sometimes neglect to invest time in cultivating a prospective customer because of the pressure to make quota. Instead, the sales rep goes for the quick sale with an established customer.

Another problem is that *performance goals can sometimes detract from an interest in the task*. People with a performance-goal orientation (focusing on being judged as competent) will sometimes lose interest in the task. The loss of interest is most likely to occur when the task is difficult. [12] Assume that your primary reason for working as an information technology specialist is to perform well enough so that you can earn a high income. If carrying out your responsibilities encounters some hurdles, you may readily become discouraged with information technology as a field. However, if your orientation is primarily to advance your knowledge about a dynamic field, you will not be readily frustrated when you encounter problems. You might even look on it as a learning opportunity.

A tight focus on goals can also encourage unethical behavior and a disregard for *how* the goals are attained. A sales representative might give kickbacks simply to gain a sale, and a CEO might lay off needed workers and neglect investing in new-product research simply to make certain profit figures.

Despite the problems that can arise in goal setting, goals are valuable tools for managing your work and personal life. Used with common sense and according to the ideas presented in this chapter, they could have a major, positive impact on your life.

What Are Some Self-Motivation Techniques?

■ Learning Objective 6

Many people never achieve satisfying careers and never realize their potential because of low motivation. They believe they could perform better but admit that "I'm simply not a go-getter" or "I'm simply not that motivated." Earlier we described how identifying your most important needs could enhance motivation. Here we describe six additional techniques for self-motivation.

1. Set goals for yourself. As shown throughout this chapter, goal setting is one of the most important techniques for self-motivation. If you set long-range goals and support them with a series of smaller goals set for shorter time spans, your motivation will increase.

2. Find intrinsically motivating work. A major factor in self-motivation is to find work that is fun or its own reward. Intrinsic motivation refers to the natural tendency to seek out novelty and challenges, to extend and use one's capacities, to explore, and to learn. [13] The intrinsically motivated person is involved in the task at hand, such as a technology enthusiast surfing the Web for hours at a time. Finding a job that offers you motivators in ample supply will help enhance your intrinsic motivation. For example, you might have good evidence from your past experience that the opportunity for close contact with people is a personal motivator. Find a job that involves working in a small, friendly department or team.

Based on circumstances, you may have to take whatever job you can find, or you may not be in a position to change jobs. In such a situation, try to arrange your work so you have more opportunity to experience the reward(s) that you are seeking. Assume that solving difficult problems excites you but that your job is 85 percent routine. Develop better work habits so that you can take care of the routine aspects of your job more quickly. This will give you more time to enjoy the creative aspects of your job.

3. Get feedback on your performance. Few people can sustain a high level of motivation without receiving information about how well they are doing. Even if you find your work challenging and exciting, you will need feedback. One reason positive feedback is valuable is that it acts as a reward. If you learn that your efforts achieved a worthwhile purpose, you will feel encouraged. For example, if a graphics display you designed was well received by company officials, you would probably want to prepare another graphics display.

Industrial psychology professors Remus Ilies of Michigan State University and Timothy A. Judge of the University of Florida conducted an experiment with management students about the effects of feedback on goal setting. The study demonstrated that participants adjusted their goals upward after receiving positive feedback and downward after negative feedback. It was also found that when the students were more emotional about the feedback, the positive and negative results were more pronounced. [14] The link here to self-motivation is that when goals are higher, motivation will be higher.

■ **Behavior modification**

system of motivation that emphasizes rewarding people for doing the right things and punishing them for doing the wrong things

4. Apply behavior modification to yourself. Behavior modification is a system of motivation that emphasizes rewarding people for doing the right things and punishing them for doing the wrong things. Many people have used behavior modification to change their own behavior. Specific purposes include overcoming eating disorders, tobacco addiction, Internet abuse, nail biting, and procrastination. To boost your own motivation through behavior modification, you would have to first decide what specific motivated actions you want to increase (such as working 30 minutes longer each day). Second, you would have to decide on a suitable set of rewards and punishments. You may choose to use rewards only because rewards are generally better motivators than punishments.

■ **Expectancy theory of motivation**

people will be motivated if they believe that their efforts will lead to desired outcomes

5. Improve your skills relevant to your goals. The **expectancy theory of motivation** states that people will be motivated if they believe that their efforts will lead to desired outcomes. According to this theory, people hold back effort when they are not confident that their efforts will lead to accomplishments. You should, therefore, seek adequate training to ensure that you have the right abilities and skills to perform your work. The training might be provided by the employer or on your own through a course of self-study. Appropriate training gives you more confidence that you can perform the work. The training also increases your feelings of self-efficacy. [15] By recognizing your ability to mobilize your own resources to succeed, your self-confidence for the task will be elevated.

6. Raise your level of self-expectation. Another strategy for increasing your level of motivation is to simply expect more of yourself. If you raise your level of self-expectation, you are likely to achieve more. Because you expect to succeed, you do succeed. The net effect is the same as if you had increased your level of motivation. The technical term for improving your performance through raising your own expectations is the Galeta effect. In one experiment, for example, the self-expectations of subjects were raised in brief interviews with an organizational psychologist. The psychologist told the subjects they had high potential to succeed in the undertaking they were about to begin (a problem-solving task). The subjects who received the positive information about their potential did better than those subjects who did not receive such encouragement. [16]

High self-expectations and a positive mental attitude take a long time to develop. However, they are critically important for becoming a well-motivated person in a variety of situations.

> "Remind yourself that you have personal power, and that you can make things happen. Erase those negative mental tapes that say 'No, I can't.'"
> —E. Carol Webster, clinical psychologist, quoted in *Black Enterprise Magazine*, September 2005, p. 157.

7. Develop a strong work ethic. A highly effective strategy for self-motivation is to develop a strong work ethic. If you are committed to the idea that most work is valuable and that it is joyful to work hard, you will automatically become strongly motivated. A person with a weak work ethic cannot readily develop a strong one because the change requires a profound value shift. Yet if a person gives a lot of serious thought to the importance of work and follows the right role models, a work ethic can be strengthened. The shift to a strong work ethic is much like a person who has a casual attitude toward doing fine work becoming more prideful.

8. Develop psychological hardiness. A comprehensive approach to becoming better self-motivated would be to develop a higher degree of **psychological hardiness**—a mental state in which the individual experiences a high degree of commitment, control, and challenge. *Commitment* is a tendency to involve oneself in whatever one is doing or encounters, such as being committed to developing a successful video game. *Control* is a tendency to feel and act as if one is influential, rather than helpless, in facing twists and turns in life. *Challenge* is a belief that change rather than stability is normal in life and that changes lead to growth and are not threats to security. (Moving in these three directions would involve substantial personal development.) A study with more than 600 college students demonstrated that those who scored higher on psychological hardiness tended to have stronger motivation to study and learn. [17] Psychological hardiness would also be helpful in work motivation.

■ **Psychological hardiness**
mental state in which the individual experiences a high degree of commitment, control, and challenge

How Do You Develop the Self-Discipline to Achieve Goals and Stay Motivated?

■ **Learning Objective 7**

Another perspective on achieving goals and staying motivated is that it requires **self-discipline,** the ability to work systematically and progressively toward a goal until it is achieved. The self-disciplined person works toward achieving his or her goals without being derailed by the many distractions faced each day. Self-discipline incorporates self-motivation because it enables you to motivate yourself to achieve your goals without being nagged or prodded with deadlines. Our discussion of how to develop self-discipline follows the model shown in Figure 3-6. You will observe that the model incorporates several of the ideas about goals already discussed in

■ **Self-discipline**
the ability to work systematically and progressively toward a goal until it is achieved

The Self-Discipline Model

this chapter. Without realizing it, you have already invested mental energy into learning the self-discipline model. To think through your own tendencies toward being self-disciplined, you are invited to take Human Relations Self-Assessment Quiz 3-2.

Component 1: *Formulate a mission statement.* Who are you? What are you trying to accomplish in life? If you understand what you are trying to accomplish in life, you have the fuel to be self-disciplined. With a mission, activities that may appear mundane to others become vital stepping-stones for you. An example would be learning Spanish grammar to help you become an international businessperson. To help formulate your mission statement, answer two questions: What are my five biggest wishes? What do I want to accomplish in my career during the next five years?

Component 2: *Develop role models.* An excellent method of learning how to be self-disciplined is to model your behavior after successful achievers who are obviously well disciplined. To model another person does not mean you will slavishly imitate every detail of that person's life. Instead, you will follow the general pattern of how the person operates in spheres related to your mission and goals. An ideal role model is the type of person whom you would like to become, not someone you feel you could never become.

Component 3: *Develop goals for each task.* Your mission must be supported by a series of specific goals that collectively will enable you to achieve your mission. Successfully completing goals eventually leads to fulfilling a mission. Each small goal achieved is a building block toward larger achievements.

Component 4: *Develop action plans to achieve goals.* Self-disciplined people carefully follow their action plans because they make goal attainment possible. It is helpful to chart your progress against the dates established for the subactivities.

Component 5: *Use visual and sensory stimulation.* A self-disciplined person relentlessly focuses on a goal and persistently pursues that goal. To accomplish this consistent focus, self-disciplined people form images of reaching their goals—they actually develop a mental image of the act of accomplishing what they want. As mysterious as it sounds, visualization helps the brain convert

Human Relations Self-Assessment Quiz 3-2

The Self-Discipline Quiz

On the following scale, indicate the extent to which each of the following statements describes your behavior or attitude by circling one number for each: disagree strongly (DS), disagree (D), neutral (N), agree (A), agree strongly (AS). Consider asking someone who knows your behavior and attitudes well to help you respond accurately.

	DS	D	N	A	AS
1. I have a strong sense of purpose.	1	2	3	4	5
2. Life is a pain when you are always chasing goals.	5	4	3	2	1
3. My long-range plans in life are well established.	1	2	3	4	5
4. I feel energized when I have a new goal to pursue.	1	2	3	4	5
5. It is difficult for me to picture an event in my mind before it occurs.	5	4	3	2	1
6. When success is near, I can almost taste, feel, and see it.	1	2	3	4	5
7. I consult my daily planner or a to-do list almost every day.	1	2	3	4	5
8. My days rarely turn out the way I had planned.	5	4	3	2	1
9. What I do for a living is not (or would not be) nearly as important as the money it pays.	5	4	3	2	1
10. Some parts of my job are as exciting to me as any hobby or pastime.	1	2	3	4	5
11. Working 60 hours per week for even a short period of time would be out of the question for me.	5	4	3	2	1
12. I have personally known several people who would be good role models for me.	1	2	3	4	5
13. So far I have never read about or known anybody whose lifestyle I would like to emulate.	5	4	3	2	1
14. My work is so demanding that it's difficult for me to concentrate fully on my personal life when I'm not working.	5	4	3	2	1
15. When I'm involved in an important work project, I can enjoy myself fully at a sport or cultural event after hours.	1	2	3	4	5
16. If it weren't for a few bad breaks, I would be much more successful today.	5	4	3	2	1
17. My best helping hand is at the end of my arm.	1	2	3	4	5
18. I get bored easily.	5	4	3	2	1
19. Planning is difficult because life is so unpredictable.	5	4	3	2	1
20. I feel that I'm moving forward a little bit each day toward achieving my goals.	1	2	3	4	5

Scoring and Interpretation:

Calculate your score by adding the numbers circled.

90–100 points: You are a highly self-disciplined person who should be able to capitalize on your skills and talents. Studying about self-discipline might help you capitalize even further on your strong self-discipline.

60–89 points: You have an average degree of self-discipline, so studying the self-discipline model could point to areas for personal improvement.

40–59 points: You may be experiencing problems with self-discipline. Start putting into practice the ideas contained in the self-discipline model.

20–39 points: If your answers are accurate, you have enough problems with self-discipline to limit achieving many of the things in life important to you. In addition to studying the self-discipline model, study about work habits and time management.

Questions: 1. How does this score agree with your evaluation of your self-discipline?

2. Who might you use as a role model of a person with high self-discipline?

> "Nothing in the world can take the place of persistence. Persistence and determination alone are omnipotent. The slogan 'press on' has solved, and always will solve, the problems of the human race."
> — Calvin Coolidge, thirtieth president of the United States

images into reality. The more senses you can incorporate into your visual image, the stronger its power. Imagine yourself seeing, tasting, hearing, smelling, and touching your goal. Can you imagine yourself sitting in your condo overlooking the ocean, eating a great meal to celebrate the fact that the business you founded now has 10,000 employees?

Component 6: *Search for pleasure within the task* .A self-disciplined person finds joy, excitement, and intense involvement in the task at hand and, therefore, finds intrinsic motivation. Instead of focusing on the extrinsic (or external) reward, the love of the task helps the person in pursuit of the goal. An axiom of becoming wealthy is not to focus on getting rich. Instead, focus on work. If the task at hand does not thrill you, at least focus on the pleasure from the most enjoyable element within the task. A bill collector might not find the total task intrinsically motivating, but perhaps he or she enjoys developing skill in resolving conflict.

Component 7: *Compartmentalize spheres of life.* Self-disciplined people have a remarkable capacity to divide up (or compartmentalize) the various spheres of their lives to stay focused on what they are doing at the moment. While working, develop the knack of concentrating on work and putting aside thoughts about personal life. In the midst of social and family activities, concentrate on them rather than half thinking about work. This approach will contribute to both self-discipline and a better integration of work and family life.

Component 8: *Minimize excuse making.* Self-disciplined people concentrate their energies on goal accomplishment rather than making excuses for why work is not accomplished. Instead of trying to justify why they have been diverted from a goal, high-achieving, self-disciplined people circumvent potential barriers.

Key Factor	Average Score on Factor for 325 Adults	Relationship to Self-Discipline Score
1. Age	34.7 years	Almost zero
2. Years of formal education	15.9	Slightly positive
3. Salary in U.S. dollars	$45,899	Slightly positive
4. Self-rating of career on scale of 1 to 7	4.9	Quite positive
5. Self-rating of goal accomplishment on scale of 1 to 7	5.6	Quite positive
6. Self-discipline score on scale of 20 to 100	76.9	------

Figure 3-7

Relationship between Self-Discipline Score and Key Factors

Score: Table derived from data presented in Andrew J. DuBrin, "Career-Related Correlates of Self-Discipline," *Psychological Reports*, 2001, Vol. 89, p. 109.

Undisciplined people, in contrast, seem to look for excuses. If you are an excuse maker, conduct a self-audit, writing down all the reasons blocking you from achieving any current goal. Be brutally honest in challenging each one of your excuses. Ask yourself, "Is this a valid excuse, or is it simply a rationalization for my getting sidetracked?"

The belief that self-discipline contributes to goal attainment and success is about as strong as the belief that a healthy diet and exercise contribute to physical health. Nonetheless, a study conducted with 325 working adults provides reassurance about the benefits of self-discipline. The study participants completed the self-discipline questionnaire previously presented, and they also answered questions about their age, education, salary, and how they felt about their career success and goal accomplishment. As shown in Figure 3-7, positive relationships were found between being self-disciplined and education, salary, career success, and goal attainment. Self-ratings of career success and goal accomplishment were the most strongly related. [18] In conclusion, self-discipline pays. Why do you think it was found that self-discipline was positively associated with years of formal education?

Concept Review and Reinforcement

Key Terms

Need, 54
Motive, 54
Need for achievement, 55
Maslow's need hierarchy, 57

Goal, 59
Action plan, 63
Intrinsic motivation, 66
Behavior modification, 66

Expectancy theory of motivation, 66
Psychological hardiness, 67
Self-discipline, 67

Summary and Review

Self-motivation is important for achieving success in work and personal life. A well-accepted explanation of human behavior is that people have needs and motives propelling them toward achieving certain goals.

- The central idea behind need theory is that unsatisfied needs motivate us until they become satisfied.
- After satisfaction of one need, the person usually pursues satisfaction of another, higher need.

Work and personal life offer the opportunity to satisfy many different needs and motives. Among the more important needs and motives are achievement, power, affiliation, recognition, and order. The need for risk taking and thrill seeking is also important for some people.

According to Maslow's need hierarchy, people have an internal need pushing them on toward self-actualization.

- Needs are arranged into a five-step ladder. Before higher-level needs are activated, certain lower-level needs must be satisfied.
- In ascending order, the groups of needs are physiological, safety, social, esteem, and self-actualization (such as self-fulfillment).

Need theory helps in self-motivation. First identify which needs you want to satisfy and then focus your efforts on an activity that will satisfy those needs.

Substantial research indicates that setting specific, reasonably difficult goals improves performance. Goals are valuable because they

- focus effort in a consistent direction
- improve your chances for success
- improve motivation and satisfaction

Goals can be aimed at either learning or performing. A learning-goal orientation means that an individual is focused on acquiring new skills and mastering new situations. A performing-goal orientation is aimed at wanting to demonstrate and validate the adequacy of your competence by seeking favorable judgments of competence. People with learning-goal orientations are more likely to

- seek feedback on how well they are performing
- have higher job performance
- improve performance and lead to skill development
- develop better relationships with their supervisors
- be innovative in solutions to problems

Goal setting is widely used on the job. Goals set by employees at lower levels in an organization are supposed to contribute to goals set at the top.

Goal setting in personal life can contribute to life satisfaction. For maximum advantage, personal goals should be integrated with career goals. Areas of life in which personal goals may be set include

- social and family
- hobbies and interests
- physical and mental health
- career
- financial

To increase their effectiveness, goals should be supported with action plans. Effective goals are

- specific and concise
- realistically challenging, yet also include stretch goals
- set for different time periods

Goals have some problems associated with them. They can create inflexibility, performing goals can detract from an interest in the task, and goals can encourage unethical behavior.

Key techniques of self-motivation include

- setting goals for yourself
- finding intrinsically motivating work
- getting feedback on your performance
- applying behavior modification to yourself
- improving your skills relevant to your job
- raising your level of self-expectation
- developing a strong work ethic
- developing psychological hardiness (a high degree of commitment, control, and challenge)

Achieving goals and staying motivated requires self-discipline. A model presented here for developing self-discipline consists of eight components:

- formulate a mission statement
- develop role models
- develop goals for each task
- develop action plans
- use visual and sensory stimulation
- search for pleasure within the task
- compartmentalize spheres of life
- minimize excuse making

A study found positive relationships between self-discipline scores and education, salary, satisfaction with career success, and satisfaction with goal attainment.

Check your Understanding

1. How would the need theory of motivation explain the fact that shortly after accomplishing an important goal many people begin thinking about their next possible goal?
2. One of the biggest issues in labor-management relations today is that workers want employers to pay more of their health-care insurance. What does this issue tell us about the importance of satisfying the lower-level needs of workers?
3. How might having a strong need for affiliation retard a person's career advancement?
4. Identify any self-actualized person you know or have heard of and explain why you think that person is self-actualized.
5. Why does a learning-goal orientation often contribute to more peace of mind than a performing-goal orientation?

6. Why is self-motivation so important even when you have a job skill that is in high demand?
7. Give examples of two jobs in your chosen field you think are likely to be intrinsically motivating. Explain your reasoning.
8. Explain how you might be able to use the Galatea effect to improve the success you achieve in your career and personal life.
9. What sacrifices might a highly self-disciplined person have to make in contrast to a lowly self-disciplined person?
10. Ask a person who has achieved career success how much self-discipline contributed to his or her success.

Web Corner

Motivation: www.beginnersguide.com

Self-discipline: www.mindperk.com

INTERNET SKILL BUILDER Anchoring

At www.InstantPower.com you will learning about the technique called *anchoring* that is designed to help you

experience your most enabling emotional state any time you want. The purpose of the anchoring program is to help you go from feeling afraid, hesitant, or depressed to confident, determined, and happy. After reading about the program, you decide if it appears promising or is simply a bunch of exaggerated promises.

Developing Your Human Relations Skills

Human Relations Application Exercises

Applying Human Relations Exercise 3-1

Goal-Setting and Action Plan Worksheet

Goal setting, along with developing action plans to support the goals, is a basic success strategy. Here you are being asked to refine a process you may have already begun. Consider entering more than one goal and accompanying action plan in each category. To clarify the meaning of the following entries, we provide examples in italics of a recent graduate entering the retail field (as illustrated in the opening case to the chapter). Before writing down your goals, consult the section "Guidelines for Goal Setting." If you are not currently employed, set up hypothetical goals and action plans for a future job.

Long-Range Goals (beyond five years)

Work: *Ultimately become CEO of a major division of a retail company, perhaps the CEO of Bloomingdales.*

(Place your entry here.)

Action plan: *Work my way up, position by position, starting as assistant merchandising manager.*

(Place your entry here.)

Personal: *Married, with children, home ownership.*

(Place your entry here.)

Action plan: *Continue to develop relationship with my boyfriend as life partner. We will both save and invest at least 10 percent of our incomes each year.*

(Place your entry here.)

Medium-Range Goals (two to five years)

Work: *Become merchandising manager for one store in a large retail chain.*

(Place your entry here.)

Action plan: *Will work hard as assistant merchandising manager, listen to and act on feedback from my* supervisors, take courses in human relations and merchandising management.

(Place your entry here.)

Personal: *Continue to develop relationship with my boyfriend and marry him within three years.*

(Place your entry here.)

Action plan: *Communicate in depth with each other regularly to build relationship. We will work on not criticizing each other so often. After he proposes marriage, we will use our business skills to plan the wedding.*

(Place your entry here.)

Short-Range Goals (within two years)

Work: *Do an outstanding job as assistant merchandising manager this month.*

(Place your entry here.)

Action plan: *Will take care of more e-mail and other routine work when not in the store. In this way I can put more time and energy into merchandising. I will ask my supervisor for feedback from time to time so I can make adjustments to my performance.*

(Place your entry here.)

Personal: *Get further into digital photography, particularly learning how to take action shots. Will go beyond the "point-and-click" approach to photography.*

(Place your entry here.)

Action plan: *I will study the camera manual more carefully and attend one of the digital photography workshops given at my former community college.*

(Place your entry here.)

Skill-Building Exercise 3-2

Need Identification among Members of Generations X and Y

Following is a list of work preferences characteristic among members of generations X and Y (collectively people born since 1965). Identify what psychological need or needs might be reflected in each work preference. Jot down the needs right after the work preference.

- They like variety, not doing the same thing every workday.
- Part of their career goals is to face new challenges and opportunities. It's not all based on money, but on growth and learning.
- They want jobs that are cool, fun, and fulfilling.
- They believe that if they keep growing and learning then that's all the security they need. Advancing their skill set and continuous learning is their top priority.
- They have a tremendous thirst for knowledge.

- Unlike many baby boomers, who tend to work independently, members of generations X and Y like to work in a team environment.
- They prefer learning by doing and making mistakes as they go along.
- They are apt to challenge established ways of doing things, reasoning that there is always a better way.
- They want regular, frequent feedback on job performance.
- Career improvement is a blend of life and job balance.

Questions

1. How well does the analysis presented apply to you? Do the statements fit your work preferences?

2. What needs are you (or will you be) attempting to satisfy on the job? How do you know?

Source: Reprinted with permission from the TemPositions Group of Companies, 420 Lexington Avenue, Suite 2100, New York, NY, 10170-0002.

Human Relations Case Study 3-1

Motivating the Staff at HRPro

Tammy Sheldon is a program manager at HRPro, a company that supplies human resource services to small and medium-size organizations, including businesses, hospitals, and a variety of nonprofit firms. The human resources services include administering payroll and employee benefits, bonus plans, and training. Sheldon is the program manager for training services, a small but growing part of client work for HRPro.

The three members of Sheldon's staff are Christina Conway, Peter Wang, and Maria Sanchez, all of whom hold the job title of human resources consultant. All three consultants are performing adequately, yet Sheldon has been thinking lately about enhancing their performance. Sheldon's immediate manager, the vice president of client programs, agrees that her staff has room for improvement in terms of effort and commitment. Sheldon's preliminary

action plan for enhancing the motivation of her staff is to interview them to search for specific motivators.

In Sheldon's words, "As an HR professional, I'm not naïve enough to think that a one-size-fits-all approach to motivation is going to work. I'm going to offer each member of my team a gift certificate to their favorite on-line shopping service as a reward for outstanding performance. Gifts are nice, but I want to try something a little more sophisticated." Excerpts from the interviews are as follows:

Sheldon: "Chris, what do you really want from working at HRPro? What would it take to get you to the next level of effort?"

Conway: "Thanks for asking me, Tammy. I haven't given the issue much thought yet. But off the top of my head, I would say I want your job and then to keep moving. I see a great future in human resource programs being outsourced, and I want to be part of that future. I'm 26 right now, and I can see myself as a CEO of a human resources outsourcing firm by the time I hit 35. So if I could see some clear signs of career advancement, I would put a little more pressure on the accelerator."

Sheldon: "Peter, what do you want to get out of working for HRPro? How could we get you to be even more strongly motivated?"

Wang: "I like what I see at the company, yet I'm falling into a little bit of a routine. I keep doing safety training and diversity training for clients. It's getting a little repetitious. I have to appear excited and enthused even if I've given the identical training program seven times in one month. I want to branch out, and maybe help install a bonus system for a client or two. I want to get into other aspects of HR.

"I don't want to feel like I'm finished growing as an HR professional. I'm only 31."

Sheldon: "Good morning Maria. How are you doing today? I wanted to learn a little bit more about what makes you happy and motivated. What do you hope to get out of working for HRPro?

What type of work would get you even more fired up?"

Sanchez: "I thought I was pretty fired up. I think I could be more committed to the company if the company was more committed to me. I feel I am only as good as my last client assignment. Suppose the company runs out of client assignments for me. Does that mean I'm out the door?

"Stable employment is pretty important for me. I have a child, and my husband is a full-time student in a field with little prospect for high-paying work. I would like to wake up every morning and feel that my job at HRPro will be there."

Case Questions

1. What needs are Conway, Wang, and Sanchez attempting to satisfy?
2. Make a suggestion to Sheldon and her manager for motivating Conway, Wang, and Sanchez.
3. Should Sheldon have asked each staff member exactly the same question in order to understand more clearly their potential motivators?

Human Relations Case Study 3-2

How Self-Disciplined Is Gus?

Cora, an office temporary, noticed that Gus, one on the professionals in the office where she was assigned, was constantly seated in front of the computer. One day when Gus returned from lunch, Cora engaged him in general conversation about the weather and the recent Winter Olympics games. Gus looked down at the time indicated on his cell phone, and said, "Excuse me, but I have to get back to work."

Cora commented, "Excuse me for saying so, but don't you get bored just sitting in front of the computer all day? I mean, don't you just want to take a break and get some fresh air? How much can a human being stare at a monitor all day?" Gus smiled and replied, "It may

look like I'm just sitting in front of a computer monitor all day just banging the key board. But the computer is a tool that helps me accomplish something very important. I'm analyzing data to help determine how our company can make products more environmentally friendly. Our company wants to be 'green.' In this way, I'm helping to improve the world."

Questions

1. Which elements of the self-discipline model is Gus applying?
2. To what extent might Cora have a self-discipline problem?

REFERENCES

1. Anne D'Innocenzio, "Retail Seeking More Top Business Grads," Associated Press, February 26, 2006.
2. For a theoretical explanation of the principle of self-interest, see Dale T. Miller, "The Norm of Self-Interest," *American Psychologist,* December 1999, pp. 1053–1060.
3. David C. McClelland and Richard Boyatzis, "Leadership Motive Pattern and Long-Term Success in Management," *Journal of Applied Psychology,* December 1982, p. 737.
4. Marvin Zuckerman, "Are You a Risk Taker?" *Psychology Today,* November/December 2000, p. 53.
5. The original statement is Abraham H. Maslow, "A Theory of Human Motivation," *Psychological Review,* July 1943, pp. 370-396. See also Maslow, *Motivation and Personality* (New York: Harper & Row, 1954).
6. Pamela Babcock, "Find What Workers Want," *HR Magazine,* April 2005, p. 53.
7. Gary P. Latham, "The Motivational Benefits of Goal Setting," *Academy of Management Executive,* November 2004, pp. 126–129.
8. Don VandeWalle and Larry L. Cummings, "A Test of the Influence of Goal Orientation on the Feedback-Seeking Process," *Journal of Applied Psychology,* June 1997, pp. 390–400; VandeWalle, William L. Cron, and John W. Slocum, Jr., "The Role of Goal Orientation Following Performance Feedback," *Journal of Applied Psychology,* August 2001, pp. 629–640.
9. Don VandeWalle, Steven P. Brown, William L. Cron, and John W. Slocum, Jr., "The Influence of Goal Orientation and Self-Regulation Tactics on Sales Performance: A Longitudinal Field Test," *Journal of Applied Psychology,* April 1999, pp. 249–259.
10. Onne Janssen and Nico W. Van Yperen, "Employee Goal Orientations, The Quality of Leader–Member Exchange, and the Outcomes of Job Performance and Job Satisfaction," *Academy of Management Journal,* June 2004, pp. 368–384.
11. Gerard H. Seijts and Gary P. Latham, "Learning versus Performance Goals: When Should Each Be Used? *Academy of Management Executive,* February 2005, p. 130.
12. VandeWalle and Cummings, "A Test of the Influence of Goal Orientation," p. 392.
13. Richard M. Ryan and Edward L. Deci, "Self-Determination Theory and the Facilitation of Intrinsic Motivation, Social Development, and Well-Being," *American Psychologist,* January 2000, p. 70.
14. Remus Ilies and Timothy A. Judge, "Goal Regulation across Time: The Effects of Feedback and Affect," *Journal of Applied Psychology,* May 2005, pp. 453–467.
15. P. Christopher Earley and Terri R. Lituchy, "Delineating Goals and Efficacy: A Test of Three Models," *Journal of Applied Psychology,* February 1992, p. 96.
16. Taly Dvir, Dov Eden, and Michal Lang Banjo, "Self-Fulfilling Prophecy and Gender: Can Women Be Pygmalion and Galatea?" *Journal of Applied Psychology,* April 1995, p. 268.
17. Michael S. Cole, Hubert S. Field, and Stanley G. Harris, "Student Learning Motivation and Psychological Hardiness: Interactive Effects on Students' Reactions to a Management Class," *Academy of Management Learning and Education,* March 2004, pp. 64–85. The definition of psychological hardiness is from citations on page 66 of the same source.
18. Andrew J. DuBrin, "Career-Related Correlates of Self-Discipline," *Psychological Reports,* 2001, Vol. 89, pp. 107–110.

4

Emotional Intelligence, Attitudes, and Happiness

Learning Objectives

After studying the information and doing the exercises in this chapter, you should be able to:

1 Explain how emotional intelligence contributes to effective human relations.

2 Understand the components of attitudes, and how they are acquired and changed.

3 Appreciate the importance of positive attitudes.

4 Pinpoint why organizational citizenship behavior is so highly valued in the workplace.

5 Understand the nature of happiness and how it can be acquired.

Outline

Andrea Jung, the chair and CEO of Avon Products told *Harvard Business Review,* "Emotional intelligence is in our DNA here at Avon because relationships are critical at every stage of our business. It starts with the relationships our 4.5 million independent sales reps have with their customers and goes right up through senior management to my office.

"So the emphasis on emotional intelligence is much greater here than it was at other companies in which I've worked. We incorporate emotional intelligence education into our development training for senior managers, and we factor in emotional intelligence competence when we evaluate employee's performance.

"Of all a leader's competencies, emotional and otherwise, self-awareness is the most important. Without it, you can't identify the impact you have on others. Self-awareness is very important for me as CEO. At my level, few people are willing to tell me the things that are hardest to hear. We have a CEO advisory counsel—10 people chosen each year from Avon offices throughout the world—and they tell me the good, the bad, and the ugly about our company. Anything can be said. It helps keep me connected to what people really think and how my actions affect them. . . . " [1]

The comments offered by top Avon lady Andrea Jung illustrate how one of the key themes of this chapter, emotional intelligence including self-awareness, figures into success in business. Other major sections of the chapter deal with related aspects of using emotion constructively: attitudes and happiness.

■ Learning Objective 1

What Is Emotional Intelligence?

Research into the functioning of the human brain has combined personality factors with wisdom and common sense, indicating that how effectively people use their emotions has a major impact on their success. The topmost layers of the brain govern intelligence functions, such as analytical problem solving. The innermost areas of the brain govern emotional functions, such as dealing with anger when being criticized by a customer.

The term *emotional intelligence* has gathered different meanings, all relating to how effectively a person makes constructive use of his or her emotions. John D. Mayer, a professor of psychology at the University of New Hampshire, along with Yale psychology professor Peter Saloey originated the concept of emotional intelligence. Mayer explains that from a scientific (rather than a popular) viewpoint, **emotional intelligence** is the "ability to accurately perceive your own and others' emotions; to understand the signals that emotions send about relationships; and to manage our own and others' emotions." [2] A person with high emotional intelligence would be able to engage in such behaviors as sizing up people, pleasing others, and influencing them.

■ **Emotional intelligence**
the ability to accurately perceive emotions, to understand the signals that emotions send about relationships, and to manage emotions

KEY COMPONENTS OF EMOTIONAL INTELLIGENCE

Four key factors included in a current analysis of emotional intelligence are as follows: [3]

1. **Self-awareness.** The ability to understand your moods, emotions, and needs as well as their impact on others. Self-awareness also includes using intuition to make decisions you can live with happily. (A person with good self-awareness knows whether he or she is pushing other people too far.) In the chapter opener, Andrea Jung emphasized the importance of self-awareness for a leader.

2. **Self-management.** The ability to control one's emotions and act with honesty and integrity in a consistent and acceptable manner. The right degree of self-management helps prevent a person from throwing temper tantrums when activities do not go as planned. Effective workers do not let their occasional bad moods ruin their day. If they cannot overcome the bad mood, they let coworkers know of their problem and how long it might last. (A person with low self-management would suddenly decide to drop a project because the work was frustrating.)

3. **Social awareness.** Includes having empathy for others and having intuition about work problems. A team leader with social awareness, or empathy, would be able to assess whether a team member has enough enthusiasm for a project to assign him to that project. Another facet of social skill is the ability to interpret nonverbal communication, such as frowns and types of smiles. [4] (A supervisor with social awareness, or empathy, would take into account the most likely reaction of group members before making a decision affecting them.)

4. **Relationship management.** Includes the interpersonal skills of being able to communicate clearly and convincingly, disarm conflicts, and build strong personal bonds. Effective workers use relationship management skills to spread their enthusiasm and solve disagreements, often with kindness and humor. (A worker with relationship management skill would use a method of persuasion that is likely to work well with a particular group or individual.)

■ **Self-awareness**
the ability to understand moods, emotions, and needs as well as their impact on others; self-awareness also includes using intuition to make decisions you can live with happily

■ **Self-management**
the ability to control one's emotions and act with honesty and integrity in a consistent and acceptable manner

■ **Social awareness**
having empathy for others and having intuition about work problems

■ **Relationship management**
the interpersonal skills of being able to communicate clearly and convincingly, disarm conflicts, and build strong personal bonds

Emotional intelligence thus incorporates many of the skills and attitudes necessary to achieve effective interpersonal relations in organizations. Many topics in human relations, such as resolving conflict, helping others develop and positive political skills would be included in emotional intelligence.

A review of many studies concluded that low emotional intelligence employees are more likely than their high emotional intelligence counterparts to experience negative emotional reactions to job insecurity, such as high tension. Furthermore, workers with low emotional intelligence are more likely to engage in negative coping behaviors, such as expressing anger and verbally abusing an immediate supervisor for the organization failing to provide job security. [5]

Tests of emotional intelligence typically ask you to respond to questions on a 1-to-5 scale (never, rarely, sometimes, often, consistently). For example, indicate how frequently you demonstrate the following behaviors:

I can laugh at myself.	1 2 3 4 5
I help others grow and develop.	1 2 3 4 5
I watch carefully the nonverbal communication of others.	1 2 3 4 5

Human Relations Self-Assessment Quiz 4-1 gives you an opportunity to measure your emotional intelligence.

Demonstrating good emotional intelligence is impressive because it contributes to performing well in the difficult arena of dealing with feelings. A worker with good emotional intelligence would engage in such behaviors as (1) recognizing when a coworker needs help but is too embarrassed to ask for help, (2) dealing with the anger of a dissatisfied customer, (3) recognizing that the boss is facing considerable pressure also, and (4) being able to tell whether a customer's "maybe" means "yes" or "no." The accompanying Human Relations in Practice provides another illustration of how a businessperson might make good use of emotional intelligence.

Human Relations Self-Assessment Quiz 4-1

What Is Your Emotional Intelligence?

Psychologists have developed various measures of emotional intelligence. The EQ (Emotional Quotient) test found by visiting www.myskillsprofile.com deals with 16 emotional competencies. The feedback report provides a chart of your emotional competencies together with a detailed description of your profile. An advantage of this quiz is that it is based on the work of two of the original researchers in emotional intelligence, not the later popularizers of the concept.

Human Relations in Practice

Colleen Barrett, president and COO of Southwest Airlines Tunes into Feelings

Reflecting on her ability to read people, Barrett said, "The other day I was talking to one of our officers, and he said, 'How did you do that?' and I said 'How do I do what?' He was referring to a meeting we'd both been at earlier. I'd asked one of the presenters at the meeting, a fellow who reported to this officer, if he was feeling OK. The officer thought the employee was fine, but, it turns out, the poor guy had a pretty traumatic experience in his personal life the night before. His presentation went well, but he seemed off to me, distracted. I suppose in order to have seen that, I must have been fairly attuned to what his fellow's presentations were usually like.

"I often communicate on a passionate, emotional level—which can be a detriment, particularly for a woman in a predominantly male leadership group, as ours was for many years."

Questions

1. Which aspect of emotional intelligence was Barrett demonstrating?
2. How might it have helped the presenter to be asked if he were doing OK?

Source: "Leading by Feel: Watch the Language," *Harvard Business Review*, January 2004, p. 29.

ACQUIRING AND DEVELOPING EMOTIONAL INTELLIGENCE

Many people believe that emotional intelligence can be acquired and developed, much like a person can learn to become more extraverted or learn to control his or her intelligence. Many consultants offer training programs for helping employees develop emotional intelligence, and school systems throughout North America provide students some training in emotional intelligence. Elkhonon Goldberg, a clinical professor of neurology at New York University School of Medicine explains that emotional intelligence can be learned to a degree, much like musical talent or numerical ability can be developed. Having the right natural talent, however, is an important starting point. The combination of biological endowment (such as being aware of your emotions) and training will enable most people to enhance their emotional intelligence. [6]

Given that emotional intelligence is composed of different components, to acquire and develop such ability would usually require working on one component at a time. For example, if a person had difficulty in self-management, he or she would study and be coached in an aspect of self-management such as anger control. Training in anger management is widespread today because so many people have difficulty in managing their anger. Skill-Building Exercise 4-1 presented later in the chapter provides a step-by-step approach to the development of emotional intelligence.

A criticism of the ideal of emotional intelligence is that it might simply be part of analytical (or traditional) intelligence. For example, if you can read the feelings of other people, aren't you just being smart? Another concern is that the popularized concept of emotional intelligence has become so broad it encompasses almost the entire study of personality.

What Are the Components of Attitudes, and How Are They Acquired and Changed?

■ Learning Objective 2

"You've got an attitude," said the supervisor to the store associate, thus emphasizing the importance of attitude to job performance. For mysterious reasons, the term *attitude* in colloquial language often connotes a *negative* attitude. More accurately, an **attitude** is a predisposition to respond that exerts an influence on a person's response to a person, a thing, an idea, or a situation. Attitudes are an important part of human relations because they are linked with perception and motivation. For example, your attitude toward a coworker influences your perception of how favorably you evaluate his or her work, and you will be better motivated if you have a positive attitude toward your work. Having and displaying positive attitudes will also help you build better relationships with coworkers, managers, and customers.

Our study of attitudes includes the components of attitudes, how attitudes are acquired, how they are changed, the importance of positive attitudes, how companies attempt to enhance positive attitudes and job satisfaction, and organizational citizenship behavior.

■ Attitude
a predisposition to respond that exerts an influence on a person's response to a person, a thing, an idea, or a situation

COMPONENTS OF ATTITUDES

Attitudes are complex, having three components as shown in Figure 4-1. The **cognitive component** refers to the knowledge or intellectual beliefs an individual might have about an object (an idea, a person, a thing, or a situation). A market researcher might have accumulated considerable factual information about statistics (such as sampling procedures) and software for running data. The researcher might, therefore, have a positive attitude toward statistics.

■ Cognitive component
(of attitude) the knowledge or intellectual beliefs an individual might have about an object (an idea, a person, a thing, or a situation)

Figure   **4-1**

The Three Components of Attitudes

Observe that the three components of attitudes influence each other and that the attitude toward a subject, person, object, or thing is the combined effect of the cognitive, affective, and behavioral components.

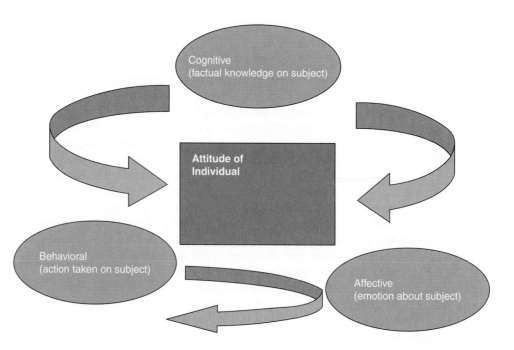

■ **Affective component**

(of attitude) the emotion connected with an object or a task

■ **Behavioral component**

(of attitude) how a person acts

■ **Cognitive dissonance**

situation in which the pieces of knowledge, information, attitudes, or beliefs held by an individual are contradictory

The feeling or **affective component** refers to the emotion connected with an object or a task. The market researcher mentioned might basically like statistical analysis because of some pleasant experiences in college associated with statistics. The **behavioral component** refers to how a person acts. The market researcher might make positive statements about statistical methods or emphasize them in his or her reports.

The cognitive, affective, and behavioral aspects of attitudes are interrelated. A change in one of the components will set in motion a change in one or more of the others. If you have more facts about an object or process (cognitive), you form the basis for a more positive emotional response to the object (affective). In turn, your behavior toward that object would probably become more favorable. For example, if you have considerable information about the contribution of feedback to personal development, you might have a positive feeling toward feedback. When receiving feedback, therefore, you would act favorably.

At times, people do not experience the type of consistency previously described and feel compelled to search for consistency. **Cognitive dissonance** is the situation in which the pieces of knowledge, information, attitudes, or beliefs held by an individual are contradictory. When a person experiences cognitive dissonance, the relationship between attitudes and behaviors is altered. People search for ways to reduce internal conflicts when they experience a clash between the information they receive and their actions or attitudes. The same process is used when a person has to resolve two inconsistent sets of information.

A typical example of cognitive dissonance on the job might occur when a worker believes that the report she submits to team members is of high quality; her teammates, however, tell her the report is flawed and requires substantial revisions. To reduce the dissonance, the worker might conveniently ignore the criticism. Or the worker might reason that she is the resident expert on the topic of the report, and her teammates, therefore, are not qualified to judge the merits of her report.

HOW ATTITUDES ARE FORMED

Attitudes usually are based on experience. Assume that you visited a convenience store, and you left your wallet on the counter without realizing it. Your wallet contained your credit cards, debit cards, driver's license, $150 in cash, and personal memories. On returning home you receive a telephone call from the clerk, informing you that he is holding your wallet for you. You most likely develop an immediate positive attitude toward the convenience store, the clerk, and perhaps toward other people of his ethnic group. Next we look more closely at the processes underlying attitude formation. [7]

A starting point in developing attitudes is to receive direct instruction from another individual. A friend whose opinion you respect tells you that e-filing of income tax is fast, efficient, and modern. You might quickly have a positive attitude toward e-filing. Similarly, you might develop a positive attitude through modeling the behavior of another person. You have seen that your trusted friend e-files her income tax, so you develop a positive attitude toward e-filing.

Conditioning, or making associations, also contributes to attitude formation, as in the example of the convenience store. The attitudes that we develop based on conditioning or associations usually develop after at least several exposures. You might develop a favorable attitude toward the human resources (HR) department if you asked for help several times, and each time you received useful advice. In contrast, you might have developed negative attitudes toward HR if a department representative was unhelpful at each visit.

The way we think about things, or our *cognitions,* can influence attitude formation. You might be quite content with your salary and benefits provided by your employer. You then visit ***www.salary.com*** and discover that you make much less than other workers in your city performing the same work. As a result your attitude toward your salary and benefits plunges.

The deepest contributor to attitude formation could be a person's standing on the personality trait of optimism. People with a high degree of optimism are predisposed toward viewing events, persons, places, and things as positive which in turn leads to a positive attitude. In contrast, people who have a high standing on pessimism will harbor many negative attitudes. Many workers who have chronically low job satisfaction are pessimistic at the core. [8]

THE IMPORTANCE OF POSITIVE ATTITUDES

■ Learning Objective 3

Positive attitudes have always been the foundation of effective human relations, as reflected in the writings of Dale Carnegie, the pioneer of the popular (rather than scientific) approach to human relations. A sampling of Carnegie's wisdom is presented in Figure 4-2. In recent years positive attitudes have also become of interest to human relations specialists, as reflected in the fields called positive psychology and positive organizational studies. A major thrust of these fields is to enhance our experiences of enjoyment of work, as well as love, and play. The assumption is that when employees are in a positive mood, they are typically more creative, better motivated to perform well, and more helpful toward coworkers. [9]

A worker who consistently maintains a *genuine* positive attitude will accrue many benefits. Being genuine is important because people with good emotional intelligence can readily detect a phony smile used as a cover up for anger. Assuming the worker with a positive attitude backs it up with good performance, he or she is more likely to (a) be liked by customers, (b) close more sales, (c) receive good performance reviews, (d) receive favorable work assignments, and (e) be promoted.

The name "Dale Carnegie" is synonymous with a popularized approach to human relations. Carnegie (1888–1955) authored several best sellers, including *How to Win Friends and Influence People* first published in 1937. More than 50 million copies of Carnegie's books have been printed and published in 38 languages. Nine of Carnegie's suggestions for becoming a positive, friendlier person follow:

1. Don't criticize, condemn, or complain.
2. Give honest, sincere appreciation.
3. Arouse in the other person an eager want.
4. Become genuinely interested in other people.
5. Smile.
6. Remember that a person's name is to that person the sweetest and most important sound in any language.
7. Be a good listener. Encourage others to talk about themselves.
8. Talk in terms of the other person's interests.
9. Make the other person feel important—and do it sincerely.

Source: *Dale Carnegie's Golden Book*, Dale Carnegie® Training, www.dalecarnegie.com, undated.

Figure 4-2

The Wisdom of Dale Carnegie

A mild note of caution is that there is a negative side to workers being too positive. As analyzed by Judge and Ilies, putting on a happy face can lead to stress, burnout, and job dissatisfaction. Workers who have an unrealistically positive self-concept might become self-centered and manipulative and think they deserve more attention and rewards than other workers. [10] Also a little negativity and cynicism is helpful in jobs such as auditor, budget analyst, tax accountant, and store detective. Sometimes being suspicious and negative contributes to a job role.

HOW ATTITUDES ARE CHANGED

In general, attitudes can be changed by reversing the processes by which they were formed. Yet, we can look at the process of attitude change more specifically. First, we might receive information from a source we trust. A manager might have negative attitudes toward the value of employee training, then reads in a reliable business magazine that IBM spends more than $100 million annually on employee training. As a consequence, the manager develops a more favorable attitude toward training. A person might also be reconditioned to bring about attitude change. A small-business owner might have a negative attitude toward e-filing income taxes because of the need to learn new skills combined with a fear of security. After trying e-filing for two consecutive years because of being almost forced to by the law, the business owner receives refunds promptly and find the process not really so complicated. So her attitude toward e-filing becomes reconditioned in a positive direction.

Another way to change attitudes is to learn to look at the positive or negative aspect of situations, if you are a pessimist or optimist, respectively. A pessimistic person should concentrate on searching for the positive elements of a situation, such as a supervisor saying to himself or herself, "Okay this employee is a pill, but maybe there is something good about him."

In contrast, a naturally optimistic person might learn to say, "I tend to fall in love with the credentials of most job candidates. So maybe I should scrutinize this candidate more carefully."

HOW COMPANIES ENCOURAGE POSITIVE ATTITUDES AND JOB SATISFACTION

From the standpoint of management it is beneficial for employees to have positive attitudes and job satisfaction. These two emotional states contribute to better customer service, less absenteeism and tardiness, less turnover, and often higher productivity. Much of the effort of human resource professionals is aimed at making employees more content. Among the hundreds of possible company initiatives to foster positive attitudes and high job satisfaction among employees are flexible working hours, recognition awards, company picnics, financial bonuses, time off for birthdays, on-site haircuts, and on-premises child-care centers. Following are three specific examples of companies voted among the 100 Best Companies to Work For (as evaluated by *Fortune* magazine) to enhance employee attitudes and satisfaction: [11]

Genetech, South San Francisco (biotechnology products). Ninety-five percent of the 8,121 employees are shareholders, giving them a stake in the success of the company. As Genetech stock has soared, employees watched the value of their investments rise also. Employees receive free cappuccino, and parties every Friday night.

W. L. Gore & Associates, Newark, Delaware (Gore-Tex fabrics, guitar string, dental floss). To encourage job satisfaction as well as innovation, there are no bosses, job titles, or organization charts. Instead there are sponsors, team members, and leaders.

Container Store, Coppell, Texas (storage retailer). Bonuses are given to full-time and part-time employees, and drivers are rewarded for long service and driver safety. One driver received a $5,000 bonus for 10 years of accident-free driving.

ORGANIZATIONAL CITIZENSHIP BEHAVIOR

An employee attitude highly valued by employers is **organizational citizenship behavior (OCB)**, the willingness to go beyond one's job description to help the company, even if such act does not lead to an immediate reward. Being a good organizational citizen is also tied in with values because the person who goes beyond the job description to help others most likely has a strong work ethic and values helping others. Several examples of good organizational citizenship follow:

■ Melissa helps an employee in another department with a currency exchange problem because she has skill in this area, but Melissa's job does not involve working with currency exchange.

■ Jeff is walking into the company from the company parking lot. He notices that a few beer bottles have been scattered on the lot. Worried about possible flat tires to employee vehicles, Jeff collects the bottles and disposes of them properly. He does not tell anybody about his good deed.

■ Penelope, an information technology gifted person, is walking down the isle toward her cubicle. She notices a worker from another department with a panicked

> "You have the capacity to choose what you think about. If you choose to think about past hurts, you will continue to feel bad. While it's true you can't change the effect past influences had on you once, you can change the effect they have on you now."
> —Gary McKay, Ph.D., psychologist

■ Learning Objective 4

■ **Organizational citizenship behavior (OCB)**
the willingness to go beyond one's job description to help the company, even if such act does not lead to an immediate reward

look on his face as he stares into his computer monitor. Penelope asks if there is anything she can do to help and proceeds to transfer valuable data from a corrupted file to a new file for the employee in panic.

Organizational citizenship behavior is so important to organizations that this set of attitudes has been the subject of many studies. A general finding has been that as a result of many workers being good organizational citizens, the organization functions more effectively in such ways as improved product quantity and quality. [12]

Three management professors from Indiana University at Bloomington, Philip M. Podsakoff, Michael Ahearne, and Scott B. MacKenzie, conducted one of the first studies about the impact of organizational citizenship behavior on work unit performance. They studied the effects of citizenship behavior on the quantity and quality of the performance of 218 people working in 40 machine crews in a paper mill in the northeastern United States that produced bond and catalog paper. Three different aspects of OCB were measured—helping behavior, sportsmanship, and civic virtue—by having the crew members fill out questionnaires about each other. An example of a questionnaire statement measuring *helping behavior* was "Help each other out if someone falls behind in his or her work." An example of a *civic virtue* statement was "Provide constructive suggestions about how the crew can improve its performance." And for *sportsmanship*, "Consume a lot of time complaining about trivial matters" (reverse scoring). All three aspects of organizational citizenship behavior were rated on a scale of 1 to 7.

Quantity was measured by the amount of paper produced as a percentage of total machine capacity for the year. Quality was measured as the percentage of paper produced that was rejected by the mill's quality department or the customer.

The results of the study showed that helping behavior and sportsmanship had a significant effect on performance quantity and that helping behavior had a significant impact on performance quality. Somehow civic virtue had no effect on quality or quantity of the work produced by the crews. [13] In conclusion, organizational citizenship behavior was associated with higher quality and quantity of paper production by mill crews.

What Is Happiness and How Can It Be Acquired?

■ **Learning Objective 5**

When asked "What is the most important thing in life?" most people respond "Happiness." Research and opinion on the topic indicate that people can take concrete steps to achieve happiness. Planning for happiness is possible because it appears to be somewhat under people's control. A recent compilation of research emphasizes the importance of happiness. Happier people have better physical health, achieve more career success, work harder, and are more caring and socially engaged. Misery can lead to self-obsession and inactivity. [14]

Our approach to the unlimited topic of understanding how to achieve happiness involves a model of happiness, a listing of keys to happiness, and the five principles of psychological functioning.

THE SPHERES OF LIFE AND HAPPINESS

A practical way of understanding happiness is that it is a by-product of having the various components of life working in harmony and synchrony. To understand this approach, visualize about six gears with teeth, spinning in unison. As long as all gears are moving properly (and no teeth are broken), a state of equilibrium and fluid motion is achieved. Similarly, imagine that life has six major components. The exact components will differ among people. For most people, the components would be approximately as follows:

1. work and career

2. interpersonal life, including loved ones and romantic life

3. physical and mental health

4. financial health

5. interests and pastimes, including reading, surfing the Internet, and sports

6. a spiritual life or belief system, including religion, science, or astrology

When a person has ample satisfactions in all six spheres, he or she achieves happiness. However, when a deficiency occurs in any of these six factors, the person's spheres are no longer in harmony, and dissatisfaction or unhappiness occurs. Yet sometimes if a person is having problems in one sphere, satisfaction in the other spheres can compensate temporarily for a deficiency in one. For the long range, a state of happiness depends on all six spheres working in harmony. In short, the theme of this book surfaces again: Work and personal life are mutually supportive. Figure 4-3 presents the spheres-of-life model of happiness.

People vary as to how much importance they attach to each sphere of life. A person with intense career ambitions, for example, might place less weight on the interests sphere than would a more leisure-oriented person. However, if any of these spheres are grossly deficient, total happiness will not be forthcoming. Another source of variation is that the importance people attach to each sphere may vary according to the stage of life. A full-time student, for example, might need just enough money to avoid worrying about finances. However, after about 10 years of full-time career experience, a person's expenses might peak. The person would then attach more importance to the financial sphere.

Figure 4-3

The Spheres-of-Life Model of Happiness

THE KEYS TO HAPPINESS

Much research has been conducted about the ingredients of happiness. If you are aware of these contributors to happiness, you might be able to enhance your happiness. The spheres-of-life model of happiness also furnishes direction for the person seeking happiness: Strive for acceptable levels of achievement in all six spheres. Here we summarize and synthesize a wide range of research and opinion on the keys to happiness. [15]

Give High Priority to the Pursuit of Happiness

Having the intention or goal of being happy will enhance your chances of being happy. A key principle is to discover what makes you happy and make the time to pursue those activities. Spending time doing what you enjoy contributes directly to happiness.

Experience Love and Friendship and Find a Life Partner

A happy person is one who is successful in personal relationships and who exchanges care and concern with loved ones. Happy people are able to love and be loved. Hugging people you like or being hugged by them is an important part of having enjoyable personal relationships. Research with hundreds of students suggests that the happiest among them spend the least time alone and the most time socializing. Married adults, in general, are happier than unmarried adults, and the results are similar for men and women. According to the Men's Health Network, married men take fewer health risks, eat better, and are involved in more health-enhancing behaviors. Furthermore, married men also earn an average of 10 to 40 percent more than those never married, even with comparable education and work experience. [16] (Good health and high income make some contribution to happiness.) Despite the consistency of this finding about marriage, it must be interpreted cautiously. It takes a satisfying marriage to bring happiness, and unmarried partners who have a long-term, caring relationship are also likely to be happy.

Develop a Sense of Self-Esteem

Self-love must precede love for others. High self-esteem enables one to love and be loved. Developing a good self-image leads to the self-esteem required for loving relationships. The importance of looking at yourself in a positive way has been expressed many times by many commentators. An early contributor to the importance of thinking positively about yourself was Emile Coué, a French psychologist, made a name for himself in the twentieth century by teaching that mental health could be achieved by repeating the sentence, "Every day and in every way I'm becoming better and better." [17]

A feeling of self-worth is important because it helps prevent being overwhelmed by criticism. An important part of developing self-esteem is to not want financial success more than other things. Insecure people seek society's approval in the form of purchasing consumer goods and accumulating investments. The accompanying Core Self-Evaluation Scale is a scientifically developed instrument that gives you an opportunity to assess how positively you think about yourself.

Work Hard at What You Enjoy and Achieve the Flow Experience

Love may be the most important contributor to happiness, with staying involved in work you enjoy coming in second. To achieve happiness, it is necessary to find a career that fits your most intense interests. In addition, it helps to achieve regularly

Human Relations Self-Assessment Quiz   4-2

The Core Self-Evaluation Scale

Below are several statements about you with which you may agree or disagree. Using the response scale below, indicate your agreement or disagreement with each item by placing the appropriate number on the line preceding that item.

1	2	3	4	5
Strongly Disagree	Disagree	Neutral	Agree	Strongly Agree

1. _____ I am confident I get the success I deserve.
2. _____ Sometimes I feel depressed.
3. _____ When I try, I generally succeed.
4. _____ Sometimes when I fail, I feel worthless.
5. _____ I complete tasks successfully.
6. _____ Sometimes, I do not feel in control of my work.
7. _____ Overall, I am satisfied with myself.
8. _____ I am filled with doubts about my competence.
9. _____ I determine what will happen in my life.
10. _____ I do not feel in control of my success in my career.
11. _____ I am capable of coping with most of my problems.
12. _____ There are times when things look pretty bleak and hopeless to me.
_____ Total score

Scoring and Interpretation:

The scoring for items 1, 3, 5, 7, 9, and 11 proceeds as follows: 5, 4, 3, 2, 1 to indicate a positive attitude toward yourself. The scoring for questions 2, 4, 6, 8, 10, and 12 proceeds as follows: 1, 2, 3, 4, 5 to indicate a positive attitude toward yourself. Add all your scores to attain your total score. The higher the score, the more positive your attitude toward yourself. Scores of 48 and higher suggest a very positive attitude, scores between 37 and 47 suggest a neutral attitude, and scores between 12 and 35 indicate a negative attitude toward yourself. The mean score for several different groups of people, including working adults and students, is 45.

Source: Timothy A. Judge, Amir Erez, Joyce E. Bono, and Carl J. Thoresen, "The Core Self-Evaluation Scale: Development of a Measure," *Personnel Psychology,* Summer 2003, p. 315. This measure is nonproprietary (free) and may be used without permission.

the flow experience of total involvement in what you are doing at the moment. Happiness stemming from flow is powerful because it is not dependent on favorable external circumstances, such as recognition or love. The individual creates the happiness that follows from flow. Hard work contributes to happiness in another important way. A fundamental secret of happiness is accomplishing things and savoring what you have accomplished. Happiness researcher David T. Lyken argues that happiness is available to anyone who develops skills, interests, and goals that he or she finds meaningful and enjoyable. [18] A log cabin dweller who lived off the land and whose goal was to be close to nature would therefore be happier than a wealthy person in a luxurious house who was not leading the lifestyle he or she wanted.

Appreciate the Joys of Day-to-Day Living

Another key to happiness is the ability to live in the present without undue worry about the future or dwelling on past mistakes. Be on guard against becoming so pre-occupied with planning your life that you neglect to enjoy the happiness of the moment. The essence of being a happy person is to savor what you have right now. As Benjamin Franklin said, "Happiness is produced not so much by great pieces of good fortune that seldom happen as by the little advantages that occur every day."

Be Fair, Kind, and Helpful, and Trust Others

The Golden Rule is a true contributor to happiness. It is also important to practice charity and forgiveness. Helping others brings personal happiness. Knowing that you are able to make a contribution to the welfare of others gives you a continuing sense of satisfaction and happiness. Related to fairness and kindness is trust of others. Happy people have open, warm, and friendly attitudes.

Have Recreational Fun in Your Life

A happy life is characterized by fun, zest, joy, and delight. When you create time for fun (in addition to the fun in many kinds of work), you add an important element to your personal happiness. However, if you devote too much time to play, you will lose on the fun of work accomplishments. In choosing fun activities, avoid overplanning. Because novelty contributes to happiness, be ready to pursue an unexpected opportunity or to try something different.

Learn to Cope with Grief, Disappointment, Setbacks, and Stress

To be happy, you must learn how to face problems that occur in life without being overwhelmed or running away. It is also important to persevere in attempting to overcome problems rather than to whine or engage in self-pity. Once you have had to cope with problems, you will be more able to appreciate the day-to-day joys of life.

Live with What You Cannot Change

Happiness guru Martin Seligman says that attempting to change conditions unlikely to change sets us up for feeling depressed about failing. Weight loss is a prime example. Nineteen out of 20 people regain weight they lost. It is, therefore, better to worry less about weight loss and concentrate on staying in good physical condition by engaging in moderate exercise. Good condition contributes much more to health than does achieving a weight standard set primarily to achieve an aesthetic standard. You can then concentrate on being happy about your good physical condition instead of being unhappy about your weight. [19]

Energize Yourself through Physical Fitness

Engage in regular physical activity, such as dancing or sports that make you aerobically fit. Whether it is the endorphins released by exercise, dopamine released by the excitement, or simply the relaxed muscles, physical fitness fosters happiness. Another important part of energizing yourself is to attain adequate rest. Happy people invest time in revitalizing sleep and solitude.

Satisfy Your Most Important Values

Based on a survey of more than 6,000 individuals, social psychologist Steven Reiss concluded that people cannot find lasting happiness by aiming to have more fun or seeking pleasure. Instead, you have to satisfy your basic values or desires and take happiness in passing. To increase your value-based happiness, you have to first identify your most important desires and then gear your life toward satisfying these values. Among these key values are curiosity, physical activity, honor, power, family, status, and romance. [20] For example, if power and romance are two of your basic values, you can achieve happiness only if your life is amply provided with power and romance. Religion also fits into the realm of values, and religious people tend to be happier than nonreligious people. [21]

Earn Enough Money to Avoid Feeling Miserable

The role of money as a contributor to happiness is the subject of endless debate. Money cannot buy happiness but having enough money to purchase the things that make you happy is important. Whether an iPod or a penthouse condominium with a view of the water would make you happy, they both require money—even though the amounts differ. However, the pursuit of money for its own sake is less likely to contribute to happiness.

According to Arthur C. Brooks, a professor at the Syracuse University Maxwell School of Public Affairs, some research by economists suggests that people with a lot of money tend to express a higher degree of subjective happiness than people with very little. Data from the National Opinion Research Center indicate that people in the top 20 percent income bracket are about 50 percent more likely to say they are "very happy" than people in the bottom 20 percent. Those in the higher bracket are also about half as likely to say they are "not too happy." [22]

Another consideration is that not being able to pay for what you consider a necessity may lead to low self-esteem and unhappiness. Even if a person does not equate money with happiness, having a car repossessed or a house foreclosed contributes to at least a temporary state of unhappiness. Yet despite this obvious truth, many people in poor countries are happy. For example, surveys taken over a 20-year period indicate that the Inuit people of northern Greenland score an average of 5.8 on a scale of 1 to 7 in response to a question about life satisfaction. Survey respondents on the list of the *Forbes* magazine wealthiest 400 also averaged 5.8 on the same scale. [23]. People in rich countries are not consistently happier than people in poor countries. Yet the underlying principle could be the same. As long as you have enough money to pay for what you consider to be necessities, money is not a factor in your happiness.

Lead a Meaningful Life

Most of the principles previously stated, as well as the spheres-of-life happiness model, all point toward the conclusion that having a meaningful life is a major contributor to happiness. A meaning or an important purpose helps a person get through periodic annoyances that temporarily lower happiness. Seligman says that the ultimate level of happiness is the meaningful life. It consists of identifying your core strengths and then using them in the services of something you perceive to be bigger than you are. [24] For example, if you are a greeting card designer and you perceive that you are contributing to improved personal relationships, you are likely to be happy.

THE FIVE PRINCIPLES OF PSYCHOLOGICAL FUNCTIONING

According to clinical psychologist Richard Carlson, the best way to achieve inner serenity (or happiness) is to follow the five principles of psychological functioning. [25] These principles act as guides toward achieving a feeling of inner happiness. The first is *thinking*, which creates the psychological experience of life. Feelings come about only after you thought about something or somebody. If you think of another person as attractive, it will lead to a warm feeling toward that person. People who learn to direct their thinking in positive directions will contribute to their own happiness. Remember that you produce your own thoughts.

The second principle is *moods,* meaning that the positive or negative content of your thinking fluctuates from moment to moment and day to day. Practice ignoring your low (bad) moods rather than analyzing them, and you will see how quickly they vanish. Developing this skill will contribute substantially to healthy psychological functioning. The third principle is *separate psychological realities.* Because each person thinks in a unique way, everyone lives in a separate psychological reality. Accept the idea that others think differently from you, and you will have much more compassion and fewer quarrels. As a result, you will be happier. Also, if you accept the principle of separate realities, you will waste less time attempting to change people. At the same time, others will like you more, thus contributing to your happiness.

The fourth principle of psychological functioning is *feelings.* Combined with emotions, feelings are a built-in feedback mechanism that tells us how we are doing psychologically. If your feelings turn negative suddenly, you know that your thinking is dysfunctional. It is then time to make a mental readjustment. If you feel discontented, for example, it is necessary to clear the head and start thinking positively. As a consequence, you will experience contentment and happiness. A key point is that the person will maintain a sense of well-being as long as he or she does not focus on personal concerns.

The fifth principle is *the present moment.* Learning to pay attention to the present moment and to your feelings enables people to live at peak efficiency without the distraction of negative thinking. Much like the flow experience, the present moment is where people find happiness and inner peace. Carlson advises, "The only way to experience genuine and lasting contentment, satisfaction, and happiness is to learn to live your life in the present moment." [26] (This supports the fifth happiness key.)

Concept Review and Reinforcement

Key Terms

Emotional intelligence, 80
Self-awareness, 81
Self-management, 81
Social awareness, 81
Relationship management, 81

Attitude, 83
Cognitive component
(of attitude), 83
Affective component
(of attitude), 84

Behavioral component
(of attitude), 84
Cognitive dissonance, 84
Organizational citizenship behavior
(OCB), 87

Summary and Review

Emotional intelligence generally refers to how effectively a person makes constructive use of his or her emotion. The four key components of emotional intelligence are

- self-awareness (understanding the self)
- self-management (emotional control)
- social awareness (includes empathy and intuition)
- relationship management (includes interpersonal skills)

The combination of biological endowment and training will enable most people to enhance their emotional intelligence.

Attitudes are complex, having three components

- cognitive (knowledge or beliefs)
- affective (emotional)
- behavioral (how a person acts)

Cognitive dissonance occurs when the three components are not consistent with each other. Attitudes are formed based on experience, including receiving instruction from another person, conditioning, and cognitions (the way we think about something). The trait of optimism versus pessimism influences attitudes strongly. A worker who maintains a genuine positive attitude will accrue many benefits, yet being too positive can have disadvantages.

Attitudes can be changed by reversing the process by which they were formed. Looking at the positive or negative aspect of a situation can also lead to attitude change. From the standpoint of management it is beneficial for employees to have positive attitudes and job satisfaction. Organizational citizenship behavior is highly valued by employers because such attitudes can lead to improved product quality and quantity.

Planning for happiness is somewhat under a person's control. A practical way of understanding happiness is that it is a by-product of having the spheres of life working in harmony and synchrony. For most people these spheres would be

- work and career
- interpersonal life, including romance
- physical and mental health
- financial health
- interests and pastimes
- spiritual life or belief system

Contributors or keys to happiness include the following:

- giving priority to happiness
- love and friendship
- self-esteem
- working hard at things enjoyed
- appreciation of the joys of day-to-day living
- fairness, kindness, helpfulness, and trust
- recreational fun
- coping with grief, disappointment, setbacks, and stress
- living with what you cannot change
- energizing yourself through physical fitness
- satisfying your most important values
- earning enough money to avoid feeling miserable

According to Richard Carlson, the best way to achieve inner serenity (or happiness) is to follow the five principles of psychological functioning.

- First is thinking which brings about feelings.
- Second is moods, including the idea that you can ignore bad moods.
- Third is separate psychological realities, meaning that each person thinks in a unique way.
- Fourth is feelings, which can be turned from negative to positive.
- Fifth is the present moment, which is where people find happiness and inner peace.

Check your Understanding

1. What has one of your professors or instructors done recently to demonstrate good emotional intelligence in dealing with students?
2. Describe what a business executive, entertainer, or well-known athlete has done recently to demonstrate low emotional intelligence. Explain your reasoning.
3. Suppose the vast majority of company managers had high emotional intelligence. How might this fact give the company a competitive advantage?
4. Imagine yourself as the human resources director of a medium-size manufacturer of airplane parts, and you have $150,000 in your training budget to spend for product training and emotional intelligence training. How would you divide your budget between the two types of training?
5. Many gerontology specialists believe that people with a positive attitude live longer. How could this possibly be true? Don't people die of *physical* causes?
6. What are some of the skills a person needs to acquire to become happy?
7. How do your "spheres of life" compare with those in Figure 4-3?
8. When you are happiest, are you more productive on the job or at school?
9. Why might being very happy prompt some people to become less competitive in their careers?
10. Many companies place posters with smiley faces around the factory and office in order to boost worker morale and happiness. How effective do you think this practice might be?

Web Corner

Emotional intelligence: www.emotionalintelligence. com; www.eiconsortium.org

The Happiness Test: www.Web.tickle.com

Positive attitudes: www.attitudeiseverything.com; www. pops.com

Internet Skill Builder

Daily Doses of Happiness on the Web

Visit *www.thehappyguy.com* to receive your "daily dose of happiness." The Daily Dose of Happiness offers you happiness quotes and suggestions for self-actualization. Happyguy promises to help you achieve such ends as becoming inspired about life, discovering the meaning of happiness, and achieving personal growth. After trying out this program of happiness and personal growth, you be the judge. Have you made strides toward becoming happier? Do you feel any better emotionally? What impact do the Daily Happiness mugs have on your personal well being? Be happy!

Developing Your Human Relations Skills

Human Relations Application Exercises

Applying Human Relations Exercise 4-1

Enhancing Your Emotional Intelligence

A realistic starting point in improving your emotional intelligence is to work with one of its four components at a time, such as the empathy aspect of social awareness. A complex behavior pattern or trait such as emotional intelligence takes considerable time to improve, but the time will most likely be a good investment. Follow these steps:

1. Begin by obtaining as much feedback as you can from people who know you. Ask them if they think you understand their emotional reactions and how well they think you understand them. It is helpful to ask someone from another culture or someone who has a severe disability how well you communicate with him or her. (A higher level of empathy is required to communicate well with somebody much different from you.) If you work with customers, ask them how well you appear to understand their position.

2. If you find any area of deficiency, work on that deficiency steadily. For example, perhaps you are not perceived as taking the time to understand a point of view quite different from your own. Attempt to understand other points of view. Suppose you believe strongly that only people with lots of money can be happy. Speak to a person with a different opinion and listen carefully until you understand that person's perspective.

3. At a minimum of a few weeks later, obtain more feedback about your ability to empathize. If you are making progress, continue to practice.

4. Prepare a document about your skill development. Describe the steps you took to enhance your empathy, the progress you made, and how people react differently to you now. For example, you might find that people talk more openly and freely with you now that you are more empathetic.

5. Then, repeat these steps for another facet of emotional intelligence. As a result you will have developed another valuable interpersonal skill.

Applying Human Relations Exercise 4-2

Achieving Happiness

The following exercises will help you develop attitudes that contribute mightily to happiness.

1. *Start the day off right.* Begin each day with five minutes of positive thought and visualization. Commit to this for one week. When and how do you plan to fit this into your schedule?

   _____

   _____

2. *Make a list of five virtues in which you believe.* Examples would include patience, compassion, and helping the less fortunate.

   _____

   _____

   _____

3. *Each week, for the next five weeks, incorporate a different virtue into your life.* On a simple index card, write this week's virtue in bold letters, such as "helping the less fortunate." Post the card in a prominent place. After you have completed one incident of helping the less fortunate, describe in about 10 to 25 words what you did. Also record the date and time.

   _____

   _____

   _____

4. *Look for good things about new acquaintances.* List three students, customers, or coworkers you have just met. List three *positive* qualities about each.

   _____

   _____

   _____

5. *List the positive qualities of fellow students or coworkers you dislike or have trouble working with.* Remember, keep looking for the good.

_____

_____

_____

6. *Think of school assignments or job tasks you dislike and write down the merits of these tasks.* Identify the benefits they bring you.

_____

_____

_____

7. *Look at problems as opportunities.* What challenges are you now facing? In what way might you view them that would inspire and motivate you?

_____

_____

_____

Source: Adapted from Stu Kamen, "Turn Negatives into Positives," *Pryor Report Success Workshop*, May 1995, pp. 1–2.

Human Relations Case Study 4-1

The Very Positive Kelly Malibu

Kelly Malibu, twenty-seven, is the manager of Deco, a woman's store that features clothing with an art deco design. Deco is one of several specialty retail stores owned by Max and Mary Lowenstein. When the store opened three years ago, Malibu was hired as the manager. Max Lowenstein said, "Kelly was a wonderful fit. She had retailing in her blood, having worked at women's stores since age seventeen. She also had supervisory experience, and is so upbeat. Our one concern was that she might be too nice to be a tough boss when needed."

Malibu is responsible for merchandising. Twice a year she makes trips to New York to buy designs imported from Asia in bulk, and also purchases some clothing online. Malibu contends that the most difficult part of her responsibilities is dealing with employees and customers. "When I deal with vendors, things usually go pretty smoothly," she says. "The vendors are usually trying to please me. We sometimes haggle a little bit about price, but we can usually work out a deal. We have the occasional dispute about returning merchandise that we cannot sell. I know that some big retailers insist on a generous return policy."

"My attitude is that our vendors are themselves small outfits operating on slim margins. So I hate to cut too deeply into their profits. If can't sell a few dresses at Deco unless we practically give them away, it's as much my

fault as that of the manufacturer or distributor. I guessed wrong on what our clientele wants. Max and Mary don't agree with my philosophy 100 percent, but they do respect my right to manage the store as I see fit."

Malibu notes that keeping her store associates productive and happy can be a challenge. Deco Style has two full-time associates and three part-time associates. One challenge is that her part-time associates make frequent requests for a change of schedule to fit their personal life or school demands. A recent Columbus Day was a good example of this problem.

She says, "Columbus Day is usually one of our best days outside of the holiday season. So I wanted to make sure we had two part-time sales associates on board to supplement the two full-time associates." Three days before Columbus Day, Tracy, one of the part-timers, told her she had to complete a mammoth project for her computer science class so she wouldn't be able to work that day. "My instinct was to tell Tracy that if she couldn't be here on Columbus Day, she could set sail for another job. Then I thought of my own experiences in college. A computer science project can suck up all your mental energy and make it difficult to concentrate on anything else. So I let Tracy off the hook.

"Kim, another one of our associates, said she would be out of town for her brother's wedding. She had given me two month's notice about the wedding, so I couldn't insist that she be here. Bruce, another one of our associates, said he couldn't work on Columbus Day because he would be running a marathon. My first thoughts were to tell Bruce that running a marathon was no excuse for missing work. However, as I thought it through I realized that completing a marathon would add considerably to Bruce's self-esteem. As a result, I simply wished Bruce the best of luck in the marathon. I know that Bruce appreciated my understanding.

"That left me with one sales associate, Nicki, who could work on Columbus Day. I made up for one of the missing sales associates with my mom, who isn't a bad last-minute substitute.

"My biggest hassle with customers is when they want to see the manager because of a dispute with the associ-

ate about a return. You know that quite often they bought the dress, blouse, or suite with the intention of using it for a special occasion, and then returning it for a full refund. I usually go along with the return as a way of building customer goodwill. But I have my limits. No returns when clothing has food or perspiration stains."

Questions

1. In what way does Malibu demonstrate empathy?
2. In what way does Malibu demonstrate a positive attitude?
3. To what extent do you think Malibu would be a more effective manager if she were less empathic and positive?

Human Relations Case Study 4-2

Does the Microsoft CEO Steve Ballmer Have a Problem?

Microsoft CEO Steve Ballmer is well regarded by many workers in his company as a strong coach, cheerleader, and motivator. In times past he has screamed so hard, his vocal cords required surgical treatment. Ballmer also has the reputation of being forceful and intimidating.

In 2005, Mark Lucovsky, a Microsoft "distinguished engineer," left the company to work at Google. Later Lucovsky participated in a court hearing about another Microsoft defector, Eric Schmidt. During a sworn statement, Lucovsky reported that Ballmer became so upset over Schmidt's departure, that he tossed a chair while

uttering the following: "[Expletive] Eric Schmidt is a [expletive] pussy [cat]. I'm going to [expletive] bury that guy. I have done it before and I will do it again. I'm going to [expletive] kill Google."

A Microsoft spokesperson denies Lucovsky's version of the incident.

Questions

1. If the incident was true, in what aspect of emotional intelligence might Ballmer be deficient?
2. If the incident was true, what kind of treatment or assistance should Ballmer be offered?

Source: Adapted and softened a little from Adam Horowitz, David Jacobson, Mark Lasswell, and Owen Thomas, "101 Dumbest Moments in Business," *Business 2.0,* January/February 2006, p. 102.

REFERENCES

1. "Leading by Feel: Seek Frank Feedback," *Harvard Business Review,* January 2004, p. 31.
2. Quoted in "Leading by Feel: Be Realistic," *Harvard Business Review,* January 2004, p. 28.
3. Daniel Goleman, Richard Boyatzis, and Annie McKee, "Primal Leadership: The Hidden Driver of Great Performance," *Harvard Business Review,* December 2001, pp. 42–51.
4. David A. Morand, "The Emotional Intelligence of Managers: Assessing the Construct Validity of a Nonverbal Measure of, 'People Skills,'" *Journal of Business and Psychology,* Fall 2001, pp. 21–23.
5. Peter J. Jordan, Neal M. Ashkanasy, and Charmine E. J. Hartel, "Emotional Intelligence as a Moderator of Emotional and Behavioral Reactions to Job Insecurity," *Academy of Management Review,* July 2002, pp. 361–372.
6. "Leading by Feel: Train the Gifted," *Harvard Business Review,* January 2004, p. 31.
7. Based to some extent on information synthesized in Dodge Fernald, *Psychology* (Upper Saddle River, NJ: Prentice Hall, 1997), pp. 562–563.
8. L. A. Burke and L. A. Witt, "Personality and High-Maintenance Employee Behavior," *Journal of Business and Psychology,* Spring 2004, pp. 349–363.
9. Timothy A. Judge and Remus Ilies, "Is Positiveness in Organizations Always Desirable?" *Academy of Management Executive,* p. 152.
10. Ibid., pp. 153–155.
11. Betsy Morris, "The Best Place to Work Now," *Fortune,* January 22, 2006, pp. 79, 89, 90.
12. Mark C. Ehrant and Stefanie E. Nauman, "Organizational Citizenship Behavior in Work Groups: A Group Norms Approach," *Journal of Applied Psychology,* December 2004, pp. 960–974.
13. Philip M. Podsakoff, Michael Ahearne, and Scott B. MacKenzie, "Organizational Citizenship Behavior and the Quantity and Quality of Work Group Performance," *Journal of Applied Psychology,* April 1997, pp. 262–270.
14. Research reported in "So What Do You Have to Do to Find Happiness?" *The Sunday Times Magazine,* available at *www.timesonline.co.uk,* October 2, 2005.
15. The major sources of information for this list are Mihaly Csikzentmihalyi, "Finding Flow," *Psychology Today,* July/August 1997, pp. 46–48, 70–71; Martin Seligman, *What You Can Change and What You Can't* (New York: Knopf, 1994); Richard Corliss, "Is There a Formula for Joy?" *Time,* January 20, 2003, pp. 72–74; David G. Meyers, "Pursuing Happiness," *Psychology Today,* available at www.psychologytoday.com/articles; retrieved, March 1, 2006. "So What Do You Have to Do to Find Happiness?" *The Sunday Times Magazine,* available at *www. times online.co.uk,* October 2, 2005.
16. Survey reported in Jennifer Wirth, "Hubbies Earn More, Study Says," Gannett New Service, October 24, 2003.
17. Quoted in George Melloan, "The Rich Are Getting Richer, but So Are Others," *The Wall Street Journal,* December 23, 2003, p. A15.
18. David T. Lyken, *Happiness: What Studies on Twins Show Us about Nature, Nurture, and Happiness Set Point* (New York: Golden Books, 1999), p. 67.
19. Martin Seligman, "Don't Diet, Be Happy," *USA Weekend,* February 4–6, 1994, p. 12.
20. Steven Reiss, "Secrets of Happiness," *Psychology Today,* January/February 2001, pp. 50–52, 55–56.
21. Corliss, "Is There a Formula for Joy?" p. 74.
22. Arthur C. Brooks, "Money Buys Happiness," *The Wall Street Journal,* December 8, 2005, p. A16.
23. Sharon Begley, "Wealth and Happiness Don't Necessarily Go Hand in Hand," (Science Journal), *The Wall Street Journal,* August 13, 2004, p. B1.
24. Quoted in Corliss, "Is There a Formula for Joy?" p. 74.
25. Richard Carlson, *You Can Be Happy No Matter What: Five Principles Your Therapist Never Told You,* revised edition (Novato, CA: New World Library, 1997).
26. Ibid., p. 71.

5 Values and Ethics

Learning Objectives

After studying the information and doing the exercise in this chapter, you should be able to:

1 Understand the nature of values and how they are learned.

2 Be able to classify values and explain generational differences in values.

3 Pinpoint the nature of value clarification and how the meshing of individual and organizational values is important.

4 Understand the importance of business ethics, the difficulty of being ethical, and the extent of ethical problems in business.

5 Identify workplace situations that often present ethical dilemmas.

6 Follow the guidelines for making ethical decisions and behaving ethically.

Outline

RadioShack Corp. chief executive officer David Edmonston—who admitted inflating his educational background—resigned by "mutual agreement," and the electronics retailer's board launched a search for a new CEO. Edmonston said in a statement released by the company: "The board and I have agreed that it is in the best interest of the company for new leadership to step forward." He will receive a severance package valued at about $1.5 million said Leonard H. Roberts, the company's executive chairperson.

A week before resigning Edmonston acknowledged misstating his educational credentials, saying he believed he had received a ThG diploma—typically a certificate with fewer requirements than a bachelor's degree—and not a bachelor of science degree as he previously claimed. But the 46-year-old CEO also acknowledged he couldn't document the ThG diploma. Another report on the same incident indicates that Edmonston claimed two degrees, one in psychology and one in theology from the Pacific Coast Bible College, with most of the work done through correspondence courses. The concerns about Edmonston falsifying his credentials came about because of an investigation by the Fort Worth, Texas, Star-Telegram.

Edmonston was awaiting trial on a charged of driving while intoxicated (DWI), his third DWI charge in 17 years. The first two didn't result in convictions, although one, in July 2000, resulted in deferred adjudication, a type of probation. [1]

The story about the disgraced retail company executive illustrates that people in high places are not always as ethical as their employers would like them to be. At the same time the story might make some people wonder how ethical it is to give a $1.5 million severance package to someone who lied on his job résumé—and who also has been charged with DWI. In this chapter we study values, an important force contributing to a person's level of ethical behavior, as well as ethics. Values and ethics are foundation topics in human relations because our values and ethics influence how we treat others, and how we are treated in return.

In What Way Are Values a Part of Understanding Human Relations?

■ **Learning Objective 1**

■ **value**

The importance a person attaches to something; values are also tied to the enduring belief that one's mode of conduct is better than another mode of conduct

■ **ethics**

The moral choices a person makes

One group of factors influencing how a person behaves on the job is that person's values and beliefs. A **value** refers to the importance a person attaches to something. Values are also tied to the enduring belief that one's mode of conduct is better than another mode of conduct. If you believe that good interpersonal relations are the most important part of your life, your humanistic values are strong. Similarly, you may think that people who are not highly concerned about interpersonal relations have poor values.

Values are closely tied in with **ethics**, the moral choices a person makes. A person's values influence which kinds of behaviors he or she believes are ethical. Ethics converts values into action. A business owner who highly values money and profits might not find it unethical to raise prices higher than needed to cover additional costs. A corporate executive who strongly values family life might suggest that the company invest company funds in an on-premises dependent care center.

HOW VALUES ARE LEARNED

People are not born with a particular set of values. Instead, people acquire values in the process of growing up, and many values are learned by the age of four. One important way we acquire values is through observing others, or modeling. Models can be teachers, friends, brothers, sisters, and even public figures. If we identify with a particular person, the probability is high that we will develop some of his or her major values, such as identifying with a parent, instructor, or coach.

Another major way values are learned is through the communication of attitudes. The attitudes that we hear expressed directly or indirectly help shape our values. Assume that using credit to purchase goods and services was considered an evil practice among your family and friends. You might, therefore, hold negative values about installment purchases.

Unstated but implied attitudes may also shape your values. If key people in life showed a lack of enthusiasm when you talked about work accomplishments, you might not place such a high value on achieving outstanding results. If, however, your family and friends centered their lives on their careers, you might develop similar values. (Or, you might rebel against such a value because it interfered with a more relaxed lifestyle.) Many key values are also learned through religion and thus become the basis for society's morals. For example, most religions emphasize treating other people fairly and kindly. To "knife somebody in the back" is considered immoral both on and off the job.

Later Life Influences on Values

Although many core values are learned early in life, our values continue to be shaped by events late in life. The media, including dissemination of information about popular culture, influence the values of many people throughout their lives. The aftermath of Hurricane Katrina intensified a belief in the value of helping less fortunate people. Volunteers from throughout the United States invested time, money, and energy into helping rebuild New Orleans and several other Gulf Coast cities. Influential people, such as NBA players, were seen on television building houses for Katrina victims. Such publicity sent a message that helping people in need is a value worth considering.

The media, particularly advertisements, can also encourage the development of values that are harmful to a person intent on developing a professional career. People featured in advertisements for consumer products, including snack food, beer, and vehicles, often flaunt rudeness and gross grammar. The message comes across to many people that such behavior is associated with success.

Changes in technology can also change our values. As the world has become increasingly digitized, more and more people come to value a *digital lifestyle* as the normal way of life. The changes in values leads to curious changes in the behavior of people. Eastman Kodak Co. chair and chief executive Antonio Perez commented on how people have shifted away from storing prints of photos in shoeboxes, thereby being in danger of losing many important memories. Perez said, "As much as we complain about the old shoebox, it was brilliant. Because it was just a matter of going through the attic. . . . This is going to be a lot more difficult in digital, as you all know. Formats are going to change. Hard drives will crash." [2] Of course, people who truly value stored memories can make prints.

The Influence of Company Values

Values can sometimes be learned later in life when we are introduced to values that did not capture our attention earlier. It is possible that the teaching and demands of an employer will help us acquire new values. A relevant example is the effort and time IBM invests in teaching company values to employees. Several years ago Chair,

President, and Chief Executive Officer Sam Palmisano wanted to update company values at IBM. He spearheaded an effort called ValuesJam in which more than 1,000 employees contributed information about the company's values into a Web site. After analyzing more than 1 million words of input, three new values emerged for IBM:

- dedication to every client's success

- innovation that matters—for our company and the world (such as using software to help develop new disease-fighting drugs)

- trust and personal responsibility in all relationships [3]

IBM employees at every level are expected to incorporate these values into interaction with coworkers and customers. A sales representative when meeting a customer might say to himself or herself, "What IBM product or service might help this company be more successful" rather than "What IBM product or service can I sell this company so I can meet my sales quota?" Figure 5-1 presents another example of company values that are supposed to guide employee behavior.

Another value that individuals may acquire as a result of being part of an organization is *corporate spiritualism*. This type of spiritualism takes place when management is just as concerned about nurturing employee well being as they are about profits. A practice such as a work/life program contributes to this style of corporate spiritualism. [4] The purpose of a work/life program is to make it easier for workers to effectively manage both work and personal life responsibilities. Flexible working hours and dependent-care assistance are prime examples, but even the presence of a dry cleaner on company premises can help workers balance the demands of work and personal life.

Our Mission

At Microsoft, we work to help people and businesses throughout the world realize their potential. This is our mission. Everything we do reflects this mission and the values that make it possible.

Our Values

As a company, and as individuals, we value:

- Integrity and honesty
- Passion for customers, for our partners, and for technology
- Openness and respectfulness
- Taking on big challenges and seeing them through
- Constructive self-criticism, self-improvement, and personal excellence
- Accountability to customers, shareholders, partners, and employees for commitment and quality

To find out more how we are living our mission and values, explore the About Microsoft Web.

Questions

1. Based on your knowledge of Microsoft, how well do company practices match up to their values?
2. If you were (or are) a Microsoft employee, how inspirational would (or do) these values inspire you toward ethical behavior and high performance?

Source: www.microsoft.com/mscorp/mission.

Figure   5-1

The Mission and Values of Microsoft Corporation.

The Methodist Hospital System based in Houston, Texas has seen many positive results from its effort to promote corporate spiritualism as a corporate value. The greater emphasis on corporate spiritualism was part of a values initiative, as guided by Cindy Vanover, the project director for spiritual care and values integration. The values initiative integrated spiritual values across the entire system, with the core values being integrity, compassion, accountability, respect, and excellence. (The values of compassion and respect fit directly the definition of corporate spiritualism presented previously.) Methodist Hospital calculates that, as a result of the values initiative, employee turnover and hospital vacancy rates decreased, while patient and employee/physician satisfaction levels increased. [5]

THE CLASSIFICATION AND CLARIFICATION OF VALUES

■ Learning Objective 2

Because values can be related to anything we believe in, a large number of values exist. Several attempts have been made to classify values, and each one is closely tied to psychological needs. If we value something strongly, such as accomplishing worthwhile activities, it leads to a need such as achievement. If we value independence, it will most likely lead to a need for autonomy. The following classification of values involves needs and is linked to both career and personal life. The basis of the value classification is to categorize people in to five types who emphasize different values and needs. [6]

■ *Humanists* are driven primarily by a need for self-awareness, personal growth, and a sense of being individual and unique. Humanism is their most important value.

■ *Strategists* highly value a sense of mastery and personal achievement. They are likely to say, "I am what I do." Strategists might believe that insight and understanding are important but they place the highest value on tangible accomplishments.

■ *Pragmatists* strive for a corner in the world anchored by power, influence, stability, and control. They search for roles and settings that provide them with formal power, respect, and prestige. A pragmatist, therefore, highly values career success in the traditional meaning of the term—high compensation and rank.

■ *Adventurers* place low value on status and conformity. Instead, they have a powerful drive for excitement and adventure. The adventurer might say, "I don't want to play it safe. I want to play often and big. Play is good. Just do it." The adventurer has high standing on the trait of risk taking and thrill seeking.

Another key value that influences both work and personal life is *conscientiousness*. As a personality trait, conscientiousness is regarded as one of the basic components of personality. However, the same trait also functions as a value, with the conscientious person striving to be industrious, well organized, self-controlling, responsible, traditional, and virtuous. [7] Dozens of studies have demonstrated that workers with a high standing on conscientiousness tend to perform well in a wide variety of positions. [8] As a result, employers look for conscientious workers when choosing among job candidates for both initial hiring and later promotion.

Differences in values among people often stem from age, or generational, differences. Workers older than age 50, in general, may have different values than people who are much younger. These age differences in values have often been seen as a clash between baby boomers and members of generation X and generation Y. According to the stereotype, boomers see generation X and generation Y as disrespectful of rules, not willing to pay their dues, and being disloyal to employers. Generation X and generation Y see boomers as worshipping hierarchy (layers of authority), being overcautious, and wanting to preserve the status quo.

Baby Boomers (1946-1964)	Generation X (1961-1980)	Generation Y (1981-2002) (Millenials)
Uses technology as necessary tool	Technosavvy	Technosavvy
Tolerates teams but values independent work	Teamwork very important	Teamwork very important
Appreciates hierarchy	Dislikes hierarchy	Dislikes hierarchy; prefers participation
Strong career orientation	Strives for work/life balance but will work long hours for now	Strives for work/life balance but will work long hours for now
More loyalty to organization	Loyalty to own career and profession	Belief in informality
Favors diplomacy	Candid in conversation	Wants to strike it rich quickly
Favors old economy	Appreciates old and new economy	Ultracandid in conversation
Expects a bonus based on performance	Would appreciate a signing bonus	Prefers the new economy
		Expected a signing bonus before the dot-com crash
Believes that issues should be formally discussed	Believes that feedback can be administered informally	Believes that feedback can be given informally, even on the fly

Source: Several of the ideas in this table are from Robert McGarvey, "The Coming of Gen X Bosses," *Entrepreneur*, November 1999, pp. 60–64; Joanne M. Glenn, "Teaching the Net Generation," *Business Education Forum*, February 2000, pp. 6–14; Anita Bruzzese, "There Needn't Be a Generation Gap," Gannett News Service, April 22, 2002; Gregg Hammill, "Mixing and Managing Four Generations of Employees," *FDUMagazine Online*, Winter/Spring 2005, p. 5.
Note: Disagreement exists about which age bracket fit baby boomers, generation X, and generation Y with both professional publications and dictionaries showing slight differences.

Figure   5-2

Value Stereotypes for Several Generations of Workers.

> "Above all, Gen Y is tech savvy. Their lifestyle is all about technology. They are consumed by entertainment and accomplished at multitasking."
> —Elizabeth Gillespie, vice president of marketing for Jones Lang LaSalle Americas Inc., a real estate firm.

■ Learning Objective 3

Figure 5-2 summarizes these stereotypes with the understanding that massive group stereotypes like this are only partially accurate because there are literally millions of exceptions. For example, many Baby Boomers are fascinated with technology, and many members of Generation Y like hierarchy.

Expanding and clarifying the list of values the members of generation Y emphasize are a fun work environment, opportunities for growth, and a wide range of projects on which to work. The same group, similar to career-oriented workers of all ages, wants opportunities to learn and develop new skills paid for by the company. In addition, the majority of generation Y employees value friendly relationships among employees. [9]

Value Clarification

The values that you develop early in life are directly related to the kind of person you are and to the quality of the relationships you form. [10] Recognition of this fact has led to exercises designed to help people clarify and understand some of their own values. At times the values you clarify will match with the value categories previously listed including company values, and generational differences in values. At other times, your personal value list will be different. The Internet Skill-Building Exercise at the end of the chapter gives you an opportunity to clarify your values.

THE MESH BETWEEN INDIVIDUAL AND JOB VALUES

Under the best of circumstances, the values of employees mesh with those required by the job. When this state of congruence exists, job performance is likely to be high. Suppose that Jacquelyn strongly values giving people with limited formal education an opportunity to work and avoid being placed on welfare. So she takes a job as a manager of a dollar store that employs many people in their stores who would ordinarily have limited opportunity for employment. Jacquelyn is satisfied because her employer and she share a similar value.

When the demands made by the organization or a superior clash with the basic values of the individual, he or she suffers from **person–role conflict**. The individual wants to obey orders but does not want to perform an act that seems inconsistent with his or her values. A situation such as this might occur when an employee is asked to produce a product that he or she feels is unsafe or of no value to society.

■ **Person–role conflict**
the demands made by the organization or a superior clash with the basic values of the individual

A manager of a commercial weight-reduction center resigned after two years of service. The owners pleaded with her to stay based on her excellent performance. The manager replied, "Sorry, I think my job is immoral. We sign up all these people with great expectations of losing weight permanently. Most of them do achieve short-term weight reduction. My conflict is that more than 90 percent of our clientele regain the weight they lost once they go back to eating standard food. I think we are deceiving them by not telling them up front that they will most likely gain back the weight they lose."

What constitutes a good fit between personal values and organizational values may change at different stages of a person's career because of a change in values. At one point in a person's career, he or she may think that founding a business is important because the new firm might create employment. At another stage of the same person's career, he or she might believe that working for the nonprofit sector is more meritorious.

A starting point in finding a good fit between individual and organizational values is to identify what type of work would be the most meaningful. Po Bronson, a writer specializing in social documentaries, observes that people "thrive by focusing on the question of who they really are—and connecting to work that they truly love (and, in so doing, unleashing a productive and creative power that they never imagined)." [11] After identifying your passion in terms of work, you would then seek an employment opportunity that provides such work. For example, a manager might discover that helping young people learn useful job skills brings her the most professional excitement. She might then seek an opportunity to manage a manufacturing apprenticeship program in her company.

Why Be Concerned About Business Ethics?

■ **Learning Objective 4**

When asked why ethics (the moral choices a person makes) is important, most people would respond something to the effect that, "Ethics is important because it's the right thing to do. You behave decently in the workplace because your family and religious values have taught you what is right and wrong." All this is true, but the justification for behaving ethically is more complex, as described next. [12]

A major justification for behaving ethically on the job is to recognize that people are motivated by both self-interest and moral commitments. Most people want to maximize gain for themselves. At the same time, most people are motivated to do something morally right. As one of many examples, vast numbers of people donate money to charity, although keeping that amount of money for themselves would provide more personal gain.

Many business executives want employees to behave ethically because a good reputation can enhance business. A favorable corporate reputation may enable firms to charge premium prices and attract better job applicants. A favorable reputation also helps attract investors, such as mutual fund managers who purchase stock in companies. Certain mutual funds, for example, invest only in companies that are environmentally friendly. Managers want employees to behave ethically because unethical behavior—for example, employee theft, lost production time, and lawsuits—is costly.

Behaving ethically is also important because many unethical acts are also illegal, which can lead to financial loss and imprisonment. A company that knowingly allows workers to engage in unsafe practices might be fined and the executives may be held personally liable. Furthermore, unsafe practices can kill people. Low ethics have also resulted in financial hardship for employees as company executives raid pension funds of other companies they purchase, sharply reducing or eliminating the retirement funds of many workers.

Extreme acts of unethical behavior can lead a company into bankruptcy, such as the famous scandals at Enron Corporation. Among the worst ethical violations were hiding financial losses by passing the losses on to phony subsidiaries, encouraging employees to invest their life savings in company stock that was doomed to failure, and creating power shortages in California to artificially inflate energy prices. Furthermore, company executives sometimes held business meetings at strip clubs—at company expense. [13]

A subtle reason for behaving ethically is that high ethics increases the quality of work life. Ethics provides a set of guidelines that specify what makes for acceptable behavior. Being ethical will point you toward actions that make life more satisfying for work associates. A company code of ethics specifies what constitutes ethical versus unethical behavior. When employees follow this code, the quality of work life improves. Several sample clauses from ethical codes are as follows:

- Demonstrate courtesy, respect, honesty, and fairness.

- Do not use abusive language.

- Do not bring firearms or knives to work.

- Do not offer bribes.

- Maintain confidentiality of records.

- Do not harass (sexually, racially, ethnically, or physically) subordinates, superiors, coworkers, customers, or suppliers.

To the extent that all members of the organization abide by this ethical code, the quality of work life will improve. At the same time, interpersonal relations in organizations will be strengthened. To help raise your awareness of your own ethical thoughts and behaviors, do Human Relations Self-Assessment Quiz 5-1.

■ Learning Objective 5

WHY BEING ETHICAL ISN'T EASY

As analyzed by Linda Klebe Treviño, an organizational behavior professor at The Pennsylvania State University, and Michael E. Brown, a management professor at Penn State–Erie, behaving ethically in business is more complex than it seems on the surface for a variety of reasons. [14] To begin with, ethical decisions are complex. For example, someone might argue that hiring children for factory jobs in overseas countries is unethical. Yet if these children lose their jobs, many would starve or turn to crime to survive. Second, people do not always recognize the moral issues involved in a decision. A handyman on a work assignment who finds a butcher knife under the bed might not think that he has a role to play in perhaps preventing murder.

Human Relations Self-Assessment Quiz   5-1

The Ethical Reasoning Inventory

Describe how well you agree with each of the following statements. Use the following scale: disagree strongly (DS), disagree (D), neutral (N), agree (A), agree strongly (AS). Circle the number in the appropriate column.

	DS	D	N	A	AS
1. When applying for a job, I would cover up the fact that I had been fired from my most recent job.	5	4	3	2	1
2. Cheating only a few dollars in one's favor on an expense account is OK if a person needs the money.	5	4	3	2	1
3. Employees should report on each other for wrongdoing.	1	2	3	4	5
4. It is acceptable to give approximate figures for expense account items when one does not have all the receipts.	5	4	3	2	1
5. I see no problem with conducting a little personal business on company time.	5	4	3	2	1
6. Simply to make a sale, I would stretch the truth about a delivery date.	5	4	3	2	1
7. I would fix up a purchasing agent with a date simply to close a sale.	5	4	3	2	1
8. I would flirt with my boss simply to get a bigger salary increase.	5	4	3	2	1
9. If I received $500 for doing some odd jobs, I would report it on my income tax return.	1	2	3	4	5
10. I see no harm in taking home a few office supplies.	5	4	3	2	1
11. It is acceptable to read the e-mail messages and faxes of coworkers, even when not invited to do so.	5	4	3	2	1
12. It is unacceptable to call in sick in order to take a day off, even if only done once or twice a year.	1	2	3	4	5
13. I would accept a permanent, full-time job even if I knew I wanted the job for only six months.	5	4	3	2	1
14. I would first check company policy before accepting an expensive gift from a supplier.	1	2	3	4	5
15. To be successful in business, a person usually has to ignore ethics.	5	4	3	2	1
16. If I felt physically attracted toward a job candidate, I would hire that person over a more qualified candidate.	5	4	3	2	1
17. On the job, I tell the truth all the time.	1	2	3	4	5
18. If a student were very pressed for time, it would be acceptable to either have a friend write the paper or purchase one.	5	4	3	2	1
19. I would authorize accepting an office machine on a 30-day trial period, even if I knew we had no intention of buying it.	5	4	3	2	1
20. I would never accept credit for a coworker's ideas.	1	2	3	4	5

Scoring and Interpretation:

Add the numbers you have circled to obtain your total score.

90–100   You are a strongly ethical person who may take a little ribbing from coworkers for being too straitlaced.

60–89   You show an average degree of ethical awareness and, therefore, should become more sensitive to ethical issues.

41–59   Your ethics are underdeveloped, but you at least have some awareness of ethical issues. You need to raise your level of awareness of ethical issues.

20–40   Your ethical values are far below contemporary standards in business. Begin a serious study of business ethics.

Sometimes language hides the moral issue involved, such as when the term *file sharing* music replaces *stealing* music.

Another complexity in making ethical decisions is that people have different levels of moral development. At one end of the scale some people behavior morally simply to escape punishment. At the other end of the scale, some people are morally developed to the point that they are guided by principles of justice and right such as wanting to help as many people as possible. The environment in which we work also influences our behaving ethically. Suppose a restaurant owner encourages such practices as serving customers food that was accidentally dropped on the kitchen floor. An individual server is more likely to engage in such behavior to obey the demand of the owner.

A SURVEY OF THE EXTENT OF ETHICAL PROBLEMS

The ethical misdeeds of executives have received substantial publicity in recent years. However, recent surveys show that ethical violations by rank-and-file employees are widespread, particularly with respect to lying. According to two separate surveys, more than one-third of workers admit to having fabricated about their need for sick days. More employees are stretching the reasons for taking time off. Job applicants reporting false or embellished academic credentials have hit a three-year high. Here are the major findings of a composite of several surveys: [15]

- 36 percent of employees call in sick when they are well

- 34 percent of employees keep quiet when they see coworker misconduct

- 19 percent of employees see coworkers lie to customers, vendors, and the public

- 12 percent of employees steal from customers or the company

- 12 percent of résumés contain at least some false information

Although these findings might suggest that unethical behavior is on the increase, another explanation is possible. Workers today might be more observant of ethical problems and more willing to note them on a survey.

Going beyond surveys of what individuals believe, some company practices of today might be considered unethical in terms of people getting harmed. Today, there is much less disgrace in a company declaring bankruptcy, thereby leaving many debts unpaid and abandoning employees pensions. (The federal government is then forced to take over the pension plan and pays the workers a small percentage of the pension for which they were hoping.) *Fortune* magazine writer Justin Fox, represents the ethical thinking of the executives who feel no guilt about bankruptcy in these words: "Chapter 11 [a type of bankruptcy] encourages risk taking, helps the economy adapt to changing times, and helps companies rebound from past mistakes. American business wouldn't be where it is today without it." [16]

Ethical violations often occur when entertaining customers or potential customers in the hopes of winning business. A case in point was the bachelor party the brokerage house the Jeffries Group held for a star trader for Fidelity Investments. (The Jeffries Group was trying to win a big chunk of Fidelity's business.) The festivities included a jet from Boston to a small airport outside New York City, the company of two presumably paid women, a flight to South Beach in Miami, a stay at the ritzy Delano Hotel, a yacht cruise, and entertainment by a dwarf. (Dwarfs are often rented as party entertainers. See ***www.ShortDwarf.com***) Regulators investigated this party and may file charges. [17]

FREQUENT ETHICAL DILEMMAS

Certain ethical mistakes, including illegal actions, recur in the workplace. Familiarizing oneself with these mistakes can be helpful in monitoring one's own behavior. Here we describe a number of common ethical problems faced by business executives as well as workers at lower job levels. [18]

The Temptation to Illegally Copy Software

A rampant ethical problem is whether to illegally copy computer software. According to the Business Software Alliance, approximately 35 percent of applications used in business are illegal. [19] The illegal copying of software deprives software developers of profits they deserve for having produced the software. Such pirating also leads to the loss of potential jobs for many software developers because the companies that produce the software have less revenue.

Treating People Unfairly

Being fair to people means equity, reciprocity, and impartiality. Fairness revolves around the issue of giving people equal rewards for accomplishing equal amounts of work. The goal of human resource legislation is to make decisions about people based on their qualifications and performance—not on the basis of demographic factors such as sex, race, or age. A fair working environment is where performance is the only factor that counts (equity). Employer–employee expectations must be understood and met (reciprocity). Prejudice and bias must be eliminated (impartiality).

> "Follow the *Platinum Rule:* Treat people the way *they* wish to be treated."
> —Eric Harvey and Scott Airitam, authors of *Ethics 4 Everyone*.

    Treating people fairly—therefore ethically—requires an underemphasis on political factors. Yet this ethical doctrine is not always easy to implement. It is human nature to want to give bigger rewards (such as fatter raises or bigger orders) to people we like.

Sexual Harassment

Sexual harassment is a source of conflict and an illegal act. Sexual harassment is also an ethical issue because it is morally wrong and unfair. All acts of sexual harassment flunk an ethics test. Before sexually harassing another person, the potential harasser should ask, "Would I want a loved one to be treated this way?"

Conflict of Interest

Part of being ethical is making business judgments only on the basis of the merits or facts in a situation. Imagine that you are a supervisor who is romantically involved with a worker within the group. When it comes time to assign raises, it will be difficult for you to be objective. A **conflict of interest** occurs when your judgment or objectivity is compromised. Conflicts of interest often take place in the sales end of business. If a company representative accepts a large gift from a sales representative, it may be difficult to make objective judgments about buying from the representative. Yet being taken to dinner by a vendor would not ordinarily cloud one's judgment. Another common example of a conflict of interest is making a hiring decision about a friend who badly needs a job, but is not well qualified for the position.

■ **Conflict of interest**
Judgment or objectivity is compromised

    Conflicts of interest have been behind some of the major business scandals in recent times, such as Enron Corporation auditors giving the company a favorable rating. Many outsiders dealing with Enron—including auditors, bankers, and even regulators—were tempted by a piece of the equity action. [20] The conflict occurs when one party paid to make objective judgments about the financial health of a second party has a personal interest in how profitable the second party looks to the public. An auditor might be hesitant to give a negative evaluation of the financial condition of a company if the auditor's firm also provides consulting services to that company. Some financial research analysts gave glowing public reports about the fiscal condition of a company when that company was a client of the analyst's own firm. The analyst's firm sold services for issuing new stock and assisting with corporate mergers and acquisitions.

Dealing With Confidential Information

An ethical person can be trusted by others not to divulge confidential information unless the welfare of others is at stake. Suppose a coworker tells you in confidence that she is upset with the company and, therefore, is looking for another job. Behaving ethically, you do not pass this information along to your supervisor even though it would help your supervisor plan for a replacement. Now suppose the scenario changes slightly. Your coworker tells you she is looking for another job because she is upset. She tells you she is so upset that she plans to destroy company computer files on her last day. If your friend does find another job, you might warn the company about her contemplated activities.

The challenge of dealing with confidential information arises in many areas of business that affect interpersonal relations. If you learned that a coworker was indicted for a crime, charged with sexual harassment, or facing bankruptcy, there would be a temptation to gossip about the person. A highly ethical person would not pass along information about the personal difficulties of another person.

Presentation of Employment History

Many people are tempted to distort in a positive direction information about their employment history on their job résumé, job application form, and during the interview. Distortion, or lying, of this type is considered unethical and can lead to immediate dismissal if discovered. A recent case in point is David Edmonston, the former chief executive officer of RadioShack Corp. who resigned amid charges that his résumé included college degrees he never earned (as described in the opening case). Similarly, Ronald Zarella, the CEO of Bausch & Lomb Inc. was discovered to have not completed a graduate degree at New York University, as was originally claimed in his biographical information. [21] Zarella paid a fine but was retained in his post because of his outstanding job performance.

Possible Ethical Violations With Computers and Information Technology

As computers dominate the workplace, many ethical issues have arisen in addition to pirating software. One ethical dilemma that surfaces frequently is the fairness of tracking the Web sites a person visits and those from which he or she buys. Should this information be sold, like a mailing list? Another issue is the fairness of having an employee work at a keyboard for 60 hours in one week when such behavior frequently leads to repetitive motion disorder. And is it ethical for workers to spend so much time doing on-line shopping and placing bets on-line during the working day?

You may have observed that these common ethical problems are not always clear-cut. Aside from obvious matters, such as prohibitions against stealing, lying, cheating, and intimidating, subjectivity enters into ethical decision making.

What Are Some Guidelines for Making Ethical Decisions and Behaving Ethically?

■ Learning Objective 6

Following guidelines for ethical behavior is the heart of being ethical. Although many people behave ethically without studying ethical guidelines, they are usually following guidelines programmed into their minds early in life. The Golden Rule exemplifies a guideline taught by parents, grandparents, and kindergarten teachers. In this section we approach ethical guidelines from six perspectives: (1) developing the right character traits, (2) following a guide for ethical decision making, (3) developing close relationships with work associates, (4) using corporate programs for ethics, (5) following an ethical role model, and (6) following an applicable professional code of conduct.

DEVELOPING THE RIGHT CHARACTER TRAITS

Character traits develop early in life, yet with determination and self-discipline many people can modify old traits or develop new ones. A **character trait** is an enduring characteristic of a person that is related to moral and ethical behavior that shows up consistently. For example, if a person has the character trait of untruthfulness, he or she will lie in many situations. Conversely, the character trait of honesty leads to behaving honestly in most situations.

■ **Character trait**
An enduring characteristic of a person that is related to moral and ethical behavior that shows up consistently

The Character Counts Coalition is an organization formed to encourage young people to develop fairness, respect, trustworthiness, responsibility, caring, and good citizenship. The coalition has developed a list of 10 key guidelines as a foundation for character development. [22] If you develop, or already have, these traits, it will be easy for you to behave ethically in business. As you read the following list, evaluate your own standing on each character trait. Remember, however, that extra effort is required to evaluate one's character traits, because most people have an inflated view of their honesty and integrity.

1. **Be honest.** Tell the truth; be sincere; do not mislead or withhold information in relationships of trust; do not steal.

2. **Demonstrate integrity.** Stand up for your beliefs about right and wrong; be your best self; resist social pressure to do wrong.

3. **Keep promises.** Keep your word and honor your commitments; pay your debts and return what you borrow.

4. **Be loyal.** Stand by family, friends, employers, community, and country; do not talk about people behind their backs.

5. **Be responsible.** Think before you act; consider consequences; be accountable and "take your medicine."

6. **Pursue excellence.** Do your best with what you have; do not give up easily.

7. **Be kind and caring.** Show you care through generosity and compassion; do not be selfish or mean.

8. **Treat all people with respect.** Be courteous and polite; judge all people on their merits; be tolerant, appreciative, and accepting of individual differences.

9. **Be fair.** Treat all people fairly; be open-minded; listen to others and try to understand what they are saying and feeling.

10. **Be a good citizen.** Obey the law and respect authority; vote; volunteer your efforts; protect the environment.

If you score high on all of the preceding character traits and behaviors, you are an outstanding member of your company, community, and school. Your ethical behavior is superior.

USING A GUIDE TO ETHICAL DECISION MAKING

A powerful strategy for behaving ethically is to follow a guide for ethical decision making. Such a guide for making contemplated decisions includes testing their

■ **Ethical screening**

Running a contemplated decision or action through an ethics test, particularly when a contemplated action or decision is not clearly ethical or unethical

ethics. **Ethical screening** refers to running a contemplated decision or action through an ethics test. Such screening makes the most sense when the contemplated action or decision is not clearly ethical or unethical. If a sales representative were to take a favorite customer to Pizza Hut for lunch, an ethical screen would not be necessary. Nobody would interpret a "veggie super" to be a serious bribe. Assume, instead, that the sales rep offered to give the customer an under-the-table gift of $600 for placing a large offer with the rep's firm. The sales representative's behavior would be so blatantly unethical that conducting an ethical screen would be unnecessary.

Several guidelines, or ethical screens, have been developed to help the leader or other influence agent decide whether a given act is ethical or unethical. The Center for Business Ethics at Bentley College has developed six questions to evaluate the ethics of a specific decision: [23]

■ **Is it right?** This question is based on the deontological theory of ethics that there are certain universally accepted guiding principles of rightness and wrongness, such as "thou shall not steal."

■ **Is it fair?** This question is based on the deontological theory of justice that certain actions are inherently just or unjust. For example, it is unjust to fire a high-performing employee to make room for a less competent person who is a relative by marriage.

■ **Who gets hurt?** This question is based on the utilitarian notion of attempting to do the greatest good for the greatest number of people.

■ **Would you be comfortable if the details of your decision or actions were made public in the media or through e-mail?** This question is based on the principle of disclosure.

■ **What would you tell your child, sibling, or young relative to do?** This question is based on the deontological principle of reversibility, which evaluates the ethics of a decision by reversing the decision maker.

■ **How does it smell?** This question is based on a person's intuition and common sense. For example, not paying overtime to employees who work through their lunch hour would "smell" bad to a sensible person.

Ethical issues that require a run through the guide are usually subtle rather than blatant, a decision that falls into the gray zone. An example would be the business plan of Krispy Kreme. Profits from company-owned stores are not large enough to cover corporate expenses. The company's real profits derive from dealing with its franchisees that pay royalties of 4.5 to 6 percent of sales plus 1 percent for advertising and public relations. All supplies must be purchased from the parent. After all the payments to the parent, it is exceedingly difficult for the franchisees to earn a profit. So is Krispy Kreme leadership being ethical?

DEVELOPING STRONG RELATIONSHIPS WITH WORK ASSOCIATES

A provocative explanation of the causes of unethical behavior emphasizes the strength of relationships among people. [24] Assume that two people have close professional ties to each other, such as having worked together for a long time or knowing each other both on and off the job. As a consequence, they are likely to behave ethically toward one another on the job. In contrast, if a weak professional relationship exists between two individuals either party is more likely to engage in an unethical relationship. The owner of an auto service center is more likely to behave unethically toward a stranger passing through town than toward a long-time customer. The opportunity for unethical behavior between strangers is often minimized because individuals typically do not trust strangers with sensitive information or valuables.

The ethical skill-building consequence of information about personal relationships is that building stronger relationships with people is likely to enhance ethical behavior. If you build strong relationships with work associates, you are likely to behave more ethically toward them. Similarly, your work associates are likely to behave more ethically toward you. The work associates we refer to are all your contacts.

USING CORPORATE ETHICS PROGRAMS

Many organizations have various programs and procedures for promoting ethical behavior. Among them are committees that monitor ethical behavior, training programs in ethics, and vehicles for reporting ethical violations. The presence of these programs is designed to create an atmosphere in which unethical behavior is discouraged and reporting on unethical behavior is encouraged.

Ethics hotlines are one of the best-established programs to help individuals avoid unethical behavior. Should a person be faced with an ethical dilemma, the person calls a toll-free line to speak to a counselor about the dilemma. Sometimes employees ask questions to help interpret a policy, such as "Is it okay to ask my boss for a date?" or "Are we supposed to give senior citizen discounts to customers who qualify but do not ask for one?" At other times, a more pressing ethical issue might be addressed, such as "Is it ethical to lay off a worker only five months short of his qualifying for a full pension?"

Sears, Roebuck and Co., has an ethics hotline the company refers to as an "Assist Line" because very few of the 15,000 calls it receives per year represent crises. Often the six full-time ethics specialists who handle the calls simply listen; at other times they intervene to help resolve the problem. The Assist Line is designed to help with these kinds of calls: guidance about company policy; company Code of Conduct issues; workplace harassment/discrimination; selling practices; theft; and human resource issues. Employees and managers are able to access information and guidance without feeling they are facing a crisis. So the Assist Line is kind of a cross between 911 and 411 calls. At times an ethical problem of such high moral intensity is presented that employee confidentiality cannot be maintained. However, the Ethics Office handles the inquiries in as confidential a manner as practical and assigns them case identification numbers for follow up. [25]

Wells Fargo & Co., a mammoth bank, emphasizes both a code of conduct and ethics training. Its Code of Ethics and Business Conduct specifies policies and standards for employees, covering a variety of topics from maintaining accurate records to participating in civic activities. Each year, employees also participate in ethics training. Any Wells Fargo employee may ask questions or report ethical breaches anonymously using an ethics hotline or dedicated e-mail address. The company will fire violators, dismissing about 100 people a year for misconduct ranging from conflicts of interest to cheating on incentive plans.

Patricia Callahan, executive vice president and director of human resources at the bank says, "I'm the biggest soft touch in the world. But when someone lies or cheats, you can't have people like that representing us to our customers, whose trust is all we have." [26]

A caution about ethics programs is that they lose their effectiveness if top-level management does not display high ethics. Executives have to communicate regularly about the importance of high ethics and corporate values. For example, when sales representatives are asked about their total sales, they should also be asked how ethically they behaved in attaining the sales. [27]

A corporate ethics program works best when placed in a corporate culture that promotes ethical behavior. When top management holds meetings at strip clubs, such as Enron executives did on occasion, it is difficult to seriously preach the

Human Relations in Practice

Supervisors at Utility Companies Teach Ethics

Public Service Co. of New Mexico (PNM) started its ethics program in the mid-1990s to comply with government guidelines and to improve its image after a public outcry over rate hikes. "We had an incentive to show a new side of ourselves," says Sarah Smith, director of business ethics and corporate compliance at the Albuquerque-based government-regulated gas and electric utility.

In 2001, Smith benchmarked other utilities' ethics programs and was impressed with one from San Francisco-based Pacific Gas and Electric. "The training involved video vignettes of employees having to make an ethical choice. [Examples of making an ethical choice would be whether to shut off the heat at the home of an unemployed single parent with infants, and dealing with an act of racial harassment by a high-performing employee.] The video pauses and the supervisor talks through the options," says Smith. PNM added a segment from the CEO talking about ethics and compliance. Employee groups received customized combinations of vignettes appropriate to their positions.

"We produced 200 videos and facilitator guides and sent them to the supervisor groups," says Smith. She encouraged the supervisors to conduct the training, but, she says, "Some weren't very confident and asked me to do it."

In 2005, PNM rolled out a refresher with a new video course and stringent requirements that supervisor conduct the training discussions. Smith believes that having supervisors guide the postvideo discussion makes it compelling. "Ethics training should be done in person. But we wanted to have a consistent message. We went the video–discussion route so that we could have a consistent message and a live dialogue."

Source: "A Consistent Message from Management," *HR Magazine*, February 2005, p. 100.

importance of ethics. A positive example of an ethical corporate culture is the Vanguard Group mutual fund company. The scandals in the mutual fund industry in recent years never touched Vanguard. Company leaders consistently talk about the client-oriented practices that are as important as legal controls. Vanguard's orientation for new employees includes a history lesson, examples of commitment to client service, and a clear warning: "Cross the line, and there's no second chance. It's clear from day one," says managing director Mike Miller. [28]

The accompanying Human Relations in Practice box insert provides and example of a corporate ethics program.

FOLLOW AN ETHICAL ROLE MODEL IN THE COMPANY

An important influence on your ethical behavior can be the behavior of other people whom you regard as ethical role models. The role model is not necessarily a top-level manager. He or she could be the purchasing agent who refuses to accept tickets to sporting events from vendors; the coworker who goes on a business trip and returns the part of the travel advance not spent; or the supervisor who tells workers the truth about company problems that might affect them. According an interview study conducted by organizational behavior and ethics professors Gary R. Weaver, Linda Klebe Treviño, and Bradley Agle, of the University of Delaware, four general categories of attitudes and behaviors characterized ethical role models in organizations:

- everyday interpersonal behaviors, such as taking responsibility for others

- high ethical expectations for oneself, such as working extra hours simply to make sure performance evaluations of group members were completed on time

- high ethical expectations for others, such as expecting others to behave ethically, including not recommending unqualified friends and relatives for jobs at the company

- fairness in dealing with others, such as getting their input on a problem situation involving them

Quite often these role models were managers the participants in the study knew well rather than distant executives. As one of the interviewees in the study responded, "I had an opportunity to interact with him on a daily basis in close confines. I had the chance to see that the actions matched the verbal message." [29]

FOLLOW AN APPLICABLE CODE OF PROFESSIONAL CONDUCT

Professional codes of conduct are prescribed for many occupational groups including physicians, nurses, lawyers, paralegals, purchasing managers and agents, and real estate sales people.

A useful ethical guide for members of these groups is to follow the code of conduct for their profession. If the profession or trade is licensed by the state or province, a worker can be punished for deviating from the code of conduct specified by the state. The code of conduct developed by the profession or trade is separate from the legal code but usually supports the same principles and practices. Some of these codes of conduct developed by the professional associations are 50 and 60 pages long, yet all are guided by the kind of ethical principles implied in the ethical decision-making guide described earlier. Figure 5-3 presents a sampling of provisions from these codes of conduct.

Professional Organization	Sample of Ethical Guidelines and Regulations
Institute of Management Accountants	1. Maintain an appropriate level of professional competence by ongoing development of their knowledge and skills. 2. Refrain from disclosing confidential information acquired in the course of their work and monitor their activities to assure the maintenance of that confidentiality. 3. Avoid actual or apparent conflicts of interest and advise all appropriate parties of any potential conflict.
National Association of Legal Assistants	1. A legal assistant (paralegal) must not perform any of the duties that attorneys only may perform nor take any actions that attorneys may not take. 2. A legal assistant may perform any task which is properly delegated and supervised by an attorney, as long as the attorney is ultimately responsible to the client, maintains a direct relationship with the client, and assumes professional responsibility for the work product. 3. A legal assistant must protect the confidences of a client and must not violate any rule or statute now in effect or hereafter enacted controlling the doctrine of privileged communications between a client and an attorney.
National Association of Purchasing Management	1. Avoid the intent and appearance of unethical or compromising practice in relationships, actions, and communications. 2. Refrain form any private business or professional activity that would create a conflict between personal interests and the interest of the employer. 3. Refrain from soliciting or accepting money, loans, credits, or prejudicial discounts, and the acceptance of gifts, entertainment, favors, or services from present or potential suppliers which might influence, or appear to influence purchasing decisions.

Figure **5-3**

Excerpts from Codes of Professional Conduct.

Source: Institute of Management Accountants Code of Ethics; National Association of Legal Assistants Professional Standards; National Association of Purchasing Management Principles and standards of Purchasing Practice.

Concept Review and Reinforcement

Key Terms

Value, 104   Person–role conflict, 109   Character trait, 115
Ethics, 104   Conflict of interest, 113   Ethical screening, 116

Summary and Review

Values and beliefs influence how a person behaves on the job, and values are closely tied in with ethics, the moral choices a person makes. Values are learned in several ways, as follows:

- observing others or modeling
- communication of attitudes by others
- unstated but implied attitudes of others
- later life influences, such as stories reported by the media
- demands of employers that may help us acquire new values, including corporate spiritualism

Values are closely tied to psychological needs. One way of categorizing values is as follows:

- humanists (includes personal growth)
- strategists (mastery and personal achievement)
- pragmatists (power and control)
- adventurers (excitement and adventure)

Conscientiousness is another value that influences both work and personal life.

Differences in values often stem from generational differences, such as members of generation X and generation Y being less concerned about hierarchy than are baby boomers. Value clarification can lead to a better understanding of your values. When individual and job values mesh, performance may be higher. A person may suffer from person–role conflict when personal and job values clash. To find a good value fit, it helps to identify the type of work that would be most meaningful to you.

Business ethics are important to study for many reasons, including the following:

- People are motivated by both self-interest and moral commitments.
- A good ethical reputation can enhance business.

- Many unethical acts are illegal.
- High ethics increases the quality of work life because they provide guidelines for acceptable behavior

Being ethical isn't easy because ethical decisions are complex, people have different levels of moral development, and our work environment influences our ethical behavior. Surveys reveal that unethical behavior is widespread. Also, much questionable unethical behavior exists including companies declaring bankruptcy and providing lavish entertainment to obtain sales.

Common ethical problems faced by business executives as well as workers at lower job levels include the following:

- the temptation to illegally copy software
- sexual harassment
- conflict of interest
- dealing with confidential information
- accurate presentation of employment history
- possible ethical violations with computers and information technology

Guidelines for making ethical decisions and behaving ethically include the following:

- Develop the right character traits (such as honesty, integrity, and loyalty).
- Use a guide to ethical decision making (the process of ethical screening).
- Develop strong relationships with work associates.
- Use corporate ethics programs.
- Follow an ethical role model in the company.
- Follow an applicable code of professional conduct.

Check Your Understanding

1. Identify several of your values that you think will help you succeed. Why do you think these values will help you?
2. What evidence would you need to conclude that there was a good fit between your values and those of your employer?
3. Get together in a brainstorming group to identify what you think might be a few values important to (a) Wal-Mart and (b) Starbucks. Support your reasoning.
4. Assume that company management brags about its values of being altruistic and humanitarian. Should such a company then shelter the homeless at night on company premises? Why or why not?
5. Give an example of an action in business that might be unethical but not illegal.
6. Based on your knowledge of human behavior, why do professional codes of conduct— such as those for doctors, paralegals, and realtors—not prevent all unethical behavior on the part of members?
7. What decision of ethical consequence have you made in the past year that you would not mind having publicly disclosed?
8. If so many successful business executives and people in public office have been charged with ethical violations, why should you worry about being ethical?
9. Is it ethical for companies to sell rubber cement in retail stores even though many young people become addicted to glue sniffing?
10. Some hospitals prohibit doctors from accepting any gift but a free lunch from pharmaceutical companies. Are these hospitals going overboard on ethics? Explain your reasoning.

Web Corner

Choosing a Career Based on Values

www.careersonline. com.au/disc/vwp.html

Learning More About Business Ethics

www.ethicsandbusiness.org/links/

Value-Based Ethics and Compliance Solutions

www. ethics.com

INTERNET SKILL BUILDER

Develop some skill and insight into assessing the values and priorities of a workplace by visiting. http://wordscapes/net.assessing.htm. Although this exercise is the most applicable if you are currently part of a workplace, you can relate the questions to any place you might have worked in the past. The questions asked on this Web site will help you understand what to look for in assessing workplace values.

Developing Your Human Relations Skills

Human Relations Application Exercises

Applying Human Relations Exercise 5-1

Value Clarification

Learning how to clarify your values can be uplifting and, at the same time, can help you make career choices based on these values. Ideally, you might pursue career opportunities that give you an opportunity to satisfy your most important career values, such as a person who highly valued "making an above-average income" pursing a career in industrial sales. And a person who valued "helping people less fortunate than me" might pursue a career in youth work.

Rank from 1 to 20 the importance of the following values to you as a person. The most important value on the list receives a rank of 1; the least important a rank of 20. Use the space next to "Other" if the list has left out an important value in your life.

_____ Having my own place to live
_____ Having one or more children
_____ Having an interesting job and career
_____ Owning a car
_____ Having a good relationship with coworkers
_____ Having good health
_____ Sending and receiving e-mail messages, and using the Web

_____ Being able to stay in frequent contact with friends by cell phone
_____ Watching my favorite television shows
_____ Participating in sports or other pastimes
_____ Following a sports team, athlete, music group, or other entertainer
_____ Being a religious person
_____ Helping people less fortunate than me
_____ Loving and being loved by another person
_____ Having physical intimacy with another person
_____ Making an above-average income
_____ Being in good physical condition
_____ Being a knowledgeable, informed person
_____ Completing my formal education
_____ Other

1. Discuss and compare your ranking of these values with the person next to you.
2. Perhaps your class, assisted by your instructor, can arrive at a class average on each of these values. How does your ranking compare to the class ranking?
3. Look back at your own ranking. Does it surprise you?
4. Are there any surprises in the class ranking? Which values did you think would be highest and lowest?

Applying Human Relations Exercise 5-2

The Ethics Game

Citicorp (now part of Citigroup) has developed an ethics game, The Work Ethic. [30] The game teaches ethics by asking small teams of employees to confront difficult scenarios such as those that follow. Discuss these ethical problems in teams. As you discuss the scenarios, identify the ethical issues involved.

Scenario 1: One of your assignments is to find a contractor to conduct building maintenance for your company headquarters. You invite bids for the job. High-Performance Cleaners, a firm staffed largely by teenagers

from troubled families who have criminal records, bids on the job. Many of these teenagers also have severe learning disabilities and cannot readily find employment. High-Performance Cleaners proves to be the second-highest bidder. You

a. advise High-Performance Cleaners that its bid is too high for consideration and that your company is not a social agency.
b. award the bid to High-Performance Cleaners and justify your actions with a letter to top management talking about social responsibility.

c. falsify the other bids in your report to management, making High-Performance Cleaners the low bidder—and thus the contract winner.

d. explain to High-Performance Cleaners that it lost the bid, but you will award the company a piece of the contract because of its sterling work with needy teenagers.

Scenario 2: You live in Texas and your company sends you on a three-day trip to New York City. Your business dealings in the Big Apple will keep you there Wednesday, Thursday, and Friday morning. You have several friends and relatives in New York, so you decide to stay there until Sunday afternoon. Besides, you want to engage in tourist activities such as taking a boat tour around Manhattan and visiting Radio City Music Hall. When preparing your expense report for your trip, you request payment for all your business-related costs up through Friday afternoon, plus

a. your return trip on Sunday.

b. the return trip and the room cost for Friday and Saturday nights.

c. the return trip, one-half of your weekend food expenses, and two extra nights in the hotel.

d. the return trip and your food costs for the weekend (which you justify because you ate at fast-food restaurants on Wednesday, Thursday, and Friday).

Scenario 3: You are the leader of a self-managing work team in a financial services company. The work of your team has expanded to the point where you are authorized to hire another team member. The team busily interviews a number of candidates from inside and outside the company. The other team members agree that one of the candidates (Pat) has truly outstanding credentials. You agree that Pat is a strong candidate. Yet you don't want Pat on the team because you and Pat were emotionally involved with each other for about one year in the past. You think

that working with Pat would disrupt your concentration and bring back hurtful memories. You decide to

a. tell the group that you have some negative information about Pat's past that would disqualify Pat for the job.

b. telephone Pat and beg that Pat find employment elsewhere.

c. tell the group that you agree Pat is qualified but explain your concerns about the disruption in concentration and emotional hurt.

d. tell the group that you agree Pat is right for the position and mention nothing about the past relationship.

Scoring and Observation

Scenario 1, about High-Performance Cleaners, raises dozens of ethical questions, including whether humanitarian considerations can outweigh profit concerns. Teams that chose "a" receive 0 points; "b," 20 points; "c," −10 points; "d," 10 points. ("D" is best here because it would not be fair to give the bid to the second-highest bidder. However, you are still finding a way to reward the High-Performance Cleaners for its meritorious work in the community. "C" is worst because you would be outright lying.)

Scenario 2 raises ethical issues about using company resources. Teams that chose "a" receive 20 points; "b," −10 points; "c," −15 points; "d," 0 points. ("A" is fairest because the company would expect to reimburse you for your round trip plus the expenses up through Friday afternoon. "C" is the worst because it would be unjustified for you to be reimbursed for your vacation in New York.)

Scenario 3 raises issues about fairness in making selection decisions. Teams that choose "a" receive −20 points; "b," −10 points; "c," 15 points; "d," 0 points. ("C" is the most ethical because you are being honest with the group about the reason you do not wish to hire Pat. "A" is the most unethical because you are telling lies about Pat. Furthermore, you might be committing the illegal act of libel.)

Human Relations Case Study 5-1

The Mortgage Field Services Specialist

Chuck Seabrease steered his pickup truck into the driveway of a two-story house on a cul-de-sac in Upper Marlboro, Maryland, a suburb of Washington, DC. He was carrying a drill and tools for picking locks. But Seabrease found on this

chilly morning that someone had kicked the door open, shattering the frame and leaving a black boot mark. Seabrease, a 36-year-old father of two who plays hockey in his spare time, stepped warily into the house and prepared to do his job: safeguarding foreclosed properties for lenders.

During a two-year period, business was generally slow for the approximately 10,000 members of Seabrease's profession, known among people in the industry as mortgage field services. Prior to 2006, home prices were rising so fast in much of the United States that most people who fell behind on their payments could easily sell their homes and thus avoid foreclosure. During the last quarter of 2005, according to the Mortgage Bankers Association, only 0.97% of all home mortgages were in the process of foreclosure, in which the lender takes ownership after the borrower defaults on payments.

Fewer foreclosures mean less business for field service operations, independent contractors hired by lenders to clean up the sometimes horrific messes left by people who lose their houses. Now the people in this little-known trade hope that a cooler housing market will create more work. House prices have fallen modestly in some places, and inventories of unsold homes are rising.

Kevin McFalls, the owner of JKM Mortgage Field Services, Baltimore, where Seabrease works, says he already has noticed an uptick in business in the Washington and Baltimore areas. McFalls expects a surge in assignments from lenders over the next few years. Rick Taggard, the owner of a field services company in Porterville, California, agrees: "All of us are just waiting, and when it turns around, it's rags to riches again."

During the recent lean years for foreclosure, some people in field services left the business. Others have stayed busy heading to foreclosure hot spots such as New Orleans, devastated by Hurricane Katrina, and Taggard has hired subcontractors there to inspect damaged homes and secure them against intruders.

Both McFalls and Seabrease made the 45-mile drive from their Baltimore office to the house in Upper Marlboro. Though the door had been kicked open, they were relieved to find nobody inside. Most likely, Seabrease said, it was a bored teenager who broke in and had a look around after the former owner had abandoned the house.

Most of the furnishings were gone, but a stuffed dog and other toys were strewn across stained grey carpeting. An empty bottle of Heineken sat on a coffee table. Shriveled roses, apparently from a funeral arrangement, clung to a wire stand decorated with a white ribbon inscribed with the word "Dad" in gold letters. A file cabinet contained a sixth grader's scrawled notes from Sunday school. In the kitchen, a few dirty plastic dishes remained in the sink, and the refrigerator was mottled with mold. "This house is actually pretty clean compared to a lot of them," Seabrease said.

His mission was to preserve the value of the house while the lender prepares to sell it. In the basement, Seabrease twisted a valve to turn off the water supply. He then used an air compressor to blast the remaining water out of the pipes so they wouldn't freeze. Seabrease took digital pictures of each room, fixed the door frame and installed a new lock. The total charge for about an hour's work, excluding travel time, was about $125. Taggard says that in a good year someone running a field-services business can earn a six-figure income.

Aside from the preservation work, field services companies do inspections. When borrowers fall more than a month or two behind on payments, lenders hire field services companies to check whether the home is still occupied and to note any major damage. Field services businesses also provide labor to clear out debris after evictions by sheriffs or other law enforcement people. Usually the people who lived in the house are long gone by the time the foreclosure comes.

Field services work can be dangerous. While one of McFall's crew was dragging junk from a house in Baltimore one day, three men emerged from the basement and one brandished a gun. After a scuffle during which one of the workers was cut above the eye, the gunman and his companions fled.

In crime-ridden areas, McFalls tells his crews to show up early in the morning to inspect or secure houses: "Typically, the troublemakers are still asleep or passed out then." Often, field services workers themselves are suspected of making trouble. Neighbors see them breaking in and call the police. Crew members sometimes end up in handcuffs before they can convince the police that the break-in was ordered by a bank.

McFalls notes that you need a strong stomach for his business. For one thing, people sometimes leave pets behind. Dirty needles and clogged toilets are other occupational hazards. In some homes, says Robert Preston, who runs a field services business in Grand Rapids, Michigan, his crews have found decomposed bodies. "After a time you just become desensitized," says D. Scott Smith, who ran a field services business for eight years.

McFalls says he feels sorry for some of the people whose belongings his crews cart away. But he thinks many people get into trouble simply because they have made bad choices, buying expensive cars and other luxuries instead of paying off their mortgages. "The majority of them are just living beyond their means and putting themselves in that position," he says.

Questions

1. What is your evaluation of the ethics of the field services businesses? Are they basically vultures?
2. What kind of value deficiencies (if any) do you see in the people who leave their homes in broken and filthy condition?
3. What steps do you think banks can take to grant mortgages to people who will not make it necessary for the bank to hire field service specialists?

Source: Abridged and adapted from James R. Hagerty, "For This Industry, Rising Foreclosures Are Good for Business," *The Wall Street Journal*, March 1, 2006, pp. A1, A13.

The Highly Rated but Expendable Marsha

Department manager Nicholas had thought for a long time that Marsha, one of his financial analysts, created too many problems. Although Marsha performed her job in a satisfactory manner, she required a lot of supervisory time and attention. She frequently asked for time off when her presence was needed the most because of a heavy workload in the department. Marsha sent Nicholas many long and complicated e-mail messages that required substantial time to read and respond. When Nicholas responded to Marsha's e-mail message, she would typically send another e-mail back asking for clarification.

Marsha's behavior during department meetings irritated Nicholas. She would demand more time than any other participant to explain her point of view on a variety of issues. At a recent meeting she took 10 minutes explaining how the company should be doing more to help the homeless and invest in the development of inner cities. Nicholas coached Marsha frequently about the problems she was creating, but Marsha strongly disagreed

with his criticism and concerns. At one time, Nicholas told Marsha that she was a high-maintenance employee. Yet Marsha perceived herself as a major contributor to the department. She commented once, "Could it be Nick, that you have a problem with an assertive woman working in your department?"

Nicholas developed a tactic to get Marsha out of the department. He would give her outstanding performance evaluations, emphasizing her creativity and persistence. Marsha would then be entered into the company database as an outstanding employee, thereby making her a strong candidate for transfer or promotion. Within six months, a manager in a new division of the company took the bait. She requested that Marsha be recruited into her department as a senior financial analyst. Nicholas said to the recruiting manager, "I hate to lose a valuable contributor like Marsha, but I do not want to block her career progress."

Two months later, Marsha's new manager telephoned Nicholas, and asked, "What's the problem with Marsha? She's kind of a pill to have working with us. I thought she was an outstanding employee."

Nicholas responded, "Give Marsha some time. She may be having a few problems adjusting to a new environment. Just give her a little constructive feedback. You'll find out what a dynamo she can be."

Questions

1. How ethical was Nicholas in giving Marsha a high-performance evaluation for the purposes of attracting her to other departments?
2. What should the manager do who was hooked by Nicholas's bait of the high-performance evaluation?
3. What might the company do to prevent more incidents of inflated performance evaluations for the purpose of transferring an unwanted employee?

Skill-Building Exercise

Confronting the Ethical Deviant

One student plays the role of the manager who transferred Marsha into his or her department. The new manager has become suspicious that Nicholas might have manipulated Marsha's performance evaluations to make her appear like a strong candidate for transfer or promotion.

In fact, the new manager thinks he may have caught an ethical deviant. Another student plays the role of Nicholas who wants to defend his reputation as an ethical manager. During the role play, pay some attention to ethical issues. As usual, other students will provide feedback on the effectiveness of the interaction they observed.

REFERENCES

1. Gary McWilliams, "RadioShack CEO Agrees to Resign," *The Wall Street Journal*, February 21, 2006, p. A3.; Heather Landy, "Pastor Can't Verify RadioShack CEO's Account on Diploma," Forth Worth, Texas, *Star-Telegram* available at Star-Telegram.com retrieved February 15, 2006.
2. Ben Rand, "'On Track' at Kodak," Rochester, New York, *Democrat and Chronicle*, May 21, 2006, p. 4E.
3. Paul Hemp and Thomas A. Stewart (interview with Samuel J. Palmisano), "Leading Change When Business Is Good," *Harvard Business Review*, December 2004, p. 63.
4. Joanne Cole, "Building Heart and Soul," *HRfocus*, October 1998, pp. 9–10.
5. Matthew Gilbert, "At Methodist Hospital, A Values Initiative Makes True Believers of Workers," *Workforce Management*, February 2005, pp. 67–69.
6. Douglas B. Richardson, "Know Thyself: An Easy Approach," www.CareerJournal.com as reproduced in www.shrm.org/jobs/043/May.
7. Brent W. Roberts, Oleksandr S. Chernyshenko, Stephen Stark, and Lewis R. Goldberg, "The Structure of Conscientiousness: An Empirical Investigation Based on Seven Major Personality Questionnaires," *Personnel Psychology*, Spring 2005, pp. 103–139.
8. A recent review of the evidence is Nicole N. Dudley et al., "A Meta-Analytic Investigation of Conscientiousness in the Prediction of Job Performance: Examining the Intercorrelations and the Incremental Validity of Narrow Traits," *Journal of Applied Psychology*, January 2006, pp. 40–57.
9. Christine Lupporter, "Understanding Y: Learn How to Recruit Generation Y Workers and How to Make Them Stay," available at www.WomenConnect; March 1, 2006 "Get Ready for 'Millennials' at Work," *Manager's Edge*, January 2006, p. 1.
10. David C. McClelland, "How Motives, Skills, and Values Determine What People Do," *American Psychologist*, July 1985, p. 815.
11. Po Bronson, "What Should I Do with My Life?" *Fast Company*, January 2003, p. 72.
12. Linda K. Treviño and Katherine A. Nelson, *Managing Business Ethics: Straight Talk about How to Do It Right* (New York: Wiley, 1995), pp. 24–35; O. C. Ferrell, John Fraedrich, and Linda Ferrell, *Business Ethics: Ethical Decision Making and Cases*, 4th ed. (Boston: Houghton Mifflin, 2000) pp. 13–16; Anita Bruzzese, "Tools Take Ethics to the Real World," Gannett News Service, May 16, 2005.
13. Matt Kempner, *The Atlanta Journal-Constitution* (ajc.com), February 13, 2006; Erin Kelly, "Unethical Behavior Is on Rise, Experts Fear," Gannett News Service, March 5, 2006.
14. Linda Klebe Treviño, "Managing to Be Ethical: Debunking Five Business Ethics Myths," *Academy of Management Executive*, May 2004, pp. 69–72.
15. Data from Ethics Resource Center and Kronos Inc., reported in Sue Shellenbarger, "How and Why We Lie at the Office: From Pilfered Pens to Padded Accounts," *The Wall Street Journal*, March 24, 2005, p. D1.
16. Justin Fox, "Three Cheers for Bankruptcy," *Fortune*, October 17, 2005, p. 34.
17. Susanne Craig and John Hechinger, "A Wall Street Affair: The Bachelor Party Gets Lots of Attention," *The Wall Street Journal*, July 18, 2005, p. A1.
18. Treviño and Nelson, *Managing Business Ethics*, pp. 47–64.
19. Data reported in "McAfee Anti-Piracy Information," available at *www.networkassociates.com/us/antipircacy_policy.htm*, retrieved May 25, 2005.
20. Bruce Nussbaum, "Can You Trust Anybody Anymore?" *Business Week*, January 28, 2002, p. 32.
21. Erin Kelly, "Unethical Behavior Is on Rise, Experts Fear," Gannett News Service, March 5, 2006.
22. Michael S. Josephson, "Does Character Still Count?" *USA Weekend*, September 23–25, 1994, p. 20.
23. James L. Bowditch and Anthony E. Buono, *A Primer of Organizational Behavior* (New York: Wiley, 2001), p. 4.
24. Daniel J. Brass, Kenneth D. Butterfield, and Bruce C. Skaggs, "Relationships and Unethical Behavior: A Social Network Perspective," *Academy of Management Review*, January 1998, pp. 14–31.
25. "Extolling the Virtues of Hot Lines," *Workforce*, June 1998, pp. 125–126; Daryl Koehn, "An Interview with William Griffin," available at *www.stthom.edu/cbes/griffin.html*, retrieved March 8, 2006, May 27, 2005.
26. Quoted in "The Optima Awards: They've Got Game," *Workforce Management*, March 2005, p. 44.
27. Kathryn Tyler, "Do the Right Thing: Ethics Training Programs Help Employees Deal with Ethical Dilemmas," *HR Magazine*, February 2005, pp. 99–102.
28. Quoted in Jonathan Pont, "Doing the Right Thing to Instill Business Ethics," *Workforce Management*, April 2005, p. 27.
29. Gary R. Weaver, Linda Klebe Treviño, and Bradley Agle, "'Somebody I Look Up To': Ethical Role Models in Organizations," *Organizational Dynamics*, Issue 4, 2005, pp. 313–330.
30. The concept of the game is from Karen Ireland, "The Ethics Game," *Personnel Journal*, March 1991, p. 74. The scenarios are original.

6 Problem Solving and Creativity

Learning Objectives

After studying the information and doing the exercises in this chapter, you should be able to:

1 Understand how personal characteristics influence the ability to solve problems and make decisions.

2 Apply the problem-solving and decision-making steps to complex problems.

3 Summarize the characteristics of creative people.

4 Describe various ways of improving your creativity.

Outline

Peter Labaziewicz, an Eastman Kodak Co. scientist, was riding on the train to work one day in Japan when he reached back across the decades for an idea that could push the digital era to new frontiers. He started thinking about the old "turret" film cameras—beastly looking models containing multiple lenses on a "plate" that rotates in front of a shutter. His concept: building similar flexibility in choice of lenses into a digital camera. "Wouldn't it be interesting?" Labaziewicz says he wondered.

> It's not only interesting but also possible, and very, very successful, as Labaziewicz and his colleagues have found out. His musings helped trigger the creation of the Kodak imaging into an important new phase. The V750 is the first camera with two lenses and image sensors—one for wide-angle picture taking, the other for regular zoom. It's considered the first attempt by an industry mainstay to design digital products with attributes that are unique in their own right, free of the constraints of the film era.
>
> Since its introduction in early January 2006, the V750 has become a miniphenomenon, capturing the imagination of snap shooters and celebrities alike. It has drawn thousands of e-mails and numerous requests for product placements and donations. Kodak gave out diamond-encrusted models of the V750 to nominees for best actress at the 2006 Academy Awards. The attention is largely because of its sleek, unusual, space-age look and the allure of the camera offering something different. [1]

■ **Problem**

gap between what exists and what you want to exist

■ **Decision making**

choosing one alternative from the various alternative solutions that can be pursued

The new turret digital camera may not rival the light bulb or the computer as creative brilliance. Yet it does illustrate a few basic facts about problem solving, decision making, and creativity. The inventor of the new camera found a **problem,** a gap between what exists and what you want to exist. His employer was looking to push the digital era to new frontiers. Part of being a creative problem solver is to rely on a storehouse of information, such as knowledge about old turret film cameras. **Decision making** refers to choosing one alternative from the various alternative solutions that can be pursued. The developers of the new camera undoubtedly were sifting through hundreds of new product ideas to find a breakthrough camera.

The general purpose of this chapter is to help you become a more effective and creative problem solver when working individually or in groups. Whether you are solving problems by yourself or as part of a group, the principles apply equally well.

What Are Some Personal Characteristics That Influence Your Problem-Solving Ability

■ **Learning Objective 1**

Many personal characteristics and traits influence the type of problem solver and decision maker you are or are capable of becoming. Fortunately, some personal characteristics that influence your decision-making ability can be improved through conscious effort. For instance, if you make bad decisions because you do not concentrate on the details of the problem, you can gradually learn to concentrate

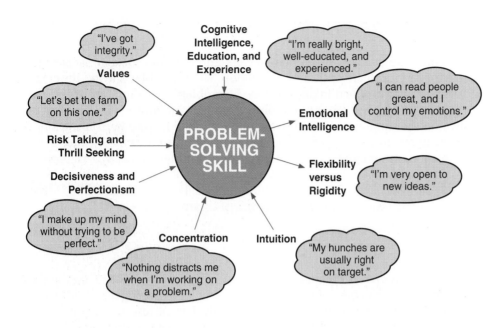

Figure 6-1

Influences on Problem-Solving Skill

better. Most of the personal characteristics described next can be strengthened through the appropriate education, training, and self-discipline. Figure 6-1 outlines these characteristics.

COGNITIVE INTELLIGENCE, EDUCATION, AND EXPERIENCE

In general, if you are intelligent, well educated, and well experienced, you will make better decisions than people without these attributes. (The term *cognitive intelligence* refers to the intellectual, or traditional, type of intelligence that is necessary for such tasks as solving math problems and conjugating verbs.) Cognitive intelligence helps because, by definition, intelligence denotes the ability to solve problems. Education improves the problem-solving and decision-making process because it gives you a background of principles and facts on which to rely.

Experience facilitates decision making because good decisions tend to be made by people who have already faced similar situations in the past. All things being equal, would you prefer to take your computer problem to an experienced or an inexperienced specialist?

EMOTIONAL INTELLIGENCE

Being able to deal effectively with your feelings and emotions and those of others can help you make better decisions. This type of intelligence has to do with the ability to connect with people and understand their emotions. A worker with high emotional intelligence would be able to engage in such behaviors as sizing up people, pleasing others, and influencing them. [2]

Emotional intelligence is important for decision making because how effective you are in managing your feelings and reading those of other people can affect the quality of your decisions. For example, if you cannot control your anger, you are likely to make decisions that are motivated by retaliation, hostility, and revenge. An example would be shouting and swearing at your team leader because of a work assignment you received. Your emotional intelligence could also influence your career decision making. If you understand your own feelings, you are more likely to enter an occupation or accept a position that matches your true attitude.

FLEXIBILITY VERSUS RIGIDITY

Some people are successful problem solvers and decision makers because they approach every problem with a fresh outlook. They are able to avoid developing rigid viewpoints. Flexible thinking enables the problem solver to think of original—and therefore creative—alternative solutions to solving a problem. Another perspective on the same issue is that being open-minded helps a person solve problems well. In recent years several major retailers have become more flexible in their thinking about inner cities as profitable locations for their stores. For example, the Kmart division of Sears Holdings Inc. has been successful with many of its new inner-city stores. The link between flexibility and creativity will be described in more detail in the discussion of the characteristics of creative people.

INTUITION

Effective decision makers do not rely on careful analysis alone. Instead, they also use their **intuition,** an experience-based way of knowing or reasoning in which weighing and balancing of evidence are done automatically. Recent research about intuition suggests that it is composed of the interplay between knowing (intuition-as-expertise) and sensing (intuition-as-feeling). The best use of intuition, therefore, involves both bring past facts in mind to deal with the situation and a sudden emotional hunch at the same time. [3] An experienced real estate developer might look at an old building and within 10 minutes decide it would be a good investment to rehabilitate the structure. Based on hundreds of property evaluations, the developer knows that rehabilitating an old building can be profitable. At the same time the developer visualizes what the old building would look like when rehabilitated.

Relying on intuition is like relying on your instincts when faced with a decision. Intuition takes place when the brain gathers information stored in memory and packages it as a new insight or solution. Intuitions, therefore, can be regarded as stored information that is reorganized or repackaged. Developing good intuition may take a long time because so much information has to be stored. Cognitive psychologist Gary Klein, the founder of Klein Associates, explains it this way:

> We sometimes think that experts are weighted down by information, by facts, by memories—that they make decisions slowly because they must search through so much data. But in fact, we've got it backward. The accumulation of experience does not weight people down—it lightens them up. It makes them fast. [4]

Intuition has become perhaps the hottest topic in decision making, including being the subject of a bestseller (*Blink* by Malcolm Gladwell). [5] Nevertheless, intuition has its drawbacks. Our hunches based on the combination of experience and emotion can sometimes lead us astray when a more analytical approach would have led to a better decision. For example, a charming and articulate job candidate might be chosen mostly on the basis of intuition. A background check based on rational analysis might have revealed that the candidate is a procrastinator and a criminal. One way to improve intuition is to get feedback on the decisions we make, so we can sharpen future decisions. [6] For example, a credit analyst in a bank profits from feedback about the future payment records of the loans he or she approved.

CONCENTRATION

Mental concentration is an important contributor to making good decisions. Many people who solve problems poorly do so because they are too distracted to immerse themselves in the problem at hand. In contrast, effective problem solvers often achieve the **flow experience**—total absorption in their work. When flow occurs, things seem to go just right. The person feels alive and fully attentive to what he or she is doing. As a by-product of the flow experience, a good solution to a problem may surface. If you fail to concentrate hard enough, you may overlook an important detail that could affect the outcome of the decision. For example, a person about to purchase an automobile might be excited about the high gas mileage but forget to check the vehicle's ability to withstand a crash.

■ **Flow experience**

total absorption in work; when flow occurs, things seem to go just right

DECISIVENESS AND PERFECTIONISM

Some people are ill suited to solving problems and making decisions because they are fearful of committing themselves to any given course of action. "Gee, I'm not sure, what do you think?" is their typical response to a decision forced on them. If you are indecisive, this characteristic will have to be modified if you are to become successful in your field. A manager has to decide which person to hire. And a photographer has to decide which setting is best for the subject. As the old saying goes, at some point "you have to fish or cut bait." The combination of being indecisive and a perfectionist can lead to procrastination. Also, being a procrastinator can make one indecisive. Perfectionism contributes to delayed decision making because the person keeps working on a project before deciding to submit it to somebody else.

RISK TAKING AND THRILL SEEKING

The need for taking risks and seeking thrills is yet another personality characteristic that influences problem-solving skill. For some types of problems, the high risk taker and thrill seeker is at an advantage. Firefighters have to take risks to save people from burning buildings and remove people trapped in collapsed buildings. An information technology specialist might have to engage in a risky maneuver to salvage data from a crashed hard drive. Risk taking and thrill seeking can also lead to poor problem solving and decision making, such as a merchandiser buying a huge inventory of a highly original fashion. The experienced decision maker needs to know when to take high risks and seek thrills and when to be more conservative.

VALUES OF THE DECISION MAKER

Values influence decision making at every step. The right values for the situation will improve problem solving and decision making, whereas the wrong values will lead to poor decisions. Ultimately, all decisions are based on values. A manager who places a high value on the well-being of employees tries to avoid alternatives that create hardships for workers. Another value that significantly influences problem solving and decision making is the pursuit of excellence. A worker who embraces the pursuit of excellence (and is, therefore, conscientious) will search for the high-quality alternative solution.

GENDER DIFFERENCES IN DECISION MAKING

Gender is a possible source of differences in the types of decisions people make, even if gender does not influence the quality of decisions. According to some research men and women in managerial positions have different decision making styles. Rita Mano-Negrin of the human services department of the University of Haifa in Israel observes that women collaborate, listen, and strive to build teamwork. Men are more likely to direct, blame others, and frequently say "I." A personality assessment by Hagberg Consulting concluded that women give most weight to two factors in making a decision: how it will affect the team and whether it will affect short-term goals. In contrast, men focus on the competitive environment and long-term results. [7] Furthermore, according to cultural stereotypes, women typically rely more on intuition when making decisions, and men tend to rely more on analytical reasoning.

What Are the Problem-Solving and Decision-Making Steps?

■ **Learning Objective 2**

Whatever complex problem you face, it is best to use the standard problem-solving and decision-making steps as a guide. These steps are similar to the systematic approach used in the scientific method. Figure 6-2 summarizes the steps involved in problem solving and decision making. It assumes that problem solving should take place in an orderly flow of steps. Paying attention to this model is important because deviating too far will often result in decision failure. Paul C. Nutt studied 356 decisions in medium to large organizations in the United States and Canada. He found that one-half of these decisions failed, meaning that the decision was not fully used after two years. The typical reason for failure is that the decision makers did not take a systematic approach, such as searching for many alternative solutions. The managers involved also committed the human relations error of not involving enough people in the decisions. [8]

Although the problem-solving and decision-making steps appear logical, we emphasize again that people are frequently not entirely rational when making decisions. Emotions and personality traits can cloud decision making. In fact, psychologist Daniel Kahneman won a Nobel Prize in economics for his research on how people often behave irrationally in ordinary situations, such as holding on to losing mutual funds or buying insurance for inexpensive appliances. [9]

Figure **6-2**

Problem-Solving and Decision-Making Steps

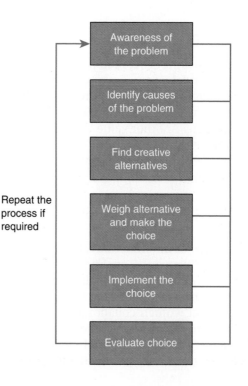

AWARENESS OF THE PROBLEM

Problem solving and decision making begin when somebody is aware that a problem exists. In most decision-making situations, problems are given to another person. At other times, people create their own problems to solve, or they find problems. Scotch Tape had its origins more than 75 years ago because somebody noticed a problem. The story goes like this:

> Richard Drew, a young engineer working for the Minnesota Mining and Manufacturing Co. (3M today), a small sandpaper manufacturer, noticed that car painters were having trouble masking one section while painting another in a different color. In 1925, Drew invented a masking tape using crepe paper with lines of pressure-sensitive glue running along the edges. Trouble was, the tape kept falling off. An automotive painter told a 3M representative to go back to his "Scotch" (negative stereotype that Scotch people are cheap) bosses and tell them to put adhesive all over the tape, not just on the edges. They did, the tape worked and the name stuck. Five years later Drew overcame numerous production hurdles and developed the clear, cellophane tape today that has become a worldwide staple. [10]

After you are aware that a problem exists or have identified it, recognize that it may represent an important opportunity. For example, if you are bothered enough by a problem facing your company, you might volunteer to be the person in charge of overcoming the problem.

IDENTIFY CAUSES OF THE PROBLEM

The causes of problems should be diagnosed and clarified before any action is taken because they are not always what they seem to be on the surface. Some may be more complicated than suspected or may even be the wrong problem you need to solve in a particular situation. Five key elements to ask questions about (along with some sample questions) are as follows:

- **People.** What do the people involved contribute to the problem? Are they competent? Do they have an attitude problem?

- **Materials.** Do we have the right materials available? Is the quality of the materials adequate?

- **Machines and facilities.** Do we have the right machines and facilities to do the job? Have the machines and facilities changed?

- **Physical environment.** Is anything wrong with the environment (such as toxic fumes making people sick)? Has the environment changed?

- **Methods.** Are the processes and procedures adequate? Have new methods been introduced that workers do not understand?

The approach to analyzing causes is often place in a cause-and-effect diagram, as shown in Figure 6-3. The approach is sometimes referred to as a *fishbone diagram* because of the angles of the lines leading to the various causes. Notice that all the causes contribute to the problem at the right. Even when you have identified the general source of a problem, you may still need to dig further as to what, when, and where a problem *did not* occur. Suppose a friend talks about a fear of public speaking. By asking a few "but not" questions, you might be able to identify a major cause of the problem. Let's try out the method:

Your friend: I'm horribly afraid of public speaking. I hate going up in front of class.

You: But have you ever not been afraid of speaking to a group of people?

Your friend:	Yes, I can remember once feeling OK speaking at a victory dinner for my high school soccer team. We came in first place in the region.
You:	What did you talk about?
Your friend:	I told a cute story about how my mother and father put a soccer ball in my crib. I hugged it every day like it was a teddy bear.
You:	So why weren't you afraid of giving that talk?
Your friend:	I knew what I was talking about. I didn't have to rehearse.
You:	What else was different about the talk?
Your friend:	It wasn't like talking to strangers. I was just there with my buddies and our coaches.
You:	What you are really telling me is that public speaking is OK when you are well prepared and you are in a comfortable surrounding?
Your friend:	Thanks for helping me understand my problem.

FIND CREATIVE ALTERNATIVES

Creativity and imagination enter into problem solving and decision making. Successful decision makers have the ability to think of different alternatives. The person who pushes to find one more alternative to a problem is often the person who finds a breakthrough solution. The more alternatives you generate, the more likely you will find a useful solution to your problem. In the words of business strategy expert and consultant Gary Hamel, "Innovation is a numbers game. It takes 1,000 wacky ideas to find 100 things worth putting any money at all on, to find 10 ideas worth really investing in, to wind up with one really great idea." [11]

WEIGH ALTERNATIVES AND MAKE THE CHOICE

This stage refers simply to examining the pros and cons of the various alternatives in the previous stages and then making a choice. In a major decision, each alternative would have to be given serious consideration. In practice, weighing alternatives often means jotting down the key good and bad points of each possible choice. The essence of decision making is selecting the right course of action to follow. You have to choose an alternative, even if it is not to go ahead with a new plan of action. For instance, after conducting a job campaign, you could decide *not* to change jobs.

Figure   6-3

Basic Cause-and-Effect Diagram

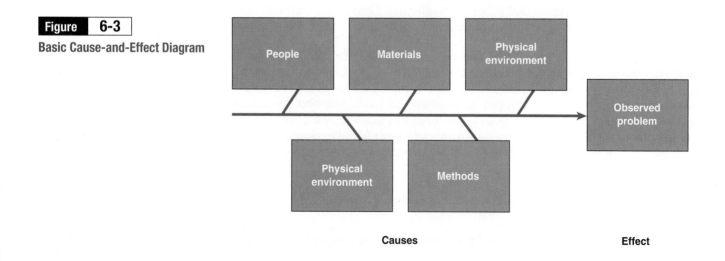

Causes   Effect

Instead of coming to a decision, some people overanalyze a problem. Do you suffer from "analysis paralysis," or do you make up your mind after a reasonable amount of thought?

In choosing an alternative, it is helpful to remember that most problems really have multiple solutions. You, therefore, do not have to be overly concerned with finding the only correct answer to your problem. For instance, there might be several effective ways of reducing the costs of running a department.

IMPLEMENT THE CHOICE

After you decide which course of action to take, you have to put the choice into effect. Some decisions are more difficult to implement than others. Decisions made by top management, for example, are sometimes so difficult to implement that they have to be reversed. An executive at a major on-line retailer announced a new policy that all customer problems would have to be resolved by e-mail and that the toll-free number for customer assistance would be disbanded. Hundreds of customers complained about the new policy by e-mail, and many customer accounts became inactive. The executive reconsidered the decision in terms of its effect on customer service and goodwill and reinstated the toll-free telephone call option. The general point is that to implement many decisions, the human element must be taken into consideration.

EVALUATE THE CHOICE

The decision-making sequence is not complete until the decision has been evaluated. Evaluation may take a considerable period of time because the results of your decision are not always immediately apparent. Suppose you receive two job offers. It might take several months to a year to determine whether you are satisfied with the job you accepted. It would be necessary to look at the factors you think are most important in a job. Among them might be "Is there opportunity for advancement?" "Are the people here friendly?" "Is the work interesting?"

Evaluating your choice would be further complicated by the difficulty of determining how you might have fared in the job you didn't accept. Now and then, you might obtain some information to suggest what that alternative held in store for you, as did a woman who turned down a job offer with a new and promising company. She questioned that decision until she read one morning a year later that the company had gone into bankruptcy.

What happens when your evaluation of a decision is negative? You go back to the drawing board, as the line and arrow on the left-hand side of Figure 6-1 indicates. Because your first decision was not a good one, you are faced with another problem situation. A helpful decision-making aid is to visualize what you would do if the alternative you chose proved to be dreadful—the **worst-case scenario**. Suppose, for example, you choose a job that proves to be unsuited to your talents. Would you resign as soon as your mistake became apparent, or would you sweat it out for a year to show some employment stability? Or would you retain the job while starting to look for a more suitable job? Developing a worst-case scenario helps prevent you from becoming overwhelmed by a bad decision. Closely related to the worst-case scenario is establishing an **exit strategy** that determines in advance how you will get out of a bad decision, such as having joined a failing family business.

▪ **Worst-case scenario**

helpful decision-making aid is that involves visualizing what you would do if the alternative chosen proved to be dreadful

▪ **Exit strategy**

determining in advance how to get out of a bad decision, such as having joined a failing family business

BRAIN TEASERS FOR IMPROVING YOUR PROBLEM-SOLVING ABILITY

A widely accepted belief is that solving difficult problems and puzzles enhances your problem-solving ability. Among these brain teasers could be crossword puzzles, some types of video games, and various types of word puzzles. Just to give

Frame Games
Source: The frame games are from
Terry Stickels, "Frame Games," *USA
Weekend*, March 10–12, 2006, p. 26.

Figure 6-4

SPINAL
SPINAL
SPINAL
SPINAL

MUCH
MUCH
DO
DO + time time

Figure 6-5

Sudoku
Fill in the Sudoko grid so that every row,
every column, and every 3 × 3 box contains the digits 1 through 9.

	6		1		4		5	
		8	3		5	6		
2								1
8			4		7			6
		6				3		
7			9		1			4
5								2
		7	2		6	9		
	4		5		8		7	

you a brief mental workout, here we present an example of a frame game (Figure 6-4) and Sudoko (Figure 6-5). Performing activities such as these regularly might sharpen your mental acuity for problem solving on the job and in school. The answers to the Sudoku and the Frame Games are presented following the References in this chapter.

What Do I Need to Know About Creativity in Decision Making?

Creativity is helpful at any stage of problem solving but is essential for being aware of problems, analyzing their causes, and searching for alternative solutions. Simply put, **creativity** is the ability to develop good ideas that can be put into action. Finding a creative idea usually involves a flash of insight as to how to solve a problem, such as that experienced by the person who thought of Scotch tape.

When many people see or hear the word *creativity,* they think of a rarefied talent. A more helpful perspective is to recognize that not all creativity requires wild

■ **Creativity**
the ability to develop good ideas that can be put into action

imagination. The emphasis here is on creativity applied to business and personal life rather than on creativity in science, technology, and the arts. Creativity is important for companies of all sizes, not only for large firms.

A major theme of this chapter is that for the vast majority of people, it is possible to improve their creativity. As explained in the *Encyclopedia of Creativity,* creativity can be taught and learned, enhanced, and mastered. Enough is known about creativity that it can be integrated into every level in the educational system [12].

MEASURING YOUR CREATIVE POTENTIAL

One way to understand creativity is to try out exercises used to measure creative potential. Begin with Human Relations Self-Assessment Quiz 6-1 that measures creativity based on verbal ability.

CHARACTERISTICS OF CREATIVE WORKERS

Creative workers tend to have different intellectual and personality characteristics from their less creative counterparts. In general, creative people are more mentally flexible than others, which allows them to overcome the traditional ways of looking at problems. This flexibility often shows up in practical jokes and other forms of playfulness, such as making up a rap song about the company's product line. The characteristics of creative workers can be grouped into three broad areas: knowledge, intellectual abilities, personality. [13]

Knowledge

Creative thinking requires a broad background of information, including facts and observations. Knowledge supplies the building blocks for generating and combining ideas. This is particularly true because, according to some experts, creativity always comes down to combining things in a new and different way. The introductory case about the scientist who linked knowledge of old turret cameras with knowledge about digital cameras illustrates how combining facts can be helpful. Taking Human Relations Self-Assessment Quiz 6-2, will help you appreciate how possessing knowledge contributes to thinking creatively.

Intellectual Abilities

In general, creative workers tend to be bright rather than brilliant. Extraordinarily high intelligence is not required to be creative, but creative people are good at generating alternative solutions to problems in a short period of time. According to Yale University professor of psychology and education, Robert Sternberg, the key to creative intelligence is **insight,** an ability to know what information is relevant, to find connections between the old and the new, to combine facts that are unrelated, and to see the "big picture." [14] Creative people also maintain a youthful curiosity throughout their lives, and the curiosity is not centered on only their own field of expertise. Instead, their range of interests encompasses many areas of knowledge, and they generate enthusiasm toward almost any puzzling problem.

Creative people are able to think divergently. They can expand the number of alternatives to a problem, thus moving away from a single solution. Yet the creative thinker also knows when it is time to think convergently, narrowing the number of useful solutions. For example, the divergent thinker might think of 27 different names for a Web site to sell high-fashion buttons. Yet at some point, he or she will have to converge toward choosing the best name, such as ***www.chicbutton.com.***

Creativity can stem from both *fluid intelligence* and *crystallized intelligence.* Fluid intelligence depends on raw processing ability, or how quickly you learn

> "Anyone who thinks or attempts to convince you that it's business as usual at Ford is wrong and would serve us all by pursuing their [his or her] interests elsewhere.... Innovative answers need to be found for every aspect of our business, from product development and manufacturing to human resources and finance. Not everyone will have the ideas that we need, but everyone can support and help implement needed innovation."
> —William C. Ford, CEO Ford Motor Company, November 28, 2005, e-mail to employees

■ Learning Objective 3

■ **Insight**
an ability to know what information is relevant, to find connections between the old and the new, to combine facts that are unrelated, and to see the "big picture"

Human Relations Self-Assessment Quiz   **6-1**

Creative Personality Test

Answer each of the following statements as Mostly True or Mostly False. We are looking for general trends, so do not be concerned that under certain circumstances your answer might be different in response to a particular statement.

	Mostly True	Mostly False
1. I think novels are a waste of time, so I am more likely to read a nonfiction book.	_____	_____
2. You have to admit, some crooks are ingenious.	_____	_____
3. I pretty much wear the same style and colors of clothing regularly.	_____	_____
4. To me most issues have a clear-cut right side or wrong side.	_____	_____
5. I enjoy it when my boss hands me vague instructions.	_____	_____
6. When I'm surfing the Internet, I sometimes investigate topics, about which I know very little.	_____	_____
7. Business before leisure activities is a hard-and-fast rule in my life.	_____	_____
8. Taking a different route to work is fun, even if it takes longer.	_____	_____
9. From time to time I have made friends with people of a different sex, race, religion, or ethnic background from myself.	_____	_____
10. Rules and regulations should be respected, but deviating from them once in a while is acceptable.	_____	_____
11. People who know me say that I have an excellent sense of humor.	_____	_____
12. I have been known to play practical jokes or pranks on people.	_____	_____
13. Writers should avoid using unusual words and word combinations.	_____	_____
14. Detective work would have some appeal to me.	_____	_____
15. I am much more likely to tell a rehearsed joke than make a witty comment.	_____	_____
16. Almost all national advertising on television bores me.	_____	_____
17. Why write letters or send e-mail greetings to friends when there are so many clever greeting cards already available in the stores or on-line?	_____	_____
18. For most important problems in life, there is one best solution available.	_____	_____
19. Pleasing myself means more to me than pleasing others.	_____	_____
20. I'm enjoying taking this test.	_____	_____

Scoring and Interpretation:

Give yourself a plus 1 for each answer scored in the creative direction as follows:

1. Mostly False	8. Mostly True	15. Mostly False
2. Mostly True	9. Mostly True	16. Mostly False
3. Mostly False	10. Mostly True	17. Mostly False
4. Mostly False	11. Mostly True	18. Mostly False
5. Mostly True	12. Mostly True	19. Mostly True
6. Mostly True	13. Mostly False	20. Mostly True
7. Mostly False	14. Mostly True	

A score of 15 or more suggests that your personality and attitudes are similar to those of a creative person. A score of between 9 and 14 suggests an average similarity with the personality and attitudes of a creative person. A score of 8 or less suggests that your personality is dissimilar to that of a creative person. You are probably more of a conformist and not highly open-minded in your thinking at this point in your life. To become more creative, you may need to develop more flexibility in your thinking and a higher degree of open-mindedness.

Human Relations Self-Assessment Quiz   **6-2**

Rhyme and Reason

A noted creativity expert says that exercises in rhyming release creative energy; they stir imagination into action. While doing the following exercises, remember that rhyme is frequently a matter of sound and does not have to involve similar or identical spelling. This exercise deals with light and frivolous emotions. After each "definition," write two rhyming words to which it refers.

Examples

1.	Large hog	Big	pig
2.	Television	Boob	tube
3.	A computer command tool for the home	House	mouse

Now try these:

1. Happy father
2. False pain
3. Formed like a simian
4. Highest-ranking police worker
5. Voyage by a large boat
6. Corpulent feline
7. Melancholy fellow
8. Clever beginning
9. Heavy and unbroken slumber
10. Crazy custom
11. Lengthy melody
12. Weak man
13. Instruction at the seashore
14. Criticism lacking in effectiveness
15. A person who murders for pleasurable excitement
16. Musical stringed instrument with full, rich sounds
17. Courageous person who is owned as property by another
18. Mature complaint
19. Strange hair growing on the lower part of a man's face
20. Drooping marine crustacean
21. A computer whiz with a ridiculous sense of humor
22. You make one up now for the most important question of all

Answers and Interpretation:

The more of these rhymes you were able to come up with, the higher your creative potential. You would also need an advanced vocabulary to score very high (for instance, what is a *simian* or a *crustacean*?). Ten or more correct rhymes would tend to show outstanding creative potential, at least in the verbal area. Here are the answers:

1.	Glad dad	**3.**	Ape shape	**5.**	Ship trip
2.	Fake ache	**4.**	Top cop	**6.**	Fat cat

(continued)

Human Relations Self-Assessment Quiz   6-2   (*Continued*)

7. Sad lad	**13.** Beach teach	**18.** Ripe gripe
8. Smart start	**14.** Weak critique	**19.** Weird beard
9. Deep sleep	**15.** Thriller killer	**20.** Limp shrimp
10. Mad fad	**16.** Mellow cello	**21.** Absurd nerd
11. Long song	**17.** Brave slave	**22.** Two bonus points
12. Frail male		

If you can think of a sensible substitute for any of these answers, give yourself a bonus point. For example, for number 21, how about a freak geek?

Source: The current test is an updated version of Eugene Raudsepp with George P. Hough, Jr., *Creative Growth Games* (New York: Harcourt Brace Jovanovich, 1977). Reprinted with permission.

information and solve problems. Like raw athletic ability, fluid intelligence begins to decline by age 30, particularly because our nerve conduction slows. Crystallized intelligence is accumulated knowledge that increases with age and experience.

Personality

The emotional and other nonintellectual aspects of a person heavily influence creative problem solving. Creative people tend to have a positive self-image without being blindly self-confident. Because they are self-confident, creative people are able to cope with criticism of their ideas. Creative people have the ability to tolerate the isolation necessary for developing ideas. Talking to others is a good source of ideas. Yet at some point, the creative problem solver has to work alone and concentrate.

Creative people are frequently nonconformists and do not need strong approval from the group. Many creative problem solvers are thrill seekers who find developing imaginative solutions to problems to be a source of thrills. Creative people are also persistent, which is especially important for seeing that a new idea is implemented. Selling a creative idea to the right people requires considerable follow-up. Creative people enjoy dealing with uncertainty and chaos. A creative person, for example, would enjoy the challenge of taking over a customer service department that was way behind schedule and ineffective. Less creative people become frustrated quickly when their jobs are unclear and disorder exists.

Self-reflection and a concentration on feelings are characteristic of many creative people. The quiet thinking is helpful in finding useful ideas, as in thinking of how to solve a difficult problem while walking alone or taking a shower. Creative people are also open and responsive to feelings and emotions in the world around them.

THE CONDITIONS NECESSARY FOR CREATIVITY

Creativity is not simply a random occurrence. Well-known creativity researcher and professor of business administration at Harvard Business School Teresa M. Amabile has summarized 22 years of her research about creativity in the workplace. Her findings are also supported by others. [15] Creativity takes place when three components come together: expertise, creative thinking skills, and the right type of motivation. *Expertise* refers to the necessary knowledge to put facts together. The more ideas floating around in your head, the more likely you are to combine them in some useful way, as already described.

Creative thinking refers to how flexibly and imaginatively individuals approach problems. If you know how to keep digging for alternatives and to avoid getting stuck in the status quo, your chances of being creative multiply. Along these same lines, you are much more likely to be creative if you are intentionally seeking ideas, such always being on the lookout for money-saving ideas. Persevering, or sticking with a problem to a conclusion, is essential for finding creative solutions. A few rest breaks to gain a fresh perspective may be helpful, but the creative person keeps coming back until a solution emerges.

The right type of *motivation* is the third essential ingredient for creative thought. A fascination with or passion for the task is much more important then searching for external rewards. People will be the most creative when they are motivated primarily by the satisfaction and challenge of the work itself. A Dutch psychologist attempted to analyze what separated chess masters from chess grand masters. He subjected groups of each to a variety of mental ability tests but found no difference between the two groups. The only difference was found in motivation: grand masters simply loved chess more and had more passion and commitment for the game. [16]

Passion for the task and high intrinsic motivation contribute to a total absorption in the work and intense concentration, resulting in the flow experience. A creative businessperson, such as an entrepreneur developing a plan for worldwide distribution of a product, will often achieve the experience of flow. One analysis of creativity suggests that hard work and the love of the task can be at least as important as raw talent in ensuring creative success. [17] In addition to the internal conditions that foster creativity, five factors outside the person are key:

1. **An environmental need must stimulate the setting of a goal.** This is another way of saying, "Necessity is the mother of invention." For example, several years ago independent hardware stores were faced with the challenge of large chains, such as Home Depot and Lowe's, driving them out of business. Many of these independent stores survived by forming buying alliances with each other so that they could purchase inventory in larger quantities—and, therefore, lower prices. The independents also emphasize doing home repairs, such as fixing ripped screens and broken windows.

2. **Another condition that fosters creativity is enough conflict and tension to put people on edge.** Robert Sutton advises managers to prod happy people into fighting among themselves to stimulate creativity. The fights should be about ideas, not personality conflicts and name calling. For example, a group member should be given time to defend his or her work, and then the ideas should be sharply criticized by the other group members. [18] Cirque du Soleil, the world-famous circus, capitalizes on the importance of conflict for creativity. Cirque officials generally ensure there is a mix of nationalities and viewpoints when they assemble a creative team. Daniel Lamarre, the troupe's president, says that easy consensus is the enemy of groundbreaking ideas. The ideas, in this context, usually refer to fascinating acts. [19]

3. **Another external factor for creativity is encouragement, including a permissive atmosphere that welcomes new ideas.** A manager or team leader who encourages imagination and original thinking and does not punish people for making honest mistakes is likely to receive creative ideas from people. 3M is highly regarded as a company with many innovations in addition to Scotch tape and Post-it® notes. The company encourages creativity in many ways, such as granting people time off from regular responsibilities simply to think about new ideas. W. L Gore is often cited among the world's most innovative companies. You may be familiar with their waterproof fabrics and guitar strings. The cornerstone of Gore's innovative culture has been a permissive atmosphere. In the words of human resources associate, Jackie Brinton, "We believe in the power of the individual who is given the freedom to do great things and in the beauty of small teams, even though we're now operating on a global, coordinated scale." [20]

4. Humor is a key environmental condition for enhancing creativity. Humor has always been linked to creativity. Humor gets the creative juices flowing, and effective humor requires creativity. Thomas Edison started every workday with a joke-telling session. Mike Vance, chair of the Creative Thinking Association of America, says, "Humor is unmasking the hypocritical. What makes us laugh often is seeing how things are screwed up—then sometimes seeing how we can fix them. Whenever I go into a company and don't hear much laughter, I know it's not a creative place." [21]

5. A final key environmental condition to be considered here is how much time pressure the problem solver should face to trigger creativity. Conventional wisdom says that people produce the best when pressure is highest, for example, thinking of ways to keep a business running after a disaster, such as a fire, flood, or terrorist attack. Yet studies show that the more workers feel pressed for time, the less likely they are to produce creative output, such as solving a tricky problem or envisioning a new product, or to have other such "aha" experiences that result in innovation. Time pressures may diminish creativity because they limit a worker's freedom to think through different options and directions. A subtle finding, however, is that time pressures may help creativity if the worker is focused on a single task he or she considers important. [22] So if you are under heavy time pressure to arrive at a creative solution, focus on one task.

Despite the theme of permissiveness in several of the conditions for enhancing creativity, constraints also have their place. Individuals or teams with budget constraints and time constraints sometimes find that these constraints help them rise to the occasion. Marissa Ann Mayer, the vice president for search products and user experience at Google contends that constraints can actually speed product development. Google often gets a sense of just how good a new concept is if they simply prototype it (try it out) for a single day or week. Another constraint would be limiting team size to two or three people. [23]

How Do I Improve My Creativity?

■ Learning Objective 4

Because of the importance of creative problem solving, many techniques have been developed to improve creativity. Here we look at both specific techniques and general strategies for becoming more creative. The goal of these experiences is to think like a creative problem solver. Such a person lets his or her imagination wander. He or she ventures beyond the constraints that limit most people. The result of thinking more creatively is to bring something new into existence. *Something new* can be a totally new creation or a combination of existing things and ideas. To focus again on the subject, when we refer to creativity in business we are not necessarily thinking of revolutionary ideas that create a new industry. The new design of containers for prescription medicine is a representative example. Old prescription bottles are difficult to open and read, whereas the new prescription bottles are color-coded to specific medicines and easy to read and open. [24]

CONCENTRATE INTENSELY ON THE TASK AT HAND

The ability to concentrate was mentioned earlier as a characteristic that contributes to effective problem solving in general. The ability to eliminate distractions also contributes mightily to generating new ideas. At times we think we are thinking intently about our problem yet in reality we may be thinking about something that interferes with creativity. Among the office distractions that interfere with concentration are phone calls, a computer beep informing you of an incoming message, a person in the next cubicle talking loudly on the phone, and a friendly hello from a work associate walking past your cubicle. All the methods that follow for creativity enhancement require concentration.

OVERCOME TRADITIONAL MENTAL SETS

An important consequence of becoming more intellectually flexible is that you can overcome a **traditional mental set,** a fixed way of thinking about objects and activities. Overcoming traditional mental sets is important because the major block to creativity is perceiving things in a traditional way. All creative examples presented so far in this chapter involved this process, and here is another one. You may be familiar with the Nalgene sports bottle for carrying water and other fluids. Aside from its decorative colors, a key feature is its durability. The bottle had its origins in chemical laboratories—the traditional use for a durable plastic bottle. However, by the 1970s, managers at Nalgene noticed that scientists were using the durable bottles to hold water for camping and hiking. The company soon started a division to market its "laboratory" bottles to Boy Scouts and other hikers. [25] Today, the company is challenged to keep up with the demand for the Nalgene bottle.

An effective way of overcoming a traditional mental set (or thinking outside the box) is to challenge the status quo. If you want to develop an idea that will impress your boss or turn around an industry, you must use your imagination. Question the old standby that things have always been done in a particular way.

> ■ **Traditional mental set**
> fixed way of thinking about objects and activities

DISCIPLINE YOURSELF TO THINK LATERALLY

A major challenge in developing creative thinking skills is to learn how to think laterally in addition to vertically. **Vertical thinking** is an analytical, logical process that results in few answers. The vertical thinker is looking for the one best solution to a problem, much like solving an equation in algebra. In contrast, **lateral thinking** spreads out to find many different alternative solutions to a problem. In short, critical thinking is vertical, and creative thinking is lateral. A vertical thinker might say, "I must find a part-time job to supplement my income. My income is not matching my expenses." The lateral thinker might say, "I need more money. Let me think of the various ways of earning more money. I can find a second job, get promoted where I am working, cut my expenses, run a small business out of my home. . . ."

To learn to think laterally, you have to develop the mental set that every problem has multiple alternative solutions. Do not leave the problem until you have sketched out multiple alternatives. Use a pencil or pen and paper or a computer screen, but do not walk away from your problem until you have thought of multiple alternatives. The accompanying Human Relations in Practice box insert provides an industrial example of lateral thinking.

> ■ **Vertical thinking**
> analytical, logical process that results in few answers; the vertical thinker looks for the one best solution to a problem, much like solving an equation in algebra
>
> ■ **Lateral thinking**
> process of spreading out to find many different alternative solutions to a problem

CONDUCT BRAINSTORMING SESSIONS

The best-known method of improving creativity is **brainstorming**, a technique by which group members think of multiple solutions to a problem. Using brainstorming, a group of six people might sit around a table generating new ideas for a product. During the idea-generating part of brainstorming, potential solutions are not criticized or evaluated in any way. In this way, spontaneity is encouraged. Brainstorming continues as a standard procedure for producing creative ideas in all types of organizations. IDEO, the famous design firm that now teaches other companies how to be innovative, uses brainstorming to design products and improve

> ■ **Brainstorming**
> technique by which group members think of multiple solutions to a problem

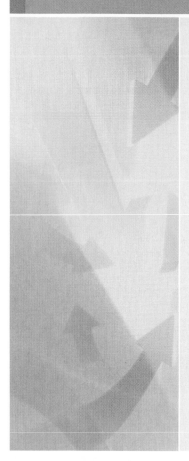

Human Relations in Practice

Robot Maker Thinks Laterally to Find New Use for Product

The KR 500, designed to lift car parts, is sold by Kuka Robotics, Europe's largest manufacturer of automated industrial machines. In 2000, several Kuka engineers wondered aloud whether the KR 500 could also lift people. "We could attach a chair to the end of it," one said. "It could make a fun ride." At any other industrial manufacturer, such an idea might have been laughed at and forgotten. But at Kuka, which has long built robots not only to perform but also to delight, it breathed new life into the company.

Only five years ago, Kuka was a century-old supplier of manufacturing equipment whose profits were disappearing because of its overreliancce on automakers. By taking on its engineers challenge to break down the barrier between man and machine, Kuka has found lucrative customers in a range of new industries and made its robots the stars of internationally renowned movies (for example, *Die Another Day*) and theme parks. Says Donald Vincent, executive vice president of Robotic Industries Association, "Kuka has stretched the envelope in growing new markets."

Questions

1. Why is the new use for an industrial robot an example of lateral thinking?
2. Why are Kuka's ideas for new uses for their products more about business creativity than scientific creativity?

Source: Siri Schubert, "Taking Robots for a Ride," *Business 2.0*, August 2005, p. 46.

---

consumer services for clients. Among its successes are the stand-up toothpaste tube for Procter & Gamble Co.'s Crest and the Oral-B toothbrush for children. [26] Rules for brainstorming are presented in Figure 6-6. Brainstorming has many variations, including an electronic approach and brainwriting.

An important strategy for enhancing the outcome of brainstorming is to have intellectually and culturally diverse group members. Some group leaders purposely choose people of different problem-solving styles (such as sensation types and intuitive types) to encourage more diverse thinking. The sensation type might have more "brainstorms" based on facts, whereas the intuitive type might have more brainstorms based on hunches. Cultural diversity is likely to improve brainstorming because people with different cultural experiences often bring different viewpoints to bear on the problem. A basic example is that when developing new food products, members with different ethnic backgrounds are chosen for a brainstorming group. You will recall that Cirque du Soleil relies on heterogeneous groups to produce new ideas.

Electronic Brainstorming

In electronic brainstorming, group members simultaneously enter their suggestions into a computer. The ideas are distributed to the screens of other group members. Although the group members do not talk to each other, they are still able to build on each other's ideas and combine ideas. Electronic brainstorming helps overcome

1. Use groups of about five to seven people.
2. Encourage the spontaneous expression of ideas. All suggestions are welcome, even if they are outlandish or outrageous. The least workable ideas can be edited out when the idea-generation phase is completed.
3. Quantity and variety are very important. The greater the number of ideas, the greater the likelihood of a breakthrough idea.
4. Encourage combination and improvement of ideas. This process is referred to as *piggybacking* or *hitchhiking*.
5. One person serves as the secretary and records the ideas, perhaps posting them on a whiteboard or a computer with a projection device.
6. Do not overstructure by following any of the preceding rules too rigidly. Brainstorming is a spontaneous process.

Figure   6-6

Rules and Guidelines for Brainstorming

certain problems encountered in traditional brainstorming. Shyness, domination by one or two members, and participants who loaf tend to be less troublesome than in face-to-face situations.

Brainwriting

In many situations, brainstorming by yourself produces as many or more useful ideas than does brainstorming in groups. **Brainwriting** is arriving at creative ideas by jotting them down yourself. The creativity-improvement techniques discussed so far will help you develop the mental flexibility necessary for brainstorming. After you have loosened up your mental processes, you will be ready to tackle your most vexing problems. Self-discipline is very important for brainwriting because some people have a tendency to postpone something as challenging as thinking alone. A variation of brainwriting is for group members to pass along their ideas from working alone to another member who reads them and adds his or her own ideas.

■ **Brainwriting**
arriving at creative ideas by jotting them down

In the various types of brainstorming just discussed, collecting wild ideas is only the start of the process. After ideas are collected, the group or each member carefully evaluates and analyzes the various alternatives. (You also need to refine your ideas from brainwriting.) It is usually important to also specify the implementation details. For example, how do you actually convert an industrial robot into an amusement park ride?

Borrow Creative Ideas

Copying the successful ideas of others is a legitimate form of creativity. Be careful, however, to give appropriate credit. Knowing when and which ideas to borrow from other people can help you behave as if you were an imaginative person. Creative ideas can be borrowed through such methods as the following:

speaking to friends, relatives, classmates, and coworkers

reading newspapers, newsmagazines, trade magazines, textbooks, nonfiction books, and novels and surfing the Internet

watching television and listening to radio programs

subscribing to computerized information services (expensive but worth it to many ambitious people)

■ **Benchmarking**
business firms borrowing ideas from each other regularly as part of quality improvement and improving productivity; representatives from one company visiting another to observe firsthand the practices of the other company

Business firms borrow ideas from each other regularly as part of quality improvement and improving productivity. The process is referred to as **benchmarking** because another firm's product, service, or process is used as a standard of excellence. Benchmarking involves representatives from one company visiting another to observe firsthand the practices of another company. The company visited is usually not a direct competitor. It is considered unethical to visit a competitor company for the purpose of appropriating ideas.

ESTABLISH IDEA QUOTAS FOR YOURSELF

To enhance creativity, many companies assign idea quotas to workers. For example, workers might be instructed to bring one good idea for earning or saving money to every meeting. Establishing idea quotas is similar to brainwriting with a goal in mind. An easy way of getting started is to establish a monthly minimum quota of one creative idea to improve your personal life and one to improve your job or school performance. Although this exercise might only take about five minutes of thinking each month, it could have a tremendous impact on your life.

A strategy for producing ideas is similar to the techniques for borrowing ideas previously described. To force-feed your creative thinking, follow the suggestion of science fiction writer Ray Bradbury: Read something daily that stimulates your imagination. "If you stuff yourself full," says Bradbury, "you will automatically explode every morning like Old Faithful." [27]

PLAY THE ROLES OF EXPLORER, ARTIST, JUDGE, AND LAWYER

A method for improving creativity has been proposed that incorporates many of the suggestions already made. The method calls for you to adopt four roles in your thinking. [28]

1. **Be an explorer.** Speak to people in different fields and get ideas that you can use. For example, if you are a telecommunications specialist, speak to salespeople and manufacturing specialists.

2. **Be an artist by stretching your imagination.** Strive to spend about 5 percent of your day asking "what if" questions. For example, a sales manager at a fresh-fish distributor might ask, "What if some new research suggests that eating fish causes intestinal cancer in humans?" Also, remember to challenge the commonly perceived rules in your field. A bank manager challenged why customers needed their canceled checks returned each month. This questioning led to some banks not returning canceled checks unless the customer paid an additional fee for the service. (As a compromise, most banks send customers photocopies of about 10 checks on one page.)

3. **Know when to be a judge.** After developing some wild ideas, at some point you have to evaluate them. Do not be so critical that you discourage your own imaginative thinking. However, be critical enough to prevent attempting to implement weak ideas.

4. **Achieve results by playing the role of a lawyer.** Negotiate and find ways to implement your ideas within your field or place of work. The explorer, artist, and judge stages of creative thought might take only a short time to develop a creative idea. Yet you may spend months or even years getting your brainstorm implemented. For example, it took a long time for the developer of the electronic pager to finally get the product manufactured and distributed on a large scale.

Concept Review and Reinforcement

Key Terms

Summary and Review

Problem solving occurs when you try to remove an obstacle that is blocking a path you want to take or when you try to close the gap between what exists and what you want to exist. Decision making takes place after you encounter a problem and you select one alternative from the various courses of action that can be pursued. Many traits and characteristics influence the type of problem solver you are now or are capable of becoming. Among them are:

- cognitive intelligence, education, and experience
- emotional intelligence
- flexibility versus rigidity
- intuition
- concentration
- decisiveness and perfectionism
- risk taking and thrill seeking
- values of the decision maker

Gender differences may exist in decision making, including the fact that women are more concerned about how a decision will affect the team and short-term results, whereas men focus more on the competitive environment and long-term results.

The decision-making process outlined in this chapter uses both the scientific method and intuition for making decisions in response to problems. Decision making follows an orderly flow of events:

1. You are aware of a problem or create one of your own.
2. You identify causes of the problem.
3. You find creative alternatives.
4. You weigh the alternatives and make a choice.
5. You implement the choice.

6. You evaluate whether you have made a sound choice. If your choice was unsound, you are faced with a new problem, and the cycle repeats itself.

Creativity is the ability to look for good ideas that can be put into action. Creative workers tend to have different intellectual and personality characteristics than their less creative counterparts. In general, creative people are more mentally flexible than others, which allows them to overcome the traditional way of looking at problems.

- **Knowledge.** Creative thinking requires a broad background of information, including facts and observations.
- **Intellectual abilities.** Creative workers tend to be bright rather than brilliant. The key to creative intelligence is insight. Creativity can stem from both fluid (raw) intelligence and crystallized (accumulated) intelligence.
- **Personality.** The emotional and other nonintellectual aspects of a person heavily influence creative problem solving. For example, creative people are frequently nonconformists and thrill seekers.

Creativity takes place when three components come together:

- expertise
- creative thinking skills (being flexible and imaginative)
- right type of motivation (passion for the task and intrinsic motivation)

Four factors outside the person play a key role in fostering creativity: an environmental need, enough conflict and tension to put people on edge, encouragement from management, and the presence of humor. Unless a person is working on a highly focused task, time pressures are likely to diminish creativity. Constraints, such as time and budgets, can often enhance creativity.

Methods of improving your creativity include the following:

- Concentrate intensely on the task at hand.
- Overcome traditional mental sets.
- Discipline yourself to think laterally.
- Conduct brainstorming sessions, including electronic brainstorming and brainwriting.
- Borrow creative ideas.
- Establish idea quotas for yourself.
- Play the roles of explorer, artist, judge, and lawyer.

Check Your Understanding

1. What would be some of the symptoms or signs of a "rigid thinker"?
2. Furnish an example from your own life in which you became aware of a problem. What led to this awareness?
3. Why does concentration improve problem solving?
4. Why is intuition often referred to as a "sixth sense"?
5. Why does knowledge lead to creativity?
6. How can a person still be creative in his or her work without having much talent?
7. Provide an example of how a supervisor or teacher of yours encouraged you to be creative. How effective was this encouragement?
8. Give an example of one work problem and one personal problem for which brainstorming might be useful.
9. Why is being passionate about the task at hand almost essential for being creative?
10. Ask an experienced manager or professional how important creative thinking has been in his or her career. Be prepared to report back to class with your findings.

Web Corner

Problem solving techniques: WWW.MNDTOOLS.COM

Development of Creative Thinking: WWW.CRE8NG.COM

Internet Skill Builder

Many Web sites offer creativity training. One such site is www.before-after.com, which mentions many reasons for improving creativity, including "Bring greater creativity to our sales process," "Infuse our meeting with creative energy," and "I'm just looking for creative inspiration." We especially recommend going to the two-minute Creative IQ test. How do the results of this test compare to the creativity test you took in this chapter? If before-after.com is no longer in operation, insert "creativity training" in your search engine to find a comparable site.

Applying Human Relations Exercise 6-1

Using the Problem-Solving Process

Imagine that you have received $2 million in cash with the income taxes already paid. The only stipulation is that you will have to use the money to establish some sort of enterprise, either a business or a charitable foundation. Solve this problem using the following worksheet. Describe what thoughts you have or what actions you will take for each step of problem solving and decision making.

I. *Identify causes of the problem.* Have you found your own problem, or was it given to you?

II. *Diagnose the problem.* What is the true decision that you are facing? What is your underlying problem?

III. *Find creative alternatives.* Think of the many alternatives facing you. Let your imagination flow and be creative.

IV. *Weigh alternatives and make the choice.* Weigh the pros and cons of each of your sensible alternatives.

Alternatives	Advantages	Disadvantages
1.		
2.		
3.		
4.		
5.		

V. Based on your analysis in step IV, choose the best alternative.

VI. *Implement the choice.* Outline your action plan for converting your chosen alternative into action.

VII. *Evaluate the choice.* Do the best you can here by speculating how you will know if the decision you reached was a good one.

Applying Human Relations Exercise 6-2

Choose an Effective Domain Name

Using conventional brainstorming or one of its variations, huddle in small groups. Your task is to develop original domain names for several products or services. An effective domain name is typically one that is easy to remember and will capture potential customers in an uncomplicated Web search. One reason this exercise is difficult is that "cybersquatters" grab unclaimed names they think business owners might want, and then sell these names later. For example, a cybersquatter (or domain name exploiter) might develop or buy the domain name www.dogfood.com, hoping that an e-tailer of dog food will want this name in the future. The owner of dogfood.com would charge a company such as Pet Smart every time a surfer looking to purchase dog food over the Internet, entered www.dogfood.com and was then linked to Pet Smart.

After your team has brainstormed a few possible domain names, search the Internet to see if your domain name is already in used. Simply enter www plus the name you have chosen into your browser. Or visit the site of a company such as DomainCollection.com Inc. After you have developed your list of domain names not already in use, present your findings to the rest of the class.

■ Funeral homes
■ Replacement parts for antique or classic autos

- A used-car chain
- Personal loans for people with very poor credit ratings
- Clothing for cross-dressers
- A dating (introduction) service
- You choose one of your own

Questions

1. Suppose the domain names you come up with are also developed by other groups in the class. What might this tell you about the creative process?

2. What do you think of the ethics of cybersquatters holding the rights to obvious domain names such as www.usedautoparts or www.asthmatreatment.com?

3. Why not become a cybersquatter and attempt to sell your domain names, sharing the profits with the group?

Source: Several of the facts for this skill-building exercise (but not the exercise) stem from Kelly K. Spors, "Pick a Domain Name," *The Wall Street Journal*, May 9, 2005, p. R8.

Human Relations Case Study 6-1

L.L. Bean Changes Its Mind

A few years ago, outdoor-clothing retailer L.L. Bean Inc. began building a call center near Waterville, Maine. Then, in November, mobile-phone carrier T-Mobile USA Inc. said it would build its own call center next door. Within a week, Bean chief executive Christopher McCormick halted construction—literally stopping bull-dozers in their tracks. A few weeks later, Bean said it would abandon the Waterville site; it ultimately chose to open the new call center in Bangor, about 55 miles away.

McCormick wasn't concerned about appearing wishy-washy. He simply wanted to make the best decision for the closely held Freeport, Maine, retailer. A 23-year veteran who was named CEO in 2001, 50-year-old McCormick is the first chief executive from outside the founding family.

Bean, which does much of its business through cat-alog telephone sales, opened a call center in an old Wa-terville shopping center in 1997. But the storefront was cramped and offered limited parking, so Bean executives in early 2004 began scouting for another site. By summer, they had settled on the FirstPark business center in nearby Oakland. Bean purchased the land, drew up the plans for a 50,000-square-foot office that could accom-modate up to 800 workers and began grading the site.

Then T-Mobile disclosed plans for a 77,000 square-foot center in FirstPark, housing 700 or more employees. McCormick says he worried immediately whether Wa-terville, a city of 16,000 had enough workers to supply both companies. He was especially concerned because much of Bean's workforce is seasonal, peaking near the Christmas holidays. He feared that experienced call-center workers would prefer relatively stable year-round employment with T-Mobile, leaving Bean out in the cold.

Within days, he called a meeting of his top lieu-tenants and told them he wanted to stop work at First-Park. "You want to do what?" he recalls one asking. "There were certainly some shocked looks." It didn't help that the reappraisal came at Bean's busiest time of the year, when executives were already stretched thin to ac-commodate holiday sales. Moreover, McCormick wanted the new call center ready by the fall of 2005, then only about nine months away.

McCormick says he has never before reversed such a significant decision. Beyond the land cost, Bean had al-ready sunk more than $500,000 into plans and prelimi-nary construction. But he also wanted to send a signal to other executives. "I want my people to consider all the options. I want objective decision making," he says. "I don't want them to be a champion of one point of view."

Bean began searching for a new call-center site, em-ploying the same real estate broker that had steered T-Mobile to FirstPark. By spring, Bean executives settled on a vacant office building in Bangor, where the city of-fered the company a break on the rent. When it came time to formally abandon the Waterville deal and com-mit to Bangor, McCormick says the Bean executive team agreed unanimously.

In disagreement with state officials, McCormick says he couldn't take the chance on moving forward with the Waterville call center. "It was too risky to build this huge building" without more confidence about the potential labor supply. McCormick briefly considered locating the call center outside Maine. He says Bean could have saved money, but he rejected the move because Bean's connection to the state is crucial to the company's branding.

Questions

1. To what extent did McCormick use the problem-solving and decision-making steps described in the chapter?

2. How will CEO McCormick know if he made a good decision?
3. What is your opinion of the ethics of McCormick backing off on the deal to construct a call center in Waterville?

Source: Adapted from Scott Thurm, "Seldom-Used Executive Power: Reconsidering," *The Wall Street Journal*, February 6, 2006, p. B3.

Human Relations Case Study 6-2

Hanging on to a Vulnerable Account

Henry Sanderson is an outsourcing manager at Mercury Products, an office equipment manufacturer. He manages 17 customer sites and 35 employees who work at the sites. Sanderson described a recent problem his group faced. Business was good in that the customers were pleased with the management of their office equipment but had concerns over their monthly costs, which ranged from $37,000 to $43,000. It seemed like a great deal of money to them.

About two years before the five-year account was going to be up for renewal, Alice Reuben, an on-site technician telephoned Sanderson and said there had been a couple of sales reps from one of their competitors in to visit with a customer. Furthermore, the customer had agreed to allow them to make a formal presentation the following week.

Sanderson realized that this account could be taken by a worthy outsourcing competitor, so he listed this major account as vulnerable in his customer database. The consequences of losing an account were tremendous because of lost revenues and layoffs of the on-site employees.

Sanderson decided to conduct a brainstorming session to deal with possible loss of the account. After this the brainstorming began, Betty Yang acted as the scribe to capture every thought on a flip chart. The big question the team sought answers to was, "What can we do better with the customer?" The ideas thrown out included the following: (A few of the ideas were accompanied by action plans.)

■ We need to do better training of end users. A lot of the service calls were needed because the end users

did not know how to perform certain functions on our copiers. Although all end users had been trained three years earlier when the equipment was installed, this growing business had added a lot of new employees who didn't know how to use the equipment. Fewer calls to service meant techs would spend less time at this site. This would have a positive effect on their overall performance and budget.
■ Improve overall customer service.
■ Seek an early renewal to the contract.
■ Find a way to lock out the competition. One of the sales strategies for the new contract was to remove the labor component. This would bring the cost down by $3,800 per month.
■ Take the misery out of billing.
■ Create a roles and responsibilities document. The document will help organize our individual efforts so we can present a unified organization to the customer.
■ Give more value to the customer. The sales team, led by Shawn Elliot will determine the appropriate new equipment for the account and determine the pricing with the standard net profit margin. The monthly charge to the customer will probably be higher because of the buyout and the fact that installing networked equipment costs more. However, it will be the task of sales and technical to present a value-added solution that also saves the customer money in terms of time-in-motion, while increasing their productivity.
■ Respond more quickly to service problems. Stephanie Johnson reported that the group's average response time to service calls has been 2.4 hours.

This is at the very high end of acceptability as the industry average is more than 7 hours.

- Find some quick ways to delight the customer. Mercury's invoice would be put on "auto-pay," meaning it did not need any corporate-level approval and the company could be paid immediately.
- Go for seven-year contracts instead of the traditional five-year contract.

Sanderson scheduled another day for solution presentations in one week. The sales group was asked to present their results. Based on a seven-year contract, we would accomplish all of our goals:

- The on-site labor component would remain at 100 percent.
- The cost to the customer would be reduced by $1,719 per month.
- The biggest possible savings for the customer would be $8,000 per month.

The customer would save approximately four cents for each print. The sales group concluded that the customer was printing about 200,000 prints to desktop printers per month, at a cost of about five cents per print; $10,000 for printing documents. The cost of printing with our products would only be one cent, or $2,000 per month, representing a new savings of $8,000 per month. Additional savings would come through the removal of the desktop printers and the supplies and service that accompanied them. A new contract was signed four days after this presentation.

Questions

1. In what way did the Mercury group make effective use of brainstorming?
2. In what way did the Mercury group deviate from traditional brainstorming?
3. What advice can you offer Sanderson when he conducts his next brainstorming session?

Source: Case researched by Henry Soric, Liverpool, New York, March 2006.

REFERENCES

1. Ben Rand, "Kodak Seeks Digital's Future via Past: V570's Dual Lenses Harken to 'Turret' Cameras," Rochester, New York, *Democrat and Chronicle*, March 12, 2006, pp. 1E, 4E.
2. Daniel Goleman, *Working with Emotional Intelligence* (New York: Bantam, 1998).
3. Eugene Sadler-Smith and Erella Shefy, "The Intuitive Executive: Understanding and Applying 'Gut Feel' in Decision-Making," *Academy of Management Executive*, November 2004, p. 76.
4. Quoted in Bill Breen, "What's Your Intuition?" *Fast Company*, September 2000, p. 300.
5. Malcolm Gladwell, *Blink: The Power of Thinking without Thinking* (New York: Little, Brown, 2005).
6. Lea Winerman, "What We Know without Knowing," *Monitor on Psychology*, March 2005, p. 52.
7. Research cited in Janet Guyon, "The Art of the Decision," *Fortune*, November 14, 2005, p. 144.
8. Paul C. Nutt, "Surprising but True: Half the Decision in Organizations Fail," *Academy of Management Executive*, November 1999, pp. 75–90; Nutt, *Why Decisions Fail* (San Francisco: Berrett-Koehler, 2002).
9. Peter Coy, "Laurels for an Odd Couple: A Psychologist and a Traditionalist Share This Year's Nobel," *BusinessWeek*, October 21, 2002, p. 50.
10. Carol Polsky, "This Invention Is So Useful, It Has Stuck around for 75 Years," *Newsday* syndicated story, May 13, 2000.
11. Quoted in Ann Pomeroy, "Cooking Up Innovation," *HR Magazine*, November 2004, pp. 49–50.
12. Mark A. Runco and Steven R. Pritzker, eds., *Encyclopedia of Creativity*, vol. 1 (San Diego: Academic Press, 1999), p. xv.
13. Richard W. Woodman, John E. Sawyer, and Ricky W. Griffin, "Toward a Theory of Organizational Creativity," *Academy of Management Review*, April 1993, pp. 293–321; Greg R. Oldham and Anne Cummings, "Employee Creativity: Personal and Contextual Factors at Work," *Academy of Management Journal*, June 1996, pp. 607–634; Robert J. Sternberg, "Creativity as a Decision," *American Psychologist*, May 2002, p. 376; Zak Stambor, "Self-Reflection May Lead Independently to Creativity, Depression," *Monitor on Psychology*, June 2005, p. 13.
14. Robert J. Sternberg, ed., *Handbook of Creativity* (New York: Cambridge University Press, 1999).
15. Teresa M. Amabile, "How to Kill Creativity," *Harvard Business Review*, September–October 1998, pp. 78–79.
16. Research cited in "What Happens in the Brain of an Einstein in the Throes of Creation?" *USA Weekend*, January 1–3, 1999, p. 11.
17. Teresa M. Amabile, "Beyond Talent: John Irving and the Passionate Craft of Creativity," *American Psychologist*, April 2001, p. 335.
18. Robert I. Sutton, "The Weird Rules of Creativity," *Harvard Business Review*, September 2001, p. 101.
19. Linda Tischler, "Join the Circus," *Fast Company*, July 2005, p. 56.
20. Patrick J. Kiger, "Small Groups: Big Ideas," *Workforce Management*, February 27, 2006, p. 2
21. Cited in Robert McGarvey, "Turn It On," *Entrepreneur*, November 1996, pp. 156–157.
22. Research cited in Bridget Murray, "A Ticking Clock Means a Creativity Drop," *Monitor on Psychology*, November 2002, p. 24; Interview with Teresa M. Amabile in Bill Breen, "The 6 Myths of Creativity," *Fast Company*, December 2004, pp. 77–78.
23. Marissa Ann Mayer, "Creativity Loves Constraints," *Business Week*, February 13, 2006, p. 102.
24. Bruce Nussbaum, "Get Creative! How to Build Innovative Companies," *Business Week*, August 1, 2005, pp. 66, 67.
25. "Sports Bottles Oh So Cool," *Rochester (NY) Democrat and Chronicle*, August 23, 2003, p. 14D.
26. Bruce Nussbaum, "The Power of Design," *Business Week*, May 17, 2004, p. 88.
27. "Leadership Tips," *Executive Leadership*, December 2005, p. 8.
28. "Be a Creative Problem Solver," *Executive Strategies*, June 6, 1989, pp. 1–2.

Answers to brain teasers are as follows:

The answers to the Frame Games are (1) Spinal column and (2) Too much to do and too little time. The Sudoko solution is presented in the grid.

9	6	3	1	7	4	2	5	8
1	7	8	3	2	5	6	4	9
2	5	4	6	8	9	7	3	1
8	2	1	4	3	7	5	9	6
4	9	6	8	5	2	3	1	7
7	3	5	9	6	1	8	2	4
5	8	9	7	1	3	4	6	2
3	1	7	2	4	6	9	8	5
6	4	2	5	9	8	1	7	3

7

Personal Communication Effectiveness

Learning Objectives

After studying the information and doing the exercises in this chapter, you should be able to:

1 Explain the basic communication process.

2 Explain the relationship-building aspect of interpersonal communication.

3 Describe the nature and importance of nonverbal communication in the workplace.

4 Identify roadblocks to communication.

5 Know how to build bridges to communication.

6 Overcome many gender communication barriers.

7 Enhance your listening skills.

Outline

ast year, Buck Baker came close to getting three job offers but didn't get hired. Then a friend suggested that Baker, who had been laid off as the head of marketing for a Milwaukee staffing agency, might be having trouble because of his communication style, not for any lack in his credentials. He advised Baker, then 47, to pay a few visits to Patricia Smith-Pierce, an executive coach, to hone his communication skills.

Baker did just that—and made some eye-opening discoveries. For example, Smith-Pierce showed him how his relaxed posture and habit of picking up anything within reach made him appear indecisive. So Baker practiced sitting more upright and keeping his hands at his side. After two sessions and some phone consultations on this and other issues, he landed a job as a management consultant for the Detroit office of Hewitt Associates. Baker says the cost of his training sessions were worth every penny. [1]

The story of the professional who landed the job he wanted in part because he strengthened his communication skills illustrates how these skills contribute to success at the individual level. Effective communication skills are also important for many other reasons. Communication is so vital that it has been described as the glue that holds organizations and families together. Most job foul-ups and marital disputes are considered to be a result of communication problems. Furthermore, to be successful in work or personal life, you usually have to be an effective communicator. You can't make friends or stand up against enemies unless you can communicate with them. And you can't accomplish work through others unless you can send and receive messages effectively.

In this chapter we explain several important aspects of interpersonal communication, such as the communication process and overcoming various communication barriers. Many factors contribute to enhanced communication, leading in turn to more effective human relations. Explanation should also lead to skill improvement. For example, if you understand the steps involved in getting a message across to another person, you may be able to prevent many communication problems.

How Does Communication Take Place?

■ Learning Objective 1

■ **Communication**
the sending and receiving of messages

A convenient starting point in understanding how people communicate is to look at the steps involved in communicating a message. **Communication** is the sending and receiving of messages. A diagram of how the process takes place is shown in Figure 7-1. The theme of the model is that two-way communication involves three major steps and that each step is subject to interference or noise. Assume that Crystal, a customer, wishes to inform Tony, a used-car sales representative, that she is willing to make an offer of $8,000 on a used car. The price tag on the car is $8,750.

■ **Encoding**
the process of organizing ideas into a series of symbols, such as words and gestures, designed to communicate with a receiver

Step 1.   Sender encodes the message. Encoding is the process of organizing ideas into a series of symbols, such as words and gestures, designed to communicate with the receiver. Word choice has a strong influence on communication effectiveness. The better a person's grasp of language, the easier it is for him or her to encode. Crystal says, "Tony, this car obviously is not in excellent condition, but I am willing to give you $8,000 for it."

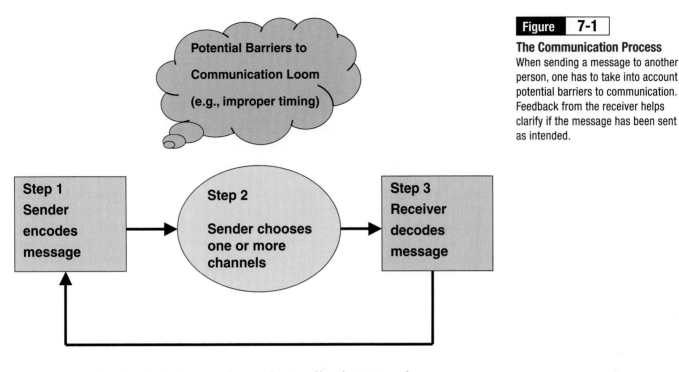

Figure   7-1

The Communication Process
When sending a message to another person, one has to take into account potential barriers to communication. Feedback from the receiver helps clarify if the message has been sent as intended.

Step 2.   Sender chooses one or more channels. The message is sent via a communication channel or medium, such as voice, telephone, paper, e-mail, or messaging. It is important to select a medium that fits the message. It would be appropriate to use the spoken word to inform a coworker that he swore under his breath at a customer. It would be less appropriate to send the same message through e-mail. Many messages on and off the job are sent nonverbally through the use of gestures and facial expressions. For example, a smile from a superior during a meeting is an effective way of communicating the message "I agree with you." Crystal has chosen the oral medium to send her message.

Step 3.   Receiver decodes the message. In **decoding,** the receiver interprets the message and translates it into meaningful information. Decoding is the process of understanding a message. Barriers to communication are most likely to surface at the decoding step. People often interpret messages according to their psychological needs and motives. Tony wants to interpret Crystal's message that she is very eager to purchase this car. Therefore, he may listen attentively for more information demonstrating that she is interested in purchasing the car.

■ **Decoding**
the process of understanding a message; the receiver interprets the message and translates it into meaningful information

Decoding the message leads naturally to action—the receiver does something about the message. If the receiver acts in the manner the sender wants, the communication has been successful. If Tony says, "It's a deal," Crystal had a successful communication event. Many missteps can occur between encoding and decoding a message. **Barriers to communication** or unwanted interference or **noise** can distort or block a message. If Crystal has an indecisive tone and raises her voice at the end of her statement, it could indicate that she is not really serious about offering a maximum of $8,000 for the car.

■ **Barriers to communication (or noise)**
missteps that can occur between encoding and decoding a message; unwanted interference that can distort or block a message

■ **Learning Objective 2**

How Does Interpersonal Communication Relate to Relationship Building?

Another way of understanding the process of interpersonal communication is to examine how communication is a vehicle for building relationships. According to Texas Tech business communication professors Rich Sorenson, Grace De Bord, and Ida Ramirez, we establish relationships along two primary dimensions: dominate–subordinate and cold–warm. In the process of communicating we attempt to *dominate or subordinate*. When we dominate, we attempt to control communication. When we subordinate, we attempt to yield control, or think first of the wishes and needs of the other person. Dominators expect the receiver of messages to submit to them; subordinate people send a signal that they expect the other person to dominate. [2]

We indicate whether we want to dominate or subordinate by the way we speak or write, or by the nonverbal signals we send. The dominator might speak loudly or enthusiastically; write forceful messages filled with exclamation points; or gesture with exaggerated, rapid hand movements. He or she might write a harsh e-mail message such as, "It's about time you started taking your job seriously and put in some real effort."

In the subordinate mode, we might speak quietly and hesitantly, in a meek tone, being apologetic. A subordinate person might ask, "I know you have better things on your mind than to worry about me, but I was wondering when I can expect my reimbursement for travel expenses?" In a work setting we ordinarily expect people with more formal authority to have the dominant role in conversations. However, in more democratic, informal companies, workers with more authority are less likely to feel the need to dominate conversations.

The *cold–warm dimension* also shapes communication because we invite the same behavior that we send. Cold, impersonal, negative messages evoke similar messages from others. In contrast, warm verbal and nonverbal messages evoke similar behavior from others. Getting back to the inquiry about the travel-expense check, here is a colder versus warmer response by the manager:

Colder: Travel vouchers really aren't my responsibility. You'll just have to wait like everybody else.

Warmer: I understand your problem. Not getting reimbursed on time is a bummer. I'll follow up on the status of your expense check sometime today or tomorrow.

The combination of dominant and cold communication sends the signal that the sender of the message wants to control and to limit, or even withdraw from, a personal relationship. A team leader might say that she cannot attend a Saturday morning meeting because she has to go out of town for her brother's wedding. A dominant and cold manager might say, "I don't want to hear about your personal life. Everyone in this department has to attend our Saturday meeting."

Subordinate actions combined with warm communication signal a desire to maintain or build the relationship while yielding to the other person. A manager communicating in a warm and subordinate manner in relation to the wedding request might say, "We'll miss you on Saturday morning because you are a key player in our department. However, I recognize that major events in personal life sometimes take priority over a business meeting."

Figure 7-2 summarizes how the dual dimensions of dominant–subordinate and cold–warm influence the relationship building aspects of communication. Rather

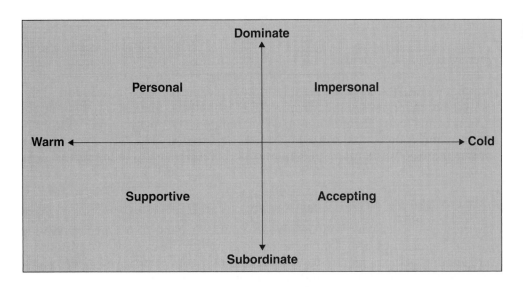

Figure **7-2**

Communication Dimensions of Establishing a Relationship
Source: Adapted with permission from Rich Sorenson, Grace De Bord, and Ida Ramirez, *Business and Management Communication: A Guide Book*, 4th ed. (Upper Saddle River, NJ: Prentice Hall, 2001), p. 7.

than regarding these four quadrants of relationships as good or bad, think of your purposes. In some situations you might want to dominate and be cold, yet in most situations you might want to submit a little and be warm in order to build a relationship. For example, being dominant and cold might be necessary for a security officer who is trying to control an unruly crowd at a sporting event.

Observe that the person in the quadrant *dominate–cold* has an impersonal relationship with the receiver, and the person in the *warm–subordinate* quadrant has a supportive relationship with the receiver. Being *dominant and warm* leads to a personal relationship, whereas as being *subordinate and cold* leads to an accepting relationship. The combinations of *dominate–cold* and *warm–subordinate* are more likely to produce the results indicated.

What Is Nonverbal Communication (Sending and Receiving Silent Messages)?

■ Learning Objective 3

So far we have been considering mostly spoken communication. However, much of the communication among people includes nonspoken and nonwritten messages. These nonverbal signals are a critical part of everyday communication. As a case in point, *how* you say "Thank you" makes a big difference in the extent to which your sense of appreciation registers. In **nonverbal communication,** we use our body, voice, or environment in numerous ways to help put a message across. Sometimes we are not aware how much our true feelings color our spoken message.

■ **Nonverbal communication**
using the body, voice, or environment in numerous ways to help get a message across

One problem of paying attention to nonverbal signals is that they can be taken too seriously. Just because some nonverbal signals (such as yawning or looking away from a person) might reflect a person's real feelings, not every signal can be reliably connected with a particular attitude. Jason may put his hand over his mouth because he is shocked. Lucille may put her hand over her mouth because she is trying to control her laughter about the message, and Ken may put his hand over his mouth as a signal that he is pondering the consequences of the message. Here we look at eight categories of nonverbal communication that are generally reliable indicators of a person's attitude and feelings.

ENVIRONMENT OR SETTING

Where you choose to deliver your message indicates what you think of its importance. Assume that your supervisor invites you over for dinner to discuss something with you. You will think it is a more important topic under these circumstances than if it were brought up when the two of you met in the supermarket. Other important environmental cues include room color, temperature, lighting, and furniture arrangement. A person who sits behind an uncluttered large desk, for example, appears more powerful than a person who sits behind a small, cluttered desk.

DISTANCE FROM THE OTHER PERSON

How close you place your body relative to another person's also conveys meaning when you send a message. If, for instance, you want to convey a positive attitude toward another person, get physically close to him or her. Putting your arm around someone to express interest and warmth is another obvious nonverbal signal. However, many people in a work setting abstain from all forms of touching (except for handshakes) because of concern that touching might be interpreted as sexual harassment. Cultural differences must be kept in mind in interpreting nonverbal cues. A French male is likely to stand closer to you than a British male, even if they had equally positive attitudes toward you. A set of useful guidelines has been developed for estimating how close to stand to another person (at least in many cultures). [3] They are described here and diagrammed in Figure 7-3.

> *Intimate distance* covers actual physical contact to about 18 inches. Usually, it is reserved for close friends and loved ones or other people you feel affectionate toward. Physical intimacy is usually not called for on the job, but there are exceptions. For one, confidential information might be whispered within the intimate distance zone.

> *Personal distance* covers from about 1.5 to 4 feet. In this zone it is natural to carry on friendly conversations and discussions. When people engage in a heated argument, they sometimes enter the personal distance zone. One example is a baseball coach getting up close to an umpire and shouting in his face.

> *Social distance* covers from 4 to 12 feet and, in general, is reserved for interaction that is businesslike and impersonal. We usually maintain this amount of distance between ourselves and strangers, such as retail sales associates.

> *Public distance* covers from 12 feet to the outer limit of being heard. This zone is typically used in speaking to an audience at a large meeting or in a classroom, but a few insensitive individuals might send ordinary messages by shouting across a room. The unstated message suggested by such an action is that the receiver of the message does not merit the effort of walking across the room.

People sometimes manipulate personal space in order to dominate a situation. A sales representative might move into the personal or intimate circle of a customer simply to intimidate him or her. Many people become upset when you move into a closer circle than that for which a situation calls. They consider it an invasion of their personal space, or their "territorial rights."

POSTURE

Certain aspects of your posture communicate a message. Leaning toward another individual suggests that you are favorably disposed toward his or her message. Leaning backward communicates the opposite. Openness of the arms or legs serves

Figure | **7-3**

Four Circles of Intimacy

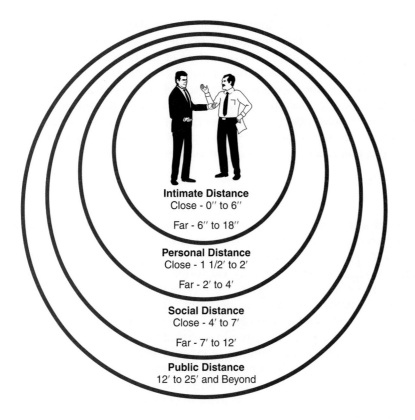

Intimate Distance
Close - 0″ to 6″

Far - 6″ to 18″

Personal Distance
Close - 1 1/2′ to 2′

Far - 2′ to 4′

Social Distance
Close - 4′ to 7′

Far - 7′ to 12′

Public Distance
12′ to 25′ and Beyond

as an indicator of liking or caring. In general, people establish closed postures (arms folded and legs crossed) when speaking to people they dislike. Standing up straight generally indicates high self-confidence. Stooping and slouching could mean a poor self-image. In any event, there is almost no disadvantage to standing up straight.

Related to posture are the nonverbal signals sent by standing versus sitting. Sitting down during a conversation is generally considered to be more intimate and informal than standing. If you do sit down while conversing, be sure to stand up when you wish the conversation to end. Standing up sends a message to the other person that it is time to leave. It also gives you the chance to be more attentive and polite in saying good-bye.

HAND GESTURES

An obvious form of body language is hand gestures. Hand gestures are universally recognized as conveying specific information to others. If you make frequent hand movements, you will generally communicate a positive attitude. If you use few gestures, you will convey dislike or disinterest. An important exception here is that some people wave their hands vigorously while arguing. Some of their hand movements reflect anger. Another example is that open-palm gestures toward the other person typically convey positive attitudes.

FACIAL EXPRESSIONS AND EYE CONTACT

When used in combination, the head, face, and eyes provide the clearest indications of attitudes toward other people. Lowering your head and peering over your glasses, for instance, is the nonverbal equivalent of the expression, "You're putting me on." As is well known, maintaining eye contact with another person improves communication with that person. To maintain eye contact, it is usually necessary to correspondingly move your head and face. Moving your head, face, and eyes away from another person is often interpreted as a defensive gesture or one suggesting a lack of self-confidence. Would you hire a job candidate who didn't look at you directly?

The face is often used as a primary source of information about how we feel. We look for facial clues when we want to determine another person's attitude. You can often judge someone's current state of happiness by looking at his or her face. The expression "sourpuss" attests to this observation. Happiness, apprehension, anger, resentment, sadness, contempt, enthusiasm, and embarrassment are but a few of the emotions that can be expressed through the face.

VOICE QUALITY

More significance is often attached to the *way* something is said than to *what* is said. A forceful voice, which includes a consistent tone without vocalized pauses, connotes power and control. Closely related to voice tone are volume, pitch, and rate of speaking. Anger, boredom, and joy can often be interpreted from voice quality. Anger is noted when the person speaks loudly, with a high pitch and at a fast rate. Boredom is indicated by a monotone. A tip-off to joy is when the person speaks loudly with a high pitch and fast rate. Joy is also indicated by loud volume.

Avoiding an annoying voice quality can make a positive impact on others. The research of voice coach and founder of Jacobi Voice, Jeffrey Jacobi provides some useful suggestions. A while back he surveyed a nationwide sample of 1,000 men and women and asked, "Which irritating or unpleasant voice annoys you the most?" His results are still valid today. The most irritating quality was a whining, complaining, or nagging tone.

Jacobbi notes that we are judged by the way we sound. He also contends that careers can be damaged by voice problems, such as those indicated in the survey. "We think about how we look and dress. And that gets most of the attention. But people judge our intelligence much more by how we sound than how we dress." [4] Human Relations Self-Assessment Quiz 7-1 provides more details about his findings.

Human Relations Self-Assessment Quiz   7-1

Voice Quality Checkup

The study of voice quality (cited in the text) ranked voice quality, in decreasing order of annoyance, as follows:

- Whining, complaining, or nagging tone—44.0 percent
- High-pitched, squeaky voice—15.9 percent
- Mumblers—11.1 percent
- Very fast talkers—4.9 percent
- Weak and wimpy voice—3.6 percent
- Flat, monotonous tone—3.5 percent
- Thick accent—2.4 percent

Ask yourself and two other people familiar with your voice if you have one or more of the preceding voice-quality problems. If your self-analysis and feedback from others does indicate a serious problem, get started on self-improvement. Record your voice and attempt to modify the biggest problems. Another avenue of improvement is to consult with a speech coach or therapist.

PERSONAL APPEARANCE

Your external image plays an important role in communicating messages to others. Job seekers show recognition of this aspect of nonverbal communication when they carefully groom for a job interview. People pay more respect and grant more privileges to people they perceive as being well dressed and attractive. The meaning of being well dressed depends heavily on the situation and the culture of the organization. In an information technology firm, neatly pressed jeans, a stylish T-shirt, and clean sport shoes might qualify as being well dressed. The same attire worn in a financial service firm would qualify as being poorly dressed. In recent years, more formal business attire has made a comeback, as reflected in more space in department stores being devoted to suits for men and women.

Common sense and research indicate that a favorable personal appearance leads to higher starting salaries and, later, salary increases. One study showed that people perceived to be physically attractive tend to receive salaries 8 to 10 percent higher. A possible explanation offered for the results is that employers might attribute other positive attributes to employees they perceive as physically attractive. [5]

NONVERBAL COMMUNICATION AND AIRPORT SECURITY

An advanced workplace application of nonverbal communication is to help combat drug trafficking and terrorism. The art of spotting nervous or threatening behavior has gained respect among airport security officials. Since the terrorist attacks on September 11, 2001, the Federal Bureau of Investigation (FBI) started teaching nonverbal behavior analysis to all new FBI recruits. In the past, passengers were selected to be interrogated mostly on the basis of what they looked like, such as a negative ethnic stereotype. Customs agents are now trained to observe what people do and to ask pointed questions when suspicious nonverbal behavior surfaces. Among the indicators of suspicious behavior are darting eyes, hand tremors, a fleeting style, and an enlarged carotid artery (indicating the rapid blood flow associated with anxiety). Failure to make eye contact with the customs official is a strong red flag. [6]

What Are Some Frequent Roadblocks to Communication?

■ **Learning Objective 4**

Communication rarely proceeds as effectively as we would like. Many different factors filter out a message on its way to the intended receiver, shown as potential barriers in Figure 7-1. In this section we look at some of the human roadblocks to communication. If you are aware of their presence, you will be better able to overcome them.

Routine or neutral messages are the easiest to communicate. Communication roadblocks are most likely to occur when a message is complex, is emotionally arousing, or clashes with the receiver's mental set. An emotionally arousing message would deal with such topics as job security or money. A message that clashes with a receiver's mental set requires that person to change his or her familiar pattern of receiving messages. The next time you order a meal in a restaurant, order dessert first and an entrée second. The server will probably not "hear" your dessert order because it deviates from the normal ordering sequence. The roadblocks or barriers described here are as follows:

1. Limited understanding of people

2. One-way communication

3. Different interpretation of words (semantics)

4. Credibility of the sender and mixed signals

5. Distortion of information

6. Different perspectives and experiences

7. Emotions and attitudes

8. Communication overload

9. Improper timing

10. Poor communication skills

11. Cultural and language barriers

LIMITED UNDERSTANDING OF PEOPLE

If you do not understand people very well, your communication effectiveness will be limited. To take a basic example, if you frame your message in terms of what can be done for you, you may be in trouble. It's much more effective to frame your message in terms of what you can do for the other person. Suppose a person in need of money wants to sell food supplements to a friend. Mentioning financial need is a very self-centered message. It could be made less self-centered:

> *Very self-centered.* "You've got to buy a few food supplements from me. I can't meet my credit card payments."

> *Less self-centered.* "Would you be interested in purchasing a few food supplements that would bring you more energy and help you live longer? If your answer is yes, I can help you."

Limited understanding of people can also take the form of making false assumptions about the receiver. The false assumption serves as a communication roadblock. A supervisor might say to a telemarketer (a person who sells over the phone), "If you increase sales by 15 percent, we will promote you to lead telemarketer." When the telemarketer does not work any harder, the supervisor thinks the message did not get across. The false assumption the supervisor made was that the telemarketer wanted a position with supervisory responsibility. What false assumptions have you made lately when trying to communicate with another person?

ONE-WAY COMMUNICATION

Effective communication proceeds back and forth. An exchange of information or a transaction takes place between two or more people. Person A may send messages to person B to initiate communication, but B must react to A to complete the communication loop. One reason written messages sometimes fail to achieve their purpose is that the person who writes the message cannot be sure how it will be interpreted. One written message that is subject to many interpretations is "Your idea is of some interest to me." (How much is *some*?) Face-to-face communication helps clarify meanings.

Instant messaging helps overcome the one-way barrier because the receiver reacts immediately to your message. An example: "You said ship the first batch only to good customers. Who do you consider to be a *good* customer?" Ten seconds later comes the reply, "A good customer bought at least $4,000 worth of goods last year and is up to date on payments." Three seconds later, the first person writes, "Got it." E-mail is also widely used to clarify messages and engage in two-way communication.

DIFFERENT INTERPRETATION OF WORDS (SEMANTICS)

Semantics is the study of the meaning and changes in the meaning of words or symbols. These different meanings can create roadblocks to communication. Often the problem is trivial and humorous; at other times, semantic problems can create substantial communication barriers. Consider first an example of trivial consequence.

Two first-time visitors to Montreal, Quebec (the French-Canadian province), entered a restaurant for dinner. After looking over the menu, the husband suggested they order the shrimp cocktail *entrées*. He said to his wife, "A whole shrimp dinner for $11.95 Canadian is quite a deal. I guess it's because Montreal is a seaport." When the entrées arrived, the visitors were sadly disappointed because they were the size of an *appetizer*.

The husband asked the server why the entrées were so small in Montreal. With a smile, the server replied, "You folks must be Americans. In French-speaking countries the entrée is the beginning of the meal, like the word *enter*. In the United States it's just the reverse—the entrée is the main meal. Are you now ready to order your main meal?"

Of greater consequence is the experience of a trainer of airplane pilots who inadvertently contributed to a crash. As a rookie pilot navigated down the runway, the trainer shouted, "Takeoff power." The pilot shut off the engine and skidded off the runway. What the trainer really meant was to *use* takeoff power—a surge of energy to lift the airplane off the ground. He was using *takeoff* as an adjective, not a verb. [7]

■ **Semantics**
the study of the meaning and changes in the meaning of words or symbols

CREDIBILITY OF THE SENDER AND MIXED SIGNALS

The more trustworthy the source or sender of the message, the greater the probability that the message will get through clearly. In contrast, when the sender of the message has low credibility, many times it will be ignored. Communications can also break down for a subtle variation of low credibility. The disconnect occurs from **mixed signals,** a type of message in which the sender might recommend one thing to others yet behave in another way himself or herself. A team leader might tell others that a tidy worker is a productive worker. However, his or her own cubicle contains a four-month supply of empty soft-drink cans, and old papers consume virtually every square inch of his or her desk.

Mixed signals also refers to sending different messages about the same topic to different audiences. For example, company representatives might brag about the high quality of its products in its public statements. Yet on the shop floor and in the office, the company tells its employees to cut costs whenever possible to lower costs.

■ **Mixed signals**
type of message in which the sender might recommend one thing to others yet behave in another way

DISTORTION OF INFORMATION

A great problem in sending messages is that people receiving them often hear what they want to hear. Without malicious intent, people modify your message to bolster their self-esteem or improve their situation. An incident that occurred between Danielle and her supervisor is fairly typical of this type of communication roadblock. Danielle asked her supervisor when she would be receiving a salary increase. Regarding the request as far-fetched and beyond the budget at the time, Danielle's supervisor replied, "Why should the company give you a raise when you are often late for work?"

Danielle *heard* her supervisor say, "If you come to work on time regularly, you will receive a salary increase." One month later Danielle said to her supervisor that she had not been late for work in a month and should now be eligible for a raise. Her supervisor replied, "I never said that. Where did you get that idea?"

DIFFERENT PERSPECTIVES AND EXPERIENCES

People perceive words and concepts differently because their experiences and vantage points differ. On the basis of their perception of what they have heard, many Latino children believe that the opening line of the "Star-Spangled Banner" is "José, can you see. . . ." (note that few children have *seen* the national anthem in writing). Cultural differences create different perspectives and experiences, such as workers from Eastern cultures tending to have high respect for authority. A worker from India might more readily accept a message from the boss than would his or her counterpart from California or Sweden. In the last two places, workers have a more casual attitude toward authority.

EMOTIONS AND ATTITUDES

Have you ever tried to communicate a message to another person while that person is emotionally aroused? Your message was probably distorted considerably. Another problem is that people tend to say things when emotionally aroused that they would not say when calm. Similarly, a person who has strong attitudes about a particular topic may become emotional when that topic is introduced. The underlying message here is try to avoid letting strong emotions and attitudes interfere with the sending or receiving of messages. If you are angry with someone, for example, you might miss the merit in what that person has to say. Calm down before proceeding with your discussion or attempting to resolve the conflict. Emotional intelligence makes a key contribution in this situation.

COMMUNICATION OVERLOAD

■ **Communication overload**
phenomenon that occurs when people are so overloaded with information that they cannot respond effectively to messages

A major communication barrier facing literate people is being bombarded with information. **Communication overload** occurs when people are so overloaded with information that they cannot respond effectively to messages. As a result, they experience work stress. Workers at many levels are exposed to so much printed, electronic, and spoken information that their capacity to absorb it is taxed. The problem is worsened when low-quality information is competing for your attention. An example is a flashing pop-up ad informing you that you have just won a free laptop computer, and all you have to do is follow a link to claim your prize. The human mind is capable of processing only a limited quantity of information at a time.

IMPROPER TIMING

Many messages do not get through to people because they are poorly timed. You have to know how to deliver a message, but you must also know *when* to deliver it. Sending a message when the receiver is distracted with other concerns or is rushing to get somewhere is a waste of time. Furthermore, the receiver may become discouraged and, therefore, will not repeat the message later.

The art of timing messages suggests not to ask for a raise when your boss is in a bad mood or to ask a new acquaintance for a date when he or she is preoccupied. However, do ask your boss for a raise when business has been good, and do ask someone for a date when you have just done something nice for that person and have been thanked.

POOR COMMUNICATION SKILLS

A message may fail to register because the sender lacks effective communication skills. The sender might garble a written or spoken message so severely that the receiver finds it impossible to understand. Also, the sender may deliver the message so poorly that the receiver does not take it seriously. A common deficiency in sending messages is to communicate with low conviction by using *wimpy* words, backpedaling, and qualifying. Part of the same idea is to use affirmative language, such as saying "when" instead of "if." Also, do not use phrases that call your integrity into question, such as "to be perfectly honest" (implying that you usually do not tell the truth). [8] To illustrate, here are three statements that send a message of low conviction to the receiver: "I think I might be able to finish this project by the end of the week." "It's possible that I could handle the assignment you have in mind." "I'll do what I can."

Another communication skill deficiency that can serve as a communication barrier is to have a regional accent so strong that it detracts from your message. Your regional accent is part of who you are, so you may not want to modify how you speak. Nevertheless, many public personalities and salespeople seek out speech training or speech therapy to avoid having an accent that detracts from their message. [9]

Communication barriers can result from deficiencies within the receiver. A common barrier is a receiver who is a poor listener. Improving listening skills is such a major strategy for improving communication skills that it receives separate mention later in this chapter.

CULTURAL AND LANGUAGE BARRIERS

Communication barriers in work and personal life can be created when the sender and receiver come from different cultures are not fluent in each other's language. Quite often cultural differences and language differences exist at the same time. An example of a cultural difference creating a barrier to communication often takes this form: A supervisor from a culture that emphasizes empowering (giving power to) employees is giving instructions to an employee from a culture that believes the boss should make all the decisions. In response to a question from the subordinate, the supervisor says, "Do what you think is best." The subordinate has a difficult time understanding the message because he or she is waiting for a firm directive from the boss.

A language communication barrier is sometimes amusing, such as an American worker complimenting another by saying "You have been working like a dog" on this project. The second person might interpret the comment as suggesting he or she must be punished to work hard. At other times language barriers cause accidents. Many foreign-language speaking construction workers in the United States encounter accidents because they do not clearly understand the instructions about danger.

To help overcome cultural and language barriers, many companies invest considerable time and money into cross-cultural training. For example, the semiconductor giant Intel has made firsthand exposure to different cultures a key part of its midlevel management training program. Under the program, about 800 midlevel managers fly to weeklong seminars in countries outside their home region. [10] In addition to learning more about another culture, many of the managers are able to enhance a second language in which they already have some proficiency.

What Are Some Ways to Build Bridges to Communication?

■ **Learning Objective 5**

With determination and awareness that communication roadblocks and barriers do exist, you can become a more effective communicator. It would be impossible to remove all barriers, but they can be minimized. The following nine techniques are helpful in building better bridges to communication.

1. Appeal to human needs and time your messages.

2. Repeat your message, using more than one channel.

3. Have an empowered attitude and be persuasive.

4. Discuss differences in frames of reference.

5. Check for comprehension and feelings through feedback.

6. Minimize defensive communication.

7. Combat communication overload.

8. Use mirroring to establish rapport.

9. Engage in small talk and constructive gossip.

APPEAL TO HUMAN NEEDS AND TIME YOUR MESSAGES

People are more receptive to messages that promise to do something for them. In other words, if a message promises to satisfy a need that is less than fully satisfied, you are likely to listen. The person in search of additional money who ordinarily does not hear low tones, readily hears the whispered message, "How would you like to earn $500 in one weekend?"

Timing a message properly is related to appealing to human needs. If you deliver a message at the right time, you are taking into account the person's mental condition at the moment. A general principle is to deliver your message when the person might be in the right frame of mind to listen. The right frame of mind includes such factors as not being preoccupied with other thoughts, not being frustrated, being in a good mood, and not being stressed out. (Of course, all this severely limits your opportunity to send a message!)

REPEAT YOUR MESSAGE, USING MORE THAN ONE CHANNEL

You can overcome many roadblocks to communication by repeating your message several times. It is usually advisable not to say the same thing so as to avoid annoying the listener with straight repetition. Repeating the message in a different form is effective in another way: The receiver may not have understood the message the first way in which it was delivered. Repetition, like any other means of overcoming communication roadblocks, does not work for all people. Many people who repeatedly hear the message "drinking and driving do not mix" are not moved by it. It is helpful to use several methods of overcoming roadblocks or barriers to communication.

A generally effective way of repeating a message is to use more than one communication channel. For example, follow up a face-to-face discussion with an e-mail message or telephone call or both. Your body can be another channel or medium to help impart your message. If you agree with someone about a spoken message, state your agreement and also shake hands over the agreement. Can you think of another channel by which to transmit a message?

HAVE AN EMPOWERED ATTITUDE AND BE PERSUASIVE

According to Sharon Lund O'Neil, University of Houston professor of business education, a person's communication effectiveness is directly proportional to his or her attitude. The point is that a positive attitude helps a person communicate better in speaking or writing or nonverbally. Being positive is a major factor in being persuasive, as mentioned previously in avoiding wimpy words. *Empowerment* here refers to the idea that the person takes charge of his or her own attitude. [11] Developing a positive attitude is not always easy. A starting point is to see things from a positive perspective, including looking for the good in people and their work. If your work is intrinsically motivating, you are likely to have a positive attitude. You would then be able to communicate about your work with the enthusiasm necessary. Figure 7-4 summarizes key ideas about persuasive communication, a topic most readers have most likely studied in the past. [12] If you can learn to implement most of the nine suggestions, you are on your way toward becoming a persuasive communicator. In addition, you will need solid facts behind you, and you will need to make skillful use of nonverbal communication.

DISCUSS DIFFERENCES IN FRAMES OF REFERENCE

Another way of understanding differences in perspectives and experiences is to recognize that people often have different frames of reference that influence how they interpret events. A **frame of reference** is a model, viewpoint, or perspective. When two people with different frameworks look at a situation, a communication

■ **Frame of reference**
model, viewpoint, or perspective

Figure   7-4

Key Principles of Persuasive Communication

1. *Know exactly what you want.* Clarify ideas first in your own mind.
2. *Never suggest an action without telling its end benefit.* Explain how your message will benefit the receiver.
3. *Get a yes response early on.* It is helpful to give the persuading session a positive tone by establishing a "yes pattern" at the outset.
4. *Use powerful words.* Sprinkle your speech with words such as *bonding with customers*, and *vaporizing the competition*.
5. *Minimize raising your pitch at the end of sentences.* Part of being persuasive is to not sound unsure and apologetic.
6. *Back up conclusions with data.* You will be more persuasive if you support your spoken and written presentations with solid data, but do not become an annoyance by overdoing it.
7. *Minimize "wimp" phrases.* (As discussed earlier in this chapter.)
8. *Avoid or minimize common language errors.* Do not say "could care less" when you mean "couldn't care less," or "orientated" when you mean "oriented."
9. *Avoid overuse of jargon and clichés.* To feel "in" and hip many workers rely heavily on jargon and clichés, such as referring to their "fave" (for *favorite*) product, or that "At the end of the day," something counts. [12]

problem may occur. For instance, one person may say, "I have just found the *ideal* potential mate." To this person, an *ideal* mate would be a person who was kind, caring, considerate, in good health, gainfully employed, and highly ethical. The listener may have a perception of an *ideal* potential mate as someone who has a superior physical appearance and is wealthy (a traditional stereotype). Until the two people understand each other's frame of reference, meaningful communication about the prospective mate is unlikely. The solution to this communication clash is to discuss the frame of reference by each side defining the perception of an *ideal* mate.

CHECK FOR COMPREHENSION AND FEELINGS THROUGH FEEDBACK

Don't be a hit-and-run communicator. Such a person drops a message and leaves the scene before he or she is sure the message has been received as intended. It is preferable to ask for feedback. Ask receivers for their understanding or interpretation of what you said. For example, you might say after delivering a message, "What is your understanding of our agreement?" Also use nonverbal indicators to gauge how well you delivered your message. A blank expression on the receiver's face might indicate no comprehension. A disturbed, agitated expression might mean that the receiver's emotions are blocking the message.

A comprehension check increases in importance when possible cultural and language barriers exist. A simple direct inquiry about comprehension is often effective, such as "Is what I said OK with you" or "Tell me what I said." A friendly facial expression should accompany such feedback checks, otherwise your inquiry will come across like a challenge.

In addition to looking for verbal comprehension and emotions when you have delivered a message, check for feelings after you have received a message. When a person speaks, we too often listen to the facts and ignore the feelings. If feelings are ignored, the true meaning and intent of the message is likely to be missed, thus creating a communication barrier. Your boss might say to you, "You never seem to take work home." To clarify what your boss means by this statement, you might ask, "Is that good or bad?" Your boss's response will give you feedback on his or her feelings about getting all your work done during regular working hours.

When you send a message, it is also helpful to express your feelings in addition to conveying the facts. For example, "Our defects are up by 12 percent [fact], and I'm quite disappointed about those results [feelings]." Because feelings contribute strongly to comprehension, you will help overcome a potential communication barrier.

MINIMIZE DEFENSIVE COMMUNICATION

■ **Defensive communication**

tendency to receive messages in such a way that one's self-esteem is protected

Distortion of information was described previously as a communication barrier. Such distortion can also be regarded as **defensive communication,** the tendency to receive messages in such a way that our self-esteem is protected. Defensive communication is also responsible for people sending messages to look good. For example, when criticized for achieving below-average sales, a store manager might shift the blame to the sales associates in her store. Overcoming the barrier of defensive communication requires two steps. First, people have to acknowledge the existence of defensive communication. Second, they have to try not to be defensive when questioned or criticized. Such behavior is not easy because of **denial,** the suppression of information we find uncomfortable. For example, the store manager previously cited would find it uncomfortable to think of herself as being responsible for below-average performance.

■ **Denial**

the suppression of information one finds uncomfortable

Defensive communication sometimes takes the form of answering the wrong question. Being touchy about a particular issue, you might regard a request for information as a criticism. David's manager might say to him, "Have you collected the data yet that we need for the trade show?" Angrily defensive because he feels criticized, David might say, "You know that I'm covering for two employees who are out ill." If he had simply said no, the boss might have said, "Oh, I just wanted to offer my help." [13]

COMBAT COMMUNICATION OVERLOAD

You can decrease the chances of suffering from communication overload by such measures as carefully organizing and sorting information before plunging ahead with reading. Speed reading may help, provided that you stop to read carefully the most relevant information. Or you can scan through hard-copy reports, magazines, and Web sites looking for key titles and words that are important to you. Recognize, however, that many subjects have to be studied carefully to derive benefit. It is often better to read thoroughly a few topics than to skim through lots of information.

Being selective about your e-mail and Internet reading goes a long way toward preventing information overload. Suppose you see an e-mail message titled "Car Lights Left On in Parking Lot." Do not retrieve the message if you distinctly remember having turned off your lights or you did not drive to work. E-mail programs and Internet search software are available to help users sort messages according to their needs. You can help prevent others from suffering from communication overload by being merciful in the frequency and length of your messages. Also, do not join the ranks of pranksters who send loads of jokes on e-mail and who widely distribute their personal blogs.

USE MIRRORING TO ESTABLISH RAPPORT

Another approach to overcoming communication barriers is to improve rapport with another person. A form of nonverbal communication called **mirroring** can be used to establish such rapport. To mirror someone is to subtly imitate that individual. The most successful mirroring technique for establishing rapport is to imitate the breathing pattern of another person. If you adjust your own breathing rate to someone else's, you will soon establish rapport with that person. Mirroring sometimes takes the form of imitating the boss in order to communicate better and win favor. Many job seekers now use mirroring to get in sync with the interviewer. Is this a technique you would be willing to try?

Mirroring takes practice to contribute to overcoming communication barriers. It is a subtle technique that requires a moderate skill level. If you mirror (or match) another person in a rigid, mechanical way, you will appear to be mocking that person. And mocking, of course, erects rather than tears down a communication barrier.

■ **Mirroring**
form of nonverbal communication to overcoming communication barriers by subtly imitating another; used to improve rapport with another person

ENGAGE IN SMALL TALK AND CONSTRUCTIVE GOSSIP

The terms *small talk* and *gossip* have negative connotations for the career-minded person with a professional attitude. Nevertheless, the effective use of small talk and gossip can help a person melt communication barriers. Small talk is important because it contributes to conversational skills, and having good conversational skills enhances interpersonal communication. Trainer Randi Fredeig says, "Small talk helps build rapport and eventually trust. It helps people find common ground on which to build conversation." [14] A helpful technique is to collect tidbits of information to use as small talk to facilitate work-related or heavy-topic conversation in personal life. Keeping informed about current events, including sports, television, and films, provides useful content for small talk.

Being a source of positive gossip brings a person power and credibility. Workmates are eager to communicate with a person who is a source of not-yet-verified developments. Having such inside knowledge enhances your status and makes you a more interesting communicator. Positive gossip would include such tidbits as mentioning that the company will be looking for workers who would want a one-year assignment in Europe or that more employees will soon be eligible for stock options. In contrast, spreading negative gossip will often erode your attractiveness to other people. [15]

How Do You Overcome Gender Barriers to Communication?

■ **Learning Objective 6**

Another strategy for overcoming communication barriers is to deal effectively with potential cultural differences. Two types of cultural differences are those related to gender (male versus female role) and those related to geographic differences. Of course, not everybody agrees that men and women are from different cultures. Here we describe gender differences, whereas cultural differences are a separate topic.

Despite the movement toward equality of sexes in the workplace, substantial interest exists in identifying differences in communication style between men and women. The basic difference between women and men, according to the research of Deborah Tannen, professor of sociolinguistics at Georgetown University, is that men emphasize and reinforce their status when they talk, whereas women downplay their status. As part of this difference, women are more concerned about building social connections. [16] People who are aware of these differences face fewer communication problems between themselves and members of the opposite sex.

As we describe these differences, recognize that they are group stereotypes. Individual differences in communication style are usually more important than group (men versus women). Here we will describe the major findings of gender differences in communication patterns. [17]

1. **Women prefer to use conversation for rapport building.** For most women, the intent of conversation is to build rapport and connections with people. It has been said that men are driven by transactions, whereas women are driven by relations. Women are, therefore, more likely to emphasize similarities, to listen intently, and to be supportive.

2. **Men prefer to use talk primarily as a means to preserve independence and status by displaying knowledge and skill.** When most men talk, they want to receive positive evaluations from others and maintain their hierarchical status within the group. Men are, therefore, more oriented to giving a *report,* whereas women are more interested in establishing *rapport.*

3. **Women want empathy, not solutions.** When women share feelings of being stressed out, they seek empathy and understanding. If they feel they have been listened to carefully, they begin to relax. When listening to the woman, the man may feel blamed for her problems or that he has failed the woman in some way. To feel useful, the man might offer solutions to the woman's problem.

4. **Men prefer to work out their problems by themselves, whereas women prefer to talk out solutions with another person.** Women look on having and sharing problems as an opportunity to build and deepen relationships. Men are more likely to look on problems as challenges they must meet on their own. The communication consequence of these differences is that men may become uncommunicative when they have a problem.

5. **Men tend to be more directive and less apologetic in their conversation, whereas women are more polite and apologetic.** Women are, therefore, more likely to frequently use the phrases "I'm sorry" and "Thank you," even when there is no need to express

apology or gratitude. Men less frequently say they are sorry for the same reason they rarely ask directions when they are lost while driving: They perceive communications as competition, and they do not want to appear vulnerable.

6. Women tend to be more conciliatory when facing differences, whereas men become more intimidating. Again, women are more interested in building relationships, whereas men are more concerned about coming out ahead.

7. Men are more interested than women in calling attention to their accomplishments or hogging recognition. One consequence of this difference is that men are more likely to dominate discussions during meetings. Another consequence is that women are more likely to help a coworker perform well. In one instance, a sales representative who had already made her sales quota for the month turned over an excellent prospect to a coworker. She reasoned, "It's somebody else's turn. I've received more than my fair share of bonuses for the month."

8. Women are more likely to use a gentle expletive, whereas men tend to be harsher. For example, if a woman locks herself out of the car, she is likely to say, "Oh dear." In the same situation, a man is likely to say, "Oh _____." (Do you think this difference really exists?)

How can this information just presented help overcome communication problems on the job? As a starting point, remember that gender differences often exist. Understanding these differences will help you interpret the communication behavior of people. For example, if a male coworker is not as polite as you would like, remember that he is simply engaging in gender-typical behavior. Do not take it personally.

A woman can remind herself to speak up more in meetings because her natural tendency might be toward holding back. She might say to herself, "I must watch out to avoid gender-typical behavior in this situation." A man might remind himself to be more polite and supportive toward coworkers. The problem is that, although such behavior is important, his natural tendency might be to skip saying thank you.

Men and women should recognize that when women talk over problems, they might not be seeking hard-hitting advice. Instead, they may simply be searching for a sympathetic ear so they can deal with the emotional aspects of the problem.

A general suggestion for overcoming gender-related communication barriers is for men to improve communication by listening with more empathy. Women can improve communication by becoming more direct.

How Can You Enhance Your Listening Skills?

▥ Learning Objective 7

Improving your receiving of messages is another part of developing better face-to-face and telephone communication skills. Unless you receive messages as they are intended, you cannot perform your job properly or be a good companion. Listening is a particularly important skill for anybody whose job involves solving problems for others because you need to gather information to understand the nature of the problem. Improving employee listening skills is important because insufficient listening is extraordinarily costly. Listening mistakes lead to reprocessing letters, rescheduling appointments, reshipping orders, and recalling defective products. Effective listening also improves interpersonal relationships because people listen to feel understood and respected. Human Relations Self-Assessment Quiz 7-2 gives you the opportunity to think through possible listening traps you may have developed. The accompanying Human Relations in Practice illustrates how being a good listener can enrich the lives of others.

Human Relations Self-Assessment Quiz **7-2**

Listening Traps

Communication specialists have identified certain behavior patterns that interfere with effective hearing and listening. After thinking carefully about each trap, check how well the trap applies to you: Not a Problem or Need Improvement. To respond to the statements accurately, visualize how you acted when you recently were in a situation calling for listening.

	Not a Problem	Need Improvement
1. **Mind reader.** You will receive limited information if you constantly think "What is this person really thinking or feeling?"	❏	❏
2. **Rehearser.** Your mental rehearsals for "Here's what I'll say next" tune out the sender.	❏	❏
3. **Filterer.** You engage in selective listening by hearing only what you want to hear. (Could be difficult to judge because the process is often unconscious.)	❏	❏
4. **Dreamer.** You drift off during a face-to-face conversation, which often leads you to an embarrassing "What did you say?" or "Could you repeat that?"	❏	❏
5. **Identifier.** If you refer everything you hear to your experience, you probably did not really listen to what was said.	❏	❏
6. **Comparer.** When you get sidetracked sizing up the sender, you are sure to miss the message.	❏	❏
7. **Derailer.** You change the subject too quickly, giving the impression that you are not interested in anything the sender has to say.	❏	❏
8. **Sparrer.** You hear what is said but quickly belittle or discount it, putting you in the same class as the derailer.	❏	❏
9. **Placater.** You agree with everything you hear just to be nice or to avoid conflict By behaving this way, you miss out on the opportunity for authentic dialogue.	❏	❏

Interpretation:

If you checked "Need Improvement" for five or more of the above statements, you are correct—your listening needs improvement! If you checked only two or fewer of the above traps, you are probably an effective listener and a supportive person.

Source: Reprinted with permission from *Messages: The Communication Skills Book* (Oakland, CA: New Harbinger Publications, 1983).

■ **Active listener**

person who listens intensely, with the goal of empathizing with the speaker

■ **Empathy**

understanding another person's point of view

A major component of effective listening is to be an **active listener.** The active listener listens intensely, with the goal of empathizing with the speaker. **Empathy** means understanding another person's point of view. If you understand the other person's paradigm, you will be a better receiver and sender of messages. Empathy does not necessarily mean that you sympathize with the other person. For example, you may understand why some people are forced to beg in the streets, but you may have very little sympathy for their plight.

A useful way of showing empathy is to accept the sender's figure of speech. By so doing, the sender feels understood and accepted. Also, if you reject the person's figure of speech by rewording it, the sender may become defensive. Many people use the figure of speech "I'm stuck" when they cannot accomplish a task. You can facilitate smooth communication by a response such as, "What can I do to help you get unstuck?" If you respond with something like, "What can I do to help you think more clearly?" the person is forced to change mental channels and may become defensive. [18]

Human Relations in Practice

Big Success Tony Wainwright Listened Well

Barry Farber, top-rated sales, management, and motivation speaker, reflects fondly about a person he admired, in these terms: "I met Tony Wainwright, chairman of a $2.5 billion corporation, author, playwright, incredible philanthropist, and one of the world's foremost salespeople. He became my greatest mentor and one of my best friends.

"Tony passed away not long ago. I miss him every day. Shortly after he died, I began to wonder: What set him apart from the other people who tried to do what he did but failed? As I thought about Tony's life—not just his sales life, but about everything he did—I realized that what made him great was his uncanny ability to listen. He listened—truly listened to everyone he met.

"When you had a conversation with Tony, he made you feel as if your ideas were worth their weight in gold. (Not that everything you said was right—if you were on the wrong track, he would let you know.) He would make you feel special, as if you were the most important appointment he had in his life, and his only purpose was to find out what was on your mind. Then he'd tell you how you could make your idea 20 times larger than anything you'd conceived. His belief in you was so strong that you had to believe it, too. That's what made him such a great salesperson: He sold you on yourself."

Source: Abridged from Barry Farber, "All Ears? Sales Success: In Business and in Life, Learning to Listen Is One of the Most Important Skills You Can Develop," *Entrepreneur,* April 2004, pp. 83–84.

As a result of listening actively, the listener can feed back to the speaker what he or she thinks the speaker meant. Feedback of this type relies on both verbal and nonverbal communication. Feedback is also important because it facilitates two-way communication. To be an active listener, it is also important to **paraphrase,** or repeat in your own words what the sender says, feels, and means. You might feel awkward the first several times you paraphrase. Therefore, try it with a person with whom you feel comfortable. With some practice, it will become a natural part of your communication skill kit. Here is an example of how you might use paraphrasing:

■ **Paraphrase**

repeating in one's own words what a sender says, feels, and means

Other Person: I'm getting ticked off at working so hard around here. I wish somebody else would pitch in and do a fair day's work.

You: You're saying that you do more than your fair share of the tough work in our department.

Other Person: You bet. Here's what I think we should be doing about it. . . .

Life coach Sophronia Scott advises that, after you have paraphrased, it is sometimes helpful to ask the person you listened to whether your impression of what he or she said is correct. Your goal is not to make others repeat themselves but to extend the conversation so you can obtain more useful details. [19]

To help become an active listener, consider several additional suggestions. If feasible, keep papers and your computer screen out of sight when listening to somebody else. Having distractions in sight creates the temptation to glance away from the message sender. Avoid answering a cell telephone call unless you are anticipating an emergency call. At the start of your conversation, notice the other person's eye color to help you establish eye contact. (But don't keep staring at his or her eyes!) A major technique of active listening is to ask questions rather than making conclusive statements. Asking questions provides more useful information. Suppose a teammate is late with data you need to complete your analysis. Instead of saying, "I must have your input by Thursday afternoon," try, "When will I get your input?"

Be sure to let others speak until they have finished. Do not interrupt by talking about yourself, jumping in with advice, or offering solutions unless requested. [20] A final suggestion is not to smile continuously during your conversation. Although you may appear friendly, the smiling could also be interpreted as you not taking the other person seriously. [21]

Research with employees from a Swedish insurance company provides some evidence that listening skills can be improved. A small group of employees received 24 hours of training in *reflective listening* that involves empathizing with the listener and then paraphrasing what he or she said (as in active listening). A 27-year-old female undergraduate psychology student was paid to act as a customer in evaluations of the listening skills before and after training. She acted in the roles of (1) a customer who was waiting for the results of whiplash injury investigation and (2) a person who had been accused by her insurance agent of having staged a burglary. The student dealt with both the trained group and an untrained, or comparison, group. She rated the listening skills of the employees, using a scale provided by the experimenters.

Later, the employees were also rated on their listening skills based on audiotapes with actual customers. The judges this time were a group of 54 psychology students. The results of the study showed that training increased reflective listening and that these skills were transferred to work with live customers. However, training did not result in higher evaluations of their conversation skills. [22] The training in reflective listening provided some assistance to the insurance agents, even if their conversational skill did not appear to be better.

In this chapter we have described many aspects of how people communicate, including gender-specific tendencies. How you combine verbal and nonverbal communication becomes part of your **personal communication style,** or your unique approach to sending and receiving information. Your personal communication style is a major component of your personality because it differentiates you from others. Hundreds of styles are possible, including the following:

■ **Personal communication style**
verbal and nonverbal communication style
for a unique approach to sending and
receiving information

- Katherine speaks loudly, smiles frequently, and moves close to people when speaking. Her communication style might be described as aggressive.

- Oscar speaks softly, partially covers his mouth with his hand while talking, and looks away from others. His communication style might be defined as passive or wimpy.

- Tim speaks rapidly, uses a colorful vocabulary, smiles frequently, and makes sweeping gestures. His communication style might be defined as flamboyant.

Concept Review and Reinforcement

Summary and Review

Communication is the sending and receiving of messages. Therefore, almost anything that takes place in work and personal life involves communication. The steps involved in communication are sending, transmission over a channel, and decoding.

Nonverbal communication, or silent messages, are important parts of everyday communication. Nonverbal communication includes the following:

- environment or setting in which the message is sent
- distance from the other person
- posture
- hand gestures
- facial expressions and eye contact
- voice quality
- personal appearance

An advanced application of nonverbal communication is to help combat drug trafficking and terrorism by spotting nervous or threatening behavior.

Communication is a vehicle for building relationships. We establish relationships along two primary dimensions: dominate–subordinate and cold–warm.

- In the process of communicating, we attempt to dominate or subordinate.
- We indicate whether we want to dominate or subordinate by the way we speak or write, or by nonverbal signals we send.
- The four combinations of dominate–subordinate, and cold–warm lead to different types of relationships—impersonal, accepting, supportive, or personal.

Roadblocks to communication are most likely to occur when messages are complex or emotional or clash with the receiver's mental set. Communication roadblocks include

- limited understanding of people
- one-way communication
- semantics
- credibility of the sender and mixed signals
- distortion of information
- different perspectives and experiences
- emotions and attitudes
- communication overload
- improper timing
- poor communication skills
- cultural and language barriers

Strategies to overcome communication roadblocks include

- appealing to human need and timing your messages
- repeating your message using more than one channel
- having an empowered attitude and being persuasive
- discussing differences in paradigms
- checking for comprehension and feelings
- minimizing defensive communication
- combating communication overload
- using mirroring to establish rapport
- engaging in small talk and constructive gossip

Some opinion and evidence exists about gender differences in communication style. For example, women prefer to use conversation for rapport building, and men prefer to use talk primarily as a means to preserve independence and status by displaying knowledge and skill. Understanding gender differences will help you interpret the communication behavior of people.

Improving your receiving of messages is another part of developing better communication skills. Unless you receive messages as intended, you cannot perform your job properly or be a good companion. A major component of effective listening is to be an active listener. The active listener uses empathy and can feed back to the speaker what he or she thinks the speaker meant. Active listening also involves paraphrasing what the speaker says, feels, and means. After paraphrasing it is helpful to clarify if your impression was correct. Another major technique of active listening is to ask questions rather than making conclusive statements.

How you combine verbal and nonverbal communication becomes your personal communication style.

Check your Understanding

1. Based on Figure 7-1, describe one way in which you could use interpersonal communication to build a better relationship.
2. How can knowing the three major steps in communication help a person communicate more effectively?
3. Many people contend they communicate much more formally when on the job and much more informally (including using a more limited vocabulary) when among family members and friends. What do you see as the potential advantages and disadvantages of using two communication styles?
4. Why is nonverbal communication so important for the effectiveness of a manager or sales representative?
5. In what way is a handshake a form of nonverbal communication?
6. What potential problems do you see in security personnel at airports and border crossings relying heavily on nonverbal communication indicators to bring people in for additional questioning?
7. In what way might an e-mail message contain nonverbal communication?
8. Based on your own observations, identify a term or phrase in the workplace that creates semantic problems.
9. So what if differences in communication patterns between men and women have been identified? What impact will this information have on your communication with men and women?
10. How would you rate the persuasive communication skills of the current president of the United States? Have you any suggestions as to how he or she could improve?

Web Corner

Effective listening: www.womensmedia.com/seminar-listening.html

Exploring nonverbal communication: http://nonverbal.ucsc.edu/

Internet Skill Builder

Infoplease offers some practical suggestions for improving your listening skills that both support and supplement the ideas offered in this chapter. Infoplease divides listening into three basic steps: hearing, understanding, and judging. Visit the site at www.infoplease.com/homework/listeningskills1.html.

Developing Your Human Relations Skills

Human Relations Application Exercises

Applying Human Relations Exercise 7-1

I Want a Raise

The purpose of this exercise is to practice your persuasive skills using a topic of interest to many people—obtaining a salary increase. One by one, students make a presentation in front of the class, presenting a persuasive argument why they merit a salary increase. The instructor will decide whether to use a handful of volunteers or the entire class. The audience represents the boss. The student will first explain his or her job title and key responsibilities. (Use your imagination here.) Next, make a three-minute convincing argument as to why you merit a salary increase and perhaps indicate how much you want. You will probably have about 15 minutes to prepare, inside or outside of class.

After the presentations, volunteers will offer feedback on the effectiveness of selected presentations. During the presentations of the other students, make a few notes about the presenter's effectiveness. You may need a couple of minutes between presenters to make your notes. Consider these factors:

- Overall, how convincing was the presenter? If you were the boss, would you give him or her the requested salary increase?
- Which techniques of persuasion did he or she use?
- What aspect of the presentation was unconvincing or negative?

What lessons did you take away from this exercise about persuasive communication?

Applying Human Relations Exercise 7-2

Active Listening

Before conducting the following role plays, review the suggestions for active listening in this chapter. The suggestion about paraphrasing the message is particularly relevant because the role plays involve emotional topics.

The elated coworker

One student plays the role of a coworker who has just been offered a promotion to supervisor of another department. She will be receiving 10 percent higher pay and be able to travel overseas twice a year for the company. She is eager to describe the full details of her good fortune to a coworker. Another student plays the role of the coworker to whom the first coworker wants to describe her

good fortune. The second worker decides to listen intently to the first worker. Other class members will rate the second student on his or her listening ability.

The discouraged coworker

One student plays the role of a coworker who has just been placed on probation for poor performance. His boss thinks that his performance is below standard and that his attendance and punctuality are poor. He is afraid that if he tells his girlfriend, she will leave him. He is eager to tell his tale of woe to a coworker. Another student plays the role of a coworker he corners to discuss his problems. The second worker decided to listen intently to his problems but is pressed for time. Other

181

class members will rate the second student on his or her listening ability.

When evaluating the active listening skills of the role players, consider using the following evaluating factors, on a scale of 1 (low) to 5 (high):

Evaluation Factor	Rating 1 2 3 4 5
1. Maintained eye contact	
2. Showed empathy	
3. Paraphrased what the other person said	
4. Focused on other person instead of being distracted	
5. Asked questions	
6. Let other person speak until he or she was finished	

Total Points: _____

Human Relations Case Study 7-1

The Scrutinized Team Member Candidate

HRmanager.com is a human resources management firm that provides human resource services such as payroll, benefits administration, affirmative action programs, and technical training to other firms. By signing up with HRmanager, other firms can outsource part or all of their human resources functions. During its seven years of operation, HRmanager has grown from 3 to 50 employees and last year had total revenues of $21 million.

Teams perform most of the work, led by a rotating team leader. Each team member takes an 18-month turn at being a team leader. CEO and founder Jerry Clune regards the four-person new ventures team as vital for the future of the company. In addition to developing ideas for new services, the team members are responsible for obtaining clients for any new service they propose that Clune approves. The new ventures team thus develops and sells new services. After the service is launched and working well, the sales group is responsible for developing more clients.

As with other teams at HRmanager, the team members have a voice as to who is hired to join their team. In conjunction with Clune, the new ventures team decided it should expand to five members. The team posted the job opening for a new member on an Internet recruiting service, ran classified ads in the local newspaper, and also asked present employees for referrals. One of the finalists for the position was Gina Cleveland, a 27-year-old business graduate. In addition to interviewing with Clune and the two company vice presidents, Cleveland spent one-half day with the new ventures team, breakfast and lunch

included. About two-and-one-half hours of the time was spent in a team interview in which Gina sat in a conference room with the four team members.

The team members agreed that Cleveland appeared to be a strong candidate on paper. Her education and experience were satisfactory, her résumé was impressive, and she presented herself well during a telephone-screening interview. After Cleveland completed her time with the new ventures team, Lauren Nielsen, the team leader, suggested that the group hold a debriefing session. The purpose of the session would be to share ideas about Cleveland's suitability for joining the team.

Nielsen commented, "It seems like we think that Gina is a strong candidate based on her credentials and what she said. But I'm a big believer in nonverbal communication. Studying Gina's body language can give us a lot of valuable information. Let's each share our observations about what Gina's body language tells us she is *really* like. I'll go first."

Lauren: I liked the way Gina looked so cool and polished when she joined us for breakfast. She's got all the superficial movements right to project self-confidence. But did anybody else notice how she looked concerned when she had to make a choice from the menu? She finally did choose a ham-and-cheese omelet, but she raised her voice at the end of the sentence when she ordered it. I got the hint that Gina is not very confident.

I also noticed Gina biting her lips a little when we asked her how creative she thought she was. I know that Gina said she was creative and gave us an example of a creative project she completed. Yet nibbling at her lips like that suggests she's not filled with firepower.

Michael: I didn't make any direct observations about Gina's being self-confident or not, but I did notice something that could be related. I think Gina is on a power trip, and this could indicate high or low self-confidence. Did anybody notice how Gina put her hands on her hips when she was standing up? That's a pure and clear signal of somebody who wants to be in control. Her haircut is almost the same length and style as most women who've made it to the top in Fortune 500 companies.

Another hint I get of Gina's power trip is the way she eyed the check in the restaurant at lunch. I could see it in her eyes that she really wanted to pay for the entire team. That could mean a desire to control and show us that she is very important. Do we want someone on the team with such a strong desire to control?

Brenda: I observed a different picture of Gina based on her nonverbal communication. She dressed just right for the occasion—not too conservatively, not too far business casual. This tells me she can fit into our environment. Did you notice how well groomed her shoes were? This tells you she is well organized and good at details. Her attaché case was a soft, inviting leather. If she were really into power and control, she would carry a hard vinyl or aluminum attaché case. I see Gina as a confident and assertive person who could blend right into our team.

Larry: I hope that because I'm last, I'm not too influenced by the observations that you three have shared so far. My take is that Gina looks great

on paper but that she may have a problem in being a good team player. She's too laid back and distant. Did you notice her handshake? She gave me the impression of wanting to have the least possible physical contact with me. Her handshake was so insincere. I could feel her hand and arm withdrawing from me as she shook my hand.

I also couldn't help noticing that Gina did not lean much toward us during the round-table discussion. Do you remember how she would pull her chair back ever so slightly when we got into a heavy discussion? I interpreted that as a sign that Gina does not want to be part of a close-knit group.

Lauren: As you have probably noticed, I've been typing as fast as I can with my laptop, taking notes on what you have said. We have some mixed observations here, and I want to summarize and integrate them before we make a decision. I'll send you an e-mail with an attached file of my summary observations by tomorrow morning. Make any changes you see fit and get back to me. After we have finished evaluating Gina carefully, we will be able to make our recommendations to Jerry [Clune].

Questions

1. To what extent are new ventures team members making an appropriate use of nonverbal communication to size up Gina Cleveland?
2. Which team member do you think made the most realistic interpretation of nonverbal behavior? Why?
3. Should Lauren, the team leader, have told Gina in advance that the team would be scrutinizing her nonverbal behavior? Justify your answer.

Human Relations Case Study 7-2

The Dental Floss Communication Challenge

Claudia Telfair has worked as a dental hygienist for five years in the same large dental practice in suburban Columbus, Ohio. She treats patients about 25 hours per week. In

her words, "If I work too much more than 25 hours per week I'm liable to get tendonitis and carpal tunnel syndrome. All that precision scraping takes a toll on my right hand, and to some extent on my left hand. Hovering over patients can also give me back pains, if I do it for too long each week.

"I feel that my work is so important that I am willing to put up with a little physical pain to help my patients have healthy teeth and gums."

"You would then say that the biggest frustration in your work is its physical demands?" asked the case researcher.

"I never said that. You said that," replied Telfair. "The part of my job with the biggest impact on the health of patients is getting across my message about healthy habits to prevent tooth decay and gum disease. I lecture my patients. I demonstrate how they should be brushing and flossing, and how they should use soft wood plaque removers [such as Stim-u-Dents]. I give out samples.

"I do everything I can think of to convince my patients to take good care of their teeth and gums between cleaning appointments."

"What is so frustrating about what you have just described?"

"The frustration is that my patients don't seem to listen. They smile, they nod in agreement, and they pack the samples. Yet four months later when the patients return, it appears that most of them are engaging in the same old sloppy dental habits. They continue with superficial brushing with an old toothbrush instead of using an electric one. It looks like they forgot my message about using wooden plaque removers. Yet flossing is the least used preventive treatment of them all."

"When you ask patients why they neglect flossing between their cleaning appointments, what do they say?" asked the case researcher.

"I hear more excuses than you get from violators in traffic court," said Telfair. "Some of the typical excuses are that the patients forget, that they are too busy, and that flossing is too painful. A patient told me the other day that he dislikes flossing because the ritual is so ugly and weird."

"What do you tell the patients when you observe that they are not following your advice?"

"I usually just tell them that are doing a poor job of taking care of their teeth and gums. Also, I will usually give them more samples of floss and plaque remover so they will be reminded to do better. Sometimes I give them another brochure about an electric tooth brush.

"I guess you could say that I'm doing a much better job treating tooth and gum problems than preventing them."

Questions

1. What communication problems is Claudia Telfair facing in her role as a dental hygienist?
2. What communication errors might Telfair be making?
3. Offer Telfair a couple of suggestions to help her accomplish her goal of being more effective at preventing dental and gum problems, based on your knowledge of interpersonal communication.

Skill-Building Exercise

The Dental Hygienist and Dental Patient Role Play

One student sits on a chair pretending to be a dental patient who does a sloppy job of dental care, such as brushing regularly and flossing. Another student plays the role of dental hygienist Claudia. (She can use a pencil or pen to simulate a metal gum scraper.) With the patient in the chair, engage in a dialogue about the importance of using dental floss. Claudia wants this patient to practice much better dental hygiene, whereas the patient is somewhat skeptical about her advice. Perhaps two or three different pairs can conduct the role play in front of the class. Other class members will observe the effectiveness of the communication episode in terms of Claudia getting her message across. Here are several questions you might include in your analysis of Claudia's communication effectiveness:

■ Did she attempt to listen carefully to that patient's side of the story?

■ Did she give ask the question while the patient was being scraped and, therefore, had difficulty in responding?

■ Did she do an effective job of selling the patient on the benefits of her message?

■ Did she establish a warm supportive climate for communication?

REFERENCES

1. Adapted from Anne Field, "Coach, Help Me Out with This Interview," *Business Week*, October 22, 2001, p. 134E2.
2. Rich Sorenson, Grace De Bord, and Ida Ramirez, *Business and Management Communication: A Guide Book*, 4th ed. (Upper Saddle River, NJ: Prentice Hall, 2001), pp. 6–10.
3. Edward T. Hall, "Proxemics—A Study of Man's Spatial Relationships," in *Man's Image in Medicine and Anthropology* (New York: International Universities Press, 1963); Pauline E. Henderson, "Communication without Words," *Personnel Journal*, January 1989, pp. 28–29.
4. Jeffrey Jacobi, *The Vocal Advantage* (Upper Saddle River, NJ: Prentice Hall, 1996).
5. Genviève Coutu-Bouchard, "L'effet Pygmalion," *Montréal Campus*, April 24, 2002, p. 11.
6. Ann Davis, Joseph Pereira, and William M. Bulkeley, "Silent Signals: Security Concerns Bring New Focus on Body Language," *The Wall Street Journal*, August 15, 2002, pp. A1, A6.
7. Although this story has been widely circulated, its origin has yet to be identified.
8. "Weed Out Wimpy Words," *WorkingSMART*, March 2000, p. 2; George Walther cited in "Power Up Your Persuasiveness," *Executive Leadership*, July 2003, p. 1.
9. Joe Neumaier, "Sweet Sounds of Success: Dialect Coach Sam Chwat Accents Hollywood's Best," *USA Weekend*, July 12–14, 2002, p. 12.
10. Ed Frauenheim, "Crossing Cultures," *Workforce Management*, November 21, 2005, pp. 1, 26.
11. Sharon Lund O'Neill, "An Empowered Attitude Can Enhance Communication Skills," *Business Education Forum*, April 1998, pp. 28–30.
12. For more details about point 9 see Brian Fugere, Chelsea Hardaway, and Jon Warshawsky, *Why Business People Speak Like Idiots* (New York: Free Press, 2005).
13. Suzette Haden Elgin, *Genderspeak* (New York: Wiley, 1993).
14. Quoted in Jacquelyn Lynn, "Small Talk, Big Results," *Entrepreneur*, August 1999, p. 30.
15. Nancy B. Kurland and Lisa Hope Pelled, "Passing the Word: Toward a Model of Gossip and Power in the Workplace," *Academy of Management Review*, April 2000, pp. 428–438; Samuel Greengard, "Gossip Poisons Business: HR Can Stop It," *Workforce*, July 2001, pp. 24–28.
16. Deborah Tannen, *Talking from Nine to Five* (New York: William Morrow, 1994).
17. Deborah Tannen, *You Just Don't Understand* (New York: Ballentine, 1990); John Gray, *Men Are from Mars, Women Are from Venus* (New York: HarperCollins, 1992); Deborah Tannen, "The Power of Talk: Who Gets Heard and Why," *Harvard Business Review*, September–October 1995, pp. 138–148.
18. Daniel Araoz, "Right-Brain Management (RBM): Part 2," *Human Resources Forum*, September 1989, p. 4.
19. Cited in "Five Keys to Effective Listening," *Black Enterprise*, March 2005, p. 113.
20. Deb Koen, "Work World Needs Good Listeners," *Rochester (NY) Democrat and Chronicle*, November 3, 2002, p. 14E.
21. "Train Yourself in the Art of Listening," *Positive Leadership*, sample issue, Summer 2000, p. 10.
22. Erik Rautalinko and Hans-Olof Lisper, "Effects of Training Reflective Listening in a Corporate Setting," *Journal of Business and Psychology*, Spring 2004, pp. 281–299.

8

Communication in the Workplace

Learning Objectives

Outline

After studying the information and doing the exercises in this chapter, you should be able to:

1 Describe the formal channels of communication within organizations.

2 Describe the informal channels of communication within organizations.

3 Identify the challenges to interpersonal communication created by information technology.

4 Be ready to do an effective job of conducting or participating in a business meeting.

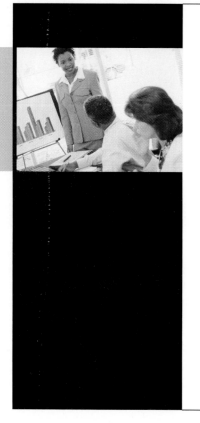

The youngest CEO in the National Basketball Association (NBA), Brett Yormark, 39, is arguably the hardest-working too. He has signed 84 new corporate sponsors in slightly more than a year on the job. The East Rutherford, New Jersey, team brought in an estimated $86 million in a recent season. On a typical workday morning, he wakes up at 3:35 A.M. in his Franklin, New Jersey, home after about three hours sleep. He stops at Dunkin' Donuts during his commute. Clad in gym gear, he arrives at Nets' corporate office. At 4:10 A.M. he responds to 60 messages and reads through a thick stack of yesterday's e-mails, which his assistant has printed out for him. After running 3.4 miles on the treadmill downstairs while watching ESPN, he showers and gets dressed. At 7:35 A.M. he has a biweekly direct-report meeting. At 9:25 A.M., over the phone, he placates a disgruntled season ticket holder. At 12:30 P.M. he checks his Blackberry and then has lunch.

At 1:15 P.M. Yormark has a meeting at NBA headquarters in midtown to brainstorm ways to increase the rate of renewals on season tickers. At 8:40 P.M. he is watching tonight's game against Orlando in the Meadowlands arena. At 9 P.M. he does some work in his basement office, checking more messages. Toward the end of the game he gathers his key team members to have a strategy meeting under the stands. At 10 P.M. he checks his Blackberry at Chill, a night club in Mill Valley. There's an e-mail from a tech staffer working to solve a customer problem. [1]

The dizzying workday of the energetic CEO described illustrates many aspects of human relations. Of particular relevance here, the story illustrates how communications is such a key part of a businessperson's life, from checking e-mails to resolving conflicts over the phone.

Effective communication contributes to organization success in many ways, such as keeping employees informed as to what needs to be accomplished and identifying problems before they cripple a company. For example, a lab technician might quickly warn her manager that a new food supplement being sold by the company had an unacceptably high level of mercury, thereby avoiding a recall and lawsuits. Another example of the benefit of effective communication is that workers kept up to date about key issues that affect them are much more likely to stay on the job. According to a survey of 2,600 employees by Mercer Human Resources Consulting, only 15 percent of those who enjoy good workplace communication are thinking about finding new employment. In contrast, 41 percent of employees in companies that limit communication are thinking of leaving. [2]

In this chapter we study communication in organizations from several perspectives: formal and informal communication channels, the communication challenges created by information technology, and dealing effectively with meetings.

What Are the Formal Channels of Communication Within Organizations?

■ **Learning Objective 1**

■ **Formal communication channels**
the official pathways for sending information inside and outside an organization

Messages in organizations are sent over both formal (official) and informal (unofficial) channels. **Formal communication channels** are the official pathways for sending information inside and outside an organization. The primary source of information about formal channels is the organization chart. It indicates the channels the messages are supposed to follow. By carefully following an organization chart, an entry-level worker would know how to transmit a message to someone in the executive suite. Formal communication channels are often bypassed through information technology. Using e-mail, anybody can send a message to anybody else in the organization. During an emergency, workers are also likely to bypass formal channels, such as a technician telephoning the plant manager directly about a chemical spill.

Two relatively recent formal channels of communication are procedures for crisis management and blogs. We also look at communication directions.

COMMUNICATION CHANNELS FOR MANAGING CRISES

Many companies have developed formal communication channels for managing crises, such as fires and explosions, massive product recalls, financial scandals, and terrorist attacks. One of the most crucial parts of a disaster plan is how to communicate with the company's workforce during a crisis. A key part of the challenge is to locate and reestablish contact with employees who may be scattered in the streets or stranded in airports around the world. Aon Corporation, an international insurance, risk-management, and consulting company, improvised to use its Web site as an official communication channel during the crisis of September 11. A company official said, "With everything else down, we decided to use the company Web site. That seemed like the only option we had." [3]

Web sites have now become the premier formal crisis communication channel. Formal channels during a crisis are necessary for informing employees about a disaster, work assignments, health services and grief counseling, and assistance in returning to work. Other formal communication channels during a crisis include the television or radio.

COMPANY BLOGS AS FORMAL CHANNELS

The company blog (or more precisely a Web log or journal) is a rapidly growing form of formal communication, paralleling the surging use of blogs in private life. Blogs originated by consumers are often used to complain about products or services and less often to compliment a company. Blogs were first used by business to communicate with customers in a personal, direct manner and perhaps form a bond with them. [4]

The blog communicates business information but with a soft, human touch. For example, a product manager for bicycle helmets might write, "Just the other day, I heard from a mother of a six year old in our housing development. Little Jason complained about having to wear a helmet simply to ride his tricycle around the neighborhood. But then he was hit lightly by a car and thrown five feet. He escaped with a few scratches and bruises but no head injury. I'm so happy for Jason and so thankful to our fine staff who built that bike helmet to get the job done."

A company might also use a blog to communicate its side of the story in response to outside criticism, such as the ***http://blogs.sun.com*** launched by Jonathan Schwartz, president and chief operating officer (COO) of Sun Microsystems. For example, one time he complained about a negative magazine article written about the company and criticism by Intel executives. [5]

The company blog can also be used to communicate with employees in a relaxed, casual tone. Employees, as well as customers, can interact with the Web log by providing comments that can be a source of valuable feedback to management and communicated directly to other visitors to the site.

An individual who establishes a blog on his or her own to chat about the employer creates an *informal* rather than a formal channel—when the blog is not authorized by the company. Bloggers who publish negative information about their employer, or publish unprofessional photos of themselves, are liable to being fired. The rationale behind these firings is that the employee is making unwarranted use of his or her association with the company. To prevent problems of negativity appearing on personal blogs by employees, many companies now establish guidelines, such as "no disclosure of negative information about the company," "no nude photos," or "no profanity."

COMMUNICATION DIRECTIONS

■ **Downward communication**
the transmission of messages from higher to lower levels in an organization

■ **Upward communication**
the transmission of messages from lower to higher levels in an organization

■ **Open-door policy**
communication channel that is structured upward that allows employees to bring a gripe to top management's attention without first checking with the employee's manager

Another aspect of formal communications in the directions messages follow in the organization. Messages in organizations travel in four primary directions: downward, upward, horizontally, and diagonally. **Downward communication** is the flow of messages from one level to a lower level. It is typified by a middle manager giving orders to a lower-level supervisor or by top management sending announcements to employees. Information is sometimes transmitted from a higher level to a lower one without the sender inviting a response. When this occurs, the feedback built into two-way communication is lost.

Upward communication is the transmission of messages from lower to higher levels in an organization. It is the most important channel for keeping management informed about problems within the organization. Simply talking regularly to employees improves upward communication. An **open-door policy** is a more structured upward communication channel that allows employees to bring a gripe to top management's attention without first checking with their manager. Managers who are willing to listen to bad news without becoming upset at the messenger are more likely to receive upward communication. Alan Lafley, the chief executive at Procter & Gamble is recognized for his ability to listen to problems without becoming vindictive. As a result, he often receives early warning of impending problems. Upward communication is more widely used in less bureaucratic firms than in highly bureaucratic firms. Almost all executives contend that they value upward communication, regardless of whether the majority employees agree.

Horizontal communication is sending messages among people at the same organization level. It often takes the form of coworkers from the same department talking to one another. Horizontal communication is the basis for cooperation. When coworkers are not sharing information with and responding to one another, they are likely to fall behind schedule. Also, efforts are duplicated and quality suffers. Another type of horizontal communication takes place when managers communicate with other managers at the same level.

Diagonal communication is the transmission of messages to higher or lower organizational levels in different departments. Because these pathways are infrequently spelled out on the organization chart, diagonal communication is usually an *informal* channel. A typical diagonal communication event occurs when a manager from one department contacts a lower-ranking person from a department outside of his or her chain of command. Diagonal communication becomes an *informal* pathway.

What Are the Informal Channels of Communication Within Organizations

■ **Learning Objective 2**

■ **Informal communication channels**
unofficial networks of channels that supplement the formal channels

Informal communication channels are the unofficial network of channels that supplements the formal channels. Most of these informal channels arise out of necessity. For example, people will sometimes depart from the official communication channels to consult with a person with specialized knowledge. Suppose an administrative professional in the inventory control department spoke and wrote fluent German. Employees from other departments would regularly consult her when they were dealing with a customer from Germany. Here we study several aspects of informal communication channels: networks of contacts, the grapevine, rumors, chance encounters, and management by walking around.

NETWORKS OF CONTACTS

Perhaps the most useful aspect of informal communication channels is that they enable workers to accomplish many tasks they would not be able to if they relied exclusively on formal channels. The network of contacts often means in practice that an individual worker might be in touch with people in his or her formal and informal channels to get work accomplished. However, the emphasis is on the informal communication channels.

Some observers believe that the network of contacts explains how work really gets accomplished. According to this viewpoint, all companies have hidden **shadow organizations** where much of the real work gets accomplished. The shadow organization is revealed by *network analysis* which traces who talks to whom. [6] For example, in most firms there are "tech fixers" who supplement—but do not replace—the technical support center. Suppose a worker is stuck with an information technology problem, such as a document being filled with mysterious codes that he or she cannot eliminate. The worker might get in immediate contact with a tech fixer (whose formal job responsibilities do not include solving technical problems outside his or her department) for help with the problem.

Your network of contacts can also extend outside the organization. A real estate developer, for example, might have contacts inside a bank who inform him of upcoming foreclosures. In this way the developer can make an early appraisal of the property to be ready with an effective bid on the foreclosed property. The mortgage specialist in the bank is part of the real estate developer's network of contacts.

At Fannie Mae, a private, shareholder-owned company based in Washington, DC, network analysis is used to enhance collaboration among workers. "We want to break down silos (separate self-contained departments)," says David Flaxman, an executive in charge of eSolutions products and services. "By analyzing their personal networks, employees establish new relationships across the organization. This helps employees to be more effectively share information and solve complex problems." [7] An important output of network analysis is to find an employee working someplace else in the organization who might have skills or knowledge that can help perform your work well. A Fannie Mae specialist who purchases mortgages from banks with many customers with poor credit ratings might need the expertise of someone else at Fannie Mae who has faced this challenge.

The networks under discussion help explain why changes in organizational structure (which specifies the formal communication channels) sometimes do not change the quantity and quality of work that gets accomplished. The same pattern of networks that workers use to accomplish their tasks may not change despite the changes on the organization chart. [8]

THE GRAPEVINE

The **grapevine** is the major informal communication channel in organizations. The grapevine refers to the tangled pathways that can distort information. The term referred originally to the snarled telegraph lines on the battlefield during the U.S. Civil War. The grapevine is often thought to be used primarily for passing along negative rumors and negative gossip. Gossips sometimes use the Internet and e-mail as

■ **Shadow organizations**
where much of the real work gets accomplished, the shadow organization is revealed by network analysis, which traces who talks to whom

■ **Grapevine**
major informal communication channel in organizations; the grapevine refers to the tangled pathways that can distort information

channels for transmitting negative gossip. When left to fester, gossip can cause individuals chagrin and also lead to turnover, conflict, and lawsuits. Gossip often increases when workers are bored or lack ample information about company events. Managers can often stop negative gossip by confronting the source of the gossip, demanding that he or she stop. Positive gossip, however, makes a contribution to the organization because trading information strengthens ties among workers and humanizes the workplace. Gossip can be viewed as the glue that binds social groups together. [9] An example of positive gossip would be, "I heard management is considering adding a paid holiday next year. Everyone with five or more service years gets his or her birthday off from work."

The grapevine is sometimes used purposely to disseminate information along informal lines. For example, top management might want to hint to employees that certain work will be outsourced (sent to another company or outside the country) unless the employees become more productive. Although the plans are still tentative, feeding them into the grapevine may result in improved motivation and productivity.

Rumors

Rumors are an important informal communication force within organizations, and they tend to thrive in organizations with poor corporate communication, such as a penitentiary. Respondents to a worldwide survey agreed that rumors are an important early source of information. To ensure that rumors are more helpful than harmful, management might do the following:

- Be wary of vague communication, which fosters misinterpretation and anxiety.

- Promote healthy, accurate communication. Encourage employees to discuss rumors with their manager.

- Avoid concealing bad news. Promise employees that they will receive accurate information as soon as it becomes available.

- Correct erroneous communications that relate to organizational policies, practices, and strategic plans. [10]

Consultant and author Tom E. Jones reinforces the importance of open communication to combat rumors. He recommends that unless the company is bound by some legal restriction, top-level management should tell everyone what they know about the facts. "Don't wait until you have all the details. Just get the truth out there fast." [11]

A problem with inaccurate rumors is that they can distract workers, create anxiety, and decrease productivity. A frequent by-product of false rumors about company relocation or a pending merger is that some of the more talented workers leave in the hopes of more stable employment.

CHANCE ENCOUNTERS AND MANAGEMENT BY WALKING AROUND

Another informal channel of significance is *chance encounters.* Unscheduled informal contact between managers and employees can be an efficient and effective communication channel. John P. Kotter, professor of leadership at Harvard Business School, found that effective managers do not confine their communication to formal meetings. [12] Instead, they collect valuable information during chance encounters. Spontaneous communication events may occur in the cafeteria, near the water fountain, in the halls, and on the elevator. In only two minutes, the manager might obtain the information that would typically be solicited in a 30-minute meeting or through a series of e-mail exchanges. A representative question might be, "What seems to be the buzz on our newest product?"

One important communication channel can be classified as either formal or informal. **Management by walking around** involves managers intermingling freely with workers on the shop floor or in the office, as well as with customers. By spending time in personal contact with employees, the manager enhances open communication. During contacts with employees the manager will often ask questions such as, "How are you enjoying your work?" or "What bottlenecks have you encountered today?" Because management by walking around is systematic, it could be considered formal. However, a manager who circulates throughout the company is not following the formal paths prescribed by the organization chart. Management by walking around differs from chance encounters in that the latter are unplanned events; the former occur intentionally.

Another perspective on management walking around is that it is similar to a physician making rounds to visit his or her hospital patients. Instead of visiting patients, the manager drops by to see employees and engages in brief, informal conversations. Sample questions to ask on rounds include, "What is working well today?" "Do you have the tools and equipment you need to do your job?" "Is there anything I could do better?" [13] Recognizing the nature of the rounds, the employees are likely to respond with brief, spontaneous, and useful feedback—assuming the manager making the rounds is trusted!

■ **Management by walking around**
managers intermingle freely with workers on the shop floor or in the office, as well as with customers; enhances open communication

What Are the Challenges to Interpersonal Communication Created by Information Technology?

■ **Learning Objective 3**

Rapid advances in information technology may enable workers to communicate more easily, rapidly, and quickly than they could even a few years ago. Quite often the influence has been positive, but at other times the effectiveness of interpersonal communication has decreased. Five developments that illustrate the impact of information technology on interpersonal communication are e-mail, presentation technology, telephones and voice mail, telecommuting, and multitasking. (The author realizes that telephones are not usually considered part of information technology, but they too are electronic devices that create communication challenges.)

E-MAIL AND COMMUNICATION AMONG PEOPLE

E-mail is the information technology system with the most dramatic impact on interpersonal communication in the current era. For both work and personal life, e-mail is typically less formal than a letter but more formal than a telephone conversation. The major impact of e-mail on interpersonal communication is that written messages replace many telephone and in-person exchanges. Team members often keep in regular contact with each other without having lengthy meetings or telephone conversations.

E-mail, including instant messaging, has become the dominant form of communication on the job. The same technology is likely to expand into a form of communication that will incorporate not only still drawings and photographs but also audio, video, and chunks of voice mail. The biggest threat to e-mail, however, is that about 50 percent of e-mails are classified as *spam,* or unwanted and uninvited messages, often of a commercial nature. Several potential communication problems that e-mail and instant messaging create should be kept in mind to minimize these problems. [14]

A major problem with e-mail is that it encourages indiscriminate sending of messages Some professional workers receive an average of 300 e-mail messages per day. Some of these workers make cynical comments such as, "My job is answering e-mail" or "I answer e-mail during the day and do my work at night and on weekends." Some workers conduct virtual joke-telling contests over e-mail, with some of the jokes being perceived as offensive by many other workers. The proliferation of electronic junk mail (spam) has prompted some company officials to take corrective action, such as the installation of spam filters.

Although many people contend that they are overloaded with e-mail, one study suggests that e-mail is being used wisely and is under control. As revealed in a survey of close to 2,500 workers, the majority of e-mail users find that it is a manageable part of their job. The typical work user of e-mail spends approximately 30 minutes during the workday processing e-mail, receives about 10 incoming messages, and sends five messages. A subgroup of these e-mailers, labeled power e-mailers, spends two hours or more daily on e-mail. They handle between 30 and 50 messages per day, yet only 11 percent say they feel overwhelmed by processing e-mail. [15]

To minimize feeling overwhelmed by e-mail, it is best to schedule blocks of time for sending and answering e-mail—assuming you have the type of work that allows you to limit e-mail. Many successful people control e-mail, rather than letting it control them. Jeff Bezos, founder and CEO of Amazon.com, is besieged by people sending him e-mails. To protect his creativity and time for interacting with his staff, Bezos reserves part of every Tuesday for reading and responding to e-mail messages. [16] (Of course, the customer service rep does not have this luxury of time blocking.)

The informal style of many e-mail exchanges can lead a person to believe that incorrect spelling, poor grammar, and disconnected thoughts are acceptable in all forms of business communication. The opposite is true. To appear professional and intelligent, writers of business e-mail messages should use correct spelling, grammar, capitalization, and punctuation.

E-mail has become a new tool for office politicians who search for ways to look good themselves and make others look bad. Many office politicians use e-mail to give credit to themselves for their contributions to a project, perhaps using a companywide distribution list. When something goes wrong, such as a failed project, the office politician will inform hundreds of people that it was not his or her fault.

Many supervisors and other workers use e-mail to reprimand others because, by sending a message over the computer, they can avoid face-to-face confrontation. E-mail is well suited for managers who would prefer to avoid face-to-face contact with group members. Harsh messages sent over e-mail create several problems. First, it is shocking to be reprimanded or insulted in writing. Second, the person cannot offer a defense except by writing back an e-mail message explaining his or her position. Third, the recipient, not knowing what to do about the harsh message, may brood and become anxious.

The use of e-mail and instant messaging during negotiations points to the strengths and limitations of this form of communication. E-mail should be used to supplement, not substitute for face-to-face negotiations. Professor Janet Nadler of Northwestern University School of Law conducted a study in which students paired up to negotiate a commercial transaction. Half of the students used e-mail exclusively, and half conducted a brief phone conversation before beginning the negotiation via e-mail. The students who first interacted by phone were four times more likely to reach an agreement than those who relied only on e-mail. The problem highlighted by the experiment is that there are no audio or visual cues (such as facial expressions or voice tone) to establish rapport when using e-mail. [17] Figure 8-1 presents suggestions for good etiquette when using e-mail, including messaging. The good etiquette leads to more productive use of e-mail.

Some business firms have counterattacked the problems associated with e-mail by shifting to related technologies. The major problem counterattacked is the time drain of sending and responding to e-mail messages. Workers at such well known organizations as Disney, Eastman Kodak, and the U.S. military are replacing e-mail with

Observing the following tips will enhance your e-mail etiquette and electronic communication effectiveness.

Keep it simple. Each message should have only one piece of information or request for action so that it's easier for the executive to respond. However, avoid sending an e-mail with an attachment without some type of greeting or explanation. Do not allow e-mail threads longer than a football field. E-mail messages longer than one screen often are filed instead of read.

Include an action step. Clearly outline what type of reply you're looking for as well as any applicable deadlines.

Use the subject line to your advantage. Generic terms such as "details" or "reminder" do not describe the contents of your message or whether it's time sensitive. So the executive may delay opening it. Do not forward a long chain of e-mails without changing the subject; otherwise, you might have a confusing subject line, such as "RE: FW: RE: FW: RE: FW."

Take care in writing e-mails. Clearly organize your thoughts; avoid sending e-mails with confusing, incomplete, or missing information. Never use profane or harsh language (referred to as *flaming*). Use business writing style and check carefully for grammatical and typographical errors. (Also, avoid the trend of spelling "I" in lowercase.)

Be considerate. Use "please" and "thank you" even in brief messages. Part of being considerate, or at least polite, is to begin you e-mail with a warm salutation, such as "Hello Gina," rather than jumping into the subject with no greeting.

Don't include confidential information. E-mail is occasionally forwarded to unintended recipients. If your message is in any way sensitive or confidential, set up a meeting or leave a voice mail in which you request confidentially.

Do not use e-mail to blast a coworker, and send copies to others. Criticizing another person with e-mail is equivalent to blasting him or her during a large meeting.

When in doubt, send plain text e-mail, not HTML. Not everybody can receive e-mails with fancy formatting, and some receivers dislike nontraditional formatting.

Ask before sending huge attachments. Do not clog e-mail systems without permission.

Avoid passing along chain letters. Few people believe that if they pass along your e-mail letter to 10 friends, they will ultimately become rich or avoid bad luck. In a work setting, chain letters make the sender appear unprofessional.

Instant messaging requires a few additional considerations for practicing good electronic etiquette:

Don't be Big Brother. Some bosses use instant messaging to check up on others, to make sure they are seated at their computer. Never intrude on workers unless it is urgent.

Lay down the instant messaging law. Make sure your message has some real value to the recipient before jumping right in front of someone's face. Instant messaging is much like walking into someone's office or cubicle without an appointment or without knocking.

Take it off-line. When someone on your buddy list becomes too chatty, don't vent your frustration. By phone, in-person, or through regular e-mail, explain tactfully that you do not have time for processing so many instant messages. Suggest that the two of you might get together for lunch or coffee soon.

Set limits to avoid frustration. To avoid constant interruptions, use a polite custom status message, such as "I will be dealing with customers today until 4:40."

Source: Todd Grady, "Even via E-Mail, Courtesy Matters," *Rochester Democrat and Chronicle,* May 1, 2000, p. 1F; Andrea C. Poe, "Don't Touch That 'Send' Button!" *HR Magazine*, July 2001, pp. 76, 80; Heinz Tschabitscher, "The Ten Most Important Rules of E-mail Etiquette," available at http://email.about.com/cs/netiquettetips/tp/core_netiquette.htm, retrieved September 9, 2003: Monte Enbysk, "Bosses: Ten Tips for Better E-Mails," *Microsoft Small Business Center,* available at www.microsoft.com/smallbusiness/resources/technology/communications/bosses_10, 2006.

Figure 8-1

E-Mail and Messaging Etiquette

other software tools that function in real time. Among them are private workplace wikis, blogs, instant messaging, RSS, and more elaborate forms of groupware that allow workers to create Web sites for the team's use on a specific project. A *wiki* is a site allows a group of people to comment on and edit each other's work. *RSS* is the acronym for really simple, syndication that enables people to subscribe to the information they need. E-mail will probably remain strong for one-to-one communication, but the tools just mentioned will be relied on more heavily for collaboration. [18]

USE PRESENTATION TECHNOLOGY TO YOUR ADVANTAGE

Speakers in all types of organizations supplement their talk with computer slides and overhead transparencies and often organize their presentation around them. Many people want presentations reduced to bulleted items and eye-catching graphics. (Have you noticed this tendency among students?) The communication challenge here is that during an oral presentation the predominant means of connection between sender and receiver is eye contact. When an audience is constantly distracted from the presenter by movement on the screen, sounds from the computer, or lavish colors, eye contact suffers, as does the message.

One of the biggest challenges is to learn how to handle equipment and maintain frequent eye and voice contact at all times. Several professionals in the field of business communication offer these sensible suggestions for overcoming the potential communication barrier of using presentation technology inappropriately: [19]

- **Reveal points only as needed.** Project the overhead transparencies or computer slides only when needed and use a cursor, laser pointer, or metal pointer for emphasis.

- **Talk to the audience and not the screen.** A major problem with computer slides is that the presenter as well as the audience is likely to focus continually on the slide. If the presenter minimizes looking at the slide and spends considerable time looking at the audience, it will be easier to maintain contact with the audience.

- **Keep the slide in view until the audience gets the point.** A presenter will often flash a slide or transparency without giving the audience enough time to comprehend the meaning of the slide. It is also important for presenters to synchronize the slides with their comments.

- **Reduce the text on each page of your PowerPoint presentation to a bare minimum.** Few people can really listen to you and read your slides at the same time, even if they think they are effective at multitasking.

- **Make sure to triple-check your presentation for spelling errors.** A spelling error projected on a screen can quickly become a joke passed around the room.

The point again is not to avoid the new technologies for communication but to use them to your advantage skillfully.

IMPROVE YOUR TELEPHONE, VOICE MAIL, AND SPEAKERPHONE COMMUNICATION SKILLS

A direct way of overcoming communication barriers is to use effective telephone and voice mail communication skills because these two communication media often create communication problems. Also, many businesses attract and hold on to customers because their representatives interact positively with people through the telephone and voice mail. Many other firms lose money, and nonprofit organizations irritate the public because their employees have poor communication and voice mail skills. Furthermore, despite the widespread use of computer networks, a substantial amount of work among employees is still conducted via telephone and voice mail. For example, investment firms, such as Merrill Lynch, do not want to send sensitive financial information by e-mail but instead encourage telephone conversations.

Speakerphones present some of their own communication challenges. Small noises, such as crumpling paper, eating crunchy food, and placing a handset on a hard desk, magnify when broadcast over a speakerphone. If other people are present in the office, advise the person you are telephoning at the beginning of the conversation. [20] Doing so may save a lot of embarrassment, such as the caller making negative comments about your boss or coworker. Most of the previous comments about overcoming communication barriers apply to telephone communications including speakerphones. Keep in mind these three representative suggestions for improving telephone effectiveness:

■ Vary your voice tone and inflection to avoid sounding bored or uninterested in your job and the company.

■ Smile while speaking on the phone—somehow a smile gets transmitted over the telephone wires or optic fibers!

■ Although multitasking has become the mode, when speaking on a telephone do not conduct a conversation with another person simultaneously and do not have a television or radio playing in the background. (The last point is a challenge for people who work from home.) Business callers expect your undivided attention.

> "Say your phone number slowly. I can't tell you how many people have zipped through it."
> —Michael Shepley, the owner of a public relations firm in New York City

TELECOMMUTING AND THE DISTRIBUTED WORKFORCE

A **telecommuter** is an employee who works at home full time or part time and sends output electronically to a central office. An estimated 22.5 million people in the United States work at home, out of their cars, or from customer premises as corporate employees. Collectively, they are referred to as the distributed workforce. Technology companies rely the most heavily on the distributed workforce. For example, at IBM, 40 percent of employees have no office at the company. [21] The majority of people who work at home do so only a day or two per week at their residence. Also, millions of people work from their homes in self-employment. Concerns about terrorists threats, contagious diseases, and the high cost of gasoline have made working at home even more attractive for many workers in recent years. Some people believe that the pollutants from driving a gasoline-powered vehicle contribute to global warming. Furthermore, some people find workplaces to have too many interruptions and distractions, such as conversations with coworkers, superiors, and meetings.

■ **Telecommuter**

employee who works at home full time or part time and sends output electronically to a central office

Telecommuters can communicate abundantly via electronic devices, but they miss out on the face-to-face interactions so vital for dealing with complex problems. Another communication problem telecommuters face is feeling isolated from activities at the main office and missing out on the encouragement and recognition that take place in face-to-face encounters. (Of course, many telecommuters prefer to avoid such contact.) Many telecommuters have another communications problem: Because they have very little face-to-face communication with key people in the organization, they believe they are passed over for promotion. Most telecommuters spend some time in the traditional office, yet they miss the day-by-day contact.

Another communication problem with telecommuting is that it lacks a solid human connection. As one telecommuting marketing consultant put it, face time is critical for building empathy. "It's a human connection. It takes time, and human beings need visual cues, the symbols of being together and caring for one another." [22] The accompanying Human Relations in Practice illustrates how far working away from the traditional office has become integrated into the modern workplace.

Human Relations in Practice

The Distributed Workforce at Sun Microsystems

Charlie Grantham, a cofounder of Work Design Collaborative LLC, was asked how do workplaces change with distributed workers. He responded as follows:

"Sun Microsystems has a program called iWork, a network of 127 remote work sites around the world. Employees can go to one of these locations for part of the workweek to plug in. Once Sun gave people this opportunity, getting them to come back to their assigned workplace was very difficult. These workplaces look and feel more residential. We're already starting to see housing developments with separate community offices attached in places like suburban Atlanta."

Source: Interview by Christopher Percy Collier, "Workplace 1.5: Managing Teleworkers—At Home, at Work, at Starbucks," *Fast Company*, November 2005, p. 105.

THE MULTITASKING MOVEMENT

A major consequence of electronic communication devises is that they encourage multitasking, for good or for bad. It has become standard communication practice for many workers to read e-mail while speaking on the phone, to surf the Internet while in a business meeting, and to check text messages while listening to a presentation. Some customer contact workers even conduct cell phone conversations with friends while serving customers. Many workers are now using two computer monitors so they can write reports while attending to e-mail. Multitasking has become a way of life for many members of generation Y, who grew up studying while watching television and chatting with their friends on a cell phone.

Advocates of multitasking contend that it increases productivity, such as accomplishing two or more tasks at once. A prime example is Marissa Mayer, vice president, Search Products and User Experience, Google (and a former computer science major). Among the comments she makes in describing the "secrets of her greatness" are as follows:

> I don't feel overwhelmed with information. I really like it. I use Gmail for my personal e-mail—15 to 20 e-mails a day—but on my work e-mail I get as many as 700 to 800 a day, so I need something really fast. I use an e-mail application called Pine, a Linux-based utility I started using in college. . . . I do marathon e-mail catch-up sessions, sometimes on a Saturday or Sunday. I'll just sit down and do e-mail for 10 to 14 hours straight. I almost always have the radio or my TV on. Sometimes it's the news. Sometimes it's a sitcom. I actually like the two streams of information. I guess I'm a typical 25 to 35 year old who's now really embracing the two-screen experience. [23]

Although many workers can multitask successfully, the bulk of scientific evidence is that performing more than one demanding cognitive activity at once lowers accuracy and productivity. Would you want a brain surgeon to operate on a loved one while he or she chatted on the cell phone with an investment consultant? While flying a commercial airline, would you want the pilot to be surfing the Internet? Or to take a less than life-and-death situation, would you want your tax accountant to e-file your return while making calculations on someone else's return?

Decades of research indicate that the quality of mental output and depth of thought deteriorate as a person attends to more than one task simultaneously. One of the problems is that the brain does not handle multitasking well. The brain rapidly toggles (an on-an-off switch effect) among tasks rather than performing true simultaneous processing. The problem is more acute for complex and demanding tasks that require action planning, such as deciding how to respond to a customer complaint or solve an accounting problem. Highly practiced and routine tasks, such as sealing an envelope, suffer less from multitasking.

David E. Meyer, the director of the Brain, Cognition and Action Laboratory at the University of Michigan, notes that when people attempt to perform two or more related tasks at the same time or alternating rapidly—instead of doing them sequentially—two negative consequences occur. Errors increase substantially, and the amount of time required to perform the task may double. [24]

The scientific findings just mentioned support the complaints of many professional and managerial workers that the constant inflow of electronic information hampers their creativity and analytical thinking ability. A practical antidote is to reserve multitasking for routine, well-rehearsed activities and to focus on one tasks at a time for creative and analytical work. Yet this conclusion does not mean that everybody is incapable of multitasking and producing good results.

Whether communication in the workplace is formal or informal, electronic or printed, the human touch should be included for the highest level of effectiveness. Many of the points already made about informal communication illustrate this point. Consider also that an adhesive note (Post-It style) is useful in obtaining a quick response from a colleague. A study by psychology professor Randy Garner at Sam Houston University in Texas examined response rates to a questionnaire. Volunteers who were asked to fill out a survey were more likely to comply, and give more complete answers, if it included a handwritten sticky note. Writing on the survey cover page was not as effective. Garner believes that the sticky note is perceived as a request for a personal favor, even between strangers. [25]

How Does One Do An Effective Job of Conducting or Participating in a Business Meeting?

■ **Learning Objective 4**

Much of workplace communication, including group decision making, takes place in meetings. Among the many purposes of meetings are problem solving, including brainstorming; disseminating information; training; and building team spirit. When conducted properly, meetings accomplish the purpose. Yet when conducted poorly, meetings represent a substantial productivity drain. The following suggestions apply to those who conduct physical and electronic meetings, and some are also relevant for participants. Videoconferencing is sometimes used to conduct meetings with people in dispersed locations, as is teleconferencing. The globalization of business is increasing the demand for videoconferencing. [26] By following these nine suggestions, you increase the meeting's effectiveness as a communication vehicle.

1. **Meet only for valid reasons.** Many meetings lead to no decisions because they lacked a valid purpose in the first place. Meetings are necessary only in situations that require coordinated effort and group decision making. Memos can be substituted for meetings when factual information needs to be disseminated and discussion is unimportant. When looking to meet for valid reasons, be aware of possible cultural differences in the motives for having a meeting. In many cultures, meetings are conducted to build relationships. For example, a

key to doing business in Asia is to get to know work associates on a personal level before getting down to problem solving, buying, or selling. [27] So for an Asian manager, conducting a meeting to build personal relationships *is* a valid reason.

2. **Start and stop on time, and offer refreshments.** Meetings appear more professional and action oriented when the leader starts and stops on time. If the leader waits for the last member to show up, much time is lost and late behavior is rewarded. Stopping the meeting on time shows respect for the members' time. Offering refreshments is another tactic for emphasizing the importance of the meeting and also enhances satisfaction with the meeting. Agree in advance on when and if there will be a break to reduce anxiety about when the break will occur.

3. **Keep comments brief and to the point.** A major challenge facing the meeting leader is to keep conversation on track. Verbal rambling by participants creates communication barriers because other people lose interest. An effective way for the leader to keep comments on target is to ask the contributor of a non sequitur, "In what way does your comment relate to the agenda?"

4. **Encourage critical feedback and commentary.** Meetings are more likely to be fully productive when participants are encouraged to be candid with criticism and negative feedback. Openness helps prevent groupthink and also brings important problems to the attention of management.

5. **Strive for wide participation.** One justification for conducting a meeting is to obtain a variety of input. Although not everybody is equally qualified to voice a sound opinion, everyone should be heard. A skillful leader may have to limit the contribution of domineering members and coax reticent members to voice their ideas. Asking participants to bring several questions to the meeting will often spur participation. The meeting leader should not play favorites by encouraging the participation of some members, and ignoring others. If the meeting leader spends the entire time making a PowerPoint presentation, participation will be discouraged. The slides should supplement the meeting and be starting points for discussion.

6. **Solve small issues ahead of time with e-mail.** Meetings can be briefer and less mundane when small issues are resolved ahead of time. E-mail is particularly effective for resolving minor administrative issues and also for collecting agenda items in advance.

7. **Consider "huddling" when quick action is needed.** A huddle is a fast-paced, action-oriented way to bring workers together into brief meetings to discuss critical performance issues. A department store manager might bring together five floor managers 10 minutes before opening to say, "We have a line-up of about 500 customers waiting to get in because of our specials today. Is everybody ready for the rush of excitement? What problems do you anticipate?" The huddle is particularly important when it would be difficult for the workers to attend a long meeting. [28]

8. **Ensure that all follow-up action is assigned and recorded.** All too often, even after a decision has been reached, a meeting lacks tangible output. Distribute a memo summarizing who is responsible for taking what action and by what date.

9. **Minimize distractions during the meeting.** The group should agree on whether meeting participants will be allowed to use laptop computers for purposes other than recording information in the meeting. If handouts are used, allow participants enough time to read them so one person is not presenting while the others are reading. Ensure beforehand that computer-related equipment, such as the projector, is working and that it is compatible with the presenter's software.

Concept Review and Reinforcement

Key Terms

Formal communication
  channels, 188
Downward communication, 190
Upward communication, 190

Open-door policy, 190
Informal communication
  channels, 190
Shadow organizations, 191

Grapevine, 191
Management by walking
  around, 193
Telecommuter, 197

Summary and Review

Messages in organizations are sent over both formal (official) and informal (unofficial) channels. Three key aspects of the formal channels are as follows:

- Many companies have developed formal communication channels for managing crises, such as fires and terrorist attacks.
- The company blog is a rapidly growing type of formal communication. It communicates business information with a soft, human touch.
- Messages in organizations travel in four primary directions: downward, upward, horizontally, and diagonally. An open-door policy facilitates upward communication.

An informal communication channel supplements the formal channel.

- A major informal communication channel is the network of contacts that employees use to accomplish work, sometimes referred to as the shadow organization.
- The grapevine is the major informal communication channel, and it carries rumors and gossip.
- Chance encounters between managers and employees foster informal communication as does management by walking around.

Information technology creates challenges for interpersonal communication, despite all its advantages.

- E-mail has the most dramatic impact on interpersonal communication in organizations. Some workers are overwhelmed by e-mail, whereas others have the system under control.

- E-mail encourages informal, unprofessional communication, and the system is too often used to play office politics.
- E-mail should be used to supplement, not substitute, face-to-face negotiations.
- Some business firms have counterattacked the problems associated with e-mail by shifting to related technologies.

Presentation technology creates challenges of its own, including the need to learn how to handle equipment and maintain eye contact at the same time. It is important to talk to the audience and not the screen and reduce the text on each page to a bare minimum.

Effective telephone and voice mail communication skills are helpful in overcoming communication problems. Remember to vary your voice tone and avoid multitasking while speaking.

Telecommuters are now referred to as the distributed workforce.

- Telecommuters may miss out on the face-to-face interactions necessary for dealing with complex problems.
- Telecommuting is also a challenge because it lacks a solid human connection.

Electronic communication facilitates the multitasking that is so popular with generation Y.

- Advocates of multitasking claim it enhances productivity.
- The bulk of scientific evidence is that performing more than one demanding cognitive activity at

once lowers accuracy and productivity. Mental output and depth of thought deteriorate while multitasking.

Much of workplace communication takes place in meetings. Among the many suggestions for productive meetings are:

- Meet only for valid reasons.
- Start and stop on time and offer refreshments.
- Solve small issues ahead of time with e-mail.
- Minimize distractions during the meeting.

Check your Understanding

1. The CEO of a professional basketball team described in the opening case has somebody print out his e-mail messages so he can read them. What might be his problem?
2. Suppose you thought that the CEO of your company was moving the company in the wrong direction, and you want to tell him or her. Explain which communication channel you would choose to deliver your message.
3. In what ways does diagonal communication make an organization more flexible?
4. In what way might management by walking around undermine the authority of the supervisor?

5. How might an e-mail message contain nonverbal communication?
6. Give three examples of business situations in which telephone conversations still play a key role.
7. Give an example from your own life in which multitasking has enhanced your performance?
8. Give an example from your own life in which multitasking has lowered your performance.
9. Why are face-to-face meetings still so popular even in high-technology companies?
10. Why do people complain so much about meetings on the job?

Web Corner

Suggestions for writing better e-mails:

www.microsoft.com/smallbusiness/resources/technolgy/communication/bosses_10

How to run an effective business meeting:

www.allbusiness.com/business_advice/articles/11341.html

Internet Skill Builder:

Use your preferred search engine or engines to identify three different negative rumors about business companies.

You might even find a Web site or two devoted to combating a particular rumor launched about a company. Attempt to identify how any of these rumors started or whether they had any validity. Do you have any thoughts as to what the companies involved might have done to combat these rumors?

Developing Your Human Relations Skills

Human Relations Application Exercises

Applying Human Relations Exercise 8-1

Designing an Office for a Virtual Customer Agent

Work in a team to design a home office for a virtual customer agent, a worker whose responsibilities are to fill orders for merchandise for three different companies. The agent receives calls through a toll-free number and then uses the computer to enter the order. He or she also processes orders on-line. The office in question will be placed somewhere in a three bedroom house that also has a family room, kitchen, basement, and enclosed porch.

While designing the office, include such factors as the layout of the furniture and equipment, the equipment needed, and any decorations. Keep in mind ergonomic factors that focus on making the equipment easy to use and with low risk for physical problems such as carpal tunnel syndrome and backaches. Because the virtual agent will have to pay for the office setup, derive a tentative budget.

Draw your design on any convenient format including a flip chart, whiteboard, blackboard, or computer screen. Your team leader might be asked to present the design to the rest of the class so class members can compare the effectiveness of each design. Class members evaluating the home office design might use the following evaluation factors in addition to whatever their intuition suggests:

- To what extent does the office design help reduce possible conflict with other people living in the same household?
- How might this design offer productivity advantages over a conventional office?
- When and if customers or company representatives call into this office, how professional the will setup sound?
- How will this office design contribute to job satisfaction?

Applying Human Relations Exercise 8-2

Evaluating a Business Meeting

The class organizes into teams of about six students to conduct a meeting to formulate plans for building temporary housing for homeless people downtown in your city or a nearby city. Three other students, or the entire class, will observe the meeting. This exercise should take about 35 minutes; it can be done inside or outside of class. Each team takes on the assignment of formulating plans for building temporary shelters for the homeless. The dwellings you plan to build, for example, might be two-room cottages with electricity and indoor plumbing. During the time allotted to the task, formulate plans for going ahead with Shelters for the Homeless. Consider dividing up work by assigning certain tasks to each team member. Sketch out tentative answers to the following questions: (1) How will you obtain funding for your venture? (2) Which homeless people will you help? (3) Where will your shelters be? (4) Who will do the actual construction?

After the meeting is completed, the three observers will provide feedback to the team members about the effectiveness of the meeting, using the following criteria:

1. How effective was the teamwork? Support you conclusion with an example of specific behavior.
2. How well did group members stay on track in terms of focusing on their goal?
3. Did the team members make any introductory warm-up comments to help build rapport?
4. To what extent was the participation among team members balanced?
5. Did the team move toward any conclusions or action plans?
6. Choose another criterion you think might be relevant.

Human Relations Case Study 8-1

Can Microsoft Groups Communicate with Each Other?

In March 2005, Microsoft Corp. consolidated six divisions into three, with each division having its own president, as shown in the accompanying organization chart. The hope of the new structure was that Microsoft will be able to more efficiently deliver products by combining technology from divisions that previously had difficulty in working together because they were in separate organizational units (divisions of the company). Robe Enderle, principal analyst for the research firm the Enderle Group in San Jose, California, said, "The company had become almost unmanageable. In the past two and a half years, it felt like you just couldn't get anything done. The turf wars became more pronounced."

Enderle used the example of the handheld gaming machines. "Microsoft couldn't build one because you have to bring together a bunch of different groups that don't work together," he said. An issue like this is capable of being resolved under the reorganization. One reason is that it aligns different groups that previously were sep- arate divisions. Also, workers now have an approachable throat to choke—in the form of a division president—in case there are collaboration problems among the teams, Enderle said.

"Before you kind of had to go up to CEO Steve Ballmer, and you don't want to go up to him and say people aren't working together because Steve will start picking up bodies and hurling them around. Microsoft has built the company in a way that makes sense," said Enderle.

Questions

1. In what way is the Microsoft reorganization a way of improving organizational communications?
2. Why will communication among the various groups now likely be better?
3. What suggestions can you offer Microsoft to obtain good communication among the three divisions?
4. Comment on the communication effectiveness of CEO Steve Ballmer.

Source: Chart derived from information presented in Robert A. Guth, "Microsoft to Restructure Businesses," *The Wall Street Journal*, September 21, 2005, pp. A3, A5; Elizabeth Montalbano, *IDG New Service*, San Francisco Bureau, September 21, 2005 (redistributed in *IT World.com*) www.microsoft.com; Allison Linn, "Microsoft Realigns Execs as Windows Update Lags," The Associated Press, March 24, 2006. As with any organization chart, the arrangement of people and the names of units are subject to frequent change.

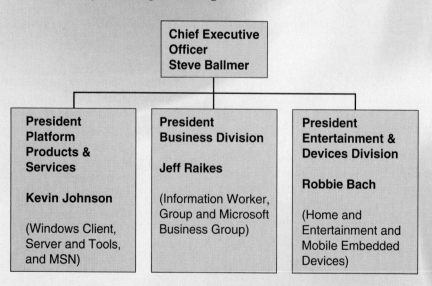

Overall organization structure at Microsoft Corp.

Human Relations Case Study 8-2

Is Telecommuting Good for Us?

Susan Lepsch and Russell Stratton, co-owners of Lepsch and Stratton Travel Agency, met for breakfast on the first Monday in July. "Either we take decisive action or we stop complaining about too little office space and too much turnover," said Russ. "We've expanded despite people making their own travel arrangements over the Internet. Our focus on giving advice that you don't get with the on-line travel agencies has helped us grow. We should expand our office from 4,000 to 5,000 square feet. Our volume of business is good, but not good enough to cover that much increase in expenses."

Sue responded, "I've read that one of the best ways to keep good office staff is to give them a work schedule that makes life easy. If we allowed our staff to telecommute, we could get by without the additional space. This would save us a lot of money."

"I'm willing to try the program on a voluntary basis," said Russ. "Who should we start with?"

"The likely candidates are the support specialists and one direct-mail specialists. Those people could do a substantial portion of their work at home if they had the right equipment. Our staff members all have PCs or laptops at home, but they might not have powerful enough equipment to run our software. They would need upgrades." Sue and Russ later identified five volunteers for the telecommuting program.

The telecommuting program was launched September 1. During mid-November, Sue and Russ decided to evaluate the new system. Neither partner had heard of any substantial complaint about the program from the employees or from travel clients because of poor service. If the program were working well, the present space could be retained, thus avoiding the expense and effort of relocation.

Sue began her evaluation of telecommuting by describing her experiences in supervising the work of Kim and Betty. "I was worried about the possibility of Kim not doing her job because she wasted time on the telephone and with e-mail. That proved to be not a problem. Kim did all the work that was required."

Russ spoke to Kristin, the direct-mail specialist, about her experiences as a teleworker. Kristin replied, "My reaction has been mixed. I enjoy being treated like a true professional. Nobody has to watch over me to see that I get my work done. Besides, our work is driven by clients anyway. I like saving commuting time, so I have a little more time for reading the newspaper and taking care of errands."

"What I don't like is being so alienated from the office. I want to move up to supervisor as our agency expands substantially. If you two hardly ever see me, I could easily be passed over for promotion. Another problem I didn't anticipate is the distraction at home. My daughter asks me for rides, and my friends drop by. People simply don't take working at home as seriously as working in an office building."

Sue asked Cindy, one of the support specialists, for her reaction to working at home. With a gleam in her eye and a smile, Cindy replied, "Telecommuting has helped make my life work. My biggest problem before working at home was that I had a latchkey child. Trevor, my son, is too old for child care yet too young to go home unsupervised. He gets home at around 3:15 in the afternoon. When he arrives, he knows that I'm working, but it's better than my not being on the premises. By not worrying so much about Trevor on my working days, I feel much less stressed and better able to concentrate on my work."

Russ interviewed Tony, another support specialist, about his telecommuting experiences. "On a scale of 1 to 10," said Tony, "I would rate teleworking a 5. I like being able to avoid commuting on a day when road conditions are bad. And I like getting home from work at 4:31 after having stopped work at 4:30. The pay is the same so I have no complaints there."

"What reservations do you have?" Russ asked.

"I miss the interaction with the office buddies," said Tony. "I never wanted to be a loner. I like people. I like taking coffee breaks with coworkers. At home, I drink my coffee at my desk. For a break, I take out the garbage. If I'm lucky, I say hello to the mail carrier."

After this round of interviews, Sue and Russ had not made up their minds about the effectiveness of the telecommuting program. Sue mentioned, however, "I don't know how far we will go with telecommuting. But I do know that we will always need somebody around the office to talk to our clients both in person and on the phone."

Questions

1. What is your opinion of the effectiveness of the telecommuting program at the travel agency so far?
2. What evidence should Sue and Russ be seeking to know if the telecommuting program is beneficial to the travel agency?
3. What recommendations do you have for Tony so his teleworking will become a more positive experience for him?

REFERENCES

1. Adapted from Secrets of Success: All in a Day's Work," *Fortune,* March 20, 2006, pp. 97–105.
2. "Keep Workers in the Loop or They'll Say Goodbye," *Employee Recruitment & Retention,* Sample Issue, 2004.
3. Patrick Kiger, "Lessons from a Crisis: How Communication Kept a Company Together," *Workforce,* November 2001, p. 28.
4. Michelle Conlin and Andrew Park, "Blogging with the Boss's Blessing," *Business Week,* June 28, 2004, p. 102.
5. "It's Hard to Manage If You Don't Blog," *Fortune,* October 4, 2004, p. 46.
6. Mark Hendricks, "The Shadow Knows," *Entrepreneur,* January 2000, p. 110.
7. Rob Cross and Sally Colella, "Building Vibrant Employee Networks," *HR Magazine,* December 2004, pp. 101–104.
8. Interview with Bob Rosner, "Studying the World Beneath the Org Chart," *Workforce,* September 2001, p. 65.
9. Sameul Greengard, "Gossip Poisons Business: HR Can Stop It," *Workforce,* July 2001, pp. 26–27; Lea Winerman, "Have Your Heard the Latest?" *Monitor on Psychology,* April 2006, pp. 56–57.
10. "Make the Rumor Mill Work for You," *Executive Leadership,* May 2003, p. 7.
11. Anne Fisher, "Psst! Rumors Can Help at Work," *Fortune,* December 12, 2005, p. 202.
12. John P. Kotter, *The General Managers* (New York: Free Press, 1991).
13. "'Making Rounds' Like a Physician," *Manager's Edge,* February 8, 2006. As adapted from Quint Studer, *Hardwiring Excellence* (Gulf Breeze, FL: Fire Starter Publishing, 2005).
14. "Using E-Mail and Voice Mail Effectively," *Business Education Forum,* October 1998, pp. 6–9, 51; Andrew Blackman, "Spam's 'Easy Target,'" *The Wall Street Journal,* August 19, 2003, pp. B1, B4.
15. Survey reported in Carol Monaghan, "Inbox Glutted? Maybe You're a Power E-Mailer," *Chicago Tribune,* December 15, 2002.
16. Letitia Baldrige, "How to Cope with E-mails," Briefings Publishing Group, available at *www.briefings.com.* Retrieved February 15, 2003.
17. Janice Nadler, "Rapport in Legal Negotiation: How Small Talk Can Facilitate Email Dealmaking," *Harvard Negotiation Law Review,* Vol. 9, 2004, pp. 225–253.
18. Michelle Conlin, "E-Mail Is So Five Minutes Ago: It's Being Replaced by Software That Promotes Real-Time Collaboration," *Business Week,* November 28, 2005, pp. 111–112.
19. Jean Mausehund and R. Neil Dortch, "Presentation Skills in the Digital Age," *Business Education Forum,* April 1999, pp. 30–32; Michael Patterson, "The Pitch Coach," *Business Week SmallBiz,* Fall 2005, p. 61.
20. John T. Adams, III, "When You're on a Speakerphone, Don't Make Noise," *HR Magazine,* March 2001, p. 12.
21. Based on U.S. Bureau of Labor statistics and data reported in Michelle Conlin, "The Easiest Commute of All," *Business Week,* December 12, 2005, p. 79.
22. "Work à la Modem," *Business Week,* October 4, 1999, p. 176.
23. "Secrets of Greatness: How I Work," *Fortune,* March 20, 2006, p. 68.
24. The scientific information about multitasking is reviewed in Claudia Wallis, "The Multitasking Generation," *Time,* March 27, 2006, pp. 48–55. See also Joshua Rubinstein, David Meyer, and Jeffrey Evans, "Human Perception and Performance," *Journal of Experimental Psychology,* no 4, 2001.
25. Research reported in "Post-It Persuasion: Read Me Now!" *Psychology Today,* December 2005, p. 32.
26. Martha McKay, "Face-to-Face Meetings Gain Remote Possibilities," *The Bergen, N.J. Record,* March 20, 2006.
27. Ed Frauenheim, "Custom-Fit Communication," *Workforce Management,* November 21, 2005, p. 30.
28. Pamela Babcock, "Sending the Message," *HR Magazine,* November 2003, p. 70.

9

Getting Along with Your Manager, Coworkers, and Customers

Learning Objectives

Outline

After reading the information and doing the exercises in this chapter, you should be able to:

1 Select several tactics for developing a good relationship with your manager or team leader.

2 Deal effectively with a problem manager.

3 Describe methods of getting along with coworkers.

4 Identify tactics that help a person become a good team player.

5 Pinpoint tactics for dealing effectively with difficult people.

6 Specify approaches to building good relationships with customers.

When Sue Nokes joined T-Mobile as a senior vice president of customer service a few years back, the cell phone company had a little problem: Lousy customer service was driving T-Mobile users crazy. Calling with a question or complaint, they got put on hold for what seemed like eons. Users then spoke with customer service reps who weren't much help. J. D. Power's customer satisfaction surveys ranked T-Mobile dead last in the industry.

Nokes launched a total overhaul. The first step: getting T-Mobile's human resources people and its marketing department to sit down and talk. The idea was to revamp the company's hiring practices, thus increasing the odds of selecting customer service staffers willing and able to follow through on the marketing maven's promises.

A new set of hiring criteria at T-Mobile emphasized traits such as empathy and quick thinking. Nokes then set up a rigorous evaluation process. "In our business, customers want their problems resolved fast, in one phone call—and courtesy matters," she says. "So we created a system that gives a lot of weight to those two elements. And we made sure that everyone knows exactly how he'll be evaluated. Nokes started an employee-rewards program called Do More, Get More, which bestows restaurant dinners and exotic trips on workers who meet stringent standards for courtesy and speed.

With all the improvements, J. D. Power has ranked T-Mobile number one in customer service for two consecutive years. [1]

The story about upgrading the cell phone company customer service representatives illustrates once again that unless front-line workers have good human relations skills a company's reputation can go downhill rapidly. Developing effective relationships with work associates, including customers, has been seen as having good **political skills,** an interpersonal style that combines awareness of others with the ability to communicate well. People with political skill are charming and engaging, which inspires confidence, trust, and sincerity. [2] Based on these attributes, the person with political skill effectively influences others. This chapter presents information about developing productive relationships with three major groups of work associates: managers, coworkers, and customers. Along the way, we include information about coping with difficult bosses and coworkers.

■ Political skills

an interpersonal style that combines awareness of others with the ability to communicate well; developing effective relationships with work associates, including customers

How Do You Develop a Good Relationship With Your Manager or Team Leader?

■ Learning Objective 1

Getting along well with your manager is the most basic strategy of getting ahead in your career. If you cannot gain favor with the boss, it will be difficult to advance to higher positions or earn much more money. Obtaining good performance reviews and receiving favorable work assignments also depends on a good relationship with the person to whom you report. The boss might be more of a traditional boss, such as a person with the title of manager or supervisor. Or the boss might be a team leader who typically has less formal authority than a manager or supervisor. Your manager or team leader is always the person who is contacted first when someone wants to determine what kind of employee you are. Usually this information is sought when you are being considered for transfer, promotion, or a position with another firm.

Getting along with the boss is particularly important when the economy is sluggish or when the threat of outsourcing exists. Workers who have good relationships with their manager have more job security than those with poor relationships. Vince Waldron, a researcher in workplace relationships, observes that employees must tend to their workplace relationships, going out of their way to communicate with managers and seek feedback on their performance. [3] In this section we present a variety of approaches that lead to constructive relationships with an immediate superior. The goal is to be legitimately perceived as a strong contributor to your work unit.

ACHIEVE GOOD JOB PERFORMANCE

Good job performance remains the most effective strategy for impressing your manager. When any rational manager evaluates a group member's performance, the first question asked is, "Is this employee getting the job done?" And you cannot get the job done if you are not competent. Many factors contribute to whether you can become a competent performer. Among them are your education, training, personality characteristics, job experience, and special skills, such as being able to organize your work.

An advanced way of displaying good job performance is to assist your manager with a difficult problem he or she faces. Your manager, for example, might need to operate equipment outside his or her area of expertise. If you show the manager how to operate the equipment, he or she will think highly of your job performance. Another example would be helping your manager get ready for an important meeting with higher management by preparing attention-getting PowerPoint slides.

DISPLAY A STRONG WORK ETHIC

A strong **work ethic** is a firm belief in the dignity and value of work and, therefore, is important for favorably impressing a manager. An employee with a strong work ethic will sometimes be excused if his or her performance is not yet exceptional. This is true because the manager assumes that a strong work ethic will elevate performance eventually. Six suggestions follow for demonstrating a strong work ethic.

> ■ **Work ethic**
> a firm belief in the dignity and value of work and, therefore, important for favorably impressing a manager

1. Work hard and enjoy the task. By definition, a person with a strong work ethic works diligently and has strong internal motivation. The person may appreciate external rewards yet appreciates the importance of any work that adds value to society.

2. Demonstrate competence even on minor tasks. Attack each assignment with the recognition that each task performed well, however minor, is one more career credit. A minor task performed well paves the way for your being given more consequential tasks.

3. Assume personal responsibility for problems. An employee with a problem will often approach the manager and say, "We have a tough problem to deal with." The connotation is that the manager should be helping the employee with the problem. A better impression is created when the employee says, "I have a tough problem to deal with, and I would like your advice." This statement implies that you are willing to assume responsibility for the problem and for any mistake you may have made that led to the problem.

4. Assume responsibility for free-floating problems. A natural way to display a strong work ethic is to assume responsibility for free-floating (nonassigned) problems. Taking on even a minor task, such as ordering lunch for a meeting that is running late, can enhance the impression one makes on a manager.

5. Get your projects completed promptly. A by-product of a strong work ethic is an eagerness to get projects completed promptly. People with a strong work ethic respect deadlines imposed by others. Furthermore, they typically set deadlines of their own more tightly than those imposed by their bosses.

6. Accept undesirable assignments willingly. Look for ways to express the attitude, "Whether this assignment is glamorous and fun is a secondary issue. What counts is that it is something that needs doing for the good of the company."

DEMONSTRATE GOOD EMOTIONAL INTELLIGENCE

Dealing effectively with feelings and emotions is a big challenge in the workplace. Demonstrating good emotional intelligence is impressive because it contributes to performing well in the difficult arena of dealing with feelings. A worker with good emotional intelligence would engage in such behaviors as (1) recognizing when a coworker needs help but is too embarrassed to ask for help, (2) dealing with the anger of a dissatisfied customer, (3) recognizing that the boss is facing considerable pressure also, and (4) being able to tell whether a customer's "maybe" means "yes" or "no."

Many of the competencies described throughout this chapter are facilitated by emotional intelligence. Nevertheless, being aware of strategies and tactics for dealing effectively with others helps your capitalize on your emotional intelligence.

BE DEPENDABLE AND HONEST

Dependability is a critical employee virtue. If an employee can be counted on to deliver as promised and to be at work regularly, that employee has gone a long way toward impressing the boss. A boss is uncomfortable not knowing whether an important assignment will be accomplished on time. If you are not dependable, you will probably not get your share of important assignments. Honesty is tied to dependability because a dependable employee is honest about when he or she will have an assignment completed. Dependability and honesty are important at all job levels. One of the highest compliments a manager can pay an employee is to describe the employee as dependable. Conversely, it is considered derogatory to call any employee undependable. As one company president put it when describing a subordinate, "When he's great, he's terrific; but I can't depend on him. I'd rather he be more consistent even if he delivered fewer peak successes—at least I could rely on him." [4]

BE A GOOD ORGANIZATIONAL CITIZEN

An especially meritorious approach to impressing key people is to demonstrate organizational citizenship behavior. An effective way of being a good organizational citizen is step outside your job description. Job descriptions are characteristic of a well-organized firm. If everybody knows what he or she is supposed to be doing, there will be much less confusion, and goals will be achieved. This logic sounds impressive, but job descriptions have a major downside. If people engage only in work included in their job description, an "it's not my job" mentality pervades. An effective way to impress your manager, therefore, is to demonstrate that you are not constrained by a job description. If something needs doing, you will get it done regardless of whether it is your formal responsibility.

An impressive way of stepping outside your job description is to anticipate problems, even when the manager had not planned to work on them. Anticipating problems is characteristic of a resourceful person who exercises initiative. Instead of working exclusively on problems that have been assigned, the worker is perceptive enough to look for future problems. Anticipating problems impresses most managers because it reflects an entrepreneurial, take-charge attitude.

CREATE A STRONG PRESENCE

A comprehensive approach to impressing your manager or team leader and other key people in the workplace is to create a strong presence, keeping yourself in the forefront. Such actions impress key people and simultaneously help advance your career. Stephanie Sherman, a career consultant, offers this advice for creating a strong presence:

- Get involved in high-visibility projects, such as launching a new product or re-designing work methods. Even an entry-level position on such a project can help a worker get noticed.

- Get involved in teams because they give you an opportunity to broaden your skills and knowledge.

- Get involved in social and community activities of interest to top management, such as those sponsored by the company. Behave professionally and use your best manners.

- Create opportunities for yourself by making constructive suggestions about earning or saving money. Even if an idea is rejected, you will still be remembered for your initiative.

- Show a willingness to take on some of the tasks that your manager doesn't like to do but would be forced to do if you did not step in. [5]

FIND OUT WHAT YOUR MANAGER EXPECTS OF YOU

You have little chance of doing a good job and impressing your manager unless you know what you are trying to accomplish. Work goals and performance standards represent the most direct ways of learning your manager's expectations. A **performance standard** is a statement of what constitutes acceptable performance. These standards can sometimes be inferred from a job description. Review your work goals and ask clarifying questions. An example would be, "You told me to visit our major customers who are 60 days or more delinquent on their accounts. Should I also visit the three of these customers who have declared bankruptcy?" In addition to having a clear statement of your goals, it is helpful to know the priorities attached to them. In this way you will know which task to execute first.

A subtle aspect of understanding the expectations of your boss is adapting to his or her preferred style of work. Managers vary in terms of wanting written versus oral briefings. Some managers prefer to receive e-mail messages from you regularly, others once a week. Some managers want to be treated informally, much like being a coworker. A minority of managers wanted to be treated as if they were royalty. Matching your work style to the work style of your boss can help build a strong relationship between the two of you.

■ **Performance standard**
a statement of what constitutes acceptable performance

MINIMIZE COMPLAINTS

Being open and honest in expressing your feelings and opinions is part of having good human relations skills. Nevertheless, this type of behavior, when carried to excess, could earn you a reputation as a whiner. Few managers want to have a group member around who constantly complains about working conditions, coworkers, working hours, pay, and so forth. An employee who complains too loudly and frequently quickly becomes labeled a pill or a pest.

Another important reason a boss usually dislikes having a direct report (subordinate) who complains too much is that listening to these complaints takes up considerable time. Most managers spend a disproportionate amount of time listening to the problems of a small number of ineffective or complaining employees. Consciously or unconsciously, a manager who has to listen to many of your complaints may find a way to seek revenge.

How, then, does an employee make valid complaints to the manager? The answer is to complain only when justified. And when you do offer a complaint, back it up with a recommended solution. Anyone can take potshots at something. The valuable employee is the person who supports these complaints with a constructive action plan. An example follows of a complaint, supported by action plans for its remedy:

> *We have a difficult time handling emergency requests when you are away from the department. I would suggest that when you will be away for more than one or two hours, one of us can serve as the acting supervisor. It could be done on a rotating basis to give each of us some supervisory experience.*

One possibility for minimizing the need for complaints is to attempt to look at decisions from the boss's point of view. The company might decide to prohibit workers from using instant messaging for personal reasons during working hours. Instead of complaining that the prohibition on instant messages is unjust, the worker might attempt to understand why company management thinks instant messages lower productivity.

AVOID BYPASSING YOUR MANAGER

A way to embarrass and sometimes infuriate your manager is to repeatedly go to his or her superior with your problems, conflicts, and complaints. Such bypasses have at least three strongly negative connotations. One is that you don't believe your boss has the power to take care of your problem. Another is that you distrust his or her judgment in the matter at hand. A third is that you are secretly launching a complaint against your manager.

The boss bypass is looked on so negatively that most experienced managers will not listen to your problem unless you have already discussed it with your immediate superior. There *are* times, however, when running around your manager is necessary, such as when you have been unable to resolve a conflict directly with him or her (see the following major section). Should your manager be involved in highly immoral or illegal actions, such as sexual harassments or taking kickbacks from vendors, a boss bypass might be warranted. But even under these circumstances, you should politely inform your manager that you are going to take up your problem with the next level of management.

In short, if you want to keep on the good side of your manager, bring all problems directly to him or her. If your boss is unable or unwilling to take care of the problem, you might consider contacting your boss's superior. Nonetheless, considerable tact and diplomacy are needed. Do not imply that your manager is incompetent but merely that you would like another opinion about the issues at stake. If an organization has a formal system for filing complaints, such as an open-door policy, it can be used to substitute for a boss bypass but should be used only when you are unable to resolve a problem with your boss.

ENGAGE IN FAVORABLE INTERACTIONS WITH YOUR MANAGER

The many techniques described previously support the goal of engaging in favorable interactions with your manager. A study of interactions between bank employees and their supervisors showed that purposely trying to create a positive impression on the supervisor led to better performance ratings. [6] Although the finding is not surprising, it is reassuring to know that it is backed by quantitative evidence. Human Relations Self-Assessment Quiz 9-1 contains a listing of behaviors used by employees in the study to create positive interactions with their supervisors. Use these behaviors as a guide for skill building.

According to a synthesis of findings by organizational behavior professor Cecily D. Cooper at the University of Miami, an effective way of ingratiating yourself to your boss, as well as to others in the workplace, is to make effective use of humor. **Ingratiating** is an attempt to increase one's attractiveness to others, so as to influence their behavior. The most effective type of humor for building a relationship with the boss should be work related and hint at a strength of the boss, department, or company. If the humor is well received, it helps build a relationship with the manager (or other targets of the humor as well). [7] Here's an attempt at ego-building humor that worked well with one vice president. The department administrative assistant said, "Herb, we all know what a reputation you've developed in the company. When you are promoted to CEO, will you take the old gang for a ride in your corporate jet?"

■ **Ingratiating**
an attempt to increase one's attractiveness to others to influence their behavior

Human Relations Self-Assessment Quiz   9-1

Supervisor Interaction Checklist

Use the following behaviors as a checklist for achieving favorable interactions with your present manager or a future one. The more of these actions you are engaged in, the higher the probability that you are building a favorable relationship with your manager.

1. Agree with your supervisor's major opinions outwardly even when you disagree inwardly.   _____
2. Take an immediate interest in your supervisor's personal life.   _____
3. Praise your supervisor on his or her accomplishments.   _____
4. Do personal favors for your supervisor.   _____
5. Do something as a personal favor for your supervisor even though you are not required to do it.   _____
6. Volunteer to help your supervisor on a task.   _____
7. Compliment your supervisor on his or her dress or appearance.   _____
8. Present yourself to your supervisor as being a friendly person.   _____
9. Agree with your supervisor's major ideas.   _____
10. Present yourself to your supervisor as being a polite person.   _____

Source: Adapted from Sandy J. Wayne and Gerald R. Ferris, "Influence Tactics, Affect, and Exchange Quality in Supervisor–Subordinate Interactions: A Laboratory Experiment and Field Study," *Journal of Applied Psychology*, October 1990, p. 494.

Although favorable interactions with a manager are valuable for relationship building, there are times when a group member has to deliver bad news. For example, you might have to inform the manager about a burst water pipe in the mainframe computer room or a bunch of customer complaints about a new product. You want to avoid being the messenger who is punished because he or she delivered bad news. Attempt to be calm and businesslike. Do not needlessly blame yourself for the problem. Mention that *we are* or *the company is* facing a serious challenge. If possible, suggest a possible solution, such as, "I have already investigated a backup computer service we can use until the damage is repaired."

When working to establish a good relationship with your manager, keep in mind that cultural factors could influence how a given tactic should be modified for best effectiveness. An example would be that displaying strong work ethic to a supervisor from Japan would be different from displaying the same ethic to a manager from France. The Japanese manager might think that working 55 hours a week indicates a strong work ethic, whereas the French manager might think that 40 hours a week of hard work is exceptional. Another cultural factor in establishing a good relationship could be the amount of respect shown to the manager. A typical American manager might expect an informal, friendly relationship, with the two of you acting like equals. However, a manager from China might expect much more respect. In one situation a manager from China in charge of a chemistry lab in the United States became angry when workers addressed him by his first name. He expected to be addressed as "Dr." plus his last name.

How Do You Cope with a Problem Manager?

■ **Learning Objective 2**

Up to this point we have prescribed tactics for dealing with a reasonably rational boss. At some point in their careers, many people face the situation of dealing with a problem manager—one who makes it difficult for the subordinate to get the job done. The problem is sometimes attributed to the boss's personality or incompetence. At other times, differences in values or goals could be creating the problem. Our concern here is with constructive approaches to dealing with the delicate situation of working for a problem manager.

REEVALUATE YOUR MANAGER

Some problem managers are not really a problem. Instead, one or more group members have been misperceived by them. Some employees think they have problem managers when those bosses simply have major role, goal, or value differences. (A role in this context is the expectations of the job.) The problem might also lie in conflicting personalities, such as being outgoing or shy. Another problem is conflicting perspectives, such as being detail oriented as opposed to taking an overall perspective. The differences just noted can be good or bad, depending on how they are viewed and used. For example, a combination of a detail-oriented group member with an "overall perspective" boss can be a winning combination. [8]

Another approach to being more cautious in evaluating your manager is to judge slowly and fairly. Many decisions your manager makes may prove to be worthwhile if you give the decisions time. [9] Top management at your company might issue an order that employees cannot surf the Web for personal reasons on the job. You might think this rule is unfair and treats workers like adolescents. If you wait for the result of the decisions, you might find that productivity improves. Another benefit might be that many workers no longer have to work late because they save time by not surfing.

CONFRONT YOUR MANAGER ABOUT THE PROBLEM

A general-purpose way of dealing with a problem manager is to confront the problem, then look for a solution. Because your manager has more formal authority than you, the confrontation must be executed with the highest level of tact and sensitivity. A beginning point in confronting a manager is to gently ask for an explanation of the problem. Suppose, for example, you believed strongly that your team leader snubs you because he or she dislikes you. You might inquire gently, "What might I be doing wrong that is creating a problem between us?"

Another situation calling for confrontation would be outrageous behavior by the manager, such as swearing at and belittling group members. For example, a worker reported that in meetings his manager openly belittles his peers and the people higher in the organization. The worker was concerned that this behavior fosters poor morale and unprofessional attitudes among team members and hurts productivity. [10] Because several or all group members are involved in the example cited, a group discussion of the problem might be warranted. You and your coworkers might meet as a group to discuss the impact of the manager's style on group morale and productivity. This tactic runs the risk of backfiring if the manager becomes defensive and angry. Yet confrontation is worth the risk because the problem of abuse will not go away without discussion.

Confrontation can also be helpful in dealing with the problem of **micromanagement,** the close monitoring of most aspects of group member activities by the manager. "Looking over your shoulder constantly" is an everyday term for micromanagement. If you feel that you are being supervised so closely that it is difficult to perform well, confront the situation. Say something of this nature, "I notice that you check almost everything I do lately. Am I making so many errors that you are losing confidence in my work?" [11] As a consequence, the manager might explain why he or she is micromanaging or begin to check on your work less frequently.

■ **Micromanagement**
the close monitoring of most aspects of group member activities by the manager

LEARN FROM YOUR MANAGER'S MISTAKES

Just as you can learn from watching your manager do things right, you can also learn from watching him or her do things wrong. In the first instance, we are talking about using your manager as a positive model. "Modeling" of this type is an important source of learning on the job. Using a superior as a negative model can also be of some benefit. As an elementary example, if your manager criticized you in public and you felt humiliated, you would have learned a good lesson in effective supervision: Never criticize a subordinate publicly. By serving as a negative example, your manager has taught you a valuable lesson.

Learning from a problem manager's mistakes can also occur when a manager is fired. Should your manager be fired, analyze the situation to avoid the mistakes he or she made. Enlist the help of others in understanding what went wrong. Did the manager get along poorly with higher-level managers? Was the manager lacking in technical expertise? Did the manager work hard enough? Did the manager commit ethical or legal violations, such as sexual harassment or stealing company property? Whatever the reason, you will learn quickly what behavior the company will not tolerate. If your manager was fired simply as a way to cut costs, there is still a lesson to be learned. Attempt to prove to the company that your compensation is a good investment for the company because your work is outstanding.

How Do You Build Good Coworker Relationships?

Anyone with work experience is aware of the importance of getting along with coworkers. If you are unable to work cooperatively with others, it will be difficult to hold on to your job. Poor relationships with coworkers can lead to frustration, stress, and decreased productivity, whereas getting along with them makes the workplace more satisfying. [12] You need their cooperation and support, and they need yours. Furthermore, the leading reason employees are terminated is not poor technical skills but rather inability or unwillingness to form satisfactory relationships with others on the job. In this section we describe a handful of basic tactics for developing and maintaining good coworker relationships.

DEVELOP ALLIES THROUGH BEING CIVIL

People who are courteous, kind, cooperative, and cheerful develop allies and friends in the workplace. Practicing basic good manners, such as being pleasant and friendly, is also part of being civil. Being civil helps make you stand out because many people believe that crude, rude, and obnoxious behavior has become a national problem. A poll of nearly 800 U.S. workers found that 10 percent witnessed incivility every day on the job, and 20 percent said they were direct targets of incivility at least once a week. [13] Examples of incivility include the following:

■ A salesperson makes sarcastic comments about another employee in front of a customer.

■ A coworker initiates cell phone calls while listening to a presentation at a meeting.

■ One worker continues responding to e-mail messages while another is talking to him in person.

■ A person whistles or sings constantly in the office (an intensely annoying behavior for many people). [14]

Being civil also involves not snooping; not spreading malicious gossip; and not weaseling out of group presents, such as shower or retirement gifts. In addition, it is important to be available to coworkers who want your advice as well as your help in times of crisis.

Closely related to being civil is maintaining a positive outlook. Everyone knows that you gain more allies by being optimistic and positive than by being pessimistic and negative. Nevertheless, many people ignore this simple strategy for getting along well with others. Coworkers are more likely to solicit your opinion or offer you help when you are perceived as a cheerful person.

MAKE OTHER PEOPLE FEEL IMPORTANT

A fundamental principle of fostering good relationships with coworkers and others is to make them feel important. Leadership and change consultant Sheila Murray Bethel advises us to make use of the please-make-me-feel-important concept. Visualize that everyone in the workplace is wearing a small sign around the neck that says, "Please make me feel important." [15] Although the leader has primary responsibility for satisfying this recognition need, coworkers also play a key role. One approach to making a coworker feel important would be to bring a notable accomplishment of his or hers to the attention of the group. Human

Relations Self-Assessment Quiz 9-2 gives you an opportunity to think through your tendencies to make others feel important.

MAINTAIN HONEST AND OPEN RELATIONSHIPS

In human relations we attach considerable importance to maintaining honest and open relationships with other people. The mechanism underlying openness is **self-disclosure,** the process of revealing your inner self to others. A person with a high degree of self-disclosure is open, whereas a person with a low degree of self-disclosure is closed. Nevertheless, you must be careful of excessive self-disclosure. Many people feel uneasy if another person is too self-revealing. The overly candid person risks beign rejected. For instance, if you communicate all your negative feelings and doubts to another person, that person may become annoyed and pull away from you. It would be too open to tell an office mate, "I am ticked off that the manager has us sharing the same office, but I'll put up with it until you quit or are fired."

Giving coworkers frank but tactful answers to their requests for your opinion is one useful way of developing open relationships. Assume that a coworker asks your

■ **Self-disclosure**

the process of revealing one's inner self to others

Human Relations Self-Assessment Quiz **9-2**

How Important Do I Make People Feel?

Indicate on a 1-to-5 scale how frequently you act (or would act if the situation presented itself) in the ways indicated: very infrequently (VI), infrequently (I), sometimes (S), frequently (F), very frequently (VF). Circle the number underneath the column that best fits your answer.

	VI	I	S	F	VF
1. I do my best to correctly pronounce a coworker's name.	1	2	3	4	5
2. I avoid letting other people's egos get too big.	5	4	3	2	1
3. I brag to others about the accomplishments of my coworkers.	1	2	3	4	5
4. I recognize the birthdays of friends in a tangible way.	1	2	3	4	5
5. It makes me anxious to listen to others brag about their accomplishments.	5	4	3	2	1
6. After hearing that a friend has done something outstanding, I shake his or her hand.	1	2	3	4	5
7. If a friend or coworker recently received a degree or certificate, I would offer my congratulations.	1	2	3	4	5
8. If a friend or coworker finished second in a contest, I would inquire why he or she did not finish first.	5	4	3	2	1
9. If a coworker showed me how to do something, I would compliment that person's skill.	1	2	3	4	5
10. When a coworker starts bragging about a family member's accomplishments, I do not respond.	5	4	3	2	1

Total score _____

Scoring and Interpretation:

Total the numbers corresponding to your answers. Scoring 40 to 50 points suggests that you typically make people feel important; 16 to 39 points suggests that you have a moderate tendency toward making others feel important; 10 to 15 points suggests that you need to develop skill in making others feel important. Study this chapter carefully.

opinion about a document he intends to send to his boss. As you read it, you find it somewhat incoherent and filled with spelling and grammatical errors. An honest response to this document might be, "I think your idea is a good one. But I think your memo needs more work before that idea comes across clearly."

Accurately expressing your feelings also leads to constructive relationships. If you arrive at work upset over a personal problem and appearing obviously fatigued, you can expect some reaction. A peer might say, "What seems to be the problem? Is everything all right?" A dishonest reply would be, "Everything is fine. What makes you think something is wrong?" In addition to making an obviously untrue statement, you would also be perceived as rejecting the person who asked the question.

If you prefer not to discuss your problem, an honest response on your part would be, "Thanks for your interest. I am facing some problems today. But I think things will work out." Such an answer would not involve you in a discussion of your personal problems. Also, you would not be perceived as rejecting your coworker. The same principle applies equally well to personal relationships.

■ Learning Objective 4

BE A TEAM PLAYER

■ **Team player**
one who emphasizes group accomplishment and cooperation rather than individual achievement and not helping others

An essential strategy for developing good relationships with coworkers is to be a team player. A **team player** is one who emphasizes group accomplishment and cooperation rather than individual achievement and not helping others. Team play has surged in importance because of the emphasis on having teams of workers decide how to improve productivity and quality. You will also have to be a team player if you reach the pinnacle of power in your organization. Executives are expected to be good team players as well as individual decision makers. However, team play is even more important on the way to becoming an executive because impatience and making unilateral decisions is more tolerated in the executive suite.

Being an effective team player is important because without such capability, collaborative effort is not possible. Being an effective team player is also important because of managerial perceptions. A survey of 15 business organizations in 34 industries indicates that employers rate "team player" as the most highly ranked workplace behavior. Approximately 40 percent of the managers surveyed ranked team player as number one among seven desirable traits. [16]

Here we describe a representative group of behaviors that contribute to team play. In addition, engaging in such behavior helps you be perceived as a team player.

1. Share credit with coworkers. A direct method of promoting team play is to share credit for good deeds with other team members. Instead of focusing on yourself as the person responsible for a work achievement, point out that the achievement was a team effort.

2. Display a helpful, cooperative attitude. Working cooperatively with others is virtually synonymous with team play. Cooperation translates into such activities as helping another worker with a computer problem, covering for a teammate when he or she is absent, and making sure a coworker has the input required from you on time. A helpful cooperative attitude is the main component of organizational citizenship behavior.

3. To establish trust, keep confidential information private and give honest opinions. Trust is important for teamwork because trust is a major contributor to cooperation. [17] Confidential information shared with you by a teammate should not be shared with others. Trust is exceedingly difficult to regain after a person has been betrayed. Giving honest opinions helps develop trust because the recipient of your honesty will regard you as a person of integrity. However, tact and diplomacy are still important. A dishonest opinion can often be detected through your nonverbal cues, such as discomfort in your voice tone. Assume that a friend of yours is starting a business selling antique toys over the Internet. She asks you if you like her proposed domain name, "www.OldjunkRus.com." You think the name is both ridiculous and an infringement on the Toys R Us name; yet you say, "Hey, terrific" with a sickened look on your face. You might lose some of your friend's trust.

4. Share information and opinions with coworkers. Teamwork is facilitated when group members share information and opinions. This is true because one of the benefits of group effort is that members can share ideas. The result is often a better solution to problems than would have been possible if people worked alone. The group thus achieves **synergy,** a product of group effort whereby the output of the group exceeds the output possible if the members worked alone.

■ **Synergy**
a product of group effort whereby the output of the group exceeds the output possible if the members worked alone

5. Provide emotional support to coworkers. Good team players offer each other emotional support. Such support can take the form of verbal encouragement for ideas expressed, listening to a group member's concerns, or complimenting achievement. An emotionally supportive comment to a coworker who appears to be experiencing stress might be, "This doesn't look like one of your better days. What can I do to help?" According to a one study, emotionally supporting coworkers facilitates their being able to service customers better. [18] Perhaps when workers feel emotionally supported, it is easier for them to have a positive attitude toward customers.

New research suggests that you may have to remind yourself to be supportive as you become more experienced at work. A study of 2,300 workers conducted by the human capital assessment firm PsyMax Solutions found that the longer someone holds the same job the less likely he or she will be supportive of others in the workplace. The study found a steady decline in supportive behavior as a person's tenure increased. According to Wayne Nemeroff, the CEO of PsyMax, "While someone's work style might ordinarily be expected to stay the same, we learned that in respect to one behavior there is a definite change. After three to five years on the job, there's less willingness to show concern, assist others, or even to act in a welcoming manner." [19] Apparently over time workers become more focused on the task at hand, and less interested in others. Could it also be that a little bit of burnout is entering the picture?

6. Follow the Golden Rule. The ancient adage "Treat others the way you would like them to treat you" provides a firm foundation for effective teamwork. Although some may dismiss the Golden Rule as a syrupy platitude, it still works. For example, you would probably want someone to help you with a perplexing problem, so you take the initiative to help others when you have the expertise needed.

7. Avoid actions that could sabotage or undermine the group in any way. Frequently criticizing group members directly or complaining about them to outsiders works against the best interest of the group. Members within the group, as well as the team leader, will most likely hear that you criticized them to an outsider, thus doing severe damage to your ability to work cooperatively with them.

8. Attend company-sponsored social events. A worker's reputation as a team player is often judged both on the job and in company-sponsored social events, such as parties, picnics, and athletic events. If you attend these and participate fully, your reputation as a team player will be enhanced. Company-sponsored social events are also important because they provide an opportunity to build rapport with coworkers. Rapport, in turn, facilitates teamwork.

9. Share the glory. You will make a poor team player if you try to grab all the glory for ideas that work and distance yourself from ideas that do not work. An effective team member wants all other members to succeed. You will stand out by praising the people you work with rather than hogging any praise for the team.

10. Avoid backstabbing. A special category of disliked behavior is **backstabbing,** an attempt to discredit by underhanded means such as innuendo, accusation, or the like. A backstabber might drop hints to the boss, for example, that a coworker

■ **Backstabbing**
an attempt to discredit by underhanded means such as innuendo, accusation, or the like

performs poorly under pressure or is looking for a new job. Sometimes the back-stabber assertively gathers information to backstab a coworker. He or she might engage another worker in a derogatory discussion about the boss and then report the coworker's negative comments back to the boss. A person who develops a reputation as a backstabber will receive poor cooperation from coworkers. The person might also be considered untrustworthy by management, thus retarding his or her own career.

These 10 points contribute specifically to effective team play. Recognize also that all other actions directed toward good coworker relationships will enhance team play.

FOLLOW GROUP STANDARDS OF CONDUCT

■ **Group norms**

unwritten set of expectations for group members—what people ought to do; basic principle to follow in getting along with coworkers

■ **Organizational culture**

values and beliefs of the firm that guide people's actions

The basic principle to follow in getting along with coworkers is to follow **group norms.** These refer to the unwritten set of expectations for group members—what people ought to do. Norms become a standard of what each person should do or not do within the group. Norms also provide general guidelines for reacting constructively to the behavior of coworkers. Norms are a major component of the **organizational culture,** or values and beliefs of the firm that guide people's actions. In one firm, the norms and culture may favor hard work and high quality. In another firm, the norms and culture may favor a weaker work ethic.

Group norms also influence the social aspects of behavior on the job. These aspects of behavior relate to such things as the people with whom to have lunch, getting together after work, joining a company team, and the type of clothing to wear to work. Sharing laughter, such as poking positive fun at coworkers, is another example of an important social behavior linked to a group norm.

Workers learn about norms through both observation and direct instruction from other group members. If you do not deviate too far from these norms, the group will accept much of your behavior. If you deviate too far, you will be subject to much rejection and feelings of isolation. In some instances, you might even be subjected to verbal abuse if you make the other employees look bad.

Getting along too well with coworkers has its price as well. The risk of conforming too closely to group norms is that you lose your individuality. You become viewed by your superiors as "one of the office gang" rather than a person who aspires to move up in the organization. It is important to be a good team player, but to advance in your career you must also find a way to distinguish yourself, such as through creative thinking and outstanding performance.

EXPRESS AN INTEREST IN THE WORK AND PERSONAL LIFE OF COWORKERS

Almost everyone is self-centered to some extent, as suggested by the what's-in-it-for-me (WIIFM) principle. Thus, topics that are favored are ones closely related to themselves, such as their children, friends, hobbies, work, or possessions. Sales representatives rely heavily on this fact in cultivating relationships with established customers. They routinely ask the customer about his or her hobbies, family members, and work activities. You can capitalize on this simple strategy by asking coworkers and friends questions such as these:

How is your work going? *(highly recommended)*

How did you gain the knowledge necessary for your job?

How does the company use the output from your department?

How did your son enjoy computer camp?

Closely related to expressing interest in others is to investigate what you have in common, both professionally and personally, with peers. You might identify common interests, such as a focus on the company's market share, or a personal interest, such as hiking. [20]

A danger in asking questions about other people's work and personal life is that some questions may not be perceived as well intentioned. There is a fine line between honest curiosity and snooping. You must stay alert to this subtle distinction.

USE APPROPRIATE COMPLIMENTS

An effective way of developing good relationships with coworkers and friends is to compliment something with which they closely identify, such as their children, spouses, hobbies, or pets. Paying a compliment is a form of positive reinforcement, rewarding somebody for doing something right. The right response is therefore strengthened or reinforced. A compliment is a useful multipurpose reward.

Another way of complimenting people is through recognition. The suggestions made earlier about making people feel important are a way of recognizing people and, therefore, compliments. Investing a small amount of time in recognizing a coworker can pay large dividends in terms of cultivating an ally. Recognition and compliments are more likely to create a favorable relationship when they are appropriate. *Appropriate* in this context means that the compliment fits the accomplishment. Praise that is too lavish may be interpreted as belittling and patronizing.

Let's look at the difference between an appropriate and an exaggerated compliment over the same issue. An executive secretary gets a fax machine operating that was temporarily not sending messages.

> *Appropriate compliment.* Nice job, Stephanie. Fixing the fax machine took considerable skill. We can now resume sending important fax messages.

> *Exaggerated compliment.* Stephanie, I'm overwhelmed. You're a world-class fax machine specialist. Are there no limits to your talents?

Observe that the appropriate compliment is thoughtful and is proportionate to what Stephanie accomplished. The exaggerated compliment is probably wasted because it is way out of proportion to the magnitude of the accomplishment.

Cultural factors can mediate (influence) the most effective approach for getting along with coworkers. Although there is a strong tendency for people from another country to quickly adapt to the culture of your country, you still have to be sensitive to cultural differences for rapport building. An example would be for an American not to be disappointed when a British coworker offers modest, instead of effusive, compliments for a job well done. The American might have just won a sales contest, and informs her British coworker of the feat. He responds, "Certainly, in the right direction." (Your disappointment might come across as a frown or some other subtle rejection.)

DEAL EFFECTIVELY WITH DIFFICULT PEOPLE

■ **Learning Objective 5**

A major challenge in getting along well with coworkers is dealing constructively with **difficult people.** A coworker is classified as difficult if he or she is uncooperative, touchy, defensive, hostile, or even very unfriendly. Three examples of difficult people follow:

■ **Difficult people**
a coworker is classified as difficult if he or she is uncooperative, touchy, defensive, hostile, or even very unfriendly

■ **The lone wolf.** Can't stand being part of anything: a team, a project, or group functions. Independent to a fault—makes no attempt to hide solitary preferences.

■ **Chicken Little.** No matter how sunny things seem to be, he or she will always find a cloud to cast a shadow. ("What a great Web site we have. Twenty thousand visitors in the first week." "Yeah, but are more than 1 percent buying anything?") [21]

■ **The high-maintenance person.** Requires so much assistance, special attention, and extra help that it wears you down. No matter what type of help you offer, they want a little more. If you bring a high-maintenance worker a soft drink, he or she is likely to say, "Didn't they have any decaffeinated soft drinks?"

■ **The office magpie.** Always eager to chat and assumes that other workers want to do likewise. Whenever he or she is not faced with a pressing deadline barges into your workspace to shoot the breeze. Also known to send dozens of e-mails, along with chatty personal comments, over the same issue. [22]

■ **Personality disorder**

pervasive, persistent, inflexible, maladaptive pattern of behavior that deviates from expected cultural norms

In dealing with difficult coworkers, as well as difficult bosses, it is important to recognize that their problems could go much deeper than those of the types of individuals mentioned. Such individuals could be suffering from one or more of the personality disorders summarized in Figure 9-1. A **personality disorder** is a pervasive, persistent, inflexible, maladaptive pattern of behavior that deviates from expected cultural norms. The disorder is learned early in life and cause distress to the person or conflicts with others. Individuals with personality disorders range from harmless eccentrics to dangerous, aggressive individuals. [23] If your difficult coworker has a severe personality disorder, the techniques described in the following paragraphs will not work as well as they would with a difficult person who has a mild disorder. About 5 to 10 percent of the population suffers from a personality disorder, and the negative behavior is the most likely to be triggered by heavy stress.

Rather than attempt to list different tactics for dealing with specific types of difficult people, here we present five widely applicable approaches for dealing with such individuals.

Take Problems Professionally, Not Personally

A key principle in dealing with difficult people is to take what they do professionally, not personally. Difficult people are not necessarily out to get you. You may simply represent a stepping stone for them to get what they want. [24] For example, if a coworker insults you because you need his help Friday afternoon, he probably has nothing against you personally. He just prefers to become mentally disengaged from work that Friday afternoon. Your request distracts him from mentally phasing out of work as early as he would like.

Give Ample Feedback

The primary technique for dealing with counterproductive behavior is to feed back to the difficult person how his or her behavior affects you. Focus on the person's behavior rather than on characteristics or values. If a Chicken Little type is annoying you by constantly pointing out potential disasters, say something to this effect: "I have difficulty maintaining my enthusiasm when you so often point out the possible negatives." Such a statement will engender less resentment than saying, "I find you to be a total pessimist, and it annoys me."

Listen and Respond

Closely related to giving feedback is listening and responding. Give the difficult person ample opportunity to express his or her concerns, doubts, anger, or other feelings. Then acknowledge your awareness of the person's position. [25] An example: "OK, you tell me that management is really against us and, therefore, we shouldn't work so hard." After listening, present your perspective in a way such as this: "Your viewpoint may be valid based on your experiences. Yet so far, I've found management here to be on my side." This exchange of viewpoints is less likely to lead to failed communication than if you are judgmental with a statement such as, "You really shouldn't think that way."

The 10 personality disorders recognized by the American Psychiatric Association are grouped into three clusters. Many difficult people may in reality suffer from a personality disorder, such as the "control freak" who is experiencing an obsessive-compulsive disorder.

Cluster A: The Odd or Eccentric Group
   1. *Paranoid Personality.* Pattern of distrust and suspiciousness with a tendency to attribute evil motives to others.
   2. *Schizoid Personality.* Pervasive pattern of detachment from social relationships and restriction of emotion in interpersonal settings.
   3. *Schizotypal* Behavior, appearance, or thinking that is consistently strange or odd.

Cluster B: The Dramatic, Emotional, and Erratic Group
   4. *Antisocial.* Chronic maladaptive behavior that disregards the rights of others.
   5. *Borderline.* Instability of interpersonal relationships, self-image, and mood.
   6. *Histrionic.* Excessive emotionality and attention-seeking behavior.
   7. *Narcissistic.* Behavior includes grandiosity, need for admiration, and lack of empathy.

Cluster C: The Anxious and Fearful Group
   8. *Avoidant.* Pattern of social inhibition, feelings of inadequacy, and hypersensitivity to negative evaluation.
   9. *Dependent.* Predominantly dependent and submissive behavior.
  10. *Obsessive-compulsive.* Preoccupation with orderliness, perfectionism, and control at the expense of flexibility and efficiency.

Figure	9-1

Ten Major Personality Disorders
Source: Michael S. Beeson, "Personality Disorders," available at www.emedicine.com/emerg/topic418.html, retrieved March 26, 2006 "Personality Disorders," in *DSM*-IV (Washington, DC: American Psychiatric Association, 1966), pp. 629–674. ("DSM" refers to *Diagnostic and Statistical Manual*.)

Use Tact and Diplomacy in Dealing with Annoying Behavior

Coworkers who irritate you rarely do annoying things on purpose. Tactful actions on your part can sometimes take care of these annoyances without your having to confront the problem. Close your door, for example, if noisy coworkers are gathered outside. Or try one woman's method of getting rid of office pests: She keeps a file open on her computer screen and gestures to it apologetically when someone overstays a visit.

Sometimes subtlety doesn't work, and it may be necessary to diplomatically confront the coworker who is annoying you. A useful approach is to precede a criticism with a compliment. Here is an example of this approach: "You're one of the best people I've ever worked with, but one habit of yours drives me bananas. Do you think you could let me know when you're going to be late getting back to the office after lunch?" [26]

Use Humor

Nonhostile humor can often be used to help a difficult person understand how his or her behavior is blocking others. Also, the humor will help defuse conflict between you and that person. The humor should point to the person's unacceptable behavior yet not belittle him or her. Assume that you and a coworker are working jointly

> "Having dealt with both of them [Steve Jobs and Bill Gate] personally, I can tell you it's a challenge to work with brilliance. You've got to get their respect and prove you're up to dealing with them."
> —Dave House,
>
> former head of Bay Networks, and also former Intel executive. Quoted in Carol Hymowitz, "To Some Executives, Football Star's Battle Is Like Office Games," *The Wall Street Journal*, August 23, 2005, p. B1.

on a report. For each idea that you submit, your coworker gets into the know-it-all mode and informs you of important facts that you neglected. An example of non-hostile humor that might jolt the coworker into realizing that his or her approach is annoying is at follows:

> *If there is ever a contest to choose the human with a brain that can compete against a Zip file, I will nominate you. But even though my brain is limited to human capacity, I still think I can supply a few facts for our report.*

Your humor may help the other person recognize that he or she is attempting to overwhelm you with facts at his or her disposal. You are being self-effacing and thereby drawing criticism away from your coworker. Self-effacement (self-criticism) is a proven humor tactic.

Avoid Creating a Dependency on You

A trap to avoid with many difficult people, and especially the high-maintenance person, is to let him or her become too dependent on you for solutions to problems. In your desire to be helpful and supportive to coworkers, you run the risk of creating a dependency. A difficult person might be pestering you to regularly help solve some of his or her most challenging work problems. The high-maintenance worker might ask you to look up a number in the phone book, reboot a stalled computer, or help scrape ice from the windshield and windows of his or her auto. You may want to be a good organizational citizen, yet you also need more time for your own work, and you do not want to make the person too dependent on you. [27] As an antidote to the problem, make frequent statements such as, "You have a telephone directory," "I know you can reboot your computer," and "Perhaps you can scrape the ice yourself because I have to do the same thing with my SUV."

Reinforce Civil Behavior and Good Moods

In the spirit of positive reinforcement, when a generally difficult person is behaving acceptably, recognize the behavior in some way. Reinforcing statements would include, "It's fun working with you today" and "I appreciate your professional attitude."

The tactics for dealing with difficult people described require practice to be effective. Also, you may have to use a combination of the seven tactics described in this section to deal effectively with a difficult person. The point of these tactics is not to outmanipulate or subdue a difficult person but to establish a cordial and productive working relationship.

FACE MATURELY THE CHALLENGE OF THE OFFICE ROMANCE

Office romances can be disruptive to morale and productivity. Coworker romances are a more widespread potential problem because more romances take place between coworkers on the same level than between superiors and subordinates. As more women have entered the workforce in professional positions and as professionals work longer hours, the office has become a frequent meeting place. People often work closely in teams and other joint projects, thus creating the conditions for romance to take place. Another basic reason why office romances are so frequent is that familiarity builds emotional and physical attraction. Based on research spanning 20 years, Cindy Hazan, an associate professor of human development at Cornell University, concludes that people need attachment. And proximity breeds attachment. "Proximity is really the core of attachment. Familiar people have a calming, soothing effect on us." [28]

Many companies have policies against managers dating people below them in the hierarchy, but few companies attempt to restrict same-level romantic relationships.

About 72 percent of companies do not have written policies about dating, yet about 14 percent have an unwritten understanding. [29] Managers widely accept the idea of employees dating each other, with nearly 68 percent of managers of all ages saying it is acceptable, according to an American Management Survey. [30] Nevertheless, sensitivity is required to conduct an office romance that does not detract from your professionalism.

Many companies are concerned about information leakage within their organization. If you date a person who has access to confidential information (such as trade secrets), management might be concerned that you are a security risk. You, therefore, might miss out on some opportunities for better assignments. Companies also worry about negative consequences stemming from office romances, such as sexual harassment claims, low morale of coworkers, lowered productivity from the couple involved in the romance, and an unprofessional atmosphere. Yet an important positive consequence to employers from an office romance is that while the relationship is working well, the couple may have a heightened interest in coming to work. Also, romance can trigger energy that leads to enhanced productivity.

It is important not to abuse company tolerance of the coworker romance. Do not invite the person you are dating to meals at company expense, take him or her on nonessential business trips, or create projects to work on jointly. Strive to keep the relationship confidential and restricted to after hours. Minimize talking to coworkers about the relationship. Such behavior as holding hands or kissing in public view is regarded as poor office etiquette. Disappearing acts together during working hours are taboo.

Should your coworker romance terminate, you face a special challenge. You must now work together cooperatively with a person toward whom you may have angry feelings. Few people have the emotional detachment necessary to work smoothly with a former romantic involvement. Extra effort, therefore, will be required on both your parts.

What should you do if you and your boss seem suited for a long-term commitment? Why walk away from Mr. or Ms. Right? My suggestion is that if you do become romantically involved, one of you should request a transfer to another department. Many office romances do lead to happy marriages and other long-term relationships. At the start of the relationship, however, use considerable discretion. Engaging in personal conversations during work time or holding hands in the company cafeteria is unprofessional and taboo.

To help deal with the complexity and the positive and negative aspects of office romance, some companies have established policies covering such relationships. To prevent charges of sexual harassment, a policy about office romance is likely to emphasize that both parties must mutually and voluntarily consent to the social relationship. Furthermore, the policy states that the social relationship must not affect job performance or negatively impact the company's business. [31] The accompanying Human Relations in Practice box offers some additional professional advice about the conduct of office romances.

How Do You Build Good Relationships with Customers?

■ Learning Objective 6

Success on the job also requires building good relationships with both external and internal customers. Business success is built on good relationships, as emphasized again and again by business advisors. [32] *External customers* fit the traditional definition of customer that includes clients and guests. External customers can be classified as either retail or industrial. The latter represents one company buying from another, such as purchasing steel. *Internal customers* are the people you serve

Human Relations in Practice

Human Resources Specialist Advises on Office Romance

Professionals who advise company owners and managers about office romances say the owner or manager, on learning of the relationship, needs to talk to the couple. "You should immediately meet with those people and set some guidelines for appropriate workplace behavior," says Arlene Vernon, a human resources consultant in Eden Prairie, Minnesota. "You need to tell them, 'This is not your place for any of the fooling around that might go on—sneaking, hand-holdings, hugging in the corner, passing little notes.'"

But you shouldn't try to forbid the couple from having the relationship. As lawyer, John Robinson puts it, "You can't stop biology." And Vernon said that trying to force an end to a relationship can create an unpleasant atmosphere for everyone, including other employees who wouldn't want similar interference in their personal lives. She suggests telling the couple, "I'm glad you met and that things are going well, but this is what I expect in the workplace."

Source: Excerpted from Joyce M. Rosenberg, "Office Romances Can Pose Problems," Associated Press, February 6, 2004.

within the organization or those who use the output from your job. For example, if you design computer graphics, the other people in the company who receive your graphics are your internal customers.

The information already presented about getting along with your manager and coworkers dealt with internal customers. Here we emphasize providing good service (or delight) to external customers. An employee whose thoughts and actions are geared toward helping customers has a **customer service orientation.** Good service is the primary factor that keeps customers coming back. This is important because profits jump considerably as the customer is retained over time. Some techniques described here for serving external customers would also work well with internal customers and vice versa.

■ **Customer service orientation**
approach of employee whose thoughts and actions are geared toward helping customers

An overall approach to dealing effectively with customers is to be a good organizational citizen with respect to customer relationships. You gear a lot of your out-of-the-way effort into customer relationships. Specific behaviors of this type are presented in Figure 9-2. Time-tested suggestions for high-level customer service are presented next. [33] Taken together, these suggestions will help you bond with a customer, referring to a close and valued ongoing relationship. You will be able to implement principles of good service more readily if you are treated well by your employer. When workers feel valued, and are adequately compensated, they usually spread the sunshine to customers. Satisfied employees create satisfied customers. [34] One of the key reasons for the enviable success of JetBlue airlines is that all workers are treated well, and they, in turn, treat customers well.

1. **Establish customer satisfaction goals.** Decide jointly with your manager how much you intend to help customers. Find answers to questions such as the following: "Is your company attempting to satisfy every customer within 10 minutes of his or her request?" "Are you striving to provide the finest customer service in your field?" "Is your goal zero defections to competitors?" Your goals will dictate how much and the type of effort you put into pleasing customers.

2. **Understand your customer's needs and place them first.** The most basic principle of selling is to identify and satisfy customer needs. Many customers may not be able

1. Tells outsiders this is a good place to work.
2. Says good things about the organization to others.
3. Generates favorable goodwill for the company.
4. Encourages friends and family to use the firm's products and services.
5. Actively promotes the firm's products and services.
6. Follows customer service guidelines with extreme care.
7. Conscientiously follows guidelines for customer promotions.
8. Follows up in a timely manner to customer requests and problems.
9. Performs duties with unusually few mistakes.
10. Always has a positive attitude at work.
11. Regardless of circumstances, exceptionally courteous and respectful to customers.
12. Encourages coworkers to contribute ideas and suggestions for service improvement.
13. Contributes many ideas for customer promotions and communications.
14. Makes constructive suggestions for service improvement.
15. Frequently presents to others creative solutions to customer problems.
16. Takes home brochures to read up on products and services.

Figure 9-2

Service-Oriented Organizational Citizenship Behaviors
Source: Portion of a table from Lance A. Bettencourt, Kevin P. Gwinner, and Matthew L. Meuter, "A Comparison of Attitude, Personality, and Knowledge Predictors of Service-Oriented Organizational Citizenship Behaviors," *Journal of Applied Psychology*, February 2001, p. 32.

to express their needs clearly. Also, they may not be certain of their needs. To help identify customer needs, you may have to probe for more information. For example, an associate in a consumer electronics store may have to ask, "What uses do you have in mind for your television receiver aside from watching regular programs? Will you be using it to display digital photographs?" Knowing such information will help the store associate identify which television receiver will satisfy the customer's needs.

After you have identified customer needs, focus on satisfying them rather than doing what is convenient for you or the firm. Assume, for example, that the customer says, "I would like to purchase nine reams of copier paper." The sales associate should not respond, "Sorry, the copying paper comes in boxes of 10, so it is not convenient to sell you nine reams." The associate might, however, offer a discount for the purchase of the full 10-ream box if such action fits company policy.

3. Show care and concern. During contacts with your customer, show concern for his or her welfare. Ask questions such as the following: "How have you enjoyed the television set you bought here awhile back?" "How are you feeling today?" After asking the question, project a genuine interest in the answer. A strictly business approach to showing care and concern is to follow up on requests. A telephone call or e-mail message to the requester of your service is usually sufficient follow-up. A follow-up is effective because it completes the communication loop between two people.

4. Communicate a positive attitude. A positive attitude is conveyed by factors such as appearance, friendly gestures, a warm voice tone, and good telephone communication skills. If a customer seems apologetic about making a heavy demand, respond, "No need to apologize. My job is to please you. I'm here to serve." One reason a positive attitude is important is that hostility by the customer contact person leads to customer dissatisfaction. Lorna Doucet, a professor of organizational behavior at the University of Illinois, conducted a study in the telephone service center for a large retail bank. She found that hostility by the service provider had the strongest negative effect on customers when it was combined with low technical performance (poor answers) by the call center representative. (Perceived hostility was measured by questionnaires.) Hostility was more tolerated if the customers received the answers they needed. [35]

5. Make the buyer feel good. A fundamental way of building a customer relationship is to make the buyer feel good about himself or herself. Also, make the buyer feel good because he or she has bought from you. Offer compliments about the customer's healthy glow or a report that specified vendor requirements (for an industrial customer). Explain how much you value the customer's business. An effective feel-good line is, "I enjoy doing business with you." Smiling is a useful technique for making the customer feel good. Also, smiling is a natural relationship builder and can help you bond with your customer. Smile several times during each customer contact, even if your customer is angry with your product or service. Yet guard against smiling constantly or inappropriately because your smile then becomes meaningless. False smiling if carried out regularly is stressful, so look for opportunities to smile genuinely.

6. Display strong business ethics. Ethical violations receive so much publicity that you can impress customers by being conspicuously ethical. Look for ways to show that you are so ethical that you would welcome making your sales tactics public knowledge. Also, treat the customer the same way you would treat a family member or a valued friend.

7. Be helpful rather than defensive when a customer complains. As described earlier, look at a complaint professionally rather than personally. Listen carefully and concentrate on being helpful. The upset customer cares primarily about having the problem resolved and does not care whether you are at fault. Use a statement such as, "I understand this mistake is a major inconvenience. I'll do what I can right now to solve the problem." Remember also that complaints that are taken care of quickly and satisfactorily will often create a more positive impression than mistake-free service. Another way of being helpful is to ask for enough details about what went wrong so that you can begin resolving the problem. Explain as soon as possible how you are going to fix the problem.

8. Invite the customer back. The southern U.S. expression "Y'all come back, now!" is well suited for good customer service. Specific invitations to return may help increase repeat business. The more focused and individualized the invitation, the more likely it will have an impact on customer behavior. ("Y'all come back, now!" is sometimes used too indiscriminately to be effective.) Pointing out why you enjoyed doing business with the customer and what future problems you could help with is an effective technique. Another way of encouraging the customer to return is to explain how much you value him or her.

9. Avoid rudeness. Although rudeness to customers is obviously a poor business practice, the problem is widespread. Rudeness by customer contact personnel is a major problem from the employer's standpoint. Be aware of subtle forms of rudeness, such as complaining about your job or working hours in front of customers. To elevate your awareness level about rudeness among customer contact personnel, do Human Relations Self-Assessment Quiz 9-3.

The preceding nine points emphasize the importance of practicing good human relations with customers and having a customer service orientation. Good customer service stems naturally from practicing good human relations.

Human Relations Self-Assessment Quiz 9-3

Am I Being Rude?

Following is a list of behaviors of customer contact workers that would be interpreted as rude by many customers. Indicate whether you have engaged in such behavior in your dealings with customers or whether you are likely to do so if your job did involve customer contact.

	Yes	No
1. I talk to a coworker while serving a customer.	_____	_____
2. I conduct a telephone conversation with someone else while serving a customer.	_____	_____
3. I address customers by their first names without having their permission.	_____	_____
4. I address customers as "You guys."	_____	_____
5. I chew gum or eat candy while dealing with a customer.	_____	_____
6. I laugh when customers describe an agonizing problem they are having with one of our company's products or services.	_____	_____
7. I minimize eye contact with customers.	_____	_____
8. I say the same thing to every customer, such as "Have a nice day," in a monotone.	_____	_____
9. I accuse customers of attempting to cheat the company before carefully investigating the situation.	_____	_____
10. I hurry customers when my break time approaches.	_____	_____
11. I comment on a customer's appearance in a flirtatious, sexually oriented way.	_____	_____
12. I sometimes complain about or make fun of other customers when I am serving another customer.	_____	_____

Interpretation:

The more of these behaviors you have engaged in, the ruder you are and the more likely you are losing potential business for your company. If you have not engaged in any of these behaviors, even when faced with a rude customer, you are an asset to your employer. You are also tolerant.

As you deal with customers in our culturally diverse and enriched workplace, remember also to be aware of possible cross-cultural differences. Be alert to customs that could make a difference in terms of the customer feeling good about his or her experience with you. An illustrative cultural difference is that in the typical Asian family, older family members accompany younger members when a major purchase, such as a home, is being contemplated. Although the older family members may stay in the background, they might be a major financial and emotional influence on the purchase. So the eager real estate agent should not act as if the older family members are simply along for the ride. Instead, the agent should show respect by presenting vital details to all the family members, not only the couple making the purchase.

Concept Review and Reinforcement

Key Terms

Summary and Review

Adequate interpersonal skills are necessary for success in business. Developing a favorable relationship with your manager is the most basic strategy of getting ahead in your career. Specific tactics for developing a good relationship with your manager include the following:

- Achieve good job performance.
- Display a strong work ethic. (Use such means as demonstrating competence on even minor tasks, assuming personal responsibility for problems, and completing projects promptly.)
- Demonstrate good emotional intelligence. (Deal effectively with the emotional responses of coworkers and customers.)
- Be dependable and honest.
- Be a good organizational citizen. (Be willing to work for the good of the organization even without the promise of a specific reward.)
- Create a strong presence (keep yourself in the forefront).
- Find out what your manager expects of you.
- Minimize complaints.
- Avoid bypassing your manager.
- Engage in favorable interactions with your manager.

Coping with a manager you perceive to be a problem is part of getting along with him or her.
Consider the following approaches:

- Reevaluate your manager to make sure you have not misperceived him or her.
- It is important to confront your manager about your problem. Often this problem is a case of being micromanaged.
- Learning from your problem manager's mistakes (even if he or she gets fired) is recommended.

Methods and tactics for building coworker relationships include the following:

- Develop allies through being civil, including maintaining a positive outlook.
- Make other people feel important.
- Maintain honest and open relationships (including self-disclosure).
- Be a team player.
- Follow group standards of conduct.
- Express an interest in the work and personal life of coworkers.
- Use appropriate (nonexaggerated) compliments.

Deal effectively with difficult people, including the following:

- Take problems professionally.
- Give ample feedback.
- Listen and respond.
- Use tact and diplomacy.
- Use humor.
- Avoid creating a dependency on you.
- Reinforce civil behavior and good moods.
- Face maturely the challenge of the office romance.

Team player approaches include sharing credit, maintaining a cooperative attitude, establishing trust, sharing information and opinions, providing emotional support, practicing the Golden Rule, avoiding sabotaging or undermining actions, sharing the glory, and avoiding backstabbing.

Job success also requires building good relationships with both internal and external customers. Techniques for providing high-level customer service include:

- Establishing customer satisfaction goals.
- Understanding your customer's needs and placing them first.
- Showing care and concern.
- Communicating a positive attitude.
- Making the buyer feel good.

- Displaying strong business ethics.
- Being helpful rather than defensive when a customer complains.
- Inviting the customer back.
- Avoiding rudeness.

Check your Understanding

1. If team leaders don't have as much power as a regular manager, why is it still important to build a good relationship with your team leader?
2. In what way does emotional intelligence contribute to getting along with managers, coworkers, and customers?
3. How can a worker implement the tactic "engage in favorable interactions with your manager" without appearing to be "kissing up" to the boss?
4. Why is "creating a strong presence" considered a key strategy for getting ahead in the workplace?
5. Why study about getting along with coworkers and customers? Isn't common sense good enough to develop smooth working relationships with people?
6. Give an example of a technique you think would make a coworker feel important.

7. Many customer contact workers routinely say, "Have a nice day" when the customer's transaction has been completed. How effective is this expression in building customer relationships?
8. Suppose you thought the reason that a coworker of yours was a difficult person was because he or she had a true personality disorder. Would you recommend that he or she seek mental health treatment? Explain your reasoning.
9. If rudeness is so widespread today, why bother being polite and considerate on the job?
10. Ask a person who has achieved job success what he or she thinks are two important ways of getting along with coworkers and customers. Compare notes with classmates.

Web Corner

Getting along with your coworkers:
http://careerplanning.about.com/od/bosscoworkers/

Managing relationships:
www.howtoadvice.com/BossRelations.

Getting along with customers: www.smallbizresource.com

Internet Skill Builder:

Visit http://careers.homedepot.com, and proceed to "Living our values." Identify which skills mentioned relate to workplace relationships, including communication skills and self-understanding. Reflect back on any time you have visited a Home Depot or a competitor's store. How realistic is Home Depot about the interpersonal and personal skills required for a sales associate? If you happen to know a Home Depot employee, obtain his or her input in formulating your answer to the preceding question.

Developing Your Human Relations Skills

Human Relations Applications Exercises

Applying Human Relations Exercise 9-1

Giving Good Customer Service

Role players in this exercise will demonstrate two related techniques for giving good customer service: show care and concern and make the buyer feel good. The role players will carry out the scenarios in front of the class. For both role plays, the provider of customer service should think through before starting the role play what specifically he or she is attempting to accomplish. For example, the role player might ask himself or herself, "How am I going to show care and concern?" or "What am I going to do to make the buyer feel good."

Scenario 1: Show care and concern. A sales representative meets with two company representatives to talk about installing a new information system for employee benefits. One of the company representatives is from the human resources department and the other is from the information technology department. The sales representative will attempt to show care and concern for both company representatives during the same meeting.

Scenario 2: Make the buyer feel good. A couple, played by two role players, enters a new-car showroom to examine a model they have seen advertised on television. Although they are not in urgent need of a new car, they are strongly interested. The sales representative is behind quota for the month and would like to close a sale today. The rep decides to use the tactic "make the buyer feel good" to help form a bond.

The rest of the class will provide some constructive feedback, and perhaps compliments, to the role players.

Use the following evaluation dimensions to help you evaluate the effectiveness of the customer service providers and customers. Use a scale of 1 to 5 in making your ratings: 1 = very poor, 2 = poor, 3 = average, 4 = good, and 5 = very good.

Customer Service Evaluation Factors	1 VP	2 P	3 A	4 G	5 VG
1. Maintained eye contact					
2. Was warm and supportive					
3. Smiled appropriately					
4. Displayed positive attitude					
5. Showed genuine concern					
6. Made buyer feel good					

Customer Evaluation Dimensions	1 VP	2 P	3 A	4 G	5 VG
1. Behaved realistically					
2. Showed respect for service provider					
3. Treated provider like a professional					
4. Showed appreciation for service provider's effort.					

Other comments about the role players:

Applying Human Relations Exercise 9-2

The Elevator 30-Second Speech

A long-standing tip in career development and impressing higher ups is to make a 30-second impromptu presentation when you have a chance encounter with a key person in your organization. If you work in an office tower, the chance encounter is likely to take place on an elevator—and it is generally frowned on to have long conversations in an elevator. So the term "elevator speech" developed to describe a brief opportunity to impress a key person. Imagine that you have a chance encounter with a high-ranking executive in your area on the elevator or escalator, in the parking lot, during a company picnic, or at some other location. You then give that person a 30-second pitch geared to make a positive impression. Because you must boil your pitch down to 30 seconds, you will need to prepare for a long time. (Credit President Abraham Lincoln for that insight.)

About six different pairs (impresser and person to be impressed) will carry out this role play in front of the class. The evaluators will put themselves in the role of the target key person of the 30-second evaluation. Consider using the following scale and answering the two questions:

_____ Wow, I was impressed. (5 points)

_____ I was kind of impressed with the person I ran into. (4 points)

_____ He or she left me with at least an average impression. (3 points)

_____ I found the person to be somewhat annoying. (2 points)

_____ That person I met left with a terrible impression. (1 point)

1. What I liked about person's 30-second pitch:
2. What I saw as possible areas for improvement:

Find a mechanism to feed back some of your observations to the role players. Volunteer to present the findings in class, give the person your comments on note paper, or send him or her an e-mail.

Human Relations Case Studies 9-1

The Downhill Insurance Office

A large insurance company established a small sales office in the Detroit, Michigan, area. In addition to sales, the office would also provide the field staff with training in new product knowledge and sales skills. The four key people in the office were transferred from both inside and outside the geographic area of the office. The group worked well together, and within several months the sales and training goals established for the office were met. As the goals were reached, the office was expanded to a total of 30 staff members, most of whom were sales agents. Soon the office was producing $300,000 monthly in insurance premiums. In addition to commissions for the initial sale, the agents would receive residuals, or additional commissions, as the policies were renewed.

Tim Draper, the vice president who established the new office, suddenly decided to return to his hometown so he could spend more time with his family. The company then appointed Gordon Bracker, an experienced sales manager with the company, to replace Draper. Bracker created a strong initial impression within the office. He appeared ambitious, powerful, and socially smooth. He remarked in a sales meeting that about one-half of the agents were producing 85 percent of the sales volume, but he never brought up the matter again or took action on the problem. The previous vice president would make sure that low-producing sales agents had more training.

Soon Bracker began to behave quite differently from how he had at first. During the late morning and early afternoon, Bracker was often seen with an open bottle of Jack Daniels on his desk. He made no attempt to hide the bottle when visitors entered his office. The office staff also noticed that porn sites were regularly displayed on his desktop computer. Bracker began inviting others into the office to visit porn sites with him. The agents and trainers became increasingly uncomfortable with the behavior and actions of the new vice president.

The first person to quit was Bracker's secretary who told others she could no longer support her boss and that she would not work for a boss for whom she had lost respect. Two other sales agents soon quit. The volume of commissions in the office was declining steeply, and new policies being issued were often lost. Insufficient information was being furnished to the home office for the agents to receive their proper commissions. When a trainer invited field sales reps into the office, she was often greeted with wisecracks about "Hard-drinking, Gordon, the porno guy."

The three remaining staff members got into a huddle one afternoon to decide what they should do about the office and their livelihoods falling apart.

Source: Case researched by Tammy Riggs, Rochester Hills, Michigan, March 2006.

Questions

1. In what way is Gordon Backer a problem manager?
2. What should the remaining staff members do to restore a professional workplace?
3. Is bypassing the boss in this situation a possibility?

Human Relations Case Studies 9-2

What to Do about Brian?

Brian is one of 10 home mortgage refinance specialists working in his department of Cypress Finance, a substantially sized financial services firm. Most of the customer contact work of the mortgage refinance department is conducted over the telephone (using a toll-free number), even when potential customers initiate their inquiries through the company Web site. Each refinance specialist does considerable individual work—including interacting with customers and potential customers and evaluating the mortgage applicant's credit worthiness. Credit checks are made with computerized databases, but occasionally clarifying information is sought.

Refinance specialists have to cooperate with each other on complex cases. The cooperation often takes the form of asking a teammate's opinion on the creditworthiness of the risk. A member of management, however, gives final approval to all but the most routine refinance applications.

At times, the supervisor of the group, Nina, makes assignments to balance the workload among the specialists. However, the work piles up so quickly that the specialists are supposed to look for ways to spread the work out evenly among themselves to prevent delays in processing refinance applications.

Nina perceives Brian to be a superior performer. His most recent performance evaluation stated that he was an outstanding refinance specialist with potential for promotion to a supervisory position in the future. Nina also rated Brian's sales performance to be outstanding. A "sale" means that an inquiry over the telephone or Web site is converted into an application to refinance that becomes approved. Despite his outstanding performance,

Nina did mention that Brian could strengthen his teamwork skills. She specifically mentioned that Brian was sometimes so busy with his individual cases that he neglected to help out other team members.

During a recent team meeting, Nina told the group, "Once again I am pleased to announce that Brian has been the outstanding producer in the department. I know that we work together as a team yet still have our individual goals. Brian is great at closing applicants with good credit risks, and he still contributes his share as a team player."

Kenny, one of the other refinance specialists, gave a gentle nudge with his elbow to Cindy, a specialist seated to his right. Kenny murmured, "What a kiss-up this guy is. Nina should know what an annoyance Brian is in the office."

After the meeting, Kenny, Cindy, and Lindsay, a third specialist, were standing together near the elevator. Lindsay said, while giggling, "Did you see the look on Brian's face? All smiles, like he was voted the MVP of the Super Bowl. Brian sometimes forgets that we help him with his trickiest applications, and then he grabs the glory. But ask Brian for a little help, and he will say something to the effect that he is too busy closing a major deal. You would think he was refinancing the Sears Tower in Chicago." Kenny, Cindy, and Lindsay giggled simultaneously.

The next workday at Cypress was one of the busiest ever. Newspaper and television reports throughout the country announced that mortgage rates were expected to climb by 1.5 percent the following month. The number of applicants for refinancing doubled as many home owners were eager to lock in the present low rates for refinancing. The refinance specialists were asked to put in 60-hour weeks until the workload drifted back to normal.

During the lunch break on one of the peak-load days, Brian approached the three other specialists taking the break at the same time as he with this proposition. "As everyone in this office knows, I am really talented at closing deals. And the more deals we close as a group, the bigger will be the group bonus at the end of the year. So I'm suggesting that when I have a couple of big deals on the hook, I send my minnows over to you. (Minnows refer to small deals.) Also, I would like your cooperation in doing some of the detail work, such as lengthy credit inquiries for major deals. My time is better invested in reeling in the big deals."

One of the specialists said, "Sounds good to me." Cindy took an opposite approach, as she told Brian, "Happy fishing, but you're not my boss. Why should I volunteer to help you when you never volunteer to help me?"

Brian retorted, "Cindy, you may be a nice person, but I think you're a rotten team player. We have to divide up responsibilities for the good of the team."

Later that day, Cindy chatted with Kenny and Lindsay about the incident during the lunch break. She said, "We've got to do something about Brian, but I don't know what. It's tough when you have to do battle with the boss's pet."

Questions

1. Is Brian a *difficult person?* Explain.
2. What steps should the refinance specialists take who object to Brian's work style?
3. How might a system of peer evaluation (workers contributing to the evaluation of each other) help Nina in her supervision of the department?
4. Do you think Cindy is being a rotten team player?

REFERENCES

1. Anne Fisher, "For Happier Customers, Call HR," *Fortune,* November 28, 2005, p. 272.
2. Gerald R. Ferris, Pamela L. Perrewé, William P. Anthony, and David C. Gilmore, "Political Skill at Work." *Organizational Dynamics,* Spring 2000, p. 25.
3. Quoted in Janie Magruder, "Getting Along with Boss Best Strategy," *Arizona Republic,* June 23, 2003.
4. Quoted in William A. Cohen and Nuritt Cohen, "Get Promoted Fast," *Success,* July/August 1985, p. 6.
5. Quoted in Anita Bruzzese, "Get the Boss to Take Notice of You," Gannett News Service, April 21, 1997.
6. Sandy J. Wayne and Gerald R. Ferris, "Influence Tactics, Affect, and Exchange Quality in Supervisor–Subordinate Interactions: A Laboratory Experiment and Field Study," *Journal of Applied Psychology,* October 1990, pp. 487–499.
7. Cecily D. Cooper, "Just Joking Around? Employee Humor Expression as Ingratiatory Behavior," *Academy of Management Review,* October 2005, pp. 765–776.
8. J. Kenneth Matejka and Richard Dunsing, "Managing the Baffling Boss," *Personnel,* February 1989, p. 50.
9. "So You're Smarter Than the Boss? Yeah, Right," *Executive Leadership,* June 2000, p. 5.
10. Cited in "Ask Annie," *Fortune,* April 1, 2002, p. 171.
11. "How's the View Back There?" *Working Smart,* December 1996, p. 1.
12. "Getting Along with Your Coworkers," available at *www.irishjobs.ie/advice/getting/along.html,* retrieved January 7, 2006.
13. Christine M. Pearson and Christine L. Porath, "On the Nature, Consequences and Remedies of Workplace Incivility: No time for 'nice'? Think Again," *Academy of Management Executive,* February 2005, pp. 7–18;
14. Jared Sandberg, "Office Minstrels Drive the Rest of Us Nuts but Are Hard to Silence," *The Wall Street Journal,* February 14, 2006, p. B1+.
15. Shelia Murray Bethel, *Making a Difference* (New York: G. P. Putnam's Sons, 1989).
16. "Team Player Gets Top Spot in Survey" (undated sample copy distributed by Dartnell Corporation), p. 3.
17. Andrew C. Wicks, Shawn L. Berman, and Thomas M. Jones, "The Structure of Optimal Trust: Moral and Strategic Implications," *Academy of Management Review,* January 1999, p. 99.
18. Alex M. Susskind, K. Michele Kacmar, and Carl P. Borchgrevink, "Customer Service Providers' Attitudes Relating to Customer Service and Customer Satisfaction in the Customer-Server Exchange," *Journal of Applied Psychology,* February 2003, pp. 179–187.
19. "Employee's Eagerness to Help Colleagues Drops over Time," Press Release from PsyMax Solutions, available at *www.psymaxsolutions.com/psymax-pressroom/supportive.asp* retrieved March 29, 2006.
20. "Build Allies for Personal Support," *Manager's Edge,* January 2003, p. 8
21. The first two types are from a brochure for ETC w/Career Track, 3085 Center Green Drive, Boulder, CO 80301–5408.
22. Matt Vilano, "How to Shush the Office Magpie," *The New York Times,* available at nytimes.com, retrieved December 25, 2005.
23. Charles G. Morris and Albert A. Maisto, *Psychology: An Introduction,* 11th ed. (Upper Saddle River, NJ: Prentice Hall, 2002), p. 537; Michael S. Beeson, "Personality Disorders," available at *www.emedicine.com/emerg/topic418.htm,* retrieved March 25, 2006.
24. Dru Scott, *Customer Satisfaction: The Other Half of Your Job* (Los Altos, CA: Crisp Publications, 1991), p. 16.
25. Sam Deep and Lyle Sussman, *What to Say to Get What You Want* (Reading, MA: Addison-Wesley, 1995).
26. Jane Michaels, "You Gotta Get Along to Get Ahead," *Woman's Day,* April 3, 1984, p. 58.
27. Lin Grensing-Pophal, "High-Maintenance Employees," *HR Magazine,* February 2001, p. 89.
28. Carlin Flora, "Close Quarters: Why We Fall in Love with the One Nearby," *Psychology Today,* January/February 2004, p. 15.
29. Charlene Marmer Solomon, "The Secret's Out: How to Handle the Truth of Workplace Romance," *Workforce,* July 1998, p. 45.
30. Survey cited in Stephanie Armour, "Cupid Finds Work as Office Romance No Longer Taboo," *USA Today,* February 11, 2003.
31. Policy developed by law firm of Gutierrez, Preciado & House, LLP, available at *www.gutierrez-preciado.com/Memos/romance.htm,* retrieved April 15, 2003.
32. For example, see Barry Farber, "Means to a Friend," *Entrepreneur,* April 2005, p. 80.
33. Linda Thornburg, "Companies Benefit from Emphasis on Superior Customer Service," *HR Magazine,* October 1993, pp. 46–49; Theodore Garrison, III, "The Value of Customer Service," in Rick Crandall, ed., *Celebrate Customer Service* (Corte Madera, CA: Select Press, 1999), pp. 3–22; Hal Hardy, "Five Steps to Pleasing Difficult, Demanding Customers," *First Rate Customer Service* (sample issue distributed by Briefings Publishing Group, 2002).
34. Anne Fisher, "A Happy Staff Equals Happy Customers," *Fortune,* July 12, 2004, p. 52.
35. Lorna Doucet, "Service Provider Hostility and Service Quality," *Academy of Management Journal,* October 2004, pp. 761–771.

10 Managing Conflict

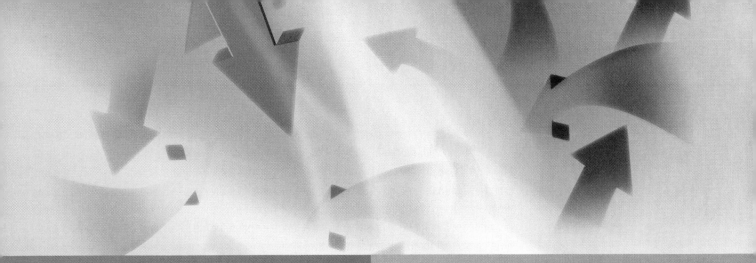

Learning Objectives

Outline

After studying the information and doing the exercises in this chapter, you should be able to:

1 Identify reasons why conflict between people takes place so often.

2 Pinpoint several helpful and harmful consequences of conflict.

3 Choose an effective method of resolving conflict.

4 Improve your assertion skills.

5 Improve your negotiating skill.

6 Develop anger management skills.

W hen Susan Siverson quit her Wall Street human resource job at a banking concern to stay home with her twin toddlers, she had no intention of returning for years. If asked then, she says, "I would have said, 'You'd have to drag me back kicking and screaming.'" But a campaign by Lehman Brothers to woo at-home mothers like Siverson—inviting her to an executive luncheon for ex-Wall Streeters, contacting her repeatedly, and offering flexible work—changed her attitude. She thought, "Maybe this is a tenable option for me," she says. She became a part-time consultant for the firm just recently. [1]

■ **Conflict**

condition that exists when two sets of demands, goals, or motives are incompatible

The situation just described illustrates a reality about the workplace and personal life. Conflict takes place frequently, and being able to manage it well contributes to your feeling of well-being. In this situation, the company helped the human resource professional resolve her conflict by offering her flexible work as a part-timer. **Conflict** is a condition that exists when two sets of demands, goals, or motives are incompatible. For example, if a person wants a career in retailing yet also wants to work a predictable eight-hour day with weekends off, that person faces a conflict. He or she cannot achieve both goals. A conflict can also be considered a dispute, feud, or controversy.

Our approach to studying conflict includes explaining why so much conflict exists, constructive approaches to resolving conflict, and the management of anger.

■ **Learning Objective 1**

Why Does So Much Conflict Exist?

Many reasons exist for the widespread presence of conflict in all aspects of life. All these reasons are related to the basic nature of conflict—the fact that not every person can have what he or she wants at the same time. As with other topics in this book, understanding conflict helps you develop a better understanding of why people act as they do. Here we describe seven key sources of conflict.

COMPETITION FOR LIMITED RESOURCES

A fundamental reason you might experience conflict with another person is that not everybody can get all the money, material, supplies, or human help they want. Conflict also ensues when employees are asked to compete for prizes, such as bonuses based on individual effort or company-paid vacation trips. Because the number of awards is so limited, the competition becomes intense enough to be regarded as conflict. Conflict stemming from limited resources has become prevalent as so many companies attempt to reduce expenses. Many units of the organization have to compete for the limited money available to hire new people or purchase new technology.

■ **Personality clash**

antagonistic relationship between two people based on differences in personal attributes, preferences, interests, values, and styles

PERSONALITY CLASHES

Various value and personality differences among people contribute to workplace conflict. Many disagreements on the job stem from the fact that some people simply dislike each other. A **personality clash** is thus an antagonistic relationship between two people based on differences in personal attributes, preferences, interests, values, and styles. People involved in a personality clash often have difficulty specifying why they dislike each other. The end result, however, is that they cannot maintain an amiable work relationship. A strange fact about personality clashes is that people who get along well may begin to clash after working together for a number of years. Many business partnerships fold because the two partners eventually clash.

AGGRESSIVE PERSONALITIES INCLUDING BULLIES

Coworkers naturally disagree about topics, issues, and ideas. Yet some people convert disagreement into an attack that puts down other people and damages their self-esteem. As a result, conflict surfaces. **Aggressive personalities** are people who verbally and sometimes physically attack others frequently. Verbal aggression takes the form of insults, teasing, ridicule, and profanity. The aggression may also be expressed as attacks on the victim's character, competence, background, and physical appearance. When people are verbally abused, they are put on the defensive making them feel uncomfortable. [2]

▮ **Aggressive personalities**
people who verbally and sometimes physically attack others frequently

Aggressive personalities are also referred to as *bullies*. Among their typical behaviors are interrupting others, ranting in a loud voice, and making threats. A typical attitude of a bullying boss is "My way or the highway," sending the message that the employee's suggestions are unwelcome. One bullying manager would frequently ask people, "Are you going to be stupid the rest of your life?" Bullied workers complain of a range of psychological and physical ailments such as the following: anxiety, sleeplessness, headache, irritable bowel syndrome, skin problems, panic attacks, and low self-esteem. Human relations specialist Gary Namie of The Work Doctor—a firm that works with companies to help reduce hostility—says that bullying can have negative effects on employees and the organization. Bullying reduces morale and productivity by increasing absenteeism and sick leave. "If you have been pummeled and denigrated long enough, you will not be a peak performer," he said. [3]

Aggressiveness can also take the extreme form of the shooting or knifing of a former boss or colleague by a mentally unstable worker recently dismissed from the company. Violence has become so widespread that homicide is the second-highest cause of workplace deaths, with about 550 workplace homicides each year in the United States. [4] Most of these deaths result from a robbery or commercial crime. Many of these killings, however, are perpetrated by a disgruntled worker or former employee harboring an unresolved conflict. As companies have continued to reduce their workforce despite being profitable, these incidents have increased in frequency.

CULTURALLY DIVERSE TEAMS AND FACTIONAL GROUPS

Conflict often surfaces as people work in teams whose members vary in many ways. Ethnicity, religion, and gender are three of the major factors that lead to clashes in viewpoints. Differing educational backgrounds and work specialties can also lead to conflict. Workers often shut out information that doesn't fit comfortably with their own beliefs, particularly if they do not like the person providing the information. When these conflicts are properly resolved, diversity lends strength to the organization because the various viewpoints make an important contribution to solving a problem. Groups that are reminded of the importance of effective communication and taught methods of conflict resolution that usually can overcome the conflict stemming from mixed groups. [5]

Another form of diversity occurs when groups contain different factions, such as those representing two different companies that merged. Often the factional group consists of two subgroups, each with several representatives, such as a cost-cutting task force consisting of three representatives each from marketing, operations, and finance. The potential for conflict within factional groups increases when the subgroups differ substantially in demographic characteristics such as age, gender, and educational levels. Professors Jiatao Li of Hong Kong University of Science and Technology and Donald C. Hambrick of the Pennsylvania State University studied factional groups at 71 Sino-foreign ventures in China. Five hundred and thirty-five managers completed surveys in either English or Chinese. Among the findings were that when there were large demographic differences between members of the joint venture teams, stereotyping, distrust, and discord mounted. These negative emotions led to conflict and a decrease in performance. [6]

COMPETING WORK AND FAMILY DEMANDS

Balancing the demands of work and family life is a major challenge facing workers at all levels. Yet achieving this balance and resolving these conflicts is essential for being successful in career and personal life. The challenge of achieving balance is particularly intense for employees who are part of a two-wage-earner family. **Work–family conflict** occurs when the individual has to perform multiple roles: worker, spouse or partner, and often parent. From the standpoint of the individual, this type of conflict can be regarded as work interfering with family life. From the standpoint of the employer, the same conflict might be regarded as family life interfering with work.

■ **Work–family conflict**

conflict that occurs when an individual has to perform multiple roles: worker, spouse or partner, and often parent

Attempting to meet work and family demands is a frequent source of conflict because the demands are often incompatible. Imagine having to attend your child's championship soccer game and then being ordered at the last minute to attend a late-afternoon meeting. A survey revealed the following evidence of work–family conflict and the potential of such conflict:

■ About 45 percent of students say their top consideration in selecting a first employer is the opportunity to achieve a balance between work and life outside of work.

■ Approximately 80 percent of workers consider their effort to balance work and personal life as their first priority.

■ More than one-third of employed Americans are working 10 or more hours a day, and 39 percent work on weekends.

■ One-third of employees say that they are forced to choose between advancing in their jobs or devoting attention to their family or personal lives. [7]

The conflict over work versus family demands intensifies when the person is serious about both work and family responsibilities. The average professional working for an organization works approximately 55 hours per week, including five hours on weekends. Adhering to such a schedule almost inevitably results in some incompatible demands from work versus those from family members and friends. Conflict arises because the person wants to work sufficient hours to succeed on the job yet still have enough time for personal life.

The chapter opener described how one employer uses flexible work to help key workers deal with work–family conflict. Later in the chapter we present more information about what employers are doing to help resolve such conflict.

MICROINEQUITIES AS A SOURCE OF CONFLICT

■ **Microinequity**

small, semiconscious message sent with a powerful impact on the receiver

Growing attention is being paid to snubbing, or ignoring others, as a source of conflict. A **microinequity** is a small, semiconscious message we send with a powerful impact on the receiver. A microinequity might also be considered a subtle slight.

Conflict occurs because a person's feelings are hurt, and he or she feels trivialized. Two examples of workplace microinequities follow:

- You check your messages on a cell phone, Blackberry, or computer screen while a coworker is talking to you. [You are devaluing the other person's time, and trivializing his or her importance.]

- A manager dismisses the first idea offered in a meeting by responding, "Okay, so who would like to get the ball rolling?" [The person who offered the idea feels like his or her suggestion is not even worth consideration and, therefore, has hurt feelings]

Many companies, including IBM and Wells Fargo, offer training seminars to help managers avoid microinequities, including those already mentioned as well as mispronouncing the name of subordinates and looking at a watch while someone else is talking. [8]

SEXUAL HARASSMENT: A SPECIAL TYPE OF CONFLICT

Many employees face conflict because they are sexually harassed by a supervisor, coworker, or customers. **Sexual harassment** is an unwanted sexually oriented behavior in the workplace that results in discomfort or interference with the job. It can include an action as violent as rape or as subdued as telling a sexually toned joke. Sexual harassment creates conflict because the harassed person has to make a choice between two incompatible motives. One motive is to get ahead, keep the job, or have an unthreatening work environment. But to satisfy this motive, the person is forced to sacrifice the motive of holding on to his or her moral values or preferences. For example, a person might say, "I want a raise; but to do this, must I submit to being fondled by my boss?" Here we focus on the types and frequency of sexual harassment and guidelines for dealing with the problem.

- **Sexual harassment**
unwanted sexually oriented behavior in the workplace that results in discomfort or interference with the job

Types and Frequency of Harassment

Two types of sexual harassment are legally recognized. Both are violations of the Civil Rights Acts of 1964 and 1991 and are, therefore, a violation of your rights. In quid pro quo sexual harassment, the individual suffers loss (or threatened loss) of a job benefit as a result of his or her response to a request for sexual favors. The demands of a harasser can be blatant or implied. An implied form of quid pro quo harassment might take this form: A manager casually comments to one of his or her employees, "I've noticed that workers who become very close to me outside of the office get recommended for bigger raises."

The other form of sexual harassment is hostile-environment harassment. Another person in the workplace creates an intimidating, hostile, or offensive working environment. No tangible loss or psychological injury has to be suffered under this form of sexual harassment.

A major problem in controlling sexual harassment in the workplace is that most workers understand the meaning and nature of quid pro quo harassment but are confused about what constitutes the hostile-environment type. For example, some people might interpret the following behaviors to be harassing, whereas others would regard them as friendly initiatives: (1) calling a coworker "sweetie" and (2) saying to a subordinate, "I love your suit. You look fabulous."

An employee who is continually subjected to sexually suggestive comments, lewd jokes, or requests for dates is a victim of hostile-environment harassment. When the offensive behavior stems from customers or vendors, it is still harassment. Although the company cannot readily control the actions of customers or vendors, the company may still be liable for such harassment. According to several legal decisions, it is a company's job to take action to remedy harassment problems involving employees.

Surveys as well as the opinions of human resource professionals suggest that somewhere between 50 and 60 percent of women are sexually harassed at least once in their career. Aside from being an illegal and immoral act, sexual harassment has negative effects on the well-being of its victims. The harassed person may experience job stress, lowered morale, severe conflict, and lowered productivity. A study with both business and university workers found that even at low levels of frequency, harassment exerts a significant impact on women's psychological well-being and productivity. High levels of harassment, however, had even more negative effects. [9]

A related study of the long-term effects of sexual harassment indicated that the negative effects remained two years after the incident. For example, 24 months after an incident of sexual harassment, many women still experienced stress, a decrease in job satisfaction, and lowered productivity. [10]

Although much of the research on the consequences of sexual harassment has focused on the individual, one study indicates that harassment can negatively affect the team also. Professors of organizational psychology Jana L. Raver of Queen's University and Michele J. Gelfand of the University of Maryland studied sexual harassment in 35 teams within a food-service organization. It was found that the presence of sexual harassment in the form of insulting verbal and nonverbal behavior led to conflict about tasks (work to be performed) and people. The same type of harassment also led to lower group cohesion (team spirit) and lower financial performance. Another finding was that sexual harassment was more prevalent in the larger teams, suggesting that some workers feel they might be able to get away with misbehavior in a crowd. [11]

Guidelines for Preventing and Dealing with Sexual Harassment

A starting point in dealing with sexual harassment is to develop an awareness of the type of behaviors that are considered sexual harassment. Often the difference is subtle. Suppose, for example, you placed copies of two nudes painted by Renoir, the French painter, on a coworker's desk. Your coworker might call that harassment. Yet if you took that same coworker to a museum to see the originals of the same nude paintings, your behavior would usually not be classified as harassment. This example illustrates that the setting of the words or behavior influences whether they are harassing. College courses in understanding and dealing with pornography have grown in popularity, and these courses often show adult (sexually explicit) films as part of the curriculum. [12] If an accounting professor in a college of business showed the same films to accounting students, he or she would most likely be charged with sexual harassment.

Education about the meaning of sexual harassment is, therefore, a basic part of any company program to prevent sexual harassment. The situation and your tone of voice, as well as other nonverbal behavior, contribute to perceptions of harassment. For example, the statement "You look wonderful" might be perceived as good natured versus harassing, depending on the sender's voice tone and facial expression.

The easiest way to deal with sexual harassment is to speak up before it becomes serious. The first time it happens, respond with statements such as, "I won't tolerate that kind of talk." "I dislike sexually oriented jokes." "Keep your hands off me." Write the harasser a stern letter shortly after the first incident. Confronting the harasser in writing dramatizes your seriousness of purpose in not wanting to be sexually harassed. If the problem persists, say something to the effect, "You're practicing sexual harassment. If you don't stop, I'm going to exercise my right to report you to management." Don't leave any room for doubt that the behavior or words you heard were unwelcome.

The Good and Bad Sides of Conflict

Conflict over significant issues is a source of stress. We usually do not suffer stress over minor conflicts such as having to choose between wearing one sweater or another. Like stress in general, we need an optimum amount of conflict to keep us mentally and physically energetic. Handled properly, moderate doses of conflict can be beneficial. Some of the benefits that might arise from conflict can be summarized around the following key points. Figure 10-1 outlines the positive, as well as the negative consequences of conflict.

1. Talents and abilities may emerge in response to conflict. When faced with a conflict, people often become more creative than they are in a tranquil situation. Assume that your employer told you that it would no longer pay for your advanced education unless you used the courses to improve your job performance. You would probably find ways to accomplish such an end.

2. Conflict can help you feel better because it satisfies a number of psychological needs. By nature, many people like a good fight. As a socially acceptable substitute for attacking others, you might be content to argue over a dispute on the job or at home.

3. As an aftermath of conflict, the parties in conflict may become united. Two warring supervisors may become more cooperative toward each other in the aftermath of confrontation. A possible explanation is that the shared experience of being in conflict with each other *sometimes* brings the parties closer.

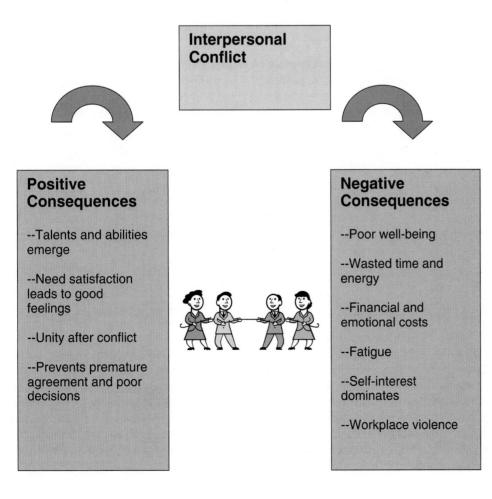

| **Figure** | **10-1** |

The Good and Bad Side of Conflict
Conflict between people and groups can have both positive and negative consequences.

4. Conflict helps prevent people in the organization from agreeing too readily with each other, thus making some very poor decisions. Groupthink is the situation that occurs when group members strive so hard to get along that they fail to critically evaluate each other's ideas.

Despite the positive picture of conflict just painted, it can also have detrimental consequences to the individual, the organization, and society. These harmful consequences of conflict make it important for people to learn how to resolve conflict:

1. Prolonged conflict can be detrimental to some people's emotional and physical well-being. As a type of stress, prolonged conflict can lead to such problems as heart disease and chronic intestinal disorders. President Lyndon B. Johnson suffered his first heart attack after an intense argument with a young newspaper reporter.

2. People in conflict with each other often waste time and energy that could be put to useful purposes. Instead of fighting all evening with your roommate, the two of you might fix up your place. Instead of writing angry e-mail messages back and forth, two department heads might better invest that time in thinking up ideas to save the company money.

3. The aftermath of extreme conflict may have high financial and emotional costs. Sabotage—such as ruining machinery—might be the financial consequence. At the same time, management may develop a permanent distrust of many people in the workforce, although only a few of them are saboteurs.

4. Too much conflict is fatiguing, even if it does not cause symptoms of emotional illness. People who work in high-conflict jobs often feel spent when they return home from work. When the battle-worn individual has limited energy left over for family responsibilities, the result is more conflict. (For instance, "What do you mean you are too tired to visit friends?" or "If your job is killing your interest in having friends, find another job.")

5. People in conflict will often be much more concerned with their own interests than with the good of the family, organization, or society. An employee in the shipping department who is in conflict with his supervisor might neglect to ship an order. And a gang in conflict with another might leave a park or beach strewn with broken glass.

6. Workplace violence erupts, including the killing of managers, previous managers, coworkers, customers, as well as spouses and partners. Intense conflict can release anger, leading to aggressive behavior and violence. Disgruntled employees, such as those recently fired, may attempt revenge by assassinating work associates. [13] People involved in an unresolved domestic dispute sometimes storm into the partner's workplace to physically attack him or her. Unresolved conflict and frustration from financial, marital, or other domestic problems increase the odds of a person "going ballistic" at work.

What Are Some Techniques for Resolving Conflicts?

■ **Learning Objective 3**

Because of the inevitability of conflict, a successful and happy person must learn effective ways of resolving conflict. An important general consideration is to face conflict rather than letting conflict slide or smoothing over it. Ignoring or smoothing over conflict does little to resolve the real causes of conflict and seldom leads to an effective long-term solution. [14] Here we concentrate on methods of conflict resolution that you can use on your own. Most of them emphasize a collaborative or win–win philosophy. Several of the negotiating and bargaining tactics described may be close to the competitive orientation. Human Relations Self-Assessment Quiz 10-1 gives you the opportunity to think through your style of managing conflict.

BEING ASSERTIVE

■ Learning Objective 4

Several of the techniques for resolving conflict described here require assertiveness. Learning to express your feelings to make your demands known is also an important aspect of becoming an effective individual in general. Expressing your feelings helps you establish good relationships with people. If you aren't sharing your feelings and attitudes with other people, you will never get close to them. Here we examine the nature of assertiveness and then describe several techniques for building assertiveness.

Assertive, Nonassertive, and Aggressive Behavior

As implied previously, **assertive** people state clearly what they want or how they feel in a given situation without being abusive, abrasive, or obnoxious. People who are assertive are open, honest, and "up-front" because they believe that all people have an equal right to express themselves honestly. Assertive behavior can be understood

■ Assertive

characteristic of people who state clearly what they want or how they feel in a given situation without being abusive, abrasive, or obnoxious; open, honest, and "up-front" people who believe that all people have an equal right to express themselves honestly

---

Human Relations Self-Assessment Quiz **10-1**

Collaborative versus Competitive Styles of Conflict Management

Answer on a 1-to-5 scale how well you agree with each of the following statements: disagree strongly, disagree, neutral, agree, agree strongly.

	Disagree Strongly	Disagree	Neutral	Agree	Agree Strongly
1. I like to see the other side squirm when I resolve a dispute.	5	4	3	2	1
2. Winning is everything when it comes to settling conflict.	5	4	3	2	1
3. After I have successfully negotiated a price, I like to see the seller smile.	1	2	3	4	5
4. I have a "smash-mouth" attitude toward resolving conflict.	5	4	3	2	1
5. In most conflict situations one side is clearly right, and the other side is clearly wrong.	1	2	3	4	5
6. I think there are effective alternatives to strikes for settling union versus management disputes.	1	2	3	4	5
7. The winner should take all.	5	4	3	2	1
8. Conflict on the job is like a prize fight: The idea is to knock out the opponent.	5	4	3	2	1
9. I like the idea of tournaments in which first-round losers receive another opportunity to play.	1	2	3	4	5
10. Nice guys and gals usually finish first.	1	2	3	4	5

Scoring and Interpretation:

Add the point value of your scores to obtain your total. Scores of 40 and higher suggest that you prefer a *collaborative*, or *win–win*, approach to resolving conflict. You tend to be concerned about finding long-term solutions to conflict that will provide benefits to both sides. Scores of 39 and lower suggest that you prefer a *competitive* approach to resolving conflict. You want to maximize gain for yourself, with little concern about the welfare of the other side.

■ **Nonassertive**

characteristic of people who let things happen to them without letting their feelings be known

■ **Aggressive**

characteristic of people who are obnoxious and overbearing; they push for what they want with almost no regard for the feelings of others

more fully by comparing it to that shown by two other types of people. **Nonassertive** people let things happen to them without letting their feelings be known. **Aggressive** people are obnoxious and overbearing. They push for what they want with almost no regard for the feelings of others.

Another representative assertive behavior is to ask for clarification rather than contradicting a person with whom you disagree. The assertive person asks for clarification when another person says something irritating, rather than hurling insults or telling the other person he or she is wrong. For example, assume someone says to you, "Your proposal is useless." Aggressively telling the person, "You have no right to make that judgment," shuts out any possible useful dialogue. You will probably learn more if you ask for clarification, such as "What is wrong with my proposal?"

Gestures as well as words can communicate whether the person is being assertive, nonassertive, or aggressive. Figure 10-2 illustrates these differences.

Becoming More Assertive and Less Shy

Shyness, or not being assertive, is widespread, and about 50 percent of the U.S. population is shyer than they want to be. The personality trait of shyness has positive aspects, such as leading a person to think more deeply and become involved in ideas and things. (Where would the world be today if Bill Gates weren't shy as a youth?) However, shyness can also create discomfort and lower self-esteem. [15] There are a number of everyday actions a person can take to overcome being nonassertive or shy. Even if the actions described here do not elevate your assertiveness, they will not backfire and cause you discomfort. After reading the following five techniques, you might be able to think of others that will work for you. [16]

1. Set a goal. Clearly establish in your mind how you want to behave differently. Do you want to speak out more in meetings? Be able to express dissatisfaction to coworkers? You can overcome shyness only by behaving differently; feeling differently is not enough.

2. Appear warm and friendly. Shy people often communicate to others through their body language that they are not interested in reaching out to others. To overcome this impression, smile, lean forward, uncross your arms and legs, and unfold your hands.

Assertive	Nonassertive	Aggressive
Well-balanced	Covering mouth with hand	Pounding fists
Straight posture	Excessive head nodding	Stiff and rigid posture
Hand gestures, emphasizing key words	Tinkering with clothing or jewelry	Finger waving or pointing
	Constant shifting of weight	Shaking head as if other person isn't to be believed
	Scratching or rubbing head or other parts of the body	
	Wooden body posture	Hand on hips
Moderately loud voice	Voice too soft with frequent pauses	Voice louder than needed, fast speech

Figure 10-2

Assertive, Nonassertive, and Aggressive Gestures

3. **Conduct anonymous conversations.** Try starting a conversation with strangers in a safe setting, such as a sporting event, the waiting room of a medical office, or a waiting line at the post office or supermarket. Begin the conversation with the common experience you are sharing at the time. Among them might be

"How many people do you estimate are in the audience?"

"How long does it usually take before you get to see the doctor?"

"Where did you get that shopping bag? I've never seen one so sturdy before."

4. **Greet strangers.** For the next week or so, greet many of the people you pass. Smile and make a neutral comment such as "How ya doing?" or "Great day, isn't it." Because most people are unaccustomed to being greeted by a stranger, you may get a few quizzical looks. Many other people may smile and return your greeting. A few of these greetings may turn into conversations. A few conversations may even turn into friendships. Even if the return on your investment in greetings is only a few pleasant responses, it will boost your confidence.

5. **Practice being decisive.** An assertive person is usually decisive, so it is important to practice being decisive. Some nonassertive people are even indecisive when asked to make a choice from a restaurant menu. They communicate their indecisiveness by asking their friend, "What are you going to have?" or asking the server, "Could you please suggest something for me?" or "What's good?" Practice quickly sizing up the alternatives in any situation and reaching a decision. This will help you be assertive and also project an image of assertiveness.

CONFRONTATION AND PROBLEM SOLVING LEADING TO WIN–WIN

The most highly recommended way of resolving conflict is **confrontation and problem solving.** It is a method of identifying the true source of conflict and resolving it systematically. The confrontation in this approach is gentle and tactful rather than combative and abusive. It is best to wait until your anger cools down before confronting the other person to avoid being unreasonable. Reasonableness is important because the person who takes the initiative in resolving the conflict wants to maintain a harmonious working relationship with the other party. Also, both parties should benefit from the resolution of the conflict.

■ **Confrontation and problem solving** the most highly recommended way of resolving conflict; method of identifying the true source of conflict and resolving it systematically

Assume that Jason, the person working at the desk next to you, whistles loudly while he works. You find the whistling to be distracting and annoying; you think Jason is a noise polluter. If you don't bring the problem to Jason's attention, it will probably grow in proportion with time. Yet you are hesitant to enter into an argument about something a person might regard as a civil liberty (the right to whistle in a public place). An effective alternative is for you to approach Jason directly in this manner:

You: Jason, there is something bothering me that I would like to discuss with you.

Jason: Go ahead, I don't mind listening to other people's problems.

You: My problem concerns something you are doing that makes it difficult for me to concentrate on my work. When you whistle, it distracts me and grates on my nerves. It may be my problem, but the whistling does bother me.

Jason: I guess I could stop whistling when you're working next to me. It's probably simply a nervous habit. Maybe I can find a less disruptive habit, such as rolling my tongue inside my mouth.

An important advantage of confrontation and problem solving is that you deal directly with a sensitive problem without jeopardizing the chances of forming a constructive working relationship in the future. One reason that the method works so effectively is that the focus is on the problem at hand and not on the individual's personality.

The intent of confrontation and problem solving is to arrive at a collaborative solution to the conflict. The collaborative style reflects a desire to fully satisfy the desires of both parties. It is based on an underlying philosophy of **win–win,** the belief that after conflict has been resolved, both sides should gain something of value. The user of win–win approaches is genuinely concerned about arriving at a settlement that meets the needs of both parties or at least that does not badly damage the welfare of the other side. When collaborative approaches to resolving conflict are used, the relationships among the parties are built on and improved.

Here is an example of a win–win approach to resolving conflict. A manager granted an employee a few hours off on an occasional Friday afternoon because she was willing to be on call for emergency work on an occasional weekend. Both parties were satisfied with the outcome, and both accomplished their goals.

The opposite approach to win–win conflict resolution is *win–lose* in which one side attempts to maximize gain at the expense of the other side. Win–lose is also referred to as a *zero-sum game* in which one side wins nothing, and the other side wins everything. Common sense tells us that win–lose is the best approach to resolving conflict—and that is one reason so much conflict goes unresolved in the form of physical attacks on people and bankruptcies. A person with a competitive orientation is likely to engage in power struggles in which one side wins and the other loses. "My way or the highway" is a win–lose strategy. An extreme example of a win–lose strategy would be to bad-mouth a rival so he or she gets fired.

If faced with an adversary who has a win–lose orientation, a plausible defense is to keep on pointing out the benefits of finding a solution that fits both sides. A sales representative for a company that makes steel buildings (often used for warehousing) was about to be laid off because of poor business. He proposed to his boss, "Please give me one more chance. Give me just enough salary to pay my rent and feed our newborn child. All the rest of my income will come from commissions on the sales I make." The owner conceded, and the sales rep did earn his way, so a win–lose situation emerged into a win–win.

DISARM THE OPPOSITION

When in conflict, your criticizer may be armed with valid negative criticism of you. The criticizer is figuratively clobbering you with knowledge of what you did wrong. If you deny that you have made a mistake, the criticism intensifies. A simple technique has been developed to help you deal with this type of manipulative criticism. **Disarm the opposition** is a method of conflict resolution in which you disarm the criticizer by agreeing with his or her criticism of you. The technique assumes that you have done something wrong. Disarm the opposition generally works more effectively than counterattacking a person with whom you are in conflict. Another reason this technique is effective is that it implies you are apologizing for a mistake or error you have made. An apology often gets the other person on your side, or at least softens the animosity.

Agreeing with criticism made of you by a manager or team leader is effective because, by so doing, you are in a position to ask that manager's help in improving your performance. Most managers and team leaders recognize that it is their responsibility to help employees to overcome problems, not merely to criticize them. Imagine that you have been chronically late in submitting reports during the past six months. It is time for a performance review and you know you will be reprimanded for your tardiness. You also hope that your boss will not downgrade

---

Margin notes:

■ **Win–win**

belief that after conflict has been resolved both sides should gain something of value

> "Many people avoid confronting day-to-day issues because they're not certain how to open the door to conversation in a productive manner that will preserve the relationship."
> —Deb Koen, vice president of Career Development Services, Rochester, New York

■ **Disarm the opposition**

method of conflict resolution in which you disarm the criticizer by agreeing with his or her criticism all other aspects of your performance because of your tardy reports. Here is how disarming the situation would work in this situation:

Your boss: Have a seat. It's time for your performance review, and we have a lot to talk about. I'm concerned about some things.

You: So am I. It appears that I'm having a difficult time getting my reports in on time. I wonder if I'm being a perfectionist. Do you have any suggestions?

Your boss: I like your attitude. I think you can improve on getting your reports in on time. Maybe you are trying to make your reports perfect before you turn them in. Try not to figure out everything to four decimal places. We need thoroughness around here, but we don't want to overdo it.

COGNITIVE RESTRUCTURING

An indirect way of resolving conflict between people is to lessen the conflicting elements in a situation by viewing them more positively. According to the technique of **cognitive restructuring,** you mentally convert negative aspects into positive ones by looking for the positive elements in a situation. The original purpose of cognitive restructuring was to help people overcome automatic, negative thinking about themselves or situations. An example would be recognize that a challenging situation, such as making a presentation in front of a group, is not as bad as it first seems. The idea is to overcome unhealthy thoughts. How you frame or choose your thoughts can determine the outcome of a conflict situation. Your thoughts can influence your actions. If you search for the beneficial elements in a situation, there will be less area for dispute. Although this technique might sound like a *mind game* to you, it can work effectively.

■ **Cognitive restructuring**
technique of mentally converting negative aspects into positive ones by looking for the positive elements in a situation

Imagine that a coworker of yours, Jennifer, has been asking you repeated questions about how to carry out a work procedure. You are about ready to tell Jennifer, "Go bother somebody else, I'm not paid to be a trainer." Instead, you look for the positive elements in the situation. You say to yourself, "Jennifer has been asking me a lot of questions. This does take time, but answering these questions is valuable experience. If I want to become a manager, I will have to help group members with problems."

After having completed this cognitive restructuring, you can then deal with the conflict more positively. You might say to Jennifer, "I welcome the opportunity to help you, but we need to find a mutually convenient time. In that way, I can better concentrate on my own work."

APPEAL TO A THIRD PARTY

Now and then you may be placed in a conflict situation in which the other party either holds most of the power or simply won't budge. Perhaps you have tried techniques such as confrontation and problem solving or disarming the opposition, yet you cannot resolve your conflict. In these situations you may have to enlist the help of a third party with power—more power than you or your adversary has. Among such third parties is your common boss, union stewards, or human resource managers. Filing a lawsuit against your adversary is another application of the third-party technique, such as filing an age discrimination charge.

In some situations, simply implying that you will bring in a third party to help resolve the conflict situation is sufficient for you to gain advantage. One woman felt she was repeatedly passed over for promotion because of her sex. She hinted that if she were not given fairer consideration, she would speak to the Equal Employment Opportunity Commission (EEOC). She was given a small promotion shortly thereafter. Many conflicts about sexual harassment, as well as ethnic and racial harassment, are resolved through third-party appeal.

THE GRIEVANCE PROCEDURE

■ **Grievance procedure**

formal process of filing a complaint and resolving a dispute within an organization

The formal process of filing a complaint and resolving a dispute within an organization is the **grievance procedure.** It can also be regarded as a formal method of resolving conflict, in which a series of third parties are brought into the picture. The third-party appeal described previously skips the step-by-step approach of a formal grievance procedure. In a unionized firm, the steps in the grievance procedure are specified in the written contract between management and labor. The grievance procedure is a key part of a labor agreement because one of the union's goals is to obtain fair treatment for union members. An example of a grievance about favoritism would be, "I get the worst assignments because I'm not one of the boss's fishing buddies." An example of a grievance about discrimination would be, "I didn't get the transfer to the receptionist job because I'm 55 years old."

The steps in the grievance procedure may vary from one to six, depending on the labor agreement or company procedures. A summary of the typical steps in a grievance procedure is presented next and outlined in Figure 10-3. If the company does not have a labor union, a specialist from the human resources department might serve as a third party.

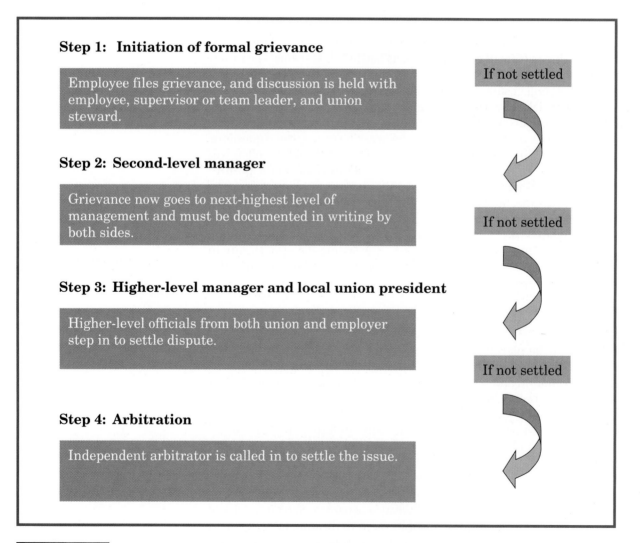

Figure   10-3

The Grievance Procedure

Step 1. Initiation of the formal grievance. Suppose that an employee feels that he or she has been treated unfairly or that his or her rights have been violated in some way. The employee then files a grievance with the supervisor (or team leader). Most grievances end at step 1 by conversation among the employee, union steward, and the supervisor. At this stage, it makes sense to use some of the techniques for resolving conflict already described.

Step 2. Second level of management. If the steward, supervisor or team leader, and employee cannot reach a satisfactory solution to the conflict, it goes to the next-highest level in the organization. At this point, the grievance must be documented in writing by both sides. Which people are involved at this level depends on the size of the firm. In a small firm, a high-ranking manager might be involved in step 2.

Step 3. A higher-level manager and the local union president. If the grievance is not resolved at step 2, higher-level officials from both the union and the employer become involved in settling the dispute. A general principle is that at each higher step in the grievance process, comparable levels of management from both company and union face each other, or a higher-level representative from the human resources department might be involved.

Step 4. Arbitration. If the grievance cannot be settled at lower steps, an independent arbitrator may be called in to settle the issue. Only about 1 percent of grievances go all the way to arbitration. Arbitration is often used as an alternative to a strike. The arbitrator has the authority to settle the dispute and must be a person acceptable to both sides.

In a small organization, step 2 is sometimes omitted. After the grievance is discussed with the union steward, and it is not resolved, the grievance is taken to chief executive or business owner, and then to arbitration if necessary. [17]

Mediation is often confused with arbitration. A mediator is a third party who enters a controversy but holds no power of decision. The mediator helps the two sides find a resolution to their conflict. Relatively few labor agreements allow for mediation, yet mediation might be used to settle a strike. A mediator works like a marriage counselor by helping both sides come to agreement by themselves.

A grievance procedure used in many firms without a union is the **jury of peers,** whereby unresolved grievances are submitted to a panel of coworkers. The panel chosen is similar to a jury in a criminal case. Panel members weigh evidence and, after group discussion, vote for or against the grievant. The jury-of-peers method works well when the jury members are knowledgeable about organizational justice.

The grievance processes described are formal and legalistic. Nevertheless, to represent your interests well, it is helpful to use the informal conflict resolution techniques described earlier, such as confrontation and problem solving. Grievances are less likely to lead to labor strikes in the current business environment partly because labor unions in manufacturing (not in the public service sector) are less powerful than in the past. As more and more manufacturing jobs are being outsourced to lower-wage regions, including other countries, employees fear job loss. Worldwide competition has taken a lot of bargaining power away from workers and unions in the manufacturing sector. [18] Also, an increasing number of manufacturing jobs are being automated, making workers feel more vulnerable.

■ **Jury of peers**
grievance procedure used in many firms without a union whereby unresolved grievances are submitted to a panel of coworkers

COMPANY PROGRAMS FOR LESSENING WORK–FAMILY CONFLICT

Employers have taken major steps in recent years to help employees balance the competing demands of work and family. One reason for giving assistance in this area is that balancing work and family demands helps both the worker and the company. Reducing work–family conflict is likely to reduce Workers' Compensation claims, medical expenses, absenteeism, and turnover. A study conducted with faculty members at 23 universities suggested that the positive effects of work–family programs are most likely to be forthcoming when the programs are administered in a just manner. Justice would include figuring out who needs the most help and avoiding favoritism. Furthermore, workers receiving assistance with work–family conflict should have a say as to what types of programs would be the most beneficial. [19]

A sampling of these work/family programs and practices follow. The accompanying Human Relations in Practice provides another example of how a company might help employees reduce work–family conflict.

1. Flexible work schedules. Many employers allow employees to work flexible hours, provided that they work the full 40-hour schedule and are present at certain core times. A related program is the compressed workweek, whereby the person works 40 hours in four days or less. Some employees prefer the compressed workweek because it gives them longer weekends with their families. Yet compressed workweeks can also be family unfriendly and create major conflicts. An example is that for some workers, having to work three 12-hour days in one week creates family problems.

2. Dependent-care programs. Assistance in dealing with two categories of dependents, children and elderly parents, lies at the core of programs and policies to help employees balance the demands of work and family. At one end of child-care assistance is a fully equipped nursery school on company premises. At the other end is simply a referral service that helps working parents find adequate child care. Many companies offer financial assistance for child care, including pretax expense accounts that allow employees to deduct dependent-care expenses.

■ **Job sharing**

work arrangement in which two people who work part time share one job

3. Job sharing. Another way to reduce work–family conflict is to give workers half a job, a variation of part-time work. **Job sharing** is a work arrangement in which two people who work part time share one job. The sharers divide up the work according to their needs, including the family situation. Each may work selected days of the workweek. Or, one person might work mornings and the other afternoons. If you want to job share, workplace consultant Shari Rosen Ascher suggests approaching the arrangement from the employer benefit perspective. Among these benefits would be more coverage of a single job, twice the knowledge and expertise, increased productivity, and enhanced employee satisfaction and retention. [20]

4. Employee sabbaticals. An extreme measure some companies offer to help selected employees reduce work–family conflict is to offer them paid sabbaticals—time off to recharge and reconnect with the family. A representative arrangement would be six weeks of leave after four years of employment. Sabbaticals are also thought to reduce turnover and retain wisdom that would be lost if a valuable worker burned out and quit. Among the companies offering these sabbaticals (usually after five years of service) are Intel Corp., McDonald's Corp., and women's clothing designer Eileen Fisher, Inc. [21]

5. Compassionate attitudes toward individual needs. An informal policy that facilitates balancing work and family demands is for the manager to decide what can be done to resolve individual conflicts. Yet the manager cannot make arrangements with employees who would violate company policy. Being sensitive to individual situations could involve such arrangements as allowing a person time off to deal with a personal crisis. After the crisis is resolved, the employee makes up the lost time in small chunks of extra work time. In this way the manager helps the worker achieve success both on and off the job.

■ **Learning Objective 5**

■ **Negotiating and bargaining**

situation of conferring with another person to resolve a problem

NEGOTIATION AND BARGAINING TACTICS

Conflicts can be considered situations calling for **negotiating and bargaining,** conferring with another person to resolve a problem. When you are trying to negotiate

Human Relations in Practice

Best Buy Helps Employees Resolve Work–Family Conflicts

Cali Ressler, manager of the work–life balance program for Best Buy, helped a troubled division of the retail group in Minneapolis deal with sinking employee morale. Ressler encouraged the manager to try flexible scheduling, trusting his team to work as it suited them. "He said, 'Well, trust doesn't cost me anything,'" she recalls. The innovation was that the whole team did it together. Although the sample size was fewer than 300 employees, the early results were promising. Turnover in the first three months of employment fell from 14 to 0 percent, job satisfaction rose 10 percent, and their team-performance scores rose 13 percent.

When Jody Thompson, Best Buy's "organizational change" guru, heard about Ressler's work, she pushed the company's management to make total flexibility available to everyone. No one is forced into it; teams sign up when they're ready. Best Buy expects that ROWE (results-oriented work environment) one day will apply to the whole company. Under ROWE, headquarters employees can work when and where they like, as long as they get the job done. At the moment, it is working on a version for the 100,000 retail employees in its stores, a much more difficult task because most of those employees are hourly, and their work is regulated by federal law.

Source: Jyoti Thottam, "Reworking Work," *Time*, July 25, 2005, pp. 51, 52.

a fair price for an automobile, you are also trying to resolve a conflict. At first the demands of both parties seem incompatible. After haggling for a while, you will probably reach a price that is satisfactory to both sides. Negotiation has many applications in the workplace, including buying, selling, arriving at a starting salary or raise, and deciding on a relocation allowance. Negotiation may also take place with coworkers when you need their assistance. For example, you might need to strike a bargain with a coworker to handle some of your responsibilities if you are faced with a temporary overload.

A sampling of negotiating tactics to help you resolve conflict is presented next. As with other techniques of resolving conflict already presented, choose those that best fit your style and the situation. Many people feel awkward at the prospects of negotiating with a stranger, yet speaker and attorney Marc Deiner says that by learning and practicing new skills most people can become better negotiators. [22]

Create a Positive Negotiating Climate

Negotiation proceeds much more swiftly if a positive tone surrounds the session, so it is helpful to initiate a positive outlook about the negotiation meeting. A good opening line in a negotiating session is, "Thanks for fitting this meeting into your hectic schedule." Nonverbal communication such as smiling and making friendly gestures helps create a positive climate. A calm voice helps build the trust necessary for creating a positive climate.

In negotiating with coworkers for assistance, a positive climate can often be achieved by phrasing demands as a request for help. Most people will be more accommodating if you say to them, "I have a problem that I wonder if you could help me with." The problem might be that you need the person's time and mental energy.

By giving that person a choice of offering you help, you have established a much more positive climate than by demanding assistance. [23]

Allow Room for Compromise, but Be Reasonable

The basic strategy of negotiation is to begin with a demand that allows room for compromise and concession. Anyone who has ever negotiated the price of an automobile, house, or used furniture recognizes this vital strategy. If you are a buyer, begin with a low bid. (You say, "I'll give you $60 for that painting" when you are prepared to pay $90.) If you are the seller, begin with a high demand. (You say, "You can have this painting for $130" when you are ready to sell it for as low as $100.) As negotiations proceed, the two of you will probably arrive at a mutually satisfactory price. This negotiating strategy can also be used for such purposes as obtaining a higher starting salary or purchasing excess inventory.

Common sense propels many negotiators to allow *too much* room for compromise. They begin negotiations by asking way beyond what they expect to receive or offering far less than they expect to give. As a result of these implausible demands, the other side may become hostile, antagonistic, or walk away from the negotiations. Beginning with a plausible demand or offer is also important because it contributes to a positive negotiating climate.

Focus on Interests, Not Positions

Rather than clinging to specific negotiating points, keep your overall interests in mind and try to satisfy them. A negotiating point might be a certain amount of money or a concession that you must have. Remember that the true object of negotiation is to satisfy the underlying interests of both sides. Among the interests you and the other side might be trying to protect include money, lifestyle, power, or the status quo. For example, instead of negotiating for a particular starting salary, your true interests might be to afford a certain lifestyle. If the company pays all your medical and dental coverage, you can get by with a lower salary. Or your cost of living might be much lower in one city than in another. Therefore, you can accept a lower starting salary in the city with a lower cost of living.

Make a Last and Final Offer

In many circumstances, presenting a final offer will break a deadlock. You might frame your message something like this. "All I can possibly pay for your guitar is $250. You have my number. Call me when it is available at that price." Sometimes the strategy will be countered by a last and final offer from the other side: "Thanks for your interest. My absolute minimum price for this guitar is $300. Call us if that should seem OK to you." One of you will probably give in and accept the other person's last and final offer.

Role-Play to Predict What the Other Side Will Do

An advanced negotiating technique is to prepare in advance by forecasting what the other side will demand or offer. Two marketing professors from New Zealand, J. Scott Armstrong and Kesten Green, have discovered that when people role-play conflicts their ability to predict outcomes jumps remarkably. The researchers presented 290 participants with descriptions of six actual conflicts and asked them to choose the most likely eventual decisions. The conflicts involved labor–management, commercial, and civil disputes. Five of these conflicts were chosen for role playing. Without the use of role playing, the participants did not much better than chance, with a 27 percent success ratio. Next, the researchers asked 21 international game theorists (specialist in predicting outcomes of events) to forecast the conflict outcomes. The game theorists were correct only 28 percent of the time. (Chance here would be one-fifth, or 20 percent.)

Next, 352 students were instructed to role-play the conflicts in the five situations. The average correct decision was 61 percent versus 27 percent for the comparable group. The authors note that in more than 40 years of studying forecasting, they have never seen a technique that led to such improvement in predictive accuracy. [24]

The implication for making you a better negotiator is to role-play with a friend in advance of the negotiating session you will be facing. The role-play should help you predict what the other side and you will do so you will be better prepared. For example, if your role-play suggests that the company would be willing to give you a 15 percent bonus for incredible performance, ask for a 15 percent bonus.

Allow for Face-Saving

We have saved one of the most important negotiating and conflict resolution strategies for last. Negotiating does not mean that you should try to squash the other side. You should try to create circumstances that will enable you to continue working with that person if it is necessary. People prefer to avoid looking weak, foolish, or incompetent during negotiation or when the process is completed. If you do not give your opponent an opportunity to save face, you will probably create a long-term enemy.

Face-saving could work in this way. A small-business owner winds up purchasing a network system for about twice what he originally budgeted. After the sale is completed, the sales rep says, "I know you bought a more professional networking rig than you originally intended. Yet I know you made the right decision. You will be able to do boost productivity enough with the networked PCs to pay back the cost of the networking system in two years."

What Are Some Suggestions for Managing Anger?

■ Learning Objective 6

Limited ability to manage anger damages the careers and personal lives of many people. The ability to manage your anger, and the anger of others, is an important human relations skill now considered to be part of emotional intelligence. A person who cannot manage anger well cannot take good advantage of his or her intellectual intelligence. As an extreme example, a genius who swears at the manager regularly will probably lose his or her job despite being so talented. Concerns about employees becoming violent have prompted many companies to offer employees training in anger management. Also, employees who become verbally abuse on the job are often sent to such training. [25] Anger-management training is likely to encompass most of the suggestions presented next. Our concern here is with several tactics for managing your own anger and that of others effectively.

MANAGING YOUR OWN ANGER

A starting point in dealing with your anger is to recognize that at its best, anger can be an energizing force. Instead of letting it be destructive, channel your anger into exceptional performance. If you are angry because you did not get the raise you thought you deserved, get even by performing so well that there will be no question you deserve a raise next time. Develop the habit of expressing your anger before it reaches a high intensity. Tell your coworker that you do not appreciate his or her listening to an iPod while you are having dinner together the first time the act of rudeness occurs. If you wait too long, you may wind up grabbing the iPod and slamming it to the floor.

As you are about to express anger, *slow down.* (The old technique of counting to 10 is still effective.) Slowing down gives you the opportunity to express your anger in a way that does not damage your relationship with the other person. Following your first impulse, you might say to the other person, "You're a stupid fool." If you slow down, this might translate into "You need training on this task."

Closely related to slowing down is a technique taught in anger-management programs: Think about the consequences of what you do when you are worked up. Say to yourself as soon as you feel angry, "Oops, I'm in the anger mode now. I had better calm down before I say something or do something that I will regret later." To gauge how effectively you are expressing your anger, ask for feedback. Ask a friend, coworker, or manager, "Am I coming on too strong when I express my negative opinion?" [26]

MANAGING ANGER IN OTHER PEOPLE

A variation of confrontation and problem solving has developed specifically to resolve conflict with angry people: confront, contain, and connect. *Confront* in this context means that you jump right in and get agitated workers talking to prevent future blowups. The confrontation, however, is not aimed at arguing with the angry person. If the other person yells, you talk more softly. *Contain* refers to moving an angry worker out of sight and out of earshot. At the same time you remain impartial. The supervisor is advised not to choose sides or appear to be a friend.

You *connect* by asking open-ended questions such as "What would you like us to do about your concern?" to get at the real reasons behind an outburst. Using this approach, one worker revealed he was upset because a female coworker got to leave early to pick up her daughter at daycare. The man also needed to leave early one day a week for personal reasons but felt awkward making the request. So instead of being assertive (explicit and direct) about his demands, he flared up.

An important feature of the confront–contain–connect technique is that it provides angry workers a place where they can vent their frustrations and report the outbursts of others. Mediator Nina Meierding says, "Workers need a safe outlet to talk through anger and not feel they will be minimized or put their job in jeopardy." [27]

CHOOSING A TACTIC FOR RESOLVING A CONFLICT OR MANAGING ANGER

How does a person know which of the tactics or strategies presented in this chapter will work best for a given problem? The best answer is to consider both your personality and the situation. With respect to your personality, or personal style, pick a tactic for resolving conflict that you would feel comfortable using. One person might say, "I would like the tactic of make a last and final offer because I like to control situations." Another person might say, "I prefer confrontation because I'm an open and up-front type of person." Still another person might say, "I'll avoid disarming the opposition for now. I don't yet have enough finesse to carry out this technique."

In fitting the strategy to the situation, it is important to assess the gravity of the topic for negotiation or the conflict between people. A woman might say to herself, "My boss has committed such a blatant act of sexual harassment that I had best take this up with a higher authority immediately." Sizing up your opponent can also help you choose the best strategy. If she or he appears reasonably flexible, you might try to compromise. Or if your adversary is especially upset, give that person a chance to simmer down before trying to solve the problem.

Concept Review
and Reinforcement

Key Terms

Summary and Review

Conflict occurs when two sets of demands, goals, or motives are incompatible. Such differences often lead to a hostile or antagonistic relationship between people. A conflict can also be considered a dispute, feud, or controversy. Among the reasons for widespread conflict are

- competition for limited resources
- personality clashes
- aggressive personalities, including bullies
- culturally diverse teams and factional groups
- competing work and family demands
- microinequities (semiconscious slights)
- sexual harassment

Sexual harassment is one of two types: quid pro quo (a demand for sexual favors in exchange for job benefits) and creating a hostile environment. It is important for workers to understand what actions and words constitute sexual harassment and how to deal with the problem.

The benefits of conflict include the emergence of talents and abilities, constructive innovation and change, and increased unity after the conflict is settled. Among the detrimental consequences of conflict are physical and mental health problems, wasted resources, the promotion of self-interest, and workplace violence.

Techniques for resolving conflicts with others include the following:

- Being assertive. To become more assertive, set a goal, appear warm and friendly, conduct anonymous conversations, greet strangers, and practice being decisive.
- Confrontation and problem solving leading to win–win. Get to the root of the problem

and resolve it systematically. The intention of confrontation and problem solving is to arrive at a collaborative solution to the conflict. The opposite of win–win is win–lose, where each side attempts to maximize gain at the expense of the other.

- Disarm the opposition. Agree with the criticizer and enlist his or her help.
- Cognitive restructuring. Mentally convert negative aspects into positive ones by looking for the positive elements in a situation.
- Appeal to a third party (such as a government agency).
- Use the grievance procedure (a formal organizational procedure for dispute resolution), used extensively in unionized companies
- Use company programs to help reduce work–family conflict including flexible work schedules, dependent-care programs, job sharing, employee sabbbitacals, and compassionate attitudes toward individual needs. Such programs increase productivity.
- Use negotiation and bargaining tactics, including creating a positive negotiating climate; allowing room for compromise but being reasonable; focusing on interests, not positions; making a last and final offer; role-playing to predict what the other side will do; and allowing for face-saving.

Limited ability to manage anger damages the careers and personal lives of many people. The ability to manage anger is part of emotional intelligence. In managing your own anger, remember that anger can be an energizing force.

- Express your anger before it reaches a high intensity.
- As you are about to express your anger, slow down.
- Ask for feedback on how you deal with anger.
- In dealing with the anger of others, use the confront, contain (move the angry worker out of sight),

and connect (ask open-ended questions to get at the real reason behind the outburst) method.

In choosing a tactic for resolving conflict, consider both your personality or style and the nature of the situation facing you. The situation includes such factors as the gravity of the conflict and the type of person you are facing.

Check Your Understanding

1. Many former students of human relations or organizational behavior contend that the most useful information they learned in the course pertained to conflict resolution. Why might their contention be true?
2. Give an example from your own life of how competition for limited resources can breed conflict.
3. Some conflicts go on for decades without being resolved, such as disputes between countries that last for up to 100 years. Why is it so difficult to resolve such conflicts?
4. Imagine that after two weeks on a new job that you want, your boss begins to treat you in a bullying, intimidating manner. What would you say to that boss?
5. Many male managers who confer with a female worker in their offices leave the door open to avoid any charges of sexual harassment. Are these managers using good judgment, or are they being overly cautious?

6. Why is it that during a game, same-sex professional athletes touch (even on the buttocks), hug, and kiss each other yet such behavior is frowned on or forbidden in other workplaces, such as the office or factory?
7. Identify several occupations in which conflict resolution skills are particularly important.
8. How might a person use cognitive restructuring to help deal with the conflict of having received a below-average raise yet expecting an above-average raise?
9. What is your explanation of the research showing that role-playing a negotiation scenario helps people make more accurate predictions about the outcome of conflicts?
10. Ask a successful person how much conflict he or she experiences in balancing the demands of work and personal life. Be prepared to report your findings in class.

Web Corner

Cognitive restructuring: http://www.mindtools.com/stress/rt/CognitiveRestructuring.htm

Assertiveness training: http://www.psychologyinfo.com/treatment/asssertiveness.html

Shyness: www.shyness.com (self-quizzes about shyness, plus the opportunity to participate in research about shyness)

INTERNET SKILL BUILDER:

WWW.NEGOTIATORS.COM/60SECONDS.HTM presents a teaser of a program that suggests you can learn to

negotiate within one minute, based on slides presented. As you read the presentation, identify the concepts and skills that you think would be the most beneficial to you. What else would you have to do in addition to absorbing the presentation on this Web site to enhance your negotiating skills? Compare the techniques in the 60-second presentation to those described in the text. What similarities do you see?

Applying Human Relations Exercise 10-1

Win–Win Conflict Management

The class is organized into groups of six, with each group being divided into conflict resolution teams of three each. The members of the team would like to find a win–win solution to the issue separating each side. The team members are free to invent their own pressing issue or choose among the following:

- Management wants to control costs by not giving cost-of-living adjustments in the upcoming year. The employee group believes that a cost-of-living adjustment is absolutely necessary.
- The marketing team claims it could sell 250,000 units of a toaster large enough to toast bagels if the toasters could be produced at $15 per unit. The manufacturing

group says it would not be feasible to get the manufacturing costs below $20 per unit.
- Starbucks Coffee would like to build in a new location, adjacent to a historic district in one of the oldest cities in North America. The members of the town planning board would like the tax revenue and the jobs that the Starbucks store would bring, but they still say they do not want a Starbucks store adjacent to the historic district.

After the teams have developed win–win solutions to the conflicts, the creative solutions can be shared with teammates. Explain why each of your solutions should be classified as win–win. Describe the benefits each side received from the resolution of conflict and why you classified the outcome as a benfit.

Applying Human Relations Exercise 10-2

Learning to Manage Anger

The next few times you are really angry with somebody or something, use one or more of the following good mental health statements. Each statement is designed to remind you that you are in charge, not your anger. To begin, visualize something that has made you angry recently. Practice making the following statements in relation to that angry episode.

- I'm in charge here, not my emotional outbursts.
- I'll breathe deeply a few times and then deal with this.
- I feel _____ when you _____.
- I can handle this.
- I'm going to take time out to cool down before I deal with this.
- Yes, I'm angry and I'll just watch what I say or do.

Now describe the effect making these statements had on your anger.

Source: Based on Lynne Namka, "A Primer on Anger: Getting a Handle on Your Mads," available at http://members.aol.com/AngriesOut/grown2.htm, p. 4, retrieved April 21, 1998.

Applying Human Relations Exercise 10-3

Conflict Resolution

Imagine that Heather in the case presented, next decides that her job is taking too big a toll on her personal life.

However, she still values her job and does not want to quit. She decides to discuss her problem with her team leader, Tyler. From Tyler's standpoint, a professional person must stand ready to meet unusual job demands and cannot expect an entirely predictable work schedule. One person plays the role of Heather and another the role of Tyler as they attempt to resolve this incident of work–family conflict.

Observers will look for (a) how well the conflict appears to have been resolved and (b) which techniques of conflict resolution Heather and Tyler used. Other feedback observations will also be welcome.

Human Relations Case Study 10-1

Caught in a Squeeze

Heather Lopez is a product development specialist at a telecommunications company. For the past seven months she has worked as a member of a product development team composed of people from five different departments within the company. Heather's previously worked full time in the marketing department. Her primary responsibilities were to research the market potential of an idea for a new product. The product development team is now working on a product that will integrate a company's printers and copiers.

Heather's previous position in the marketing department was a satisfactory fit for her lifestyle. Heather thought that she was able to take care of her family responsibilities and her job without sacrificing one for the other. As Heather explains, "I worked about 45 predictable hours in my other job. My hours were essentially 8:30 A.M. to 4:30 P.M. with a little work at night and on Saturdays. But I could do the work at night and on Saturdays at home.

"Brad, my husband, and I had a smooth-working arrangement for sharing the responsibility for getting our son, Christopher, off to school and picking him up from the after-school child-care center. Brad is a devoted accountant, so he understands the importance of giving high priority to a career yet still being a good family person."

In her new position as a member of the product development team, Heather is encountering some unanticipated demands. Three weeks ago, at 3 P.M. on a Tuesday, Tyler Watson, Heather's team leader, announced an emergency meeting to discuss a budget problem with the new product. The meeting would start at 4 and probably end at about 6:30. "Don't worry folks," said the team leader, "if it looks like we are going past 6:30, we will order in some Chinese food."

With a look of panic on her face, Heather responded to Tyler, "I can't make the meeting. Christopher will be expecting me at about 5 at the child-care center. My husband is out of town, and the center closes at 6 sharp. So count me out of today's meeting."

Tyler said, "I said that this is an emergency meeting and that we need input from all the members. You need to organize your personal life better to be a contributing member to this team. But do what you have to do, at least this once."

Heather chose to leave the office at 4:30 so she could pick up Christopher. The next day, Tyler did not comment on her absence. However, he gave her a copy of the minutes and asked for her input. The budget problem surfaced again one week later. Top-level management asked the group to reduce the cost of the new product and its initial marketing costs by 15 percent.

Tyler said to the team on a Friday morning, "We have until Monday morning to arrive at a reduced cost structure on our product development. I am dividing up the project into segments. If we meet as a team Saturday morning at 8, we should get the job done by 6 at night. Get a good night's rest so we can start fresh tomorrow morning. Breakfast and lunch will be on the company."

Heather could feel stress overwhelming her body, as she thought to herself, "Christopher is playing in the finals of his Little League soccer match tomorrow morning at 10. Brad has made dinner reservations for 6, so we can make it to the *The Lion King* at 8 P.M. Should I tell Tyler he is being unreasonable? Should I quit? Should I tell Christopher and Brad that our special occasions together are less important than a Saturday business meeting?"

Questions

1. What type of conflicts is Heather facing?
2. What should Heather do to resolve her conflicts with respect to family and work responsibilities?
3. What should the company do to help deal with the type of conflict Heather is facing? Or should the company not consider Heather's dilemma to be their problem?

Human Relations Case Study 10-2

Wal-Mart Plays Tough in Quebec

In electronics, only "Le Gros Albert" (Fat Albert) and a few other leftover DVDs remain. Over in household goods, liquidation tags dangle beside thin skillets as the Wal-Mart in Jonquiere, Quebec (Canada), prepares to close. The company shut the doors here May 6, 2005, after workers voted to make this the first unionized Wal-Mart in North America.

The closure left 190 bitter employees out of work and the town uneasy over the future of unions. Supporters of organized labor also say it serves as a warning for workers at other Wal-Mart stores who might contemplate defying founder Sam Walton's sharp distaste for unions. The world's largest retail chain has fiercely and successfully resisted unionization attempts at its 3,600 stores in the United States.

In Canada, the battle has been pitched, pitting the country's still-healthy union movement against what is now its largest retailer. Wal-Mart Stores Inc. now takes 52 percent of the retail market share in Canada and is opening about 30 stores a year. Jonquiere was the first store to be unionized.

Andrew Pelletier, head of corporate affairs for Wal-Mart Canada Corp., said that, although the union may have succeeded in organizing a store in Jonquiere, Wal-Mart workers have on five other occasions voted against unionization. "I think that says we are a good employer," Pelletier said.

Jonquiere, 120 miles north of Quebec City, is a French-speaking mill town of 60,000. Its bland neighborhoods of square clapboard homes attest to its origins a century ago as a center for the pulp-and-paper industry. The Wal-Mart here is one of three in the area, and it was welcomed when it opened more than three years ago. The town's manufacturing legs are getting old: The two paper mills closed lines in their plants in 2004, costing 1,200 jobs. "Economically, it's not a good time for us," said the mayor of the Saguenay area, Jean Tremblay. The new Wal-Mart was swamped with applications, and those who were hired thought themselves lucky.

"I never had a job as good as this before," said Lynn Morissette, 44, who tracks inventory in the store. "I worked in the daytime. I thought I had a good wage, and I was a shareholder, too, so I could save up some money. I was going to retire here." But others were not so thrilled about Wal-Mart's pay—starting at about $6.20 (U.S.) an hour, its floating shifts for part-timers, or the rules that limited some full-time employees to 28 hours of work a week. In an area built on union jobs, with higher wage scales, it wasn't long before some employees tried to organize.

Those involved in the organizing effort claim they were harassed by the company. "We were targeted fairly quickly by Wal-Mart," said Pierre Martineau, a 60-year-old maintenance man who helped organize the union. He said he was humiliated and ridiculed by managers at a storewide meeting and followed around by supervisors who made implied threats.

Those who did not want a union, say organizers, harassed them to join. "People signed the cards just to get some peace" from the union organizers, said Noella Langlois, 53, who works in the clothing department. "They thought they would vote against it in a secret vote." In fact, there was a vote last April that rejected the union. But under Quebec labor laws, the organizers could try again. When they collected signed union cards from 51 percent of the employees, the law declared the Jonquiere Wal-Mart a union shop.

Pelletier, the Wal-Mart spokesperson, says the Quebec laws are unfair, and only a secret ballot would show the true feelings of the workers. "Signing a union card, when there's someone on your doorstep at night saying, 'Sign this card,' should not be the last word," he said. "A democratic, secret vote is the only way to avoid intimidation by either the union or an employer."

But it became moot in February, when Wal-Mart announced it would close the store. Company officials said it was losing money, and the demands of the union would have made it even less tenable. "You can't take a store that is a struggling store anyway and add a bunch of people and a bunch of work rules," said Wal-Mart chief executive H. Lee Scott, Jr.

Some here in Jonquiere don't believe the company's claim that the store was losing money. They say the chain sacrificed the store to make a point to its employees across Canada and the United States, where union organizers are involved in dozens of organizing drives and court battles. "They closed it to be a threat to other unions," said Tremblay, the mayor. "We know that for Wal-Mart, Jonquiere is nothing. They wanted to close it to make a lesson to other Wal-Marts."

The announcement deepened animosities among the employees. Those who liked their jobs and said they were happy at Wal-Mart are bitter at the union for its tactics, which they blame for the store closure.

Sylvie Lavoie, 40, said she is unsure how, as a single mother, she will support herself and her 10-year-old daughter after the store closes. But the backup cashier, who earns $7.55 an hour, said she does not regret joining the union drive. "We can't regret trying to make our lives better," she said at the union hall. "I don't know what I'll do, but I know my daughter will be proud of me."

Questions

1. Which technique of conflict resolution might have made it possible for Wal-Mart to stay open in Jonquiere?
2. How might the Wal-Mart workers who opposed the union and those that favored the union have approached their differences?
3. What has this case got to do with human relations skills?

Source: Excerpted from Doug Struck, "Wal-Mart Leaves Bitter Chill: Quebec Store Closes after Vote to Unionize," *Washington Post Foreign Service*, April 14, 2005, p. E01.

REFERENCES

1. Sue Shellenbarger, "Employers Step Up Efforts to Lure Stay-at-Home Mothers Back to Work," *The Wall Street Journal*, February 9, 2006, p. D1.
2. Dominic A. Infante, *Arguing Constructively* (Prospects Heights, IL: Waveland Press, 1992); Siobhan Leftwich, "Hey, You Can't Say That! How to Cope with Verbally Abusive People," *Black Enterprise*, January 2006, p. 95.
3. Julie Ellis, "Knock Down Workplace Bullying; Improve Office Morale," *Managing Workplace Conflict* (The Dartnell Corporation sample issue, 2002), p. 6.
4. "Safety and Health Topics: Workplace Violence," U.S. Department of Labor, Occupational Safety and Health Administration, available at www.osha.gov, retrieved April 2, 2006.
5. Angela Pirisi, "Teamwork: The Downside of Diversity," *Psychology Today*, November/December 1999, p. 18.
6. Jiatao Li and Donald C. Hambrick, "Factional Groups: A New Vantage on Demographic Faultlines, Conflict, and Disintegration in Work Teams," *Academy of Management Journal*, October 2005, pp. 794–813.
7. "When Work and Private Lives Collide," *Workforce*, February 1999, p. 27.
8. The examples, but not the interpretations, are from Julie Fawe, "Why Your Boss May Start Sweating the Small Stuff," *Time*, March 20, 2006, p. 80. See also, Joann S. Lublin, "How to Stop the Snubs that Demoralize You and Your Colleagues," *The Wall Street Journal*, December 7, 2004, p. B1.
9. Kimberly T. Schneider, Suzanne Swan, and Louise F. Fitzgerald, "Job-Related and Psychological Effects of Sexual Harassment in the Workplace: Empirical Evidence in Two Organizations," *Journal of Applied Psychology*, June 1997, p. 406
10. Theresa M. Glomb, Liberty J. Munson, and Charles L. Hulin, "Structural Equation Models of Sexual Harassment: Longitudinal Explorations and Cross-Sectional Generalizations," *Journal of Applied Psychology*, February 1999, pp. 14–28.
11. Jana L. Raver and Michele J. Gelfand, "Beyond the Individual Victim: Linking Sexual Harassment, Team Processes, and Team Performance," *Academy of Management Journal*, June 2005, pp. 387–400.
12. Lisa Takeuchi Cullen, "Sex in the Syllabus," *Time*, April 3, 2006, pp. 80–81.
13. Data reported in Anne Fisher, "How to Prevent Violence at Work," *Fortune*, February 21, 2005.
14. "Right and Wrong Ways to Manage Conflict," *Manager's Edge*, October 2001, p. 5
15. Bernardo J. Carducci, *Shyness: A Bold Approach* (New York: HarperCollins, 1999).
16. Philip Zimbardo, *Shyness: What It Is, What to Do about It* (Reading, MA: Addison-Wesley, 1977), pp. 220–226; Mel Silberman with Freda Hansburg, *PeopleSmart* (San Francisco: Berrett-Koehler, 2000), pp. 75–76.
17. Stephen P. Robbins and David A. DeCenzo, *Supervision Today!* 4th ed. (Upper Saddle River, NJ: Pearson Prentice Hall, 2004), p. 438.
18. David Welch, "Twilight of the UAW," *Business Week*, April 10, 2006, p. 62.
19. Timothy A. Judge and Jason A. Colquitt, "Organizational Justice and Stress: The Mediating Role of Work–Family Conflict," *Journal of Applied Psychology*, June 2004, pp. 395–404.
20. Cited in Marcia A. Reed-Woodward, "Share and Share Alike: A New Option for Work/Life Balance." *Black Enterprise*, April 2006, p. 63.
21. Michael Arndt, "Nice Work If You Can Get It," *Business Week*, January 9, 2006, pp. 56–57.
22. Marc Deiner, "Speak Up: Hate to Negotiate? That's Still No Excuse to Avoid Learning the Skill," *Entrepreneur*, September 2004, p. 79.
23. Joseph D'O'Brian, "Negotiating with Peers: Consensus, Not Power," *Supervisory Management*, January 1992, p. 4.
24. J. Scott Armstrong, "Forecasting in Conflicts: How to Predict What Your Opponents Will Do," *Knowledge@ Wharton*, February 13, 2002, p.1.
25. Linda Wasmer Andrews, "When It's Time for Anger Management," *HR Magazine*, June 2005, pp. 131–135.
26. Fred Pryor, "Is Anger Really Healthy?" *The Pryor Management Newsletter*, February 1996, p. 3.
27. The quote and technique are both from Kathleen Doheny, "It's a Mad, Mad Corporate World," *Working Woman*, April 2000, pp. 71–72.

11 Becoming an Effective Leader

Learning Objectives

Outline

After studying the information and doing the exercises in this chapter, you should be able to:

1 Identify personal traits and characteristics of effective leaders.

2 Identify behaviors of effective leaders.

3 Understand the nature of leadership style and the importance of the leader adapting to the situation.

4 Know what needs to be done to get along well with group members.

5 Map out a tentative program for developing your leadership potential and skills.

A few years ago, R. Todd Bradley was sitting on the beach near his San Diego home when his mobile phone rang. A friend was calling to urge him to get in touch with Mark V. Hurd, the newly appointed chief executive of Hewlett-Packard Co. (HP). The computer and printer giant was looking for someone to run its $25 billion PC unit. Bradley, fresh off a tough turnaround at handheld maker Palm Inc., was a reluctant recruit. "I was ready to lay on the beach for a while—both literally and figuratively," he says.

Just weeks later, Bradley signed on. The primary reason for his change of heart? HP's new boss. Like Bradley, Hurd is a straight-talking, number-crunching operations wonk. Hurd seemed intent on ending the high drama that had distracted many at HP during the tenure of his predecessor, Carleton S. "Carly" Fiorina. He wanted to bear down on the numbers, spreadsheets, and execution. "Mark seemed like a genuine, focused guy—far more focused on creating value through operational performance than just pitching grand visions," says Bradley. [1]

■ Leadership

the process of bringing about positive changes and influencing others to achieve worthwhile goals

The story about Mark Hurd illustrates several of the many characteristics of effective leaders: They attract the support of others, are trustworthy, and have good knowledge of the business. **Leadership** is the process of bringing about positive changes and influencing others to achieve worthwhile goals. (In a work setting, the worthwhile goals would relate to what the company wanted to accomplish.) The key words in understanding leadership are *change* and *influence*. A leader often challenges the status quo and brings about improvements. A leader also influences people to do things, such as achieve higher performance that they would not do otherwise.

Effective leadership at the top of organizations is necessary for their prosperity and even survival. Effective leadership is also important throughout the organization, particularly in working with entry-level workers. Good supervision is needed to help employees deal with customer problems, carry out their usual tasks, and maintain high quality.

The study of leadership warrants your attention because today people at all levels in the organization are expected to exert some leadership. Organizations seek people to exert leadership at all levels by giving many people an opportunity to engage in such tasks as motivating others and setting goals. [2] Even if your job title does not include the mention of management responsibility, you will often be called on to be a temporary leader, such as being appointed the head of a committee or project. Our approach to the vast topic of leadership encompasses the attributes and behaviors of leaders, leadership style, getting along with subordinates, and developing your leadership potential.

What Are Some Traits and Characteristics of Effective Leaders?

■ Learning Objective 1

■ Leadership effectiveness

inner quality of a leader who helps the group accomplish its objectives without neglecting satisfaction and morale

A major thrust to understanding leaders and leadership is to recognize that effective leaders have the "right stuff." In other words, certain inner qualities contribute to leadership effectiveness in a wide variety of situations. **Leadership effectiveness** in this situation means that the leader helps the group accomplish its objectives without neglecting satisfaction and morale. The characteristics that contribute to effectiveness depend somewhat on the situation. A supervisor in a meatpacking plant and one in an information technology department will need different sets of personal characteristics. The situation includes such factors as the people being supervised, the job being performed, the company, and the cultural background of employees.

In the next several pages, we describe some of the more important traits and characteristics of leaders. Many of these traits and characteristics are capable of development and refinement. Figure 11-1 outlines the seven key traits.

SELF-CONFIDENCE AND COURAGE

Self-confidence is necessary for leadership because it helps assure group members that activities are under control. Assume you are a manager in a company that is facing bankruptcy. At a meeting you attend, the chief executive officer sobs, "I'm sorry, I'm just no good in a crisis. I don't know what's going to happen to the company. I don't think I can get us out of this mess. Maybe one of you would like to try your hand at turning around the company." You would probably prefer that the CEO behave in a confident, assured manner.

In other leadership situations as well, the leader who functions best is self-confident enough to reassure others and to appear in control. But if the leader is so self-confident that he so she will not admit errors, listen to criticism, or ask for advice, that too creates problems. Being too self-confident can lead to the person to ignore potential problems, thinking, "I can handle whatever comes my way."

One of many possible examples of a self-confident leader is W. James McNerney, Jr., whose latest major executive position is chair, president, and CEO of Boeing Co. His record of high-level leadership accomplishments suggest that he projects self-confidence and feels self-confident. Further attesting to his confidence, when

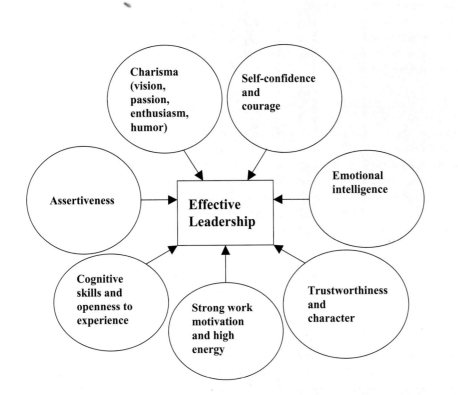

Figure   11-1

Seven Key Leadership Traits

McNerney started his new role at Boeing, he said, "This job will test more things about me than almost any job I can think of. I like a challenge—and I've got one." [3]

Self-confidence often takes the form of the courage to face the challenges of taking prudent risks and taking initiative in general. Courage comes from the heart, as suggested by the French word for heart, *le coeur.* Leaders must be able to face up to responsibility and be willing to put reputations on the line, even if this means taking a course of action others would not advise.

EMOTIONAL INTELLIGENCE

Emotional intelligence is considered a major contributor to leadership effectiveness. In review, the concept refers to managing ourselves and our relationships effectively with an emphasis on dealing with emotion. Intelligence of this type can be developed through working on some of its components, such as learning to control your temper and developing empathy by listening to people carefully. It is also important to develop the habit of looking to understand the feelings and emotions of people around you. Also, ask yourself, "How do I feel about what's going on here?" When you have a hunch about people's motives, look for feedback in the future to see if you were right. Here is an example of applying emotional intelligence:

> Visualize yourself as a team leader. Vanessa, one of the team members, says to you, "I'm worried about Rick. I think he needs help. He looks like he has a drinking problem." If you have good emotional intelligence, you might think to yourself, "I wonder why Vanessa is telling me this. Is she simply being helpful? Or is she out to backstab Rick?" So you seek some tangible evidence about Rick's alleged problem before acting. You would also seek to spend more time with Vanessa so you can better understand her motives. Your investigation might reveal that Vanessa and Rick are rivals and have a personality clash.

With much less emotional intelligence, you would immediately get in touch with Rick, accuse him of having a drinking problem, and tell him to get help or get fired.

Many business leaders encounter difficulties for what appears to be a deficit in emotional intelligence. A case in point is former Coca-Cola president Stephen J. Heyer. Despite his marketing brilliance, he was passed over for the CEO position. Among the reasons were his confrontational style, including his tendency to belittle other executives and staffers. Heyer rebounded and became the CEO of Starwood Hotels and Resorts. [4]

TRUSTWORTHINESS AND CHARACTER

Considerable evidence exists that being trustworthy or honest contributes to being an effective leader. An effective leader is supposed to *walk the talk*, thereby showing a consistency between deeds (walking) and words (talking). Group members consistently believe that leaders must display honesty, integrity, and credibility. Leaders themselves believe that honesty and integrity make a difference in their effectiveness. [5] In this context, **trust** is defined as a person's confidence in another individual's intentions and motives and in the sincerity of that individual's words. Leaders must be trustworthy, and they must also trust the group members.

■ **Trust**
a person's confidence in another individual's intentions and motives and in the sincerity of that individual's words

It takes a leader a long time to build trust, yet one brief incident of untrustworthy behavior can destroy it. An example of untrustworthy behavior would be using company money for private purposes or sexually harassing a team member. Leaders are usually allowed a fair share of honest mistakes. In contrast, dishonest mistakes quickly erode leadership effectiveness. Meg Whitman, the CEO of eBay, exemplifies a leader who many people—employees and members of the eBay community—trust. Part of the trust comes from her being self-effacing and low key, and the fact that she responds directly to e-mail messages from buyers and sellers.

[6] The small percentage of frauds who prey on eBay users have not diminished trust in Whitman because the criminals are not eBay employees.

Having certain character traits contributes to being trustworthy and being perceived as a trustworthy person. **Character** in this context refers to doing the right things despite outside pressures to do the opposite. Being of good character also includes leaving enduring marks that set one apart from another. [7] To be of good character is to be moral. The U.S. Air Force has developed a list of 12 attributes that are part of its character program. Air Force leaders are expected to have many of these attributes, and leaders in other organizations will benefit as well. Figure 11-2 lists and defines these 12 traits.

■ **Character**

doing the right things despite outside pressures to do the opposite; includes leaving enduring marks that set one apart from another; being moral

STRONG WORK MOTIVATION AND HIGH ENERGY

Leadership positions tend to be both physically and mentally demanding. A successful leader must be willing to work hard and long to achieve success. Many business leaders often work 70-hour weeks, including Robert Nardelli, the top executive at Home Depot, who treats most Saturdays and Sundays as ordinary business days. (See the case about Nardelli at the end of the chapter.) Many leaders appear to be driven by a need for self-fulfillment. Another fundamental reason strong work motivation is required for effectiveness is that a person has to be willing to accept the heavy responsibility that being a supervisor entails. As one department manager said, "Whoever thought being a manager would mean that I would have to fire a single parent who has three children to feed and clothe?"

1. *Integrity.* Consistently adhering to a moral or ethical code or standard. A person who consistently chooses to do the "right thing" when faced with alternate choices.
2. *Honesty.* Consistently being truthful with others.
3. *Loyalty.* Being devoted and committed to one's organization, supervisors, coworkers, and subordinates.
4. *Selflessness.* Genuinely concerned about the welfare of others and willing to sacrifice one's personal interest for others and their organization.
5. *Compassion.* Concern for the suffering or welfare of others and their organization.
6. *Competency.* Capable of performing tasks assigned in a superior fashion and excels in all task assignments. Is effective and efficient.
7. *Respectfulness.* Shows esteem for and consideration and appreciation of other people.
8. *Fairness.* Treats people in an equitable, impartial, and just manner.
9. *Responsibility and self-discipline.* Can be depended on to make rational and logical decisions and to do tasks assigned. Can perform tasks assigned without supervision.
10. *Decisiveness.* Capable of making logical and effective decisions in a timely manner. Does not "shoot from the hip" but does promptly make a good decision after considering data appropriate to the decision.
11. *Spiritual appreciation.* Values the spiritual diversity among individuals with different backgrounds and cultures and respects all individuals rights to differ from others in their beliefs.
12. *Cooperativeness.* Willingness to work or act together with others in accomplishing a task or some common end or purpose.

What is your standing on the above character dimensions? Do you have enough self-awareness to find some room for improvement?

Source: Copyright © 2000 by William H. Hendrix.

Figure 11-2

Character Attributes of Leaders

COGNITIVE SKILLS AND OPENNESS TO EXPERIENCE

■ **Cognitive skills**
problem-solving and intellectual skills

Cognitive skills, as well as personality, are important for leadership success. Problem-solving and intellectual skills are referred to collectively as **cognitive skills.** The term *cognition* refers to the mental process of faculty by which knowledge is gathered. To inspire people, bring about constructive changes, and solve problems creatively, leaders need to be mentally sharp. A synthesis of 151 different studies examining the relationship between intelligence and leadership performance found a slight positive relationship between the two variables. However, when the leader's job emphasized playing an active role in making decisions about the work of the group (such as helping solve technical problems), intelligence showed a higher relationship with performance. [8]

A cognitive skill of major importance is *knowledge of the business,* or technical competence. An effective leader has to be technically or professionally competent in some discipline, particularly when leading a group of specialists. It is difficult for the leader to establish rapport with group members when he or she does not know what they are doing. A related damper on leadership effectiveness is when the group does not respect the leader's technical skill. Having good practical intelligence (*street smarts*) is also part of an effective leader's intellectual makeup. A leader with high practical intelligence could size up a good opportunity without spending an extensive amount of time analyzing what could possibly go wrong.

■ **Openness to experience**
personality characteristic of positive orientation toward learning; people with considerable openness to experience have well-developed intellects

Closely related to cognitive skills is the personality characteristic of **openness to experience,** a positive orientation toward learning. People who have considerable openness to experience have well-developed intellects. Traits commonly associated with this dimension of the intellect include being imaginative, cultured, curious, original, broad-minded, intelligent, and artistically sensitive.

ASSERTIVENESS

Assertiveness is a widely recognized leadership trait. If you are self-confident, it is easier to be assertive with people. An assertive leader might say, "I know that the ice storm put us out of business for four days, but we can make up the time by working smart and pulling together. Within 30 days, we will have met or surpassed our goals for the quarter." This statement reflects self-confidence in leadership capabilities and assertiveness in expressing thoughts.

Assertiveness helps leaders perform many tasks and achieve goals. Among them are confronting group members about their mistakes, demanding higher performance, and setting high expectations. An assertive leader will also make demands on higher management, such as asking for equipment needed by the group.

CHARISMA

■ **Charisma**
type of charm and magnetism that inspires others; important quality for leaders at all levels

An important quality for leaders at all levels is **charisma,** a type of charm and magnetism that inspires others. Not every leader has to be charismatic, yet to be an effective leader you often need some degree of this personality quality. Being charismatic helps leaders form better relationships with workers, who might then work harder for them. A leader's charisma is determined by the subjective perception of him or her by other people. Therefore, it is impossible for even the most effective leaders to inspire and motivate everyone. Even popular business leaders are disliked by some of their employees. For example, Steven Jobs, cofounder of Apple Computer, is regarded as charismatic and inspirational by many employees and company outsiders. Yet, he is also perceived to be arrogant and obnoxious by many others who work with him because of his explosive temper and second-guessing their decisions. Charisma encompasses many traits and characteristics. Here we focus on vision, passion, enthusiasm, excitement, and humor.

Vision

Top-level leaders need a visual image of where the organization is headed and how it can get there. The person with vision can help the organization or group establish a vision. The progress of the organization depends on the executive having a vision, or an optimistic version of the future. Effective leaders project ideas and images that excite people and, therefore, inspire employees to do their best. Leadership positions of lesser responsibility also call for some vision. Each work group in a progressive company might be expected to form its own vision, such as "We will become the best accounts receivable group in the entire auto replacement parts industry."

Passion, Enthusiasm, and Excitement

Charismatic leaders are passionate about their work and their group members. Part of the reason charismatic leaders can readily be passionate, enthusiastic, and excited is that they tend to be extraverted. The extraversion is most strongly associated with the type of charismatic leader who brings about major changes in the organization or an organizational unit. [9] The charismatic business owner is likely to think about the company's product or service day and night. Because of their contagious excitement, charismatic leaders stimulate group members. Workers respond positively to enthusiasm, especially because enthusiasm may be perceived as a reward for good performance. Enthusiasm is also effective because it helps build good relationships with group members. Spoken expressions of enthusiasm include such statements as "great job" and "I love it." Andrea Jung, the stylish and inspirational chief executive officer of Avon Products, tells Avon representatives at company meetings that she loves them. The leader can express enthusiasm nonverbally through gestures, nonsexual touching, and so forth.

Sense of Humor

Humor is a component of charisma and a contributor to leadership effectiveness. Humor helps leaders influence people by reducing tension, relieving boredom, and defusing anger. The most effective form of humor by a leader is tied to the leadership situation. It is much less effective for the leader to tell rehearsed jokes. A key advantage of a witty, work-related comment is that it indicates mental alertness. A canned joke is much more likely to fall flat.

A sales manager was conducting a meeting about declining sales. He opened the meeting by saying, "Ladies and gentlemen, just yesterday I completed a spreadsheet analysis of our declining sales. According to my spreadsheet analysis, if we continue our current trend, by the year 2014 we will have sales of negative $3,750,000. No company can support those figures. We've got to reverse the trend." The manager's humor helped dramatize the importance of reversing the sales decline.

A caution about charisma is that it is not entirely dependent on personal characteristics but also on what a person accomplishes. Achieving outstanding results may lead to being perceived as charismatic. An example would be if an almost-forgotten coach suddenly has an outstanding season and is then described as charismatic. A study of 128 CEOs of major U.S. corporations found that when the corporation performed well, the CEO was perceived as charismatic by members of his or her team. In contrast, when the CEOs were perceived as charismatic by the top management team, the organization did not necessarily perform better. [10]

Although inherited characteristics, such as energy, contribute to charisma, most people can develop some charismatic qualities. Figure 11-3 presents suggestions for becoming more charismatic.

Following are a number of suggestions for behaving charismatically, all based on characteristics and behaviors often found among charismatic leaders and other charismatic persons as well.

1. *Communicate a vision.* A charismatic leader offers an exciting image of where the organization is headed and how to get there. A vision is more than a forecast because it describes an ideal version of the future of an entire organization or an organizational unit, such as a department. The supervisor of paralegal services might communicate a vision such as, "Our paralegal group will become known as the most professional and helpful paralegal group in Arizona."

2. *Make frequent use of metaphors and analogies.* To inspire people, the charismatic leader uses colorful language and exciting metaphors and analogies. Develop metaphors to inspire people around you. To pick up the spirits of her maintenance group, a maintenance supervisor told the group, "We're a lot like the heating and cooling system in a house. A lot of people don't give us much thought, but without us their lives would be very uncomfortable."

3. *Inspire trust and confidence.* Make your deeds consistent with your promises. As mentioned earlier in this chapter, being trustworthy is a key leadership trait. Get people to believe in your competence by making your accomplishments known in a polite, tactful way.

4. *Be highly energetic and goal oriented.* Impress others with your energy and resourcefulness. To increase your energy supply, exercise frequently, eat well, and get ample rest. You can also add to an image of energy by raising and lowering your voice frequently and avoiding a slow pace.

5. *Be emotionally expressive and warm.* A key characteristic of charismatic leaders is the ability to express feelings openly. In dealing with team members, refer to your feelings at the time, such as "I'm excited because I know we are going to hit our year-end target by mid-October." Nonverbal emotional expressiveness, such as warm gestures and frequent touching (nonsexual) of group members, also exhibits charisma.

6. *Make ample use of true stories.* An excellent way of building rapport is to tell stories that deliver a message. Storytelling adds a touch of warmth to the teller and helps build connections among people who become familiar with the same story.

7. *Smile frequently, even if you are not in a happy mood.* A warm smile seems to indicate a confident, caring person, which contributes to a perception of charisma.

8. *Be candid.* Practice saying directly what you want rather than being indirect and evasive. If you want someone to help you, don't ask, "Are you busy?" Instead, ask, "Can you help me with a problem I'm having right now?"

9. *Make everybody you meet feel that he or she is quite important.* For example, at a company social gathering, shake the hand of every person you meet. Also, thank people frequently both orally and by written notes.

10. *Stand up straight and also use other nonverbal signals of self-confidence.* Practice having good posture. Minimize fidgeting, scratching, foot tapping, and speaking in a monotone. Walk at a rapid pace without appearing to be panicked. Dress fashionably without going to the extreme that people notice your clothes more than they notice you. Shake hands firmly without creating pain and make enough eye contact to notice the color of the other person's eyes. When you take that much trouble, you project care and concern.

11. *Be willing to take personal risks.* Charismatic leaders are typically risk takers, and risk taking adds to their charisma. Risks you might take include suggesting a bright but costly idea and recommending that a former felon be given a chance in your firm.

Figure   **11-3**

Suggestions for Becoming More Charismatic

■ **Learning Objective 2**

What Are Some Behaviors and Skills of Effective Leaders?

The personal traits, skills, and characteristics just discussed help create the potential for effective leadership. A leader also has to *do* things that influence group members to achieve good performance. The behaviors or skills of leaders described next contribute to productivity and morale in most situations. Before studying the behaviors and skills of effective leaders, do Human Relations Self-Assessment Quiz 11-1.

Human Relations Self-Assessment Quiz **11-1**

Readiness for the Leadership Role

Indicate the extent to which you agree with each of the following statements. Use a 1-to-5 scale:
(1) disagree strongly, (2) disagree, (3) neutral, (4) agree, (5) agree strongly. If you do not have
leadership experience, imagine how you might react to the questions if you were a leader.

1. It is enjoyable having people count on me for ideas and suggestions.	1	2	3	4	5
2. It would be accurate to say that I have inspired other people.	1	2	3	4	5
3. It's a good practice to ask people provocative questions about their work.	1	2	3	4	5
4. It's easy for me to compliment others.	1	2	3	4	5
5. I like to cheer up people even when my own spirits are down.	1	2	3	4	5
6. What my team accomplishes is more important than my personal glory.	1	2	3	4	5
7. Many people imitate my ideas.	1	2	3	4	5
8. Building team spirit is important to me.	1	2	3	4	5
9. I would enjoy coaching other members of the team.	1	2	3	4	5
10. It is important to me to recognize others for their accomplishments.	1	2	3	4	5
11. I would enjoy entertaining visitors to my firm even if it interfered with my completing a report.	1	2	3	4	5
12. It would be fun for me to represent my team at gatherings outside our department.	1	2	3	4	5
13. The problems of my teammates are my problems, too.	1	2	3	4	5
14. Resolving conflict is an activity I enjoy.	1	2	3	4	5
15. I would cooperate with another unit in the organization even if I disagreed with the position taken by its members.	1	2	3	4	5
16. I am an idea generator on the job.	1	2	3	4	5
17. It's fun for me to bargain whenever I have the opportunity.	1	2	3	4	5
18. Team members listen to me when I speak.	1	2	3	4	5
19. People have asked to me to assume the leadership of an activity several times in my life.	1	2	3	4	5
20. I've always been a convincing person.	1	2	3	4	5

Total score: _____

Scoring and Interpretation:

Calculate your total score by adding the numbers circled. A tentative interpretation of the scoring is as follows:

90–100   High readiness for the leadership role

60–89   Moderate readiness for the leadership role

40–59   Some uneasiness with the leadership role

39 or less Low readiness for carrying out the leadership role

   If you are already a successful leader and you scored low on this questionnaire, ignore your score. If you scored surprisingly low and you are not yet a leader, or are currently performing poorly as a leader, study the statements carefully. Consider changing your attitude or your behavior so that you can legitimately answer more of the questions with 4s or 5s. Studying the rest of this chapter will give you additional insight into the leader's role that may be helpful in your development as a leader.

The exercise will help you understand how ready you are to assume a leadership role. Taking the quiz will also give you insight into the type of thinking that is characteristic of leaders.

PRACTICE STRONG ETHICS

Being trustworthy facilitates a leader practicing strong (or good) ethics, the study of moral obligation, or separating right from wrong. Ethics deals with doing the right thing by employees, customers, the environment, and the law. [11] Practicing good ethics contributes to effective leadership for several reasons. Workers are more likely to trust an ethical than an unethical leader, which helps the leader gain the support of the group. Good ethics serves as a positive model for group members, thus strengthening the organization. Also, ethical leaders help group members avoid common ethical pitfalls in the workplace. Many of these unethical practices, as listed next, can lead to lawsuits against the company:

- lying or misrepresenting facts

- blaming others for your mistakes

- divulging personal or confidential information to others in the company to promote yourself

- permitting or failing to report violations of legal requirements

- protecting substandard performers from proper discipline

- condoning or failing to report theft or misuse of company property

- suppressing grievances and complaints

- covering up accidents and failing to report health and safety hazards

- ignoring or violating higher management's commitments to employees

- taking credit for the ideas of others [12]

To simplify a complex issue, an effective leader practices the Golden Rule: *Do unto others as you would have others do unto you.* Similarly, popular author Steven Covey encourages leaders to follow natural principles, such as doing only good things. [13] He urges corporate executives, for example, to establish only those goals that will benefit people. Warren G. Bennis, distinguised professor of business administration at the University of California and former university president, emphasizes that leaders have to "rely on a moral compass, a set of principles, a belief system, a set of convictions." [14]

DIRECTION SETTING

Given that leaders are supposed to bring about change, they must point people in the right direction. Setting a direction includes the idea of establishing a vision for the organization or a smaller group. An example of direction setting by a top-level manager would be for the chief executive officer of a toy company to decide that the company should now diversify into the bicycle business. Direction setting by a team leader would include encouraging the group to strive toward error-free work from this point forward or to collaborate more with each other to form a true team.

DEVELOP PARTNERSHIPS WITH PEOPLE

Leadership is now regarded as a long-term relationship, or partnership, between leaders and group members. According to consultant and trainer Peter Block, in a

partnership the leader and group members are connected in such a way that the power between them is approximately balanced. To form a partnership, the leader has to allow the group members to share in decision making. Four conditions are necessary to form a true partnership between the leader and group members:

1. **Exchange of purpose.** The leader and team member should work together to build a vision.

2. **A right to say no.** In a partnership, each side has the right to say no without fear of being punished.

3. **Joint accountability.** Each person takes responsibility for the success and failure of the group.

4. **Absolute honesty.** In a partnership, not telling the truth to each other is an act of betrayal. When group members recognize that they have power, they are more likely to tell the truth because they feel less vulnerable to punishment. [15]

■ **Partnership**
the leader and group members are connected in such a way that the power between them is approximately balanced

HELP GROUP MEMBERS REACH GOALS AND ACHIEVE SATISFACTION

Effective leaders help group members in their efforts to achieve goals according to the path-goal theory of leadership. [16] In a sense, they smooth out the path to reaching goals. One important way to do this is to provide the necessary resources to group members. An important aspect of a leader's job is to ensure that subordinates have the proper tools, equipment, and human resources to accomplish their objectives.

Another way of helping group members achieve goals is to reduce frustrating barriers to getting work accomplished. A leader who helps group members cut through minor rules and regulations would be engaging in such behavior. In a factory, a supervisory leader has a responsibility to replace faulty equipment, make sure unsafe conditions are corrected, and see that troublesome employees are either rehabilitated or replaced.

Another important general set of actions characteristic of an effective leader is looking out for the satisfaction of the group. Small things sometimes mean a lot in terms of personal satisfaction. One office manager fought for better beverage facilities for her subordinates. Her thoughtfulness contributed immensely to job satisfaction among them. Giving group members emotional support is another effective way of improving worker satisfaction. An emotionally supportive leader would engage in activities such as listening to group members' problems and offering them encouragement and praise. Again, basic human relations skills contribute to leadership effectiveness.

SET HIGH EXPECTATIONS

In addition to making expectations clear, it is important for leaders to set high expectations for group members. Effective leaders consistently hold group members to high standards of performance. The owner of a Toyota dealership might say, "I see that our customer satisfaction ratings have been about 80 percent. From now on, I want to hear back from regional headquarters that our ratings average 95 percent. We'll figure out together how to do it." If you as a leader expect others to succeed, they are likely to live up to your expectations. This mysterious phenomenon has been labeled the **Pygmalion effect.** According to Greek mythology, Pygmalion was a sculptor and king of Cyprus who carved an ivory statue of a maiden and fell in love with the statue. The statue was soon brought to life in response to his prayer. (Pygmalion wished so hard for the statue to become alive that the statue was transformed into a living woman to love.)

■ **Pygmalion effect**
leader's ability to elevate worker performance by the simple method of expecting them to perform well; the manager's high expectations become a self-fulfilling prophecy

The point of the Pygmalion effect is that the leader can elevate performance by the simple method of expecting others to perform well. The manager's high expectations become a self-fulfilling prophecy. Why high expectations lead to high performance could be linked to self-confidence. As the leader expresses faith in the group members' abilities to perform well, they become more confident of their skills. Also, when a managerial leader believes that a group member will succeed, the manager communicates this belief without realizing it.

GIVE FREQUENT FEEDBACK ON PERFORMANCE

Effective leaders inform employees how they can improve and praise them for things done right. Often, a simple e-mail message can be effective feedback, such as "Sue, the financial analysis you prepared for our client today was exactly the information he needed to purchase a $300,000 variable annuity. Thanks so much." Less effective leaders, in contrast, often avoid confrontation and give limited positive feedback. An exception is that some ineffective leaders become involved in many confrontations—they are masters at reprimanding people!

MANAGE A CRISIS EFFECTIVELY

When a crisis strikes, that's the time to have an effective leader around. When things are running very smoothly, you may not always notice whether your leader is present. Effectively managing a crisis means giving reassurance to the group that problems will soon be under control, specifying the alternative paths for getting out of the crisis, and choosing one of the paths. Showing compassion for those directly affected by the crisis is also quite helpful. After Hurricane Katrina, for example, managers at McDonald's made a concentrated effort to be in touch with as many employees as possible to communicate concern about their welfare and to discuss their employment situation.

ASK THE RIGHT QUESTIONS

Leaders do not need to know all the answers. Instead, a major contribution can be to ask the right questions. Although being knowledgeable about the group task is important, there are many times when asking group members penetrating questions is more important. In today's complex and rapidly changing business environment, the collective intelligence of group members is needed to solve problems. [17] Quite often a leader does not have the answer to a problem, so asking questions is important. Also, asking questions rather than giving answers is the natural method of helping group members become better problem solvers. Here are sample questions a leader might ask group members to help them meet their challenges:

- What are you going to do differently to reduce by 50 percent the time it takes to fill a customer order?

- Top management is thinking of getting rid of our group and subcontracting the work we do to outside vendors. What do you propose we do to make us more valuable to the company?

- Can you figure out why the competition is outperforming us?

BE A SERVANT LEADER

■ **Servant leader**

one who serves group members by working on their behalf to help them achieve their goals, not the leader's goals

A humanitarian approach to leadership is to be a **servant leader,** one who serves group members by working on their behalf to help them achieve their goals, not the leader's goals. The idea behind servant leadership, as developed by Robert K. Greenleaf, is that leadership stems naturally from a commitment to service. Serving others, including employees, customers, and the community, is the primary motivation for the servant leader. The servant leader is passionate about the people he or she works with and for. [18] Servant leadership encompasses many different acts, all designed to make life easier or better for group members. Among the emphases included are collaboration, trust, listening, and the ethical use of power and empowerment (sharing power). Several acts of servant leadership are mentioned next.

A good starting point is for the leader to see himself or herself as a humble servant. ("I'm here to serve you.") The leader downplays his or her ego to support the talents of others. Servant leaders also look for the opportunity to lend assistance directly to employees, such as a supermarket manager bagging groceries during an unanticipated rush of business. A servant leader would also provide the tools people needed to accomplish their work, such as fighting for enough money for the budget to purchase expensive new equipment.

Although a servant leader is idealistic, he or she recognizes that one individual cannot accomplish everything. So the leader listens carefully to the array of problems facing group members and then concentrates on a few. As the head of a nurses' union told the group, "I know you are hurting in many ways. Yet I think that the work overload issue is the biggest one, so we will head into negotiations working on obtaining sensible workloads. After that we will work on job security."

Servant leadership has been put into practice by many managers as well as business corporations. Such companies as Southwest Airlines, The Toro Company, Men's Warehouse, and Starbucks have adapted the philosophy of servant-leadership into their cultures and mission statements (a statement of purpose). All of these firms emphasize treating employees humanely, and allowing for profit sharing. [19]

The accompanying Human Relations in Practice box describes a leader who embodies many of the leadership traits, characteristics, and behaviors already described in this chapter. The leader in question has succeeded mightily in business and entertainment.

> "Three words leaders have trouble dealing with: "I don't know." I think good leadership will often start with questions whose answer is: 'I don't know, but we're going to find out.'"
> —Warren G. Bennis, whose name is practically synonymous with leadership. Quoted in "Viewpoint: Warren Bennis: Leading Managers to Adapt and Grow," in *Business: The Ultimate Resource* (Cambridge, MA: Perseus Publishing, 2002), p. 212.

What Is Leadership Style, and What Is Style Flexibility?

■ Learning Objective 3

Understanding the traits, behaviors, skills, as well as attitudes of leaders, points to another major approach to explaining leadership. A **leadership style** is a leader's characteristic way of behaving in a variety of situations. Here we look at the classic dimensions of leadership style, participative leadership, and style flexibility or adaptability.

■ **Leadership style**
a leader's characteristic way of behaving in a variety of situations

THE CLASSIC DIMENSIONS OF CONSIDERATION AND INITIATING STRUCTURE

Leadership styles have been characterized in many ways, beginning in the 1950s with studies at the Ohio State University conducted with factory supervisors and military personnel. [20] Most approaches to leadership style are variations, refinements, and expansions of this pioneering work. The researchers asked group members to describe their supervisors by responding to the questionnaires. Leaders were also asked to rate themselves on leadership dimensions (activities they performed). Two main dimensions were identified that accounted for the vast majority of a leader's activity: "consideration" and "initiating structure."

Consideration is the degree to which the leader creates an environment of emotional support, warmth, friendliness, and trust. The leader creates this environment by being friendly and approachable, and looking out for the welfare of the group. He or she also keeps the group informed about new developments and does small

■ **Consideration**
the degree to which the leader creates an environment of emotional support, warmth, friendliness, and trust

Human Relations in Practice

Jerri DeVard Exercises Leadership at Verizon

Industry watchers view Jerri DeVard as a shepherd of technology. DeVard oversees a staff of 400 nationwide and she guides a flock of 47.4 million Verizon customers to use the company's services to enrich their personal and professional lives. DeVard ultimately seeks the answer to one simple question: "How are we enabling technology to allow you to do the things that are important to you?" Her response is to bolster the Verizon brand and communicate its value across its three business units: wireless, broadband, and information services. And by leveraging technology in marketing, DeVard has helped transform the telecommunications giant into the brand leader in this ultra-competitive sector.

Since joining the company in 2003, DeVard has pushed Verizon's innovative technology with advertising campaigns such as "Richer, Deeper, Broader," which touted how the company's broadbrand capabilities impact people's everyday lives. Another campaign, "Realize Your Dream," targeted would-be entrepreneurs.

The marketing whiz joined Verizon after stints at Citigroup, where she served as chief marketing officer of its e-consumer business, and Revlon, where she rose to vice president of marketing for color cosmetics. Her secret for success, she says, is being a student of human behavior—understanding how people choose one brand over another. She developed an interest in creating consumer demand while completing her MBA at Clark Atlanta University Graduate School of Management. "I was able to hone that craft by going to work for Pillsbury, a consumer-packaged-good company," says DeVard. At Pillsbury she learned one of her most important career lessons: "There's no substitute for performance, because at the end of the day, you had to deliver." She also worked for about 18 months with the Minnesota Vikings as head of their private suites marketing.

She serves on the boards of Tommy Hilfiger Corp., the Association of National Advertisers, the Executive Leadership Council, and the Pepsi African American Advisory Board.

Source: Carolyn M. Brown, "50 Most Powerful Black Women in Business," *Black Enterprise*, February 2006, p. 128. A few additional facts are from "AAPRC Weekly, Jerri DeVard, Senior Vice President, Marketing and Brand Management, Verizon Communications," *The Crusade.net*, September 19, 2006, http://thecrusade.net/2006/02/vaprc-weakly:jeri-devard.

■ **Initiating structure**

organizing and defining relationships in the group by engaging in such activities as assigning specific tasks, specifying procedures to be followed, scheduling work, and making expectations clear

favors for the group, such as getting the break area repainted. In other words, the leader focuses on the human relations aspect of work.

Initiating structure means organizing and defining relationships in the group by engaging in such activities as assigning specific tasks, specifying procedures to be followed, scheduling work, and making expectations clear. In other words, the leader provides structure for the group and focuses on the work.

Leaders have been categorized with respect to how much emphasis they place on the two dimensions of consideration and initiating structure. As implied by Figure 11-4, the two dimensions are not mutually exclusive. A leader can achieve high or low status on both dimensions. For example, an effective leader might contribute to high productivity yet still place considerable emphasis on warm human relationships. Mark Hurd, the HP honcho described at the outset of this chapter emphasizes initiating structure in his style, whereas servant leaders tend to emphasize consideration. A leader's style could be characterized in terms of which one of the four boxes he or she fits in Figure 11-4. Later approaches to classifying leadership style, such as the leadership grid and the path-goal theory of leadership build on these dimensions.

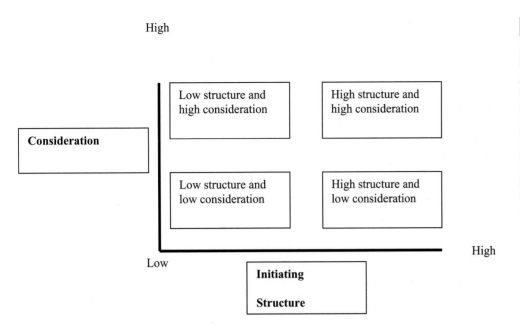

High

	Low structure and high consideration	High structure and high consideration
Consideration		
	Low structure and low consideration	High structure and low consideration

Low

Initiating

Structure

High

Figure 11-4

Four Combinations of Initiating Structure and Consideration
A leader's behavior can be described in terms of four different combinations of consideration and initiating structure. For example, a leader who emphasized both giving group members a high degree of structure and paying close attention to their needs would be characterized as "high structure and high consideration," the upper right box.

THE PARTICIPATIVE (TEAM) LEADERSHIP STYLE

For the past 25 years, the participative leadership style has received the most attention because this style enables the leader to share decisions with the group and capitalize on the talents of the group. By definition, a **participative leader** shares decision-making authority with the group. At his or her best, the participative leader motivates group members to work as a team toward high-level goals. Encouraging employees to participate in making decisions is the major approach to empowerment. Participative leadership is often favored because workers are more willing to implement decisions when they are involved in formulating the decisions. Participative leadership encompasses so many different behaviors that it is useful to divide it into three subtypes: consultative, consensus, and democratic.

■ **Participative leader**
leader who shares decision-making authority with the group; motivates group members to work as a team toward high-level goals

Consultative Leaders

A **consultative leader** solicits opinions from the group before making a decision yet does not feel obliged to accept the group's thinking. Leaders of this type make it clear that they alone have authority to make the final decisions. A standard way to practice consultative leadership would be to call a group meeting and discuss an issue before making a decision.

■ **Consultative leader**
leader who solicits opinions from the group before making a decision, yet does not feel obliged to accept the group's thinking; this type leader makes it clear that he or she alone has authority to make the final decisions

Consensus Leaders

A **consensus leader** encourages group discussion about an issue and then makes a decision that reflects the consensus of the group members. Consensus-style leaders thus turn over more authority to the group than do consultative leaders. The consensus style results in long delays in decision making because every party involved has to agree.

■ **Consensus leader**
leader who encourages group discussion about an issue and then makes a decision that reflects the consensus of the group members

Democratic Leaders

A **democratic leader** confers final authority on the group. He or she functions as a collector of opinion and takes a vote before making a decision. Democratic leaders turn over so much authority to the group that they are sometimes referred to as free-rein leaders. The group usually achieves its goals when working under a democratic leader. Democratic leadership has more relevance for community activities than for most work settings.

■ **Democratic leader**
leader who confers final authority on the group; functions as a collector of opinion and takes a vote before making a decision (sometimes referred to as a free-rein leader)

Participative leadership is also referred to as *trickle-up* leadership because suggestions flow from workers to management. Part of trickle-up leadership is for group members to step in when they perceive that the leader is having difficulty. According to Wharton School professor of organizational behavior Michael Useem, as technology evolves and organizations decentralize, frontline workers have more independence and responsibility. They are more aware of customer demands and how to manufacture a product or provide a service. These same workers can often see what the leaders are missing and can, therefore, step in to help a faltering leader. In the U.S. Marines, when a superior issues a flawed order, officers are expected to point out the flaws before the order is implemented. For example, four-star general Peter Pace ends his meetings by asking subordinates to tell him what they each think. By encouraging the group members to challenge him, Pace reinforces a culture of trickle-up leadership. [21]

In contrast to the participative leader is the leader/manager who makes decisions more independently. An **autocratic leader** attempts to retain most of the authority granted to the group. Autocratic leaders make all the major decisions and assume subordinates will comply without question. Leaders who use this style give minimum consideration to what group members are likely to think about an order or decision. Group members sometimes see an autocrat as rigid and demanding.

Although the autocratic leadership style is not in vogue, many successful leaders are autocratic. Among them are *turnaround managers*—those who specialize in turning around failing organizations or rescuing them from crises. Other situations calling for crisis management include earthquakes, product recalls, and workplace violence. The autocratic style generally works best in situations where decisions have to be made rapidly or when group opinion is not needed. One situation calling for autocratic leadership would be extinguishing an oil rig fire at sea. Another would be when a company is undergoing liquidation and bankruptcy.

A positive application of participative leadership and management took place at Royal/Dutch Shell—one of the world's largest business firms. To help revitalize the company, top-level management embarked on a program of grassroots leadership involving employees in all lines of businesses, including automobile service stations and dozens of other product lines. The basic approach to participative leadership was to bring six- to eight-person teams from a half dozen operating companies worldwide in to an intense "retailing boot camp." Team members would be introduced to the participative leadership model so they could bring it to employees back home. Participants were also taught a model for improving business that they used as a framework for solving problems locally.

The results were better than the top-level management had anticipated. Cross-functional teams in dozens of locations throughout the world came up with ways to improve their local business. Producing a video proved to be the best training exercise for getting teams to participate in decisions about business improvement. Teams were told: "Here's a video camera. In the next 90 minutes, make a five- or six-minute video that illustrates the old Shell and the new Shell." [22]

Human Relations Self-Assessment Quiz 11-2 gives you the opportunity to measure your present or potential leadership style.

STYLE FLEXIBILITY AND ADAPTABILITY

Although leadership style refers to a person's characteristic approach to dealing with leadership tasks, effective leaders adapt their style to fit the situation. For example, a leader might typically user a consensus style, yet when managing a crisis he or she might become more authoritarian—giving subordinates directions in a hurry without waiting to achieve agreement among group members. A study with 3,000 executives revealed that leaders who get the best results do not rely on one style. Instead, they use several different styles in one week, such as being autocratic in

Human Relations Self-Assessment Quiz 11-2

What Style of Leader Are You or Would You Be?

Answer the following questions, keeping in mind what you have done, or think you would do, in the scenarios and attitudes described.

	Mostly True	Mostly False
1. I am more likely to take care of a high-impact assignment myself than turn it over to a group member.	_____	_____
2. I would prefer the analytical aspects of a manager's job rather than working directly with group members.	_____	_____
3. An important part of my approach to managing a group is to keep the members informed almost daily of any information that could affect their work.	_____	_____
4. It's a good idea to give two people in the group the same problem and then choose what appears to be the best solution.	_____	_____
5. It makes good sense for the leader or manager to stay somewhat aloof from the group, so he or she can make a tough decision when necessary.	_____	_____
6. I look for opportunities to obtain group input before making a decision, even on straightforward issues.	_____	_____
7. I would reverse a decision if several of the group members presented evidence that I was wrong.	_____	_____
8. Differences of opinion in the work group are healthy.	_____	_____
9. I think that an activity to build team spirit, such as the team fixing up a poor family's house on a Saturday, is an excellent investment of time.	_____	_____
10. If my group were hiring a new member, I would like the person to be interviewed by the entire group.	_____	_____
11. An effective team leader today uses e-mail for about 98 percent of communication with team members.	_____	_____
12. Some of the best ideas are likely to come from the group members rather than the manager.	_____	_____
13. If our group were going to have a banquet, I would get input from each member on what type of food should be served.	_____	_____
14. I have never seen a statue of a committee in a museum or park, so why bother making decisions by a committee if you want to be recognized?	_____	_____
15. I dislike it intensely when a group member challenges my position on an issue.	_____	_____
16. I typically explain to group members what method they should use to accomplish an assigned task.	_____	_____
17. If I were out of the office for a week, most of the important work in the department would get accomplished anyway.	_____	_____
18. Delegation of important tasks is something that would be (or is) very difficult for me.	_____	_____
19. When a group member comes to me with a problem, I tend to jump right in with a proposed solution.	_____	_____
20. When a group member comes to me with a problem, I typically ask that person something such as, "What alternative solutions have you thought of so far?"	_____	_____

Scoring and Interpretation:

The answers in the participative/team-style leader direction are as follows:

1. Mostly false	8. Mostly true	15. Mostly false
2. Mostly false	9. Mostly true	16. Mostly false
3. Mostly true	10. Mostly true	17. Mostly true
4. Mostly false	11. Mostly false	18. Mostly false
5. Mostly false	12. Mostly true	19. Mostly false
6. Mostly true	13. Mostly true	20. Mostly true
7. Mostly true	14. Mostly false	

(continued)

Human Relations Self-Assessment Quiz **11-2** (Continued)

If your score is 15 or higher, you are most likely (or would be) a participative/team-style leader. If your score is 5 or lower, you are most likely (or would be) an authoritarian style leader.

Skill Development:

The quiz you just completed is also an opportunity for skill development. Review the 20 items and look for implied suggestions for engaging in participative leadership. For example, item 20 suggests that you encourage group members to work through their own solutions to problems. If your goal is to become an authoritarian leader (one who makes decisions primarily on his or her own), the items can also serve as useful guidelines. For example, item 19 suggests than an authoritarian leader looks first to solve problems for group members.

some situations and democratic in others. [23] Furthermore, a more recent analysis of hundreds of studies suggests that leadership should be defined as "doing the right thing at the right time." [24] The leader makes the decision or chooses the action that fits the circumstances. An example might be transferring a valuable worker to a temporary assignment rather than firing him or her because of too little work for that individual at the moment.

A rule of thumb for attaining style flexibility is to give considerable guidance, direction, and coaching to a worker who has low motivation or capability in terms of accomplishing the task. In contrast, give less guidance, direction, and coaching to a worker with high motivation and capability. The preceding is perhaps the best established finding about providing leadership to others.

■ Learning Objective 4

How Does a Leader Get Along Well with Subordinates?

The concepts already mentioned in this chapter, as well as other information you have studied about getting along with people, apply to a leader getting along well with subordinates. We spotlight this topic by presenting a well-documented theory about leader–member relationships, as well as a few illustrative principles.

THE LEADER–MEMBER EXCHANGE MODEL

■ **Leader–member exchange (LMX) model**
leadership model that focuses on the quality of leader–member relations; recognizes that leaders develop unique working relationships with each group member

George Graen, a professor of organizational behavior at the University of Louisiana, and his associates have developed a leadership model that focuses on the quality of leader–member relations. The **leader–member exchange (LMX) model** recognizes that leaders develop unique working relationships with each group member. [25] A leader might be considerate and compassionate toward one team member yet rigid and unfeeling toward another.

Each relationship between the leader/manager differs in quality. One subset of employees, the in-group, is given additional rewards, responsibility, and trust in exchange for their loyalty and performance. In contrast, another subset of employees (the out-group) is treated in accordance with a more formal understanding of the supervisor–subordinate relationship. The leader's first impression of a group member's competency heavily influences whether he or she becomes a member of the in-group or out-group.

In-group members have attitudes and values similar to the leader and interact frequently with the leader. Out-group members have less in common with the leader and operate somewhat detached from the leader. The one-to-one relationships have a major influence on the subordinate's behavior in the group. Members of the in-group become part of a smoothly functioning team headed by the formal leader. Out-group members are less likely to experience good teamwork. Being a member of the in-group facilitates achieving high productivity and satisfaction. Out-group members receive less challenging assignments and are more likely to quit because of job dissatisfaction. [26]

The specific relevance of the LMX model for getting along with group members is that if the leader establishes good relationships with group members, higher productivity and satisfaction is likely to occur.

SUGGESTIONS FOR ATTAINING GOOD RELATIONSHIPS WITH SUBORDINATES

A key part of leadership is forming good relationships with people, so getting along with subordinates is essential. If you are a leader and your subordinates do not like you, it will be difficult for the group to achieve high productivity and satisfaction. A sampling follows of time-tested principles for attaining good relationships with subordinates.

1. Solicit opinions before taking action. In the spirit of participative leadership, find out what group members think of your potential action, even on relatively small matters such as selecting a restaurant for a department banquet. Subordinates will be pleased that their input matters, and they will be more cooperative in implementing your decision.

2. Fight for their demands. An axiom of effective management is for the supervisor to bring forth the demands of group members to higher management and then fight for these demands, such as needing new equipment. Carrying out this principle enhances your stature among group members and helps you win their support.

3. Give out recognition. Most people are recognition deprived, so being a boss who recognizes the contributions of subordinates goes a long way toward building positive relationships with them. Effective forms of recognition include thank-you notes and face-to-face comments, such as, "You really helped us out in a jam, and I appreciate it." You will learn more about recognition in your study of motivation.

4. Listen to the problems and suggestions of group members. Listening is an essential tool of the participative leader or manager, and it is also an excellent way of cultivating subordinates. You will recall that listening is an important component of servant leadership. To be listened to is to be respected and considered important.

5. Be courteous. Many managers are rude to subordinates, so showing courtesy will help you build relationships with your direct reports. Being courteous to subordinates would include such acts as responding quickly to e-mail messages, returning phone calls, not multitasking when subordinates are talking to you, not keeping people waiting for you, and not belittling them.

In short, getting along well with subordinates involves the practice of good human relations, in addition to recognizing that you need the support of your subordinates as much as they need you.

How Do You Develop Your Leadership Potential?

■ **Learning Objective 5**

How to improve your potential for becoming a leader is a topic without limits. Almost anything you do to improve your individual effectiveness will have some impact on your ability to lead others. If you strengthen your self-confidence, improve your memory for names, study this book carefully, read studies about leadership, or improve your physical fitness, you stand a good chance of improving your leadership potential. Eight strategies might be kept in mind if you are seeking to improve your leadership potential:

1. **General education and specific training.** Almost any program of career training or education can be considered a program of leadership development. Courses in human relations, management, or applied psychology have obvious relevance for someone currently occupying or aspiring toward a leadership position. Many of today's leaders in profit and nonprofit organizations hold formal degrees in business. Specific training programs will also help you improve your leadership potential. Among them might be skill development programs in interviewing, employee selection, listening, assertiveness training, budgeting, planning, improving work habits, resolving conflict, and communication skills. After acquiring knowledge through study, you then put the knowledge into practice as a leader.

Warren G. Bennis emphasizes that becoming a leader involves continual learning, development, and the reinvention of the self. [27] "Reinvention" in this sense could mean rethinking your assumptions about people or even changing careers into one you found that was a better fit with your values.

2. **Leadership development programs.** A focused way of improving your leadership potential is to attend development programs designed specifically to improve your ability to lead others and develop self-confidence. A popular type of leadership development program called *outdoor training* places people in a challenging outdoor environment for a weekend or up to 10 days. Participants are required to accomplish physical feats, such as climbing a mountain, white-water canoeing, building a wall, or swinging between trees on a rope. Participants in these outdoor programs learn such important leadership skills and attitudes as teamwork and trusting others and gain confidence in their abilities to accomplish the seemingly impossible.

3. **Acquire broad experience.** Because leadership varies somewhat with the situation, a sound approach to improving leadership effectiveness is to attempt to gain supervisory experience in different settings. A person who wants to become an executive is well advised to gain supervisory experience in at least two different organizational functions, such as customer service and finance.

First-level supervisory jobs are an invaluable starting point for developing your leadership potential. It takes considerable skill to manage a fast-food restaurant effectively or to direct a public playground during the summer. First-level supervisors frequently face situations in which subordinates are poorly trained, poorly paid, and not well motivated to achieve company objectives. Taking a turn as a team leader is also valuable experience for developing leadership skills.

4. **Modeling effective leaders.** Are you committed to improving your leadership skill and potential? If so, carefully observe a capable leader in action and incorporate some of his or her approaches into your own behavior. You may not be able to or want to become that person's clone, but you can model (imitate) what the person does. For instance, most inexperienced leaders have a difficult time confronting others with bad news. Observe a good confronter handle the situation and try his or her approach the next time you have some unfavorable news to deliver to another person. Studying the biography or autobiography of a leader whom you admire is another source of ideas for modeling an effective leader.

5. **Self-development of leadership characteristics and behavior.** Study the leadership characteristics and behaviors described in this chapter. As a starting point, identify several attributes you think you could strengthen within yourself given some self-determination. For example, you might decide that with effort you could improve your passion and enthusiasm. You might also believe that you could be more emotionally supportive of others. It is also helpful to obtain feedback from reliable

sources, such as a trusted manager, about which traits and behaviors you particularly need to develop.

6. Practice a little leadership. An effective way to develop your leadership skills is to look for opportunities to exert a small amount of helpful leadership in contrast to waiting for opportunities to accomplish extraordinary deeds. [28] A "little leadership" might involve such behaviors as mentoring a struggling team member, coaching somebody about how to use a new high-tech device, or making a suggestion about improving a product.

7. Practice self-leadership. One of the most effective ways of becoming a leader is to begin by leading yourself, or practicing **self-leadership.** According to this concept, all organizational members are capable of leading themselves to some extent. You influence yourself without waiting for an external leader to lead you, much like taking the initiative to accomplish something worthwhile or being a good organizational citizen. According to Charles C. Manz, a professor of business leadership at the University of Massachusetts, self-leadership extends as far as setting your own standards and objectives. "It addresses what should be done, and why it should be done, in addition to how to do it." Recognize, however, you still have to accomplish what your leader wants you to accomplish, but you can go beyond the minimum required in your job. One company that promotes self-leadership is W. L. Gore and Associates where employees are regarded as knowledge workers who have the capacity for identifying successful new products. Self-leadership enters the picture because workers make the discoveries themselves without being instructed to do so. [29]

■ **Self-leadership**

leading oneself; influencing oneself without waiting for an external leader to lead one; all organizational members are capable of leading themselves to some extent

8. Become an integrated human being. A philosophical approach to leadership suggests that the model leader is first and foremost a fully functioning person. According to this belief, the type of person you are determines whether you will be an effective leader. According to William D. Hitt, mastering the art of leadership comes with self-mastery. Leadership development is the process of self-development. As a result, the process of becoming a leader is similar to the process of becoming an integrated human being. For example, you need to develop values that guide your behavior before you can adequately guide the behavior of others, and you also need courage. [30]

Concept Review and Reinforcement

Key Terms

Leadership, 270
Leadership effectiveness, 270
Trust, 272
Character, 273
Cognitive skills, 274
Openness to experience, 274
Charisma, 274
Partnership, 279

Pygmalion effect, 279
Servant leader, 280
Leadership style, 281
Consideration, 281
Initiating structure, 282
Participative leader, 283
Consultative leader, 283
Consensus leader, 283

Democratic leader, 283
Autocratic leader, 284
Leader–member exchange (LMX) model, 286
Self-leadership, 289

Summary and Review

Leadership is the process of bringing about positive changes and influencing others to achieve worthwhile goals. Effective leadership is needed at the top of organizations, but supervisors and team leaders also need to provide effective leadership. Effective leaders have the "right stuff." Certain traits and characteristics contribute to leadership effectiveness in many situations. Among them are

- self-confidence and courage
- emotional intelligence
- trustworthiness and character
- strong work motivation and high energy
- cognitive skills and openness to experience
- assertiveness
- charisma (vision, passion, enthusiasm, excitement, and humor)

Behaviors and skills of an effective leader (one who maintains high productivity and morale) include

- practicing strong ethics
- direction setting
- developing partnerships with people (emphasizing power sharing)
- helping group members reach goals and achieve satisfaction
- setting high expectations (the Pygmalion effect)
- giving frequent feedback on performance
- managing a crisis effectively
- asking the right questions
- being a servant leader

Leadership style is a leader's characteristic way of behaving in a variety of situations. Most approaches to understanding leadership style stem from the two dimensions of consideration and initiating structure. Leaders can be characterized with respect to how much emphasis they place on these two dimensions.

Participative leaders share decisions with the group and capitalize on the talents of the group. The subtypes of participative leadership are consultative, consensus, and democratic. In contrast to the participative leader is the autocratic leader/manager who makes decisions more independently.

Effective leaders tend to adapt their style to the situation, such as a consensus leader becoming authoritarian during a crisis. The effective leader does the right thing at the right time. In general, workers with low motivation and capability need more guidance, direction, and coaching.

According to the leader–member exchange (LMX) model, leaders develop unique working relationships with each group member. If the leader establishes good relationships with group members, higher productivity and satisfaction is likely to occur.

Time-tested principles for attaining good relationships with subordinates include

- soliciting opinions before taking action
- fighting for their demands
- giving out recognition
- listening to the problems and suggestions of group members
- being courteous

Many activities in life can in some way contribute to the development of a person's leadership potential. Eight recommended strategies for improving your leadership potential or leadership skills are

- general education and specific training
- participating in leadership development programs
- acquiring broad experience
- modeling effective leaders
- self-development of leadership characteristics and behavior
- practicing a little leadership
- practicing self-leadership
- becoming an integrated human being

Check your Understanding

1. Provide an example of something a leader motivated or inspired you to do that you would not have done without his or her presence.
2. Why is the "ability to perform the group task" essential for a team leader?
3. What is the relationship between a vision and a goal?
4. Why does being charismatic often make a leader more effective?
5. Rate the charisma of the current president of the United States on a scale of 1 to 10. Explain the basis for your rating.
6. Provide an example of how you might use the Pygmalion effect in working with subordinates or with a child you have or might have.
7. What might a person do to become part of the leader's in-group?
8. Give an example of a specific action taken by a present or former boss that helped cultivate good relationships with subordinates. Also identify an action that hurt relationships with subordinates.
9. Imagine yourself in either your present job or a job of your choice. How would you practice self-leadership in this job?
10. In what way does your program of study contribute to your development as a leader?

Web Corner

Overview of leadership:
www.ccl.org

Leadership development programs:
www.academy leadership.com/programs

Servant leadership:
http://greenleaf.org

Internet Skill Builder:

You have already received in this chapter suggestions for developing your charisma. Visit WWW.CORE-EDGE. COM to search for additional ideas for charisma development. Go to the section on *charismatology*, and read a couple of the case histories to uncover ideas you might try to enhance your charisma. After digging through core-edge.com, list two concrete ideas you might implement to enhance your charisma.

Applying Human Relations Exercise 11-1

Developing Your Charisma

An effective way of developing your leadership potential is to project a more charismatic image, even if you do not truly make over your personality. If you appear more charismatic to others, they are more likely to respond to your leadership. Also, if your project a more charismatic image, you are more likely to be nominated for leadership positions and assignments. Following is a checklist of the suggestions for becoming more charismatic presented in Figure 11-3. As you go through the list, select two or three ideas that you would be willing to try in the next two weeks. Note that some of the suggestions are much easier than others to implement in the short range.

Charisma Suggestions
(see Figure 11-3 for explanations)   Yes, I will try it

1. Communicate a vision. ❑

2. Make frequent use of metaphors and analogies. ❑

3. Inspire trust and confidence. ❑

4. Be highly energetic and goal oriented. ❑

5. Be emotionally expressive and warm. ❑

Charisma Suggestions
(see Figure 11-3 for explanations)   Yes, I will try it

6. Make ample use of true stories. ❑

7. Smile frequently, even if not in happy mood. ❑

8. Be candid. ❑

9. Make everybody you meet feel that he or she is important. ❑

10. Multiply the effectiveness of your handshake. ❑

11. Stand up straight and use other nonverbal signals of self-confidence. ❑

12. Be willing to take personal risks. ❑

13. Be self-promotional. ❑

Now that you have made your choice of suggestions, try them out with other people including students, athletic team members, coworkers, or members of a community group. Answer the following questions:

1. How did people react to me when I attempted to be more charismatic?
2. How can I use this approach more effectively next time? (How should I fine-tune my approach?)
3. Are these approaches to charisma enhancement making any contribution to my development as a leader?

Applying Human Relations Exercise 11-2

My Personal Leadership Journal

A potentially important assist in your development as a leader is to maintain a journal or diary of your leadership experiences. Make a journal entry within 24 hours after you carried out a leadership action of any kind, or failed to do so when the opportunity arose. You will, therefore, have entries dealing with leadership opportunities both capitalized on and missed. An example, "A few of my neighbors were complaining about trash flying around the neighborhood on trash pick-up days, particularly when the wind was strong. I took the initiative to send e-mails and flyers to neighborhood residents discussing what could be done about the problem. I suggested that people pack their recycling boxes more tightly. I also suggested ever-so-politely that people should pick up their own flying trash. Soon the problem nearly disappeared."

Also include in your journal such entries as comments you receive on your leadership ability, leadership traits that you appear to be developing, and leadership ideas about which you learn. Also, keep a list of leadership articles and books you intend to read. You might also want to record observations about significant acts of leadership or leadership blunders that you have observed in others, either firsthand or through the media.

Review your journal monthly, and make note of any progress you think you have made in developing your leadership skills. Also consider preparing a graph of your progress in developing leadership skills. The vertical axis can represent skill level on a 1-to-100 scale, and the horizontal axis might be divided into time intervals, such as calendar quarters.

Human Relations Case Study 11-1

Tough as Nails Leadership at Home Depot

Military analogies are commonplace at Home Depot Inc. these days. Five years after his arrival, Chief Executive Robert L. Nardelli is putting his stamp on what was long a decentralized, entrepreneurial business. And if his company starts to look and feel like an army, that's the point. Nardelli loves to hire soldiers. In fact, he seems to love almost everything about the armed services. The military, to a large extent, has become the management model for his entire enterprise. Of the 1,142 people hired into the Home Depot's store leadership program, a two-year training regimen for store managers, almost half are junior military officers. More than 100 of them now run Home Depots. Military recruits "understand the mission," says Nardelli. "It's one thing to have faced a tough customer. It's another to face the enemy shooting at you. So they probably will be pretty calm under fire.

Nardelli is a detail-obsessed, diamond-cut precise manager. Importing ideas, people, and platitudes from the military is a key part of Nardelli's sweeping move to re-shape Home Depot, the world's third-largest retailer, into a more centralized organization. That may be an untrendy idea in management circles, but Nardelli couldn't care less. It's a critical element of his strategy to rein in an unwieldy 2,048-store chain and prepare for its next leg of growth.

Nardelli is trying to build a disciplined corps, one predisposed to following orders, operating in high-pressure environments and executing with high standards. Although he has yet to win all the hearts and minds of his employees, and probably never will, Nardelli's feisty spirit is rekindling stellar financial performance. During a five-year period, he achieved an average annual growth rate of 12 percent. Profits have more than doubled during Nardelli's tenure. He has achieved this feat largely by squeezing more out of each orange box (store) through centralized purchasing and a $1.1 billion invest-

ment in technology, such as self-checkout aisles and in-store Web kiosks.

Before Nardelli arrived, managers ran Home Depot's stores on "tribal knowledge," based on years of experience about what sold and what didn't. Now they nervously click through Blackberrys at the end of each week, hoping they "made plan," a combination of sales and profit targets. The once-heavy ranks of full-time Home Depot store staff have been replaced with part timers to drive down labor costs. Underperforming executives are routinely culled from the ranks. As a manager, Nardelli is relentless, demanding, and determined to prove wrong every critic of Home Depot. He treats Saturdays and Sundays as ordinary working days and often expects those around him to do the same. Some of the 11 former Home Depot executives interviewed by *Business Week* say that the staff is demoralized, and "a culture of fear" is causing customer service to wane.

Nardelli's cultural transformation has prompted some new lingo among Home Depot workers including the following:

- ■ "Home Despot." For the most disenchanted workers, the moniker bestowed on the mighty home-improvement chain.
- ■ "Bob's Army." Slang for the store leadership program wherein almost 50 percent of the trainees hired are ex-military personnel.
- ■ "Bobaganda." The always-on Home Depot television channel, a.k.a. HD-TV, shown in rooms where employees take their breaks.

Questions

1. Identify what you perceive to be both Bob Nardelli's positive and negative leadership traits and behaviors.
2. How would you describe Nardelli's leadership style?
3. What advice can you offer Nardelli for becoming an even more effective leader?

Source: Adapted from Brian Grow, "Renovating Home Depot," *Business Week*, March 6, 2006, pp. 50–58.

Human Relations Case Study 11-2

So Is This How You Learn Leadership?

Len Olsen, age 23, was proud to be selected as part of the leader's program at a national chain of family restaurants. Workers selected for the leadership program are considered to be in line for running individual restaurants and as potential candidates in the long run for leadership positions in corporate headquarters. Before entering the key phase of the leadership program, all candidates must first work a minimum of one year as a server or bartender at one of the company stores (restaurants).

Olsen worked one year as a server in a downtown Chicago restaurant and then was assigned to another Chicago restaurant to begin his formal leadership training as an assistant manager. Olsen's assignments as an assistant manager included scheduling the wait staff, conducting preliminary screening interviews of job applicants, and resolving problems with customers. After three months on the job, Olsen was asked by a member of the corporate human resources staff how his leadership training program was going. Olsen replied, "I'm a little bit skeptical. I don't think I'm learning much about leadership."

When asked why he didn't think he was learning much about leadership, Olsen listed what he considered three recent examples of the type of responsibilities he faced regularly:

■ At 11 yesterday morning, I received a phone call from Annie, one of the servers. She told me she wouldn't be to work that afternoon because her Labrador retriever had become quite ill and she had to take the Lab to the vet. I told Annie that we desperately needed her that afternoon because of a large luncheon party. Annie told me her dog was more important to her than the job.

■ Two weeks ago, Gus, one of our salad chefs showed up to work absolutely drunk. I told him that working while drunk was absolutely against company rules. He got a little belligerent, but I did get him to take a taxi home at company expense.

■ Two days ago a customer in the restaurant spilled a cup of hot coffee on herself while answering a call on her cell phone. She told me that the coffee was too hot and that she was going to sue the restaurant. I explained to her tactfully that unless she was truly burned, she had no claim. I offered to have the restaurant pay for her dry cleaning, and then she calmed down.

Olsen then said to the human resources manager, "What has stuff like this got to do with leadership? I mean, I'm not creating great visions or inspiring hordes of people. In what way am I becoming a leader?"

Questions

1. What is your opinion of the contribution of Olsen's representative experiences to his development as a leader?

2. What else can the restaurant chain do to help Olsen, and others in the leadership program, develop as leaders?

REFERENCES

1. Peter Burrows, "HP Says Goodbye to Drama: Five Months in, CEO Hurd's No-nonsense Approach Is Being Felt in a Big Way," *Business Week*, September 12, 2005, p. 83.

2. Joseph A. Raelin, *Creating Leaderful Organizations: How to Bring Out Leadership in Everyone* (San Francisco: Berrett-Koehler, 2003).

3. Stanley Holmes, "I Like Challenge—And I've Got One: Fixing Boeing's Image and Assuring Future Growth Won't Be Easy for Jim McNerney," *Business Week*, July 18, 2005, p. 44.

4. Dean Foust, "Coke: Time for a Shakeup," *Business Week*, March 8, 2004, p. 40; "Starwood to Open More Than 70 Hotels in the Next Two Years," available at Hotel-Online.com, retrieved February 22, 2005.

5. Gareth R. Jones and Jennifer M. George, "The Experience and Evolution of Trust: Implications for Cooperation and Teamwork," *Academy of Management Review*, July 1998, pp. 531–546; Jenny C. McCune, "That Elusive Thing Called Trust," *Management Review*, August 1998, pp. 10–16.

6. Chris Taylor, "Builders & Titans," *Time*, April 26, 2004, pp. 74–75.

7. Cassie R. Barlow, Mark Jordan, and William H. Hendrix, "Character Assessment: An Examination of Leadership Levels," *Journal of Business and Psychology*, Summer 2003, p. 563.

8. Timothy A. Judge, Amy E. Colbert, and Remus Ilies, "Intelligence and Leadership: A Quantitative Review and Test of Theoretical Positions," *Journal of Applied Psychology*, June 2004, pp. 542–552.

9. Joyce E. Bono and Timothy A. Judge, "Personality and Transformational and Transactional Leadership: A Meta-Analysis," *Journal of Applied Psychology*, October 2004, pp. 901–910.

10. Bradley R. Agle, Nandu J. Nagarajan, Jeffery A. Sonnenfeld, and Dhinu Srinivasan, "Does CEO Charisma Matter? An Empirical Analysis of the Relationships among Organizational Performance, Environmental Uncertainty, and Top Management Team Perceptions of CEO Charisma," *Academy of Management Journal*, February 2006, pp. 161–174.

11. "Ethics—Business Educators Teach Students to . . . Do the Right Thing!" *Keying In*, January 1997, p. 1.

12. Robert B. Maddux and Dorothy Maddux, *Ethics in Business: A Guide for Managers* (Los Altos, CA: Crisp, 1994).

13. George W. Fotis, "Interactive Personal Ethics," *Management Review*, December 1996, p. 46, and "Covey Proposes Principle-Based Leadership," *Management Review*, September 1995, pp. 20–21.

14. "Viewpoint: Warren Bennis," in *Business: The Ultimate Resource* (Cambridge, MA: Perseus, 2002), p. 213.

15. Peter Block, *Stewardship: Choosing Service over Self-Interest* (San Francisco: Berrett-Koehler, 1993), pp. 27–32.

16. Robert T. Keller, "A Test of the Path-Goal Theory of Leadership with Need for Clarity as a Moderator in Research and Development Organizations," *Journal of Applied Psychology*, April 1989, pp. 208–212.

17. Ronald A. Heifetz and Donald L. Laurie, "The Work of Leadership," *Harvard Business Review*, January–February 1997, p. 124.

18. Robert K. Greenleaf, *The Power of Servant Leadership: A Journey into the Nature of Legitimate Power and Greatness* (San Francisco: Berrett-Koehler, 1998); James C. Hunter, *The World's Most Powerful Leadership Principle: How to Become a Servant Leader* (New York: Crown Business, 2004).

19. Book review of Larry Spears and Michelle Lawrence (eds.), *Practicing Servant-Leadership: Succeeding through Trust, Bravery, and Forgiveness* (San Francisco: Jossey-Bass, 2004). The review by Frank Hamilton, appears in *Academy of Management Review*, October 2005, pp. 875–877.

20. Ralph M. Stogdill and Alvin E. Coons (eds.), *Leader Behavior: Its Description and Measurement* (Columbus: The Ohio State University Bureau of Business Research, 1957); Carroll L. Shartle, *Executive Performance and Leadership* (Upper Saddle River, NJ: Prentice Hall, 1956).

21. Cited in Bill Breen, "Trickle-Up Leadership," *Fast Company*, November 2001, p. 90.

22. Richard Pascale, "Change How You Define Leadership, and You Change How You Run a Company," *Fast Company*, April–May 1988, pp. 114–120.

23. Daniel Goleman, "Leadership That Gets Results," *Harvard Business Review*, March–April 2000, pp. 78–90.

24. Gary Yukl and Richard Lepsinger, *Flexible Leadership: Creating Value by Balancing Multiple Challenges and Choices* (San Francisco: Jossey-Bass, 2004).

25. George Graen and J. F. Cashman, "A Role-Making Model of Leadership in Formal Organizations: A Developmental Approach," in J. G. Hunt and L. I. Larson (eds.), *Leadership Frontiers* (Kent, OH: Kent State University Press, 1975), pp. 143–165; Robert P. Vecchio, "Leader–Member Exchange, Objective Performance, Employment Duration, and Supervisor Ratings: Testing for Moderation and Mediation," *Journal of Business and Psychology*, Spring 1998, pp. 327–341.

26. Robert P. Vecchio, "Are You In or Out with Your Boss?" *Business Horizons*, vol. 29, 1987, pp. 76–78.

27. "Warren G. Bennis, Leadership Guru," in *Business: The Ultimate Resource*, p. 969.

28. Michael E. McGill and John W. Slocum, Jr., "A Little Leadership Please?" *Organizational Dynamics*, Winter 1998, p. 48.

29. Craig L. Pearce and Charles C. Manz, "The New Silver Bullet of Leadership: The Importance of Self- and Shared Leadership in Knowledge Work," *Organizational Dynamics*, no. 2, 2005, p. 133. The quote is from the same source.

30. William D. Hitt, *The Model Leader: A Fully Functioning Person* (Columbus, OH: Battelle Press, 1993).

Motivating Others and Developing Teamwork

Learning Objectives

After studying the information and doing the exercises in this chapter, you should be able to:

1 Understand how to diagnose what motivates people to perform well.

2 Recognize the contribution of two classical motivation theories to understanding work motivation.

3 Understand how to motivate others through empowerment and job design, including interesting work.

4 Understand how positive reinforcement, including financial incentives, recognition, and praise are used for employee motivation.

5 Describe strategies and tactics for developing teamwork.

6 Understand group dynamics in terms of the development of groups and group roles.

7 Identify the characteristics of effective work groups, and be aware of the problem of groupthink.

Outline

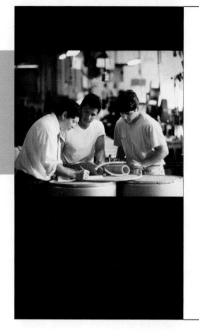

usiness is good at la Madeline Bakery, Café & Bistro chain. The privately held firm is opening new stores. Profits are growing. And they're even planning to boost raises for restaurant managers this year—but mainly for a slice of high-performing employees. The Dallas-based company's top performers will get about 3 to 5 percent, average performers 2 to 3 percent, and poor performers 1.5 percent or less, says human resources director Tina Hebert. Last year, "everybody probably got around 3.5 percent," she says.

Management at la Madeline felt pressure from rising costs of ingredients because of fuel surcharges, Ms. Hebert said, and so the company needed to control payroll expenses. To ease the transition to the new payroll system, executives told the restaurant managers about it at a conference roughly one year before awarding the new system of raises. They also added a midyear performance review so that the managers would have a better idea of where they stood. "We did come from a little bit of the entitlement mentality," Ms. Hebert said. "It's a different world." [1]

The story about the café and bistro chain illustrates that cost control may be important to make a profit in the restaurant industry. The story also presents an underlying message about using money as a motivator—salary increases are linked to how well workers perform. In this chapter we describe a variety of theories and practices for motivating others, including financial motivators. We also describe the closely related topic of developing teamwork because a group of people working together as a team are motivated to perform well.

How Do You Diagnose What Motivates Others Toward Good Performance?

■ **Learning Objective 1**

■ **Motivation**
concept with two widely used meanings: (1) an internal state that leads to effort expended toward objectives and (2) an activity performed by one person to get another to accomplish work

An eternal challenge for people responsible for the work of others is to get them to perform at a high level. **Motivation** has two widely used meanings: (1) an internal state that leads to effort expended toward objectives and (2) an activity performed by one person to get another to accomplish work. Usually the manager is doing the motivating, yet many people in the workplace have a need to motivate others. To accomplish their work, people must motivate individuals who report to them, coworkers, supervisors, and customers. Understanding how to motivate others, therefore, is essential to your success. Keep in mind also, that it is often important to motivate groups of people, such as a team, in addition to motivating people one at a time.

Knowledge of motivation is particularly important in the current era because so many workers do not feel identified with their work or their employers. According to one large study, about 70 percent of the U.S. workforce show up, do what is expected of them, but do not invest the additional energy necessary to excel. Often these workers would like to contribute more but they feel there is a disconnect with an immediate supervisor or that the organization does not care about them. "We're running an economy at 30 percent efficiency" because so many workers are not contributing at their best, says Curt Coffman, the employee engagement global practice leader for the consulting division of the Gallup Organization. [2] Note here that satisfaction is thought to be tied in with motivation because if these disengaged workers were more satisfied with the supervisor and company they might be more motivated.

A starting point in being able to motivate people and groups is to understand what outcomes or payoffs they want from their work. If you know what a person wants—and the person knows what he or she wants—you are in a better position to motivate that person. Questions can be asked in person or through a survey. [3] Basic questions might include:

- What could this job offer you that would make you work at your best?
- What factors about this job would bring out your best?
- What might the company do to make you excited about your job?
- How can I (or we) make your job a wonderful experience for you?
- What would make you feel really good about your job?

The answers to these questions are often surprising. For example, star performers often mention being give additional difficult assignments rather than a financial bonus. [4] Another worker might say, "If I could work at home only two days a month, I would work like crazy."

A person's behavior is often more revealing than what he or she says. You might, therefore, also gain some diagnostic insights by observing what elements of the job or work situation strongly interest the subordinate. For example, one group member might display enthusiasm primarily when there is an opportunity to do exciting work. Another group member might be excited primarily when a weekend or holiday approaches. You could tentatively conclude that the first person is motivated by exciting work and the second by time off from work.

What Are Two Classic Approaches to Understanding Work Motivation?

■ Learning Objective 2

In review, Maslow's need hierarchy arranges human needs into a pyramid-shaped model with basic physiological needs at the bottom and self-actualization needs at the top. According to the model or theory, people have an internal need pushing them toward self-actualization and personal superiority. However, before higher-level needs are activated, physiological needs must be satisfied. When a person is generally satisfied at one level, he or she looks for satisfaction at a higher level. The five level of needs in ascending order are (1) physiological, (2) safety, (3) social, (4) esteem, and (5) self-actualization. [5]

Maslow's need hierarchy provided an exciting beginning to recognizing the importance of understanding human needs to better motivate others. A practical application of the need hierarchy is that when a manager wants to motivate a group member, he or she must offer the individual a reward that will satisfy an important need.

The study of the needs hierarchy led to the **two-factor theory of work motivation**. According to the research of industrial psychologist Frederick Herzberg, there are two different sets of job factors. [6] One set, the motivators or satisfiers, can motivate and satisfy workers. The other set, dissatisfiers, or hygiene factors, can only prevent dissatisfaction. Motivators relate to higher-order needs, whereas hygiene factors relate to lower-order needs.

■ Two-factor theory of work motivation
two different sets of job factors—one set, the motivators, or satisfiers, can motivate and satisfy workers; the other set, dissatisfiers, or hygiene factors, can only prevent dissatisfaction

The two-factor theory explains how to design jobs to make them motivational. The motivational elements are the intrinsic, or job content, factors that make a job exciting. Motivator factors include achievement, recognition, advancement, responsibility, the work itself, and personal growth possibilities. The extrinsic, or job context, factors are hygienic. Although they are health maintaining and desirable, they are not motivational. Examples of hygiene factors are pay, status, job security, working conditions, and quality of leadership. Herzberg believed that motivation increases when one combines pay with a motivator such as challenging work.

According to the two-factor theory, only the presence of motivator factors leads to more positive energized behavior. For example, challenging work will motivate many people to exert increased effort. If intrinsic factors, such as challenging work, are not present, the result is neutral rather than negative, and the worker will feel bland rather than angry or unhappy. Although the presence of hygiene (or extrinsic) factors is not motivational, their absence can cause dissatisfaction as in the following illustration. A police captain reported that when officers were assigned old patrol cars, they complained frequently. However, when assigned brand new patrol cars, they did not express much appreciation. Nor did they increase their productivity as measured by the number of citations issued.

The two-factor theory has made two lasting contributions to work motivation. First, it has helped managers realize that money is not always the primary motivator. Second, it has spurred much of the interest in designing jobs to make them more intrinsically satisfying, as described later in this chapter.

A major problem with the two-factor theory is that it deemphasizes individual differences and glosses over the importance of hygiene factors in attracting and retaining workers. Hygiene factors such as good benefits and company management satisfy and motivate many people. Many working parents will work extra hard to keep their jobs at a company that offers on-site child care or flexible working hours. Furthermore, benefits such as company-subsidized health insurance and dental insurance, and a retirement pension would motivate many workers today to work hard and stay with a firm. The reason is that some private and public employers have drastically reduced benefits in recent years.

Another problem with the two-factor theory is that some workers show no particular interest in such motivators as opportunities for growth and advancement. They work primarily so they can pay their bills and enjoy their time with family and friends.

Because of their historical importance, and the fact that the theories of Maslow and Herzberg still influence modern thinking, the two theories are compared in Figure 12-1.

How Do You Motivate Through Empowerment and Job Design, Including Interesting Work?

■ Learning Objective 3

In this section we discuss three standard approaches to employee motivation: granting them more power, providing them interesting work, and recognizing them for their efforts.

EMPOWERMENT

A comprehensive strategy for employee motivation is to grant workers more power by enabling them to participate in decisions affecting themselves and their work. Empowerment basically involves passing decision-making authority and

Maslow's Need Hierarchy	Herzberg's Two-Factor Theory *Satisfiers or Motivators*	Managerial Action
Self-actualization Self-esteem	Achievement Recognition Work itself Responsibility Advancement Growth	Allow these factors to be present to increase satisfaction and motivation
	Dissatisfiers or Hygiene Factors	
Social (love, belonging) Safety and security Physiological	Company policy and administration Supervision Working conditions Salary Relationship with coworkers Personal life Status Job security	Keep these factors at adequate level to prevent dissatisfaction and demotivation.

Figure 12-1

Comparison of the Need Hierarchy and Two-Factor Theory

responsibility from managers to employees. A key point is that the leader shares power with group members. Because group members have some power, they can influence the manager, such as giving him or her guidance. [7]

Workers experience a greater sense of self-efficacy and ownership of their jobs when they share power. According to this logic, **empowerment** is the process by which a manager shares power with team members, thereby enhancing their feelings of self-efficacy. Because the worker feels more effective, empowerment contributes to intrinsic motivation. The individual has a choice in initiating and regulating actions, such as in deciding how to perform a particular task. [8] Sharing power with team members enables them to feel better about themselves and perform at a higher level. Teams as well as individuals can be empowered. An example of empowering a team would be to give it responsibility for developing a new product.

Employee empowerment is commonplace in the service industry in companies such as Marriott and Federal Express. It takes the form of giving customer contact employees more freedom in making decisions. At the same time, the employees are encouraged to exercise initiative and imagination (such as figuring how to satisfy an unusual customer demand), and they are rewarded for doing so. Package carrier UPS empowers its managers to deal with crises at the local level so they can respond quickly. Immediately following the 9/11 terrorist attacks, UPS in lower Manhattan was left with thousands of undeliverable packages to World Trade Center addresses. The UPS managers decided on their own to first sort out all those packages containing medical and

■ **Empowerment**

process by which a manager shares power with team members, thereby enhancing their feelings of self-efficacy pharmaceutical supplies, so the supplied would be available immediately to treat the wounded. Decisions were made later about what to do with packages addressed to demolished addresses.

Although employees are empowered, they are still given overall direction and limits to the extent of their authority. For example, a customer service worker cannot overturn a company rule, thereby creating a health or safety hazard. At a New York City hotel, a young woman wanted to check in with a boa constrictor draped around her shoulders. The snake lover insisted that her boa did not fit the ordinary pet category such as a dog, cat, or bird. The hotel associate replied firmly, "Sorry, I'm not empowered to allow boa constrictors into our hotel."

Many managers and human relations specialists assume that empowering individuals and groups leads to higher motivation and, therefore, to higher performance. A team of researchers including management professors and a human resource specialist at Siemens demonstrated that empowering a team does improvement effectiveness. The participants in the study were Canadian customer service engineers who worked for a major office equipment and technology organization. One-hundred and twenty-one recently empowered teams, comprising 521 service engineers participated in the study. The results of the study indicated that being empowered enhanced such performance measures as the reliability of the machines serviced and how long it took the service engineers to respond to calls for service. [9]

MOTIVATION THROUGH JOB DESIGN AND INTERESTING WORK

Many management experts contend that, if you make jobs more interesting, there may be less need for motivating people with external rewards. Also, attempting to motivate people by external rewards may not be sufficient. Motivating people through interesting work is based on the principle of **intrinsic motivation,** which refers to a person's beliefs about the extent to which an activity can satisfy his or her needs for competence and self-determination. Instead of looking to somebody else for rewards, a person is motivated by the intrinsic, or internal, aspects of the task.

Job enrichment refers to making a job more motivating and satisfying by adding variety and responsibility. A job is considered enriched to the extent that it demands more of an individual's talents and capabilities. As the job becomes more meaningful to you, you become better motivated and, it is hoped, more productive. Unless you want an enriched job, these positive results may not be forthcoming. Substantial research and practical experience has gone into enriching jobs. Frederick Herzberg, for example, has supervised programs for enriching the jobs of more than 100,000 employees in both the military and private industry. Three noteworthy characteristics of an enriched job are direct feedback, client relationships, and new learning. [10]

Direct feedback occurs when a worker receives immediate knowledge of the results he or she is achieving. This evaluation of performance can be built into the job (such as a highway patrol officer catching a speeder) or provided by a supervisor. *Client relationship* refers to an employee having a client or customer to serve, whether that client is inside or outside the organization. In this regard, both a customer service representative and a hairstylist have enriched jobs. *New learning* takes place when a job incumbent feels that he or she is growing psychologically. In contrast, an impoverished job allows for no new learning. The information technology component built into most jobs provides ample opportunity for new learning, as would learning a second language to relate better to customers in another country.

Going beyond the formal theory of job enrichment, interesting work also includes having a sense of purpose as you may have studied in relation to self-motivation and goal setting. The interesting work is often at the team level. Jack Welch, the former

■ **Intrinsic motivation**

a person's beliefs about the extent to which an activity can satisfy his or her needs for competence and self-determination; instead of looking to somebody else for rewards, a person is motivated by the intrinsic, or internal, aspects of the task

■ **Job enrichment**

making a job more motivating and satisfying by adding variety and responsibility chair of GE, and his wife Suzy Welch, a former *Harvard Business Review* editor, say that a bold mission allows bosses to say: "There's the hill. Let's take it together." [11] An example of a bold mission leading to interesting work for most people would be working on a community redevelopment project or finding a cure for childhood leukemia.

How Do You Motivate Through Positive Reinforcement, Including Financial Incentives, Recognition, and Praise?

■ **Learning Objective 4**

Rewarding a worker for achieving a certain result or behaving in a particular way is a widely used motivational tactic. **Positive reinforcement** means increasing the probability that behavior will be repeated by rewarding people for making the desired response. The phrase *increasing the probability* means that positive reinforcement improves learning and motivation but is not 100 percent effective. The phrase *making the desired response* is also noteworthy. To use positive reinforcement properly, a reward must be contingent on doing something right. Simply paying somebody a compliment or giving the person something of value is not positive reinforcement. Because financial incentives, recognition, and praise are given for attaining a given goal, they function as positive reinforcement.

■ **Positive reinforcement**
increasing the probability that behavior will be repeated by rewarding people for making the desired response; improves learning and motivation

Positive reinforcement is easy to visualize with well-structured jobs, such as data entry or producing parts. Yet positive reinforcement is also used to encourage desired behavior for those in highly paid, complex jobs. An accountant who developed a new method of the company getting paid faster might be rewarded with two extra days of vacation.

RULES FOR EFFECTIVE USE OF POSITIVE REINFORCEMENT

To use positive reinforcement effectively, certain rules and procedures must be followed. Although using rewards to motivate people seems straightforward, positive reinforcement requires a systematic approach. The rules are specified from the standpoint of the person trying to motivate another individual, such as a group member, coworker, supervisor, or customer. The same rules also apply to motivating a work group.

Rule 1: State Clearly What Behavior Will Lead to a Reward

The nature of good performance, or the goals, must be agreed on by the manager and group member. Clarification might take this form: "We need to decrease by 40 percent the number of new credit card customers who have delinquent accounts of 60 days or more."

Rule 2: Choose an Appropriate Reward

An appropriate reward is effective in motivating a given person and feasible from the standpoint of the individual or the company. If one reward does not motivate the person, try another. One person might be motivated by time off from work, another by an interesting assignment, and a third by an e-mail note of praise with a copy to a high-ranking executive. The importance of choosing the right reward underscores that fact that not all rewards are reinforcers. A reward is something of perceived value by the person giving the reward. However, if the reward does not strengthen the desired response (such as wearing safety goggles), it is not a true reinforcer. [12]

Rule 3: Supply Ample Feedback

Positive reinforcement cannot work without frequent feedback to individuals. Feedback can take the form of simply telling people they have done something right or wrong. Brief e-mail messages or handwritten notes are other forms of feedback. Many effective motivators, including Jack Welch, made extensive use of handwritten thank-you notes.

Rule 4: Schedule Rewards Intermittently

■ **Intermittent rewards**

sustaining desired behaviors longer and slowing down the process of behaviors fading away when they are not rewarded

Rewards should not be given on every occasion of good performance. **Intermittent rewards** sustain desired behaviors longer and also slow down the process of behaviors fading away when they are not rewarded. If each correct performance results in a reward, the behavior will stop shortly after a performance in which the reward is not received. Another problem is that a reward given continuously may lose its impact. A practical value of intermittent reinforcement is that it saves time. Few managers or team leaders have enough time to dispense rewards for every correct action by group members.

Rule 5: Make the Rewards Follow the Observed Behavior Closely in Time

For maximum effectiveness, people should be rewarded soon after doing something right. A built-in, or intrinsic, feedback system, such as software working or not working, capitalizes on this principle. E-mail and instant message are again useful here because it would be difficult for the manager or team leader to congratulate in person team members who work in another location.

Rule 6: Make the Reward Fit the Behavior

People who are inexperienced in applying positive reinforcement often overdo the intensity of spoken rewards. When an employee does something of an ordinary nature correctly, a simple word of praise such as "Good job" is preferable to something like "Fantastic performance." A related idea is that the magnitude of the reward should vary with the magnitude of the accomplishment.

Rule 7: Make the Rewards Visible

Another important characteristic of an effective reward is the extent to which it is visible, or noticeable, to other employees. When other workers notice the reward, its impact multiplies because other people observe what kind of behavior is rewarded. [13] Assume that you are being informed about a coworker having received an exciting assignment because of high performance. You might strive to accomplish the same level of performance. Rewards should also be visible, or noticeable, to the employee. A reward of five dollars per week added to a person's paycheck might be hardly noticeable, after payroll deductions. However, a bonus check for $200 might be very noticeable.

Rule 8: Change the Reward Periodically

Rewards do not retain their effectiveness indefinitely. Employees and customers lose interest in striving for a reward they have received many times in the past. This is particularly true of a repetitive statement such as "Nice job" or "Congratulations." It is helpful for the person giving out the rewards to study the list of potential rewards and try different ones from time to time.

A general approach applying to the previous rules is to look for creative ways to apply positive reinforcement. The creativity might be in the selection of the reward, or how the reward is administered. Several illustrative ideas include

- **Applause.** Choose an especially effective employee, and at the end of the week or month have coworkers gather and clap for the person.

- **Giraffe award.** Give a certificate saying, "Thanks for sticking your neck out." The name of the reward and the certificate reward risk taking.

- **Safety jackpot.** Managers give five "lotto" cards to employees who follow safety practices. Workers scratch off the cards to learn how many points they have won. Points are then redeemed via a gift catalog or Web site. [14]

FINANCIAL INCENTIVES AS POSITIVE REINFORCEMENT

Money is a natural motivator, and no program of motivation can exclude the role of financial compensation. Even the most ardent critics of the motivational power of money recognize that nonfinancial motivators are effective only when compensation is considered to be fair and adequate. When workers are preoccupied with not being paid fairly, they are less likely to respond to other approaches to motivation. When money is used as a motivator, it becomes a positive reinforcer because a person receives more money for performing well.

Financial incentives have multiplied in importance as companies struggle to stay afloat in worldwide competition. David Gregory, a labor law professor at St. John's University in New York, says that as wages spiral downward in basic industries, such as automotive, most employers will need to rely on performance-based compensation to retain skilled workers and keep them motivated. Furthermore, money as positive reinforcement will help attract the next generation of workers to the automotive industry. [15]

A challenge in understanding the role of money and other forms of compensation is that they are not pure concepts. High pay is also closely associated with other outcomes such as status and recognition. Thus, a person may work hard to earn more money as a way of achieving more status and recognition. Here we describe programs making pay partially contingent on performance, individual factors that influence the effectiveness of financial incentives, and problems with financial incentives.

Linking Compensation to Performance

Many employers make a systematic effort to link some portion of pay to performance to make pay more motivational. To relate pay to performance, many companies use variable pay as a method of motivating people with money. **Variable pay** is an incentive plan that intentionally pays good performers more money than poor performers. Employees receive more money by excelling on performance measures such as number of sales or number of computer programs completed. Variable pay is also referred to as *merit pay*. Whatever the specific plan, employees receive a base level of pay along with a bonus related to performance. The better your performance as measured by your employer, the higher your pay.

■ **Variable pay**
incentive plan that intentionally pays good performers more money than poor performers

Another approach to relating pay to performance is to link bonuses to results obtained by the work group or the entire company. Two such approaches are bonuses based on company profits and employee stock ownership. A companywide bonus plan ties individual merit pay to overall company or division performance, such as a year-end bonus based on company profits. The financial results on which the bonuses are determined can be measured at the division, group, business-unit, or company level. Sometimes the bonus is based on a combination of the levels mentioned. [16]

Nucor Corp. represents one of the most dramatic examples of the power of financial incentives tied to performance. Nucor is the most successful steel company in the United States from the standpoint of profits, employee morale, and low turnover. The company claims to have 0 percent turnover and has been profitable for 130 consecutive quarters, says Jim Coblin, vice president of human resources. "That's a huge feat in an industry as cyclical as ours is," he says. [17] On average, two-thirds of a steelworker's pay is based on a companywide production bonus. In addition, workers receive profit sharing. For 2005, the average worker received $91,293. However, three years earlier the average compensation was $58,931 because of a steel slump. Executive pay is similarly tied to attaining performance goals. [18]

Employee stock ownership plans encourage employees to purchase company stock, often at a discount. In this way the employees are part owners of the company, so they should be motivated to work hard and minimize waste. If the company prospers, the stock is likely to elevate in price, earning the employees a profit. W. Jack Duncan, professor of organizational behavior at the University of Alabama, Birmingham, among others, believes that ownership for all employees is an important key to high-performing individuals and companies. A stock that rises in values reinforces employee behaviors, such as giving good customer service and cutting costs. [19] A stock ownership plan can lead to employee discouragement if the stock declines in value and employees believe that they have made a poor investment.

As illustrated in the opening case to this chapter, many employers are widening the pay gap between high and low performers in order to boost productivity. The amount of money available for salary increases may be stable, but the pool is being distributed more unevenly as a form of variable pay. According to a survey by the consulting firm Hewitt Associates, in 2005 the best nonexecutive white-collar workers received an average raise of 9.9 percent. Average performers received 3.6 percent, and low performers received 1.4 percent. [20] "Performance" in these situations is often based on a supervisor's judgment, and at other times by more objective measures such as sales performance or number of units of work completed.

Personal Factors Influencing the Power of Financial Incentives

Individual differences influence profoundly the motivational power of financial incentives. Workers who attach a high value to financial incentives will be more motivated by money than those who attach a low value. A major influencing factor is that money is a good motivator when you need it badly enough. Money has a motivational pull for most people who perceive themselves to have a strong need for money. Once people have enough money to pay for all those things they think are important in life, money may lose its effectiveness. There are tremendous individual differences in what people classify as necessities. If, for example, somebody thinks owning three cars and having two residences is a necessity, that person will be motivated by money for a long time.

Problems Created by Financial Incentives

Despite their effectiveness as motivators, financial incentives also create problems. A major concern is that financial rewards can lead a person to focus on rewards rather than the joy built into exciting work. Another problem is that after people receive several increases based on performance, merit pay comes to be perceived as a right or entitlement. A person who does not receive a merit increase one quarter often feels that he or she has been punished. Another problem with cash awards is that they sometimes interfere with teamwork as employees concentrate on individual financial rewards. Professor of public administration at Rutgers University Marc Holzer observes, "Pay-for-performance programs do more harm than good. They set up competition between people. They emphasize the individual rather than the team. Virtually all innovations are group efforts. Yes, the exceptional person should be rewarded. But that exceptional person is dependent on others, on support services, which is often ignored." [21]

MOTIVATION THROUGH RECOGNITION AND PRAISE

The workplace provides a natural opportunity to satisfy the **recognition need,** the desire to be acknowledged for one's contributions and efforts and to feel important. A manager can thus motivate many employees by making them feel important. Employee needs for recognition can be satisfied both through informal recognition and by giving formal recognition programs. If the recognition prize is made contingent on achievement, the recognition program functions like positive reinforcement.

■ **Recognition need**

the desire to be acknowledged for one's contributions and efforts and to feel important

Praising workers for good performance is closely related to informal recognition. An effective form of praise describes the worker's performance rather than merely making an evaluation. Describing good performance might take this form: "You turned an angry customer into an ally who referred new business to us." A more general evaluation would be "You are great with angry customers."

Although praise costs no money and requires only a few minutes of time, many workers rarely receive praise. One researcher found that out of 1,500 workers surveyed, more than 50 percent said they seldom or never receive spoken or written thanks for their efforts. [22] Managers and team leaders, therefore, have a good opportunity to increase motivation by the simple act of praising good deeds. Other informal approaches to recognizing good performance include taking an employee to lunch, a handshake from the manager or team leader, and putting flowers on an employee's desk.

> "Recognition is an action, not an item."
> —Lynne Eskil, human resources specialist, Boeing's engineering group, Puget Sound, Washington.

An advanced use of praise is to tailor the praise to the needs of the person being praised, much like the diagnostic approach to motivation. A study with 103 working adults found that people who perceived themselves to be technically oriented have a more negative attitude toward being flattered (a strong form of praise). Instead, they prefer a laid-back, factual statement of how they made a contribution. (An example: "Your solution to the problem saved us 30 percent in raw material costs.") Conversely, people who perceived themselves to be less technically oriented, were more positively disposed toward being flattered. (An example: "I love it. What a fantastic solution to our problem.") Also, women had a more positive attitude toward being flattered than did men. [23] So it would appear that nontechnically oriented women would be the most receptive to praise and flattery!

Another example of individual differences in response to recognition in praise is that not every employee wants to receive the accolade of "employee of the month" or to receive public recognition. Many Asian workers, for example, prefer that praise be given privately or shared with the group publicly. [24]

Formal recognition programs are more popular than ever as companies attempt to retain the right employees and keep workers productive who worry about losing their jobs or having no private work area. Company recognition programs include awarding watches and jewelry for good service, plaques for good performance, and on-the-spot cash awards (about $25 to $50) for good performance. Because so many workers are not in face-to-face contact with their managers, managers often deliver verbal recognition by e-mail or telephone. Furthermore, some recognition programs are administered through Web sites in which the employee can choose from among a list of possible awards. [25]

A form of group recognition that fits many workers is to have a meal together, particularly on company time. A representative example is Central Hudson Gas and Electric in Poughkeepsie, New York. Tom Brocks, the assistant vice president for human resources says the utility uses meals on a routine basis to say thank you. "We give gift certificates for Culinary Institute of America meals as rewards in our suggestion program, as door prizes during our annual holiday party, and as miscellaneous rewards throughout the year." [26] (Observe here that meals are sometimes given to all employees, and at other times meals are used more as a form of positive reinforcement [rewards] for a job well done.)

The accompanying Human Relations in Practice insert illustrates several of the possible components of a company recognition program.

Human Relations in Practice

AFLAC Gets Mileage out of Employee Recognition Programs

At AFLAC, the Columbus, Georgian-based, insurance company (with the quacking duck advertising campaign), recognition programs are designed to reinforce a "strong sense of family" that is the company's culture, says Sharon Douglas, AFLAC's chief people officer. The founder's philosophy was to "treat people as you would like to be treated," she says, based on the conclusion that "if you treat the employees well, they will take care of the business."

AFLAC recognizes all employees' birthdays with a card and present they can select through a vendor. AFLAC's employee appreciation week serves as a focal point for recognition and rewards, and includes family-friendly events. "It's just a big rah-rah time," says Douglas.

In addition to employee appreciation week, AFLAC sponsors other recognition programs that Douglas describes as hybrid because they comprise multiple components. The program includes cash rewards for innovative ideas, with the top three winners honored at the end of the employee appreciation week. Also, throughout the year, division heads are encouraged to reward employees who perform "above and beyond the call of duty." The rewards can include stock options, cash, or time off.

Source: Adapted from Charlotte Garvey, "Meaningful Tokens of Appreciation: Cash Awards Aren't the Only Way to Motivate Your Workforce," *HR Magazine*, August 2004, pp. 102, 103.

What Are Some Strategies and Tactics for Building Teamwork?

■ **Learning Objective 5**

■ **Teamwork**

work done with an understanding and commitment to group goals on the part of all team members

> "Teamwork is the ability to work together toward a common vision. The ability to direct individual accomplishments toward organizational objectives. It is the fuel that allows common people to attain uncommon results."
> —Andrew Carnegie, famous 19th-century steel manufacturer and philanthropist.

So far in this chapter we have studied how leaders and managers can influence subordinates by direct use of motivational techniques. Team leaders, as well as other managers, also need to use techniques that influence subordinates to work well together in a team. In this section we describe methods for building **teamwork**—work done with an understanding and commitment to group goals on the part of all team members. [27] Figure 12-2 provides a bulleted list of methods for building teamwork mentioned here. In the following sections we describe more about how groups function because such knowledge can indirectly help the manager or leader do a better job of developing teamwork. An analogy is that if a professor understands how people learn, he or she can be more effective at teaching.

Good teamwork enhances, but does not guarantee, a successful team. For example, a group with excellent teamwork might be working on improving a service no longer valued by the company or customers. No matter what the output of the team, it will probably be ignored.

A starting point in developing good teamwork is to select members for the team who are interested in and qualified to be strong team members. The hiring manager or team leader should look for individuals who have enjoyed and performed well on teams in the past, both on and off the job. A study conducted in a manufacturing organization with highly interdependent teams found that being conscientious, extraverted, and having knowledge about teamwork were positively related to good job performance as a team member. [28]

- Select members interested in teamwork.
- Agree on what constitutes success.
- Compete against a common enemy external to the group.
- Make working together effectively an expected norm.
- Use consensus decision making.
- Use language that fosters cohesion and commitment, such as in-group jargon.
- Minimize micromanagement (managing too closely).
- Reward the team as well as individuals.
- Publish a team book, including one-page biographies of members.
- Show respect for all team members.
- Use experiential learning, such as outdoor training.
- Use the right technology so virtual team members can communicate with each other.

Figure **12-2**

Methods for Building Teamwork

Gordon Bethune, the CEO who helped rebuild Continental Airlines from "worst to first" offers a good early step for building teamwork. He maintains that the entire team must agree on what constitutes success. Every team member has to say: "Yes, that's it." [29] Another early step is to help team members believe they have an urgent, constructive purpose. A demanding performance challenge helps create and sustain the team. Rewards should stem from meeting the challenge.

Competing against a common enemy is one of the best-known methods of building team spirit. It is preferable that the adversary is external, such as an independent diner competing against franchised family restaurants. A primary strategy for teamwork promotes the attitude that working together effectively is an expected norm. Developing such a culture of teamwork generally proves difficult when a strong culture of individualism exists within the firm. The team leader can communicate the norm of teamwork by making frequent use of words and phrases that support teamwork. Emphasizing the words *team members* or *teammates*, and deemphasizing the words *subordinates* and *employees* helps communicate the teamwork norm. The norm of teamwork is also fostered by having a code of conduct to which members agree. Provisions of the code might include, "Never abandon a teammate" and "Never humiliate a teammate."

Using the consensus decision-making style provides another way to reinforce teamwork. A sophisticated approach to enhancing teamwork, it feeds team members valid facts and information that motivate them to work together. New information prompts the team to redefine and enrich its understanding of the challenge it is facing, thereby focusing on a common purpose. A subtle yet potent method of building teamwork emphasizes the use of language that fosters cohesion and commitment. In-group jargon bonds a team and sets the group apart from others. For example, a team of computer experts says "Give me a core dump" to mean "Tell me your thoughts." The culture at Microsoft heavily emphasizes using hip jargon to build teamwork. Using the term *bandwidth* as a synonym for *intelligence* appears to have been invented by CEO Bill Gates.

To foster teamwork, the manager should minimize micromanagement, or supervising group members too closely and second-guessing their decisions. Micromanagement can hamper a spirit of teamwork (potency) because team members do not feel in control of their own work.

One high-impact strategy for encouraging teamwork rewards the team as well as individuals. The most convincing team incentive is to calculate compensation partially on the basis of team results. For a more general reward strategy, managers apply positive reinforcement whenever the group or individuals engage in behavior that supports teamwork. For example, team members who took the initiative to have an information-sharing session can be singled out and praised for this activity.

To enhance team spirit, the manager can publish a team book containing a one-page biography of each team member. The biography can include a photo, a list of hobbies, personal interests, and family information. As team members look through the book, they become better acquainted with each other, leading to feelings of closeness.

Showing respect for team members is a general technique for building teamwork. Respect can be demonstrated in such ways as asking rather than demanding something be done, For example, "Jason could you investigate our developing a Web site for the team?" Giving team members your undivided attention when they come to you with a problem is another demonstration of respect. Making positive comments about other team members and not talking behind their backs are other ways of showing respect.

Another option available to organizations for enhancing teamwork comes through experiential learning, such as sending members to outdoor training. Participants acquire leadership and teamwork skills by confronting physical challenges and exceeding their self-imposed limitations. In rope activities, which are typical of outdoor training, participants attached to a secure pulley with ropes climb ladders and jump off to another spot. Another form of outdoor training for elite teams, a day at an auto-racing track, provides team members with an opportunity to drive at racecar speeds in some kind of cooperative venture. All of these challenges require teamwork rather than individual effort, hence their contribution to team development. Outdoor training generally offers the most favorable outcomes when the trainer helps the team members comprehend the link between such training and on-the-job behavior.

A special challenge in developing good teamwork is when the members are geographically dispersed, as in a virtual team. Because the members communicate with each other mostly by e-mail and group software, they lose out on the face-to-face interaction useful for building teamwork. A technologically advanced approach is for the virtual team members to use on-line team rooms where everyone can see the state of work in progress and interact with each other simultaneously. [30] (The setup is much like a Web log for team member use.) Bringing the group together for an occasional face-to-face meeting is also helpful in building teamwork.

Effective managers pick and choose from strategies as appropriate to build teamwork. Relying too heavily on one tactic, such as establishing a mission statement or outdoor training, limits the development of sustained teamwork. The accompanying Human Relations in Practice illustrates how an ordinary activity can sometimes be used to build teamwork in the workplace.

How Does Understanding Group Dynamics Contribute To Teamwork Development?

■ **Learning Objective 6**

■ **Group Dynamics**
the forces operating in groups that affect how members work together

An indirect way of a leader being effective at developing teamwork is to be knowledgeable about how groups operate. **Group dynamics** refers to the forces operating in groups that affect how members work together. To help zero in on this vast body

Human Relations in Practice

Distributorship Owner Builds Teamwork by Cleaning Up

Shortly after Leo Brewer purchased a Cummins distributorship in St. Louis, he knew that cleaning up the filthy and neglected shop area would have to be his first priority. But he also knew that he couldn't afford to pay the crew extra for the unpleasant task. So he gathered them together and simply said that he, his wife, and his children were coming in on Saturday morning to clean, and that anyone who wanted to could show up and pitch in. Not only did the employees come in to help, but they also helped Brewer repaint the shop the following weekend as well.

Brewer's direct approach resulted in more than simply a clean shop. The team developed camaraderie during those two weekends that formed the basis of a new, more productive culture.

Source: "Four Powerful Words That Build Teamwork," *Manager's Edge*, February 2006, as adapted from *The Driving Force*, Peter Schutz, Harris and Schutz, Inc., available at www.harrisandschutzinc.com. Retrieved April 14, 2006.

of knowledge, we feature three practical topics: the stages of group development, team member roles, and the characteristics of an effective work group including the problem of groupthink.

STAGES OF GROUP DEVELOPMENT

Key to understanding the nature of work groups is to know what the group does (the content) and how it proceeds (the process). A key group process is the group's development over time. To make this information more meaningful, relate it to any group to which you have belonged for at least one month. Understanding the stages of group development can lead to more effective group leadership or membership. The five group stages are shown in Figure 12-3 and described next. [31]

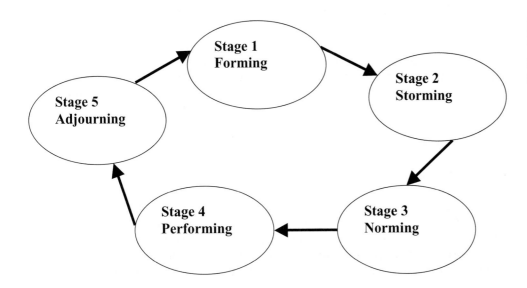

Figure **12-3**

The Stages of Group Development: Most Groups Follow a Predictable Sequence of Stages

Stage 1. Forming. At the outset, members are eager to learn what tasks they will be performing, how they can benefit from group membership, and what constitutes acceptable behavior. Members often inquire about rules they must follow. Confusion, caution, and communality are typical during the initial phase of group development.

Stage 2. Storming. During this "shakedown" period, individual styles often come into conflict. Hostility, infighting, tension, and confrontation are typical. Members may argue to clarify expectations of their contributions. Coalitions and cliques may form within the group, and one or two members may be targeted for exclusion. Subgroups may form to push for an agenda of interest to them. (Despite the frequency of storming, many workplace groups work willingly with one another from the outset, thus skipping stage 2.)

Stage 3. Norming. After storming comes the quieter stage of overcoming resistance and establishing group standards of conduct (norms). Cohesiveness and commitment begin to develop. The group starts to come together as a coordinated unit, and harmony prevails. Norms stem from three sources. First, the group itself quickly establishes limits for members, often by effective use of glares and nods. For example, the team member who swears at the leader might receive angry glances from other members. Second, norms may also be imposed that are derived from the larger organization and from professional codes of conduct. A third source of norms might be an influential team member who inspires the group to elevate its performance or behavior. The head of an audit team might say, "Let's develop the reputation of an audit team that is the most professional and objective in the industry."

Stage 4. Performing. When the group reaches the performing stage, it is ready to focus on accomplishing its key tasks. Issues concerning interpersonal relations and task assignment are put aside as the group becomes a well-functioning unit. Intrinsic motivation and creativity are likely to emerge as the group performs. At their best, members feel they are working "for the cause," much like a political campaign team or a team bringing a breakthrough product to market.

Stage 5. Adjourning. Temporary work groups are abandoned after their task has been accomplished, much like a project team to erect an office tower. The same group members, however, have developed important relationships and understandings they can bring with them should they be part of the same team in the future. The link between adjourning and forming shown in Figure 12-3 is that many groups do reassemble after one project is completed. The link between stages 1 and 5 would not apply for a group that disbanded and never worked together again.

A key managerial challenge is to help the group move past the first three stages into performing. At times, group members may have to be confronted that they are spending too much time on process issues and not enough on the task at hand.

TEAM MEMBER ROLES

■ Role

tendency to behave, contribute, and relate to others in a particular way

A major challenge in learning to become an effective team member is to choose the right roles to occupy. A **role** is a tendency to behave, contribute, and relate to others in a particular way. It is helpful for the leader to understand these roles as he or she attempts to get the group working together smoothly. For example, the leader might want to make sure that all positive roles are filled. If you carry out positive roles, you will be perceived as a contributor to team effort. If you neglect carrying out these roles, you will be perceived as a poor contributor. Human Relations Self-Assessment Quiz 12-1

Human Relations Self-Assessment Quiz 12-1

Team Player Roles

For each of the following statements about team activity, check *mostly agree* or *mostly disagree.* If you have not experienced such a situation, imagine how you would act or think if placed in that situation. In responding to the statements, assume that you are taking the questionnaire with the intent of learning something about yourself.

	Mostly Agree	Mostly Disagree
1. It is rare that I ever miss a team meeting.	_____	_____
2. I regularly compliment team members when they do something exceptional.	_____	_____
3. Whenever I can, I avoid being the note taker at a team meeting.	_____	_____
4. From time to time, other team members come to me for advice on technical matters.	_____	_____
5. I like to hide some information from other team members so I can be in control.	_____	_____
6. I welcome new team members coming to me for advice and learning the ropes.	_____	_____
7. My priorities come first, which leaves me with very little time to help other team members.	_____	_____
8. During a team meeting, it is not unusual for several other people at a time to look toward me for my opinion.	_____	_____
9. If I think the team is moving in an unethical direction, I will say so explicitly.	_____	_____
10. Rarely will I criticize the progress of the team even if I think such criticism is deserved.	_____	_____
11. It is not unusual for me to summarize the progress in a team meeting, even if not asked.	_____	_____
12. To conserve time, I attempt to minimize contact with my teammates outside of our meetings.	_____	_____
13. I intensely dislike going along with a consensus decision if the decision runs contrary to my thoughts on the issue.	_____	_____
14. I rarely remind teammates of our mission statement as we go about our work.	_____	_____
15. Once I have made up my mind on an issue facing the team, I am unlikely to be persuaded in another direction.	_____	_____
16. I am willing to accept negative feedback from team members.	_____	_____
17. Simply to get a new member of the team involved, I will ask his or her opinion.	_____	_____
18. Even if the team has decided on a course of action, I am not hesitant to bring in new information that supports another position.	_____	_____
19. Quite often I talk negatively about one team member to another.	_____	_____
20. My teammates are almost a family to me because I am truly concerned about their welfare.	_____	_____
21. When it seems appropriate, I joke and kid with teammates.	_____	_____
22. My contribution to team tasks is as important to me as my individual work.	_____	_____
23. From time to time I have pointed out to the team how we can all improve in reaching our goals.	_____	_____
24. I will fight to the last when the team does not support my viewpoint and wants to move toward consensus.	_____	_____
25. I will confront the team if I believe that the members are thinking too much alike.	_____	_____

Total score _____

Scoring and Interpretation:

Give yourself one point (+1) for each statement you gave in agreement with the keyed answer. The keyed answer indicates carrying out a positive, as opposed to a negative, role.

1. Mostly agree
2. Mostly agree
3. Mostly disagree
4. Mostly agree

(continued)

Human Relations Self-Assessment Quiz 12-1 *(Continued)*

5. Mostly disagree

6. Mostly agree

7. Mostly disagree

8. Mostly agree

9. Mostly agree

10. Mostly disagree

11. Mostly agree

12. Mostly disagree

13. Mostly disagree

14. Mostly disagree

15. Mostly disagree

16. Mostly agree

17. Mostly agree

18. Mostly agree

19. Mostly disagree

20. Mostly agree

21. Mostly agree

22. Mostly agree

23. Mostly agree

24. Mostly disagree

25. Mostly agree

20–25   You carry out a well above average number of positive team roles. Behavior of this type contributes substantially to being an effective team player. Study the roles in this chapter to further build your effectiveness as a team member.

10–19   You carry out an average number of positive team roles. Study carefully the roles described in this chapter to search for ways to carry out a greater number of positive roles.

0–9   You carry out a substantially above average number of negative team roles. If becoming an effective team player is important to you, you will have to diligently search for ways to play positive team roles. Study the information about roles in this chapter carefully.

will help you evaluate your present inclinations toward occupying effective roles as a team member. In this section we describe a number of the most frequently observed positive roles played by team members. We also mention a group of negative roles.

According to the role theory developed by Meredith Belbin and his group of researchers at Belbin Associates, there are nine frequent roles occupied by team members. [32] All of these roles are influenced to some extent by an individual's personality.

1. **Plant.** The plant is creative, imaginative, and unorthodox. Such a person solves difficult problems. A potential weakness of this role is that the person tends to ignore fine details and becomes too immersed in the problem to communicate effectively.

2. **Resource investigator.** The resource investigator is extroverted, enthusiastic, and communicates freely with other team members. He or she will explore opportunities and develop valuable contacts. A potential weakness of this role is that the person can be overly optimistic and may lose interest after the initial enthusiasm wanes.

3. **Coordinator.** The coordinator is mature, confident, and a natural team leader. He or she clarifies goals, promotes decision making and delegates effectively. A downside to occupying this role is that the person might be seen as manipulative and controlling. Some coordinators delegate too much by asking others to do some of the work they (the coordinators) should be doing.

4. **Shaper.** The shaper is challenging, dynamic, and thrives under pressure. He or she will use determination and courage to overcome obstacles. A potential weakness of the shaper is that he or she can be easily provoked and may ignore the feelings of others.

5. **Monitor-evaluator.** The monitor-evaluator is even tempered, engages in strategic (big picture and long-term) thinking, and makes accurate judgments. He or she sees all the options and judges accurately. A potential weakness of this role occupant is that he or she might lack drive and the ability to inspire others.

6. **Team worker.** The team worker is cooperative, focuses on relationships, and is sensitive and diplomatic. He or she is a good listener who builds relationships, dislikes confrontation, and averts friction. A potential weakness is that the team worker can be indecisive in a crunch situation or crisis.

7. **Implementer.** The implementer is disciplined, reliable, conservative and efficient. He or she will act quickly on ideas, and convert them into practical actions. A potential weakness is that the implementer can be inflexible and slow to see new opportunities.

8. **Completer-finisher.** The completer-finisher is conscientious and anxious to get the job done. He or she has a good eye for detail and is effective at searching out errors. He or she can be counted on for finishing a project and delivering on time. A potential weakness is that he or she can be a worrier and reluctant to delegate.

9. **Specialist.** The specialist is a single-minded self-starter. He or she is dedicated and provides knowledge and skill in rare supply. A potential weakness of the specialist is that he or she can be stuck in a niche with little interest in other knowledge and may dwell on technicalities.

The weaknesses in the first nine roles point to problems the team leader or manager can expect to emerge, and, therefore, allowances should be made. Belbin refers to these potential problems as *allowable weaknesses* because allowances should be made for them. To illustrate, if a team worker has a tendency to be indecisive in a crisis, the team should not have high expectations of the team worker when faced with a crisis. Team workers will be the most satisfied if the crisis is predicted and decisions involving them are made before the pressure mounts. [33]

Another perspective on team roles is that team members will sometimes engage in *self-oriented roles*. Members will sometimes focus on their own needs rather than those of the group. The individual might be overly aggressive because of a personal need, such as wanting a bigger budget on his or her project. The individual might hunger for recognition or power. Similarly, the person might attempt to dominate the meeting, block others from contributing, or serve as a distraction. One of the ploys used by distracters recently is to engage in cell phone conversations during a meeting and blaming it on "those people who keep calling me."

The many roles just presented overlap somewhat. For example, the implementer might engage in specialist activities. Do not be concerned about the overlap. Instead, pick and choose from the many roles as the situation dictates—regardless of whether overlap exists.

The behavior associated with the roles just described is more important than remembering the labels. For example, remembering to be creative and imaginative is more important than remembering the specific label plant.

THE PROBLEM OF GROUPTHINK (TOO MUCH CONSENSUS)

For a team to be truly effective, somebody has to step forth and say "the emperor has no clothes" when the group is making an outrageously bad decision. Often

■ **Groupthink**

a deterioration of mental efficiency, reality testing, and moral judgment in the interest of group solidarity; extreme form of consensus

the shaper or monitor-evaluator plays this role. **Groupthink** is a deterioration of mental efficiency, reality testing, and moral judgment in the interest of group solidarity. Simply put, groupthink is an extreme form of consensus. The group atmosphere values getting along more than getting things done. [34] The group thinks as a unit, believes it is impervious to outside criticism, and begins to have illusions about its own invincibility. As a consequence, the group loses its powers of critical analysis.

One historically important example of groupthink took place in relation to the explosion of the space shuttle *Challenger*. According to several analyses of the incident, NASA managers were so committed to reaching space program objectives that they ignored safety warnings from people both within and outside the agency. As reported in the internal NASA briefing paper dated July 20, 1986, both astronauts and engineers expressed concern that the agency's management had a groupthink mentality. Of related significance, the management style of NASA managers is characterized by a tendency not to reverse decisions and not to heed the advice of people outside the management group. The analysis of their styles was conducted by a series of management-style tests administered several years prior to the *Challenger* explosion. [35]

A high-level business example of groupthink took place during 2001 when a group of top executives at the energy company Enron Corporation created an artificial shortage of electricity in order to raise prices. [36] Ultimately, the scam was publicly exposed. We can assume that such a large decision was a group decision and that nobody on the executive team attempted to stop the outrageous scheme or to inform the federal government.

The negative aspects of groupthink can often be prevented if the team leader, or a member, encourages all team members to express doubts and criticisms of proposed solutions to the problem or suggested courses of action. It is also helpful to periodically invite qualified outsiders to meet with the group and provide suggestions.

What Are the Characteristics of an Effective Work Group?

■ **Learning Objective 7**

Groups, like individuals, have characteristics that contribute to their uniqueness and effectiveness. Effectiveness includes such factors as objective measures of production (e.g., units produced), favorable evaluations by the manager, and worker satisfaction. For a group to be effective, the members must strive to act like a group or team. Also, the task given to the group or team should require collective effort instead of being a task that could be better performed by individuals. For example, many customers would prefer to be called on by an individual sales representative rather than by a sales team, so for some customers the rep should work individually rather than in a team effort. As shown in Figure 12-4, and based on dozens of different studies, effective work group and team characteristics can be grouped into eleven characteristics or factors. [37]

- The team has clear-cut goals linked to organizational goals so that group members feel connected to the entire organization. Group members are empowered so they learn to think for themselves rather than expecting a supervisor to solve all the difficult problems. At the same time, the group believes it has the authority to solve a variety of problems without first obtaining approval from management.
- Group members are assigned work they perceive to be challenging, exciting, and rewarding. As a consequence, the work is self-rewarding.
- Members depend on one another to accomplish tasks and work toward a common goal. At the same time, the group believes in itself and that it can accomplish an interdependent task.
- Members learn to think "outside the box" (are creative).
- Members receive extensive training in technical knowledge, problem-solving skills, and interpersonal skills.
- Group size is generally about six people, rather than 10 or more.
- Team members have good intelligence and personality factors, such as conscientiousness and pride, that contribute to good performance.
- There is honest and open communication among group members and with other groups in the organization.
- Members have the philosophy of working as a team—25 brains, not only 50 hands.
- Members are familiar with their jobs, coworkers, and the work environment. This experience adds to their expertise. The beneficial effects of experience may diminish after awhile because the team needs fresh ideas and approaches.
- The team has emotional intelligence in the sense that it builds relationships both inside and outside the team. Included in emotional intelligence are norms that establish mutual trust among members, a feeling of group identity, and groups efficacy.

Sources: Michael A. Campion, Ellen M. Papper, and Gina Medsker, "Relations between Work Team Characteristics and Effectiveness: A Replication and Extension," *Personnel Psychology*, Summer 1996, p. 431; Stanley M. Gulley, Kara A. Incalcaterra, Aparna Joshi, and J. Matthew Beaubien, "A Meta-Analysis of Team Efficacy, Potency, and Performance: Interdependence and Level of Analysis as Moderators of Observed Relationships," *Journal of Applied Psychology*, October 2002, pp. 819–832; Vanessa Urch Druskat and Steven B. Wolff, "Building the Emotional Intelligence of Groups," *Harvard Business Review*, March 2001, pp. 80–90; Clause W. Langred, "Too Much of a Good Thing? Negative Effects of High Trust and Individual Autonomy in Self-Managing Work Teams, " *Academy of Management Journal*, June 2004, pp. 385–399.

Figure 12-4

Key Characteristics of Effective Teams and Work Groups

Concept Review and Reinforcement

Key Terms

Motivation, 298
Two-factor theory of work
  motivation, 299
Empowerment, 301
Intrinsic motivation, 302

Job enrichment, 302
Positive reinforcement, 303
Intermittent rewards, 304
Variable pay, 305
Recognition need, 307

Teamwork, 308
Group dynamics, 310
Role, 312
Groupthink, 316

Summary and Review

Motivating others toward good performance begins with the diagnosis of motivation. Diagnostic questions might include, "What could this job offer you that would make you work at your best?" Diagnosis should also include observing the subordinate's behavior in terms of what interests him or her.

Two classic theories of worker motivation are Maslow's need hierarchy and Herzberg's two-factor theory of motivation.

- A practical application of the need hierarchy is that when a manager wants to motivate a group member, he or she must offer the individual a reward that must satisfy an important need.
- According to the two-factor theory of work motivation, one set of factors, the motivators or satisfiers, can motivate and satisfy workers. The other set, dissatisfiers or hygiene factors, can only prevent dissatisfaction.

Empowerment is a comprehensive motivational strategy that grants workers more power by enabling them to participate in decisions affecting themselves and their work.

- Empowerment contributes to intrinsic motivation.
- Empowerment is commonplace in the service industry.
- Empowered employees must still be given overall direction and limits to the extent of their authority.

Motivation can take place through job design and interesting work, based on the principle of intrinsic motivation. Job enrichment makes a job more motivating and satisfying through means such as

- direct feedback to the job incumbent
- the opportunity for client relationships
- new learning

Rules for effectively using positive reinforcement to motivate employees include the following:

- State clearly what behavior will lead to a reward.
- Choose an appropriate reward.
- Supply ample feedback.
- Schedule rewards intermittently.
- Make the rewards follow the observed behavior closely in time.
- Make the reward fit the behavior.
- Make the rewards visible.
- Change the reward periodically.

Financial incentives are a natural motivator and are a form of positive reinforcement. Such incentives have multiplied in importance as companies struggle to stay afloat in worldwide competition. Money is also tied in with recognition. Key issues about financial incentives include the following:

- To make pay more motivational, many employers link pay to performance such as in variable pay.
- Employee stock ownership may contribute to motivation because employees become part owners of the business.
- Personal factors influence the power of financial incentives including the value the worker attaches to money and the need for money.
- Financial incentives can cause problems including a focus more on rewards than the joy built into exciting work.

Motivation through recognition and praise is an important motivational strategy because the workplace provides a natural opportunity to satisfy the recognition need. Praising workers for good performance is closely related to informal recognition. Many workers rarely receive praise. An advanced use of praise is to tailor the praise to the needs of the person. Formal recognition programs are important for employee retention as well as motivation.

Team leaders as well as other managers need to use techniques that influence subordinates to work well together as a team. Among the many suggestions presented in the chapter for building teamwork are the following:

- Select members for the team who are interested in and qualified to be strong team members.
- Help team members believe they have an urgent, constructive purpose.
- Use the consensus decision-making style.
- Reward the team as well as individuals.
- Show respect for team members.

Understanding how groups operate (group dynamics) helps a leader effectively build teamwork. One useful concept is the stages of group development: forming, storming, norming, performing, and adjourning. Team members occupy various roles, including the following:

- resource investigator
- coordinator
- monitor-evaluator
- completer-finisher
- specialist

A key potential problem with group effort is groupthink, or extreme consensus. The problem can be lessened by team members occupying a critical role.

An effective work group has characteristics that contribute to its uniqueness and effectiveness, as outlined in Figure 12-4. For a group to be effective the members must strive to be a team and work on a task that requires collective effort.

Check your Understanding

1. How could diagnosing the motivational wishes and needs of employees save a company a lot of money when launching motivational programs?
2. Why is empowerment considered to be a method of motivating employees?
3. In what way might a program of job enrichment help reduce turnover?
4. What are several ways an instructor uses positive reinforcement to motivate students?
5. What type of recognition on the job would be motivational for you? How do you know?
6. Assume that Jennifer from the tech support center gets rid of a nasty virus in your desktop computer. What is likely to be an effective statement of praise for her?
7. Explain why cooking a gourmet meal together might be an effective form of developing teamwork.
8. Reflect on any group you currently belong to or were a member of in the past. Describe how the group went through the stages of group development.
9. What are several group norms that exist in the class for which you are studying this text?
10. Identify several of the characteristics of an effective work group that one of your favorite athletic team possesses. Justify your reasoning the best you can.

Web Corner

Diagnosing how to motivate somebody:
www.workforce.com/motivation_survey

Bowling As A Team Building Exercise:
http://management.about.com/

Teamwork quotes and proverbs:
www.heartquotes.net/teamwork-quotes.html

Internet Skill Builder

Visit www.nelson-motivation.com to watch a five-minute videoclip of one of Bob Nelson's talks. After watching the video, answer the following questions:

1. What have I learned that I could translate into a skill for motivating employees?
2. Which theory, or approach, to motivation does Nelson emphasize in his presentation.

Developing Your
Human Relations Skills

Human Relations Application Exercises

Applying Human Relations Exercise 12-1

The Job Enrichment Squad

Work individually in small groups to develop skill in enriching several standard jobs by making them more interesting, challenging, and responsibility oriented. As part of your analysis, see if you can find someone who has held such a job (either you or a group member), and interview the job incumbent for some ideas. You might use e-mail or instant messaging as an alternative or supplement to telephone or face-to-face interviews. Choose three from among the following positions:

- supermarket cashier
- highway toll collector
- custodial worker at an educational institution

- home health aide
- car wash attendant
- call center operator for service with desktop and personal computers

In your problem-solving activity and in your interviews, seek answers to these basic questions: (1) What is the most boring part of this job? (2) What is the most exciting part of this job? (3) What is the most demotivating part of the job? (4) What is the most motivating part of the job? (5) Find an answer to any other question or question you think are relevant.

After you have completed your analysis, prepare a report of about two brief paragraphs as to how the specific job can be more motivational through job design.

Applying Human Relations Exercise 12-2

Team Member Roles

A team of approximately six people is formed to conduct a 20-minute meeting on a significant topic of their choosing. The possible scenarios follow:

Scenario A: Management Team A group of managers are pondering whether to lay off one-third of the workforce in order to increase profits. The company has had a tradition of caring for employees and regarding them as the company's most precious asset. However, the CEO has said privately that times have changed in our competitive world, and the company must do whatever possible to enhance profits. The group wants to think through the advisability of laying off one-third the workforce, as well as explore other alternatives.

Scenario B: Group of Sports Fans A group of fans have volunteered to find a new team name to replace "Redskins" for the local basketball team. One person among the group of volunteers believes that the name "Redskins" should be retained because it is a compliment, rather than an insult, to Native Americans. The other members of the group believe that a name change is in order, but

they lack any good ideas for replacing a mascot team name that has endured for more than 50 years.

Scenario C: Community Group A community group is attempting to launch an initiative to help battered adults and children. Opinions differ strongly as to what initiative would be truly helpful to these people. Among the alternatives are establishing a shelter for battered people, giving workshops on preventing violence, and self-defense training. Each group member with an idea strongly believes that he or she has come up with a workable possibility for helping with the problem of battered people.

While the team members are conducting their heated discussion, other class members make notes on which team members carry out which roles. Watching for the nine different roles, as well as the self-oriented roles, can be divided among class members. For example, the people in the first row might look for examples of the plant. Use the role worksheet that follows to help make your observations. Summarize the comment that is indicative of the role. An example would be noting in the shaper category: "Linda said naming the team the 'Washington Rainbows' seems like too much of an attempt to be politically correct."

Plant _____

Team worker _____

Resource investigator _____

Implementer _____

Co-ordinator _____

Completer-finisher _____

Shaper _____

Specialist _____

Monitor-evaluator _____

Self-oriented roles _____

Human Relations Case Study 12-1

Procter & Gamble Gives Time Off for Good Behavior

On a Monday morning in late March a few years ago, A. G. Lafley, chair of Procter & Gamble (P&G), thrashed out a business decision with other key executives. By the first Wednesday in May, the plan had been orchestrated, and managers were directed to announce it at staff meetings at 11 A.M. Cincinnati time so that most of the company's 98,000 employees would find out at once.

The announcement wasn't a merger, a crucial new product rollout, or a reformulation of Tide. Instead, it was a sort of corporate parole: time off for good behavior. In their meetings, P&G workers learned they had been granted a two-day vacation bonus, a reward for the company's sustained excellent performance over the previous four years, during which time P&G's stock nearly doubled in price. "We've never before offered a company performance award such as this, but you've earned it," Lafley wrote to employees in an e-mail.

Employees will have the option of taking two days pay instead of the time off, but that was hardly men-tioned in newspaper headlines across the country that trumpeted the announcement.

Terry Loftus, a spokesperson for P&G says that the cost of the bonus "will be in the millions, though it isn't material from an accounting standpoint." The cash involved would be equivalent to less than 1 percent bonus, Loftus says. Nevertheless, P&G's gesture had people pondering the value of time off as a motivational tool.

Questions

1. How effective do you think the reward of two days off from work will be in motivating P&G employees to higher levels of performance?
2. How effective do you think the reward of two days pay will be in motivating P&G employees to higher levels of performance?
3. How will P&G know if time off from work (or two days pay) is actually an effective motivator?
4. What employee needs might be satisfied by having two days off from work?

Source: Joe Mullich, "Giving Employees Something They Can't Buy with a Bonus Check," *Workforce Management*, July 2004, p. 66.

Human Relations Case Study 12-2

The Unbalanced Team

Mercury Printing is one of the largest commercial printing companies in the city where it is located, with annual sales of $30 million. Two years ago, Alvera Velasquez, the vice president of marketing, reorganized the sales force. Previously the sales force consisted of inside sales representatives, who took care of phone-in and Internet orders, and outside sales representatives, who called on accounts. The reorganization divided the outside sales force into two groups: direct sales and major accounts. The direct sales representatives were responsible for small- and medium-size customers. As before, they would service existing customers and prospect for new accounts.

Four of the direct sales representatives were promoted to major account executives. The account executives were supposed to work together on strategy for acquiring new accounts. If a particular account executive did not have the expertise to handle his or her customer's problems, another account executive was supposed to offer help. For example, Darcy Wentworth was the resident expert on printing packages and inserts for packages. If invited, Darcy would join another account executive to call on a customer with a complex request for package printing.

After the new sales organization had been in place for 18 months, Ann Osaka, an account executive, was having lunch with Garth Lewis, a production superintendent at Mercury Printing. "I've about had it," said Ann. "I'm tired of single-handedly carrying the team."

"What do you mean you are single-handedly carrying the team?" asked Garth.

"You're a trusted friend, Garth. So let me lay out the facts. Each month the group is supposed to bring in 16 new sales. If we don't average those 16 sales per month, we don't get our semiannual bonus. That represents about 25 percent of my salary. So a big chunk of my money comes from group effort.

"My average number of new accounts brought in for the past 12 months has been nine. And we are averaging about 14 new sales per month. This translates into the other three account execs averaging five sales among them. I'm carrying the group, but overall sales are still below quota. This means I didn't get my bonus last month.

"The other account execs are friendly and helpful in writing up proposals. But they simply don't bring in their share of accounts."

Garth asked, "What does Alvera say about this?"

"I've had several conversations with him about the problem. He tells me to be patient and to remember the development of a fully functioning team requires time. He also tells me that I should develop a stronger team spirit. My problem is that I can't pay my bills with team spirit."

Questions

1. What does this case illustrate about effective teamwork?
2. What steps, if any, should Alvera Velasquez take, if any, to remedy the situation of unequal contribution of account representatives?
3. What steps, if any, should Velasquez take to improve the teamwork in the sales group?
4. To what extent are Ann Osaka's complaints justifiable?

REFERENCES

1. Adapted from Erin White, "The Best versus the Rest," *The Wall Street Journal*, January 30, 2006, p. B1.
2. Steve Bates, "Getting Engaged," *HR Magazine*, February 2004, pp. 44, 46.
3. John Sullivan, "Personalizing Motivation," *Workforce Management*, March 27, 2006, p. 50.
4. Anne Fisher, "Turn Star Employees into Superstars," *Fortune*, December 13, 2004, p. 70.
5. Abraham Maslow, *Motivation and Personality*, 3rd ed. (New York: Harper & Row, 1987).
6. Frederick Herzberg, Bernard Mausner, and Barbara Synderman, *The Motivation to Work*, 2nd ed. (New York: Wiley, 1959); Herzberg, *Work and the Nature of Man* (Cleveland: World Publishing, 1966).
7. Craig L. Pearce and Jay A. Conger, (ed.)., *Shared Leadership: Reforming the How and Why of Leadership* (Thousand Oaks, CA: Sage, 2003).
8. Gretchen M. Spreitzer, "Psychological Empowerment in the Workplace: Dimensions, Measurement, and Validation," *Academy of Management Journal*, October 1995, pp. 1443–1444.
9. John E. Mathieu, Lucy L. Gilson, and Thomas M. Ruddy, "Empowerment and Team Effectiveness: An Empirical Test of an Integrated Model," *Journal of Applied Psychology*, January 2006, pp. 97–108.
10. Frederick Herzberg, "The Wise Old Turk," *Harvard Business Review*, September–October 1974, pp. 70–80.
11. Jack and Suzy Welch, "Keeping Your People Pumped," *Business Week*, March 27, 2006, p. 122.
12. Fred Luthans and Alexander Stajkovic, "Reinforce for Performance: The Need to Go Beyond Pay and Even Rewards," *Academy of Management Executive*, May 1999, p. 52.
13. Steven Kerr, *Ultimate Rewards: What Really Motivates People to Achieve* (Boston: Harvard Business School Publishing, 1997).
14. "Simple Rewards Are Powerful Motivators," *HRfocus*, August 2001, p. 10.
15. Jessica Marquez, "Premium on Productivity," *Workforce Management*, November 2005, p. 22.
16. Patricia K. Zingheim and Jay R. Schuster, "Value Is the Goal," *Workforce*, February 2000, p. 57.
17. Nanette Byrnes, "The Art of Motivation," *Business Week*, May 1, 2006, p. 59.
18. Marquez, "Premium on Productivity," p. 22.
19. W. Jack Duncan, "Stock Ownership and Work Motivation," *Organizational Dynamics*, Summer 2001, pp. 1–11.
20. White, "The Best versus the Rest," p. B1.
21. Quoted in Janet Wiscombe, "Can Pay for Performance Really Work?" *Workforce*, August 2001, p. 32.
22. Research by Gerald Graham reported in "Motivating Entry-Level Workers," *WorkingSMART*, October 1998, p. 2.
23. Andrew J. DuBrin, "Self-Perceived Technical Orientation and Attitudes toward Being Flattered," *Psychological Reports*, Vol. 96, 2005, pp. 852–854.
24. Charlotte Garvey, "Meaningful Tokens of Appreciation: Cash Awards Aren't the Only Way to Motivate Your Workforce," *HR Magazine*, August 2004, p. 103.
25. Bob Nelson, "Long-Distance Recognition," *Workforce*, August 2000, pp. 50–52.
26. Diane Cadrain, "Just Desserts: Free Meals Can Create Camaraderie While Thanking Employees for a Job Well Done," *HR Magazine*, March 2005, pp. 97–100.
27. Jon R. Katzenbach and Douglas K. Smith, "The Discipline of Teams," *Harvard Business Review*, March–April 1993, p. 112; John Syer and Christopher Connolly, *How Teamwork Works: The Dynamics of Effective Team Development* (London: McGraw-Hill, 1966); "Fly in Formation: Easy Ways to Build Team Spirit," *Executive Strategies*, March 2000, p. 6; Regina Fazio Maruca (ed.), "Unit of One: What Makes Teams Work?" *Fast Company*, November 2000, pp. 109–114; "Improve Teamwork with a 'Code of Conduct'," *Manager's Edge*, February 2005, p. 1.
28. Frederick P. Morgeson, Matthew H. Reider, and Michael A. Campion, "Selecting Individuals in Team Settings: The Importance of Social Skills, Personality Characteristics, and Teamwork Knowledge," *Personnel Psychology*, Autumn 2005, pp. 583–611.
29. Shelia M. Puffer, "Continental Airlines' CEO Gordon Bethune on Teams and New Product Development," *Academy of Management Executive*, August 1999, p. 30.
30. Ann Majchrzak, Arvind Malhgotra, Jeffrey Stamps, and Jessica Lipnack, "Can Absence Make a Team Grow Stronger?" *Harvard Business School*, May 2004, pp. 131–137.
31. J. Steven Heinen and Eugene Jacobsen, "A Model of Task Group Development in Complex Organizations and a Strategy of Implementation," *Academy of Management Review*, October 1976, pp. 98–111.
32. "R. Meredith Belbin," in *Business: The Ultimate Resource* (Cambridge, MA: Perseus, 2002), pp. 966–967; Belbin® Team-Roles, available at *http://www.belbin.com/belbin-teamroles.htm*. Retrieved March 12, 2005.
33. From a review of Meredith Belbin, *Management Teams*, by Colin Thomson appearing in *http://www.accountingweb.co.uk*. Retrieved March 13, 2005.
34. Irving L. Janis, *Victims of Groupthink: A Psychological Study of Foreign Policy Decisions and Fiascos* (Boston: Houghton Mifflin, 1972), 39–40; Glenn Whyte, "Groupthink Reconsidered," *Academy of Management Review*, January 1989, pp. 40–56.
35. Kenneth A. Kovach and Barry Bender, "NASA Managers and *Challenger*: A Profile of Possible Explanations," *Personnel*, April 1987, p. 40.
36. Paaul Kienitz, "Enron and Friends," available at *www.paulkienitz.net/enron*. Retrieved April, 15, 2006.
37. Synthesized from Michael A. Campion, Ellen M. Papper, and Gina Medsker, "Relations between Work Team Characteristics and Effectiveness: A Replication and Extension," *Personnel Psychology*, Summer 1996, p. 431; Brian D. Janz, Jason A. Colquitt, and Raymond A. Noe, "Knowledge Worker Team Effectiveness: The Role of Autonomy, Interdependence, Team Development, and Contextual Support Variables, *Personnel Psychology*, Winter 1997, pp. 877–904; Bradley L. Kirkman and Benson Rosen, "Powering Up Teams," *Organizational Dynamics*, Winter 2000, pp. 48–52; Gerben S. Van Der Vegt, et al., "Patterns of Interdependence in Work Teams: A Two-Level Investigation of the Relations with Job and Team Satisfaction," *Personnel Psychology*, Spring 2001, pp. 51–69.

13 Diversity and Cross-Cultural Competence

Learning Objectives

Outline

After studying the information and doing the exercises in this chapter, you should be able to:

1 Explain some of the major ways in which cultures differ from one another.

2 Pinpoint barriers to cross-cultural relations.

3 Describe techniques for improving cross-cultural relations.

4 Be sensitive to potential cultural bloopers.

5 Be prepared to overcome cross-cultural communication barriers.

6 Recognize and understand gender differences in leadership style.

7 Be aware of some of the legal aspects of working in a culturally diverse environment.

S oon after he arrived at the Wegmans Food Market Stores in Dulles, Virginia, executive chef Llewellyn Correia discovered that many of the 120 employees he supervised had not been attending the company's mandatory safety and sanitation classes. The reason he said: "The courses were in English, and many of my employees don't speak English."

Correia said some of his Asian cooks needed training in U.S. food handling standards, which are more rigorous than the ones in their home countries and more likely to be enforced by government inspectors. "It's very hard to break old habits," he said. The lack of training also was raising safety issues. "We had lots of issues like slips and falls," he said.

Today, the Dulles Wegmans offers a Web-based version of its safety and sanitation courses in Mandarin and Spanish in addition to English—only one nod the supermarket says it is making to a multilingual workplace in which more than 200 of its 650 employees do not speak English as their primary language. Wegmans has hired language instructors for its Dulles and Fairfax, Virginia, stores to teach employees a bit more English and their managers un poco Espagñol [a little Spanish].

Having a diverse workforce can boost sales and build loyalty among non-English–speaking customers who can ask a question—Are the Pepsi's 12-packs still on sale?—in their native languages. [1]

The supermarket experience described illustrates how people from different cultures can learn to work together, sometimes by using a basic technique such as offering training in several languages to facilitate learning. Being able to work well with people from other cultures, both outside and inside your own country, is important for career success. Being able to relate to a culturally diverse customer base is also necessary for success. Not only is the workforce becoming more diverse but also business has become increasingly international. Small and medium-size firms, as well as corporate giants, are increasingly dependent on trade with other countries. Furthermore, as an increasing number of jobs are sent overseas, more U.S. workers will have contact with personnel in foreign countries.

This chapter presents ideas and techniques you can use to sharpen your ability to work effectively with people from diverse backgrounds. The buzzword for this activity is to be *inclusive* in your relationships with people. We also include a discussion of antidiscrimination legislation that protects the rights of workers.

What Are the Major Dimensions of Differences in Cultural Values?

■ **Learning Objective 1**

Everything we do in work and personal life is influenced by a combination of heredity and culture, or nature and nurture. You might be thirsty at this moment because a genetically produced mechanism in your brain tells you it is time to ingest fluid. However, if you choose to drink a Diet Pepsi or papaya juice with a coworker, you are engaging in culturally learned behavior. **Culture** is a learned and shared system of knowledge, beliefs, values, attitudes, and norms. As such, culture includes an enormous amount of behavior. Here we describe seven dimensions (or facets) of cultural values that help us understand how cultures differ from each other. [2] In other words, various cultures value different types of behavior.

■ **Culture**

a learned and shared system of knowledge, beliefs, values, attitudes, and norms

Recognize that these dimensions are stereotypes, representing a typical value for a person in a given culture. You might find, for example, that most Chinese people are oriented more toward the group than seeking individual recognition. However, you might meet some Chinese people who are egotistical and self-centered.

1. **Individualism versus collectivism.** At one end of the continuum is individualism, a mental set in which people see themselves first as individuals and believe that their own interests take priority. Members of a society who value individualism are more concerned with their careers than with the good of the firm. Members of a society who value collectivism, in contrast, are typically more concerned with the organization or the work group than with themselves. An example of individualistic behavior would be to want to win an employee-of-the month award; an example of collectivisitic behavior would be to want to win an award for the team. Highly individualistic cultures include the Unites States, Canada, and the Netherlands. Japan and Mexico are among the countries that strongly value collectivism. However, with the increasing emphasis on teamwork in American culture, more U.S. workers are becoming collectivistic.

2. **Acceptance of power and authority.** People from some cultures accept the idea that members of an organization have different levels of power and authority. In a culture that believes in concentration of power and authority, the boss makes many decisions simply because he or she is the boss. Group members readily comply because they have a positive orientation toward authority, including high respect for elders. In a culture with less acceptance of power and authority, employees do not recognize a power hierarchy. They accept directions only when they think the boss is right or when they feel threatened. Cultures that readily accept power and authority include France, China, and India. Countries that have much less acceptance of power and authority are the United States and, particularly, the Scandinavian countries (e.g., Sweden).

3. **Materialism versus concern for others.** In this context, materialism refers to an emphasis on assertiveness and the acquisition of money and material objects. It also means a deemphasis on caring for others. At the other end of the continuum is concern for others, an emphasis on personal relations, and a concern for the welfare of others. Materialistic countries include Japan and Italy. The United States is considered to be moderately materialistic, as evidenced by the high participation rates in charities. Scandinavian countries all emphasize caring as a national value.

4. **Formality versus informality.** A country that values formality attaches considerable importance to tradition, ceremony, social rules, and rank. At the other extreme, informality refers to a casual attitude toward these same aspects of culture. Workers in Latin American countries highly value formality, such as lavish public receptions and processions. Americans, Canadians, and Scandinavians are much more informal. Casual observation suggests that most of the industrialized world is becoming more informal through such practices as an emphasis on using the first name only during business introductions.

5. **Urgent time orientation versus casual time orientation.** Individuals and nations attach different importance to time. People with an urgent time orientation perceive time as a scarce resource and tend to be impatient. People with a casual time orientation view time as an unlimited and unending resource and tend to be patient. Americans are noted for their urgent time orientation. They frequently impose deadlines and are eager to get started doing business. Asians and Middle Easterners, in contrast, are patient negotiators. Many corporate workers and entrepreneurs engaged in international business recognize the importance of building relationships slowly overseas.

6. **Work orientation versus leisure orientation.** A major cultural difference is the number of hours per week and weeks per year people expect to invest in work versus

leisure or other nonwork activities. American corporate professionals typically work about 55 hours per week, take 45-minute lunch breaks, and take two weeks of vacation. Japanese workers share similar values with respect to time invested in work. In contrast, many European countries have steadily reduced the workweek in recent years while lengthening vacations.

7. High-context versus low-context cultures. Cultures differ in how much importance they attach to the surrounding circumstances, or context, of an event. People from a high-context culture place more emphasis on *how* something is said rather than *what* is said. (They emphasize nonverbal communication.) For example, a person from a high-context culture is not likely to take you seriously if you smile when you say that you do not like his or her service.

High-context cultures make more extensive use of body language as part of their emphasis on nonverbal communication. Some cultures, such as the Hispanic and African American cultures, are high context. In contrast, northern European cultures are low context and make less use of body language. The Anglo American culture is considered to be medium-low context. People in low-context cultures seldom take time in business dealings to build relationships and establish trust.

MULTICULTURAL IDENTITIES AND THE CULTURAL MOSAIC

■ **Multicultural identities**

individuals who incorporate the values of two or more cultures because they identify with both their primary culture and another culture or cultures

Another complexity about understanding cultural differences is that many people have **multicultural identities** because they identify with both their primary culture and another culture or cultures. As a consequence, these people may incorporate the values of two cultures. Young people develop a global identity that gives them a feeling of belonging to a worldwide culture. The feeling of belongingness enables them to communicate with people from diverse places when they travel, when others travel to where they live, and when they communicate globally using e-mail and the telephone. Television and movies also help us develop a global identity.

Further, according to this theory, people retain a local identity along with their global identity. Young people in India provide an apt example. The country has a rapidly growing high-tech sector led mostly by young people. Yet most of these well-educated young people still cling to local traditions, such as a marriage arranged by the parents and the expectation that they will care for their parents in old age. [3]

Another complexity of culture is that a person's country is but one cultural influence. For example, people from the upper-socioeconomic group within one country or ethnic group might value education and the use of grammatically correct speech more than people from a lower-socioeconomic group.

■ **Cultural mosaic**

an individual's unique mixture of multiple cultural identities that yields a complex picture of the cultural influences on that person

The fact of multicultural identities and different values among people from the same country and ethnic groups has recently been labeled the cultural mosaic by management professors Georgia T. Chao from Michigan State University and Henry Moon of Emory University. The **cultural mosaic** refers to an individual's unique mixture of multiple cultural identities that yields a complex picture of the cultural influences on that person. Rather than choosing a particular "tile" such as race, gender, or country of origin, people develop an identity based on a mix of smaller tiles. [4] Every reader of this book is probably an example of a cultural mosaic. One of thousands of possible examples is that one person could derive a cultural identity from being a (1) U.S. citizen, (2) African American, (3) Baptist, (4) male, (5) musician, (6) football player, (7) accountant, and (8) southerner.

The religious value part of the cultural mosaic often affects when people are willing to work or not work. One potential cultural clash is that the rights of an individual to freely practice and observe religious beliefs sometimes collide with company goals. Differences in religious practices must be recognized because the number of religions in the workplace has increased substantially.

Religious diversity can create problems as more companies move to 24/7 (around-the-clock, seven-days-per-week) schedules. Employers, therefore, need more flexibility from employees, yet religious beliefs often limit times at which employees are willing to work. The message for improved understanding is that employers must recognize workers' religious beliefs. At the same time, workers must understand the importance of a company meeting the demands of the marketplace, such as having 24-hour customer service support. Workers, for example, can trade off working on each others' religious holidays.

APPLYING KNOWLEDGE OF CULTURAL DIFFERENCES IN VALUES

How might you use this information about cultural differences to improve interpersonal relationships on the job? A starting point would be to recognize that a person's national values might influence his or her behavior. Assume that you wanted to establish a good working relationship with a person from a high-context culture. Make sure your facial expression fits the content of your words. For example, do not smile when, as a supervisor, you say, "No, you cannot take off tomorrow afternoon to have your French Poodle groomed." You would also want to emphasize body language when communicating with that individual. A related point is that people from high-context cultures are more likely to touch and kiss strangers. As Fernando, who was raised in the Dominican Republic and is studying in the United States, said, "In my country I hug people I meet for the first time. When I do it here, they think I'm very rude."

What Are Some Barriers to Good Cross-Cultural Relations?

■ Learning Objective 2

Many logical reasons exist as to why people often encounter difficulties in developing good relations and communicating with people from different cultures. The fact that cultures differ in key dimensions creates some friction in cross-cultural relations. A go-getter from Brooklyn, New York, might say to himself, "Why do I have to spend three days here in Hong Kong wining and dining customers just so I can sell them an enterprise software system?"

Here we look at several of the underlying factors that create problems in developing smooth cross-cultural relations. Not being aware of the type of barriers presented next blocks effective cross-cultural relations because such lack of awareness often leads to misunderstandings. The techniques presented in the following section of the chapter are designed to overcome some these barriers. To get you started thinking about your readiness to work in a culturally diverse environment, as well as to minimize cross-cultural barriers, take Human Relations Self-Assessment Quiz 13-1.

PERCEPTUAL EXPECTATIONS

Achieving good cross-cultural relations is hampered somewhat by people's predisposition to discriminate. They do so as a perceptual shortcut, much like stereotyping. A bank customer, for example, might be communicating with a 24-year-old man about a mortgage application. Dissatisfied with his concerns about her creditworthiness, the customer might say, "Let me speak to a mortgage officer." In reality, the man *is* a mortgage officer, but the woman expects an older person to be occupying such a position. The message in this anecdote about perceptual

Human Relations Self-Assessment Quiz 13–1

Cross-Cultural Skills and Attitudes

Following are various skills and attitudes that various employers and cross-cultural experts think are important for relating effectively to coworkers in a culturally diverse environment.

	Applies to Me Now	Not There Yet
1. I have spent some time in another country.	_____	_____
2. At least one of my friends is deaf or blind or uses a wheelchair.	_____	_____
3. Currency from other countries is as real as the currency from my own country.	_____	_____
4. I can read in a language other than my own.	_____	_____
5. I can speak in a language other than my own.	_____	_____
6. I can write in a language other than my own.	_____	_____
7. I can understand people speaking in a language other than my own.	_____	_____
8. I use my second language regularly.	_____	_____
9. My friends include people of races different from my own.	_____	_____
10. My friends include people of different ages.	_____	_____
11. I feel (or would feel) comfortable having a friend with a sexual orientation different from mine.	_____	_____
12. My attitude is that although another culture may be very different from mine, that culture is equally good.	_____	_____
13. I would be willing to (or already do) hang art from different countries in my home.	_____	_____
14. I would accept (or have already accepted) a work assignment of more than several months in another country.	_____	_____
15. I have a passport.	_____	_____

Interpretation:

If you checked Applies to Me Now to 10 or more of the preceding items, you most likely function well in a multicultural work environment. If you answered Not There Yet to 10 or more of the preceding items, you need to develop more cross-cultural awareness and skills to work effectively in a multicultural work environment. You will notice that being bilingual gives you at least five points on this quiz.

Source: Several ideas for statements on this quiz are derived from Ruthann Dirks and Janet Buzzard, "What CEOs Expect of Employees Hired for International Work," *Business Education Forum*, April 1997, pp. 3–7; Gunnar Beeth, "Multicultural Managers Wanted," *Management Review*, May 1997, pp. 17–21.

expectations is important. We have to overcome this form of discrimination to enhance cross-cultural relations.

Positive expectations or stereotypes can also create some barriers to cross-cultural relations. Two company representatives were entertaining Sophie, a work associate from Jamaica. They assumed that because Sophie was black and Jamaican, she enjoyed dancing, so they invited her to a dance club. Sophie was a little taken back and said, "What makes you think I like to dance? Not every Jamaican lady has natural rhythm." Similarly, on the job, we sometimes think that everybody from a certain national group has the characteristics of that group. For example, not all

Chinese workers are methodical or precise or have good eye–hand coordination and exceptional math skills.

ETHNOCENTRISM

A key barrier to good cross-cultural relations is **ethnocentrism,** the assumption that the ways of one's culture are the *best* ways of doing things. Another part of ethnocentrism is to believe that our own way of living is essentially the only way. Most cultures consider themselves to be the center of the world, such as the French believing that any cultivated person must appreciate French painters and French wine. One consequence of ethnocentrism is that people from one culture prefer people from other cultures similar to themselves. English people, therefore, would have more positive attitudes toward Australians than they would toward Mexicans. Despite this generalization, some countries that appear to have similar cultures are intense rivals. Many Japanese and Korean people dislike each other, as do the French and Belgians. In what way do you feel your country's way of doing something is the best?

■ **Ethnocentrism**
the assumption that the ways of one's culture are the *best* ways of doing things

STEREOTYPES IN INTERGROUP RELATIONS

We described perceptual expectations as a form of stereotype that could interfere with effective cross-cultural relations. Stereotypes, in general, create some problems. As a result of stereotypes, people overestimate the probability that a given member of a group will have an attribute of his or her category. People tend to select information that fits the stereotype and reject inconsistent information. As a consequence, we readily draw conclusions about people from another cultural group without carefully listening and observing. As an Indian American business graduate reports

> I took a job with a systems consulting company. The job was supposed to involve a lot of contact with users. But because I look and sound Indian, the managers just assumed that I'm heavy into information technology. Writing code all day gives me a headache. I try to explain my preferences, but all I get is a puzzled look from my manager. [The problem here is that being placed in the wrong job can lead to dissatisfaction and costly turnover.]

DIFFERENT NORMS AND CODES OF CONDUCT

Various cultural groups have norms of their own, such as in some countries men walking ahead of the women. Also, what is permissible conduct in one group may be frowned on and even punished in another group. In the United States it is permissible for people to publish nasty (even X-rated) cartoons about political leaders without fear of reprisal by the government. In some countries such behavior will lead to long-term imprisonment. In some countries copying the products and ideas of others is an accepted business strategy, but it is considered illegal piracy in another country.

At times, we may make the mistake that others are similar to us and from become confused when they act differently from our expectations. We may unknowingly insult others from a different culture, or they many unknowingly insult us. If you are from a culture that highly values time, such as the Americans and the English (James Bond is always on time), you may be angry when your new Brazilian acquaintance arrives 30 minutes late for a party. Because most Brazilians do not adhere to rigid time schedules for social events, you have just experienced a clash of different cultural norms.

MICROINEQUITIES

Many barriers to effective cross-cultural relations surface because a person is unaware that he or she is slighting another individual, according to Mary Row, a researcher on gender and racial differences. These slights are referred to as microinequities, as you may have studied in relation to interpersonal conflict. Understanding microinequities can lead to changes in one-on-one relationships that may profoundly irritate others. [5] For example, a manager was introducing a new office assistant to the group, mentioning the name of each member one by one. However, the manager omitted mentioning the name of the one Philippine American group member.

As part of a training program in understanding microinequities, the people who are slighted are taught to confront the issue rather than let resentment build. The Philippine American worker might say tactfully to the manager, "Diane, the new assistant, was introduced to everybody but me. And I am the only Philippine in the department. Was this a coincidence?"

■ Learning Objective 3

What Are Some Approaches to Improving Cross-Cultural Relations?

By now you are probably already aware of how to improve cross-cultural relations by avoiding some of the mistakes already mentioned or implied, such as relying too heavily on group stereotypes. In this section, we take a systematic look at approaches you can use on your own along with training programs designed to improve cross-cultural relations. [6] The methods and techniques for such improvement are outlined in Figure 13-1.

DEVELOP CULTURAL SENSITIVITY AND CULTURAL INTELLIGENCE

In order to relate well to someone from a foreign country, a person must be alert to possible cultural differences. When working in another country, one must be willing to

Figure 13-1

Improving Cross-Cultural Relations

Methods and techniques

1. Develop cultural sensitivity and cultural intelligence.
2. Focus on the individual rather than groups.
3. Respect all workers and cultures.
4. Value cultural differences.
5. Minimize cultural bloopers.
6. Participate in cultural training.
7. Participate in diversity training.

Improved cross-cultural relations

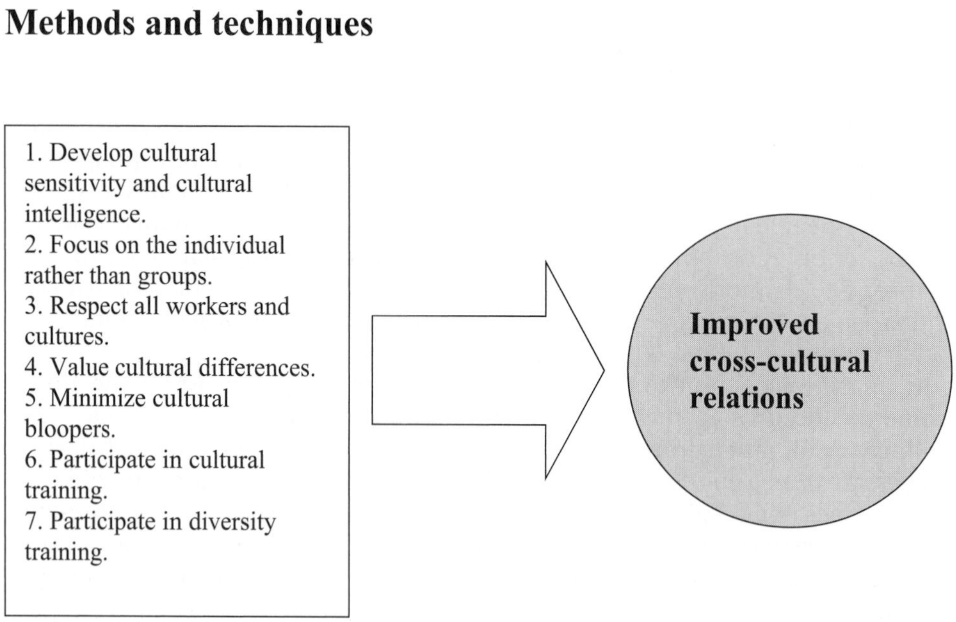

acquire knowledge about local customs and learn how to speak the native language, at least passably. When working with people from different cultures, even from one's own country, the person must be patient, adaptable, flexible, and willing to listen and learn.

These characteristics mentioned are part of **cultural sensitivity,** an awareness of and a willingness to investigate the reasons why people of another culture act as they do. [7] A person with cultural sensitivity will recognize certain nuances in customs that will help build better relationships with people from cultural backgrounds other than his or her own. A culturally sensitive person will also recognize that humor does not easily translate from one culture to another, and that some types of humor might be offensive in another culture. Assume, for example, you are having lunch with a group of Japanese workers on a trip to Japan. You begin your joke with, "This old guy walks into a bar. . . . " The Japanese workers might take offense because older people are highly respected in Japan.

One approach to enhancing cultural sensitivity is to keep in mind the types of cultural differences mentioned throughout this chapter, even down to such details as holding a fork in your left hand when dining in England and India. Another approach is to raise your antenna and observe carefully what others are doing. Suppose you are on a business trip to a different region of your country and are invited to have dinner at the plant general manager's house. You notice that she takes off her street shoes on entering the house. You do likewise to establish better rapport, even if your host says, "Oh, please don't bother." It is obvious from your host's behavior that she observes a "shoe code" in her house.

An advanced aspect of cultural sensitivity is to be able to fit in comfortably with people of another culture by observing the subtle cues they give about how a person should act in their presence. **Cultural intelligence (CQ)** is an outsider's ability to interpret someone's unfamiliar and ambiguous behavior the same way that person's compatriots would. [8] (CQ refers to a cultural quotient.) With high cultural intelligence a person would be able to figure out what behavior would be true of all people and all groups, such as rapid shaking of a clenched fist to communicate anger. Also, the person with high cultural intelligence could figure out what is peculiar to this group, and those aspects of behavior that are neither universal nor peculiar to the group. These ideas are so abstract, that an example will help clarify.

> *An American expatriate manager served on a design team that included two German engineers. As other team members floated their ideas, the engineers condemned them as incomplete or underdeveloped. The manager concluded that the Germans in general are rude and aggressive.*
>
> *With average cultural intelligence the American would have realized he was mistakenly equating the merit of an idea with the merit of the person presenting it. The Germans, however, were able to make a sharp distinction between the two. A manager with more advanced cultural intelligence might have tried to figure out how much of the two German's behavior was typically German and how much was explained by the fact that they were engineers.*

Similar to emotional intelligence, cultural intelligence encompasses several different aspects of behavior. The three sources of cultural intelligence relate to the cognitive, emotional/motivational, and the physical, explained as follows: [9]

1. **Cognitive (the head).** The cognitive part of CQ refers to what a person knows and how he or she can acquire new knowledge. Here you acquire facts about people from another culture such as their passion for football (soccer in North America), their business practices, and their promptness in paying bills. Another aspect of this source of cultural intelligence is figuring out how you can learn more about the other culture.

2. **Emotional/motivational (the heart).** The emotional/motivational aspect of CQ refers to energizing one's actions and building personal confidence. You need

■ Cultural sensitivity

an awareness of and a willingness to investigate the reasons why people of another culture act as they do

> "We have somehow been tabbed with the term Ugly Americans. It's a bad rap. I don't think we are Ugly Americans, but we are often Unprepared Americans."
> —Roger Axtell, author of eight books on business etiquette.

■ Cultural intelligence (CQ)

an outsider's ability to interpret someone's unfamiliar and ambiguous behavior the same way that person's compatriots would both confidence and motivation to adapt to another culture. A man on a business trip to the Ivory Coast in Africa might say to himself, "When I greet a work associate in a restaurant, can I really pull off kissing him on both cheeks. What if he thinks I'm weird?" With strong motivation, the same person might say, "I'll give it a try. I kind of greet my grandfather the same way back in the United States."

3. **The body (physical).** The body aspect of CQ is the action component. The body is the element for translating intentions into actions and desires. Kissing the same-sex African work associates on both cheeks is the *physical* aspect previously mentioned. We often have an idea of what we should do, but implementation is not so easy. You might know, for example, that when entering an Asian person's home you should take off your shoes, yet you might not actually remove them—thereby offending your Asian work (or personal life) associate.

To practice high cultural intelligence, the mind, heart, and body would have to work together. You would have to figure out how you have to act with people from another culture; you would need motivation and confidence to change; and you would have to translate your knowledge and motivation into action. So when you are on a business trip to Tokyo, go ahead and bow when you are introduced to the plant manager.

FOCUS ON INDIVIDUALS RATHER THAN GROUPS

Understanding broad cultural differences is a good starting point in building relationships with people from other cultures. Nevertheless, it is even more important to get to know the individual rather than relying exclusively on an understanding of his or her cultural group. Instead of generalizing about the other person's characteristics and values (such as assuming that your Mexican American coworker chooses to be late for meetings), get to know his or her personal style. You might find that this particular Mexican American values promptness and becomes anxious when others are late for a meeting. A consultant in the area of cross-cultural relations suggests that the best way to know individuals is to build personal relationships with people and not to generalize. [10]

RESPECT ALL WORKERS AND CULTURES

An effective strategy for achieving cross-cultural understanding is to simply respect all others in the workplace, including their cultures. An important component of respect is to believe that although another person's culture is different from yours, it is equally good. Respect comes from valuing differences, such as one person speaking standard English and the other favoring American Sign Language. Respecting other people's customs can translate into specific attitudes, such as respecting one coworker for wearing a yarmulke on Friday or another for wearing an African costume to celebrate Kwanzaa. Another way of being respectful would be to listen carefully to the opinion of a senior worker who says the company should never have converted to voice mail in place of assistants answering the phone (even though you disagree). An aspect of respecting all workers is the importance of respecting the rights of majorities, including white males.

Another way of showing respect for all workers and cultures is to develop supportive peer relations in the workplace with people from different cultural groups. A supportive relationship includes a feeling of closeness and trust, the sharing of thoughts and feelings, and the feeling that one is able to seek assistance from another. Such respect in the form of support doubles in importance because the creativity advantage of a diverse group is more likely to surface when there is a supportive relationship among coworkers who differ demographically. A study with

New York state employees found that peer support tends to decline when the proportion of racially different others increases. [11] A tentative interpretation of these findings is that workers find it easier to support somebody culturally different when they can focus their supportive efforts on only a few coworkers.

A major consequence of lack of respect is that it can lead to job discrimination intentionally or unintentionally. In 2006, the trendy retailer Abercrombie & Fitch settled sex discrimination and racial lawsuits. The company agreed to modify its well-known collegiate, All-American, mostly white, image by adding more African Americans, Hispanics, and Asians to its marketing materials. Abercrombie paid $40 million in fines, and agreed to hire 25 diversity recruiters and a vice president for diversity so that its hiring and promotion of minorities and women was in proportion to its applicant pool. The settlement also called for the company to increase diversity not only in hiring and promotions but also in advertisements and in catalogs.

When Abercrombie & Fitch was sued in June 2003, several Hispanic, African American, and Asian plaintiffs said that when they applied for jobs, they were steered toward backroom operations rather than sales positions. [12] If these charges were true, it would reflect lack of respect for the affected groups.

VALUE CULTURAL DIFFERENCES

Recognizing cultural differences is an excellent starting point in becoming a **multicultural worker,** one who can work effectively with people of different cultures. More importantly, however, is to *value* cultural differences. The distinction goes well beyond semantics. If you place a high value on cultural differences, you will perceive people from other cultures to be different but equally good. Gunnar Beeth, an executive placement specialist in Europe, notes that you cannot motivate anyone, especially someone of another culture, until that person first accepts you. A multilingual sales representative has the ability to explain the advantages of a product in other languages. In contrast, a multicultural sales rep can motivate foreigners to make the purchase. The difference is substantial. [13]

■ **Multicultural worker**
one who can work effectively with people of different cultures

A challenge in showing respect for other cultures is not to act revolted or shocked when a member of another culture eats something that lies outside your area of what is acceptable as food. Some westerners are shocked and repelled to find that some easterners eat insects, cats, dogs, sheep's eyeballs, chicken soup containing the feet, and rattlesnakes. Some easterners are shocked and repelled to find that westerners eat a sacred animal such as cow and are surprised about popcorn. [14]

Other cross-cultural differences in customs also represent a challenge when trying to respect another culture. An American might find it difficult to respect the Pakistani practice of having young children work in factories. In contrast, the Pakistani might find it difficult to respect the American practice of putting old relatives in nursing homes and hospices. Sometimes it takes careful reflection on one's own culture to be able to respect another culture.

A current trend in valuing cultural differences, as well as showing respect, is to be mindful of the rights of gay, lesbian, bisexual, and transgender (GLBT) employees. A leading example is Eastman Kodak Company that has earned an award from the Human Rights Campaign, a gay rights organization. Kodak executives believe that providing equitable treatment toward gay employees makes its products more appealing to the 15 million domestic gay consumers who tend to be brand-loyal. [15]

MINIMIZE CULTURAL BLOOPERS

■ **Learning Objective 4**

An effective way of being culturally sensitive is to minimize actions that are likely to offend people from another culture based on their values and customs. Cultural bloopers are most likely to take place when you are visiting another country. The same bloopers, however, can also be committed with people from a different culture within your own country. To avoid these bloopers, you must carefully observe persons from another culture. Studying another culture through reading is also helpful. Even small behaviors, such as while in France asking for ketchup to accompany an omelet, can strain a business relationship.

E-commerce and other forms of Internet communication have created new opportunities for creating cultural bloopers. The Web site developers and the workers responsible for adding content must have good cross-cultural literacy, including an awareness of how the information might be misinterpreted. Here is a sampling of potential problems:

- Numerical date formats can be readily misinterpreted. To an American, 4/9/08 would be interpreted as April 9, 2008 (or 1908!). However, many Europeans would interpret the same numerical expression as September 4, 2008.

- Colors on Web sites must be chosen carefully. For example, in some cultures purple is the color of royalty, whereas in Brazil purple is associated with death.

- Be careful of metaphors that may not make sense to a person for whom your language is a second language. Examples include "We've encountered an ethical meltdown" and "Our biggest competitor is over the hill."

International business specialist Rick Borelli recommends that being able to communicate your message directly in your customer's mother tongue provides a competitive advantage. [16] Consumers are four times more likely to purchase from a Web site written in their native language. The translator, of course, must have good knowledge of the subtleties of the language to avoid a blooper. An English-to-French translator used the verb *baiser* instead of *baisser* to describe a program of lowering prices. *Baisser* is the French verb "to lower," whereas *baiser* is the verb "to kiss." Worse, in everyday language, *baiser* is a verb that refers to having an intimate physical relationship!

Keep two key facts in mind when attempting to avoid cultural mistakes. One is that members of any cultural group show individual differences. What one member of the group might regard as an insensitive act another might welcome. Recognize also that one or two cultural mistakes will not peg you permanently as a boor. Figure 13-2 will help you minimize certain cultural bloopers.

PARTICIPATE IN CULTURAL TRAINING

■ **Cultural training**

set of learning experiences designed to help employees understand the customs, traditions, and beliefs of another culture

For many years companies and government agencies have prepared their workers for overseas assignments. The method most frequently chosen is **cultural training,** a set of learning experiences designed to help employees understand the customs, traditions, and beliefs of another culture. In today's diverse business environment and international marketplace, learning about individuals raised in different cultural backgrounds has become more important. Many industries, therefore, train employees in cross-cultural relations. Cultural training is considered essential for international workers involved with people from other cultures because negotiating styles differ across cultures. For example, the Japanese prefer an exchange of information to confrontation. Russians, in contrast, enjoy combat in negotiations. [18] (Again, we are dealing with cultural stereotypes.)

Much of the information presented in this chapter, such as understanding cultural values and bloopers, is often incorporated into cultural training. Here we describe some of the learning skills emphasized in cultural training as well as one of its frequent components, language training.

Western Europe

Great Britain	• Asking personal questions. The British protect their privacy.
	• Thinking that a business person from England is unenthusiastic when he or she says, "Not bad at all." English people understate positive emotion.
	• Gossiping about royalty.
France	• Expecting to complete work during the French two-hour lunch.
	• Attempting to conduct significant business during August—*les vacances* (vacation time).
	• Greeting a French person for the first time and not using a title such as "sir" or "madam" (or *monsieur*, *madame*, or *mademoiselle*).
Italy	• Eating too much pasta, as it is not the main course.
	• Handing out business cards freely. Italians use them infrequently.
Spain	• Expecting punctuality. Your appointments will usually arrive 20 to 30 minutes late.
	• Make the American sign for "OK" with your thumb and forefinger. In Spain (and many other countries) this is vulgar.
Scandinavia (Denmark, Sweden, Norway)	• Being overly rank conscious in these countries. Scandinavians pay relatively little attention to a person's place in the hierarchy.
	• Introducing conflict among Swedish work associates. Swedes go out of their way to avoid conflict.
Greece	• Waving good-bye by using the American hand shake. Greeks regard this practice to be an insult.

Asia

All Asian countries	• Pressuring an Asian job applicant or employee to brag about his or her accomplishments. Asians feel self-conscious when boasting about individual accomplishments and prefer to let the record speak for itself. In addition, they prefer to talk about group rather than individual accomplishments.
Japan	• Shaking hands or hugging Japanese (as well as other Asians) in public. Japanese consider the practices to be offensive.
	• Looking directly in the eye of a business acquaintance for more than a few seconds.
	• Not interpreting "We'll consider it" as a *no* when spoken by a Japanese businessperson. Japanese negotiators mean *no* when they say, "We'll consider it."
	• Not giving small gifts to Japanese when conducting business. Japanese are offended by not receiving these gifts.
	• Giving your business card to a Japanese businessperson more than once. Japanese prefer to give and receive business cards only once.
China	• Using black borders on stationary and business cards because black is associated with death.
	• Giving small gifts to Chinese when conducting business. Chinese are offended by these gifts.
	• Making cold calls on Chinese business executives. An appropriate introduction is required for a first-time meeting with a Chinese official.
Korea	• Saying *no*. Koreans feel it is important to have visitors leave with good feelings.
India	• Telling Indians you prefer not to eat with your hands. If the Indians are not using cutlery when eating, they expect you to do likewise.

Mexico and Latin America

Mexico	• Flying into a Mexican city in the morning and expecting to close a deal by lunch. Mexicans build business relationships slowly.
Brazil	• Attempting to impress Brazilians by speaking a few words of Spanish. Portuguese is the official language of Brazil.
Most Latin American countries	• Wearing elegant and expensive jewelry during a business meeting. Most Latin Americans think people should appear more conservative during a business meeting.

Note: A cultural mistake for Americans to avoid when conducting business in most countries outside the United States and Canada is to insist on getting down to business quickly. Other stereotyped American traits to avoid are aggressiveness, impatience, and frequent interruptions to get your point across. North Americans in small towns also like to build a relationship before getting down to business. Another general mistake for Americans is to use a familiar, laid-back style in locales where "business casual" is unacceptable and first names are reserved for family and friends.[17]

Figure 13-2

Cultural Mistakes to Avoid with Selected Cultural Groups

Learning Skill Dimensions of Cross-Cultural Training Program

Cultural training includes a wide variety of information and skill development, and cultural training programs vary considerably in terms of what knowledge and skills they teach. Two professors of organizational behavior, Yoshitaka Yamazaki of the International University of Japan and D. Christopher Kayes of the George Washington University, have synthesized what goes into cultural training. They identified 73 skills that are useful for expatriates (those people who live in a foreign land) in adapting to another culture. As part of their analysis, the researchers organized the 73 skills into five learning skill dimensions. [19] Figure 13-3 highlights and summarizes some of the competencies and knowledge or skill associated with the five dimensions. You will observe that much of cultural training relates to the development of human relations skills, including cultural sensitivity and cultural intelligence.

Learning Skill Dimension	Cross-Cultural Competency Cluster	Knowledge or Skill Required
Interpersonal	Building relationships	Ability to gain access to and maintain relationships with members of host culture
	Valuing people of different cultures	Empathy for differences; sensitivity to diversity
Information	Listening and observation	Knows cultural history and reasons for cultural actions and customs
	Coping with ambiguity	Recognizes and interprets implicit behavior, especially nonverbal cues
Analytical	Translating complex information	Knowledge of local language, symbols, or other forms of verbal language and written language
Action	Taking action and initiative	Understands intended and potentially unintended consequences of actions
	Managing others	Ability to manage details of a job including maintaining cohesion in a group
Adaptive	Adaptability and flexibility	Views change from multiple perspectives
	Managing stress	Understands own and other's mood, emotions, and personality

Figure 13-3

Competencies for Successful Cross-Cultural Adaptation of Expatriates
Source: Abridged from Yoshitaka Yamazaki and D. Christopher Kayes, "An Experiential Approach to Cross-Cultural Learning: A Review and Integration of Competencies for Successful Expatriate Adaptation," *Academy of Management Learning and Education*, December 2004, p. 372.

Foreign Language Training

Learning a foreign language is often part of cultural training yet can also be a separate activity. Knowledge of a second language is important because it builds better connections with people from other cultures than does relying on a translator. Many workers aside from international business specialists also choose to develop skills in a target language. Speaking another language can help build rapport with customers and employees who speak that language. Almost all language training has elements similar to taking a course in another language or self-study. Companies invest heavily in helping employees learn a target language because it facilitates conducting business in other countries. Medical specialists, police workers, and firefighters also find second-language skills to be quite helpful. Clients under stress, such as an injured person, are likely to revert to their native tongue.

Many multinational companies have downplayed the importance of American workers being fluent in a second language because English has become the standard language of commerce. [20] Despite the merits of this observation, speaking and writing well in the language of your target can help establish rapport. Furthermore, from the standpoint of career management it is worth noting that more and more highly placed managers in large companies are bilingual. Another value of foreign-language training is to better communicate with subordinates, coworkers, and customers. For example, it is estimated that in the United States, nearly two-thirds of U.S. construction workers do not speak English as their primary language. Construction supervisors who speak Spanish can prevent many accidents. [21]

As with any other skill training, these investments can only pay off if the trainee is willing to work hard developing the new skill outside the training session. It is unlikely that almost anyone can develop conversational skills in another language by listening to foreign language cassette tapes or taking classes for 30 days. The quick training program, however, helps you develop a base for further learning. Allowing even 10 days to pass without practicing your target language will result in a sharp decline in your ability to use that language.

PARTICIPATE IN DIVERSITY TRAINING

The general purpose of cultural training is to help workers understand people from other cultures. Understanding can lead to dealing more effectively with them as work associates or customers. **Diversity training** has a slightly different purpose. It attempts to bring about workplace harmony by teaching people how to get along with diverse work associates. Quite often the program is aimed at minimizing open expressions of racism and sexism. Diversity training takes a number of forms. Nevertheless, all center on increasing awareness of and empathy for people who are different in some noticeable way from oneself.

A starting point in diversity training is to emphasize that everybody is different is some way and that all these differences should be appreciated. The subtle point here is that cultural diversity does not refer exclusively to differences in race, ethnicity, age, and sex. As the United States Office of Civil Rights explains, "Diversity is a term used broadly to refer to many demographic variables, including but not limited to race, religion, color, gender, national origin, disability, sexual orientation, age, education, geographic origin, and skill characteristics." [22]

Diversity training emphasizes *inclusion*, or including everybody when appreciating diversity. The accompanying Human Relations in Practice illustrates both the scope of diversity, and how much importance companies attach to having a diverse workforce. Figure 13-4 presents a broad sampling of the ways in which workplace associates can differ from one another. All these differences are tucked under the welcoming *diversity umbrella*. Studying this list can help you anticipate the type of differences to understand and appreciate in a diverse workplace. The differences

■ **Diversity training**
program that attempts to bring about workplace harmony by teaching people how to get along with diverse work associates; often aimed at minimizing open expressions of racism and sexism

Human Relations In Practice

The Corporate Diversity Policy of Alliant Energy

A core corporate value of Alliant Energy is to be a responsible corporate citizen, caring for the environment and the communities where we do business and **encouraging diversity** in our employee and supplier ranks.

Diversity includes, but is not limited to, race, gender, age, physical and mental abilities, lifestyles, culture, education, ideas and background.

At Alliant Energy we recognize, respect, and appreciate the valuable and different perspectives that each of us bring to the work environment, our company and our customers.

Our goal is to break down barriers and create an environment that maximizes the contributions of all employees.

Source: "Corporate Diversity Policy," available at www.alliantenergy.com. (Madison, Wisconsin) Retrieved April 24, 2006.

- Race
- Sex or gender
- Religion
- Age (young, middle aged, and old)
- Generation differences, including attitudes (e.g., baby boomers versus the Net generation)
- Ethnicity (country of origin)
- Education
- Abilities
- Mental disabilities (including attention deficit disorder)
- Physical status (including hearing status, visual status, able-bodied, wheelchair user)
- Values and motivation
- Sexual orientation (heterosexual, homosexual, bisexual, transsexual)
- Marital status (married, single, cohabitating, widow, widower)
- Family status (children, no children, two-parent family, single parent, grandparent, opposite-sex parents, same-sex parents)
- Personality traits
- Functional background (area of specialization, such as marketing, manufacturing)
- Technology interest (high tech, low tech, technophobe)
- Weight status (average, obese, underweight, anorexic)
- Hair status (full head of hair, bald, wild hair, tame hair, long hair, short hair)
- Style of clothing and appearance (dress up, dress down, professional appearance, casual appearance, tattoos, body piercing including multiple earrings, nose rings, lip rings)
- Tobacco status (smoker versus nonsmoker, chewer versus nonchewer)
- Your creative suggestion

Figure 13-4

The Diversity Umbrella

include cultural as well as individual factors. Individual factors are also important because people can be discriminated against for personal characteristics as well as group characteristics. Many people who are disfigured believe they are held back from obtaining a higher-level job because of their disfigurement, such as a facial birthmark.

Another important part of diversity training is to develop empathy for diverse viewpoints. To help training participants develop empathy, representatives of various groups explain their feelings related to workplace issues. In one segment of such a program, a minority group member was seated in the middle of a circle. The other participants sat at the periphery of the circle. First, the coworkers listened to a Vietnamese woman explain how she felt excluded from the in-group composed of whites and African Americans in her department. "I feel like you simply tolerate me. You do not make me feel that I am somebody important. You make me feel that because I am Vietnamese I don't count." The next person to sit in the middle of the circle was Muslim. He complained about people wishing him Merry Christmas. "I would much prefer that my coworkers would stop to think that I do not celebrate Christian holidays. I respect your religion, but it is not my religion."

A criticism of many diversity training programs is that too many angry feelings are expressed and that negative stereotypes are reinforced, leading to strained relationships. Another criticism is that the program might be considered patronizing because the majority of participants are already respectful of people different from themselves and know how to work harmoniously with a wide variety of people.

Support for the importance of diversity training comes from a five-year study of the impact of diversity on business results conducted by Thomas A. Kochan, a professor of both management and engineering systems, at the Massachusetts Institute of Technology. He concludes that a culturally diverse workforce enhances business performance only when proper training is provided to employees. An organizational culture that supports diversity, meaning that the values and atmosphere of the firm welcome inclusion, is also required.[23] Also, a study by the Urban League found that at eight companies where diversity is a fact of life, productivity growth during the four-year period studied, exceeded that of the economy as a whole by 18 percent. "Getting serious about workforce diversity isn't just the right thing to do," notes League President Marc Morial, "It's the smart thing to do." [24]

An example of a company in the service industry that emphasizes diversity is the MGM Mirage. One of its many initiatives is the Management Associate Program, a six-month training program to prepare recent minority college graduates for careers in management. The program includes mentors, classroom instruction, job shadowing (following around a mentor) and hands-on experience. [25]

How Do You Overcome Cross-Cultural Communication Barriers?

■ **Learning Objective 5**

A key part of developing good cross-cultural relations is to overcome or prevent communication barriers stemming from cultural differences. Personal life, too, is often more culturally diverse today than previously, leading to culturally based communication problems. The information about avoiding cultural bloopers presented in this chapter might also be interpreted as a way to prevent communication barriers. Here we describe eight additional strategies and tactics to help overcome cross-cultural communication barriers.

1. Be alert to cultural differences in customs and behavior. To minimize cross-cultural communication barriers, recognize that many subtle job-related differences in customs and behavior may exist. For example, Asians typically feel uncomfortable when asked to brag about themselves in the presence of others. From their perspective, calling attention to yourself at the expense of another person is rude and unprofessional.

2. Use straightforward language and speak slowly and clearly. When working with people who do not speak your language fluently, speak in an easy-to-understand manner. Be patient for many reasons including the fact that your accent in your native tongue may not be the same as the person from whom your target learned your language. (For example, English as learned in India is quite different from English as learned in Ohio.) Minimize the use of idioms and analogies specific to your language. For example, in North America the term "over the hill" means outdated or past one's prime. A person from another culture may not understand this phrase yet be hesitant to ask for clarification. Speaking slowly is also important because even people who read and write a second language at an expert level may have difficulty catching the nuances of conversation. Facing the person from another culture directly also improves communication because your facial expressions and lips contribute to comprehension.

3. When the situation is appropriate, speak in the language of the people from another culture. Americans who can speak another language are at a competitive advantage when dealing with businesspeople who speak that language. The language skill, however, must be more advanced than speaking a few words and phrases. A new twist in speaking another language has surged recently: As more deaf people have been integrated into the workforce, knowing American Sign Language can be a real advantage to a worker when some of his or her coworkers or customers are deaf.

4. Observe cultural differences in etiquette. Violating rules of etiquette without explanation can erect immediate communication barriers. A major rule of etiquette is that in some countries older people in high-status positions expect to be treated with respect. Formality is important, unless invited to do otherwise. When visiting a company in Asia, for example, it is best to be deferent (appeal to the authority of) to company dignitaries. Visualize yourself as a company representative of a high-tech American firm that manufactures equipment for legally downloading music over the Internet. You visit Sony Corporation in Japan to speak about a joint venture. On meeting the marketing vice president, bow slightly and say something to the effect; "Mr. _____, it is my honor to discuss doing business with Sony." Do not commit the etiquette mistake of saying something to the effect, "Hi Charlie, how's the wife and kids?" (An American actually said this at a Japanese company shortly before being escorted out the door.)

5. Be sensitive to differences in nonverbal communication. Stay alert to the possibility that a person from another culture may misinterpret your nonverbal signal. To use positive reinforcement, some managers will give a sideways hug to an employee or will touch an employee's arm. People from some cultures resent touching from workmates and will be offended. Koreans in particular dislike being touched or touching others in a work setting. (Refer back to the discussion of cultural bloopers.)

6. Do not be diverted by style, accent, grammar, or personal appearance. Although all these superficial factors are related to business success, they are difficult to interpret when judging a person from another culture. It is, therefore, better to judge the merits of the statement or behavior. [26] A brilliant individual from another culture may still be learning your language and thus make basic mistakes in speaking your language. He or she might also not have developed a sensitivity to dress style in your culture.

7. Listen for understanding, not agreement. When working with diverse teammates, the differences in viewpoints can lead to conflict. To help overcome such conflict, follow the *LUNA rule:* Listen for Understanding, Not Agreement. In this way you gear yourself to consider the viewpoints of others as a first resort. For example; some older workers may express some intense loyalty to the organization, whereas their younger teammates may speak in more critical terms. By everyone listening to understand, they can begin to appreciate each others' paradigms and accept differences of opinion. [27] Listening is a powerful tool for overcoming cross-cultural communication barriers.

8. Be attentive to individual differences in appearance. A major cross-cultural insult is to confuse the identity of people because they are members of the same race or ethnic group. Psychological research suggests that people have difficulty seeing individual differences among people of another race because they code race first, such as thinking, "He has the nose of an African American." However, people can learn to search for more distinguishing features, such as a dimple or eye color.[28]

Why Are Gender Differences in Leadership Style Regarded as Cultural Differences?

■ **Learning Objective 6**

Differences in the way men and women lead can be interpreted as cultural differences because gender is one of the factors contributing to the cultural mosaic. A number of factors may contribute to a person's cultural identity, with maleness or femaleness being one contributor. Several researchers and writers argue that women have certain acquired traits and behaviors that suit them for a people-oriented leadership style. [29] Consequently, women leaders frequently exhibit a cooperative, empowering style that includes nurturing team members. According to this same perspective, men are inclined toward a command-and-control, somewhat militaristic leadership style. Women find participative management more natural than do men because they feel more comfortable interacting with people. Furthermore, it is argued that women's natural sensitivity to people gives them an edge over men to encouraging group members to participate in decision making.

The gender differences in leadership style that do exist could be attributable in part to differences in communication style between men and women. Men are more concerned about transmitting information and gaining status while they communicate, whereas women are more concerned about building social connections.

Assume that these differences in the preferred leadership style between men and women were generally true. Women managers, therefore, would be better suited for organizations that have shifted to participation and empowerment. It may be true that more women than men gravitate naturally toward the consultative, consensus, and democratic leadership styles, and men toward the autocratic. Nevertheless, there are many male leaders who find the participative style to be a good fit, and many women who are autocratic.

Even if gender differences in leadership style exist, this type of cultural difference requires a minimum of adaptation by most people. Fewer and fewer people in the workforce find it unusual or difficult to work with members of the opposite sex, even if they have a preference for working with members of their own sex.

What Are Some of the Legal Aspects of Working in a Culturally Diverse Environment?

■ **Learning Objective 7**

In this chapter we have emphasized the interpersonal aspects of building good relationships with work associates who are demographically and culturally diverse. The legal side of diversity focuses on such matters as protecting workers from being discriminated against, such as not being denied a job you are qualified for because of race, gender, age, or physical disability. However, legislation does not require workers to develop constructive relationships with each other or to develop cultural intelligence. Here we look briefly at relevant employment legislation, as well as affirmative action.

FEDERAL LAWS PROHIBITING JOB DISCRIMINATION

Workers are protected by a series of federal laws that prohibit job discrimination. In addition, states, provinces (Canada), and municipalities have their own laws governing fair treatment of employees. Furthermore, many employment lawyers bring forth law suits for discrimination not specifically mentioned in federal laws. For example, a job candidate might claim that he was denied a position for which he was qualified because he was obese. A state or local judge could then decide whether the claim was justified. The general purpose of job discrimination laws is to protect individuals who have been disadvantaged in the past because of demographic (not cultural) characteristics. Employment legislations began with prohibiting employment discrimination based on race, color, religion, sex, or national origin. Figure 13-5 summarizes Federal Equal Employment Opportunity (EEO) Laws. These laws apply to all private employers, state and local governments, and educational institutions that employ 15 or more individuals.

An effective way of understanding how these laws might affect the individual is to specify the discriminatory practices prohibited by these laws. Under Title VII, the ADA, and the ADEA, it is illegal to discriminate in any aspect of employment, including hiring and firing; compensation, assignment, or classification of employees; transfer, promotion, layoff, or recall; job advertisements; recruitment; testing; use of company facilities; training and apprenticeship programs; fringe benefits; pay, retirement plans, and disability leave; or other terms and conditions of employment. Discriminatory practices under these laws also include the following:

- Title VII of the Civil Rights Act of 1964 (Title VII) prohibits employment discrimination based on race, color, religion, sex, or national origin.
- The Equal Pay Act of 1963 (EPA) protects men and women who perform substantially equal work in the same establishment from sex-based wage discrimination.
- The Age Discrimination in Employment Act of 1967 (ADEA) protects individuals who are 40 years of age or older.
- Title I and Title V of the Americans with Disabilities Act of 1990 (ADA) prohibits employment discrimination against qualified individuals with disabilities in the private sector, and in state and local governments.
- Sections 501 and 505 of the Rehabilitation Act of 1973 prohibits discrimination against qualified individuals with disabilities who work in the federal government.
- The Civil Rights Act of 1991, among other things, provides monetary damages in cases of intentional employment discrimination.

The U.S. EEOC enforces all of these laws. EEOC also provides oversight and coordination of all federal equal employment opportunity regulations, practices, and policies.

Source: Available at www.eeoc.gov/facts/ganda.html.

Figure 13-5

Federal Laws Prohibiting Job Discrimination

1. Harassment on the basis of race, color, religion, sex, national origin, disability, or age;

2. Retaliation against an individual for filing a charge of discrimination, participating in an investigation, or opposing discriminatory practices;

3. Employment decisions based on stereotypes or assumptions about the abilities, traits, or performance of individuals of a certain sex, race, age, religion, or ethnic group, or individuals with disabilities; and

4. Denying employment opportunities to a person because of marriage to, or association with, an individual of a particular race, religion, national origin, or an individual with a disability. Title VII also prohibits discrimination because of participation in schools or places of worship associated with a particular racial, ethnic, or religious group.

Although all of these forms of discrimination may appear clear-cut, a good deal of interpretation is required to decide whether a given employee is the subject of discrimination. For example, assume that a woman files a charge of sexual harassment. Later, she is bypassed for promotion. She claims she is now the victim of discrimination, yet the company claims that she did not have the appropriate interpersonal skills to be promoted to a supervisory position.

Among the remedies awarded to individuals judged to be discriminated against are back pay, promotion, reinstatement, and the employer paying attorney's fees, and court costs. Compensatory and punitive damages are also possible.

AFFIRMATIVE ACTION

A key aspect of implementing the spirit and letter of antidiscrimination law in the United States has been affirmative action programs. **Affirmative action** consists of complying with antidiscrimination laws and correcting past discriminatory practices. Under an affirmative action program, employers actively recruit, employ, train, and promote minorities and women who have been discriminated against by an employer in the past. As a result, women and minority group members are underrepresented in certain positions. Part of an affirmative action plan might be to actively recruit Hispanic business graduates to place them in a company management training program.

> ■ **Affirmative action**
> programs that comply with antidiscrimination laws and attempt to correct past discriminatory practices

Affirmative action has been the subject of continuing debate. Proponents of affirmative action believe that it provides the opportunity many people need to prove their capability and earn just rewards. Opponents of affirmative action believe that it provides preferential treatment for certain groups and winds up discriminating against workers who are qualified but do not fit an affirmative action category. The National Leadership Network of Black Conservatives is an example of a group strongly opposed to affirmative action. The National Leadership Network supports the position that affirmative action is wrong because it is "a system rooted in the belief that blacks and certain other minorities cannot hope to win if they have to compete on a level playing field." [30] What is your opinion about the merits of affirmative action?

Concept Review and Reinforcement

Key Terms

Summary and Review

Being able to work well with people from other cultures, both outside and inside your own country, is important for career success. Seven dimensions of cultural values that help us understand how cultures differ from one another are as follows:

- individualism versus collectivism
- acceptance of power and authority
- materialism versus concern for others
- formality versus informality
- urgent time orientation versus casual time orientation
- work orientation versus leisure orientation
- high-context versus low-context cultures (with an emphasis on body language)

Many people have multicultural identities because they identify with their own culture as well as other cultures. Similarly, according to the cultural mosaic, people have a rich mixture of cultural identities. The religious value part of the cultural mosaic often affects when people are willing to work or not work. It is important to be alert to possible cultural differences.

Certain underlying factors create problems in developing smooth cross-cultural relations, including communication problems.

- Perceptual expectations are much like stereotypes that lead to misunderstandings.
- Ethnocentrism, or thinking that one's culture is best, leads to misunderstandings.
- Misunderstandings also come about from stereotypes in intergroup relations.
- Different cultural norms and codes of conduct can lead to confusion.
- Microinequities also create problems.

Six specific methods and techniques for improving cross-cultural relations are as follows:

- Develop cultural sensitivity (being aware of differences) and cultural intelligence (cognitive, emotional, and body components).
- Focus on individuals rather than groups.
- Respect all workers and cultures.
- Value cultural differences (this also involves showing respect).
- Minimize cultural bloopers (embarrassing mistakes).
- Participate in cultural training, including language training. (The skill dimensions of cross-cultural training are interpersonal, information, analytic, action, and adaptive.)
- Participate in diversity training, or learning to get along with diverse work associates.

Cross-cultural communication barriers can often be overcome by the following:

- being alert to cultural differences in customs and behavior
- using straightforward language and speaking slowly and clearly
- speaking in the language of the other group
- observing cultural differences in etiquette
- being sensitive to differences in nonverbal communication
- not being diverted by style, accent, grammar, or personal appearance
- listening for understanding, not agreement
- being attentive to individual differences in appearance.

Gender differences in leadership style have been observed that could be interpreted as cultural differences between men and women. Women tend toward a cooperative, empowering style that includes nurturing team members. It is argued that men lean toward a command-and-control autocratic style.

The legal side of diversity focuses on such matters as protecting workers from discrimination, but is not part of developing cross-cultural competence. Workers are protected by a series of federal, state, and municipal laws that govern fair treatment of employees. It is illegal to discriminate in any aspect of employment including hiring and firing, compensation, and recruitment. Affirmative action programs consist of complying with antidiscrimination laws and correcting past discriminatory practices.

Check your Understanding

1. What does it really mean to say that every member of the workforce is different in some way?
2. In what way might having a high acceptance for power and authority make it difficult for a person to work well on a team that has very little supervision?
3. Identify three positive stereotypes about cultural groups that are related to job behavior. (An example would be the observation that Mexican laborers are known for their hard work and dependability.)
4. When you meet someone from another culture, what can you do to demonstrate that you respect that person's culture?
5. Provide an example of cultural insensitivity of any kind that you have seen, read about, or could imagine.
6. Imagine that you are trying hard to "Do as Romans do when in Rome" in a foreign country. You are attending a business dinner and your host invites you to eat a meal that is composed of an animal you consider to be a household pet. How would you handle this situation?
7. All the cultural bloopers presented in Figure 13-2 dealt with errors people make in regard to people who are not American. Give an example of a cultural blooper that a person from another country might make in the United States.
8. In an era of welcoming cultural diversity, does a company have the right to exclude employees with visible body piercings from any type of positions?
9. Suppose a company wants to promote cross-cultural understanding. Should the executives then discourage students from one racial or ethnic group from forming a club or sitting together in the company cafeteria? Explain your position.
10. Many people speak loudly to deaf people, blind people, and those who speak a different language. Based on the information presented in this chapter, what mistakes are these people making?
11. Why are gender differences in leadership style referred to as cultural differences?

Web Corner

Cultural training:
www.berlitz.com; www.culturalsavvy.com (Click on/ "Tips & Info.")

Cultural diversity:
www.DiversityInc.com

Internet Skill Builder: Developing Your Multicultural Skills

A useful way of developing skills in a second language and learning more about another culture is to create a cover page (the page that appears when you open a Web site) written in your target language. In this way, each time you go the Internet on your own computer, your cover page will contain fresh information in the language you want to develop.

Assume that your target language is French. Enter a phrase such as "French language newspaper" or "French current events" in the search probe. Once you find a suitable choice, insert that newspaper as your cover page. The search engine might have brought you to www.france2.fr or www.cyberpresse.ca. These Web sites keep you abreast of French and French Canadian international news, sports, and cultural events—written in French. Now every time you access the Internet, you can spend a few minutes becoming multicultural. You can save lot of travel costs and time using the Internet to help you become multicultural.

Developing Your Human Relations Skills

Human Relations Application Exercises

Applying Human Relations Exercise 13–1

Avoiding Cultural Mistakes

Refer back to Figure 13-2, Cultural Mistakes to Avoid with Selected Cultural Groups. Review the list of cultural groups mentioned. After you have chosen one or two cultural groups, imagine how and where you might have an opportunity to relate to someone from one of these culture groups. During the next 30 days, look for an opportunity to relate to a person from another culture in the way described in these suggestions. You may have to be creative to find a target with whom you can practice your cross-cultural skills. Before approaching your target, answer these questions:

1. What would be my usual approach to dealing with a person from that culture? (An example here would be as follows: "Usually when I visit the neighborhood convenience store operated by a Korean family, I attempt to place the money for purchases directly in the hands of the cashier.)

2. What will I do differently after studying the suggestions in Figure 13-2? (Because touching a Korean's hand might be uncomfortable for him or her, I will lay the money on the counter and let the cashier pick it up.)

Observe the reaction of the other person for feedback on your cross-cultural effectiveness. Then assess whether your approach to improving cross-cultural relations had any effect on your target.

Applying Human Relations Exercise 13–2

Developing Empathy for Differences

Class members come up to the front of the room one by one and give a brief presentation (perhaps even three minutes) of any way in which they have been perceived as different and how they felt about this perception. The difference can be of any kind, relating to characteristics such as ethnicity, race, major field of study, physical appearance, height, weight, hair color, or body piercing. (Here is an example repeatedly heard from very tall people: "I am so tired of the same old stupid comment, 'How is the weather up there.' It also annoys me that so many people ask me to change a light bulb in a highly placed fixture. Even worse, because I'm tall, people think I would want to help them move furniture." An example heard frequently from information technology students is as follows: "When I'm out socially, people are forever asking me about some software problem they are facing. They think I know all about every software package ever written. Even worse, they think I have no life outside of computers. Why should I want to talk about computer problems when I'm partying?"

After each member of the class has presented (perhaps even the instructor), class members discuss what they learned from the exercise. Points to look for include the following:

- What pattern do you see in the ways people perceive themselves to be different?
- What is the most frequent difference reported by class members?
- What kind of perceptions by others seem to hurt the most?

It is also important to discuss how this exercise can improve relationships on the job. What would be at least one take-away from the exercise?

Human Relations Case Study 13–1

Are Americans Abroad Really That Bad?

Trying to combat anti, U.S. sentiment abroad, a campaign is underway to give the "ugly American" a makeover and improve the business manners of business travelers overseas. Employees and executives of some big corporations who are bound for other countries will receive a "World Citizens Guide" brochure with 16 tips to improve the image of the United States, such as trying to speak a little of foreign languages and refraining from too much talk about wealth, power, status, or American pride. The program began in May 2006 and expanded in the fall of that year to include a one-day seminar.

"We are broadly seen throughout the world as an arrogant people, totally self-absorbed and loud," said Keith Reinhard, chair emeritus of DDB Worldwide Inc. who is leading the effort through a group called Business for Diplomatic Action Inc., a nonprofit organization that tries to get U.S. companies to work to improve the reputation of the United States in the world.

AMR Corp.'s American Airlines, Lowe's Cos. and Novell Inc. have signed up for the program, the group says. Exxon Mobil Corp., Microsoft Corp., and Weyerhaeuser Co. have officials on the Board of Business for Diplomatic Action, and are expected to join the campaign, which is being funded by the National Business Travelers Association, a group of corporate travel managers. More than 40 large companies have been approached so far, according to NBTA, and about half expressed interest in participating.

Some companies cringe at the suggestion that their employees and executives are in need of "Miss Manners"–style lessons, and Reinhard's group runs into doubters who say personal interactions will do little to greatly shift the perception of U.S. citizens around the world. A State Department effort to enlist Madison Avenue to boost American's image globally fell flat shortly after September 11, 2001.

Business for Diplomatic Action has held discussions with the State Department about distributing its World Citizens Guide to every U.S. passport holder and putting it on the State Department's Web site. No decision has been reached.

The group's advice includes tried-and-true international travel suggestions, such as reminders that in Japan it is considered rude to look directly in the eye for more than a few seconds, and in Greece the hand-waving gesture commonly used in America for good-bye is considered an insult.

But it also covers stereotypical American traits such as boastfulness, loudness, and speed. The guide urges travelers to eat slower, speak slower, move slower, and dress up when abroad because casual dress can be a sign of disrespect. Tone down talk of religion, politics, and national pride, as well as your voice. "Listen as much as you talk," the guide says, and "save the lectures for your kids."

"Anger, impatience, and rudeness are universal turnoffs," the guide says, imploring employees to "Help your country while you travel for your country."

Reinhard, a prominent advertising executive who created slogans such as "You deserve a break today" and "Two all-beef patties. . .," said he started looking for ways to polish the image of the United States when he heard President Bush express dismay shortly after September 11 that "people did not like us" in other parts of the world.

Many of the suggestions offered in the World Citizens Guide stem from the results of a survey taken by an affiliate of DDB in 130 countries. The questions asked about how America was viewed and what Americans could do to make a better impression overseas. Business executives around the world were also interviewed for their opinion on the same topic.

Questions

1. How effective do you think the World Citizens Guide will be in fostering cross-cultural understanding?
2. How effective do you think the World Citizens Guide (and related seminars) will be in developing better relations between American businesspeople and their customers and affiliates overseas?
3. One criticism of this initiative by the Business for Diplomatic Action is that major U.S. foreign-policy decisions and events such as the Iraq war far outweigh manners when it comes to shaping the perception of Americans overseas. What do you think of this criticism?

Source: Adapted from Scott McCartney, "Teaching Americans How to Behave Abroad: Fearing Anti-U.S. Backlash, Big Companies Team Up to Offer Advice to Executives," *The Wall Street Journal*, April 11, 2006, pp. D1, D4.

Human Relations Case Study 13–2

The Multicultural Dealership

Manuel Ortiz is the owner and operator of Futura Motors, a large automobile and small-truck dealership in Brooklyn, New York. The dealership represents several Japanese and Korean vehicle manufacturers. For more than a decade, Ortiz and his management team have invested time, effort, and money into building culturally diverse sales and service staffs to better serve the many ethnic, cultural, and racial groups that make up the dealership's customer base. Ortiz brags that in total his sales staff speaks 13 different languages. "In this way we can communicate in the native tongue of almost any customer or sales prospect who shows up on the floor," says Ortiz. (A *sales prospect* is anyone who visits Futura without the full intention of purchasing a vehicle from the dealership, including the people who are "just looking.") The culturally diverse sales and service staffs apparently have contributed to the growth and profitability of Futura, although such an assertion would be difficult to prove. For example, Ortiz has not been able to compare the dollar volume of Futura to a comparable size foreign dealership in Brooklyn that has a more homogeneous workforce.

Penny Shakelford, the office manager at Futura, has recently brought a potential problem to Ortiz's attention that has caused him some concern about how well he and his staff are managing diversity. According to Shakelford, the multicultural sales staff appears to be well accepted by most customers and prospects, yet some problems are surfacing. Based on direct concerns expressed by both customers and prospects, Shakelford believes that they are being patronized on the basis of their demographic group. She explains:

"My impression is that some customers think we are bending over backwards to make them feel at home. If a person who walks on the floor appears to be an African American, immediately an African American sales rep walks up to him or her. The same goes for several other visible ethnic or racial groups. Two different Asiatic Indians wrote down on customer service survey cards that they thought it was too obvious that an Indian rushed out on the floor as soon as they appeared.

"A Mexican American woman said she thought it was a little bit much that three minutes after she and her husband walked into the dealership, a young sales rep introduced himself in Spanish. The customer said she was in Brooklyn, not Mexico City, and wanted to be treated like an American."

Ortiz said that it appears that the vast majority of customers and prospects find no problem with our attempt to make a direct appeal to their racial or ethnic group but that maybe some adjustment needs to be made.

"We need to give this problem some thought. We don't want to insult anybody, but neither do we want to lose our competitive edge of having a multicultural workforce."

Questions

1. What is your opinion of the merits of a vehicle dealership attempting to match the demographic group of a customer with a sales rep of the same demographic group?
2. What do you recommend Ortiz and his management team do about the several complaints the Futura dealership has received.
3. To help you analyze this case, get the input from a few people in your network about how they would feel about having a person from their demographic group approach them when they visited a dealership. (Perhaps a few classmates representing different ethnic groups can provide useful input.)

REFERENCES

1. Bill Brubaker, "Diverse Work Force Creates Challenges for Wegmans," *Washington Post* syndicated story, December 28, 2005.
2. Geert Hofstede, *Culture's Consequences: International Differences in Work-Related Values* (Beverly Hills, CA: Sage, 1980); updated and expanded in "A Conversation with Geert Hofstede," *Organizational Dynamics*, Spring 1993, pp. 53–61; Harry Triandis, The Many Dimensions of Culture," *Academy of Management Executive*, February 2004, pp. 88–93.
3. Jeffrey Jensen Arnett, "The Psychology of Globalization," *American Psychologist*, October 2002, pp. 777–778.
4. Georgia T. Chao and Henry Moon, "The Cultural Mosaic: A Methodology for Understanding the Complexity of Culture," *Journal of Applied Psychology*, November 2005, pp. 1128–1140.
5. Gary M. Stern, "Small Slights Bring Big Problems," *Workforce*, August 2002, p. 17.
6. Based on the contribution of Terri Geerinck in Andrew J. DuBrin and Terri Geerinck, *Human Relations for Career and Personal Success*, 2nd Canadian ed. (Toronto: Prentice Hall, 2001), p. 201. Geerinck also contributed the idea of a separate chapter on cross-cultural competency.
7. Arvind V. Phatak, *International Dimensions of Management* (Boston: Kent, 1983), p. 167.
8. P. Christopher Earley and Elain Mosakowski, "Cultural Intelligence," *Harvard Business Review*, October 2004, p. 140. The example is from the same source, same page.
9. Earley and Mosakowski, "Toward Cultural Intelligence: Turning Cultural Differences into Workplace Advantage," *Academy of Management Executive*, August 2004, pp. 154–155.
10. Todd Raphael, "Savvy Companies Build Bonds with Hispanic Employees," *Workforce*, September 2001, p. 19.
11. Samuel B. Bacharach, Peter A. Bamberger, and Dana Vashdi, "Diversity and Homophilly at Work: Supportive Relations among White and African-American Peers," *Academy of Management Journal*, August 2005, pp. 619–644.
12. Steven Greenhouse, "Abercrombie & Fitch Bias Case Is Settled," *The New York Times*, available at nytimes.com, retrieved November 17, 2004.
13. Gunnar Beeth, "Multicultural Managers Wanted," *Management Review*, May 1997, p. 17.
14. A few of these tasty morsels are from Lillian H. Chaney and Jeannette S. Martin, *Interpersonal Business Communication*, 3rd ed. (Upper Saddle River, NJ: Pearson Prentice Hall, 2004), p. 190.
15. Todd Henneman, "Acceptance of Gays, Lesbians, Is a Big Part of Kodak's Diversity Picture," *Workforce Management*, December 2004, p. 68.
16. Rick Borelli, "A Worldwide Language Trap," *Management Review*, October 1997, pp. 52–54.
17. The comment about informality is credited to Jacqueline Whitmore as cited in Michael Peltier, "Etiquette Lessons," *Time*, January 31, 2005, p. A4.
18. Marc Diener, "Culture Shock," *Entrepreneur*, July 2003, p. 77.
19. Yoshitaka Yamazaki and D. Christopher Kayes, "An Experiential Approach to Cross-Cultural Learning: A Review and Integration of Competencies for Successful Expatriate Adaptation," *Academy of Management Learning & Education*, December 2004, pp. 362–379.
20. Gretchen Weber, "English Rules," *Workforce Management*, May 2004, p. 48.
21. Donna M. Owens, "Multilingual Workforces," *HR Magazine*, September 2005, p. 127.
22. Definition from the U.S. Department of the Interior, Office of Civil Rights, as quoted in Janet Perez, "Diversity Inside-Out," *Hispanic Business*, April 2006, p. 64.
23. Research reported in Fay Hansen, "Diversity's Business Case Doesn't Add Up," *Workforce*, April 2003, pp. 28–32.
24. Facts and quote from Anne Fisher, "How You Can Do Better on Diversity," *Fortune*, November 15, 2004, p. 60.
25. Janet Perez, "A Fresh Deck: Publicly Traded MGM Begins Dealing Diversity," *Hispanic Business*, January/February 2006, p. 62.
26. David P. Tulin, "Enhance Your Multi-Cultural Communication Skills," *Managing Diversity*, 1, 1992, p. 5.
27. "Use Team's Diversity to Best Advantage, *ExecutiveSTRATEGIES*, April 2000, p. 2.
28. Siri Carpenter, "Why Do 'They All Look Alike'?" *Monitor on Psychology*, December 2000, p. 44.
29. One example of this research is Robert J. Kabacoff, "Gender Differences in Organizational Leadership," Management Research Group, Portland, Maine, as reported in "Do Men and Women Lead Differently?" *Leadership Strategies*, Premier Issue, copyright 2001, Briefings Publishing Group.
30. The National Leadership Network of Black Conservatives, Affirmative Action Information Center, available at *www.nationalcenter.org/AA.html*; Retrieved April 23, 2006, Jeff Jacoby, "On Flattering Minorities, *townhall.com*, May 19, 2004.

14 Getting Ahead in Your Career

Learning Objectives

Outline

After studying the information and doing the exercises in this chapter, you should be able to:

1 Identify job-finding methods and use the Internet to assist you in your job search.

2 Prepare an effective cover letter and job résumé, and prepare for the job interview.

3 Select several strategies and tactics for getting ahead in your career by taking control of your own behavior.

4 Select several strategies and tactics for advancing your career by exerting control over your environment.

5 Understand networking techniques and be ready to implement them.

indy Gikas was interviewing a senior Level manager on the phone when suddenly the job candidate paused. He said he was reading an e-mail, recalls Ms. Gikas, a managing director for Ogilvy Public Relations Worldwide, a unit of WPP Group of London. "It showed me that his conversation with me wasn't very important," she explains. He wasn't invited to interview in person. [1]

You might be saying to yourself, "How could any senior level manager be so stupid when conducting a job search? Doesn't he have any common sense? Doesn't he know any telephone etiquette?" In reality, when it comes to job finding and career management many people can use a refresher about the basics. In this chapter we review a few basic ideas about conducting a job campaign as part of the major theme of getting ahead in your career. We have divided the vast information about career advancement into three sections. The first section deals with approaches to managing or taking control of your own behavior to advance or retain a good position. The second section deals with approaches to exerting control over your environment to improve your chances for success. The third section deals with networking, the most widely accepted career advancement strategy. To begin relating career development to yourself, do Human Relations Self-Assessment Quiz 14-1.

Human Relations Self-Assessment Quiz **14-1**

The Career Development Inventory

Career development activities inevitably include answering some penetrating questions about yourself, such as the 12 questions that follow. You may need several hours to do a competent job answering these questions. After individuals have answered these questions by themselves, it may be profitable to hold a class discussion about the relevance of the specific questions. A strongly recommended procedure is for you to date your completed inventory and put it away for safekeeping. Examine your answers in several years to see (1) how well you are doing in advancing your career and (2) how much you have changed.

Keep the following information in mind in answering this inventory: People are generous in their self-evaluations when they answer career development inventories. So you might want to discuss some of your answers with somebody else who knows you well.

1. How would you describe yourself as a person?
2. What are you best at doing? Worst?
3. What are your two biggest strengths or assets?
4. What skills and knowledge will you need to acquire to reach your goals?
5. What are your two biggest accomplishments?
6. Write your obituary as you would like it to appear.
7. What would be the ideal job for you?
8. What career advice can you give yourself?
9. Describe the two peak work-related experiences in your life.
10. What are your five most important values (the things in life most important to you)?
11. What goals in life are you trying to achieve?
12. What do you see as your niche (spot where you best fit) in the modern world?

What Are the Basics of Conducting a Job Search?

■ **Learning Objective 1**

The purpose of this section is to provide a review of a few key ideas you need to conduct a successful job search, including sources of job leads, preparation of a cover letter and job résumé, and performing well in a job interview. Although job search knowledge is readily available, this concise information can be used as a refresher and a reminder to be systematic in finding a new position. We also present a few fine points to help give you an edge over those who do the minimum necessary to find a new position.

TARGET YOUR JOB SEARCH

A job search begins with a reasonably flexible description of the type of job or jobs for which you are looking. Flexibility is called for because, with so many different jobs available, it is difficult to be too specific. Also, flexibility with respect to the type of employer is important. For example, many job seekers overlook the possibilities of working for the U.S. government. The federal government hires graduates in dozens of fields, and the starting pay is competitive with similar private-sector jobs. [2] Your chances of finding suitable employment are directly proportional to the number of positions that will satisfy your job objectives. One person with a degree in information technology might be interested exclusively in working in the information systems division of a major corporation. Another person with the same background is willing to work in the information technology field for a large company, a small company, a high-tech start-up, a government agency, or an educational institution. The second person has a better chance than the first of finding a job in a geographic location he or she wants.

Closely tied in with the type of work you are seeking is the type of organization in which you would prefer to work. You are much more likely to be successful in your new job and your career when you find a good **person–organization fit,** the compatibility of the individual and the organization. In other words, what type of organization culture (or atmosphere) would fit you best? Based on many studies, the evidence is strong that your job satisfaction will be higher, and you are likely to stay longer with an employer, when there is a good person–organization fit. In addition to fitting in well with the organization, it is also important to fit your job, group, and supervisor. [3]

Unless you have had exposure to different types of organizations, you may have only tentative answers to this question. Questioning people who work at different places can provide you with some useful clues. A vital source of input about a prospective employer is present and past employees. Further, plant tours open to the public can provide valuable tips about what it is like to work in a particular firm.

Visits to stores, restaurants, and government agencies will provide informal information about the general nature of working conditions in those places. Using the Internet to find facts about a company has become standard practice. The Internet search includes the firm's Web site as well as news stories about the company. Also, the time spent talking to your prospective supervisor and coworkers is time well spent.

■ **Person–organization fit**
the compatibility of the individual and the organization

JOB-FINDING THROUGH NETWORKING AND THE INTERNET

Two cornerstone principles of conducting a job campaign are to use several different methods and keep trying. These two principles should be applied because most approaches to job finding are inefficient yet effective. *Inefficient* refers to the fact that a person might have to make many contacts to find only one job. Yet the system is *effective* because it does lead to a desired outcome—finding a suitable position. He we look at two of dozens of possible methods for conducting a job search, social networking and the Internet.

Networking (Contacts and Referrals)

The most effective method of finding a job is through personal contacts. **Networking** is the process of establishing a group of contacts who can help you in your career. Networking is particularly helpful because it taps you into the "insider system" or "internal job market." The internal job market is the large array of jobs that haven't been advertised and are usually filled by word of mouth or through friends and acquaintances of employees. Traditional wisdom states that the vast majority of job openings are found in the internal job market. However, according to recruiting specialists, the insider system is no longer so dominant. Recruiter Gerry Crispin estimates that job seekers can track down as many as 80 to 90 percent of existing job openings by sifting through the career section of an employer's Web site in addition to searching other Internet sites and print media. [4]

The best way to reach the jobs in the internal market is by getting someone to recommend you for one. When looking for a job, it is, therefore, important to tell every potential contact of your job search. The more influential the person, the better. Be specific about the type of job you are seeking. When workers are in short supply, some companies give cash bonuses and prizes to employees for referring job candidates to them. To use networking effectively, it may be necessary to create contacts aside from those you already have. Networking is time consuming yet is usually well worth the effort. Potential sources of contacts for your network include the following: friends, family members, faculty and staff, athletic team members, professional associations, and career and job fairs.

A growing development in job-search networking is to join an on-line networking site, such as *LinkedIn.com* or *Friendster.com*. The major purpose of these sites is for members to help each other find jobs. Some sites emphasize professional contacts, whereas others focus on developing friendships. A growing number of employers recruit directly through these sites. The usefulness of on-line networking increases when you meet face-to-face a few of the most promising contacts.

An important caution about networking: Too many people are consuming too much of other people's time to help them with their job searches. Keep your request for assistance brief and pointed. Ask to reciprocate in any way you can. For example, you might prepare a chart or conduct research for a manager who gave you a job lead.

The Internet and Résumé Database Services

Using the Internet, for little or no cost, the job seeker can post a résumé or scroll through hundreds of job opportunities. Web sites such as Career Mosaic and E-Span are résumé database services because they give employers access to résumés submitted by job hunters. It is also helpful to look for job Web sites for a specific field, such as information technology, finance, or sales. Also, as implied previously, the employment section of company Web sites can be as effective as general job boards in finding job leads.

Job hunting on the Internet can lead to a false sense of security. Using the Internet, a résumé is cast over a wide net, and hundreds of job postings can be explored. As a consequence, the job seeker may think that he or she can sit back and wait for a job offer to come through the e-mail. In reality, the Internet is only one source of leads that should be used in conjunction with other job-finding methods. Thousands of other job seekers can access the same job openings, and many of the positions listed have already been filled.

■ **Networking**

the process of establishing a group of contacts who can help you in your career; establishing contacts to find a better position, become a customer, become a valuable supplier, solve difficult problems, or find a mentor; people in a network also offer emotional support

A major challenge of job hunting through the Internet is finding a way to speak to a company representative about your application. Telephoning the human resources department of a large company usually leads to a voice mail system with a lengthy menu and rarely a return call. A plausible approach to making a personal contact is to call the main number of your target company and tap the operator button. Ask for the department where you hope to work, and you may be able to establish a personal contact—provided that you do not encounter another lengthy menu. Marc Cenderella, the president of an electronic newsletter and job board for high-level positions, offers this advice: "Hitting 'send' is not the end. You still need to get on the phone, take people to lunch, and work your way to the top of the résumé pile the old-fashioned way." [5]

Despite the cautions mentioned, many job seekers do find jobs through job boards and company Web sites. Keep in mind that the Internet is only one approach to conducting a job search.

The T-Form Cover Letter

■ **Learning Objective 2**

We all know that a cover letter must accompany a résumé sent on-line or through the postal mail. A novel format for a cover letter to consider is one that systematically outlines how the applicant's qualifications match up against the job requirements posted in the position announcement. The T-form (or column) approach gives the reader a tabular outline of how the applicant's background fits the position description. The T-form cover letter, presented in Figure 14-1, is also recommended because it has an attention-getting format. [6]

Preparing an Effective Job Résumé

The major purpose of a résumé is to present a targeted message that will help you obtain a job interview, not a job. A résumé is needed both as an outside candidate and often when seeking a transfer within a large firm. Effective résumés are straightforward, factual presentations of a person's experiences, education, skills, and

---

Dear Sales Manager:

In response to your recent advertisement in the Atlanta Gazette and on the Monster Board for telemarketing sales professionals, please consider the following:

REQUIREMENTS	MY QUALIFICATIONS
Prior sales experience a must	Two years of full-time and part-time selling including retail and magazine subscription renewals
Great communicator	Two different managers praised my communication skills; received an A in two communication skills courses
Self-motivated	Worked well without supervision; considered to be a self-starter
Reliable	Not one sick day in two years; never late with a class assignment

Your opportunity excites me, and I would be proud to represent your company. My résumé is enclosed for your consideration.
Sincerely,

Figure 14-1

The T-Form Cover Letter

accomplishments. A challenge in preparing an effective résumé is to suit many different preferences. To add to the confusion, some people spell *résumé* with the acute accents (*résumé* is a French word) and some without.

Résumé length illustrates how employers hold different opinions about the best résumé format. For people of limited job experience, a one-page résumé is usually sufficient. For candidates with more experience, two pages may suffice. A *curriculum vitae* (CV) is used to provide a more comprehensive work and education history of the sender and can easily run to more than six pages. [7] A CV is used primarily by professors and scientists and would include such detailed information as publications, patents, and committee experience.

Information about résumé construction is readily available. For example, Microsoft Word includes job résumé templates under File | New | Other Documents. You will find there templates for contemporary, elegant, and professional résumés plus a résumé wizard that helps you construct an individualized résumé. Done properly, a résumé can lead to an interview with a prospective employer. Done poorly, it will block you from further consideration. *Poor* refers to such features as misspellings, misuse of words, disorganization, lack of accurate contact information, too many abbreviations and acronyms, and too much unaccounted for blocks of time. Job candidates who are found to have misrepresented facts (such as pretending to have graduated from a particular school) on a résumé are immediately disqualified.

Whichever style of résumé you choose, it should include a section about your job-related skills and accomplishments. A *skill* is an activity, such as preparing a PowerPoint presentation, compiling a research report on consumer preferences, or translating documents from Spanish to English. Most employers hire for skills, so being specific about your skills in a résumé is essential. (Skill description is also quite important during a job interview.) Skills can be based on academic pursuits, paid work, volunteer work, and sometimes sports such as a team captain mentioning "activity scheduling" as a skill. Remember though, a skill is something you can do now and does not refer to a course you once took, unless you have practiced the skill learned in the course.

The skills mentioned on your résumé might be incorporated into the summary section. Jeevan DeVore, vice president of operations for **Career-Perfect.com** writes that a résumé should have a brief but compelling summary to catch the potential employer's within the first 10 seconds. After that, enough depth and detail can be presented to hold the reader's interest. [8]

The Successful Job Interview

A successful job campaign results in one or more employment interviews. Screening interviews are often conducted by telephone, particularly for customer service positions requiring telephone skills. An effective way of preparing for a telephone interview is to prepare a 30-second presentation of yourself including your name, your schooling, job experience, and the type of job you want. Keep working at your presentation until you reduce it to 30 seconds of clear, useful information.

More extensive interviews are usually conducted in person. Being interviewed by one person at a time is still standard practice. Many firms, however, also conduct group interviews in which the job candidates speak to several prospective work associates at the same time. Often the group interview is conducted in a casual environment, such as a restaurant or company cafeteria. The candidate may not be aware that meeting with the group is actually an interview and that he or she is being judged.

Another important development in employee interviewing is the **behavioral interview,** in which a candidate is asked how he or she handled a particular problem in the past. Such an interview is essentially a job sample because the interviewee is asked how a problem was dealt with in the past. An example of a behavioral

■ **Behavioral interview**
a candidate is asked how he or she handled a particular problem in the past

interview questions is as follows: "Tell me how you dealt with an angry customer. What was the problem, and what was the outcome?" Behavioral interviews are used frequently because they seem more related to job behavior than personal characteristics, general interview impressions, or test scores. Of course, this assertion neglects the important fact that a person with strong potential may never have handled the type of job situation presented yet could do so in the future.

Becoming a skillful interviewee requires practice. You can acquire this practice as you go through the job-finding process. In addition, you can rehearse simulated job interviews with friends and other students. Practice answering the questions posed in Figure 14-2. You might also think of several questions you would not like to be asked and develop answers for them. Think through how you have handled difficult job situations, such as dealing with a tight deadline or resolving conflict with a customer, so you can describe these situations during an interview.

Videotaping the practice interviews is especially helpful because it provides feedback on how you presented yourself. In watching the replay, pay particular attention to your spoken and nonverbal communication skills. Then make adjustments as needed. Many colleges of business and career schools require students to be videotaped before they go out on job interviews.

A general guide for performing well in the job interview is to present a positive but accurate self-picture. Your chances of performing well in a job increase if you are suited for the job. An effective job-getting tactic is to explain to a prospective employer what you think you can do to help the company. Look for opportunities to make **skill–benefit statements**—brief explanations of how your skills can benefit the company. If you were applying for a billing specialist position in a company that you knew was having trouble billing customers correctly, you might make this skill–benefit statement: "Here is how I would apply my skill and experience in setting up billing systems to help develop a billing system with as few glitches as possible." Or, you might state that your previous employer had a billing problem and then explain how you helped solve the problem.

A final note here about job finding is to avoid widely practiced tactics that disqualify candidates. Executive coach and corporate trainer Jim Pawiak spoke to a panel of HR specialists and hiring managers on how not to get a job. His findings encompass much wisdom:

> Being rude to the receptionist or administrative assistant, "cute" e-mail account names (e.g., babygirl44@, and bookworm@); busy signals (use voice mail rather than an

■ **Skill–benefit statements**
brief explanations of how an individual's skills can benefit the company

---

The following questions are of the same basic type and content encountered in most employment interviews. Practice answering them in front of a friend, camcorder, or mirror.

1. Why did you apply for this job?
2. What are your short-term and long-term goals?
3. What are your strengths? Areas for improvement?
4. Why should we hire you?
5. What do you know about our firm?
6. Describe how well you work under pressure.
7. Here's a sample job problem. How would you handle it?

Note: Questions 6 and 7 are often asked as part of a behavioral interview.

Figure   14-2

Seven Questions Frequently Asked of Job Candidates

answering machine); taking a call waiting interruption while talking with an employer; smelling like tobacco smoke, wearing perfume or aftershave lotion when interviewing; the dead-fish handshake; not making eye contact; not asking questions; not knowing anything–asking anything about the company; not saying "Thank you" at the end of the interview. [9] (Also, complaints are surfacing of job candidates who receive cell-phone calls while being interviewed.)

■ **Learning Objective 3**

What Are Some Effective Career Advancement Strategies and Tactics?

As you look to advance your career, it is helpful to divide your approach into developing your personal qualities and developing qualities that focus more on your interaction with the environment.

TAKING CONTROL OF YOURSELF

The unifying theme to the strategies, tactics, and attitudes described in this section is that you must attempt to control your own behavior. You can advance your career by harnessing the forces under your control. Such a perspective is important because individuals have the primary responsibility for managing their own careers. The late management guru Peter Drucker placed responsibility for career and life development on the individual. He said, "The stepladder is gone, and there's not even an implied structure of an industry's rope ladder. It's more like vines, and you bring your own machete." [10] (Professor Drucker liked to exaggerate a little.)

Some companies have career development programs, but the individual is still responsible for achieving his or her goals. The following section concentrates on getting ahead by trying to control your external environment in some small way. Do not be concerned about overlap between the general categories of controlling yourself and controlling the environment. Instead, be concerned about the meaning and application of the strategies and tactics.

Develop Expertise, Passion, and Pride

A starting point in getting ahead is to develop a useful job skill. This tactic is obvious if you are working as a specialist, such as an insurance underwriter. Being skilled at the task performed by the group is also a requirement for being promoted to a supervisory position. After being promoted to a supervisor or another managerial job, expertise is still important for further advancement. It helps a manager's reputation to be skilled in such things as memo writing, computer applications, preparing a budget, and interviewing job candidates.

Athough expertise is highly recommended, the workplace also demands that a person perform a variety of tasks as is required in working on a team. A finance specialist assigned to a product development team would also be expected to know something about marketing, such as how to analyze a marketing survey. A recommended approach is to have depth in your primary field but also have breadth by having several lesser areas of expertise. A widespread example is that no matter what your specialty field, you are also expected to have information technology skills.

Passion goes hand in hand with expertise; it contributes to problem solving and is a major requirement for being an effective leader. It is difficult to sustain expertise if you are not passionate about your specialty field. A work-passionate person, for example, would regularly read printed and electronic information about his or her specialty. In support of job passion, career coach and author Cynthia Shapiro advises that "Companies are running scared. They're looking for the kind of passion that creates a competitive edge. Employers rarely get rid of cheerleaders. Even in a drastic layoff, their jobs are safe." [11]

Developing expertise and being passionate about your work leads naturally to being proud of what you produce. People who take pride in their work are likely to achieve higher quality and a good reputation. From the standpoint of management, proud workers are major contributors because their pride motivates them to excel.

Develop a Code of Professional Ethics

Another solid foundation for developing a career is to establish a personal ethical code. An ethical code determines what behavior is right or wrong, good or bad, based on values. The values stem from cultural upbringing, religious teachings, peer influences, and professional or industry standards. A code of professional ethics helps a worker deal with such issues as accepting bribes, backstabbing coworkers, and sexually harassing a work associate.

Perform Well Including Going beyond Your Job Description

Good job performance is the bedrock of a person's career. In rare instances, a person is promoted on the basis of favoritism alone. In all other situations, an employee must have received a favorable performance appraisal (evaluation) to be promoted. Before an employee is promoted, the prospective new boss asks, "How well did this person perform for you?" To be an outstanding performer, it is also necessary to go outside your job description by occasionally taking on tasks not expected of you. Going beyond your job description is part of being a good organizational citizen. Another way of looking at the same issue is that people tend to get promoted not because they perform their jobs well but because they take the initiative to do more than expected.

Performing well on all your assignments is also important because it contributes to the **success syndrome,** a pattern in which the worker performs one assignment well and then has the confidence to take on an even more difficult assignment. Each new assignment contributes to more self-confidence and more success. As you succeed in new and more challenging assignments, your reputation grows within the firm.

Develop a Proactive Personality

If you are an active agent in taking control of the forces around you, you stand a better chance of capitalizing on opportunities. Also, you will seek out opportunities such as seeing problems that need fixing. A **proactive personality** is a person relatively unconstrained by forces in the situation and who brings about environmental change. People who are highly proactive identify opportunities and act on them, showing initiative, and keep trying until they bring about meaningful change. Jeffery A. Thompson, a professor of organizational behavior at Brigham University found that one reason proactive personalities perform better is that they develop the social networks they need to help them achieve their goals. For example, the person with a proactive personality would know who to contact for help with a specific business or technical problem. [12]

A health and safety specialist with a proactive personality might identify a health hazard others had missed. She would identify the nature of the problem and urge management for funding to control the problem, making use of her network. Ultimately, her efforts in preventing major health problems would be recognized. Having a proactive personality makes it easier for a person to be a good corporate citizen because such behavior is "built into your DNA."

> "Nothing is more important than your reputation. You can't build a reputation on what you say you are going to do—you have to build it on what you do. I learned early on in this business that I was going to live or die by my reputation."
> —Jerome Henderson, team leader at HomeBanc Mortgage Corp, Raleigh, North Carolina, and defensive back for nine years in the NFL

■ **Success syndrome**
pattern in which the worker performs one assignment well and then has the confidence to take on an even more difficult assignment

■ **Proactive personality**
characteristic of a person who is relatively unconstrained by forces in a situation and who brings about environmental change; highly proactive people identify opportunities and act on them, showing initiative, and keep trying until they bring about meaningful change

Managers prefer workers with a proactive personality because these workers become proactive employees, or those who take the initiative to take care of problems. Today's employee is supposed to be enterprising. Instead of relying solely on the manager to figure out what work needs to be accomplished, he or she looks for projects to undertake. The proactive employee, however, may clash with an old-fashioned manager who believes that an employee's job is strictly to follow orders. A study conducted with close to 500 men and women workers in diverse occupations examined the relationship between career success and a proactive personality. Proactive personality, as measured by a test, was related to salary, promotions, and career satisfaction. [13] It may not be easy to develop a proactive personality, but a person can get started by taking more initiative to fix problems and attempt to be more self-starting.

Create Good First Impressions and a Favorable Appearance

Every time you interact with a new person inside or outside your company, you create a first impression. Fair or not, these first impressions have a big impact on your career. If your first impression is favorable, you will often be invited back by an internal or external customer. Your first impression also creates a halo that may influence perceptions about the quality of your work in the future. If your first impression is negative, you will have to work extra hard to be perceived as competent later on.

Looking successful contributes to a positive first impression. Your clothing, your desk and office, and your speech should project the image of a successful, but not necessarily flamboyant, person. Your standard of dress should be appropriate to your particular career stage and work environment. At the extreme, highly placed business executives often dress as if they were walking advertisements for the beauty and fashion industry.

Appropriate dress for an inventory specialist is not the same as that for an outside salesperson dealing with industrial customers. Yet in the past few years, more formal business attire, such as suits for men and women, is making a comeback. Many salespeople and managers today maintain a flexible clothing style by such means as keeping a jacket and extra jewelry in the car or office. When an unanticipated meeting with a customer or some other special occasion arises, a quick modification of clothing style is possible. Appearing physically fit is also part of the success image.

Projecting a sense of control is another key factor contributing to a positive first impression. Show that you are in control of yourself and the environment and that you can handle job pressures. Avoid letting your body language betray you—fidgeting or rubbing your face sends negative nonverbal messages. Make your gestures project self-assurance and purpose. A verbal method of appearing in control is to make a positive assertion such as, "This is a demanding assignment and I welcome the challenge."

The factors mentioned so far contribute to a favorable appearance, which can be an asset in a career. Physical attractiveness continues to play a major role in many employment decisions—especially for workers who are in contact with customers and clients. Patrick Hicks, an attorney in a Las Vegas employment law firm, notes" "Everything else being equal, certain businesses—retail is the best example—would prefer people who are physically attractive." [14]

Body art in the form of tattoos and piercing often figures into physical appearance. More companies today accept such decorations as a fact of modern culture. Tatooing is one of the faster-growing retail businesses in the United States. Ford Motor Co. permits employees from the most senior executives on down to have tattoos and piercings—except those that could endanger factory workers. Despite this general acceptance of body art, excessive decoration in visible places could be a career deterrent. [15] Visualize a man with a pierced tongue and snake tattooed on his neck applying for a sales representative position at Hewlett Packard!

Document Your Accomplishments

Keeping an accurate record of your job accomplishments can be valuable when you are being considered for promotion, transfer, or assignment to a team or project. Documenting your accomplishments can also be used to verify new learning. In addition, a record of accomplishments is useful when your performance is being evaluated. You can show your manager what you have done for the company lately. Many professional-level workers maintain a portfolio of their accomplishments, such as samples of work accomplished. The portfolio is much like that used by photographers, artists, and models when applying for a job. Here are two examples of documented accomplishments from different types of jobs:

1. A bank teller suggested that at least one person in the bank should be fluent in American Sign Language to facilitate serving deaf customers. After implementing the idea, the bank attracted many more deaf customers.

2. A maintenance supervisor decreased fuel costs in the office by 27 percent in one year by installing ceiling fans.

After documenting your accomplishments, it pays to advertise. Let key people know in a tasteful way of your tangible accomplishments. You might request an opportunity to make a presentation to your boss to review the status of one of your successful projects. Or you could use e-mail for the same purpose if it would be presumptuous for you to request a special meeting to discuss your accomplishments.

Keep Growing through Continuous Learning and Self-Development

Many employers expect employees to keep learning, either through company sponsored programs or on their own. It is particularly important to engage in new learning in areas of interest to the company, such as developing proficiency in a second language if the company has customers and employees in other countries. Continuous learning can take many forms, including formal schooling, attending training programs and seminars, and self-study. To engage in continuous learning, it is essential to remain open to new viewpoints on your established beliefs. A belief (or stereotype) that has been true for a long time may no longer hold true. A person might think, for example, that almost all workers older than 60 are simply putting in time until they reach the traditional retirement age of 65. In reality, many workers plan to continue to work well into their 70s and 80s.

Observe Proper Etiquette

Proper etiquette is important for career advancement because such behavior is considered part of acting professionally. **Business etiquette** is a special code of behavior required in work situations. Both *etiquette* and *manners* refer to behaving in an acceptable and refined way. In the digital era, etiquette is just as important as ever because of the new challenges that high-tech devices bring. For example, is it good etiquette to read the information on a coworker's computer screen when visiting his or her cubicle? The globalization of business also creates challenges, such as figuring out when visiting another country whether handshakes are acceptable.

Deciphering what constitutes proper etiquette and business manners requires investigation. One approach is to use successful people as models of behavior and sources of information. Another approach is to consult a current book about business etiquette. The basic rules of etiquette are to make the other person feel comfortable in your presence, be considerate, and strive not to embarrass anyone. Also, be cordial to

■ **Business etiquette**
special code of behavior required in work situations

all, remembering that everyone deserves our respect. Specific guidelines for practicing etiquette stem from these basic rules. Figure 14-3 presents examples of good business etiquette and manners.

Develop the Brand Called You

Well-known business consultant Tom Peters urges career-minded people to develop their credentials and their reputations to the extent that they stand out so much that they become a brand name. Although the analogy of each person becoming a recognizable brand name such as Nike is far-fetched, the idea of becoming a trusted person with value is sound. As Peters sees it, you don't belong to any company for life, and your chief affiliation isn't any particular function or department (such as accounting). You are not defined by your job title or your job description. "Starting today you are a brand." [16]

Following are 13 specific suggestions about business etiquette and manners that should be considered in the context of a specific job situation. For example, "make appointments with high-ranking people" is not so relevant in a small, informal company when the company places less emphasis on formality.

1. *Be polite to people in person.* Say "good morning" and "good evening" to work associates at all job levels. Smile frequently. Offer to bring coffee or another beverage for a coworker if you are going outside to get some for yourself. When somebody shakes your hand, stand up instead of remaining in your chair.

2. *Write polite letters and e-mail messages.* An important occasion for practicing good etiquette is the writing of business and personal letters and e-mail messages. Include the person's job title in the inside address and spell the person's name correctly. Use supportive rather than harsh statements. (For example, say "It would be helpful if you could" rather than "You must.") When writing a hard-copy letter, avoid right margin justification (block writing) because it is much harsher than indented lines. Thank-you notes for gifts should be handwritten rather than sent by e-mail, but at least an e-mail note is better than not offering thanks.

3. *Practice good table manners.* Avoid smacking your lips or sucking your fingers. If someone else is paying the bill, do not order the most expensive item on the menu (such as a $195 bottle of Dom Pérignon champagne). Offer to cut bread for the other person and do not look at the check if the other person is paying. A pet peeve of many executives is having to dine with people who eat with their mouths open.

4. *Names should be remembered.* It is good manners and good etiquette to remember the names of work associates, even if you see them only occasionally. If you forget the name of a person, it is better to admit this rather than guessing and coming up with the wrong name. Just say, "I apologize, but I have forgotten your name. Tell me once more, and I will not forget your name again."

5. *Males and females should receive equal treatment.* Amenities extended to females by males in a social setting are minimized in business settings. During a meeting, a male is not expected to hold a chair or a door for a woman, nor does he jump to walk on the outside when the two of them are walking down the street. Many women resent being treated differently from males with respect to minor social customs. In general, common courtesies should be extended by both sexes to one another. A handshake and a smile are a better greeting than a kiss on the cheek of the opposite-sex person. Yet if a client or customer initiates the light kiss, it is acceptable to follow suit.

6. *Shouting is out.* Emotional control is an important way of impressing superiors. Following the same principle, shouting in most work situations is said to detract from you image.

7. *The host or hostess pays the bill.* An area of considerable confusion about etiquette surrounds business lunches and who should pay the check—the man or the woman. The rule of etiquette is that the person who extends the invitation pays the bill.

8. *Introduce the higher-ranking person to the lower-ranking person.* Your boss's name will be mentioned before a coworker's, you introduce the older person to the younger person, and a client is introduced first to coworkers. ("Ms. CEO I would like you to meet our new custodial assistant.")

Figure   14-3

Business Etiquette and Manners

9. *Address superiors and visitors in their preferred way.* As the modern business world has become more informal, a natural tendency has developed to address people at all levels by their first names. It is safer to first address people by a title and their last names and then wait for them to correct you if they desire. You will probably find that more than 90 percent of people want to be addressed by their first name. However, important exceptions exist. J.C. Penney only recently shifted to a culture where senior managers are addressed by their first name, and many Asian executives prefer to be referred to by a title such as Mr, Mrs., Ms., or Dr.

10. *Make appointments with high-ranking people rather than dropping in.* Although the business world has become increasingly informal, it is taboo in most firms for lower-ranking employees to casually drop in to the office of an executive. Use e-mail instead to contact higher-ranking managers directly.

11. *When another person is opening a door to exit a room or building, do not jump in ahead of him or her.* Many people have developed the curious habit of quickly jumping in past another person (moving in the opposite direction) who is exiting. Not only is this practice rude, but it can also lead to an uncomfortable collision.

12. *Be sensitive to cross-cultural differences in etiquette.* When dealing with people from different cultures, regularly investigate possible major differences in etiquette. For example, using the index finger to point is considered rude in most Asian and Eastern countries. The American sign for okay (thumb and index finger forming a circle) is considered a vulgarity in most other countries. Another example is that Finns are very private people, so don't ask questions about their private life unless they bring up the topic first. Instead, talk about the safe topic of sports. Don't blow your nose in public in Belgium where it is considered an offensive gesture. (It's not too cool elsewhere, either.)

13. *Minimize social kissing in an American workplace, but welcome it in Europe.* Kissing in business is generally regarded as rude except among close acquaintances, yet is more frequent in Europe. However, European kissing amounts to pecks on both cheeks, or top of the head, and never on the lips.

Caution: Although all the points could have some bearing on the image you project, violation of any one of them would not necessarily have a negative impact on your career. It is the overall image you project that counts the most. Therefore, the general principle of being considerate of work associates is much more important than any one act of etiquette or manners.

Source: Jim Rucker and Jean Anna Sellers, "Changes in Business Etiquette," *Business Education Forum*, February 1998, p. 45; "Business Etiquette: Teaching Students the Unwritten Rules," *Keying In*, January 1996, pp. 1–2; "Meeting and Greeting," *Keying In*, January 1996, p. 3; compilation from other sources in Andrea Sachs, "Corporate Ps and Qs," *Time*, November 1, 1999, p. 23; Sachs, "Learn How to Behave," *Time*, August 2005, p. A5; Letitia Baldrige, *The Executive Advantage* (Washington, DC: Georgetown Publishing House, 1999).

You begin developing brand You by identifying the qualities or characteristics that distinguish you from coworkers. What have you done recently to make you stand out? What benefit do you offer? Do you deliver high-quality work on time? Are you a creative problem solver? Next, you would make yourself visible so you can cash in your uniqueness (your brand). Almost all the ideas in this chapter will help you develop brand You!

EXERTING CONTROL OVER THE OUTSIDE WORLD

■ Learning Objective 4

In this section we emphasize approaches that require you to exert some control over the outside environment. If you do not control it, at least you can try to juggle it to your advantage. For example, the "Find a Mentor" section suggests that you search out a friendly and supportive person in your field who can help you advance in your career.

Develop a Flexible Career Path

Planning your career inevitably involves some form of goal setting. If your goals are laid out systematically to lead to your ultimate career goal, you have established a **career path,** a sequence of positions necessary to achieve a goal. Here we describe two types of career paths. One type emphasizes climbing up the ladder in a traditional organization. The other emphasizes the horizontal movements that fit better the new model of career advancement.

■ **Career path**
sequence of positions necessary to achieve a goal

The Traditional Career Path. A traditional career path is based on the assumption that a person will occupy a series of positions, each at a higher level of responsibility than the previous one. A person thus climbs the organizational ladder or hierarchy. If a career path is laid out in one firm, it must be related to the present and future demands of that firm. If you aspire toward a high-level manufacturing position, you would need to know the future of manufacturing in that company. Many U.S. firms, for example, continue to conduct more of their manufacturing in China. If you were really determined, you might study the appropriate language and ready yourself for a global position.

Before establishing the goals on the career path, it is helpful to clarify your values. These are probably the same values that enabled you to choose a career in the first place. Questions to think about are "Can you name the three things most important to your job satisfaction? What do you really look for in a job? Do you want to be part of a team? To think creatively? Are you passionate about helping people and improving the world? Do you want to carefully follow directions, or do you want to decide which tasks are important?" [17]

While sketching out a career path, you should list your personal goals. They should mesh with your work plans to help avoid major conflicts in your life. Some lifestyles, for example, are incompatible with some career paths. You might find it difficult to develop a stable home life (spouse, children, friends, community activities, garden) if you aspired toward holding field positions in international marketing.

Your career path is a living document and may need to be modified as your circumstances change. Keep in mind changes in your company and industry. If becoming a branch manager is an important step in your career path, check to see if your company or industry still has branch managers. The changing preferences of your family can also influence your career path. A family who wanted to stay put may now be willing to relocate, which could open up new possibilities on your career path.

Contingency ("what if?") plans should also be incorporated into a well-designed career path. For instance, "If I don't become an agency supervisor by age 35, I will seek employment in the private sector." Or, "If I am not promoted within two years, I will enroll in a business school program."

Career paths can be laid out graphically, as shown in Figure 14-4. One benefit of a career path laid out in chart form is that it gives a clear perception of climbing steps toward your target position. As each position is attained, the corresponding step can be shaded in color or crosshatched.

Most goals in a career path include a time element, which is crucial to sound career management. Your long-range goal might be clearly established in your mind (such as owner and operator of a health spa). At the same time you must establish short-range goals (get any kind of job in health spa) and intermediate-range goals (manager of a health spa by age 30). Goals set too far in the future that are not supported with more immediate goals may lose their motivational value. The career path in Figure 14-4 features a steady progression of promotions yet a reasonable number of years in each position. Such planning is realistic because promotions often take a long time to achieve.

The Horizontal Career Path. Many organizations today have no fixed career paths. Instead of plotting a series of moves over a long time period, many individuals can

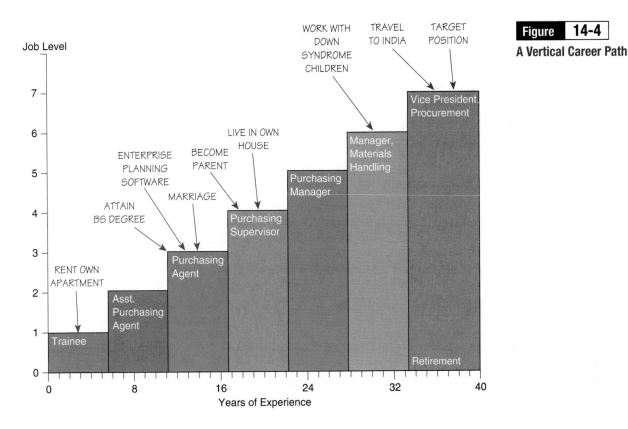

Figure **14-4**

A Vertical Career Path

only make predictions about the type of work they would like to be doing rather than target specific positions. A significant feature of the horizontal career path is that people are more likely to advance by moving sideways than moving up. Or, at least, people who get ahead will spend a considerable part of their career working in different positions at or near the same level. In addition, they may occasionally move to a lower-level position to gain valuable experience. With a horizontal career path, the major reward is no longer promotion but the opportunity to gain more experience and increase job skills. Figure 14-5 presents a horizontal career path.

A horizontal career path, as well as a traditional (or vertical) career path, does not necessarily mean the person stays with the same firm. For example, a worker might spend three years in one company as an electronics technician, three years in

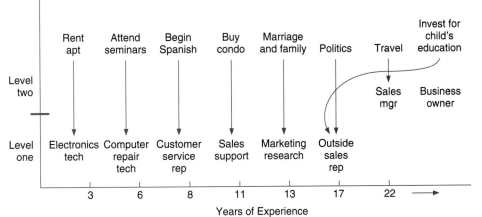

Figure **14-5**

A Horizontal Career Path

another as an e-commerce coordinator, and then three years as a customer service specialist in a third company. All three positions would be approximately at the same level. The third company then promotes the individual to a much-deserved position as the marketing team leader.

Achieve Broad Experience

Most people who land high-ranking positions usually have broad experience. Therefore, a widely accepted strategy for advancing in responsibility is to strengthen your credentials by broadening your experience. Workers who follow the alternative model of career advancement, as illustrated by the horizontal career path, are automatically achieving broad experience. It is best to achieve breadth early in your career because it is easier to transfer when an individual's compensation is not too high. Broadening can come about by performing a variety of jobs or sometimes by performing essentially the same job in different organizations. You can also achieve breadth by working on committees and special assignments.

Breadth can also be attained through self-nomination. Have the courage and assertiveness to ask for a promotion or a transfer. Your manager or team leader may not know that you are actually seeking more responsibility. An effective method of convincing him or her is to volunteer for specific job openings or for challenging assignments. A boss may need convincing because many more people will be seeking advancement than are actually willing to handle more responsibility.

A major benefit of broad experience is that you achieve more career portability, allowing you to move to another employer should the need exist. The employability derives from being a more flexible person with a broader perspective. A person, for example, who has worked in both the underwriting (setting rates for risks) and the claims aspects of insurance would be well regarded by insurance companies.

Find a Mentor

■ **Mentor**

a more experienced person who guides, teaches, and coaches another individual

The vast majority of successful career people have had one or more mentors during their careers. A **mentor** is a more experienced person who guides, teaches, and coaches another individual. In years past, mentors were almost always higher-ranking people. Today mentors can be peers and even lower-ranking individuals. A lower-ranking individual, for example, can educate you on how other parts of the organization work—something you may need to know to advance. Sometimes you are able to develop a mentor from the contacts you make on the Internet. After the person becomes your mentor, much of the mentoring can take place through e-mail and messaging. (Busier mentors may prefer e-mail because they can respond at their leisure.) E-mentoring will sometimes increase the pool of potential mentors and allow relationships to develop without social bias, such as people being suspicious of the nature of a mentoring relationship between a middle-age man and a young woman. [18]

Mentorship is an important development process in many occupations: master–apprentice, physician–intern, teacher–student, and executive–junior executive. An emotional tie exists between the less experienced person (the protégé) and the mentor. The mentor serves as a positive model and a trusted friend. In return, the person being mentored expresses appreciation, gives positive feedback to the mentor, and shares victories. It is also important to offer a concrete service in return for the mentor's advice. Possibilities include offering to collect information, prepare computer graphics, or run a few errands.

Finding a mentor involves the same process as networking (described later in this chapter). One possibility to mention for now is that you can ask people you already know if they could think of a possible mentor for you. With e-mentoring, geographic distance does not create a substantial barrier. With any prospective mentor, it is best to begin gradually by asking for some advice and then see how the relationship develops. The accompanying Human Relations in Practice box insert provides an example of e-mentoring.

The advantages of being mentored are widely accepted by managers and human relations specialists, so it is encouraging to know that data based research supports the contention that mentoring can benefit a protégé's career. A team of five researchers synthesized a group of studies covering more than 10,000 individuals. It was found that compensation and promotions were slightly higher for mentored than nonmentored individuals. Also, the mentored individuals were more satisfied with their career, felt more optimistic about promotions, and were more committed to their careers. Two key reasons that mentoring helps protégés is that they receive good suggestions from mentors about career advancement and they use the mentors as positive models. [19]

Balance Your Life

Balancing your life among the competing demands of work, social life, and personal interests can help you advance your career. Having balance gives you additional energy and vitality that will help you in your career. Without balance, a career person runs the risk of burnout and feeling that work is not worthwhile. Stephen Covey writes, "Always being the last to leave the office does not make you an indispensable employee. In fact, those who work long hours for extended periods are prone to burnout. The trick is to have your priorities clear, honor your commitments, and keep a balance in life." [20]

Human Relations in Practice

KPMG Offers Employees On-line Mentoring

KPMG LLP, a New York–based tax and audit firm with about 18,200 employees in the United States, has attained success using an on-line mentoring database. Although informal mentoring was taking place (partners mentored junior staff to help them move through the ranks), the company enacted a more formal voluntary nationwide mentoring program in 2004. "For a variety of reasons, wanted to expand on informal mentoring," says Barbara Wankoff, KPMG's director of workplace solutions which is part of HR. "We set out to encourage people and establish mentoring relationships."

The KPMG program is on the company's HR Web site and is "customized to match our competencies," says Wankoff. The system uses key words such as "boardroom skills" or "negotiation" to help find suitable mentors for employees who seek mentoring. And before accepting an assignment, a mentor agrees to terms that include confidentiality.

KPMG officials describe the on-line program as "user friendly" and easy to navigate, with information that is prominently displayed and readily accessible. "We feel the message is being put out there," says Wankoff. Employees know we support this and it's available to them if they want it. We also recognize not everyone is ready and willing to commit to mentoring, but we hope to see it grow and increase greatly." So far, there's been a positive response—about 6,000 mentoring relationships have been formed.

Source: Donna M. Owens, "Virtual Mentoring," *HR Magazine*, March 2006, p. 106.

Developing Your Networking Skills

Developing a network of contacts is important for finding a job. As a career advancement tactic, networking has several purposes. The contacts you establish can help you find a better position, offer you a new position, become a customer, become a valuable supplier, help you solve difficult problems, or find a mentor. People in your network can also offer you emotional support during periods of adversity.

A recommended approach to networking is to keep a list of at least 25 people whom you contact at least once a month. The contact can be as extensive as a luncheon meeting or as brief as an e-mail message. The starting point in networking is to obtain an ample supply of business cards. You then give a card to any person you meet who might be able to help you now or in the future. While first developing your network, be inclusive. Later, as your network develops, you can strive to include a greater number of influential and successful people. People in your network can include relatives; people you meet while traveling, vacationing, or attending trade shows; and classmates.

Community activities and religious organizations can also be a source of contacts. Golf is still considered the number one sport for networking because of the high-level contacts the sport generates. A substantial amount of social networking also takes place on the Internet. The range of potential people in your network is much greater over the Internet than if networking is done locally and in person. The people in these groups can become valuable business contacts. On-line networking includes newsgroups, mailing lists, chat rooms, and e-mail. Corporate Web sites usually have a listing of contact people for a company, and it is possible that some of these people will become part of your network. Figure 14-6 offers some additional networking suggestions, and Exercise 14-1 provides a worksheet for networking.

Networking is obviously beneficial in a field such as direct selling whereby you contact people you know to purchase your goods or services. For example, if you sell products such as financial services, Avon, or Tupperware, you are expected to capitalize on personal contacts. Almost any successful businessperson you meet uses networking, at least to some extent. A representative example is Anna Garcia, the owner of Anko Metal Services in Denver, Colorado. She attributes some of her success to networking with women. Garcia said, "Latina women used to get together in a religious setting. Now, it's in the business atmosphere." A specific event is a Latina business-development event, held throughout the United States. The gathering focuses on networking, and courting potential clients is expected behavior. [21]

We caution again to be selective about your networking. Overreliance on networking, such as contacting people who probably have no interest in hearing from you, can be annoying to the recipient. Kenneth Norton, the director of product management at Yahoo! has coined the term *snam* (a mutant of *spam*) in reference to unwanted e-mail generated by such social networking sites as Friendster, LinkedIn, and Tribe. [22]

The following networking suggestions are gathered from a number of career counselors and business writers. Select and choose from among the list those ideas that appear fit your personality and circumstances.

- Expand and diversify your network. Everyone you come in contact with is a potential resource to help you in your career. Even someone whose sole purpose is to cheer you on during downturns can be a valuable ally. Keep filling your network with new contacts because older contacts may fade away. Retired people who have had a successful careers can be a valuable source of contacts. Also, retired people typically enjoy assisting people at earlier stages in their careers.
- Add value as well as asking for assistance. Consider how you can help the other person and listen as much as you talk.
- When networking by e-mail, include your telephone number and address. The other person may want to contact you by means other than an e-mail. Also, be persistent because e-mail messages may get deleted by accident or simply disappear because of technical problems.
- When approaching someone to be part of your network, explain how you received his or her name or refresh the person's mind as to how you met previously.
- If you attend a formal networking event (such as a professional meeting), "work the room." Engage in professional conversations with as many people as feasible.
- Create good relationships with your peers and fellow students. Some of them will occupy influential positions in the future. Stay in touch with your more promising classmates. In other words, "Look at the paws on those pups."
- Strive to develop a personal relationship with at least two people at higher levels in your place of work. Keep these people informed of what you are doing and ask for their advice.
- Be memorable for positive reasons. Making a lasting positive impression is a promising way of keeping a network alive.
- When you have a change of status, such as accepting a new position, let this be an opportunity to notify network members. Let everyone know should you change your e-mail address or telephone number.

Source: Anita Bruzzese, "Restrain Yourself and Think When Networking by E-Mail," *Gannett News Service*, June 30, 2003; "Networking Isn't for Spectators: Meeting People, Discovering Trends, and Arriving Early Can Pay Dividends," Knight Ridder, February 24, 2003; Deb Koehn, "Networking Vital in Ever-Evolving Workplaces," *Rochester (NY) Democrat and Chronicle*, July 14, 2002, p. 4E; Deb Koehn, "Know Etiquette of Networking," *Rochester (NY) Democrat and Chronicle*, October 27, 2002, p. 4E; "'85 Broads' Shares Networking Tips," *Executive Leadership*, February 2002, p. 3; Anne Fisher, "How Do I Network When I Don't Even Know Anyone?" *Fortune*, July 22, 2002, p. 226.

Figure   14-6

Networking Suggestions

Concept Review and Reinforcement

Key Terms

Person–organization fit, 355
Networking, 356
Behavioral interview, 358

Skill–benefit statements, 359
Success syndrome, 361
Proactive personality, 361

Business etiquette, 363
Career path, 366
Mentor, 368

Summary and Review

The job search begins with a reasonably flexible statement of the type of job you are seeking (your job objective). Knowing what type of organization you would prefer to work for will help focus your job search. Use different methods of job searching and keep trying.

- The most effective method of finding a job is through personal contacts, or networking. Getting someone on the inside to recommend you for a job is the best way to reach the internal job market.
- Job hunting on the Internet can be done through job boards and company Web sites. Despite using the Internet, it is important to speak to a person to conclude your job search.

A novel format for a cover letter is the T-form approach that systematically outlines how the applicant's qualifications match up against the job requirements.

The major purpose of a résumé is to help you obtain a job interview. There is no one best way to prepare a résumé. Effective résumés are straightforward, factual presentations of a person's experiences, skills, and accomplishments. Avoid making untrue statements on your résumé. A résumé should include a section about your job-related skills and accomplishments.

Rehearse being interviewed and then present yourself favorably but accurately in the interview. Behavioral interviews are growing in importance.

- To perform well in an interview, present a positive but accurate self-picture.
- Look for opportunities to make a skill–benefit statement about how your skills can help the company.

One set of strategies and tactics for getting ahead can be classified as taking control of your own behavior. Included are these approaches:

- Develop expertise, passion, and pride.
- Develop a code of professional ethics.
- Perform well including going beyond your job description.
- Develop a proactive personality.
- Create good first impressions and a favorable appearance.
- Document your accomplishments.
- Keep growing through continuous learning and self-development.
- Observe proper etiquette.
- Develop the brand called You.

Another set of strategies and tactics for career advancement centers around taking control of your environment, or at least adapting it to your advantage. Included are following:

- Develop a flexible career path (including the traditional and lateral types).
- Achieve broad experience.
- Find a mentor.
- Balance your life.

Developing networking skills is a major career advancement tactic that can help you find a new position, become a customer, become a valuable supplier, solve difficult problems, find a mentor, and receive emotional support. Keep a list of at least 25 people whom you contact monthly and add value as well as asking for assistance.

Check your Understanding

1. During times when there is a shortage of skilled workers, why is it still important to study how to conduct a job campaign?
2. During a period in which there is a dire shortage of jobs available, which job-hunting tactics do you think would be the most relevant?
3. What can you do today to help you develop a contact that could someday lead to a job?
4. Visit the employment section of the Web site of three large companies of interest to you. Identify several jobs you perceive to match your qualifications or for which you have a reasonable chance of being regarded as a bona fide candidate.
5. Make up a behavioral interview question that you might be asked, and develop a good answer.
6. With the upcoming labor shortage, the future for graduates in almost all business-related specialties looks bright for at least the next 10 years. So why be concerned with strategies for career advancement?
7. Identify several jobs for which observing good business etiquette would be particularly important.
8. What similarities do you see between a person with a *proactive personality* and one who displays good *organizational citizenship behavior*?
9. Identify several tactics you would be willing to use to attract a mentor in a large company.
10. How might a person go about networking for career advancement in an airport or on an airplane?

Web Corner

Image building through image consultants:
www.aic.org

Career advice including job search and salaries:
www.vault.com.

Career advancement suggestions from The Wall Street Journal:
www.CareerJournal.com.

Find a mentor:
www.AdvanceMentoring.com

INTERNET SKILL BUILDER:

So many job boards exist on the Internet that conducting a Web-based job search can be baffling. A direct approach is to visit Yahoo! Hot Jobs (on the front page of www.Yahoo.com) and enter three specific job titles of interest to you. You will be directed to loads of job opportunities closely matching the job titles you entered. It may be helpful to enter variations of the same job title, such as both "office manager" and "administrative assistant." Your assignment is to identify five jobs for which you appear to be qualified. Even if you have no interest in conducting a job search, it is informative to be aware of job opportunities in your field. Seek answers to the following questions:

1. Do I appear to have the qualifications for the type of job I am seeking?
2. Is there a particular geographic area where the job or jobs I want are available?
3. How good are opportunities in my chosen field?

Applying Human Relations Exercise 14-1

Building Your Network

Networking can be regarded as the process of building a team that works with you to achieve success. You can start the following exercise now, but it will probably take your entire career to implement completely. To start networking or make your present networking more systematic, take the following steps:

Step 1: Jot down your top three goals or objectives for the following three months, such as obtaining a new job or promotion, starting a small business, or doing a field research study.

1. _____

2. _____

3. _____

Step 2: List family members, friends, or acquaintances who could assist you in meeting your goals or objectives. Prepare a contact card or database entry for each person on your list, including as many details as you can about the person and the person's family, friends, employers, and contacts.

Step 3: Identify what assistance you will request of your contact or contacts. Be realistic in light of your prior investment in the relationship. Remember, you have to be a friend to have a friend.

Step 4: Identify how you will meet your contact or contacts during the next month. Could it be for lunch or at an athletic field, nightclub, sports club, recreational facility on campus, cafeteria, and so forth? Learn more about your contacts during your face-to-face meetings. In some cases you may have to use the telephone or e-mail to substitute for an in-person meeting. Look for ways to mutually benefit from the relationship. At the beginning of each week, verify that you have made a small investment in building these relationships.

Step 5: Ask for the help you need. A network must benefit you. Thank the contact for any help given. Jot down on your planner a reminder to make a follow-up call, letter, or e-mail message to your contacts. In this way, you will have less work to do before you make another request for help.

Step 6: For each person in your network, think of a favor, however small, that you can return to him or her. Without reciprocity, a network fades rapidly.

Source: Adapted and expanded from Cheryl Kitter, "Taking the Work Out of Networking," Success Workshop, supplement to The Pryor Report, March 1998, pp. 1–2.

Applying Human Relations Exercise 14-2

Career Pathing

1. Each class member will develop a tentative career path, perhaps as an outside assignment. About six volunteers will then share their paths with the rest of the class. Feedback of any type will be welcomed. Class members studying the career paths of others should keep in mind such issues as the following:

a. How logical does it appear?

b. Is this something the person really wants, or is it simply an exercise in putting down on paper what the ambitious person is supposed to want?

c. How well do the individual's work plans mesh with personal plans?

2. Each class member will interview an experienced working person outside of class about his or her

career path. Most of the people interviewed will have already completed a portion of their path. Therefore, they will have less flexibility (and perhaps less idealism) than people just getting started in their careers. The conclusions reached about these interviews will make a fruitful class discussion. Among the issues raised might be the following:

a. How familiar were these people with the idea of a career path?
b. How willing were they to talk about themselves?
c. Were many actual "paths" discovered, or did a series of jobs simply come about by luck or "fate?"

Human Relations Case Study 14-1

Stacy Sings the Blues

Stacy, age 27, was proud to be an architectural technician student. She liked the idea of combining her interest in art with being part of something important. As she reasoned, "I will be helping architects erect skyscrapers, small office buildings, and houses that will last for a century. I will help provide beautiful environments in which fellow human beings will work and live."

To help fund her schooling and pay her living expenses while at career school, Stacy tended bar at the Big Boar Inn, a trendy bar frequented mostly by young people. Stacy had worked on and off as a bartender before attending career school. For several years after high school, she traveled around the world finding work at bars and resorts wherever she could. During her travels, Stacy made notes of the designs of buildings and prepared many sketches of her own ideas about building designs. She knew that she wanted someday to work in the field of architecture.

Several months before graduation, Stacy's father and several friends asked her when she would be starting her job hunt. Stacy explained that she was too busy finishing her studies at school and working at the Big Boar to get seriously involved in a job hunt. "After graduation in May, I'll take a couple of months to unwind and then begin searching for a job. Besides, most architectural firms don't get serious about hiring recent graduates until after Labor Day." Stacy's dad thought she was being a little laid back in her job-hunting approach but did not think he was in a position to tell her what to do.

After graduation, Stacy continued to work at the Big Boar about 25 hours per week. She spent a lot of time at the beach and developed a deep skin tan. One day she ran into her mentor, Professor Bill Byron, at the supermarket. Byron asked Stacy how her job search was going.

Stacy replied, "I will be getting to working on my résumé soon. With the job market for architectural technicians being soft right now, I didn't see any need to rush. Would it be OK to drop by your office to get some advice on my résumé?"

Stacy met with Mr. Byron a week later. He gave Stacy a few suggestions about résumé construction and also noted that her portfolio of architectural renderings needed more work before she could present the portfolio to prospective employers. Stacy then decided to sharpen her portfolio before beginning her job search.

At the urging of a friend, Stacy bought a few out-of-town newspapers to search the classified sections. She chose Washington, DC, Atlanta, and Miami because of their warm climates. Stacy spotted a total of three openings for architectural technicians and sent a résumé and cover letter to the addresses indicated in the ads.

Two months passed, and Stacy had not heard back from any of the firms to which she sent letters. Stacy's next approach was to give a copy of her résumé to a friend who sold furniture to an architectural firm in New Jersey. The friend said he would give the résumé to a personal contact he had at the firm.

During a work break at the Big Boar, a server asked Stacy how her job hunt was proceeding. Stacy replied, "Right now, I'm just sitting back and waiting to hear. There's not much else I can do."

Questions

1. What is your evaluation of the effectiveness of Stacy's job campaign?
2. What recommendations can you make to Stacy to help her find a position as an architectural technician?
3. You be the career counselor. Does Stacy really want to leave her job as a bartender at the Big Boar Inn and become an architectural technician?

Human Relations Case Study 14-2

San Deep Wants the Fast Track

At age 25, San Deep already had impressive leadership experience. She was the head of her Girl Scout troop at age 11, the president of the Asian Student Association in high school, and the captain of her soccer team in both high school and college. She also organized a food drive for homeless people in her hometown for three consecutive summers. Deep believed that these experiences, in addition to her formal education, were preparing her to be a corporate leader. At college, Deep majored in information systems and business administration.

Deep's first position in industry was a business analyst at a medium-size consulting firm that helped clients implement large-scale systems, such as enterprise software. She explained to her team leader at the outset that she wanted to be placed on a management track rather than a technical track because she aspired to becoming a corporate executive. Deep's team leader explained, "San, I know you are in a hurry to get ahead. Lots of capable people are looking to climb the ladder. But you first have to build your career by proving that you are an outstanding analyst."

Deep thought, "It looks like the company may need a little convincing that I'm leadership material, so I'm going to dig in and perform like a star." And Deep did dig in, much to the pleasure of her clients, her team leader, and her coworkers. Her first few performance evaluations were outstanding, yet the company was still not ready to promote San to a team leader position. Deep's team leader explained, "Bob [the team leader's manager] and I both agree that you are doing an outstanding job, but promotions are hard to come by in our company these days. The company is shrinking more than expanding, so talks about promotion are a little futile right now."

Deep decided that it would take a long time to be promoted to team leader or manager in her present company, so she began to quietly look for a new position in her field. Her job hunt proceeded more swiftly than she anticipated. Through a sports club contact, Deep was granted a job interview with a partner in a larger consulting firm offering similar services. After a series of four interviews, Deep was hired as a senior business analyst performing work on a system similar to the one she had been working with for two years. During her interviews, Deep emphasized her goals of occupying a leadership position as soon as the company believed that she was ready for such a role. Her first client assignment would be helping a team of consultants install a state income tax call center.

After a one-month-long orientation and training program, Deep was performing billable work at her new employer. At the outset, she reminded her new manager and team leader again that she preferred the managerial route to remaining in a technical position. After six months of hard work, Deep looked forward to her first formal performance evaluation. Deep's team leader informed her that her performance was better than average but short of outstanding. Deep asked for an explanation of why her performance was not considered outstanding. She informed her team leader and manager, "I need an outstanding rating to help me achieve my goals of becoming a leader in our company."

The manager replied, "Our performance evaluations are based on your contribution to the company. We care much less about writing performance evaluations to help a senior business analyst reach her career goals. Besides, San, you've made your point enough about wanting to be a leader in our firm. Let your performance speak for itself."

That evening, Deep met with her fiancé, Ryan, to discuss her dilemma. "The problem, Ryan, is that they don't get it. I'm leadership material, and they don't see it yet. I'm performing well and letting my intentions be known, but my strategy isn't working. The company is missing out on a golden opportunity by not putting me on a fast leadership track. I have to convince them of their error in judgment."

Ryan, a human resources specialist, replied, "I'm listening to you, and I want to give you good advice. Let me be objective here despite the fact that I love you. What have you done lately to prove to the company that you are leadership material?"

Questions

1. Who has the problem here, San or the consulting firm in question?
2. What advice can you offer San to help her increase her chances of being promoted to a formal leadership position in the company?
3. What is your evaluation of the validity of the advice Ryan offered San?

REFERENCES

1. Sarah E. Needleman, "Be Prepared When Opportunity Calls," *The Wall Street Journal*, February 7, 2006, p. B4.
2. Mary Ellen Slayter, "Job Hunters Take Note: Your Best Fit May Be Federal," available at *washingtonpost.com*, retrieved December 25, 2005.
3. Amy L. Kristof-Brown, Ryan D. Zimmerman, and Erin C. Johnson, "Consequences of Individuals' Fit at Work: A Meta-Analysis of Person–Job, Person–Organization, Person–Group, and Person–Supervisor Fit," *Personnel Psychology*, Summer 2005, p. 310.
4. Cited in Kris Maher, "The Jungle: Focus on Recruitment, Pay and Getting Ahead," *The Wall Street Journal*, June 17, 2003, p. B8.
5. Quoted in Anne Fisher, "How to Run an Online Job Hunt," *Fortune*, June 28, 2004, p. 43.
6. Based on form used by Garrett Associates, Alexandria, Virginia.
7. Amy Lindgren, "CV or Résumé? Depends on Purpose, Reader," *Atlanta Journal Constitution*, January 29, 2006, p. R4.
8. Laura Egodigwe, "Extreme Makeover," *Black Enterprise*, September 2004, p. 106.
9. Jim Pawlak, "Interviewing 101: How Not to Get a New Job," *The Detroit News*, available at detnews.com, retrieved September 30, 2005.
10. Peter F. Drucker, *Classic Drucker: Essential Wisdom of Peter Drucker from the Pages of Harvard Business Review* (Boston: Harvard Business School Press, 2006).
11. Quoted in Anne Fisher, "Disaster-Proofing Your Career," *Fortune*, October 3, 2005, p. 174.
12. Jeffery A. Thompson, "Proactive Personality and Job Performance: A Social Capital Perspective," *Journal of Applied Psychology*, September 2005, pp. 1011–1017.
13. Scott E. Seibert, J. Michael Crant, and Maria L. Kraimer, "Proactive Personality and Career Success," *Journal of Applied Psychology*, June 1999, pp. 416–427.
14. Quoted in Michael Barrier, "Should Looks Count: Are You Discriminating against Employees Because of Their Appearance?" *HR Magazine*, September 2004, p. 66.
15. Mielikki Org, "The Tatooed Executive: Body Art Gains Acceptance in Once-Staid Office Settings; Corporate Counsel's Yin-Yang," *The Wall Street Journal*, August 28, 2003, pp. D1, D 15; Karen Dybis, "While No Longer Taboo, Body Art Still Can Be a Sticky Issue at Work," *Detroit News*, available at detnews.com, June 21, 2005;
16. Tom Peters, "The Brand Called You: You Can't Move Up If You Don't Stand Out," *Fast Company*, August–September 1997, pp. 83–94. The quote is from p. 86.
17. Deb Koen, "Identifying Values Clarifies Career Goals," *Rochester (NY) Democrat and Chronicle*, June 4, 2000, p. D4.
18. Betti A. Hamilton and Terri A. Scandura, "E-Mentoring: Implications for Organizational Learning and Development in a Wired World," *Organizational Dynamics*, 32, no. 4, 2003, p. 388; Donna M. Owens, "Virtual Mentoring," *HR Magazine*, March 2006, pp. 105–107.
19. Tammy D. Allen et al., "Career Benefits Associated with Mentoring for Protégés: A Meta-Analysis," *Journal of Applied Psychology*, February 2004, pp. 127–136.
20. Stephen Covey, "How to Succeed in Today's Workplace," *USA Weekend*, August 29–31, 1997, pp. 4–5.
21. Will Shanley, "Latina Exec's Success Story Inspires," *Denver Post*, available at *denverpost.com*, March 21, 2005.
22. Scott Kirsner, "Networking Overload," *Fast Company*, April 2004, p. 38.

15 Learning Strategies, Perception, and Life Span Changes

Learning Objectives

After studying the information and doing the exercises in this chapter, you should be able to:

1 Understand the basic learning processes, three advanced learning processes, and e-learning.

2 Explain the meaning of learning styles, and develop insight into your own style.

3 Explain individual differences in learning ability and continuous learning.

4 Explain how perception influences behavior.

5 Identify the stages of the life cycle.

6 Understand the challenges of responding to changes in adolescence, adulthood, and late adulthood.

7 Describe the impact of the life span on life and job satisfaction.

8 Recognize the realities of dealing with a career change.

9 Be better prepared to cope with change.

Outline

Gerry Salvo, age 43, worked happily for many years as the bumper assembly supervisor for an automotive parts manufacturer in Kalamazoo, Michigan. He supervised a department of 24 skilled and unskilled workers. Over 90 percent of the company's products were sold to the three major North American automotive manufacturers. Sales volume at the company started a decline a decade ago. The decline accelerated as the Big Three automotive customers bought more auto and truck components from lower-priced overseas suppliers.

Salvo watched as his company went through a series of layoffs, hoping that he would never be "tapped." In January 2006, the unpleasant reality finally hit. Salvo's department was folded because his company could no longer compete in the sale of auto and truck bumpers. Salvo was given four months severance pay. He and his wife Michelle, a part-time home health aide, figured that the family, including two primary-age school children could last about eight months before going bankrupt. So Gerry Salvo realized he had to find new employment quickly that would pay at least 75 percent of what he was making as a supervisor.

A four-month job search turned up no job inside or outside of manufacturing that paid much more $8 per hour. Salvo thought that if obtained a degree, or even a certificate, in manufacturing such as tool design or computer-aided manufacturing, he could rebuild his own career related to what he was doing. But for now, he had to act quickly.

Looking through self-employment opportunities in magazines and on the Internet, Salvo hit on the idea of operating a window-blind franchise. His wife agreed that she could help with installations and customer contact. The Salvo's pulled together $11,000 through savings and credit-card loans to invest in a franchise. After ten days of company headquarters training, Salvo became a certified window blinds installer for homes and small businesses. Michelle's parents were their first customer, followed by an aunt of Jerry's.

Salvo thought to himself, "I never thought that in my early 40s I would be selling and installing blinds for a living. But it's no time for self-pity. Michelle and I need to focus on four installations per week to break even."

Perhaps no reader of this book is in the same boat as Gerry Salvo, but his story illustrates an important point about the world of work. It is possible that at any stage of our life cycle that we may be required to make major adaptations and changes. In this chapter we deal with a series of issues and topics that enable a person to develop career thrust and stay on track: how people learn; how perception influences their behavior, and the major challenges people face at different stages of their life, including a career change.

What Are the Major Learning Strategies and Processes?

■ **Learning Objective 1**

■ **Learning**
generally considered a lasting change in behavior based on practice and experience

Much learning takes place on the job simply because people spend such a large proportion of their lives at work. Furthermore, workers at all levels are expected to learn new job skills and technology continuously. **Learning** is generally considered to be a lasting change in behavior based on practice and experience. Yet it is possible to learn something and store it in your mind without changing your behavior. [1] For example, you read that if you press "F12" in Windows XP you open the "Save As" function. You keep it in your mind but do not use the command yet. The new knowledge is stored in your upper brain but is not yet put into action.

Here we describe several different methods of learning, beginning with classical conditioning, the simplest type. Then we describe learning of intermediate complexity, operant conditioning, followed by two ways in which more complicated skills are learned: modeling and informal learning. We conclude with e-learning because of its widespread use in delivering content for learning. Although we describe different methods of learning, most learning depends on several methods of learning. For example, in learning to operate a new vehicle you might need to develop simple reflexes to adjust to getting into the car. You would also use higher-level learning to understand how to use the computerized map.

CLASSICAL CONDITIONING: LEARNING SIMPLE HABITS AND REFLEXES

In the late 1890s a Russian physiologist, Ivan Pavlov, conducted a long series of experiments about digestion. While studying a dog, he noticed that the dog salivated not only with the presence of food in the mouth but also at the sight of the food, the sound of the food trays, and even the footsteps of the experimenter. The principles of **classical conditioning** stemming from his experiments help us to understand the most elementary type of learning—how people acquire uncomplicated habits and reflexes. Because most of work behavior involves more than reflexes and simple habits, classical conditioning itself is not of major consequence to the supervisor or individual worker. Yet its basic principles and concepts are included in more complicated forms of learning.

■ **Classical conditioning**
principles stemming from Ivan Pavlov's digestion experiments that help people understand the most elementary type of learning—how people acquire uncomplicated habits and reflexes

Classical conditioning works in this manner. Kurt takes an entry-level, unskilled job in a factory. His first day on the job a bell rings in his department at 11:34 A.M. Suddenly, every other worker stops working and opens a lunch box or heads out to the company cafeteria. Kurt says to himself, "The bell must mean it's time for lunch." By the third day on the job, Kurt develops stomach pangs and begins to salivate as soon as the bell rings. Prior to this job, Kurt was in the habit of eating lunch at 1 P.M. and did not begin to have stomach pangs until that time.

Two other conditioning concepts are also of major importance. If the department bell rings frequently when it is not time for lunch, Kurt's hunger pangs and salivation responses will gradually cease or extinguish on hearing a bell. (An important exception is that time alone or the empty feeling in his stomach can also serve as a stimulus to Kurt.) As he goes through life, Kurt will learn not to salivate or experience hunger pangs at every bell that sounds like the one used in his department. At first he may generalize his learning by salivating to many different bells and experiencing hunger pangs in response to a variety of bells. After awhile, he will discriminate and only make such responses to the bell in his department (or any other bell that signals food time).

Classical conditioning helps explain such elementary job behaviors as how people learn to avoid being conked on the head by cranes and low-hanging pipes. With classical conditioning, people also learn to avoid being burned twice by a hot pipe or not turning off a computer before saving a file.

OPERANT CONDITIONING: LEARNING THROUGH THE CONSEQUENCES OF OUR BEHAVIOR

Operant conditioning is learning that takes place as a consequence of behavior. In other words, a person's actions are instrumental in determining whether learning takes place. Operant conditioning is the cornerstone of behaviorism, as reflected first in the work of John B. Watson and then later by B. F. Skinner. The process by

■ **Operant conditioning**
learning that takes place as a consequence of behavior; a person's actions are instrumental in determining whether learning takes place

which a person learns the maximum temperature for safe operation of a personal computer illustrates operant conditioning. (The person in question lacked air conditioning.) Several times on warm days disturbing things begin to happen, such as files disappearing and unusual symbols appearing on screen. In desperation one day, the person shuts off the computer and returns late at night when the room temperature is much cooler. Because the computer now operates correctly, from that time on the person operates the computer only when the temperature is 90°F (32°C) or lower. In this case the operant is waiting for the temperature to drop or turning a fan in the direction of the computer. The person adopted checking the temperature on warm days because that person received reinforcement for the initial effort—the computer performed properly when the room temperature was lowered.

Reinforcement Strategies

The term *reinforcement* in general refers to the means by which behaviors are selected and retained. It gets at the idea that a response, such as shifting your weight on a snowboard to make a turn, is strengthened. The four reinforcement strategies are positive reinforcement, negative reinforcement (avoidance learning or motivation), punishment, and extinction.

Positive Reinforcement and Negative Reinforcement. The distinction between positive and negative reinforcement is very important. Positive reinforcement adds something rewarding to a situation, such as praise or a gift certificate. Positive reinforcement is thus receiving a reward for making a desired response. **Negative reinforcement** is effective because it takes away something unpleasant from a situation. It is a form of avoidance learning or motivation. Negative reinforcement is thus being rewarded by being relieved of discomfort. The personal computer incident described earlier included negative reinforcement. Adjusting the room temperature took away the unpleasant situation of the computer malfunctioning.

■ **Negative reinforcement**

taking away something unpleasant from a situation; being rewarded by being relieved of discomfort; form of avoidance learning or motivation

Note carefully that negative reinforcement is not the same thing as punishment. Negative reinforcement is pleasant and, therefore, a reward. Punishment, by definition, is something unpleasant, unless the person involved likes to be punished. With masochists, the reward is to be punished!

■ **Punishment**

the introduction of an unpleasant stimulus as a consequence of the learner having done something wrong

Punishment. Being punished for your mistakes can be an important part of learning. **Punishment** is the introduction of an unpleasant stimulus as a consequence of the learner having done something wrong (in the eyes of the person in control of the situation). Or the threat of punishment can be used instead of actually punishing people for the wrong response in a learning or motivational situation. Punishment assists the operant conditioning process because it weakens the particular response. You tend not to repeat a response because of its negative consequences.

■ **Extinction**

the weakening or decreasing of the frequency of undesirable behavior by removing the reward for such behavior

Extinction. The purpose of punishment is to eliminate a response. The same result can often be achieved through the reinforcement strategy of **extinction.** It refers to the weakening or decreasing of the frequency of undesirable behavior by removing the reward for such behavior. It is the absence of reinforcement. One way to stop the office clown from acting up is for coworkers to ignore that person's antics. The clown's behavior is said to be *extinguished.*

Primary and Secondary Reinforcers

■ **Primary reinforcer**

reinforcer that is rewarding by itself, without any association with other reinforcers; food, water, air, and sex are primary reinforcers

Another important distinction in operant conditioning is between primary reinforcers and secondary reinforcers. A **primary reinforcer** is one that is rewarding by itself, without any association with other reinforcers. Food, water, air, and sex are primary reinforcers. A **secondary reinforcer** is one whose value must be learned through association with other reinforcers. It is referred to as secondary not because it is less important, but because it is learned. Money is a secondary reinforcer. Although it is made of paper or metal, through its association with food, clothing, shelter, and other primary reinforcers, money becomes a powerful reward.

■ **Secondary reinforcer**
reinforcer whose value must be learned through association with other reinforcers

Schedules of Reinforcement

An important issue in operant conditioning (and in motivation) is how frequently to reward people when they make the correct response. So much experimentation has been conducted on this topic that some accurate guidelines are available. Two broad types of schedules of reinforcement are in use, continuous and intermittent.

Under a *continuous schedule*, behavior is reinforced each time it occurs, such as saying "good job" every time a bank teller comes out even at the end of the day. Continuous schedules usually result in the fastest learning, but the desired behavior quickly diminishes when the reinforcement stops. Under an *intermittent schedule* the learner receives a reward after some instances of engaging in the desired behavior but not after each instance. Intermittent reinforcement is particularly effective in sustaining behavior because the learner stays mentally alert and interested. At any point in time, the behavior might lead to the desired reward. Slot machines in gambling casinos operate on this principle.

MODELING AND INFORMAL LEARNING: LEARNING COMPLICATED SKILLS

Classical and operant conditioning provide only a partial explanation of how people learn on the job. When you acquire a complicated skill, such as speaking in front of a group, preparing a budget, or designing a store display, you learn much more than simply a single stimulus–response relationship. You learn a large number of these relationships, and you also learn how to put them together in a cohesive, smooth-flowing pattern. Two important processes that help in learning complicated skills are modeling and informal learning. Both are based on processes that are inferred to take place in the brain.

Complicated learning is called a *cognitive process* because it requires the learner to make a number of judgments and observations, or demanding mental activities. It is possible that cognitive process will someday be observed in such form as electrical charges in nerves. For now, however, scientists can only infer that these cognitive processes take place.

Modeling occurs when you learn a skill by observing another person perform the skill. Modeling is considered a form of social learning because it is learned in the presence of others. The process is classified as cognitive learning because it is a complex intellectual activity. Modeling, or imitation, often brings forth behaviors people did not previously seem to have in their repertoire. Many apprentices learn part of their trade by modeling an experienced craftsperson who practices the trade. Modeling is widely used in teaching sports through videotapes that give the viewer an opportunity to observe the skill being performed correctly. Although modeling is an effective way of learning, the learner must also have the proper capabilities and motivation.

■ **Modeling**
learning a skill by observing another person perform the skill; considered a form of social learning because it is learned in the presence of others

Informal learning is another way of learning complex skills in the workplace. It is planned or unplanned learning that occurs without a formal classroom, lesson plan, instructor, or examination. [2] The central premise of such learning is that employees acquire important information outside of a formal learning situation. The learning can be spontaneous, such as getting a tip on computer utilization while waiting in line at the cafeteria. Or the company might organize the work area to encourage such informal learning. The employees capitalize on a learning situation

■ **Informal learning**
planned or unplanned learning that occurs without a formal classroom, lesson plan, instructor, or examination; a way of learning complex skills in the workplace

in an unstructured situation where the rewards stemming from the learning are not explicit.

Informal learning can be regarded as a variation of **implicit learning,** or learning that takes place unconsciously and without an intention to learn. [3] Perhaps you have not been attempting to learn the Spanish word for *danger*, but after seeing the word *peligro* adjacent to the English word *danger* many times (such as near electric wires), you learn the Spanish word.

■ **Implicit learning**

learning that takes place unconsciously and without an intention to learn

E-LEARNING

Important innovations in learning have taken place in both schools and industry through the use of distance learning, technology-based learning, and e-learning. Here, the learner studies independently outside of a classroom setting and interacts with a computer in addition to studying course material. **E-learning** is a Web-based form of computer-based training. Many learning programs are computer based without being delivered over the Internet. For example, the tutorials included in many software packages are a form of computer-based training. An e-learning course usually is carefully structured, with specific lessons plans for the student. E-learning is more of a method of delivering content than a method of learning, yet the process helps us understand more about learning.

■ **E-learning**

studying independently outside of a classroom setting and interacting with a computer in addition to studying course material; Web-based form of computer-based training

A major impetus behind e-learning is that so many employees are geographically dispersed, making it difficult to gather them in one place for learning. A germane example is the marketing communications firm Fleishman-Hillard with 2,000 employees spread across 80 locations in 22 countries. The company uses Web-based technology to make information sharing more accessible and interactive. [4]

Although e-learning is technologically different from more traditional forms of learning, it still is based on basic methods of learning. For example, the learner will often need reinforcement to keep going. Trainers at GE Capital found that when managers gave reinforcement to employees on attendance, made them feel important, and tracked their progress, they were more likely to complete the course. [5]

Another relevant aspect of e-learning here is that its success depends on the cognitive processes of the learner, particularly self-motivation and self-discipline. Self-motivation is important because an assignment to take an e-learning course by the company often is not motivation enough to work independently. Self-discipline is necessary to create a regular time for performing class work, and it prevents distractions by work or home activities. In educational settings, successful distance learning also requires high motivation. Some students may not take e-learning seriously. Corporate e-learning programs have a high dropout rate; most students need the structure of a face-to-face instructor, a classroom, and other students to keep them focused on the course. [6]

E-learning has gained momentum, yet most companies prefer to use blended learning (Web and classroom) because it combines the personal nature of classroom training with the cost efficiencies of learning via the Internet. The cost efficiencies include decreases in travel and lodging costs, and payments to classroom instructors. [7] However, classroom training provides the difficult-to-measure benefit of employees spontaneously exchanging ideas that could lead to a creativity breakthrough. In general e-learning is most effective in delivering conceptual subject matter, such as product information, whereas classroom training is more effective for learning interpersonal skills. [8] The human touch is important for learning human relations! Furthermore, Richard E. Mayer, a psychology professor at the University of California, Irvine, conducted a review of learning studies. He concluded that learning guided by instructors is more effective than people learning on their own in most situations. [9] E-learning does provide some guidance, but an instructor adds an extra touch, such as answering questions and clarifying concepts.

What Are Several Different Learning Styles?

■ **Learning Objective 2**

Another important concept in understanding learning is **learning style,** the fact that people learn best in different ways. For example, some people acquire new material best through passive learning. Such people quickly acquire information through studying texts, manuals, magazine articles, and Web sites. They can juggle images in their mind as they read about abstract concepts such as supply and demand, cultural diversity, or customer service. Others learn best by doing rather than by studying—for example, learning hands-on about customer service by dealing with customers in many situations.

■ **Learning style**
method of coming to understand; different people learn best in different ways; some people acquire new material best through passive learning, such as acquiring information through studying texts, manuals, magazine articles, and Web sites; others learn best by doing rather than by studying; alone or cooperatively

Another key dimension of learning styles is whether a person learns best by working alone or cooperatively, such as in a study group. Learning by oneself allows for more intense concentration, and one can proceed at one's own pace. Learning in groups and through classroom discussion allows people to exchange viewpoints and perspectives. Considerable evidence has been accumulated that peer tutoring and cooperative learning are effective for acquiring knowledge. [10] Another advantage of cooperative learning is that it is more likely to lead to changes in behavior. Assume that a manager holds group discussions about the importance of achieving high customer satisfaction. Employees participating in these group discussions are more likely to assertively pursue high customer satisfaction on the job than those who only read about the topic. Learning styles have also been studied more scientifically, and one such approach is described next.

VISUAL, AUDITORY, AND KINESTHETIC LEARNING STYLES

According to the visual, auditory, and kinesthetic (VAK) learning style categorization, people learn best using one of three main sensory receivers. [11] *Visual learners* learn best by seeing, and they have two subchannels, linguistic and spatial. Learners who are *visual linguistic* prefer to learn through written language, such as reading and writing assignments. This type of learner would carefully pore over an instruction manual before using a new electronic device. Learners who are *visual spatial* prefer graphics, demonstrations, and videos or DVDs over written information.

Auditory learners prefer to learn by hearing, and they tend to move their lips and read out loud. An auditory learner would much prefer a spoken explanation of how to do something, such as using a new electronic device, than reading a manual. The same learners would prefer the interaction of a classroom over e-learning. *Kinesthetic learners* learn best while touching and moving and rely on two subchannels: kinesthetic (movement) and tactile (touch). These learners like to take notes while listening to lectures, tend to use highlighters, and frequently doodle while listening. When reading, the kinesthetic learner prefers to overview the material first to obtain the big picture and focus on details later.

Most learners combine all three styles to some degree while being dominant in one. For example, the visual learner might want to read the manual first to learn how to use a new electronic device. Yet the same learner might welcome a discussion about using the device and would also like to handle the device while reading the manual. Human Relations Self-Assessment Quiz 15-1 gives you an opportunity to measure your standing on the VAK dimensions.

LEARNING STYLES ASSOCIATED WITH PERSONALITY AS MEASURED BY THE MBTI®

Another way of understanding learning styles is to recognize that your personality can influence your learning style. You may have observed, for example, that when

Human Relations Self-Assessment Quiz 15-1

Visual, Auditory, and Kinesthetic Survey

Read each statement carefully. To the left of each statement, write the number that best describes
how each statement applies to you by using the following guide:

1	2	3	4	5
Almost never applies	Applies once in a while	Sometimes applies	Often applies	Almost always applies

Answer honestly as there are no correct or incorrect answers. It is best if you do not think about each question too long as this could lead
you to the wrong conclusion. Once you have completed all 36 statements (12 statements in three sections), total your score in the spaces
provided.

Section 1: Visual

____ **1.** I take a lot of notes and I like to doodle.

____ **2.** When talking to someone else I have the hardest time handling those who do not maintain good eye contact with me.

____ **3.** I make lists and notes because I remember things better if I write them down.

____ **4.** When reading a novel I pay a lot of attention to passages picturing the clothing, description, scenery, setting, etc.

____ **5.** I need to write down directions so I remember them.

____ **6.** I need to see the person I am talking to in order to keep my attention focused on the subject.

____ **7.** When meeting a person for the first time I notice the style of dress, visual characteristics, and neatness first.

____ **8.** When I am at a party, one of the things I love to do is stand back and "people-watch."

____ **9.** When recalling information I can see it in my mind and remember what I saw.

____ **10.** If I had to explain a new procedure or technique, I would prefer to write it out.

____ **11.** During my free time I am most likely to watch television or read.

____ **12.** If my boss has a message for me, I am most comfortable when he or she sends an e-mail or hard copy memo.

Total for Visual _____ (The minimum score is 12 and the maximum score is 60.)

Section 2: Auditory

____ **1.** When I read, I read out loud or move my lips to hear the words in my head.

____ **2.** When talking to someone else I have the hardest time handling those who do not talk back with me.

____ **3.** I do not take a lot of notes but I still remember what was said. Taking notes distracts me from the speaker.

____ **4.** When reading a novel I pay a lot of attention to passages involving conversations, talking, speaking, dialogues, etc.

____ **5.** I like to talk to myself when solving a problem or writing.

____ **6.** I can understand what a speaker says, even when I am not focused on the speaker.

___ **7.** I remember things easier by repeating them again and again.

___ **8.** When I am at a party, one of the things I love to do is talk in-depth about a subject that is important to me with a good conversationalist.

___ **9.** I would rather receive information from the radio, rather than from a newspaper (or on-line newspaper).

___ **10.** If I had to explain a new procedure or technique, I would prefer telling about it.

___ **11.** During my free time I am most likely to listen to music.

___ **12.** If my boss has a message for me, I am most comfortable when he or she calls on the phone.

Total for Auditory _____ (The minimum score is 12 and the maximum score is 60.)

Section 3: Kinesthetic

___ **1.** I am not good at reading or listening to directions. I would rather just start working on the task or project at hand.

___ **2.** When talking to someone else I have the hardest time handling those who do not show any kind of emotional support.

___ **3.** I take notes and doodle but I rarely go back and look at them.

___ **4.** When reading a novel I pay a lot of attention to passages revealing feelings, moods, action, drama, etc.

___ **5.** When I am reading, I move my lips.

___ **6.** I will exchange words and place and use my hands a lot when I can't remember the right things to say.

___ **7.** My desk appears disorganized.

___ **8.** When I am at a party, one of the things I love to do is enjoy the activities such as dancing, games, and totally losing myself in the action.

___ **9.** I like to move around. I feel trapped when seated at a meeting or a desk.

___ **10.** If I had to explain a new procedure or technique, I would prefer actually demonstrating it.

___ **11.** During my free time I am most likely to exercise.

___ **12.** If my boss has a message for me, I am most comfortable when he or she talks to me in person.

Total for Kinesthetic _____ (The minimum score is 12 and the maximum score is 60.)

Total each section: Visual _____; Auditory _____; Kinesthetic _____.

The area in which you have the highest score represents you best learning style. Note that you learn in *all* three styles, but you typically learned best using one of the three styles.

Source: "Learning Styles" (donclark@nwlink.com), available at http:www.nwlink.com/~donclark/hrd/vak.html, updated October 24, 2000, retrieved: March 20, 2005.

an impulsive person needs to learn how to use an electronic device, that person will often grab the device and start hitting the various buttons. A more reflective person will often first read the manual, or look over the device carefully before attempting to get it to function.

The MBTI® is a self-report questionnaire designed to make the theory of psychological types developed by psychoanalyst Carl Jung applicable to everyday life.

Jung developed the theory of psychological types, but he did not develop the measuring instrument in question. Katharine Cook Briggs and Isabel Briggs Myers are the authors of the MBTI® Indicator. More than 2 million Myers-Briggs® assessments are administered annually to individuals in the United States alone, for such purposes as team building, career exploration, conflict management, leadership and coaching, and retention. The administrations must be given by a certified MBTI® administrator. The developers of the MBTI® caution that the instrument should be taken voluntarily, and should not be used in the hiring or firing process.

As measured by the MBTI® instrument, four separate dichotomies direct the typical use of perception and judgment by an individual.

1. *Extraversion-Introversion dichotomy of attitudes or orientations of energy.* Extraverts direct their energy primarily toward the outer world of people and objects. In contrast, introverts direct their energy primarily toward the inner world of experiences and ideas.

2. *Sensing-Intuition dichotomy of functions or processes of perception.* People who rely on sensing focus primarily on what can be perceived by the five primary senses of vision, touch, sight, sound, and smell. People who rely on intuition focus primarily on perceiving patterns and interrelationships.

3. *Thinking-Feeling dichotomy of functions or processes of judgment.* People who rely primarily on thinking base conclusions on logical analysis and emphasize objectivity and detachment. People who rely on feelings base conclusions on personal or social values, and focus on understanding and harmony.

4. *Judging-Perceiving dichotomy of attitudes or orientations of toward dealing with the outside world.* People who use the judging process prefer to use the judging processes of Thinking or Feeling because the processes lead to decisiveness and closure. People who use one of Perceiving processes (Sensing or Intuition) do so because they prefer the flexibility and spontaneity that results from using these processes. [12]

Combining the four types with each other results in 16 personality types, such as ISTJ people who I (draw energy from and pay attention to their inner world); S (like information that is real and factual); T (use logical analysis in decision making); and J (like a structured and planned life). [13] You might want to take the MBTI® in an authorized center such as a counseling center. CPP Inc. certifies administrators of the MBTI®. Here our concern is with how your personality influences your learning style.

The third and fourth dimensions of psychological functioning are the basis for the relationship between personality and learning style. We take in information by perceiving, and we perceive in two opposite ways: sensing (S) and intuition (N). We organize the information we perceive and come to conclusions by judging. In turn, we judge in two opposite ways called thinking (T) and feeling (F). [14] The four mental processes of sensing, intuition, thinking, and feeling result in four learning styles, as shown in Figure 15-1. For example, if you have the NT learning style, you like to categorize, analyze, apply logic—and you prefer a relationship of mutual respect with your instructor!

Far too many people over-interpret Myers-Briggs Type® Inventory personality types as being definitive indicators of how an individual's personality, and therefore pigeon hole that person. In contrast, the founders of the MBTI® caution us: "You may use type to understand and forgive yourself, but not as an excuse for doing or *not* doing anything. Type should *not* keep you from considering any career, activity, or relationship." [15]

People who prefer	ST (Sensing, Thinking)	SF (Sensing, Feeling)	NF (Intuition, Feeling)	NT (Intuition, Thinking)
Interested in	Facts that supply useful information about activities encountered in everyday life	Practical information about people and a hospitable environment	Fresh ideas about how to understand people, and make use of symbols and metaphors	Hypotheses and overall explanations about why the world functions the way it does
Learn best by	Engaging in practical, hands-on activities	Engaging in practical hands-on activities with other people	Using imagination, creating in cooperation with other people, writing	Classifying and analyzing information, applying logic to problem solving
Need	Specific, step-by-step instructions; logical, practical reasons for engaging in an activity	Specific step-by-step instructions; frequent, positive interaction and approval	General direction, with freedom to choose a creative method; frequent, positive feedback	To be assigned a large problem to solve, an intellectually demanding task, and then to be allowed to solve the problem
Want from teacher	To receive fair treatment	Sympathy, emotional support, personalized recognition	Warmth, enthusiasm, humorous interactions, personalized recognition	To be respected, to respect the teacher's professional competence

Figure 15-1

Four Learning Styles Associated with the MBTI® Functions
Source: Further Information is available at http://www.cpp.com/ where you will find the full range of *Introduction to Type®* titles along other products that allow you to expand your knowledge and applications of your MBTI® type. Modified and reproduced by special permission of the Publisher, CPP, Inc., Mountain View, CA 94043. From *Introduction to Type,* 6th Edition by Isabel Briggs Myers. Copyright 1998 by Peter B. Myers and Katharine D. Myers. All rights reserved. Further reproduction is prohibited without the Publisher's written consent.

IMPROVING LEARNING AND BRAIN FUNCTIONING THROUGH REST

Interest has escalated in recent years for everyday approaches to improving a person's ability to learn and solve problems. We will return to this topic again in our discussion of cognitive challenges throughout the life span when we discuss the role of mental and physical activity to enhance learning. Here we look at the importance of *inactivity* to improve brain functioning and learning. Common wisdom suggests that it is easier to learn when you are rested, and scientific evidence supports this contention.

The potential benefits of sleep include stronger memory and better attention spans. According to James B. Maas, a psychology professor at Cornell University, good sleep is necessity rather than a luxury: "Your alertness, energy, performance, thinking, productivity, creativity, safety and health will be affected by how much you sleep," he said. Besides enhancing alertness, sleep is a way for the brain to store new information into long-term memory. The benefits are most likely to take place from rapid eye movement (REM) sleep that usually takes place during the sixth and eight hour of sleep, when people are most likely to dream.

During REM sleep the brain typically replenishes neurotransmitters, the chemical substances that transmit chemical impulses across synapses. The neurotransmitters are important because they organize the neural networks essential for remembering, learning, performance, and problem solving. So a catnap, or power nap may boost productivity but ample amounts of deep sleep is a bigger contributor to better learning and brain functioning. Sleep spindles—spikes of activity that surface during REM sleep—help people learn and remember how to perform physical tasks, such as playing golf, tennis, and basketball. [16]

■ Learning Objective 3

INDIVIDUAL DIFFERENCES RELATED TO LEARNING

The various approaches to learning, including learning styles, help us understand how people learn. How *much* people learn is another important consideration in understanding learning in the workplace. In general, people with higher mental ability and personality traits that allow them to concentrate better (such as emotional stability and conscientiousness) acquire knowledge and skills more readily.

A large-scale research study supports the idea that cognitive skills and personality traits contribute to a person profiting from training, and then using the acquired information to enhance job performance. The sample consisted of 9,793 trainees accepted into the Federal Aeronautics Association (FAA) training program for air traffic controllers. The average age of the trainee was 26 years; 84 percent were male, and 16 percent were female. Trainees took a cognitive skill test when applying for the program, whereas the personality test was administered as part of the medical examination of the air traffic control selection process.

The study found that air traffic controllers who rate high on general cognitive ability demonstrated greater skills acquisition than controllers who rate lower on general cognitive ability. A combination of personality traits, known as *Factor A (warmth)*, proved useful in predicting skill acquisition. High factor A people are warm, outgoing, attentive to others, cooperative, generous, and trusting. *Warmth* predicted skill acquisition, particularly when training was based on group work. The study also demonstrated that trainees who performed well in the training program were more likely to achieve full performance status when employed as air traffic controllers. [17]

CONTINUOUS LEARNING DURING YOUR CAREER

A reality of almost all professional, technical, and sales occupations is that career success, and even survival, depends on continuous learning. A commonplace example is that we all have to keep learning how to use new software and hardware just to perform a job. The CEO may need to understand how enterprise-level software helps the different divisions in a firm work together, and the auto-supply store associate has to learn how to track parts by computer. Acquiring human relations skills, such as working well with coworkers from different cultures, is another area of continuous learning facing many workers.

Larry D. Burns, vice president of research and strategic development for General Motors, makes the case for continuous learning during your career in these words: "Education is not a destination, it's a start. I've seen a number of students come into General Motors. They've gotten their education and think all they have to do now is to apply their skills. Universities need to prepare students for the ability to learn." [18] (Of course, this is a major intention of higher education.)

"Keeping up with the effects of globalization takes both openness and work—openness to learning, reading, and seeing the world, and work to adapt to the competitive, intellectual, and cultural shifts before they bite you in the rear."
—Kerry L. Sulkowicz, career advisor, and founder of the Boswell Group LLC. Quoted in "The Corporate Shrink," *Fast Company*, March 2006, p. 140.

How Does Perception Influence How People Interpret the World?

■ **Learning Objective 4**

Understanding learning strategies helps us cope better with the world of work, and understanding how we interpret information we receive is also important. Most of us interpret what is going on in the world outside us as we perceive it—not as it really is. You do not usually experience a mass of colors; instead, you experience a color photograph. You do not experience a thousand different vibrations in the air; instead, you hear a favorite compact disc. When we answer a question, we answer in terms of our interpretation of what we hear.

An everyday happening, such as a change in air temperature, helps to illustrate the nature of human perception. Assume that you live in Vermont. A temperature of 52° F (11.1° C) would seem warm in January. The same temperature would seem cold in July. Our perception of temperature depends on many things going on inside our mind and body.

Perceptions on the job are very important. Many studies, for example, have investigated the consequences of employee job perceptions. The results show that employees who perceive their job to be challenging and interesting have high job satisfaction and motivation. In addition, these favorable perceptions lead to better job performance. [19]

In summary, **perception** deals with the various ways in which people interpret things in the external world and how they act on the basis of these perceptions. The aspects of perception described here are (1) why perceptual problems exist, (2) agreement about perceived events, and (3) how people perceive the causes of behavior. Our discussion focuses on the social rather than the physical aspects of perception, such as taste, sound, and touch.

■ **Perception**
the various ways in which people interpret things in the external world and how they act on the basis of these perceptions

WHY PERCEPTUAL PROBLEMS EXIST

Under ideal circumstances, people perceive information as it is intended to be communicated or as it exists in reality. Suppose a company promotes a specialist to a team leader position because he or she is thought to have good potential for advancement. The manager offering the promotion hopes the specialist does not see the promotion as a plot to have the person work extra hours without being paid overtime. (Team leaders usually do not receive overtime pay.) Both characteristics of the stimulus (the idea or thing to be perceived) and the mental processes of people can lead to distorted perceptions. Figure 15-2 outlines why perceptual problems exist.

Characteristics of the Stimulus

Perceptual problems are most likely to be encountered when the stimulus or cue to be perceived has an emotional meaning. Assume that Brian, an office supervisor, announces to his staff, "I would like you to meet Brenda. She's a temporary worker here to help us out this week." Announcing the presence of an office temporary could trigger several different perceptions. The specific perceptions would depend on many motives, needs, and the knowledge of department employees. Among the possible interpretations are these:

"An office temporary? I wonder if this means the company is going to cut down the regular work force and use temporaries to help us through peak loads."

"This seems to be a sure sign that business has picked up. The front office would never authorize extra help unless business were booming. Things look good for getting a decent raise this year."

Figure **15-2**

Contributors   to   Perceptual
Problems

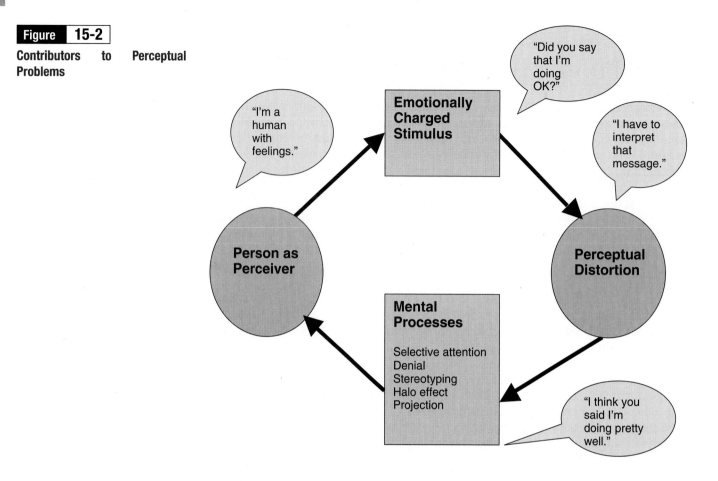

"I wonder if Brian has brought in a temporary worker to show us we had better get hustling or we could be replaced. I've heard a lot of these so-called temporaries usually wind up with full-time jobs if they like the temporary assignment."

To help reduce misperceptions, Brian should provide more complete information on why Brenda is being hired, such as pointing to a surge in orders. Reducing ambiguity helps minimize perceptual errors.

Mental Processes of People

The devices people use to deal with sensory information play a major role in creating perceptual problems. Several of these can also be classified as defensive behavior.

Selective Attention. The major contributor to perceptual distortions is the tendency for us to attend to the stimuli that are most relevant to our needs. Giving exclusive attention to something at the expense of other aspects of the environment is referred to as **selective attention.** If a stimulus fits our needs, desires, or interests we are likely to give it our attention. At the same time, we are likely to pay only minor attention to the surrounding stimuli. Thus, Joe Homeowner hears the wonderful news from the telemarketer that he is eligible to "cash out" on the equity on his home, and pay off all those high-interest debts. Only after going forward with the "cashing out" does it sink in for Joe that he now has a incurred a new long-term second mortgage on top of his existing mortgage.

Denial. If the sensory information is particularly painful to us—for example, if it hurts our self-esteem—we tend to go one step beyond selective attention. Denial is the process of excluding from awareness an important aspect of reality. This mental process is often found in the workplace, especially when people face such threats as

■ **Selective attention**

giving exclusive attention to something at the expense of other aspects of the environment job loss. As part of a downsizing, a woman was told by her manager that she would be terminated in 30 days unless somehow she could find another position in the company. That evening she informed her husband, "Our company is going through a downsizing, so it looks like I will be transferred to a different department in 30 days." By denying the reality of the message, the woman failed to search actively for another job within the company. She finally perceived the message correctly when handed her severance check.

Stereotyping. A common method of simplifying perception is to evaluate an individual or thing based on our perception of the group or class to which the person or object belongs. A perceptual disadvantage of stereotyping is that you do not look for the way in which somebody or something might be different from others in the same group. For example, a job seeker might say, "I won't look for a job in the retail field because retailing jobs have such low pay." Such stereotyping might result in the person's neglecting to investigate high-paying opportunities within the retail field based on the rapid promotions possible. Stereotypes can be positive as well as negative. For example, you might have the stereotype that all accountants are thorough and accurate. As a result, you fail to carefully review the tax return prepared by your accountant.

Halo Effect. We have a tendency to color everything that we know about a person because of one recognizable favorable or unfavorable trait. When a company does not insist on the use of objective measures of performance, it is not uncommon for a supervisor to give a favorable performance rating to people who dress well or smile frequently. The fine appearance or warm smile of these people has created a halo around them. Employees often create a negative halo about a supervisor simply because he or she is gruff or stern in manner or speech.

Projection. Another shortcut in the perceptual process is to project our own faults onto others instead of making an objective appraisal of the situation. Our feelings and thoughts are unacceptable to us, so we attribute them to another person. In this way we feel less anxious about ourselves. A manager who has a self-discipline problem himself might respond negatively to an employee's request to work at home one day per week. The manager might say, "Sorry, can't let you work at home. You would probably goof off half the day before you got down to work."

PERCEPTUAL CONGRUENCE

The discussion of perception so far has focused on perceptual errors. At times, most people in the organization perceive an event in the same way. **Perceptual congruence** refers to the degree to which people perceive things the same way. High congruence generally implies valid perception, but people can also agree on a distorted perception. For example, four members of a work team might have the authority to choose a fifth team member. All four might share the same inaccurate perception that a particular candidate is a good fit. After one month, they learn that the individual is a loner who functions poorly in a team environment.

■ **Perceptual congruence**
the degree to which people perceive things the same way

Despite the reservation cited, high congruence generally leads to more positive consequences for the organization than low congruence. A case in point is that it is beneficial for managers and group members to perceive the group members' tasks in the same manner.

ATTRIBUTION THEORY: HOW WE PERCEIVE THE CAUSES OF BEHAVIOR

An important aspect of perception is our explanation for the causes of behavior. Stated differently, to what do we *attribute* a given behavior? **Attribution theory** is the study of the process by which people ascribe causes to the behavior they

■ **Attribution theory**
the study of the process by which people ascribe causes to the behaviors they perceive

perceive. A major finding of attribution theory is that most people give relatively little weight to the circumstances in making judgments about a person's behavior. We are more likely to attribute a person's actions or results to personal characteristics than to outside forces. A supervisor who presses us to finish a project is more likely to be perceived as being impatient than as caught up in a highly competitive environment.

Another finding of attribution theory is that people have a general tendency to attribute their achievements to good inner qualities, whereas they attribute failure to adverse factors within the environment. A manager would thus attribute increased productivity to his or her leadership skills but blame low productivity on poor support from the organization.

To dig one step further into attribution theory, people attribute causes after gathering information about three dimensions of behavior: consensus, distinctiveness, and consistency. Imagine that Maria, a real estate agent, sold the highest dollar volume of real estate last year of any agent in the company nationwide. *Consensus* concerns whether other people behave similarly. If other people do not behave in the same way, we tend to attribute the cause to the person's characteristics. Because no other agent performed nearly as well, we are inclined to attribute Maria's success to her characteristics. *Distinctiveness* concerns whether the behavior in question occurred in other situations. If we had no evidence that Maria had been an outstanding performer in other situations, we might attribute her success to external factors such as luck. *Consistency* concerns the regularity of the behavior. If Maria had been a high-performing real estate agent in previous years, we would be more likely to attribute her success to personal characteristics such as high motivation and self-discipline.

The combination of all three factors helps us arrive at a final verdict of attribution. We attribute behavior to personal factors when we perceive low consensus, low distinctiveness, and high consistency. (Others aren't doing it, the person has done it in other situations, and the person acts this way consistently.) We attribute behavior to external causes when we perceive high consensus, high distinctiveness, and low consistency. (Others are doing it, the person rarely performs this way, and the person does not perform this way consistently.)

How Do We Respond to Life Span Changes and Challenges?

At different stages in life we face different challenges, beginning with the embryo struggling for enough oxygen, and ending with the 99-year-old fretting about physical well being and passing on his or her estate. Here we overview the stages of the life cycle and challenges associated with adolescence and beyond.

■ **Learning Objective 5**

STAGES OF THE LIFE CYCLE

Several approaches have been developed over the years to explain the various stages of human development, or the tasks people face at different periods in life. Among the best known is the eight stages of human development formulated by psychiatrist Erick H. Erikson in the 1950s. [20] Figure 15-3 presents an outline of these stages and the associated primary crisis for each one. According to Erikson, the socialization process consists of the "eight stages of man," with each stage representing a psychosocial crisis. The crisis must be resolved at each stage before the next stage can be satisfactorily negotiated.

Satisfactory learning and resolution of each stage is necessary if the child is to manage the next and later stages successfully. The building of a skyscraper is an

STAGES AND AGES	THE PRIMARY CRISIS AND RELATED COMMENT
1. Infancy (0–1 year)	*Learning basic trust versus basic mistrust (hope)* A well nurtured child develops trust and security.
2. Toddler (1–2 years)	*Learning autonomy versus shame (will)* The well-parented child emerges from this stage proud rather than feeling shamed.
3. Preschool (3–5 years)	*Learning initiative versus guilt (purpose)* Healthy children broaden their skills at this stage through active play.
4. Elementary school (6–12 years)	*Learning industry versus inferiority (competence)* Here the child learns the more formal life skills such as mastering reading and arithmetic, and some self-discipline.
5. Adolescence (13–19 years)	*Learning identity versus identity diffusion (fidelity)* The adolescent can now answer satisfactorily and happily the question, "Who am I?"
6. Young adulthood (20–40 years)	*Learning intimacy versus isolation (love)* The successful young adult experiences the type of intimacy that makes possible a good marriage or a genuine or enduring friendship.
7. Middle adulthood (40–65 years)	*Learning generativity (building a generation)* versus self-absorption In adulthood, the successful adult engages in a partnership and raises children.
8. Late adulthood (65 and over)	*Learning Integrity versus despair (wisdom)* The mature adult has integrity, is independent, and enjoys people and work. If the earlier psychosocial crises have not been resolve, he or she may have a self-view of disgust and despair.

Figure 15-3

Erikson's Eight Stages of Development and Associated Crisis

Source: Erick H. Erikson, *Childhood and Society* (New York: Norton, 1963); Child Development Institute, "Stages of Social-Emotional Development in Children and Teenagers," available at www.childdevelpmentinfo.com, retrieved May 10, 2006.

appropriate metaphor. Each floor, including the foundation and ground level, must be built correctly or the next floor will collapse. An example of this stage-by-stage development is that if the young adult cannot experience intimacy at stage 6, he or she will not be successful at the marriage or parenting that takes place at stage 7.

Erikson's stages of human development have prompted later investigation into how humans develop through different phases of their life. Despite these analyses of life stages, there are huge cultural and individual differences in the successful development of an adult. For example, what about Russians whose life expectancy is only about 50 years old? Do Russians never deal with Stage 8, integrity versus despair? And is it not possible to be a successful, well-adjusted adult even if you are not in a committed relationship and have no children?

Next, we summarize briefly challenges people face in adolescence, adult life, and late life. [21] The first stage, infancy and childhood is an important building block for later stages but lies outside the purview of our treatment of human relations.

RESPONDING TO CHALLENGES IN ADOLESCENCE

In its technical meaning **adolescence** is the period in life from approximately ages 13 to 20. From a biological standpoint, adolescence begins with puberty, the

■ **Learning Objective 6**

■ **Adolescence**

the period in life from approximately age 13 to 20; from a biological standpoint, adolescence begins with puberty beginning of sexual maturation marked by rising levels sex hormones and rapid growth. During adolescence many people start building work-related human skills, such as teamwork, and also engage in career choice and career preparation. Adolescents (or *teenagers*) vary considerably in their accomplishments with some teenagers being successful entrepreneurs, information technology consultants, professional athletes, and movie stars. Industries such as retailing and food service depend on the adolescent workforce, suggesting that even average teenagers occupy an important work role in society.

Cognitive Challenges

Adolescents headed for a successful career must rise to the challenge of developing logic, abstract thought, and hypothetical reasoning. Many adolescents are studying five different subjects at once and feel compelled to think well enough to perform well in school and on college entrance exams. Adolescents must also deal with the development of moral reasoning in which they attempt to learn acceptable versus unacceptable codes of conduct. According to Lawrence Kohlberg, former moral education professor at Harvard University, adolescents begin to development three levels of moral thought: [22]

■ At the *preconventional level* moral dilemmas are resolved in a self-centered way. An act is moral if it enables someone to avoid punishment or obtain reward. Obeying safety rules or returning a lost wallet might fit this category of moral development.

■ At the *conventional level* moral dilemmas are resolved in ways that reflect laws or norms set by parents and other influential adults. Making a complete stop at a stop sign on a country rode when no one else is watching would fit the conventional level of moral development.

■ At the *postconventional level* moral dilemmas are resolved by relating to abstract principles such as equality, justice, and the value of life. An adolescent at this level of moral development might start a food-and-clothing campaign for homeless people in the community.

One reason offered for the unethical behavior of many adults in executive positions in business is that they did not advance to the postconventional level of moral development.

Personality and Social Challenges

■ **Identity crisis**

adolescent struggle to establish a reliable self-concept, or personal identity, including concerns over ethnic identity, the need to keep close ties with the family or develop peer relations, sexuality, and body image

As an adolescent struggles to establish a reliable self-concept, or personal identity, he or she faces an **identity crisis.** In a multicultural world, the adolescent may need to establish an ethnic identity. Adolescents often struggle with whether to retain close ties with the family or invest more energy in developing peer relations. Adolescents struggle with sexuality, with some happily engaging in sex whereas others face unintended negative consequences such as parenthood, paternity suits, dropping out of school, and sexually transmitted diseases. Another conflict many adolescents face is one of body image, with discontent possibly leading to anorexia and excessive body piercing.

RESPONDING TO ADULT LIFE CHALLENGES

Adulthood is not marked by the same more predictable milestones as childhood and adolescence. Assuming that a person lives until about age 80, he or she spends more than half the life in the adult stage, so adults face an enormous number of challenges, including managing social life, work, and finances; raising children;

keeping a blended family working together; staying current with technology; and investing for retirement.

Cognitive Challenges

Adults face the unique challenge of applying the many cognitive skills they have acquired during study. For example, some people who performed well in math exams have no clue as to how to calculate miles per gallon on a vehicle or balance a checkbook. To prosper in a career, the adult must often learn creative-thinking skills and apply wisdom. For example, the self-employed adult must find a way to convince bankers or venture capitalists on the merits of investing in his or her idea for the launch of a new product or service. An adult faces the challenge of learning to think more flexibly rather than finding the "correct" answer to a problem—the essence of creative thinking.

Personality and Social Challenges

Adults must learn to become less self-centered and refine their interpersonal skills, including developing business etiquette. For some young people a major adjustment is to learn to take off their sports cap when eating at a restaurant or being interviewed for a job. Many adults in their forties face a **midlife crisis,** when they feel unfulfilled and search for a major shift in career or lifestyle. Adults facing a midlife crisis often wonder whether their choice of career or life partner was the right decision. During the more common **midlife transition,** adults may take stock of their life and formulate new goals, such as an engineer working for IBM deciding to teach high school math. (IBM encourages such transitions to foster math and science knowledge and skills.) Among the dozens of other personality and social challenges facing adults are the loss of a youthful appearance and a decreased reproductive or sexual capacity. Such challenges have spurred the development of plastic surgery, youth-enhancing cosmetics, and lifestyle drugs such as those designed to enhance sexual performance.

■ **Midlife crisis**
time adults in their forties face when they feel unfulfilled and search for a major shift in career or lifestyle

■ **Midlife transition**
adults taking stock of their lives and formulating new goals; among dozens of other personality and social challenges facing adults are the loss of a youthful appearance and a decreased reproductive or sexual capacity

RESPONDING TO LATE LIFE CHALLENGES

The challenges of late life have increased because more people live longer beyond the traditional retirement age, and many remain active and in good health. Yet still many other people in late life are infirmed, impoverished, and dependent on family and government to maintain their well-being.

Cognitive Challenges

Many people in late adulthood face cognitive decline, whereas many others do not. The ability to learn rapidly and reason abstractly and logically may decline through adulthood, starting at age 30. However, wisdom and judgment based on the accumulation of knowledge may increase up into the 80s. The issue of the cognitive skills of late life adults has been the subject of much opinion and research in recent years because the life span of people has increased, and so many old people hold responsible positions, drive cars, and even fly airplanes solo.

Common wisdom suggests that staying in shape mentally by such activities as doing crossword puzzles, surfing the Internet, or studying a foreign language can slow the decline of an aging brain. A long-term study called Active trained 2,832 adults 65 to 94 years old in memory, reasoning, or visual attention and perception. Although the trainees performed better on the skill they practiced, that training did not translate to improvement in the other skills. Many mentally active, late life adults show smaller cognitive decline than their less mentally active counterparts. Yet, the mentally active people most likely had a stronger cognitive reserve (mental capacity) that led them to stay mentally active. [23] Though this study did not support the use-it-or-lose-it hypothesis, it demonstrates that older adults can still master specific cognitive tasks with practice. So your grandmother who studies Mandarin Chinese may not then be able to decipher a manual for a digital camera easily, but at least she now knows Mandarin.

An optimistic note about cognitive decline is that the intake of about one alcoholic beverage a day appears to slow the decline, perhaps because moderate use of alcohol helps preserve the blood vessels in the brain. The research—not sponsored by a wine or beer distributor—was conducted by researchers from Harvard University, and Brigham and Women's Hospital in Boston. The study compared the cognitive functions in more than 11,000 nurses, ages 70 to 81, divided into alcoholic intakes of one, two, or no drinks per day. [24]

Personality and Social Challenges

A change noted in late adulthood is that people begin to value the present more because they correctly perceive that they have a shorter future than do younger adults. As a result, late life adults are less concerned about activities that may have a payoff in the long run, such as networking. Instead, they look to spend times with good friends and family already available. Practical problems for those in the most advanced years are that many friends die and family members move away. Thus, the late life adult may have to seek out new friends. Retirement communities, including assisted living, provide an opportunity for affluent older people to make new social contacts, to help compensate for the loss of friends and family members.

A challenge for some late life adults is to engage in fulfilling physical activities to replace favored activities of previous years. For example, a 75-year-old with a hip and knee replacement may not be able to play tennis or golf any longer and may have to find satisfaction in a replacement activity such as light hiking.

■ Learning Objective 7

LIFE AND JOB SATISFACTION THROUGHOUT THE LIFE SPAN

People at various stages of their life span often wonder what type of satisfaction and happiness awaits them at later stages. Typical self-questions are these: "Will I enjoy my work more in late career?" "Will I be more (or less) happy in my later years?" Although the research evidence about life and job satisfaction throughout the life span is not entirely consistent, some trends are notable.

Life Satisfaction and Age

Life satisfaction tends to increase throughout adulthood, partially because many of the major challenges in life are met as one reaches the 50s and 60s. For example, by middle age most people have completed their formal education, chosen a career, and reared children. According to a study by Daniel Mroczek, a psychology professor at Fordham University, life satisfaction for men tends to peak at age 65. His study synthesized more than 20 years of data from almost 2,000 men in the Veterans Affairs Normative Aging Study. The life satisfaction and personal traits of the subjects were measured over almost a 30-year span.

After life satisfaction peaking around 65, the men around age 95 were about as happy as they were in their mid-40s. Nevertheless, there was considerable variation among individuals with some people peaking in satisfaction early, and then experiencing a permanent decline in happiness. In contrast, some of the men in the study continued to gain in happiness. Personality factors influenced the happiness and satisfaction curve. Highly extroverted people were more likely to have high levels of life satisfaction and more stability in life satisfaction. (One interpretation of these findings is that extroversion helps a person develop friends, and positive human contact contributes to life satisfaction.) Another finding was that life satisfaction dropped considerably during the last year of life—often because a person has poor physical health during his or her final year. [25]

Women also tend to gain in life satisfaction as they become older. Psychology students Brian Scott Ehrlich and Derek Isaacowitz guided by their professors at the University of Pennsylvania, conducted a study of subjective well-being, including life satisfaction, among young, middle aged, and older people. The sample consisted of 190 women and 90 men, ranging in age from 18 to 93 years old. Young adults and middle-aged adults showed relatively the same degree of life satisfaction, and older adults tended to be the most satisfied with life. The findings about older people having higher life satisfaction were of modest magnitude, but they did support similar evidence from other studies. [26]

Not all researchers have found that life satisfaction increases with age. Yet, the bulk of evidence is at least that the ratings of life satisfaction do not *decline* with age. Apparently, as long as people have a reasonable amount of love and satisfying work, they tend to stay happy. [27]

Job Satisfaction and Age

Job satisfaction also tends to increase with age, as would be predicted because work satisfaction is such a major component of life satisfaction. A study conducted by the Conference Board in 2005 found that Americans were growing increasingly unhappy with their job in comparison to previous years. However, the smallest decline in job satisfaction took place among workers 65 and older. Overall job satisfaction slipped from 60.8 to 58.0 percent, making people in this age group the most satisfied with their jobs. [28] (It is possible that still being part of the workforce during an era of so many downsizings would add to an older person's appreciation and job satisfaction.)

A general explanation for the many studies indicating the increase in job satisfaction during a person's career is that with more work experience older workers understand better which needs work can and cannot satisfy. In addition, they have a more realistic view of life and work. [29] Experience also contributes to income, and a higher income in turn contributes to job satisfaction for many workers.

What Are Some Basic Concepts About Changing Careers?

■ **Learning Objective 8**

The new type of career emphasizes doing work that fits your major values in life, so many people switch careers to find work that fits their values. And these values could include earning enough money to support a family well and purse preferred leisure activities. A major reason for switching careers is to find better opportunities after a job loss.

A major principle of career switching is to *be thorough.* Go through the same kind of thinking and planning that is recommended for finding a first career. Obtaining valid career information is essential, such as consulting ***www. bls.gov/oco/home.htm,*** the on-line edition of the *Occupational Outlook Handbook.* The advantage for the career switcher, however, is that the experienced person often has a better understanding of the type of work he or she does not want to do. *Finding a mentor* who can help guide you through a career change is also helpful.

One of the first steps in making a career change is to *assess your likes and dislikes.* Career coach Randall S. Hansen advises that many people change careers because their dislike their job, their boss, and their company. Yet you also need to examine your likes. What work-related activities excite and energize you? [30] Many people learn more about their career preferences by taking a career assessment instrument combined with the guidance of a career counselor. Three of the most scientifically developed career inventories are as follows:

- Campbell Interest and Skill Survey *(www.pearsonassessments.com/tests/ciss.htm)*
- Myers-Briggs Type® Indicator Career Report *(www.cpp.com)*
- 16PF Personal Career Development Profile Plus *(www.Careers-By-Design.com)*

A new career should be *built gradually.* Few people are able to leave one career abruptly and step into another. For most people who switch careers successfully, the switch is more of a transition than an abrupt change. A constructive approach would be to take on a few minor assignments in the proposed new field and then search for full-time work in that field after building skill. An electronics technician, for example, might request to visit customers with sales representatives to facilitate a switch to industrial selling. To prepare for your new career, you may need to acquire the necessary education and training. Your author knew a surgeon who thought that the most interesting part of his job was talking to patients about their finances. So the good doctor took some courses in finance that helped him prepare to became a certified financial planner.

Sometimes an interim assignment can offer a person useful ideas for a complete career change or at least a different emphasis. One such possibility is to fill in for a person who is on a company-paid leave of absence, referred to as a *sabbatical.* Another possibility for an interim assignment is filling in for someone who is on family leave because of the birth or adoption of a child. Filling in for the boss, for example, can give a person a firsthand sense of managerial work.

A major reason that many employees consider a new career is that they crave more independence. As a consequence, an increasingly popular path for the career switcher is to move from salaried employment to self-employment. The prospective self-employed person needs to decide on which particular business to enter. For many people, self-employment means continuing to perform similar work, such as the company cafeteria manager entering the food catering business. Other formerly employed workers go into competition with their former employers, such as a print shop manager opening a print shop of her own. For those who lack specific plans of their own, prepackaged plans can be purchased. A sampling of these is as follows:

- cartridge printing, recharging, and repair
- check cashing service
- damage restoration
- language translations services
- bed and breakfast
- liquidated goods broker
- self-storage center

Anyone contemplating self-employment should recognize that it offers potentially high rewards as well as risks. An editor of *Entrepreneur* magazine explains the downside of being a business owner in these terms:

> Any business owner knows what deep corrections in the stock market mean for young companies. Venture capital dries up. Frustrated sellers, unable to unload shares, stop buying stock in companies like yours. Consumers resist the urge to pull the old Visas out of their wallets and buy your products. Inventories pile up, cash gets tight and pink slips appear on staffers' desks. At times like these, owning a business ranks right up there with root canals and tax audits on the list of life's undesirables. [31]

Human Relations in Practice

Dale Vnuk Switches from Airline Mechanic to Water Garden Builder

Dreams of a more satisfying life helped spur Dale Vnuk to choose a new career after more than a quarter-century in the same line of work. So did the constant grousing of coworkers. Now Vnuk is in the process of retiring early and switching from airline mechanic to water garden builder. "At 47, it's either time to do something or sit their and be miserable," said Vnuk, who opened a water garden store this year with his wife, Marcia, in suburban Fox Lake, Illinois. "It's jut a great burst of inspiration to see that you can still do something and change your life around."

Source: Dave Carpenter, "A New Career: Boomers Retire Early to Change Lives," Associated Press, October 17, 2005.

The accompanying Human Relations in Practice box insert gives a brief example of a career switch into self-employment.

Another self-employment possibility is to purchase a franchise, thus lowering the risk of a start-up business. Currently, franchises account for about one-third of retail sales in the United States and Canada. Yet franchises require a substantial financial investment, ranging from about $6,000 to $600,000. Furthermore, some of the big name franchisors, such as Dunkin Donuts, require that the franchisee purchase multiple stores simply to get started. Another caution is that some franchise operators may work about 70 hours per week to earn about $18,000 per year.

What Are Some Tactics For Coping With Change?

■ **Learning Objective 9**

We have all heard that adapting to change is necessary for career success, and even survival. A fitting conclusion to this chapter is, therefore, to present a few tactics for coping with change. To begin, *look for the personal value that could be embedded in a forced change.* [32] If you are downsized, take the opportunity to assume responsibility for your own career rather than being dependent on the organization. Many downsizing victims find a new career for themselves that better fits their interests or try self-employment in search of more job security.

When faced with a significant change, *ask "What if?" questions* such as "What if my company is sold tomorrow?" "What if I went back to school for more education?" and "What if I did accept that one-year assignment in China?" When confronting major change, *force yourself to enjoy at least some small aspect of the change.* Suppose the edict comes through the organization that purchases can now only be made over the Internet. This means you will no longer be able to interact with a few of the sales reps you considered to be buddies. With the time you save, however, you will have spare hours each week for leisure activities.

You are less likely to resist change if you *recognize that change is inevitable.* Dealing with change is an integral part of life, so why fight it? Keep in mind also to *change before you have to, which can lead to a better deal.* If your manager announces a new plan, get on board as a volunteer before you are forced to accept a lesser role. If your company has made the decision to start a Six Sigma (companywide quality improvement) program, study the subject early and ask for a role as a facilitator or team leader. Stop trying to be in control all the time because you cannot control everything. Many changes will occur that you cannot control, so relax and enjoy the ride. Finally, recognize that change has an emotional impact, which will most likely cause some inner turmoil and discomfort. Even if the change is for the better, you might remain emotionally attached to your old system—or neighborhood, car, or PC.

Continuing to acquire useful knowledge is also helpful in dealing with change because you have the new knowledge at hand to get past the change. [33] When digital photography became dominant, the operators of many portrait studios felt threatened and were too slow to offer digital services to their customers. Many of these photographers who waited too long to offer digital services were forced out of business. In contrast, many other portrait photographers were early learners of digital technology and survived the transition well.

The bestseller, *The World Is Flat: A Brief History of the Twenty-First Century* (2005) by Thomas L. Friedman, has made thousands of educators and individuals aware of the potential changes imposed on us by globalization and outsourcing. One key point of the book is that the global economic playing field has been leveled by information technology that enables people to collaborate regardless of their location. Another key point is that the success of individual workers will depend on the development of specialized skills. Furthermore, to cope with these changes workers must constantly upgrade their skills. At the same time they should search for jobs that cannot be outsourced or that are anchored because they must be done at a specific location, such as calling on an industrial customer. [34]

Many personal service jobs cannot be outsourced or sent offshore, including hair dressers, massage therapists, custodial technicians, and auto mechanics. Yet even here, some personal service workers in North America complain that residents from lower-wage countries are willing to perform these services at lower wages than the North American workers are. Some corporate professional jobs are more difficult to outsource than others. The positions less likely to be outsourced are those requiring the combination of technical (or discipline skills) plus connections with people. [35] A real estate agent with hundreds of personal contacts cannot be replaced by a Web site. An information systems specialist who performs hands-on work with internal clients cannot be replaced by an information technology specialist working 8,000 miles away in another country. The change-management lesson here is building relationships with work associates helps ward off some of the threats of the "flat world."

Concept Review and Reinforcement

Key Terms

Summary and Review

In this chapter we have studied additional knowledge that helps a person attain career thrust.

- Classical conditioning is the most elementary form of learning. It occurs when a previously neutral stimulus is associated with a natural (unconditioned) stimulus. Eventually, the neutral stimulus brings forth the unconditioned response. For example, a factory whistle blown just prior to the lunch break induces employees to salivate and experience hunger pangs.

- Operant conditioning (or instrumental learning) occurs when a person's spontaneous actions are rewarded or punished, which results in an increase or a decrease in the behavior. Much of human learning occurs through operant conditioning. The four reinforcement strategies involved in such conditioning are positive reinforcement, negative reinforcement, punishment, and extinction. A primary reinforcer is rewarding by itself, whereas the value of a secondary reinforcer must be learned through association with other reinforcers. A continuous reinforcement schedule rewards behavior each time it occurs, whereas an intermittent schedule delivers rewards periodically.

- Two important processes that help in learning complicated skills are modeling and informal learning. Modeling occurs when you learn a skill by observing another person perform that skill. Informal learning is unplanned and occurs in a setting without a formal classroom, lesson plan, instructor, or examination. Informal learning can be spontaneous, or the company might organize the work area to encourage such learning.

- E-learning is a Web-based form of computer-based training. The geographical dispersion of employees makes e-learning more important. Self-motivation and self-discipline are essential for the e-learner. Most companies continue to use blended learning (Web and classroom) to capitalize on the efficiencies of e-learning yet still rely on human contact.

- People learn best in different ways, for example, some people acquire information best through passive learning. A preference for working alone versus cooperatively is another difference in learning style. A useful classification of learning styles is the preference of visual, auditory, or kinesthetic learning. Most learners use a combination of the three styles.

- Personality type can influence learning style. According to the Myers-Briggs Type Indicator® (MBTI), two dimensions of psychological functioning are the basis for the relationship between personality and learning style. We perceive through sensing (S) and intuition (N). We judge through thinking (T) and feeling (F). The four mental processes of sensing, intuition, thinking, and feeling results in four learning styles as shown in Figure 15-2.

- In general, people with higher mental ability and personality traits that allow them to concentrate better (e.g., conscientiousness) acquire knowledge and skills more readily.

- A reality of almost all professional, technical, and sales occupations is that career success and survival depend on continuous learning.

- Perception, the organization of sensory information into meaningful experiences, influences job behavior. Perceptual problems stem from both a stimulus with an emotional meaning and the mental processes of people. These mental processes, or shortcuts, include selective attention, denial, stereotyping, the halo effect, and projection.

- Perceptual congruence refers to the degree to which people perceive things the same way. High congruence generally leads to more positive consequences for the organization than does low congruence.

- Attribution theory explains how people attribute the causes of behavior. People have a general tendency to attribute their achievements to good inner qualities, whereas they attribute failure to adverse factors within the environment. People attribute causes after gathering information about consensus (comparison among people), distinctiveness (comparison across tasks), and consistency (task stability over time). We attribute behavior to personal factors when we perceive low consensus, low distinctiveness, and high consistency.

- According to Erickson, the socialization process consists of the "eight stages of man," with each state representing a psychosocial crisis. The crisis must be resolve at each stage before the next stage can be successfully negotiated.

- The challenges of adolescence include the cognitive challenge of developing logic and abstract thought as well as developing moral reasoning. A key personality and social challenge is the identity crisis.

- The challenges of adulthood include applying cognitive skills to real-life problems. Adults must also learn to become less self-centered and refine their interpersonal skills. Adults may also face a midlife crisis and a midlife transition.

- The challenges of late adulthood include cognitive decline, even though older people can be trained to learn new, complex tasks. A change facing late life adults is more of a focus on the present.

- Life satisfaction tends to increase throughout adulthood but may peak for men at about age 65. Job satisfaction also tends to increase with age, partially because older adults understand better which needs work can and cannot satisfy.

- A major principle of career switching is to be thorough. Obtain valid career information, and assess your likes and dislikes. A new career should be built gradually, often by phasing into the new career part time. An increasingly popular path for the career switcher is to move from salaried employment to self-employment.

- Suggestions for managing change well include searching for the personal value that could be embedded in forced change, asking "What if," forcing yourself to enjoy at least some small aspect of the change, recognizing that change is inevitable, and understanding that change has an emotional impact. To help cope with possible changes caused by outsourcing and offshoring of one's job is to incorporate building relationships into one's job.

Check Your Understanding

1. Why is it that so many employers believe that a valuable skill for their employees is to "learn how to learn"?
2. Give an example of a valuable skill you have learned in life through modeling. Did you intend to learn it at the time?
3. Provide an example of knowledge that you have acquired without a conscious intention to learn.
4. What steps can a company take to encourage informal learning among employees.
5. If e-learning is so effective, why haven't most schools of higher education converted completely to distance learning?
6. Give an example of where it *is* true that perception is more important than reality.

7. How would a study of suicide rates at various ages help you understand life span challenges?
8. How do you interpret the old saying, "Youth is wasted on the young?"
9. Based on information in this chapter, what advice can you offer a person in the late 40s who is fearful of becoming old?

10. What is your strategy for dealing the biggest change you will have to face during the next 12 months?

Web Corner

Developing soft skills through e-learning: www.skill soft.com

Insight into your Myers-Briggs® Personality Type: www. cpp.com

The 10-step plan to career change: www.quintcareers.com

INTERNET SKILL BUILDER:

Although opinions vary as to the precise meaning of a *millennial,* the term generally refers to the last generation born in the twentieth century. Search the Internet to identify about 10 life span challenges facing the millenials—in other words challenges facing members of this generation attributed to their stage in life. You can probably supplement the list with reading you have done or personal observations. Did you find the World Wide Web useful for this type of search, or did you have better luck with a library database?

Developing Your Human Relations Skills

Human Relations Application Exercises

Applying Human Relations Exercise 15-1

Developing Your Brain and Learning Ability

The belief is widespread that the human brain can be developed through mental exercise. We found about 16 million entries using the search engine entry, "exercising the brain." Even when a given brain builder may work for many other people, you do not know if the technique will help you specifically. Here is an opportunity to try a brain exercise, and see what the positive consequences might be for you. You will need a few minutes a day for at least 10 days to determine whether the technique works. First, do one or both of the following exercises for 10 to 14 days:

1. Recite the alphabet backward until you are proficient. Perform the exercise a few times a day until can do the backward version almost as easily as the forward version.

2. Learn a new word in your native language or your second language every day. Visualize the new words that you have learned during this time span.

After the 10 days or two weeks are completed, reflect on your learning ability and memory. Compare your learning on new tasks today with your learning in the past. Is it easier for you to study? Do you grasp the meaning of news stories more quickly? Can you remember telephone numbers or e-mail addresses more readily? If other classmates have done this exercise, ask them about their experiences. Have these exercises resulted in more brain power for them?

If these straightforward exercises really improve brain power, what are some of the implications for human relations?

Source: The core idea for the two games is credited to http://me.essortment.com/brainexercises_rcas.htm.

Applying Human Relations Exercise 15-2

Life Span Challenges Facing Seniors

The life span challenges described in this chapter that seniors face are certainly valid. Your role in this exercise is to find out directly what challenges advanced seniors face. We refer to people 70 years old and beyond. The older the people you can find for this study, the better. Conduct interviews with parents (if they qualify), grandparents, nursing home residents, friends, and neighbors. Obtain a sample of at least four people. Ask your interviewees about the challenges and problems they face now, those in the recent past, and those they anticipate in the future. After you have collected your interview data, answer these questions:

1. What are the physical and health problems facing these seniors?
2. What are the emotional and human relations problems facing these seniors?
3. What could other people do to help these seniors with some of their most pressing concerns?

Human Relations Case Study 15-1

Nike Goes Underground to E-Train Store Associates

Seven years after his stint as a manager of a Nike store, Mike Donahue, who is in charge of e-learning at Nike, was asked to design an on-line training program that the company could offer to employees in its own stores as well as at other retailers that sell its products. He knew that he and his team would have to design a program that would convey a lot of information quickly but also would be easy to digest.

"We knew that we did a great job of advertising and that we could drive people into the stores, but ultimately the person who is talking to the customer is a 16-to 22-year-old kid," he says. "We wanted them to have a better dialogue with the consumer."

Donahue and his team knew that they wanted their program to deliver information in short increments to make it easy for associates to take in—and keep them out on the floor. "We were throwing out ideas, and someone suggested that we need to come up with something edgy, something underground," Donahue said. That's when the idea for the Sports Knowledge Underground was born. It was by pure coincidence that the acronym for the new program, SKU, also stands for the retail term, "stock keeping unit."

The layout for the Sports Knowledge Underground resembles a subway map, with different stations representing different training themes. For example, Apparel Union Station branches off into the apparel technologies line, the running products line and the Nike Pro products line. The Cleated Footwear Station offers paths to football, whereas the Central Station offers such broad lines as customer skills.

Each segment is three to seven minutes long and gives the associates the basic knowledge they need about various products. As new products are introduced each season, the training is updated and Nike customizes the program for each retailer if requested. Associates are quizzed at the end of the training and asked for feedback, which gets routed back to Donahue and his team. "If we get feedback that something is confusing, we can go back and change it immediately," we can go back and change it immediately," Donahue says.

For Nike, one of the most appealing aspects of introducing e-learning is that it sets a standard of learning for diverse workforces. The culture of one store may be vastly different from the next.

Questions

1. What would you predict will be the success of the Sports Knowledge Underground training program? Explain the basis for your prediction.
2. How well suited is e-learning of this type to the demographic group of the Nike store associates?
3. What would you think of moving some of the SKU training to handheld devices (as has been contemplated)?

Source: Excerpted from Jessica Marquez, "Faced with High Turnover, Retailers Boot up E-Learning Programs for Quick Training," *Workforce Management*, August 2005, pp. 74–75.

Human Relations Case Study 15-2

"I Know I Can Make a Contribution Somewhere"

Brad Martinez, age 43, is a senior account manager for Western Office Supply, a company that sells a wide range of products to business firms, hospitals, and schools. Western does not manufacture any products of its own, but resells the products of several hundred manufacturers, much like being a department store for other firms. His company typically sells supplies in much larger quantities than sold by giant office-supply stores such as Staples and OfficeMax. Western also sells office furniture and decorations, such as lamps and wall hangings.

Although Brad's job title is account manager, he is essentially an outside sales representative who reports to the sales manager of Western Office Supply. Brad personally calls on about 50 established accounts and solicits

new business regularly. After Brad opens an account, replacement sales for smaller items are usually made through the company Web site or telephone. However, he periodically makes in-person visits and telephone solicitations to sell office equipment such as small photocopiers, desktop computers, printers, fax machines, and office telephones.

After graduating from a career school with a major in business administration with a marketing concentration, Brad thought he would explore the world before settling on a career. He joined the U.S. Army and worked in the medical service field as a medic in several Army hospitals. Because Brad was not in the service during armed combat, he assisted in treating injuries, and injuries to dependents of Army personnel. Brad served admirably in the Army, and worked his way up to the rank of sergeant.

In Brad's words, "I left the Army proud of my service, but looking for a more promising career. No matter how much the Army liked me, they weren't going to make me the Surgeon General. I thought it was time to get started in the business field."

After the Army, Brad worked six years in the purchasing department at a machine-tool company, working his way up to a position as purchasing supervisor. After that he joined Western as a sales trainee and progressed up to his present position.

During the past several years, Brad's sales commissions have begun to decline. One problem he has faced is that many of his customers are now purchasing their supplies directly from both distributors and manufacturers over the Internet. Another problem is Western's own e-commerce initiative. Brad and the other sales representatives receive a very small commission when a new customer makes an Internet purchase or an established customer orders more supplies.

Brad has recently become discouraged with the diminishing direct people contact in his work. As he explains, "Three times during the past month I have been turned down by purchasing agents or business owners when I asked them out to lunch. Until a few years ago, I made some of my largest sales during lunch. I'm hearing more now that my customers simply want to buy over the Internet. I guess they would rather sit at the keyboard eating yogurt for lunch than discuss business in a restaurant.

"The phone has become a major headache for me also. Instead of talking to a manager or a purchasing agent, I have to conduct my business with a voice mail message. A woman told me outright the other day that when she wanted to order something from Western, she would use our Web site. She told me that phone conversations take up too much of her time."

During the past six-month period, Brad's commissions declined 45 percent from the previous six months.

For Brad, this was the last straw. He decided to change careers, as soon as he can figure out what else he could do to earn the same kind of living he did previously. For three consecutive years, Brad had even earned a six-figure income.

One Saturday morning Brad was looking at the job search site, Monster.com. He murmured to himself, "Let's see Brad, the world no longer needs a good sales rep with a personal touch. You have no more talent with the computer than most 19-year olds. Being an astronaut is out because you get motion sickness. The NFL doesn't want any 43-year-old quarterbacks without experience. My few years as an Army medic doesn't qualify me to be the chief of surgery at the Mayo Clinic.

"Oops, here's an opening for a chief financial officer for a $50 million dollar company, but they do want experience as a controller. Here's another one I like, an international marketing specialist. Except that the successful candidate must speak English, Spanish, and Italian. All I have is English, and about 20 words of Spanish I know from listening to Salsa music.

"Maybe, I should start by updating my résumé. I know I can make a contribution somewhere, but I'm not sure where to start."

Questions

1. To what extent do you think Brad Martinez really needs a career switch?
2. What approach should Brad take to finding a new career?
3. What improvements do you think Brad needs to make in his attitude before he gets down to the serious business of finding a new career?
4. What criticisms do you have of Brad's career direction so far?

REFERENCES

1. John W. Donahoe and David C. Palmer, *Learning and Complex Behavior* (Boston: Allyn & Bacon, 1994), p. 2.
2. Nancy Day, "Informal Learning Gets Results," *Workforce*, June 1998, p. 31.
3. Michael A. Stadlelr and Peter A. Frensch (eds.), *Handbook of Implicit Learning* (Thousands Oak, CA: Sage, 1998).
4. Michael A. Tucker, "E-Learning Evolves," *HR Magazine*, October 2005, p. 75.
5. Karen Frankola, "Why Online Learners Drop Out," *Workforce*, October 2001, p. 54.
6. "Assessing Online Learning: Defining the Efficacy of Online Learning," *Keying In,* March 2001, p. 3.
7. Tucker, "E-Learning Evolves," p. 78.
8. Joe Mullich, "A Second Act for E-Learning," *Workforce Management,* February 2004, p. 52.
9. Richard E. Mayer, "Should There Be a Three-Strikes Rule against Discovery Learning?" *American Psychologist,* January 2004, pp. 14–19.
10. Wanda L. Stitt-Gohdes, "Chapter 1—Teaching and Learning Styles: Implications for Business Teacher Education," in *The Twenty-First Century: Meeting the Challenges to Business Education* (Reston, VA: National Business Education Association, 1999), p. 10.
11. "Learning Styles," available at *http://www.nwlink.com/~donclark/hrd/styles.html*, pp. 4–6 March 6, 2006.
12. Isabel Briggs Myers, *Introduction to Type*®, 6th ed. (Mountain View, CA: CPP, Inc., 1998), p. 10. (Revised by Linda K. Kirby and Katharine D. Myers.)
13. Ibid., p. 11.
14. Ibid., p. 37.
15. Ibid., p. 42.
16. The quote and the content in this section are from Mark Greer, "Strengthen Your Brain by Resting It," *Monitor on Psychology,* July/August 2004, p. 60.
17. David W. Oakes et al., "Cognitive Ability and Personality Predictors of Training Program Skill Acquisition and Job Performance," *Journal of Business and Psychology,* Summer 2001, pp. 523–548.
18. Greg Livadas, "GM Official Says We Need Alternatives to Oil," *Rochester, (NY) Democrat and Chronicle*, April 30, 2006, p. 1E.
19. Ricky W. Griffin, "Effects of Work Redesign on Employee Perceptions, Attitudes, and Behavior: A Long-Term Investigation," *Academy of Management Journal*, June 1991, p.42.
20. Erick H. Erikson, *Childhood and Society* (New York: Norton, 1963); Child Development Institute, "Stages of Social-Emotional Development In Children and Teenagers,"
available at *www.childdevelpmentinfo.com*, retrieved May 6, 2006.
21. Our discussion of the challenges of adolescence and adulthood follows closely Saul Kassin, *Psychology*, 3rd ed. (Upper Saddle River, NJ: Prentice Hall, 2001), pp. 406–440; and Charles G. Morris and Albert A. Maisto, *Psychology: An Introduction*, 11th ed. (Upper Saddle River, NJ: Prentice Hall, 2002), pp. 418–441.
22. Lawrence Kohlberg, *Essays on Moral Development: Vol. 2. The Psychology of Moral Development* (New York: Harper & Row, 1984).
23. Research from *The New England Journal of Medicine* summarized in Sharon Begley, "Oops! Mental Training, Crosswords Fail to Slow Decline of Aging Brain," *The Wall Street Brain*, April 21, 2006, p. B1; Begley, "Studies on Dementia Often Confuse Causes with Consequences," *The Wall Street Journal*, April 28, 2006, p. B1.
24. Research reported in Joseph Pereira, "A Daily Drink May Help Prevent Cognitive Decline as Women Age," *The Wall Street Journal*, January 20, 2005, p. D5.
25. Research summarized in Karen Kersting, "Happiness in Men Usually Drops after Age 65, Study Finds," *Monitor on Psychology*, March 2005, p. 10.
26. Brian Scott Ehrlich and Derek Isaacowitz, "Does Subjective Well-Being Increase with Age?" *Perspectives in Psychology*, Spring 2002, pp. 20–26.
27. Kassin, *Psychology*, p. 435.
28. "U.S. Job Satisfaction Keeps Falling, The Conference Board Reports Today," available at *www.conference-board.org*, retrieved February 8, 2005.
29. Michael Drafke, *The Human Side of Organizations*, 9th ed. (Upper Saddle River, NJ: Pearson Prentice Hall, 2006), p. 335.
30. Randall S. Hansen, "Quintessential Careers: The 10-Step Plan to Career Change," *www.quintcareers.com*, retrieved April 13, 2006.
31. "The End of Entrepreneurship As We Know It?" *Entrepreneur*, September 2000, p. 18.
32. The first two items noted are from Fred Pryor, "What Have You Learned from Change?" *Managers Edge*, September 1998, p. 2.
33. Al Siebert, *The Resiliency Advantage* (San Francisco, CA: Berrett-Koehler, 2005).
34. Thomas L. Friedman, *The World Is Flat: A Brief History of the Twenty-First Century* (New York: FSG, 2005).
35. Peter Svensson, "Hands-On Jobs May Be the Safest," Associated Press, July 4, 2004.

16 Developing Good Work Habits

Learning Objectives

After studying the information and doing the exercises in this chapter, you should be able to:

1 Appreciate the importance of good work habits and time management.

2 Decrease any tendencies you might have toward procrastination.

3 Develop attitudes and values that will help you become more productive.

4 Develop skills and techniques that will help you become more productive.

5 Overcome time-wasting practices.

Outline

A nnick Baudot-Mohageg says she often had trouble saying no to her bosses and colleagues at Adobe Systems, which is probably why her workweek typically averaged 45 to 50 hours. Then her company cut its workforce, and Baudot-Mohageg, a senior marketing manager, found herself feeling even more overworked, with little energy left for her husband, Michael, and son, Lucas.

That was more than one year ago. She says she is feeling much less frazzled these days, having participated during the past year in a mentoring program sponsored by Adobe, which is based in San Jose, California. The program—intended, among other things, to help budget time—included monthly workshops with other women executives and one-to-one meetings with her own mentor from outside Adobe.

Baudot-Mohageg, 40, says she has learned to focus on details of projects that are relevant only to her, rather than trying to do other people's work for them, and to conduct staff meetings more efficiently. As a result, she estimates, her productivity has increased 50 percent. She says she also has more time to spend with her family. "Mentoring helped me set objectives in life," she said. [1]

■ **Work habits**
a person's characteristic approach to work, including such things as organization, priority setting, and handling of paper work and e-mail

■ **Productivity**
the amount of quality work accomplished in relation to the resources consumed

■ **Learning Objective 1**

As the story presented illustrates, learning to be productive, including more effective budgeting of time, is an important part of holding down an executive position as well as having time left over for personal life. Because good work habits and time management (including concentrating carefully on the task at hand) improve productivity, they contribute to success in business. **Work habits** refer to a person's characteristic approach to work, including such things as organization, priority setting, and handling of paperwork and e-mail. Good work habits and time management are more important than ever because of today's emphasis on **productivity,** the amount of quality work accomplished in relation to the resources consumed. Furthermore, a person is more likely to be fired from a job or flunk out of school because of poor work habits than because of poor aptitude.

People with good work habits tend to achieve higher career success and have more time to invest in their personal lives. They also enjoy their personal lives more because they are not preoccupied with unfinished tasks. Effective work habits are also beneficial because they eliminate a major stressor—the feeling of having very little or no control over your life. Being in control also leads to a relaxed, confident approach to work.

The goal of this chapter is to help you become a more productive person who is still flexible. Someone who develops good work habits is not someone who becomes so obsessed with time and so rigid that he or she makes other people feel uncomfortable. Ideally, a person should be well organized yet still flexible.

Information about becoming more productive is organized here into four related categories. One is overcoming procrastination, a problem that plagues almost everybody to some extent. The second is developing attitudes and values that foster productivity. The third category is the lengthiest: developing skills and techniques that lead to personal productivity. The fourth category is overcoming time wasters.

■ **Learning Objective 2**

How Does a Person Deal With Procrastination?

■ **Procrastination**
delaying a task for an invalid or weak reason

The leading cause of poor productivity and career self-sabotage is **procrastination,** delaying a task for an invalid or weak reason. Procrastination is also the major work habit problem for most workers and students. The presence of computers in the cubicle or office increases the risk of procrastination because it so easy to check e-mail or a favorite Web site just before starting almost any task. Unproductive people are the biggest procrastinators, but even productive people have problems with procrastination at times. A business owner who does not ordinarily procrastinate might delay preparing taxes knowing that she was behind in her taxes.

WHY PEOPLE PROCRASTINATE

People procrastinate for many different reasons. One is that we perceive the task to be done (such as quitting a job) as unpleasant. Another reason we procrastinate is that we find the job facing us to be overwhelming, such as assembling a computer console that arrives in a large box. To avoid an overwhelming or taxing task, some people flood their workday with small, easy-to-do tasks. As a result, these people do not appear to be procrastinators on the surface. [2] Another major cause of procrastination is a fear of the consequences of our actions.

One possible negative consequence is a negative evaluation of your work. For example, if you delay preparing a report for your boss or instructor, that person cannot criticize its quality. Bad news is another negative consequence that procrastination can sometimes delay. If you think your personal computer needs a new hard drive, delaying a trip to the computer store means you will not have to hear the diagnosis: "Your hard drive needs replacement. We can do the job for about $250."

Another reason some people procrastinate is the **fear of success.** People sometimes believe that if they succeed at an important task, they will be asked to take on more responsibility in the future. They dread this possibility. Some students have been known to procrastinate completing their degree requirements to avoid taking on the responsibility of a full-time position. People frequently put off tasks that do not appear to offer a meaningful reward. Suppose you decide that your computer files need a thorough updating, including deleting inactive files. Even if you know this task should be done, the accomplishment of updated files might not be a particularly meaningful reward.

■ **Fear of success**

belief that if one succeeds at an important task, one will be asked to take on more responsibility in the future; reason some people procrastinate

Many people procrastinate as a way of rebelling against being controlled. Procrastination, used in this way, is a means of defying unwarranted authority. [3] Rather than submit to authority, a person might tell himself, "Nobody is going to tell me when I should get a report done. I'll do it when I'm good and ready." Such people might be referred to as "anticontrol freaks."

A curious reason for procrastination is to achieve the stimulation and excitement that stems from rushing to meet a deadline. [4] Some people, for example, enjoy fighting their way through traffic or running through an airline terminal so they can make an appointment or airplane flight barely on time. They appear to enjoy the rush of adrenaline, endorphins, and other hormones associated with hurrying.

Finally, some people procrastinate because they are perfectionists. They attempt to perfect a project before being willing to admit the project is completed. As a result, the person procrastinates not about beginning a project but letting go. When asked, "Have you finished that project?" the perfectionist replies, "No, there a few small details that still need to be worked out." Being a perfectionist can also block starting new projects because the perfectionist will often want to keep working on the present project. Perfectionism comes in degrees, with slight perfectionists simply being extremely conscientious and heavy-duty perfectionists almost stalled in their actions. Human Relations Self-Assessment Quiz 16-1 gives you an opportunity to measure your degree of perfectionism.

TECHNIQUES FOR REDUCING PROCRASTINATION

To overcome or at least minimize procrastination, we recommend a number of specific tactics. A general approach, however, is simply to be aware that

Tendencies toward Perfectionism

Many perfectionists hold some of the following behaviors and attitudes. To help understand your tendencies toward perfectionism, rate how strongly you agree with each of the statements below on a scale of 0 to 4: 0=disagree strongly; 1=disagree; 2=neutral; 3=agree; 4=strongly agree.

		0	1	2	3	4
1.	Many people have told me that I am a perfectionist.	0	1	2	3	4
2.	I often correct the speech of others.	0	1	2	3	4
3.	It takes me a long time to write an e-mail because I keep checking and rechecking my writing.	0	1	2	3	4
4.	I often criticize the color combinations my friends are wearing.	0	1	2	3	4
5.	When I purchase food at a supermarket, I usually look at the expiration date so I can purchase the freshest.	0	1	2	3	4
6.	I can't stand when people use the term "remote" instead of "remote control."	0	1	2	3	4
7.	If a company representative asked me "What is your *social?*" I would reply something like, "Do you mean my *Social Security number?*"	0	1	2	3	4
8.	I hate to see dust on furniture.	0	1	2	3	4
9.	I like the Martha Stewart idea of having every decoration in the home just right.	0	1	2	3	4
10.	I never put a map back in the glove compartment until it is folder just right.	0	1	2	3	4
11.	Once an eraser on a pencil of mine becomes hard and useless, I throw the pencil away.	0	1	2	3	4
12.	I adjust all my watches and clocks so they show exactly the same time.	0	1	2	3	4
13.	It bothers me that clocks on personal computers are often wrong by a few minutes.	0	1	2	3	4
14.	I clean the keyboard on my computer at least once a week.	0	1	2	3	4
15.	I organize my e-mail messages and computer documents into many different, clearly labeled files.	0	1	2	3	4
16.	You won't find old coffee cups or soft-drink containers on my desk.	0	1	2	3	4
17.	I rarely start a new project or assignment until I have completed my present project or assignment.	0	1	2	3	4
18.	It is very difficult for me to concentrate when my work area is disorganized.	0	1	2	3	4
19.	Cobwebs in chandeliers and other lighting fixtures bug me.	0	1	2	3	4
20.	It takes me a long time to make a purchase such as a digital camera because I keep studying the features on various models.	0	1	2	3	4
21.	When I balance my checkbook, it usually comes out right within a few dollars.	0	1	2	3	4
22.	I carry enough small coins and dollar bills with me so when I shop I can pay the exact amount without requiring change.	0	1	2	3	4
23.	I throw out any underwear or T-shirts that have even the smallest holes or tears.	0	1	2	3	4
24.	I become upset with myself if I make a mistake.	0	1	2	3	4
25.	When a fingernail of mine is broken or chipped, I fix it as soon as possible.	0	1	2	3	4
26.	I am carefully groomed whenever I leave my home.	0	1	2	3	4
27.	When I notice packaged goods or cans on the floor in a supermarket, I will often place them back on the shelf.	0	1	2	3	4
28.	I think that carrying around antibacterial cleaner for the hands is an excellent idea.	0	1	2	3	4
29.	If I am with a friend, and he or she has a loose hair on the shoulder, I will remove it without asking.	0	1	2	3	4
30.	I know that I am a perfectionist.	0	1	2	3	4

Scoring and Interpretation

91 or over   You have strong perfectionist tendencies to the point that it could interfere with your taking quick action when necessary. Also, you may annoy many people with your perfectionism.

61–90   Moderate degree of perfectionism that could lead you to produce high-quality work and be a dependable person.

31–60   Mild degree of perfectionism. You might be a perfectionist in some situations quite important to you but not in others.

0–30   Not a perfectionist. You might be too casual about getting things done right, meeting deadlines, and being aware of details.

procrastination is a major drain on productivity. Being aware of the problem will remind you to take corrective action in many situations. When your accomplishment level is low, you might ask yourself, "Am I procrastinating on anything of significance?"

Calculate the cost of procrastination. You can reduce procrastination by calculating its cost. [5] One example is that you might lose out on obtaining a high-paying job you really want by not having your résumé and cover letter ready on time. Your cost of procrastination would include the difference in salary between the job you do find and the one you really wanted. Another cost would be the loss of potential job satisfaction.

Counterattack. Forcing yourself to do something overwhelming, frightening, or uncomfortable helps to prove that the task was not as bad as initially perceived. Assume that you have accepted a new position but have not yet resigned from your present one because resigning seems so uncomfortable. Set up a specific time to call your manager or send an e-mail to schedule an appointment. Force yourself further to show up for the resignation appointment. After you break the ice with the statement "I have something important to tell you," the task will be much easier.

Jump-start yourself. You can often get momentum going on a project by giving yourself a tiny assignment simply to get started. One way to get momentum going on an unpleasant or overwhelming task is to set aside a specific time to work on it. If you have to write a report on a subject you dislike, you might set aside Saturday from 3 P.M. to 4 P.M. as your time to first attack the project. If your procrastination problem is particularly intense, giving yourself even a five-minute task, such as starting a new file, might help you gain momentum. After five minutes, decide if you choose to continue for another five minutes. The five-minute chunks will help you focus your energy.

Peck away at an overwhelming task. Assume that you have a major project to do that does not have to be accomplished in a hurry. A good way of minimizing procrastination is to peck away at the project in 15- to 30-minute bits of time. Bit by bit, the project will get down to manageable size and, therefore, not seem so overwhelming. A related way of pecking away at an overwhelming task is to subdivide it into smaller units. For instance, you might break down moving into a series of tasks, such as filing change-of-address notices, locating a mover, and packaging books. Pecking away can sometimes be achieved by setting aside as little as five minutes to work on a seemingly overwhelming task. When the five minutes are up, either work five more minutes on the task or reschedule the activity for sometime soon.

Motivate yourself with rewards and punishments. Give yourself a pleasant reward soon after you accomplish a task about which you would ordinarily procrastinate. You might, for example, jog through the woods after having completed a tough take-home exam. The second part of this tactic is to punish yourself if you have engaged in serious procrastination. How about not watching any of your favorite television shows for one week?

Follow the WIFO principle. Personal effectiveness coach Shale Paul recommends that you use the technique of **worst in, first out (WIFO)** for dealing with unpleasant tasks you would prefer to avoid. After you finally get the task done, Paul says, "Chances are, you'll find that you spent nearly as much time worrying and rescheduling it as you did actually doing it." If the task fits high enough on your priorities, simply get it done and out of the way. [6] A related motivational principle is that after completing the unpleasant task, moving on to a more pleasant (or less unpleasant) task functions as a reward.

■ **Worst in, first out (WIFO)**
dealing first with unpleasant tasks you would prefer to avoid; simply getting them done and out of the way

Make a commitment to other people. Put pressure on yourself to get something done on time by making it a commitment to one or more other people. You might announce to coworkers that you are going to get a project of mutual concern completed by a certain date. If you fail to meet this date, you may feel embarrassed.

Express a more positive attitude about your intentions. Expressing a more positive attitude can often lead to changes in behavior. If you choose words that express a serious intention to complete an activity, you are more likely to follow through than if you choose more uncertain words. Imagine that a coworker says, "I *might* get you the information you need by next Friday." You probably will not be surprised if you do not receive the information by Friday. In contrast, if your coworker says, "I *will . . .* get you the information you need by next Friday," there is less likelihood the person will procrastinate. Psychologist Linda Sapadin believes that you are less likely to procrastinate if you change your "wish" to "will," your "like to" to "try to," and your "have to" to "want to." [7]

What Are Some Proper Attitudes and Values to Develop?

■ Learning Objective 3

Developing good work habits and time management practices is often a matter of developing proper attitudes toward work and time. For instance, if you think that your job is important and that time is valuable, you will be on your way toward developing good work habits. In this section we describe a group of attitudes and values that can help improve your productivity through better use of time and improved work habits.

DEVELOP A MISSION, GOALS, AND A STRONG WORK ETHIC

A mission, or general purpose in life, propels you toward being productive. Assume that a person says, "My mission is to become an outstanding professional in my career and a loving, constructive parent." The mission serves as a compass to direct your activities, such as being well organized in order to attain a favorable performance appraisal.

Goals are more specific than a mission statement. The goals support the mission statement, but the effect is the same. Being committed to a goal also propels you toward good use of time. Imagine how efficient most employees would be if they were told, "Here is five days of work facing you. If you get finished in less than five days without sacrificing quality, you can have that time to yourself." If the saved time fit your mission, such as having more quality time with family members, the impact would be even stronger.

Stephen Covey, a popularizer of time management techniques, expresses the importance of a mission of goals in his phrase, "Begin with the end in mind." He recommends you develop your mission statement by first thinking about what people who know you well would say at your funeral if you died three years from now. Also, list your various roles in life, such as spouse, child, family member, professional, and soccer player. For each role, think of one or two major lifetime goals you have in that area. Then develop a brief mission statement describing your life's purpose that incorporates these goals. [8]

A person might have the mission of becoming an outstanding professional person. Your goals to support that mission might include achieving advanced certification in your field, becoming an officer in a professional organization, and making large donations to charity. When you are deciding how to spend your time each day, give goals related to your mission top priority.

Closely related to establishing a mission and goals is develop a strong work ethic. Developing a strong work ethic may lead to even higher productivity than goal setting alone. For example, one might set the goal of earning a high income. It might lead to some good work habits but not necessarily a high commitment to quality.

VALUE GOOD ATTENDANCE AND PUNCTUALITY

On the job, in school, or in personal life, good attendance and punctuality are essential for developing a good reputation. Also, you cannot contribute to a team effort unless you are present. Poor attendance and consistent lateness are the most frequent reasons for employee discipline. Furthermore, many managers interpret high absenteeism and lateness as signs of emotional immaturity. An important myth about attendance and punctuality should be challenged early in a person's career. The myth is that a certain number of sick days are owed an employee. Some employees who have not used up their sick days will find reasons to be sick at the end of the year.

The causes of chronic lateness follow those of the causes of procrastination. Time-management specialist Diane DeLonzor says that the motivitionas are often unconscious, related to peronality characteristics such as lack of self-control and a desire for thrill-seeking. Some people are drawn to the adrenaline rush of that last minute sprint to the meeting (or class), while others receive an ego boost from over-scheduling and filling each moment with activity. Trying to get one more thing done before leaving for an appointment will often lead to being late. Keeping a time log (as described later in the chapter) can help control lateness because the result can be a more accurate estimation of the amount of time necessary to complete various activities. For example, if it takes a person 45 minutes to commute to work, he or she must leave the residence about 55 minutes before an important meeting. [9]

VALUE YOUR TIME

People who place a high value on their time are propelled into making good use of time. If a person believes that his or her time is valuable, it will be difficult to engage that person in idle conversation during working hours. Valuing your time can also apply to personal life. The yield from clipping or gathering grocery coupons is an average of $9 per hour—assuming that purchasing national brands is important to you. Would a busy professional person, therefore, be better off clipping and gathering coupons or engaging in self-development for the same amount of time? Being committed to a mission and goals is an automatic way of making good use of time.

VALUE NEATNESS, ORDERLINESS, AND SPEED

Neatness, orderliness, and speed are important contributors to workplace productivity and, therefore, should be valued. An orderly desk or work area does not inevitably signify an orderly mind. Yet orderliness does help most people become more productive. Less time is wasted and less energy is expended if you do not have to hunt for missing information. Knowing where information is and what information you have available is a way of being in control of your job. When your job gets out of control, you are probably working at less than peak efficiency. Being neat and orderly helps you achieve good performance. Frequently breaking your concentration for such matters as finding an e-mail message you printed a month ago inhibits high performance.

Neatness is linked to working rapidly because clutter and searching for misplaced items consume time. Employers emphasize speed today to remain competitive in such matters as serving customers promptly and bringing new products and services to the market. Speed is widely considered a competitive advantage. In the words of organizational consultant Price Pritchett,

> So you need to operate with a strong sense of urgency. Accelerate in all aspects of your work, even if it means living with a few more ragged edges. Emphasize *action*. Don't bog down in endless preparation trying to get things perfect before you make a move. Sure, high quality is crucial, but it must come quickly. You can't sacrifice speed. Learn to fail fast, fix it, and race on. [10]

The best approach to maintaining a neat work area and to enhance speed is to convince yourself that neatness and speed are valuable. You will then search for ways to be neat and fast, such as putting back a reference book immediately after use or making phone conversations brief. The underlying principle is that an attitude leads to a change in behavior.

WORK SMARTER, NOT HARDER

People caught up in trying to accomplish a job often wind up working hard but not in an imaginative way that leads to good results. Much time and energy, therefore, are wasted. A working-smart approach also requires that you spend a few minutes carefully planning how to implement your task. An example of working smarter, not harder, is to invest a few minutes of critical thinking before launching an Internet search. Think through carefully what might be the key words that will lead you to the information you need. In this way, you will minimize conducting your search with words and phrases that will lead to irrelevant information. For example, suppose you want to conduct research on back stabbing as negative office politics. If you simply use the term "back stabbing," the search engine will direct you to such topics as street crime and medical treatment for wounds. Working smarter is to try "back stabbing in the office."

A modern approach to working smarter is to avoid doing work that is already being accomplished in another part of the organization by using information technology designed to foster collaboration. Some programs make it easier to find out what coworkers in other parts of a far-flung company are working on, thus avoiding duplication. Company blogs can also be helpful in identifying other workers who are engaged in a similar project. For example, you might be mining data attempting to discover which customers are likely to buy a variety of products from your employer. [11] A blog might tell you that Sally in Madison, Wisconsin, is working on the same project. If you then collaborate, you will save lots of time—and work smarter.

BECOME SELF-EMPLOYED PSYCHOLOGICALLY

A distinguishing characteristic of most self-employed people is that they care deeply about what they accomplish each day. Most of their job activities directly or indirectly affect their financial health. Additionally, many self-employed people enjoy high job satisfaction because they have chosen work that fits their interests. Because of the factors previously mentioned, the self-employed person is compelled to make good use of time. Also, the high level of job satisfaction typical of many self-employed people leads them to enjoy being productive. [12]

If a person working for an employer regards his or her area of responsibility as self-employment, productivity may increase. To help regard employment by others as self-employment, keep this thought in mind. Every employee is given some assets to manage to achieve a good return on investment. If you managed the cafeteria for your company, you would be expected to manage that asset profitably.

APPRECIATE THE IMPORTANCE OF REST AND RELAXATION

A productive attitude to maintain is that overwork can be counterproductive and lead to negative stress and burnout. Proper physical rest contributes to mental alertness and improved ability to cope with frustration. Constant attention to work or study is often inefficient. It is a normal human requirement to take enough rest breaks to allow yourself to approach work or study with a fresh perspective. Napping during the day has gained in popularity as productivity booster. [13] Workers who have private offices might nap under the desk, while cubicle dwellers often nap with their head on the desk. Each person has to establish the right balance between work and leisure within the bounds of freedom granted by the situation.

Neglecting the normal need for rest and relaxation can lead to **workaholism,** an addiction to work in which not working is an uncomfortable experience. Some types of workaholics are perfectionists who are never satisfied with their work and, therefore, find it difficult to leave work behind. Career counselor Janet Salyer notes, "Workaholics put the job before family, friends, and their own health. And even if they're spending time with their families, their mind is on work." [14] Not only is the negative type of workaholic preoccupied with work but also he or she derives relatively little satisfaction from passing time with family life, friendships, health, and hobbies. [15] In addition, the workaholic who is a perfectionist may become heavily focused on control, leading to rigid behavior.

However, some people who work long and hard are classified as happy workaholics who thrive on hard work and are usually highly productive. As executives, they encourage others to work hard to achieve company goals and also pursue what matters to them in their personal life. [16] Furthermore, many people who work long and hard to be successful in their careers also intensely enjoy other activities. Warren Buffet, the legendary investor who is one of the world's richest people, carries an enormous workload although he is in his late 70s. However, he is also a fanatic about bridge and regularly interrupts his workday to play bridge on the computer.

■ **Workaholism**

neglecting the normal need for rest and relaxation that can lead to an addiction to work in which not working is an uncomfortable experience

What Are Some Effective Time-Management Techniques?

■ **Learning Objective 4**

So far we have discussed improving productivity from the standpoints of dealing with procrastination and developing the right attitudes and values. Skills and techniques are also important for becoming more productive. Here we describe some well-established methods of work habit improvement along with several new ones. For these techniques to enhance productivity, most of them need to be incorporated into and practiced regularly in our daily lives. This is particularly true because many of these techniques are habits, and habits have to be programmed into the brain through repetition.

CLEAN UP AND GET ORGANIZED

An excellent starting point for improving work habits and time management is to clean up the work area and arrange things neatly. Eliminate clutter by throwing out unnecessary paper and deleting computer files that will probably never be used again. The idea is to learn to simplify the work area so that there are fewer distractions and the brain can be more focused. In addition, finding important files becomes easier. According to the Delphi Group, a consultancy firm, about 15 percent of all paper handled in business becomes lost, and 30 percent of all employee's time is spent trying to find lost documents. [17] (We assume that the lost documents are both paper and electronic.)

Desktop search software such as Google's Desktop Search or Apple's Spotlight can help you find can help you find many missing documents. However, there is still a productivity advantage to having fewer obsolete documents and files in your computer including a front page with dozens of icons with similar-sounding names. Conducting an electronic search to find your expense report is one more task on your to-do list.

Getting organized includes sorting out which tasks need doing, including assignments and projects not yet completed. Getting organized can also mean sorting through the many small paper notes attached to the computer and on the wall. A major cleanup principle is, therefore, to discard anything that is no longer valuable. A suggestion worth considering is to throw out at least one item every day from the office and home—even if the item thrown out is as humble as a empty ball pen. Because new items come into the office and home almost daily, you will always have possessions left.

PLAN YOUR ACTIVITIES

■ **Planning**

primary principle of effective time management; deciding what to accomplish and the actions needed to make it happen

The primary principle of effective time management is **planning,** deciding what you want to accomplish and the actions needed to make it happen. The most elementary—and the most important—planning tool is a list of tasks that need doing. Almost every successful person works from a to-do list. These lists are essentially daily goals. Before you can compose a useful list, you need to set aside a few moments each day to sort out the tasks at hand. A good starting point in using to-do lists is to prepare such a list on Sunday for the rest of the week. The list can then be modified on Monday through Saturday. A list used by a working parent is presented in Figure 16-1.

Where do you put your to-do lists? Many people dislike having small to-do lists stuck in different places. One reason is that these lists are readily lost among other papers. Many people, therefore, put lists on desk calendars or printed forms called *planners,* which are also available for computers of all sizes. Planners give you an opportunity to record your activities in intervals as small as 15 minutes. Day-Timer® Planner Pads include the categories of weekly lists of activities by category, daily things to do, appointments, notes/calls, and expenses.

Another useful approach for organizing your lists is to use a notebook small enough to be portable. The notebook becomes your master list to keep track of work tasks, errands, social engagements, and shopping items. Anything else requiring action might also be recorded—even a reminder to clean up the work area again. Some people have such clear focus that they register their to-do lists in their brain, thereby skipping paper or a computer.

How do you set priorities? Faced with multiple tasks to do at the same time, it is possible to feel overwhelmed and freeze as a result. The time-tested solution is to establish a priority to each item on the to-do list. A typical system is to use *A* to signify critical or essential items, *B* to signify important items, and *C* for the least important ones. Although an item might be regarded as a *C* (for example, refilling your stapler), it still has a contribution to make to your productivity and sense of well-being. Many people obtain a sense of satisfaction from crossing an item, however trivial, off their list. Furthermore, if you are conscientious, small undone items will interfere with concentration.

How do you schedule and follow through? To be effective, a to-do list must be an action tool. To convert your list into action, prepare a schedule of when you are going to do each of the items on the list. Follow through by doing things according to your schedule, checking them off as you go along.

Figure **16-1**

A Sample To-Do List

From the Desk of Jennifer Bartow

Job

Make 10 calls to prospects for new listings.

Have "For Sale" signs put outside Hanover Blvd. house.

Set up mortgage appointment at First Federal for the Calhouns.

Update Web site listings.

Upgrade antivirus software.

Order new memo pads.

Meet with the Guptas at 5 P.M.

Set up time to show house to the Bowens.

Home

Buy new mouse for PC.

Buy running shoes for Todd.

Buy jeans for Linda.

Get defroster fixed on freezer.

Write and send out monthly bills.

Clip cat's nails.

Check out problem with hot-water tank.

Make appointment with dentist to have chipped filling replaced.

FIRST REALTY CORPORATION

Jacksonville, Florida

Jbartow@firstrealty.com

Time-and-activity charts (also referred to as Gantt Charts) have been used in factories and offices for almost 100 years to keep track of projects. Many people find these basic charts useful in scheduling their own activities, and keeping track of progress. Time-and-activity charts also reinforce the reality that much of work is calendar driven. A calendar anticipates all the dates, deadlines, and seasons essential to running a successful business firm. [18] For example, many customers want shipments by a particular date, and bills are due at a specific time. Figure 16-2 presents a time-and-activity chart you might want to use as a personal productivity booster.

GET OFF TO A GOOD START

Get off to a good beginning, and you are more likely to have a successful, productive day. Start poorly, and you will be behind most of the day. According to Douglass Merrill, people who get going early tend to be in the right place at the right time more often, thus seeming to be lucky. "When you start early, you are lucky enough to get a good parking spot. You are lucky enough to avoid traffic jams. You are lucky

A Time-and-Activity Chart for Scheduling Activities

Charting key tasks and their deadlines, along with your performance on the task, can often get you focused and organized.

Deadlines for Task Accomplishment

Task to Be Accomplished	Feb. 1	Feb. 28	Mar. 15	Mar. 31	Apr. 15	Apr. 30
Expense reports	Did it					
Antivirus treatment for PC		Two days late				
Web site installed			Blew it			
Plan office party				Did it		
File federal tax report					In the mail at midnight ☺ ☺	
Provide input to department budget						On time

enough to finish your job by the end of the day." [19] To get off to a good start regularly, it is important to start the day with the conscious intention of starting strong.

An effective way of getting off to a good start is to tackle the toughest task first because most people have their peak energy in the morning. (You will recall that a variation of this technique is useful in combating procrastination.) With a major task already completed, you are off to a running start on a busy workday.

MAKE GOOD USE OF OFFICE TECHNOLOGY

Companies now derive productivity increases from office automation. In the past, office automation was not as successful as was hoped because many office workers did not make good use of available technology. Used properly, most high-tech devices in the office improve productivity. Among the most productivity-enhancing devices are word processors, spreadsheets, voice mail, and personal digital assistants. How you use these ever-present devices is the key to increased productivity. A major consideration is that the time saved using office technology must be invested in productive activity to attain a true productivity advantage. Assume that you save two hours by ordering office equipment over the Internet. If you invest those two hours in activity such as finding ways to save the company money, you are more productive.

CONCENTRATE ON ONE KEY TASK AT A TIME

Effective people have a well-developed capacity to concentrate on the problem or person they face, however surrounded they are with potential distractions. The best results from concentration are achieved when you are so absorbed in your work that you are aware of virtually nothing else at the moment—referred to as the flow experience. Another useful by-product of concentration is that it reduces absent-mindedness. If you really concentrate on what you are doing, the chances diminish that you will forget what you intended to do.

Conscious effort and self-discipline can strengthen concentration skills. An effective way to sharpen your concentration skills is to set aside 10 minutes a day and focus on something repetitive, such as your breathing pattern or a small word. This is the same approach that is used in meditation to relieve stress. After practicing concentration in the manner just described, concentrate on an aspect of your work, such as preparing a report.

Note that the suggestion here is to concentrate on one *key* task at a time. As described later in this chapter, sometimes doing two or three minor tasks at the same time can help save time. In general younger people are more effective at multitasking than much older people, yet being distracted can lower performance for both groups. Experimental psychologists Moshe Naveh-Benjamin of the University of Missouri at Columbia, and Fergus Craik of the Rotman Research Institute in Toronto tested a group of undergraduates and a group of people averaging 70 years old on a word recall task. (For example, the participants were asked to remember "waiter–kitchen" and "paper–apple.") Half of the groups were asked to follow a green asterisk moving across a computer screen while memorizing the word pairs. The students did better than the seniors, yet both groups who learned word pairs while their attention was divided performed more poorly when recalling the words. [20]

Time management consultant Stephanie Winston also points to the problems of multitasking while performing important work. She notes that the biggest work habit problem for most people is multitasking. "Successful CEOs do not multitask. They concentrate intensely on one thing at a time," she says. [21]

The accompanying Human Relations in Practice illustrates how workers might make good use of office technology and prevent multitasking from lowering productivity.

STREAMLINE YOUR WORK AND EMPHASIZE IMPORTANT TASKS

As companies continue to operate with fewer workers than in the past despite good economic times, more nonproductive work must be eliminated. Getting rid of unproductive work is part of *reengineering*, in which work processes are radically redesigned and simplified. Every employee is expected to get rid of work that does not contribute to productivity or help customers. Another intent of work streamlining is to get rid of work that does not add value for customers. Here is a sampling of work that typically does not add value:

- e-mail or paper messages that almost nobody reads

- sending receipts and acknowledgments to people who do not need them

- writing and mailing reports that nobody reads or needs

- meetings that do not accomplish work, exchange important information, or improve team spirit

- checking up frequently on the work of competent people

In general, to streamline your work, look for duplication of effort and waste. An example of duplication of effort would be to routinely send people e-mail three times with the same question. An example of waste would be to call a meeting for disseminating information that could easily be communicated by e-mail.

Important (value-contributing) tasks are those in which superior performance could have a large payoff. No matter how quickly you took care of making sure that

Human Relations in Practice

COO John Seiple Stays Focused and Emphasizes Productive Use of Office Technology

John Seiple, president and chief operating officer of North American operations at ProLogis, a Denver-based distribution-facilities company, tries to stay focused on work that helps boost the bottom line. That means keeping paperwork to a minimum to free up time with customers. To help managers do more work with less staff, Seiple's staff streamlined work processes such as the company's accounts payable system. He discourages multitasking as unproductive. He insists that cell phones and Blackberry's are turned off during meetings. "It's so we can all focus and get through our agenda in 15 or 30 minutes instead of an hour," he says.

He checks his own e-mails early in the morning and late at night after his children go to sleep so he doesn't spend his workday in front of a computer screen. "I want to make sure we're using technology rather than have technology use us," he says. He asks managers to spend at least half their time conferring with customers. Seiple believes it's important for executives to master how to compartmentalize tasks. "When a customer presents you with a new opportunity, you give that your total focus and stop thinking about the problem you were tackling 10 minutes before," he says.

Staying focused in the moment requires discipline and some tricks. Whenever someone comes into his office to chat, Seiple moves to another chair. "That's my way of reminding myself that I'm starting a new conversation," he says.

Source: Carol Hymowitz, "Doing More with Less, Avoiding Shoddy Work and Burned-Out Staff," *The Wall Street Journal*, February 20, 2003, p. B1.

your store paid its bills on time, for example, this effort would not make your store an outstanding success. If, however, you concentrated your efforts on bringing unique and desirable merchandise into the store, this action could greatly affect your business success.

Many people respond to suggestions about emphasizing important tasks by saying, "I don't think concentrating on important tasks applies to me. My job is so filled with routine, I have no chance to work on the big breakthrough ideas." True, most jobs are filled with routine requirements. What a person *can* do is spend some time, perhaps even one hour a week, concentrating on tasks of potentially major significance.

WORK AT A STEADY PACE

In most jobs, working at a steady clip pays dividends in efficiency. The spurt worker creates many problems for management. Some employees take pride in working rapidly, even when the result is a high error rate. At home, too, a steady pace is better than spurting. A spurt houseworker is one who goes into a flurry of activity every so often. An easier person to live with is someone who does his or her share of housework at an even pace throughout the year.

Another advantage of the steady-pace approach is that you accomplish much more than someone who puts out extra effort only once in a while. The completely steady worker would accomplish just as much the day before a holiday as on a given Monday. That extra hour or so of productivity adds up substantially by the end of the year. Despite the advantages of maintaining a steady pace, some peaks and valleys in your work may be inevitable. Tax accounting firms, for example, have busy seasons.

Working at a steady pace throughout the day is difficult because it counters a natural tendency to slow down toward the end of a workday. The staffing firm, Accountemps, polled 150 senior executives on employee productivity. A third of the executives said that 4 to 6 P.M. is the least productive time of the day; another third cited the postlunch period from noon to 2 P.M. as being the least productive. Suggestions for combating the productivity dip include napping, getting fresh air, taking a short walk, and tackling the most challenging tasks early in the day. [22]

CREATE SOME QUIET, UNINTERRUPTED TIME

Many office workers find their days hectic, fragmented, and frustrating. Incessant interruptions make it difficult to get things done. The constant start–stop–restart pattern lengthens the time needed to get jobs done. Quiet time can reduce the type of productivity drain previously described. To achieve quiet time, create an uninterrupted block of time enabling you to concentrate on your work. This could mean turning off the telephone, not accessing your e-mail, and blocking drop-in visitors during certain times of the workday. Quiet time is used for such essential activities as thinking, planning, getting organized, doing analytical work, writing reports, and doing creative tasks. One hour of quiet time might yield as much productive work as four hours of interrupted time. [23] Interruptions lower productivity more for mental than physical work. This is true because interruptions break the flow of thought, and it takes time to get back into a train of thought.

Quiet time is difficult to find in some jobs, such as those involving customer contact. An agreement has to be worked out with the manager about when and where quiet time can be taken. Sometimes the quiet time can be taken at home early in the workday, or in a vacated office or conference room.

MAKE USE OF BITS OF TIME AND USE MULTITASKING FOR ROUTINE WORK

A truly productive person makes good use of miscellaneous bits of time both on and off the job. While waiting in line at a post office, you might update your to-do list; while waiting for an elevator, you might be able to read a brief report; and if you have finished your day's work 10 minutes before quitting time, you can use that time to clean out a file. When traveling for business, bring as much work as you can comfortably carry. Spare time at airports because you arrive early or because of flight delays provides a good opportunity to perform routine work. By the end of the year, your productivity will have increased much more than if you had squandered these bits of time.

Some forms of making use of bits of time, such as reviewing your to-do list as you ride the elevator, are a form of **multitasking.** Doing two or more routine chores simultaneously can sometimes enhance personal productivity. While exercising on a stationary bike, you might read work-related information; while commuting, listen to the radio for information of potential relevance for your job. Also, while reading e-mail, you might clean the outside of your computer; while waiting for a file to download, you might arrange your work area or read a brief report.

Despite searching for productivity gains through multitasking, it is important to avoid rude or dangerous acts or a combination of the two. A rude practice is doing

■ **Multitasking**
doing two or more routine chores simultaneously that can sometimes enhance personal productivity

paperwork while on the telephone or sitting in class. A dangerous practice is engaging in an intense conversation over the cell phone while driving. Checking out e-mail on a laptop or onboard computer is more dangerous because you are forced to lose full eye contact with the road.

STAY IN CONTROL OF PAPERWORK, THE IN-BASKET, AND E-MAIL

Despite the major shift to the use of electronic messages, the workplace is still overflowing with printed messages, including computer printouts. Paperwork essentially involves taking care of administrative details, such as correspondence, expense account forms, and surveys. Responding to e-mail messages, instant messages, and text messages has created additional administrative details that require handling, even if they are actually *electronic work* rather than paperwork.

Unless you handle paperwork and e-mail efficiently, you may lose control of your job or home life, which could lead to substantial negative stress. Ideally, a small amount of time should be invested in paperwork and routine e-mail every day. Non–prime time (when you are at less-than-peak efficiency but not overly fatigued) is the best time to take care of administrative routine work.

How Does One Overcome Time Wasters?

■ Learning Objective 5

Another basic thrust to improved personal productivity is to minimize wasting time. Workers wasting time is one of the most devastating problems facing work organizations of all types, probably far exceeding the cost from theft and fraud. According to a survey by America Online and **Salary.com** the average worker admits to wasting 2.09 hours per 8-hour workday, aside from lunch and scheduled breaks. **Salary.com** calculated that American employers spend $759 billion per year on salaries for which real work was expected but not actually performed. [24] One caution about this figure is that many employees who waste time during the day will speed up their work toward the end of the work day or work at home to catch up on unfinished tasks.

Many of the techniques already described in this chapter help save time. The tactics and strategies described next, however, are directly aimed at overcoming the problem of wasted time.

MINIMIZE DAYDREAMING

Allowing the mind to drift while on the job is a major productivity drain. Daydreaming is triggered when the individual perceives the task to be boring—such as reviewing another person's work for errors. Unresolved personal problems are an important source of daydreaming, thus blocking your productivity. This is especially true because effective time utilization requires good concentration. When you are preoccupied with a personal or business problem, it is difficult to give your full efforts to a task at hand.

The solution is to do something constructive about whatever problem is sapping your ability to concentrate. Sometimes a relatively minor problem, such as driving with an expired operator's license, can impair your work concentration. At other times, a major problem, such as how best to take care of a parent who has suffered a stroke, interferes with work. In either situation, your concentration will suffer until you take appropriate action.

PREPARE A TIME LOG TO EVALUATE YOUR USE OF TIME

An advanced tool for becoming a more efficient time manager is to prepare a time log of how you are currently investing your time. For five full workdays or school days, write down everything you do, including such activities as responding to e-mail and taking rest breaks. A daily planner is the tool of choice for a time log. Study your results, and look for patterns of lost time. A hospital administrative worker who used a log discovered that she was spending about 20 minutes at the start of each workday circling around the parking ramp look for a space. Her conclusion was that by arriving five minutes earlier to the hospital, she could find a space within a few minutes.

One of the most important outputs of a time log is to uncover time leaks. A **time leak** is anything you are doing or not doing that allows time to get away from you. Among them are spending too much time for lunch by collecting people before finally leaving and walking to a coworker's cubicle rather than sending an e-mail. The process of streamlining your work will also identify time leaks.

■ **Time leak**
anything you are doing or not doing that allows time to get away from you

AVOID UNPRODUCTIVE USE OF COMPUTERS

An unproductive use of computers is to tinker with them to the exclusion of useful work. Many people have become intrigued with computers to the point of diversion. They become habituated to creating new reports or exquisite graphics and making endless changes. It is easy to become diverted by the thousands of commands in a program such as Microsoft Word or PowerPoint. Some managers spend so much time with computers that they neglect leadership responsibilities, thus lowering their productivity.

In addition to these problems, Internet surfing for purposes not strictly related to the job has become a major productivity drain. According to the Accountemps survey of senior executives mentioned previously, workers spend an average of 56 minutes per day with nonwork-related Internet use. [25] Figure 16-3, based on a survey of 2,400 workers by **Cerbian.com** digs further into the specific categories of **computer surfing** unrelated to work. (Surfing in the context of the Internet refers to browsing through Web sites with no specific work goal in mind.) In defense of some of these surfers, some of the activity could enhance job performance, such as being informed of business trends.

■ **Computer surfing**
in the context of the Internet, browsing through Web sites with no specific work goal in mind; unrelated to work

The message is straightforward: To plug one more potential productivity drain, avoid using the computer for nonproductive purposes. Many companies block the use of recreational Web sites on company equipment so that workers have to resort to authorized sites, such as study equipment and supplies catalogs!

KEEP TRACK OF IMPORTANT NAMES, PLACES, AND THINGS

How much time have you wasted lately searching for such items as a telephone number you jotted down somewhere, your keys, or an appointment book? Standard solutions to overcoming these problems are to keep a wheel file (such as Rolodex) of people's names and companies. It is difficult to misplace such a file. Many managers and professionals store such information in a database or even in a word processing file. Such files are more difficult to misplace than a pocket directory, yet these files should be backed up to prevent lost data.

Two steps are recommended for remembering where you put things. First, have a parking place for everything. Put your keys and appointment book back in the same place after each use. (This tactic supports the strategy of being neat and orderly to minimize time wasting.) Second, make visual associations. To have something register in your mind at the moment you are doing it, make up a visual association about that act. Thus, you might say, "Here I am putting my résumé in the back section of my canvas bag."

Figure **16-3**

Categories of Nonjob-Related Computer Surfing

Source: "Personal Surfing and Porn Plague the Office," available at www.computertimes.com/webusageporn .htm, retrieved May 1, 2006. June 2004.

For nonjob-related surfing, where do you spend most of your time (please rank in order your top five categories)?

	Response Percentage	Response Total
News	56	1,342
Research	44	1,052
Web e-mail (e.g., hotmail)	40	969
On-line banking	33	792
Business and economy	29	704
Retail shopping	27	655
Auction (e.g., eBay)	25	595
Arts/entertainment	25	591
Sports	22	527
Travel	20	486
Education/culture	17	416
Chat/instant messaging	16	393
Brokerage/trading	13	313
Health/medical	11	276
Gaming	6	155
Pornography	3	74
Other	3	63
I'm not allowed to surf for personal reasons	2	59
Gambling	1	21

"They may be able to put their hands on that invoice, but they are using a huge amount of their memory to keep track of where everything is. That is brain power which they could use for another purpose."
—David Lewis, a British business psychologist who has made a career of mess, stress, and information overload. Quoted in Jane M. Von Bergen, "Getting Organized at the Office," available at WWW.PHILLY.COM, retrieved February 26, 2006.

SET A TIME LIMIT FOR CERTAIN TASKS AND PROJECTS

Spending too much time on a task or project wastes time. As a person becomes experienced with certain projects, he or she is able to make accurate estimates of how long a project will take to complete. A paralegal might say, "Getting this will drawn up for the lawyer's approval should take two hours." A good work habit to develop is to estimate how long a job should take and then proceed with strong determination to get that job completed within the estimated time period. A productive version of this technique is to decide that some low- and medium-priority items are worth only so much of your time. Invest that much time in the project but no more. Preparing a file on advertisements that come across your desk is one example.

SCHEDULE SIMILAR TASKS TOGETHER (CLUSTERING)

An efficient method of accomplishing small tasks is to group them together and perform them in one block of time. Clustering of this type has several applications. If you are visiting an office supply store, think of whatever you need there to avoid an unnecessary repeat visit. As long as you are visiting a particular search engine, look for some other information you will need soon. A basic way of scheduling similar tasks together is to make most of your telephone calls in relation to your job from 11:00 to 11:30 each workday morning. Or you might reserve the last hour of every workday for e-mail and other correspondence. By using this method, you develop the necessary pace and mental set to knock off chores in short order. In contrast, when you flit from one task to another, your efficiency may suffer.

BOUNCE QUICKLY FROM TASK TO TASK

Much time is lost when a person takes a break between tasks. After one task is completed, you might pause for 10 minutes to clear your work area and adjust your to-do list. After the brief pause, dive into your next important task. A compliance officer at a mutual fund says that he turns over an hourglass when he needs to decompress after handling an urgent situation. When the sand runs out, he moves to the next priority. [26]

Incorporating many of the ideas contained in this chapter will help you achieve peak performance or exceptional accomplishment.

Concept Review and Reinforcement

Key Terms

Summary and Review

People with good work habits tend to be more successful in their careers than poorly organized individuals, and they tend to have more time to spend on personal life. Good work habits are more important than ever because of today's emphasis on productivity and quality.

Procrastination is the leading cause of poor productivity and career self-sabotage. People procrastinate for many reasons, including their perception that a task is unpleasant, is overwhelming, or may lead to negative consequences. Fear of success can also lead to procrastination. Awareness of procrastination can lead to its control.

Eight other techniques for reducing procrastination are

- calculating the cost of procrastination
- counterattacking the burdensome task
- jump-starting yourself
- pecking away at an overwhelming task
- motivating yourself with rewards and punishments
- following the WIFO principle
- making a commitment to other people
- expressing a more positive attitude about your intentions

Developing good work habits and time management practices is often a matter of developing proper attitudes toward work and time. Seven such attitudes and values are

- developing a mission, goals, and a strong work ethic
- valuing good attendance and punctuality
- valuing your time

- valuing neatness, orderliness, and speed
- working smarter, not harder
- becoming self-employed psychologically
- appreciating the importance of rest and relaxation

Ten skills and techniques to help you become more productive are

- cleaning up and getting organized
- planning your activities (including the use of time-and-activity charts)
- getting off to a good start
- making good use of office technology
- concentrating on one key task at a time
- streamlining your work and emphasizing important tasks
- working at a steady pace
- creating some quiet, uninterrupted time
- making use of bits of time and using multitasking for routine work
- staying in control of paperwork, the in-basket, and e-mail

Time wasting is a major problem in the workplace. Seven suggestions for overcoming time wasting are

- minimizing daydreaming
- preparing a time log and evaluating your use of time
- avoiding unproductive use of computers
- keeping track of important names, places, and things
- setting a time limit for certain tasks and projects
- scheduling similar tasks together (clustering)
- bouncing quickly from task to task

Check your Understanding

1. In recent years, companies that sell desk planners and other time-management devices have experienced all-time peak demands for their products. What factors do you think are creating this boom?
2. What have you observed to be two of the most important areas for improvement in work habits and time management for students?
3. Many tidy, well-organized workers never attain much in the way of career success. Which principle of work habits and time management described in this chapter might they be neglecting?
4. How can preparing a personal mission statement help a person become better organized?
5. Why might drastically reducing procrastination often increase a person's income substantially?

6. What type of bad work habits might a person have who has very low tendencies toward perfectionism?
7. Give an example of any work you have ever performed or heard of someone else performing that could be eliminated because it is unproductive.
8. Identify five bits of time you could put to better use.
9. How might reducing the amount of time wasted at work help stop the flow of outsourcing of jobs?
10. What is your opinion of the honesty of the responses to the survey about non-job related computer surfing? For example, do more people spend time visiting sports Web sites and gambling Web sites than they admit?

Web Corner

Procrastination test (must take within 48 hours): www.queendom.com/testscareer/procrastination_access .html

Developing punctuality ("On Time Thinking for On-Time Results"): www.blackenterprise.com.

National Association of Professional Organizers: www.napo.net

INTERNET SKILL BUILDER:

What Are You Doing with Your Time?

Go to www.getmoredone.com/tabulator.html to find the Pace Productivity Tabulator. This interactive module enables you to enter the time you spend on 11 major activities (such as employment, eating, sleeping, and television watching) and compare your profile to others. You are also able to enter your ideal profile to see where you would like to be. Simply follow the straightforward instructions. After arriving at your personal pie chart, ask yourself, "What have I learned that will enhance my personal productivity?"

Developing Your Human Relations Skills

Human Relations Application Exercises

Applying Human Relations Exercise 16-1

The Personal Productivity Checklist

Class Project

Each class member will use the following checklist to identify the two biggest mistakes per category he or she is making in work habits and time management. The mistakes could apply to work, school, or personal life. In addition to identifying the problems, each student will develop brief action plans about how to overcome them. For instance, "One of my biggest problems is that I tend to start a lot of projects but finish very few of them. Now that I am aware of this problem, I am going to post a sign over my desk that reads, 'No one will give me credit for things I never completed.'"

Students then present their problems and action plans to the class. After each student has made his or her presentation, a class discussion is held to reach conclusions and interpretations about the problems revealed. For instance, it might be that one or two time-management problems are quite frequent.

Overcoming Procrastination	**Especially Applicable to Me**
1. Increase awareness of the problem.	_____
2. Calculate cost of procrastination.	_____
3. Counterattack.	_____
4. Jump-start yourself.	_____
5. Peck away at an overwhelming task.	_____
6. Motive yourself with rewards and punishments.	_____
7. Follow the WIFO principle.	_____
8. Make a commitment to other people.	_____
9. Express a more positive attitude about your intentions.	_____

Developing Proper Attitudes and Values

1. Develop a mission, goals, and a strong work ethic.	_____
2. Value good attendance and punctuality.	_____
3. Value your time.	_____
4. Value neatness, orderliness, and speed.	_____
5. Work smarter, not harder.	_____
6. Become self-employed psychologically.	_____
7. Appreciate the importance of rest and relaxation.	_____

Time-Management Techniques

1. Clean up and get organized.	_____
2. Plan your activities (including a to-do list with priority setting).	_____
3. Get off to a good start.	_____
4. Make good use of office technology.	_____
5. Concentrate on one key task at a time.	_____
6. Streamline your work and emphasize important tasks.	_____
7. Work at a steady pace.	_____
8. Create some quiet, uninterrupted time.	_____
9. Make use of bits of time and use multitasking for routine work.	_____
10. Stay in control of paperwork, the in-basket, and e-mail.	_____

432

Overcoming Time Wasters

1. Minimize daydreaming. _____

2. Prepare a time log to evaluate your use of time. _____

3. Avoid unproductive use of computers. _____

4. Keep track of important names, places, and things. _____

5. Set a time limit for certain tasks and projects. _____

6. Schedule similar tasks together (clustering). _____

7. Bounce quickly from task to task. _____

Applying Human Relations Exercise 16-2

My Personal Procrastination Analysis

The purpose of this exercise is to give you practice in understanding why you might have procrastinated in the past and how you might overcome a similar episode of procrastination in the future. To begin, write a 25-word or so description of some important activity on which you have procrastinated in the past. An *important* activity is one that could have a noticeable impact on your mental or financial well-being. Describe also any negative consequences that might have stemmed from the procrastination. Here is an example from an assistant manager at a health club who lives in New York state:

"I knew my vehicle inspection sticker was due in a month. But I was simply so busy with other things, I couldn't get to it. Also, I figured because it was winter time, I could spread some snow over the dated sticker, and no police office would catch me. Well, it worked out that I was pulled over for the expired sticker. Unfortunately, the officer also found out I had not renewed my driver's license. My total fines were about $500 plus having to spend loads of time at the motor vehicle bureau straightening out the mess."

Use the following table (or copy the form on your computer) to record your procrastination episode and analyze the cause. After you have checked the most likely cause or causes, make a few notes in the third column as to how you might avoid procrastinating about that situation, or similar situation, in the future.

Procrastination Episode

Reason(s) for Procrastination	Check Each Reason That Applies	Technique I Might Use to Overcome the Procrastination Next Time I Am in That Situation
1. Unpleasant task		
2. Overwhelming task		
3. Possible negative evaluation of my work		
4. Fear of success		
5. Rebelled against being controlled		
6. No meaningful reward		
7. Liked the last-minute rush		
8. I'm a perfectionist		

The assistant manager of the health club admitted that reasons 5 and 6 applied to his situation. He noted that he regards inspection stickers as a form of control over him. He noted also that having the sticker may be important, but that he doesn't feel any particular reward for complying with the law. On further reflection, he realizes that some control is necessary in a civilized society. Many uninspected vehicles are a menace on the road. So not getting a sticker has a cost to society as well as to him. He will therefore calculate the personal cost next time. He said, "Maybe I should use the WIFO next year. It takes a little time and money to get my car inspected, so I should do it first thing on the day set for the inspection."

Human Relations Case Study 16-1

A Case of Not Getting It Done

Carol Winchester sat nervously outside the office of Daniel Delvin, a time-management consultant and personal coach. She kept thinking about how self-conscious she felt about seeking professional help simply because she has a little trouble getting started on projects or finishing projects she has started. Carol said to herself, "This counselor is going to think there's something really wrong with me simply because I have a small procrastination problem."

Winchester's thought pattern was interrupted by a warm welcome from Daniel Delvin, a neatly dressed, middle-age counselor. With a smile and an extended hand, Delvin said, "Hi. You must be Carol Winchester. I'm Dan Delvin. Come in and have a seat near the coffee table. That's where we'll be talking." Delvin sat in a chair, a few feet away from Winchester.

"What kind of help do you want from me?" asked Delvin.

"The reason I'm here," answered Winchester, "is that both my boss and my boyfriend think I'm a procrastinator. Big time. I don't disagree entirely, but I don't think I'm quite the basket case they do."

Delvin replied, "I doubt you're a basket case, but I don't think you would be here if you weren't experiencing a little pain. Hurting a little bit and admitting that you have a problem are the beginning points for overcoming your problem. Let's get started, Carol, by your telling me about some of the ways in which you procrastinate."

"I've got a few horror stories to tell you," said Winchester with a nervous laugh. "A recent example is that it took me four months to make this appointment with you. [They both laugh.] I kept looking at my calendar and saying to myself that I was too busy to get help. I would pick up the phone to make an appointment. Then I would think of all the other things I needed to do. I finally set April 1 as an absolute firm date to call you.

Then I realized I only had two more weeks to prepare my income tax forms for last year. I guess you could say that I even procrastinated on my income tax. But I finally did get it in April 30, and the penalty only amounted to about $95. Those are two examples for you."

"Yes, they are two good examples. But I need more examples of your procrastination so I can better understand your problem."

"OK, you asked for it," responded Winchester. "Lance, my boyfriend, whom I love very much, proposed to me one year ago. We were in a beautiful Greek restaurant called Acropolis. He pulled a ring out of the box. The group at the table across from us were watching intently. They were ready to clap when I said yes. Lance just assumed I would say yes. I didn't say yes, but I didn't say no. I simply said I wasn't ready to make a decision that night.

"Two months later, when the engagement came up for about the tenth time in conversation, I did say yes. I know that by delaying my decision I took some of the romance out of Lance's proposal. His feelings are still a little hurt, but it didn't change his mind about wanting to marry me."

"Hold on a second," said Delvin. "Have you two agreed upon a wedding date yet?"

"Lance has been pressing me a little, but I'm simply not ready to be that specific about getting married."

"Let's switch channels now," said Delvin. "What about on the job? What has prompted your boss to think you have a major procrastination problem?"

"It would be fair to say that I need more time than most people to get my projects done. I'm the assistant sales promotion manager. I have to do things such as make some of the arrangements for trade shows and work with printers to have brochures ready. My boss says that I wait so long to make arrangements for booking hotels that we often have to pay premium rates. I think he exaggerates that problem. I'm very thorough and that can be a big asset.

"A few times I have been late in getting computer files ready to send to the printer so they can do their job on time. Yet because we're the customer, I think they should adapt to our schedule. I can think of another recent example. We were going to hire a new assistant for the office. We all agreed she was the right person to do the job. My boss had to go out of town for an important sales meeting. So he told me to contact this woman, and tell her about the job offer.

"I got so busy with other stuff that I didn't call her for a week. By that time she had accepted another job. My boss was upset and blamed losing her on my procrastination. My take on it is a little different. If that woman really wanted to work for us, she could have waited for the job offer instead of taking another position."

Delvin asked, "Carol, why do you think you procrastinate so much?"

Carol replied, "You're a little bit like my boss and my boyfriend. You assume that every time I delay doing something, it's procrastination. Sometimes something else very important comes up that prevents me from going down a particular path. At other times I might be just a little forgetful, like filing the taxes on time."

Questions

1. What do you see as some of the reason behind Winchester's procrastination?
2. What evidence do you find that Winchester might be defensive about her problem (or denying its reality)?
3. What advice can you offer Carol Winchester for overcoming her procrastination problem?

Human Relations Case Study 16-2

The Cubicle Blues

Paul Chen works as a design technician for DesignTrend, a furniture manufacturer in San Francisco. His major responsibilty is to design support devices for home and office furniture, such as the arms, legs, and frames. His employer has configured the office into cubicles, with even the company executives being assigned to cubicles. When the creative staff needs more space, such as when laying out blueprints for an office, a common area with large drawing tables is available. Because most design work is computer aided, the creative staff does most of their work in the assigned cubicles.

Previous to the reconfiguration of the office, design engineers and technicians were assigned to small private offices with doors. In this way, the engineers and technicians could work relatively uninterrupted without colleagues frequently conversing with them. The offices also closed off most sounds so a creative worker could avoid hearing office chatter, including telephone conversations.

CEO Kenneth Yang decided to change from closed offices to cubicles to enhance communication and idea sharing among all staff members. Yang opined, "Unstructured communication leads to an exchange of ideas that is vital for creativity. I don't want the staff holed up in offices and minimizing communication with each other."

Chen became increasingly troubled by life in his cubicle. He grumbled to coworkers, friends, and family members about working in a cubicle farm. He disliked the distractions, and he was having difficulty concentrating on creative tasks. One day when his supervisor dropped by his cubicle, Chen explained his problem:

"How can Yang expect the creative staff to be creative when assigned to these cubicles? I hear every conversation that's going on up to two cubicles down. When I am working on a design I need to concentrate. I need to reflect. I don't want to be interrupted by a neighbor telling her husband over the phone to pick up a pizza on the way home. I enjoy working for DesignTrend, but the cubicles have made my days insufferable."

The supervisor replied, "I'm in no position to assign you a private office. Even Ken Yang works out of a cubicle. Yet, I will give some thought to your problem."

Questions

1. Is Paul Chen offering a valid complaint that creative thought is difficult without privacy?
2. What advice can you offer Chen to help him manage interruptions better?
3. What should Chen's supervisor advise him to do?

Source: A few of the facts in this case are from Linda Tischler, "Death to the Cubicle," *Fast Company*, June 2005, pp. 29–32.

REFERENCES

1. Laura Koss-Feder, "Slowing Down the Treadmill, with Help," available at NYTimes.com, retrieved June 29, 2003.

2. Research of Timothy A. Psychl, reported in Danielle Kost, "Professor Says Putting Off Chores Is a Breakable Habit," *Rochester (NY) Democrat and Chronicle*, September 22, 2002, p. D3.

3. Theodore Kurtz, "Ten Reasons Why People Procrastinate," *Supervisory Management*, April 1990, pp. 1–2.

4. "When to Procrastinate and When to Get Going?" *Working Smart*, March 1992, pp. 1–2.

5. Alan Lakein, *How to Gain Control of Your Time and Your Life* (New York: Wyden Books, 1973), pp. 141–151.

6. Cited and quoted in "Get with It: Nip Your Procrastination Right in the Bud," *Entrepreneur*, September 1998, p. 94.

7. Linda Sapadin, *It's about Time! The Six Styles of Procrastination and How to Overcome Them* (New York: Viking, 1996).

8. Stephen R. Covey with Elaine Pofeldt, "Why Is This Man Smiling?" *Success*, January 2000, pp. 38–40.

9. Cited in Alfred A. Edmond, Jr., "Alone in Your Time Zone," *Black Enterprise*, December 2004, pp. 154–155.

10. Price Pritchett, *The Employee Handbook of New Work Habits for a Radically Changing World* (Dallas: Pritchett & Associates, undated, distributed in 2003), p. 11.

11. Michael Mandel, "The Real Reasons You're Working So Hard . . . and What You Can Do about It," *Business Week*, October 3, 2005, p. 62.

12. Raymond P. Rood and Brenda L. Meneley, "Serious Play at Work," *Personnel Journal*, January 1991, p. 90.

13. Jaed Sandberg, "Bosses May Disagree, but a Quick Nap Shows How Smart You Are," *The Wall Street Journal*, November 17, 2004, p. B1.

14. Quoted in Carrie Ferguson, "The Wages of a Workaholic," Gannett News Service, May 23, 2000.

15. Brenda Goodman, "A Field Guide to the Workaholic," *Psychology Today*, May/June 2006, p. 40.

16. Stewart D. Friedman and Sharon Lobel, "The Happy Workaholic: A Role Model for Employees," *Academy of Management Executive*, August 2003, pp. 87–98.

17. Survey reported in Jane M. Von Bergen, "Getting Organized at the Office," available at www.philly.com, retrieved February 26, 2006.

18. Joyce R. Rosenberg, "Calendar Remains a Valuable Business Tool," The Associated Press, June 20, 2005.

19. Merrill Douglass, "Timely Time Tips: Ideas to Help You Manage Your Time," *Executive Management Forum*, September 1989, p. 4.

20. Research reported in Mark Greer, "Older Adults Need Full Attention to Juggle Multiple Tasks," *Monitor on Psychology*, June 2005, p. 19.

21. Quoted in Anne Fisher "Get Organized at Work—Painlessly," *Fortune*, January 10, 2005, p. 30.

22. Survey cited in "Productivity Declines as the Workday Ends," *Rochester (NY) Democrat and Chronicle*, July 18, 2005, p. 10D.

23. Douglass, "Timely Time Tips," p. 4.

24. Dan Malachowski, "Wasted Time at Work Costing Companies Billions," available at www.salary.com, undated, retrieved May 12, 2006.

25. Survey cited in "Workers Dawdle on Net an Hour a Day, Firm Says," *Rochester (NY), Democrat and Chronicle*, August 22, 2005, p. 10D.

26. "Beating the Clock: Time Management When You Are under the Gun," *Working Smart*, March 1999, p. 1.

17 Managing Stress and Personal Problems

Learning Objectives

Outline

After studying the information and doing the exercise in this chapter, you should be able to:

1 Describe the meaning of stress and its physiology.

2 Identify several positive and negative consequences of stress.

3 Pinpoint potential stressors in personal life.

4 Pinpoint potential stressors in the workplace.

5 Describe key methods for managing the potential adverse effects of stress.

6 Develop insight into dealing with personal problems through understanding self-defeating behavior, and the importance of being resilient.

4

Considering a fourth cappuccino to get you through the day? Take it from some folks who know all about caffeine-fueled productivity: Meditation can do the work of a whole lot of java. Without the slightest nod to the inherent irony, dozens of employees at Green Mountain Coffee Roasters in Waterbury, Vermont, file into a soundproof space at company headquarters each week and sit perfectly still while being led in relaxation, visualization, and breathing exercises. The idea struck CEO Robert Stillier, who has been meditating since the 1970s, about two years ago when he realized that his 400 employees might produce better work if they occasionally did absolutely nothing. "Your best thoughts come when you're in a relaxed state like in the shower," Stillier says. "Meditation provides the space for that to happen." Now he gets word that attendees often talk about having more energy and focus; one worker, a picture of zenlike efficiency, even ditched his watch. Nonetheless, a fresh-brewed cup of 30 Green Mountain Blends is always available—just in case the guru is out. [1]

The story about the meditating coffee producers illustrates how companies are concerned about preventing and reducing stress in order to boost productivity, including having employees think more clearly. In this chapter we describe the nature and cause of stress, managing personal and work stress, and the related topic of coping with personal problems.

What Are the Physiology and Consequences of Stress?

■ **Learning Objective 1**

■ Stress
an internal reaction to any force that threatens to disturb a person's equilibrium; the internal reaction usually takes the form of emotional discomfort

■ Stressor
the external or internal force that brings about the stress

An important part of learning about stress is to understand its meaning, underlying physiology, and consequences to the person. **Stress** is an internal reaction to any force that threatens to disturb a person's equilibrium. The internal reaction usually takes the form of emotional discomfort. A **stressor** is the external or internal force that brings about the stress. Your perception of an event or thought influences whether a given event is stressful. Your confidence in your ability to handle difficult situations also influences the amount of stress you experience. If you believe you have the resources to conquer the potentially stressful event, you are much less likely to experience stress. A computer whiz, therefore, would not be stressed by the prospect of having to install a new computer operating system. Two key aspects of understanding stress are the accompanying physiological changes and the consequences—including symptoms—of stress.

PHYSIOLOGICAL CHANGES

The physiological changes taking place within the body are almost identical for both positive and negative stressors. Riding a roller coaster, falling in love, or being fired, for example, make you feel about the same inside. The stress response begins in the brain, and a number of structures, including the pituitary gland, go on alert. The experience of stress prompts the adrenal glands to release a flood of hormones that prepare the body to fight or run when faced with a challenge. This battle against the stressor is referred to as the **fight-or-flight response.** (The "response" is really a conflict because you are forced to choose between struggling with the stressor or fleeing from the scene.) It helps you deal with emergencies.

Recent studies suggest the possibility that women, along with females of other species, react differently to major stressors. Instead of the fight-or-flight response

■ Fight-or-flight response
the experience of stress prompts the adrenal glands to release a flood of hormones that prepare the body to fight or run when faced with a challenge

typical of males, they *tend and befriend.* When stress levels mount, women are more likely to protect and nurture their children (tend) and turn to social networks of supportive females (befriend). The researchers speculate that the tend-and-befriend behavior became prevalent over the centuries because women who tended and befriended would be more likely to have their offspring survive and pass on their mother's traits. Additional evidence suggests that women tend to affiliate during times of stress, whereas men do not. [2]

The activation of hormones when the body has to cope with a stressor produces a short-term physiological reaction. Among the most familiar reactions are increases in heart rate, blood pressure, and blood glucose as well as blood clotting. Digestion stops during the stress episode. To help you recognize these symptoms, try to recall the internal bodily sensations you felt if you ever were almost in an automobile accident or if you heard some wonderful news. Less familiar changes are a redirection of the blood flow toward the brain and large-muscle groups and a release of stored fluids from places throughout the body into the bloodstream.

CONSEQUENCES AND SYMPTOMS

■ Learning Objective 2

If stress is continuous and accompanied by these short-term physiological changes, annoying and life-threatening conditions can occur. A stressful life event usually leads to a high cholesterol level (of the unhealthy type) and high blood pressure. Men who respond most intensely to mental stress run a higher risk of blocked blood vessels. The result is a higher risk of heart attack and stroke. A series of studies indicated that job stressors such as a hostile work environment or excessive hours can enhance a worker's risk for cardiovascular disease. One explanation of this problem is that mental stress, over time, may injure blood vessels and foster the buildup of arterial plaques. [3] Other conditions associated with stress are migraine headaches, ulcers, allergies, skin disorders, and cancer. Stress often results in memory problems, such as forgetting where you put your keys or not remembering an appointment.

Stress symptoms vary considerably from one person to another. A sampling of common stress symptoms is listed in Figure 17-1.

| **Figure** | **17-1** |

A Variety of Stress Symptoms
Note: Anxiety is a feeling of distress or uneasiness caused by fear of an imagined or unidentified problem. For example, you might be anxious about meeting your supervisor today, but you have no specific concern in mind.

Mostly Physical

Shaking or trembling	Upper- and lower-back pain
Dizziness	Frequent headaches
Heart palpitations	Low energy and stamina
Difficulty breathing	Stomach problems
Chronic fatigue	Constant cravings for sweets
Unexplained chest pains	Increased alcohol or cigarette consumption
Frequent teeth grinding	Frequent need to eliminate
Frequent nausea and dizziness	Skin eruptions and rashes
Premature aging, including a haggard appearance	

Mostly Emotional and Behavioral

Difficulty concentrating	Anxiety or depression
Nervousness	Forgetfulness
Crying	Restlessness
Anorexia	Frequent arguments with others
Declining interest in sex and romance	Feeling high strung much of the time

A major consequence of stress is that it affects our ability to fight infection. Psychology professors Suzanne Segerstrom of the University of Kentucky and Gregory Miller of the University of British Columbia analyzed the results of 293 studies, involving 18,941 individuals, conducted over a 30-year span. Three major findings emerged from this massive analysis. First, stress does alter immunity—as has been long recognized. Second, short-term stress boosts the immune system, functioning as an adaptive response preparing for injury or infection. Giving a public speech or class presentation are examples of short-term stress for most people. Yet long-term chronic stress causes too much wear and tear, breaking down the immune system. An example of a long-term chronic stress would be long-term unemployment. Third, the immune system of older people, or those who are already ill, is more susceptible to stress-related change. [4]

Despite all the problems previously mentioned, stress also plays a positive role in our lives. The right amount of stress prepares us for meeting difficult challenges and spurs us on to peak intellectual and physical performance. (The findings about the immune system support this conclusion.) An optimum amount of stress exists for most people and most tasks. In general, performance tends to be best under moderate amounts of stress. If stress is too great, people become temporarily ineffective because they may freeze or choke. Under too little stress, people may become lethargic and inattentive. Stress can lower job performance because the stressed person makes errors in concentration and judgment.

Stress has enormous consequences to employers as well as individuals. It has been estimated that American companies lose about $200 billion annually in absenteeism, below-standard performance, tardiness, and Workers' Compensation claims linked to stress disorders. [5] A research study involving 820 truck drivers in Holland illustrates the consequence of negative job stress to employers. The drivers who suffered the negative consequences of stress (strain) were more likely to quit than drivers who experienced less strain. Furthermore, the stressed truck drivers were more likely to find another occupation after they quit. [6] We emphasize again that positive stress is not associated with negative consequences to the employer.

Figure 17-2 depicts the relationship between stress and performance. Current research adds credence to this well-established finding. In a learning situation, when the stress takes the form of challenging material, learning performance improves. In contrast, when the stress is associated with hindrances (such as not knowing what is expected of you), it lowers performance. [7] An exception to this relationship is that certain negative forms of stress are likely to lower performance even if the stress is moderate. For example, the stress created by an intimidating boss or worrying about radiation poisoning—even in moderate amounts—will not improve performance.

Multitasking contributes to the relationship between stress and performance, based on a study conducted by information technology professors Gloria Mark and Victor Gonzalez at the University of California at Irvine. The participants were 36 information technology workers at an investment firm. For most workers, as the number of tasks juggled increased, stress rose and performance decreased. However, a little multitasking raised the challenge bar and often led to enhanced performance. [8]

Where does burnout fit into the stress picture? One of the major problems of prolonged stress is that it may lead to **burnout,** a condition of emotional, mental, and physical exhaustion in response to long-term job stressors. The exhaustion aspect of burnout can be triggered by such factors as a heavy physical workload, time pressures, and shift work. [9] The burned-out person often becomes cynical. Burnout is most likely to occur among those whose jobs call for frequent and intense interactions with others, such as a social worker, teacher, or customer service representative. Yet people in other occupations also suffer from burnout, especially when not much support from others is present and the rewards are few.

Also, a hostile work environment, such as being harassed by coworkers and managers, is a major contributor to burnout. [10] Students can also experience

■ **Burnout**
a condition of emotional, mental, and physical exhaustion in response to long-term job stressors

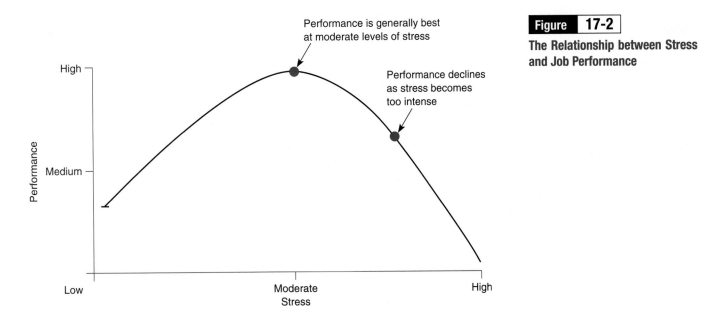

Figure   17-2

The Relationship between Stress and Job Performance

burnout because studying is hard work. Conscientiousness and perfectionism also contribute to burnout because people with these characteristics feel stressed when they do not accomplish everything they would like. Similarly, being obsessed about what you are doing can trigger burnout.

Burnout can be treated in many ways, just as with the negative effects of stress. Showing gratitude for hard work by employees is particularly helpful in preventing and treating burnout because many cases of burnout are caused by intense feelings of being unappreciated.

What Are Some Sources of Stress In Personal Life?

■ **Learning Objective 3**

Almost any form of frustration, disappointment, setback, inconvenience, or crisis in your personal life can cause stress. The list is dynamic because new sources of stress emerge continuously. For example, a prolonged downturn in the stock market can be a stressor for investors who previously paid little attention to how well their investments were performing. Our life stage also helps determine which events are stressors. A person building his or her career is more likely to be more stressed by a limited supply of jobs than a person nearing retirement. Presented next are major categories of stressful events in personal life.

1. Significant life change. A general stressor that encompasses both work and personal life is having to cope with significant change. According the research of Thomas Holmes and Richard Rahe, the necessity of a significant change in an individual's life pattern creates stress. The more significant the change you have to cope with in a short period of time, the greater the probability of experiencing a stress disorder. [11] As shown in Figure 17-3, the maximum negative change is the death of a spouse. Twenty-four other stressors created by change are listed in the table in decreasing order of impact. The rank order shown in Figure 17-3 consists of averages and does not hold true for everybody. For example, a person who could fall back into working for a family business might not find being fired from the job (item 8 in the figure) so stressful.

Figure	17-3

The Top 25 Stressors as Measured by Life-Change Units

Source: These stressors have changed over time. This version is from Thomas H. Holmes and Richard H. Rahe, "The Social Adjustment Rating Scale," *Journal of Psychosomatic Research,* 1971, *15,* pp. 210–223, with an interview updating from Sue MacDonald, "Battling Stress," *Cincinnati Enquirer,* October 23, 1995, p. C4.

1. Death of a spouse
2. Divorce
3. Marital separation
4. Jail term/imprisonment
5. Death of a family member
6. Personal injury or illness
7. Marriage
8. Fired from the job
9. Marital reconciliation
10. Retirement
11. Change in health of family member
12. Pregnancy
13. Sexual difficulties
14. Change in financial status
15. Number of arguments with spouse
16. Major mortgage
17. Foreclosure of a loan
18. Change in responsibilities at work
19. Son or daughter leaves home
20. Trouble with in-laws
21. Outstanding personal achievement
22. Spouse begins or stops work
23. Begin or end school
24. Change in living conditions
25. Revision of personal habits

2. Low self-esteem. A subtle cause of stress is low self-esteem. People who do not feel good about themselves often find it difficult to feel good about anything. Low self-esteem has several links to stress. One is that being in a bad mood continually functions as a stressor. People with low self-esteem drag themselves down into a funk, which creates stress. Another link between low self-esteem and stress proneness is that people with low self-esteem get hurt more by insults. Instead of questioning the source of the criticism, the person with self-doubt will accept the opinion as valid. [12] An insult accepted as valid acts as a stressor because it is a threat to our well-being.

Low self-esteem is linked to stress in yet another way. People with low self-esteem doubt their ability to work their way out of problems. As a result, minor challenges appear to be major problems. For example, a person with low self-esteem will often doubt he or she will be successful in conducting a job search. As a result, having to conduct a job search will represent a major stressor. A person with high self-esteem might feel better prepared mentally to accept the challenge. (As you will recall, your perception of an event influences whether it is stressful.)

3. Everyday annoyances. Managing everyday annoyances can have a greater impact on your health than major life catastrophes. Among these everyday annoyances are losing keys or a wallet, crashing a computer file, being stuck in traffic, having your car break down, and being lost on the way to an important appointment. People who have the coping skills to deal with everyday annoyances are less likely to be stressed out over them. A major reason everyday annoyances act as stressors is because they are frustrating—they block your path to an important goal, such as getting your work accomplished.

4. Social and family problems. Friends and family are the main source of love and affection in your life. But they can also be the main source of stress. Most physical acts of violence are committed among friends and family members. One of the many reasons we encounter so much conflict with friends and family is that we are emotionally involved with them.

5. Physical and mental health problems. Prolonged stress produces physical and mental health problems, and the reverse is also true. Physical and mental illness can act as stressors—the fact of being ill is stressful. Furthermore, thinking that you might soon contract a life-threatening illness is stressful. If you receive a serious injury, that too can create stress.

6. Financial problems. A major life stressor is financial problems. Although you may not be obsessed with money, not having enough money to take care of what you consider the necessities of life can lead to anxiety and tension. If you do not have enough money to replace or repair a broken or faulty personal computer or automobile, the result can be stressful. A major stressor for recent graduates who move to high cost of living areas is being able to afford a comfortable place to live.

7. School-related problems. The life of a student can be stressful. Among the stressors to cope with are exams in subjects you do not understand well, having to write papers on subjects unfamiliar to you, working your way through the complexities of registration, or having to deal with instructors who do not see things your way. Another source of severe stress for some students is having too many competing demands on their time. On most campuses you will find someone who works full time, goes to school full time, and has a family.

PERSONALITY FACTORS CONTRIBUTING TO STRESS

Some people are more stress prone than others because of personality factors. Three key personality factors predisposing people to stress are type A behavior, a belief that external forces control their life, and negative affectivity.

Type A Behavior

People with **type A behavior** characteristics have basic personalities that lead them into stressful situations. Type A behavior has two main components. One is a tendency to try to accomplish too many things in too little time. This leads the type A individual to be impatient and demanding. The other component is free-floating hostility. Because of this combined sense of urgency and hostility, trivial things irritate these people. On the job, people with type A behavior are aggressive and hard-working. Off the job, they keep themselves preoccupied with all kinds of errands to run and things to do.

Certain features of the type A behavior pattern are related to coronary heart disease. Hostility, anger, cynicism, and suspiciousness lead to heart problems, whereas impatience, ambition, and being work driven are not associated with coronary disease. One study showed that men who received a high score on a personality test about hostility were much more likely to develop coronary heart disease several years later. [13] Many work-driven people who like what they are doing—including many business executives—are remarkably healthy and outlive less competitive people.

Belief in External Locus of Control

If you believe that your fate is controlled more by external than internal forces, you are probably more susceptible to stress. People with an **external locus of control**

■ **Type A behavior**
personality characteristics that lead a person into stressful situations. Type A behavior has two main components: (1) the tendency to try to accomplish too many things in too little time and (2) free-floating hostility

■ **External locus of control**
individual's belief that external forces control their fate

believe that external forces control their fate. Conversely, people with an **internal locus of control** believe that fate is pretty much under their control. The link between locus of control and stress works in this manner: If people believe they can control adverse forces, they are less prone to the stressor of worrying about them. For example, if you believed that you can always find a job, you will worry less about unemployment. At the same time, the person who believes in an internal locus of control experiences a higher level of job satisfaction. Work is less stressful and more satisfying when you perceive it to be under your control.

The everyday problem of lost computer files illustrates the importance of an internal locus of control. When a hard drive crashes or a valuable file is lost in some other way, the "external" person blames the computer or the software for the stressful event. An "internal," in contrast, would most likely have created backup files along the way. So when a crash occurs, the person is less stressed because relatively little data have been lost.

What about your locus of control? Do you believe it to be internal? Or is it external?

Negative Affectivity

A major contributor to being stress prone is **negative affectivity,** a tendency to experience aversive (intensely disliked) emotional states. In more detail, negative affectivity is a predisposition to experience emotional stress that includes feelings of nervousness, tension, and worry. Furthermore, a person with negative affectivity is likely to experience emotional states such as anger, scorn, revulsion, guilt, and self-dissatisfaction. [14] Such negative personalities seem to search for discrepancies between what they would like and what exists. Instead of attempting to solve problems, they look for them. Although negative affectivity is a relatively stable personality characteristic, the circumstances a person faces can trigger such behavior. [15] For example, a four-hour wait in an airplane parked on the tarmac might trigger a person's mild tendencies toward negative affectivity.

What Are Some Key Sources of Work Stress?

No job is without potential stressors for some people. When work is lacking stressful elements, it may not have enough challenge to prompt employees to achieve high performance. Here we describe four major job stressors you might encounter or have already encountered, as listed in Figure 17-4.

WORK OVERLOAD OR UNDERLOAD

A heavy workload is a widely acknowledged source of job stress. According to a survey of 1,003 workers by the Family and Work Institute, one-third of employees feel highly overworked. The employees think they are handling too many tasks at the same time, have too many interruptions, or experience a combination of both. Furthermore, 54 percent of the workers surveyed felt overwhelmed at some time during the past month. [16]

Role overload, a burdensome workload, can create stress for a person in two ways. First, the person may become fatigued and thus be less able to tolerate annoyances and irritations. Think of how much easier it is to become provoked over a minor incident when you lack proper rest. Second, a person subject to unreasonable work demands may feel perpetually behind schedule, a situation that itself creates an uncomfortable, stressful feeling.

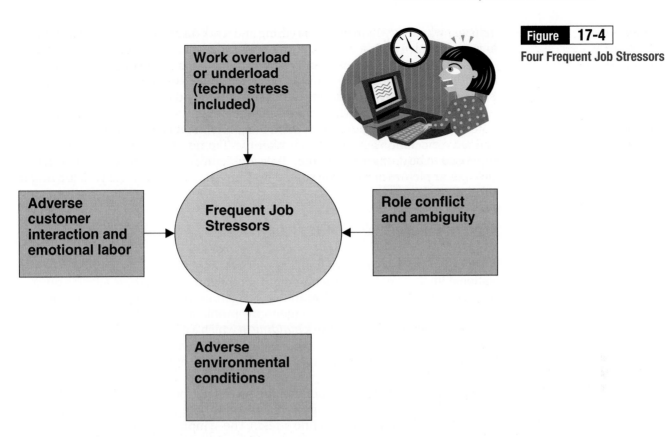

Figure **17-4**

Four Frequent Job Stressors

Another form of work overload is demanding higher and higher speed from workers. Speed is important to companies because delivering goods and services very quickly brings a competitive edge. The most stressful situation occurs when a company downsizes and the remaining workers are expected to carry a heavier workload at a faster pace than previously. The combination of additional responsibility and high speed can be a major stressor. Among the problems are that hurried employees have very little time to ask for help or to carefully study what they are doing.

A powerful stressor for knowledge workers is information overload. Workers have to process so much information in the form of e-mail messages, text messages, Web sites, written reports, and job-related news that their brain circuits become overloaded leading to stress and lowered concentration. Many workers encourage overload by multitasking while receiving information. Stress caused by information overload is sometimes referred to **techno stress,** which is caused by having to cope with ever-changing technology and the deluge of data stemming from information technology. [17] A cluttered work area, including a cluttered computer files and e-mail adds to techno stress.

A disruptive amount of stress can also occur when people experience **role underload,** or too little to do. Some people find role underload frustrating because it is a normal human desire to want to work toward self-fulfillment. Also, making a contribution on the job is one way of gaining self-esteem. Some people, however, find it relaxing not to have much to do on the job. One direct benefit is that it preserves their energy for family and leisure activities.

ROLE CONFLICT AND ROLE AMBIGUITY

Being pulled in two directions is a classic stressor. **Role conflict** refers to having to choose between two competing demands or expectations. Many workers receive conflicting demands from two or more managers. Imagine being told by your manager to give top priority to one project. You then receive a call from your manager's

■ **Techno stress**

stress caused by information overload as a result of having to cope with ever-changing technology and the deluge of data stemming from information technology

■ **Role underload**

disruptive amount of stress that can occur when people experience too little to do; one benefit is the preservation of energy for family and leisure activities

■ **Role conflict**

having to choose between two competing demands or expectations manager who tells you to drop everything and work on another project. It's often up to you to resolve such a conflict. If you don't, you will experience stress. Having to choose between taking care of job responsibilities versus personal responsibilities is another potent type of role conflict, such as having to work the night a good friend is getting married. Do you upset your boss or your good friend?

Not being certain of what they should be doing is a stressor for many people. **Role ambiguity** is a condition in which the jobholder receives confusing or poorly defined expectations. A typical complaint is "I'm not really sure I know what I'm supposed to be doing around here." Role ambiguity is related to job control. If you lack a clear picture of what you should be doing, it is difficult to get your job under control.

■ **Role ambiguity**

condition in which the jobholder receives confusing or poorly defined expectations

ADVERSE ENVIRONMENTAL CONDITIONS

A variety of adverse organizational conditions are stressors, as identified by the National Institute of Occupational Safety and Health. Among these adverse organizational conditions are unpleasant or dangerous physical conditions, such as crowding, noise, air pollution, or ergonomic problems. Enough polluted air within an office building can create a *sick building* in which a diverse range of airborne particles, vapors, molds, and gases pollute the indoor environment. The result can be headaches, nausea, and respiratory infections as well as the stress created by being physically ill.

Working at a computer monitor for prolonged periods of time can lead to adverse physical and psychological reactions. (These computer-related stressors could be considered part of techno stress.) The symptoms include headaches and fatigue, along with eye problems. Common visual problems are dry eyes and blurred or double vision. An estimated one out of five visits to vision care professionals is for computer-related problems. Another vision-related problem is that people lean forward to scan the monitor, leading to physical problems such as back strain.

■ **Carpal tunnel syndrome**

repetitive motion disorder most frequently associated with keyboarding and the use of optical scanners; occurs when repetitive flexing and extension of the wrist causes the tendons to swell, thus trapping and pinching the median nerve

A repetitive motion disorder most frequently associated with keyboarding and the use of optical scanners is **carpal tunnel syndrome.** The syndrome occurs when repetitive flexing and extension of the wrist causes the tendons to swell, thus trapping and pinching the median nerve. Carpal tunnel syndrome creates stress because of the pain and misery. The thoughts of having to permanently leave a job requiring keyboarding is another potential stressor. Repetitive motion disorders can be prevented somewhat by computer workers taking frequent rest breaks and using a well-designed combination of the worktable, chair, and monitor. Wearing elasticized wrist bands provides enough support to the wrist tendons to prevent many cases of repetitive motion disorders. Being comfortable while working prevents much physical strain. Figure 17-5 presents the basics of a workstation designed on *ergonomic* principles. (Ergonomics has to do with making machines and equipment fit human capabilities and demands.)

ADVERSE CUSTOMER INTERACTION AND EMOTIONAL LABOR

Interactions with customers can be a major stressor. Part of the problem is that the sales associate often feels helpless when placed in conflict with a customer. The sales associate is told that "the customer is always right." Furthermore, the store manager usually sides with the customer in a dispute with the sales associate. Related to adverse customer interaction is the stressor of having to control the expression of emotion to please or to avoid displeasing a customer. Imagine having to smile at a customer who belittles you or makes unwanted sexual advances.

Alicia A.Grandey, associate professor of psychology at Penn State University, defines **emotional labor** as the process of regulating both feelings and expressions to meet organizational goals. [18] The process involves both surface acting and deep

■ **Emotional labor**

process of regulating both feelings and expressions to meet organizational goals

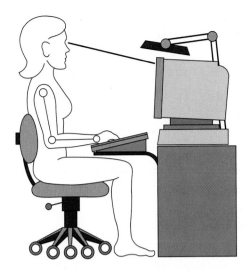

Figure **17-5**

**How to Minimize Cumulative
Trauma Disorder**

An Ergonomic Workstation

• Keep the screen below your eye level.
• Keep your elbows on the same level with home-key
  row, with your wrists and lower arms parallel to floor.
• Support your back and thighs with a well-constructed
  chair.
• Position your feet flat on the floor.
• Use lamp to supplement inadequate room lighting.

acting. Surface acting means faking expressions, such as smiling, whereas deep acting involves controlling feelings, such as suppressing anger toward a customer you perceive to be annoying. Sales workers and customer service representatives often experience emotional labor because so often they have to fake facial expressions and feelings so as to please customers. Nevertheless, according to one study, the top five occupations in terms of emotional labor demands are (1) police and sheriff's patrol officers, (2) social workers, (3) psychiatrists, (4) supervisors of police and detectives, and (5) registered nurses. Bill and account collectors ranked 15! [19]

Engaging in emotional labor for prolonged periods of time can lead to job dissatisfaction, stress, and burnout. A contributing cause is that faking expressions and emotions takes a physiological toll, such as the intestines churning. Workers who engage in emotional labor may also develop cardiovascular problems and weakened immune systems.

What Are Several Effective Approaches to Managing Stress?

■ Learning Objective 5

Because potentially harmful stressors surround us in work and personal life, virtually everybody needs a program of stress management to stay well. Stress-management techniques are placed here into four categories: attacking the source of the stress; receiving social support; relaxation techniques; and wellness through proper exercise, diet, and rest. Your challenge is to select those techniques that best fit your circumstances and preferences.

An important perspective on stress management is that you should be seeking your best stress zone—or the amount of stress that enables you to capitalize on the benefits of positive stress but not fall prey to the negative symptoms of stress. Carol Jack Scott, an emergency room doctor and executive coach, advises people to learn how to recognize when they are about to depart their best-stress zone. For some people this could mean they start misplacing their keys. For others it could mean fitful sleep. [20] After you leave your best-stress zone it is time to get on with one or more of the stress-reduction techniques described next.

DEALING WITH STRESS BY ATTACKING ITS SOURCE

Stress can be dealt with in the short range by indirect techniques such as exercise and relaxation. However, to manage stress in the long range and stay well, you must also learn to deal directly with stressors. Several of these techniques are described in the next few paragraphs.

Eliminating or Modifying the Stressor

The most potent method of managing stress is to eliminate the stressor giving you trouble. For example, if your job is your primary stressor, your stress level would be reduced if you found a more comfortable job. At other times, modifying the stressful situation can be equally helpful. Using the problem-solving method, you search for an alternative that will change the stressor. The accompanying Human Relations in Practice insert illustrates how a businessperson took constructive action against a major stressor in her life.

Placing the Stressful Situation in Perspective

Stress comes about because of our perception of the situation. If you can alter your perception of a threatening situation, you are attacking the source. A potentially stressful situation can be put into perspective by asking, "What is the worst thing that could happen to me if I fail in this activity?" The answer to this question is found by asking a series of questions, starting with the grimmest possibility. For instance, you are late with a report that is due this afternoon. Consider the following questions and answers:

- Will my reputation be damaged permanently? (*No.*)

- Will I get fired? (*No.*)

Human Relations in Practice

Business Management Consultant Digs Out from Stress

Her days of disorganization are over, but Marilyn Paul remembers them. "I tried really hard several times to do what personal organizers recommend," says Paul, a business management consultant and partner in Bridgeway Partners in Boston. "I made lists, cleaned up my desk, vowed to be on time." It didn't work. One day, Paul simply decided that "I couldn't sort through all the piles on my desk and in my office and house for the rest of my life." So Paul followed her own advice. She is a consultant to businesses undergoing changes.

It worked. Paul became what she calls organized enough to no longer face deflating clutter on her desk or stress out about being late (she has shifted to the punctual side). She filed her back taxes and paid the penalties.

Source: Bon Condor, "Cluttered Life Adds to Stress," *Chicago Tribune* syndicated story, February 25, 2004.

■ Will I get reprimanded? (*Perhaps, but not for sure.*)

■ Will my boss think less of me? (*Perhaps, but not for sure.*)

Only if the answer is yes to either of the first two questions is negative stress truly justified. This thought process allows stressful situations to be properly evaluated and kept in perspective. You, therefore, avoid the stress that comes from overreacting to a situation.

Gaining Control of the Situation

Feeling that a bothersome situation is out of control is almost a universal stressor. A key method of stress management is, therefore, to attack the stressor by gaining control of the situation. A multipurpose way of gaining control is to improve your work habits and time management. By being "on top of things," you can make heavy work and school demands less stressful. A trend related to reducing stress by gaining control is to simplify your life by getting rid of unessential activities. Andrew Weil, the natural health guru, recommends that you downsize your life. He believes that significant stress stems from the complexity of our lives, a major contributor being our material possessions. Many people have to many physical objects that require attention and maintenance. Weil recommends that you get rid of what you can spare. [21] You will gain control of your life situation by having less clutter.

A note of caution is that an oversimplified life can also be an impoverished life, creating stress of its own. Throw out or give to charity those physical possessions that contribute virtually nothing to your life. Yet save the sources of an enriched life. For example, why give up a digital camera, cell telephone, and MP3 player if all three are major sources of pleasure and satisfaction?

RECEIVING SOCIAL SUPPORT

An ideal way to manage stress is one that provides side benefits. Getting close to people falls into this category. You will reduce some stress symptoms and form healthy relationships with others in the process. By getting close to others, you build a **support system,** a group of people on whom you can rely for encouragement and comfort. The trusting relationship you have with these people is critically important. People within your support network include family members, friends, coworkers, and fellow students. In addition, some people in turmoil reach out to strangers to discuss personal problems.

The usual method of reducing stress is to talk over your problems while the other person listens. Switching roles can also help reduce stress. Listening to others will make you feel better because you have helped them. Another advantage to listening to the feelings and problems of others is that it helps you to get close to them.

■ **Support system**
a group of people on whom one can rely for encouragement and comfort

RELAXATION TECHNIQUES FOR HANDLING STRESS

"Relax" is the advice many people have always offered the stressed individual. Stress experts give us similar advice but also offer specific techniques. Here we describe three techniques that can help you relax and, consequently, help you reduce stress and its symptoms In addition, Figure 17-6 lists a variety of "stress busters," many of which are relaxation oriented. Recognize that many of these techniques contribute directly to wellness and that stress management is a major component of wellness. Pick and choose among stress-management techniques until you find several that effectively reduce your stress.

Figure **17-6**

Stress Busters

- Take a nap when facing heavy pressures. Napping is regarded as one of the most effective techniques for reducing and preventing stress.
- Give in to your emotions. If you are angry, disgusted, or confused, admit your feelings. Suppressing your emotions adds to stress.
- Take a brief break from the stressful situation and do something small and constructive, such as washing your car, emptying a wastebasket, or getting a haircut.
- Get a massage because it can loosen tight muscles, improve your blood circulation, and calm you down.
- Get help with your stressful task from a coworker, boss, or friend.
- Concentrate intensely on reading, surfing the Internet, a sport, or hobby. Contrary to common sense, concentration is at the heart of stress reduction.
- Have a quiet place at home and have a brief idle period there every day.
- Take a leisurely day off from your routine.
- Finish something you have started, however small. Accomplishing almost anything reduces some stress.
- Stop to smell the flowers, make friends with a young child or elderly person, or play with a kitten or puppy.
- Strive to do a good job but not a perfect job.
- Work with your hands, doing a pleasant task.
- Hug somebody you like and who you think will hug you back.
- Become a rag doll by standing with your arms dangling loosely at your sides. Start to shake your hands, then start shaking your arms. Next, sit and repeat the same moves with your legs.
- Find something to laugh at—a cartoon, a movie, a television show, a Web site for jokes, even yourself.
- Minimize drinking caffeinated or alcoholic beverages and drink fruit juice or water instead. Grab a piece of fruit rather than a can of beer.

Relaxation Response

A standard technique for reducing stress is to achieve the relaxation response. The **relaxation response** is a physical state of deep rest in which you experience a slower respiration and heart rate, lowered blood pressure, and lowered metabolism. By practicing the relaxation response, you can counteract the fight-or-flight response associated with stress.

According to cardiologist Herbert Benson, four things are necessary to practice the relaxation response: a quiet environment, an object to focus on, a passive attitude, and a comfortable position. You are supposed to practice the relaxation response 10 to 20 minutes, twice a day. To evoke the relaxation response, Benson advises you to close your eyes. Relax. Concentrate on one word or prayer. If other thoughts come to mind, be passive and return to the repetition. [22]

Similar to any other relaxation technique, the relaxation response is harmless and works for most people. However, some very impatient people find it annoying to disrupt their busy day to meditate. Unfortunately, these may be the people who most urgently need to learn to relax.

■ **Relaxation response**
a physical state of deep rest in which one experiences a slower respiration and heart rate, lowered blood pressure, and lowered metabolism; a standard technique for reducing stress

Meditation

Perhaps the oldest stress-management technique of all, mediation, is back in vogue as implied by the chapter opener. An estimated 10 million American adults meditate regularly. **Meditation** is a systematic method of concentration, reflection, or concentrated thinking designed to suppress the activity of the sympathetic nervous system. The relaxation response is essentially a meditation technique, and napping

■ **Meditation**
a systematic method of concentration, reflection, or concentrated thinking designed to suppress the activity of the sympathetic nervous system

provides some of the benefits of meditation. The meditator reaches a deep state of mental and physical calmness and relaxation, driving away accumulated stress. Meditation is also recommended as a way of preventing and slowing down and reducing the pain of chronic diseases, such as heart disease, AIDS, and cancer. People who meditate learn to tolerate everyday annoyances better. Meditation has been widely researched, and its key benefits in relation to stress include calming the mind and eliminating anxiety. [23]

The usual approach to meditation involves four simple steps. First, find a quiet place, with a minimum of distractions. Second, close your eyes so that you can close yourself off from the outside world. Third, pick a word whose sound is soothing when repeated. Fourth, say the word repeatedly. For most people, one 15-minute session daily will accomplish the benefits of meditation.

MANAGING STRESS BY STAYING WELL (PROPER EXERCISE, DIET, AND REST)

A far-reaching strategy for managing stress is to both prevent and reduce the negative stress by leading a healthy lifestyle, or being well. Three major components to staying well are proper exercise, diet, and rest. The three components are interrelated because each component facilitates the other: For example, if you exercise enough you tend to prefer healthy food; if you diet properly, physical exercise is easier, and so is obtaining rest. Also, if you rest well you will be in a better frame of mind to exercise, and you will not crave so much caffeine and sugar to stay energized. Proper diet and exercise are also important in helping ward off physical illness that creates stress for the individual. Poor diet and lack of exercise are responsible for almost as many deaths in the United States as smoking. [24]

EXERCISING PROPERLY INCLUDING YOGA AND TAI CHI

The right amount and type of physical exercise contributes substantially to wellness. Part of the reason exercise is useful for managing stress is that it contributes to relaxation and being better able to cope with frustration. To achieve wellness it is important to select an exercise program that is physically challenging but that does not lead to overexertion and muscle injury. Competitive sports, if taken too seriously, can actually increase a person's stress level. The most beneficial exercises are classified as aerobic because they make you breathe faster and raise your heart rate. Most of a person's exercise requirements can be met through everyday techniques such as walking or running upstairs, vigorous housework, yard work, or walking several miles per day.

A major benefit is the euphoria that often occurs when brain chemicals called *endorphins* are released into the body. The same experience is referred to as "runner's high." Other mental benefits of exercise include increased self-confidence; improved body image and self-esteem; improved mental functioning, alertness, and efficiency; release of accumulated tensions; and relief from mild depression. [25]

Millions of people seek to reduce and prevent stress though yoga, which is both physical exercise and a way of developing mental attitudes that calm the body and the mind. One of yoga's many worthwhile goals is to solder a union between the mind and body, thereby achieving harmony and tranquility. Another benefit of yoga is that it helps people place aside negative thoughts that act as stressors. [26]

Tai Chi is another popular form of physical and mental conditioning. The process is also a form of martial art that gently increases and opens internal circulation of breath, body heat, blood, and the lymph. The health training aspect of Tai Chi concentrates on relieving the physical effects of stress on the body, and the meditative aspects also reduce stress. So, the general purpose of Tai Chi is to improve health and well being, partly by reducing the negative effects of stress. [27]

The combination of moderate exercises—long, slow movements—and concentration are particularly effective stress reducers.

REST SUFFICIENTLY

Rest offers benefits similar to those of exercise, such as stress reduction, improved concentration, improved energy, and better tolerance for frustration. Achieving proper rest is closely linked to getting proper exercise. The current interest in adult napping reflects the awareness that proper rest makes a person less stress prone and enhances productivity. A growing number of firms have napping facilities for workers, and many workers nap at their desks or in their parked vehicles during lunch breaks. Naps of about 15 minutes duration taken during the workday are used both as energizers and as stress reducers. To keep the effectiveness of workday napping in perspective, workers who achieve sufficient rest during normal sleeping hours have less need for naps during working hours.

MAINTAINING A HEALTHY DIET

Eating nutritious foods is valuable for mental as well as physical health, making it easier to cope with frustrations that are potential stressors. Many nutritionists and physicians believe that eating fatty foods, such as red meat, contributes to colon cancer. Improper diet, such as consuming less than 1,300 calories per day, can weaken you physically. In turn, you become more susceptible to stress. Some non-nutritious foods, such as those laden with caffeine or sugar, tend to enhance stress levels. According to the Dietary Guidelines of the U.S. Department of Agriculture, a healthy diet is one that

- emphasizes fruits, vegetables whole grains, and fat-free or low-fat milk and milk products
- includes lean meats, poultry, fish, beans, eggs, and nuts
- is low in saturated fats, trans fats, cholesterol, salt (sodium), and added sugars

These recommendations are for the general public over two years of age. Using MyPyramid, the government personalizes a recommended diet, taking into account our age, sex, and amount of physical exercise. Consult ***http://www.mypyramid.gov***.

What Are Two Key Perspectives on Understanding and Dealing With Personal Problems?

■ Learning Objective 6

Our approach to understanding and overcoming personal problems will be to first describe self-defeating behavior in general and how to reverse the trend. We then emphasize the importance of resilience in dealing with personal problems.

SELF-DEFEATING BEHAVIOR

Many problems on the job and in personal life arise because of factors beyond our control. A boss may be intimidating and insensitive, an employer might lay you off, or your partner might abruptly terminate your relationship. Many personal problems, nevertheless, arise because of **self-defeating behavior.** A person with self-defeating tendencies intentionally or unintentionally engages in activities or harbors attitudes that work against his or her best interest. [28] A person who habitually is late for important meetings is engaging in self-defeating behavior. Dropping out of school for no reason other than being bored with studying is another of many possible examples. In short, self-defeating behavior means the same as being your own worst enemy.

To examine your present tendencies toward self-defeating behavior, take the self-sabotage quiz presented in Human Relations Self-Assessment Quiz 17-1. Taking the quiz will help alert you to many self-imposed behaviors and attitudes that could potentially harm your career and personal life.

Overcoming self-defeating behavior requires hard work and patience. Here we present four widely applicable strategies for overcoming and preventing self-defeating behavior. Pick and choose among them to fit your particular circumstance and personal style.

■ **Self-defeating behavior**

a person with self-defeating tendencies intentionally or unintentionally engages in activities or harbors attitudes that work against his or her best interest

Human Relations Self-Assessment Quiz **17-1**

The Self-Sabotage Questionnaire

Indicate how accurately each of the following statements describes or characterizes you, using a 5-point scale: (0) very inaccurately, (1) inaccurately, (2) midway between inaccurately and accurately, (3) accurately, (4) very accurately. Consider discussing some of the questions with a family member, close friend, or work associate. Another person's feedback may prove helpful in providing accurate answers to some of the questions.

Answer

1. Other people have said that I am my worst enemy. _____
2. If I don't do a perfect job, I feel worthless. _____
3. I am my own harshest critic. _____
4. When engaged in a sport or other competitive activity, I find a way to blow a substantial lead right near the end. _____
5. When I make a mistake, I can usually identify another person to blame. _____
6. I have a strong tendency to procrastinate. _____
7. I have trouble focusing on what is really important to me. _____
8. I have trouble taking criticism, even from friends. _____
9. My fear of seeming stupid often prevents me from asking questions or offering my opinion. _____
10. I tend to expect the worst in most situations. _____
11. Many times I have rejected people who treat me well. _____
12. When I have an important project to complete, I usually get sidetracked, and then miss the deadline. _____
13. I choose work assignments that lead to disappointments, even when better options are clearly available. _____
14. I frequently misplace things, such as my keys, then get very angry at myself. _____
15. I am concerned that, if I take on much more responsibility, people will expect too much from me. _____
16. I avoid situations, such as competitive sports, where people can find out how good or bad I really am. _____
17. People describe me as the "office clown." _____
18. I have an insatiable demand for money and power. _____
19. When negotiating with others, I hate to grant any concessions. _____
20. I seek revenge for even the smallest hurts. _____
21. I have an overwhelming ego. _____
22. When I receive a compliment or other form of recognition, I usually feel I don't deserve it. _____

(continued)

Human Relations Self-Assessment Quiz **17-1** (*Continued*)

23. To be honest, I choose to suffer.   _____

24. I regularly enter into conflict with people who try to help me.   _____

25. I'm a loser.   _____

Total score   _____

Scoring and Interpretation

Total your answers to all the questions to obtain your score.

0–25   You appear to have very few tendencies toward self-sabotage. If this interpretation is supported by your own positive feelings toward your life and yourself, you are in good shape with respect to self-defeating behavior tendencies. However, stay alert to potential self-sabotaging tendencies that could develop at later stages in your life.

26–50   You may have some mild tendencies toward self-sabotage. It could be that you do things occasionally that defeat your own purposes. Review actions you have taken during the past six months to decide if any of them have been self-sabotaging.

51–75   You show signs of engaging in self-sabotage. You probably have thoughts and carry out actions that could be blocking you from achieving important work and personal goals. People with scores in this category characteristically engage in negative self-talk that lowers their self-confidence and makes them appear weak and indecisive to others. People in this range frequently experience another problem. They sometimes sabotage their chances of succeeding on a project simply to prove that their negative self-assessment is correct. If you scored in this range, carefully study the suggestions offered in this chapter.

76–100   You most likely have a strong tendency toward self-sabotage. (Sometimes it is possible to obtain a high score on a test like this because you are going through an unusually stressful period in your life.) Study this section of the chapter carefully and look for useful hints for removing self-imposed barriers to your success. Equally important, you might discuss your tendencies toward undermining your own achievements with a mental health professional.

Solicit Feedback on Your Actions

Feedback is essential for monitoring whether you are sabotaging your career or personal life. A starting point is to listen carefully to any direct or indirect comments from your superiors, subordinates, coworkers, customers, and friends about how you are coming across to them. Consider the case of Bill, a technical writer:

> Bill heard three people in one week make comments about his appearance. It started innocently with, "Here, let me fix your collar." Next, an office assistant said, "Bill, are you coming down with something?" The third comment was, "You look pretty tired today. Have you been working extra hard?" Bill processed this feedback carefully. He used it as a signal that his steady late-night drinking episodes were adversely affecting his image. He then cut back his drinking enough to revert to his normal healthy appearance.

Take notes to show how serious you are about the feedback. When someone provides any feedback at all, say, "Please continue, this is very useful." Try not to react defensively when you hear something negative. You asked for it, and the person is truly doing you a favor.

Learn to Profit from Criticism

As the preceding example implies, learning to profit from criticism is necessary to benefit from feedback. Furthermore, to ignore valid criticism can be self-defeating. People who benefit from criticism are able to stand outside themselves while being criticized. It is as if they are watching the criticism from a distance and looking for its possible merits. People who take criticism personally experience anguish when receiving negative feedback.

Ask politely for more details about the negative behavior in question so that you can change if change is warranted. If your boss is criticizing you for being rude with customers, you might respond, "I certainly don't want to be rude. Can you give me a couple of examples of how I was rude? I need your help in working on this problem." After asking questions, you can better determine if the criticism is valid.

Stop Denying the Existence of Problems

Many people sabotage their careers because they deny the existence of a problem and, therefore, do not take appropriate action. Denial takes place as a defensive maneuver against a painful reality. An example of a self-sabotaging form of denial is to ignore the importance of upgrading one's credentials despite overwhelming evidence that it is necessary. Some people never quite complete a degree program that has become an informal qualification for promotion. Consequently, they sabotage their chances of receiving a promotion for which they are otherwise qualified.

Visualize Self-Enhancing Behavior

To apply visualization, program yourself to overcome self-defeating actions and thoughts. Imagine yourself engaging in self-enhancing, winning actions and thoughts. Picture yourself achieving peak performance when good results count the most. A starting point is to identify the next job situation you will be facing that is similar to ones you have flubbed in the past. You then imagine yourself mentally and physically projected into that situation. Imagine what the room looks like, who will be there, and the confident expression you will have on your face. Visualization is akin to watching a DVD or video of yourself doing something right.

DEVELOPING RESILIENCE

A master strategy for dealing with personal problems, as well as stress, is to develop resilience. The ability to overcome setback is an important characteristic of successful people. **Resilience** is the ability to withstand pressure and emerge stronger because of the experience. Being resilient also refers to being challenged and not breaking down. The ability to bounce back from a setback, or resilience, is another aspect of emotional intelligence. In the context of emotional intelligence, resilience refers to being persistent and optimistic when faced with setbacks. [29] Learning how to manage stress is an important part of developing resilience. Being resilient also closely associated with self-confidence. Human Relations Self-Assessment Quiz 17-2 gives you an opportunity to examine your tendencies toward being resilient.

■ **Resilience**
the ability to withstand pressure and emerge stronger because of an experience; being challenged and not breaking down

An important part of being resilient is to first overcome the emotional turmoil associated with the setback you have encountered, such as losing a job or being left by a spouse or good friend. Discussing your problem with a friend or counselor is a standard approach for overcoming the emotional turmoil that accompanies a setback. Selecting the right person with whom you can vent your problem is an asset in dealing with your problem. Ideally, you should find someone who can help you help yourself by listening carefully and not jumping in with advice immediately. Remember also to find a good time to discuss your problem with a confidant rather than springing it on him or her. [30]

Human Relations Self-Assessment Quiz 17-2

The Resiliency Quiz

From 1 to 5, rate how much each of the following applies to you (1 = very little, 5 = very much)

1	2	3	4	5	If I have a bad day at work or school, it does not ruin my day.
1	2	3	4	5	After a vacation, I can usually get right back into work at my regular work pace.
1	2	3	4	5	Every "no" I encounter is one step closer to a "yes."
1	2	3	4	5	The popular saying "Get over it" has a lot of merit in guiding your life.
1	2	3	4	5	The last time I was rejected for a job (or assignment) I wanted, it had no particular impact on me.
1	2	3	4	5	I enjoy being the underdog once in awhile.
1	2	3	4	5	I enjoy taking risks because I believe that the biggest rewards stem from risk taking.
1	2	3	4	5	I rarely worry about, or keep thinking about, mistakes I have made in the past.
1	2	3	4	5	If I ran for political office and were defeated, I would be willing to run again.
1	2	3	4	5	When I encounter a major problem or setback, I will talk over the situation with a friend or confidant.
1	2	3	4	5	I am physically sick much less frequently than most people I know, including friends, coworkers, and other students.
1	2	3	4	5	The last time I lost my keys (or wallet or handbag), I took care of the problem within a few days and was not particularly upset.
1	2	3	4	5	I get more than my share of good breaks.

Scoring and Interpretation:

Add numbers to get your total score.

60–70   Highly resilient with an ability to bounce back from setbacks.

45–59   Average degree of resiliency when faced with problems.

30–44   Setbacks and disappointments are a struggle for you.

1–29   You may need help in dealing with setbacks.

> "Failure is simply the opportunity to begin again, this time more intelligently."
> —Henry Ford

After some of the emotional trauma from your problem has been reduced, it is time to use your creative problem-solving skills to find a solution—those that you have developed through experience and in your study of other subjects as well as human relations.

Concept Review
and Reinforcement

Key Terms

Summary and Review

The body's battle against a stressor is the fight-or-flight response, sometimes referred to as the tend-and-befriend response in women. Stress always involves physiological changes, such as an increase in heart rate, blood cholesterol, and blood pressure. Men who respond most intensely to mental stress run a higher risk of blocked blood vessels. Stress adversely affects our ability to fight infection.

- The right amount of stress can be beneficial, such as the right amount of multitasking. Performance tends to be best under moderate amounts of stress, yet certain negative forms of stress almost always decrease performance.
- Prolonged stress may lead to burnout, a condition of emotional, mental, and physical exhaustion in response to long-term job stressors, such as a heavy workload. Occupations that require frequent and intense interaction with others often lead to burnout.
- Almost any form of frustration, disappointment, setback, inconvenience, or crisis in your personal life can cause stress. The categories of situations that can produce stress include significant life changes, low self-esteem, everyday annoyances, social and family problems, physical and mental health problems, financial problems, and school-related problems.
- Personality factors contribute to stress proneness. People with type A behavior are impatient and demanding and have free-floating hostility, all of which leads to stress. People with an external

locus of control (believing that external forces control their fate) are more susceptible to stress. Negative affectivity (a predisposition to negative mental states) also contributes to stress.
- Sources of job stress are quite varied. Among them are work overload (including techno stress) or underload, role conflict and ambiguity, adverse environmental conditions including a sick building and carpal tunnel syndrome, and adverse customer interaction and emotional labor (faking expressions and feelings).

To successfully manage stress in the long range, you have to deal with the stressors directly. Three direct approaches are to

- eliminate or modify the stressor
- place the situation in perspective
- gain control of the situation

Stress can also be reduced through social support for others, as well as relaxation techniques (including the relaxation response and meditation—a state of deep concentration and relaxation). Managing stress by staying well includes

- exercising properly including yoga and Tai Chi
- resting sufficiently
- maintaining a healthy diet

Unless personal problems are kept under control, a person's chances of achieving career and personal success diminish. Many personal problems arise out of self-defeating behavior. Approaches to overcoming and preventing self-defeating behavior include the following:

- Solicit feedback on your actions.
- Learn to profit from criticism.
- Stop denying the existence of problems.
- Visualize self-enhancing behavior.

Developing resilience is a master strategy for dealing with personal problems as well as stress. To be resilient, it is helpful to get past the emotional turmoil by talking to a confidante and then working to solve the problem.

Check Your Understanding

1. Many small-business owners complain that a major job stressor is deleting spam messages every day. Yet these business owners are afraid to use spam-blocking software because they might lose a message from a legitimate customer. What advice can you offer business owners to help them cope with the spam stressor?

2. Identify several potential stressors created by commuting a long distance to work. What can be done to reduce these stressors?

3. In what way do many sales representatives at an automobile dealership experience role underload? How do they appear to deal with the problem?

4. Assume that a professional-level worker, such as a customer service representative, is convinced that napping during the workday is an excellent way of managing stress. Where should this person nap?

5. How can a person who becomes stressed from having to interact with coworkers several hours a day compete in the modern world?

6. Speak to a person you consider to be much more relaxed than most people. Ask your contact which (if any) of the relaxation or stress-busting techniques listed in this chapter he or she uses. Report your findings to the class.

7. What is the difference between making a bad mistake once and self-defeating behavior?

8. Give an example of self-defeating behavior engaged in by a professional athlete. What appear to be the negative consequences to that athlete's career stemming from the self-defeating behavior?

9. Give an example of self-defeating behavior engaged in by a business executive or public office holder. What appear to be the negative consequences to the person's career stemming from the self-defeating behavior?

10. Imagine that a student receives an F in a course. What can he or she do to be resilient?

Web Corner

The nature of stress and stress management: www. stress.org

Evaluation of resistance to stress: www.pressanykey. com/stresstest.html

Internet Skill Builder

Use your favorite search engines to learn about employee assistance programs (EAPs). After visiting several sites,

answer these questions: (1) What type of help can an employee expect to receive from an EAP? (2) How does an EAP help with stress management? (3) Does the EAP counselor typically tell the company the nature of the problem facing the employee who sought assistance? (4) What benefits do companies expect from offering an EAP to employees?

Developing Your Human Relations Skills

Human Relations Application Exercises

Applying Human Relations Exercise 17-1

Personal Stress-Management Action Plan

Most people face a few powerful stressors in their work and personal life, but few people take the time to clearly identify these stressors or develop an action plan for remedial action. The purpose of this exercise is to make you an exception. Here is an opportunity to inventory your stressors, think through the problems they may be causing you, and develop action plans you might take to remedy the situation. Use the accompanying form or create one with a word processing table or a spreadsheet program.

Work or School Stressor	Symptoms This Stressor Is Creating for Me	My Action Plan to Manage This Stressor
1.		
2.		
3.		

Personal Life Stressor	Symptoms This Stressor Is Creating for Me	My Action Plan to Manage This Stressor
1.		
2.		
3.		

Seven days after preparing this worksheet, observe if any of your stress symptoms have diminished. Also, identify those stressors for which only a long-term solution is possible. One student reported that a major work stressor he faced was that the wanted to work in international business and emphasized doing business with Italian fashion companies. Yet he was experiencing stress because he had almost zero knowledge of the Italian language or culture. (By the way, can you offer this man any suggestions?)

Applying Human Relations Exercise 17-2

The Stress-Buster Survey

Each class member thinks through carefully which techniques he or she uses to reduce work or personal stress. Class members then come to the front of the room individually to make brief presentations of their most effective stress-reduction techniques. After the presentations are completed, class members analyze and interpret what they heard. Among the issues to explore are the following:

1. Which are the most popular stress-reduction techniques?
2. How do the stress-reduction techniques used by the class compare to those recommended by experts?
3. For each technique mentioned by a class member, indicate whether you think the method of stress busting will be helpful in the long run or is simply a short-term expedient that might even have negative consequences in the long range. Two examples of the latter are (a) "I like to drink a six pack of beer when I'm stressed out" and (b) "If I'm really uptight, I ride my bike [motorcycle] about 75 miles per hour in the middle of the night."
4. Send e-mails to three class members today or tomorrow indicating what you thought of their methods of stress reduction. If everybody in the class sends e-mail messages to three class members, it is most likely that each student will receive some feedback.

Human Relations Case Study 17-1

Not Enough to Do

Kristina Henry began her career as a government contractor in the early 1990s. Her company provided services to the U.S. government, and much of the company's work was classified. Henry was ambitious and looked to her job as a source of learning new skills and professional growth. She had heard stories about the demanding nature of government contracting, with its emphasis on precise bids and every detail of the contract spelled out carefully. Her understanding was that even the specifications for a computer mouse used for a government project had to be presented in fine detail.

Soon Henry's job left her so stressed that she started grinding her teeth and was constantly looking for new work. "My stress came from having nothing to do," she explains. "It was like Dilbert," she said. "I learned a lot about FAA regulations and flight rules. And I learned a lot of acronyms. A lot of times it was just tedious, and I was thinking, I can't believe I'm here and being paid for this."

Her coworkers were facing the same problem. Occasionally, they too sneaked out to movies and museums. And Henry brought a copy of *War and Peace* to work. She finished it in two weeks.

Questions

1. What is the technical term for the stressor Kristina Henry was facing?
2. What should Henry have done about her problem?
3. What should company management have done about Henry's problem?
4. Explain whether you think Henry really had a dream job.

Source: The basic facts in this case are from Amy Joyce, "Even at Highest Levels, Boredom on the Job Takes Toll on Workers," *Washington Post* syndicated story, August 15, 2005.

Human Relations Case Study 17-2

Geomania Naps

Geomania is a telecommunications firm based in the information technology section of New York City. Some of the several hundred employees live in Manhattan, but many have commutes of up to two hours from other cities. Having survived the downturn in the telecommunications business during the late 1990s and early 2000s, Geomania is understaffed. Many staff members in professional, technical, support, and managerial jobs are doing work that was once performed by two people.

A case researcher asked human resources manager Stephanie Cohen what impact the heavy workload was having on employees. She replied, "We've got a bunch of great soldiers here, but the overload problem is taking its toll. Some staff members are having many more fights at home. More people are having serious medical problems such as chest pains, migraine headaches, and stomach ulcers. I also think the error rate in work is going up.

Manuel Gomez, the customer service manager, tells me Geomania is receiving more complaints about our systems not working."

The case researcher pointed out that Cohen's observations were to be expected when so many people are working so hard. She was asked if she noticed any other unusual behavior in the office in recent months. Cohen said that her assistant, Bonnie Boswell, had made some observations about unusual behavior and that Boswell should be asked to participate in the interview.

Boswell got right to the heart of the matter, explaining that she has observed behaviors that could be helping productivity, hurting productivity, or a combination of both. "What I've noticed," said Boswell, "is that our people are finding more and more creative ways to take naps on the job. The motto has become, 'You snooze you win,' instead of 'You snooze you lose.'"

"There certainly is a positive side to napping. According to one NASA survey, 71 percent of corporate aviation pilots, 80 percent of regional pilots, and 60 percent of hospital workers said they took naps on the job. Another NASA study found that airline pilots who fell asleep on average for 26 minutes had 34 percent improvement in performance and 54 percent improvement in alertness. Of course, they were not sleeping while flying!

"But on the negative side, if you are sleeping you are not producing for the company. Besides that it looks so totally unprofessional to be sacked out in your cubicle, especially if you snore or scream because you are having a terrifying dream."

When asked where and how these workers were napping, both Boswell and Cohen had plenty of answers. Cohen said it has always been easy for executives to nap because they have private offices. Several keep their offices equipped with pillows so they can nap comfortably on a couch, at their desk, or on the floor under the desk. Cohen said that she had walked in on napping executives by mistakes, and an office assistant told her about the pillows.

Boswell said that cubicle dwellers have to be more creative about napping because other workers can readily see them. She explained, "Quite often they catch a nap during meetings. At some meetings half the audience is listing to one side or nap jerking (falling asleep, then quickly jerking the head to awake). One napper closes his eyes at his desk and holds a bottle of eye drops to make it appear he is in the process of self-medication. Many nappers sleep in their cars during lunch break.

"Some of the most stressed-out workers catch a few winks in the office supplies room by resting their head on a box," said Boswell.

Cohen said she was even wondering if Geomania should hire, as a consultant, psychologist Bill Anthony, who founded the Napping Company to promote productive naps in the workplace. He contends that companies do not have to set up special sleeping rooms. Instead, they can institutionalize nap breaks the way they have the coffee break.

"My concern right now," concluded Cohen, "is what to recommend to top management. I think our CEO is opposed to napping on the job (except for his little 40 winks now and then), and napping does not look professional. Yet, a formal napping program could be a real productivity booster. Maybe we could even cut down on some medical problems."

Questions

1. If you worked for Geomania and were stationed in a cubicle, explain why you would or would not nap on the job.
2. Would it be a good idea for management simply to let workers decide for themselves whether to nap on the job? Explain your reasoning.
3. As the human resources director for Geomania, develop a written policy for napping on company time. (A policy is a general guideline to follow.) Include aspects of napping such as when, where, under what circumstances, and for how long workers might nap. Mention whether Geomania should have a separate napping area. (To get a few ideas, see the information about a napping policy that follows this case.)

Source: Some of the facts in this case are from Jared Sandberg, "As Bosses Power Nap, Cubicle Dwellers Doze under Clever Disguise," *The Wall Street Journal*, July 23, 2003, p. B1.

Portions of a Sample Company Napping Policy

Our company believes that the health, wellness, and productivity of every employee is an essential part of the company's success. Part of sustaining health, wellness, and productivity is to permit employees who have no critical need to interact with a customer at the time to take a maximum of a 20-minute nap on company premises. Only one nap per eight-hour shift is permitted, except in cases of unusual fatigue. Discretion must be used as to where to take the nap, such as never napping in sight of customers or in any place that could be dangerous to the employee or other workers. This would include sleeping in an aisle or a stairwell. Bringing a blanket for napping to the workplace is discouraged, yet a small pillow is permissible. Employees must nap individually rather than in teams or with a friend, partner, or spouse. After awaking from a nap, employees are expected to ensure that their clothing is not rumpled, and to not make loud, yawning noises.

REFERENCES

1. Susanna Hamner, "Chanting the Corporate Mantra," **Business 2.0,** June 2005, p. 139.
2. Shelley E. Taylor et al., "Biobehavioral Responses to Stress in Females: Tend-and-Befriend, Not Fight-or-Flight," *Psychological Review*, 107, 2000, pp. 411–429; updated research reported in Sadie F. Dingfelder, "What Lies Behind the Female Habit of 'Tending and Befriending' during Stress," *Monitor on Psychology*, January 2004, p. 15.
3. Research reviewed in Mark Greer, "Mental Stress Wreaks Physical Havoc on Workers," *Monitor on Psychology*, May 2005, pp. 28–29.
4. Suzanne C. Sergerstrom and Gregory E. Miller, "Psychological Stress and the Human Immune System: A Meta-Analytic Study of 30 Years of Inquiry," *Psychological Bulletin*, no. 4, 2004, pp. 601–630.
5. Michele Conlin, "Meditation: New Research Shows That It Changes the Brain in Ways That Alleviate Stress," *Business Week*, August 30, 2004, p. 137.
6. Einar M. de Croon et al., "Stressful Work, Psychological Job Strain, and Turnover: A Two-Year Prospective Cohort Study of Truck Drivers," *Journal of Applied Psychology*, June 2004, pp. 442–454.
7. Jeffrey A. LePine, Marcie A. LePine, and Christine L. Jackson, "Challenge and Hindrance Stress: Relationships with Exhaustion, Motivation to Learn, and Learning Performance," *Journal of Applied Psychology*, October 2004, pp. 883–891.
8. Unpublished research reported in Claudia Wallis and Sonja Steptoe, "Help! I've Lost My Focus," *Time*, January 16, 2006, p. 75.
9. Evangelia Demerouti et al., "The Job Demands–Resources Model of Burnout," *Journal of Applied Psychology*, June 2001, p. 502.
10. Raymond T. Lee and Blake E. Ashforth, "A Meta-Analytic Examination of the Correlates of Three Dimensions of Job Burnout," *Journal of Applied Psychology*, April 1996, p. 123; Joanne Cole, "An Ounce of Prevention Beats Burnout," *HRfocus*, June 1999, pp. 1, 14–15.
11. Rabi S. Bhagat, "Effects of Stressful Life Events on Individual Performance and Work Adjustment Processes within Organizational Settings: A Research Model," *Academy of Management Review*, October 1983, pp. 660–670.
12. "Building Self-Esteem," available at *www.ashland.com/education/self-esteem/best_shot.html* retrieved May 23, 2006.
13. Research reported in Etienne Benson, "Hostility Is among Best Predictors of Heart Disease in Men," *Monitor on Psychology*, January 2003, p. 15.
14. Peter Y. Chen and Paul E. Spector, "Negative Affectivity as the Underlying Cause of Correlations between Stressors and Strains," *Journal of Applied Psychology*, June 1991, p. 398.
15. Paul E. Spector, Peter Y. Chen, and Brian J. O'Connell, "A Longitudinal Study of Relations between Job Stressors and Job Strains While Controlling for Prior Negative Affectivity and Strains," *Journal of Applied Psychology*, April 2000, p. 216.
16. "New Study Reveals One in Three Americans Are Chronically Overworked," *Families and Work Institute*, available at *www.familiesandwork.org*, retrieved March 15, 2005.
17. Keith Newman, "Information Overload—Overcoming Techno Stress," *iStart*, available at *www.istart.co.nz*. Retrieved March 4, 2006.
18. Alicia A. Grandey, "Emotion Regulation in the Workplace: A New Way to Conceptualize Emotional Labor," *Journal of Occupational Health Psychology*, 5; 1, 2000, pp. 95–110; Grandey, "When the 'Show Must Go On:' Surface Acting and Deep Acting as Determinants of Emotional Exhaustion and Peer-Related Service Delivery," *Academy of Management Journal*, February 2003, pp. 86–96.
19. Theresa M. Glomb, John D. Kammeyer-Mueller, and Maria Rotundo, "Emotional Labor Demands and Compensating Wage Differentials," *Journal of Applied Psychology*, August 2004, p. 707.
20. Cited in Chuck Salter, "Finding Your 'Best-Stress Zone,'" *Fast Company*, September 2004, p. 40.
21. Andrew Weil, "Beating Stress," *USA Weekend*, December 26–28, 1997, p. 4.
22. Herbert Benson (with William Proctor), *Beyond the Relaxation Response* (New York: Berkley Books, 1995), pp. 96–97; "Are You Working Too Hard? A Conversation with Mind/Body Researcher Herbert Benson," *Harvard Business Review*, November 2005, p. 54.
23. Evidence reviewed in Roger Walsh and Shauna L. Shapiro, "The Meeting of Meditative Disciplines and Western Psychology," *American Psychologist*, April 2006, p. 228.
24. Research reviewed in "Unhealthy Behaviors Cause Approximately One Half of U.S. Deaths," *Monitor on Psychology*, May 2004, p. 15.
25. Philip L. Rice, *Stress and Health: Principles and Practices for Coping and Wellness* (Monterey, CA: Brooks/College Publishing Company, 1987), pp. 353–354.
26. Stacy Forster, "Companies Say Yoga Isn't a Stretch," October 14, 2003. *The Wall Street Journal*, p. D4.
27. *Tai Chi Productions*, available at *www.taichiproductions.com*. Retrieved May 19, 2006.
28. Mark Goulston, *Get Out of Your Own Way at Work . . . and Help Others Do the Same* (New York: Putnam Adult, 2005); Andrew J. DuBrin, *Your Own Worst Enemy: How to Overcome Career Self-Sabotage* (New York: AMACOM, 1992).
29. Daniel Goleman, "Leadership That Gets Results," *Harvard Business Review*, March–April 2000, p. 80.
30. Robyn D. Clarke, "A Reason for Ranting," *Black Enterprise*, November 2005, p. 161.

Action plan describes how you are going to reach your goal

Active listener person who listens intensely, with the goal of empathizing with the speaker

Adolescence the period in life from approximately age 13 to 20; from a biological standpoint, adolescence begins with puberty

Affective component (of attitude) the emotion connected with an object or a task

Affirmative action programs that comply with antidiscrimination laws and attempt to correct past discriminatory practices

Aggressive characteristic of people who are obnoxious and overbearing; they push for what they want with almost no regard for the feelings of others

Aggressive personalities people who verbally and sometimes physically attack others frequently

Assertive characteristic of people who state clearly what they want or how they feel in a given situation without being abusive, abrasive, or obnoxious; open, honest, and "up-front" people who believe that all people have an equal right to express themselves honestly

Attitude a predisposition to respond that exerts an influence on a person's response to a person, a thing, an idea, or a situation

Attribution theory the study of the process by which people ascribe causes to the behaviors they perceive

Autocratic leader leader who attempts to retain most of the authority granted to the group; autocratic leaders make all the major decisions and assume subordinates will comply without question

Backstabbing an attempt to discredit by underhanded means, such as innuendo, accusation, or the like

Barriers to communication (or **noise**) missteps that can occur between encoding and decoding a message; unwanted interference that can distort or block a message

Behavior modification system of motivation that emphasizes rewarding people for doing the right things and punishing them for doing the wrong things

Behavioral component (of attitude) how a person acts

Behavioral interview a candidate is asked how he or she handled a particular problem in the past

Benchmarking business firms borrowing ideas from each other regularly as part of quality improvement and improving productivity; representatives from one company visiting another to observe firsthand the practices of the other company

Brainstorming technique by which group members think of multiple solutions to a problem

Brainwriting arriving at creative ideas by jotting them down

Burnout a condition of emotional, mental, and physical exhaustion in response to long-term job stressors

Business etiquette special code of behavior required in work situations

Career path sequence of positions necessary to achieve a goal

Carpal tunnel syndrome repetitive motion disorder most frequently associated with keyboarding and the use of optical scanners; occurs when repetitive flexing and extension of the wrist causes the tendons to swell, thus trapping and pinching the median nerve

Character doing the right things despite outside pressures to do the opposite; includes leaving enduring marks that set one apart from another; being moral

Character trait an enduring characteristic of a person that is related to moral and ethical behavior that shows up consistently

Charisma type of charm and magnetism that inspires others; important quality for leaders at all levels

Classical conditioning principles stemming from Ivan Pavlov's digestion experiments that help people understand the most elementary type of learning—how people acquire uncomplicated habits and reflexes

Cognitive component (of attitude) the knowledge or intellectual beliefs an individual might have about an object (an idea, a person, a thing, or a situation)

Cognitive dissonance situation in which the pieces of knowledge, information, attitudes, or beliefs held by an individual are contradictory

Cognitive restructuring technique of mentally converting negative aspects into positive ones by looking for the positive elements in a situation

Cognitive skills problem-solving and intellectual skills

Communication the sending and receiving of messages

Communication overload phenomenon that occurs when people are so overloaded with information that they cannot respond effectively to messages

Computer surfing in the context of the Internet, browsing through Web sites with no specific work goal in mind; unrelated to work

Conflict condition that exists when two sets of demands, goals, or motives are incompatible

Conflict of interest judgment or objectivity is compromised

Confrontation and problem solving the most highly recommended way of resolving conflict; method of identifying the true source of conflict and resolving it systematically

Consensus leader leader who encourages group discussion about an issue and then makes a decision that reflects the consensus of the group members

Consideration the degree to which the leader creates an environment of emotional support, warmth, friendliness, and trust

Consultative leader leader who solicits opinions from the group before making a decision, yet does not feel obliged to accept the group's thinking; this type leader makes it clear that he or she alone has authority to make the final decisions

Creativity the ability to develop good ideas that can be put into action

Cultural intelligence (CQ) an outsider's ability to interpret someone's unfamiliar and ambiguous behavior the same way that person's compatriots would

Cultural mosaic an individual's unique mixture of multiple cultural identities that yields a complex picture of the cultural influences on that person

Cultural sensitivity an awareness of and a willingness to investigate the reasons why people of another culture act as they do

Cultural training set of learning experiences designed to help employees understand the customs, traditions, and beliefs of another culture

Culture a learned and shared system of knowledge, beliefs, values, attitudes, and norms

Customer service orientation approach of employee whose thoughts and actions are geared toward helping customers

Decision making choosing one alternative from the various alternative solutions that can be pursued

Decoding the process of understanding a message; the receiver interprets the message and translates it into meaningful information

Defensive communication tendency to receive messages in such a way that one's self-esteem is protected

Democratic leader leader who confers final authority on the group; functions as a collector of opinion and takes a vote before making a decision (sometimes referred to as a free-rein leader)

Denial the suppression of information one finds uncomfortable

Developmental opportunity teammates rating one another on performance dimensions, such as cooperation with other members of the team, customer service attitude, productivity, and contribution to meetings

Difficult people a coworker is classified as difficult if he or she is uncooperative, touchy, defensive, hostile, or even very unfriendly

Disarm the opposition method of conflict resolution in which you disarm the criticizer by agreeing with his or her criticism

Diversity training program that attempts to bring about workplace harmony by teaching people how to get along with diverse work associates; often aimed at minimizing open expressions of racism and sexism

Downward communication the transmission of messages from higher to lower levels in an organization

E-learning studying independently outside of a classroom setting and interacting with a computer in addition to studying course material; Web-based form of computer-based training

Emotional intelligence the ability to accurately perceive emotions, to understand the signals that emotions send about relationships, and to manage emotions

Emotional labor process of regulating both feelings and expressions to meet organizational goals

Empathy understanding another person's point of view

Empowerment process by which a manager shares power with team members, thereby enhancing their feelings of self-efficacy

Encoding the process of organizing ideas into a series of symbols, such as words and gestures, designed to communicate with a receiver

Ethical screening running a contemplated decision or action through an ethics test, particularly when a contemplated action or decision is not clearly ethical or unethical

Ethics the moral choices a person makes

Ethnocentrism the assumption that the ways of one's culture are the *best* ways of doing things

Exit strategy determining in advance how to get out of a bad decision, such as having joined a failing family business

Expectancy theory of motivation people will be motivated if they believe that their efforts will lead to desired outcomes

External locus of control individual's belief that external forces control fate

Extinction the weakening or decreasing of the frequency of undesirable behavior by removing the reward for such behavior

Fear of success belief that if one succeeds at an important task, one will be asked to take on more responsibility in the future; reason some people procrastinate

Feedback information that tells one how well he or she has performed

Fight-or-flight response the experience of stress prompts the adrenal glands to release a flood of hormones that prepare the body to fight or run when faced with a challenge

Flow experience total absorption in work; when flow occurs, things seem to go just right

Formal communication channels the official pathways for sending information inside and outside an organization

Frame of reference model, viewpoint, or perspective

Galeta effect a type of self-fulfilling prophecy in which high expectations lead to high performance

Goal an event, circumstance, object, or condition a person strives to attain

Grapevine major informal communication channel in organizations; the grapevine refers to the tangled pathways that can distort information

Grievance procedure formal process of filing a complaint and resolving a dispute within an organization

Group dynamics the forces operating in groups that affect how members work together

Group norms unwritten set of expectations for group members—what people ought to do; basic principle to follow in getting along with coworkers

Groupthink a deterioration of mental efficiency, reality testing, and moral judgment in the interest of group solidarity; extreme form of consensus

Hawthorne effect applying research methods to investigate problems of employee productivity using the scientific method; in the study, employees reacted positively because management cared about them

Human relations the art of using systematic knowledge about human behavior to improve personal, job, and career effectiveness

Human relations movement movement that began as a concentrated effort by some managers and their advisors to become more sensitive to the needs of employees or to treat them in a more humanistic manner

Identity crisis adolescent struggle to establish a reliable self-concept, or personal identity, including concerns over ethnic identity, the need to keep close ties with the family or develop peer relations, sexuality, and body image

Implicit learning learning that takes place unconsciously and without an intention to learn

Informal communication channels unofficial networks of channels that supplement the formal channels

Informal learning planned or unplanned learning that occurs without a formal classroom, lesson plan, instructor, or examination; a way of learning complex skills in the workplace

Ingratiating an attempt to increase one's attractiveness to others to influence their behavior

Initiating structure organizing and defining relationships in the group by engaging in such activities as assigning specific tasks, specifying procedures to be followed, scheduling work, and making expectations clear

Insight an ability to know what information is relevant, to find connections between the old and the new, to combine facts that are unrelated, and to see the "big picture"

Intermittent rewards sustaining desired behaviors longer and slowing down the process of behaviors fading away when they are not rewarded

Internal locus of control individual's belief that fate is pretty much under a person's own control

Intrinsic motivation a person's beliefs about the extent to which an activity can satisfy his or her needs for competence and self-determination; instead of looking to somebody else for rewards, a person is motivated by the intrinsic, or internal, aspects of the task

Intuition an experience-based way of knowing or reasoning in which weighing and balancing of evidence are done automatically

Job enrichment making a job more motivating and satisfying by adding variety and responsibility

Job sharing work arrangement in which two people who work part time share one job

Jury of peers grievance procedure used in many firms without a union whereby unresolved grievances are submitted to a panel of coworkers

Lateral thinking process of spreading out to find many different alternative solutions to a problem

Leader–member exchange model (LMX) leadership model that focuses on the quality of leader–member relations; recognizes that leaders develop unique working relationships with each group member

Leadership the process of bringing about positive changes and influencing others to achieve worthwhile goals

Leadership effectiveness inner quality of a leader who helps the group accomplish its objectives without neglecting satisfaction and morale

Leadership style a leader's characteristic way of behaving in a variety of situations

Learning generally considered a lasting change in behavior based on practice and experience

Learning style method of coming to understand; different people learn best in different ways; some people acquire new material best through passive learning, such as acquiring information through studying texts, manuals, magazine articles, and Web sites; others learn best by doing rather than by studying; alone or cooperatively

Management by walking around managers intermingle freely with workers on the shop floor or in the office, as well as with customers; enhances open communication

Maslow's need hierarchy the best-known categorization of needs; according to psychologist Abraham H. Maslow, people strive to satisfy the following groups of needs in step-by-step order: physiological needs, safety needs, social needs, esteem needs, and self-actualizing needs

Meditation a systematic method of concentration, reflection, or concentrated thinking designed to suppress the activity of the sympathetic nervous system

Mentor a more experienced person who guides, teaches, and coaches another individual

Microinequity small, semiconscious message sent with a powerful impact on the receiver

Micromanagement the close monitoring of most aspects of group member activities by the manager

Midlife crisis time adults in their forties face when they feel unfulfilled and search for a major shift in career or lifestyle

Midlife transition adults taking stock of their lives and formulating new goals; among dozens of other personality and social challenges facing adults are the loss of a youthful appearance and a decreased reproductive or sexual capacity

Mirroring form of nonverbal communication to overcoming communication barriers by subtly imitating another; used to improve rapport with another person

Mixed signals type of message in which the sender might recommend one thing to others yet behave in another way

Modeling learning a skill by observing another person perform the skill; considered a form of social learning because it is learned in the presence of others

Motivation concept with two widely used meanings: (1) an internal state that leads to effort expended toward objectives and (2) an activity performed by one person to get another to accomplish work

Motive an inner drive that moves a person to do something

Multicultural identities individuals who incorporate the values of two or more cultures because they identify with both their primary culture and another culture or cultures

Multicultural worker one who can work effectively with people of different cultures

Multitasking doing two or more routine chores simultaneously that can sometimes enhance personal productivity

Need an internal striving or urge to do something, such as a need to drink when thirsty

Need for achievement the desire to accomplish something difficult for its own sake

Negative affectivity a tendency to experience aversive (intensely disliked) emotional states; predisposition to experience emotional stress that includes feelings of nervousness, tension, and worry

Negative reinforcement taking away something unpleasant from a situation; being rewarded by being relieved of discomfort; form of avoidance learning or motivation

Negotiating and bargaining situation of conferring with another person to resolve a problem

Networking the process of establishing a group of contacts who can help you in your career; establishing contacts to find a better position, become a customer, become a valuable supplier, solve difficult problems, or find a mentor; people in a network also offer emotional support

Nonassertive characteristic of people who let things happen to them without letting their feelings be known

Nonverbal communication using the body, voice, or environment in numerous ways to help get a message across

Open-door policy communication channel that is structured upward that allows employees to bring a gripe to top management's attention without first checking with the employee's manager

Openness to experience personality characteristic of positive orientation toward learning; people with considerable openness to experience have well-developed intellects

Operant conditioning learning that takes place as a consequence of behavior; a person's actions are instrumental in determining whether learning takes place

Organizational citizenship behavior (OCB) the willingness to go beyond one's job description to help the company, even if such act does not lead to an immediate reward

Organizational culture values and beliefs of a firm that guide people's actions

Organizational effectiveness the extent to which an organization is productive and satisfies the demands of interested parties, such as employees, customers, and investors

Paraphrase repeating in one's own words what a sender says, feels, and means

Participative leader leader who shares decision-making authority with the group; motivates group members to work as a team toward high-level goals

Partnership the leader and group members are connected in such a way that the power between them is approximately balanced

Peak performance exceptional accomplishment in a given task

Peer evaluations system in which teammates contribute to an evaluation of a person's job performance

Perception the various ways in which people interpret things in the external world and how they act on the basis of these perceptions

Perceptual congruence the degree to which people perceive things the same way

Performance standard a statement of what constitutes acceptable performance

Personal communication style verbal and nonverbal communication style for a unique approach to sending and receiving information

Personality clash antagonistic relationship between two people based on differences in personal attributes, preferences, interests, values, and styles

Personality disorder pervasive, persistent, inflexible, maladaptive pattern of behavior that deviates from expected cultural norms

Person–organization fit the compatibility of the individual and the organization

Person–role conflict the demands made by the organization or a superior clash with the basic values of the individual

Planning primary principle of effective time management; deciding what to accomplish and the actions needed to make it happen

Political skills an interpersonal style that combines awareness of others with the ability to communicate well; developing effective relationships with work associates, including customers

Positive reinforcement increasing the probability that behavior will be repeated by rewarding people for making the desired response; improves learning and motivation

Positive self-talk saying positive things about yourself to yourself

Positive visual imagery picturing a positive outcome in your mind

Primary reinforcer reinforcer that is rewarding by itself, without any association with other reinforcers; food, water, air, and sex are primary reinforcers

Private self the actual person an individual may be

Proactive personality characteristic of a person who is relatively unconstrained by forces in a situation and who brings about environmental change; highly proactive people identify opportunities and act on them, showing initiative, and keep trying until they bring about meaningful change

Problem gap between what exists and what you want to exist

Procrastination delaying a task for an invalid or weak reason

Productivity the amount of quality work accomplished in relation to the resources consumed

Psychological hardiness mental state in which the individual experiences a high degree of commitment, control, and challenge

Public self what a person communicates about himself or herself and what others actually perceive about the person

Punishment the introduction of an unpleasant stimulus as a consequence of the learner having done something wrong

Pygmalion effect leader's ability to elevate worker performance by the simple method of expecting them to perform well; the manager's high expectations become a self-fulfilling prophecy

Recognition need the desire to be acknowledged for one's contributions and efforts and to feel important

Relationship management the interpersonal skills of being able to communicate clearly and convincingly, disarm conflicts, and build strong personal bonds

Relaxation response a physical state of deep rest in which one experiences a slower respiration and heart rate, lowered blood pressure, and lowered metabolism; a standard technique for reducing stress

Resilience the ability to withstand pressure and emerge stronger because of an experience; being challenged and not breaking down

Role tendency to behave, contribute, and relate to others in a particular way

Role ambiguity condition in which the jobholder receives confusing or poorly defined expectations

Role conflict having to choose between two competing demands or expectations

Role overload a burdensome workload that creates stress for a person in two ways: (1) the person may become fatigued and less able to tolerate annoyances and irritations and (2) a person subject to unreasonable work demands may feel perpetually behind schedule, a situation that itself creates an uncomfortable, stressful feeling

Role underload disruptive amount of stress that can occur when people experience too little to do; one benefit is the preservation of energy for family and leisure activities

Scientific management theory that focuses on the application of scientific methods to increase individual workers' productivity

Secondary reinforcer reinforcer whose value must be learned through association with other reinforcers

Selective attention giving exclusive attention to something at the expense of other aspects of the environment

Self a complex idea generally referring to a person's total being or individuality

Self-awareness the ability to understand moods, emotions, and needs as well as their impact on others; self-awareness also includes using intuition to make decisions you can live with happily

Self-defeating behavior a person with self-defeating tendencies intentionally or unintentionally engages in activities or harbors attitudes that work against his or her best interest

Self-discipline the ability to work systematically and progressively toward a goal until it is achieved

Self-disclosure the process of revealing one's inner self to others

Self-efficacy confidence in your ability to carry out a specific task in contrast to generalized self-confidence

Self-esteem the experience of feeling competent to cope with the basic challenges in life and of being worthy of happiness

Self-leadership leading oneself; influencing oneself without waiting for an external leader to lead one; all organizational members are capable of leading themselves to some extent

Self-management the ability to control one's emotions and act with honesty and integrity in a consistent and acceptable manner

Self-respect the second component of self-esteem, refers to how you think and feel about yourself

Self-understanding gathering valid information about oneself; self-understanding refers to knowledge about oneself, particularly with respect to mental and emotional aspects

Semantics the study of the meaning and changes in the meaning of words or symbols

Servant leader one who serves group members by working on their behalf to help them achieve their goals, not the leader's goals

Sexual harassment unwanted sexually oriented behavior in the workplace that results in discomfort or interference with the job

Shadow organizations where much of the real work gets accomplished, the shadow organization is revealed by network analysis, which traces who talks to whom

Skill–benefit statements brief explanations of how an individual's skills can benefit the company

Social awareness having empathy for others and having intuition about work problems

Stress an internal reaction to any force that threatens to disturb a person's equilibrium; the internal reaction usually takes the form of emotional discomfort

Stressor the external or internal force that brings about the stress

Success syndrome pattern in which the worker performs one assignment well and then has the confidence to take on an even more difficult assignment

Support system a group of people on whom one can rely for encouragement and comfort

Synergy a product of group effort whereby the output of the group exceeds the output possible if the members worked alone

Team player one who emphasizes group accomplishment and cooperation rather than individual achievement and not helping others

Teamwork work done with an understanding and commitment to group goals on the part of all team members

Techno stress stress caused by information overload as a result of having to cope with ever-changing technology and the deluge of data stemming from information technology

Telecommuter employee who works at home full time or part time and sends output electronically to a central office

Time leak anything you are doing or not doing that allows time to get away from you

Traditional mental set fixed way of thinking about objects and activities

Trust a person's confidence in another individual's intentions and motives and in the sincerity of that individual's words

Two-factor theory of work motivation two different sets of job factors—one set, the motivators, or satisfiers, can motivate and satisfy workers; the other set, dissatisfiers, or hygiene factors, can only prevent dissatisfaction

Type A behavior personality characteristics that lead a person into stressful situations. Type A behavior has two main components: (1) the tendency to try to accomplish too many things in too little time and (2) free-floating hostility

Upward communication the transmission of messages from lower to higher levels in an organization

Value the importance a person attaches to something; values are also tied to the enduring belief that one's mode of conduct is better than another mode of conduct

Variable pay incentive plan that intentionally pays good performers more money than poor performers

Vertical thinking analytical, logical process that results in few answers; the vertical thinker looks for the one best solution to a problem, much like solving an equation in algebra

Win–win belief that after conflict has been resolved both sides should gain something of value

Work ethic a firm belief in the dignity and value of work and, therefore, important for favorably impressing a manager

Work habits a person's characteristic approach to work, including such things as organization, priority setting, and handling of paper work and e-mail

Workaholism neglecting the normal need for rest and relaxation that can lead to an addiction to work in which not working is an uncomfortable experience

Work–family conflict conflict that occurs when an individual has to perform multiple roles: worker, spouse or partner, and often parent

Worst-case scenario helpful decision-making aid is that involves visualizing what you would do if the alternative chosen proved to be dreadful

Worst in, first out (WIFO) dealing first with unpleasant tasks you would prefer to avoid; simply getting them done and out of the way

Company Index

Name and Subject Index